The Craft of
Information Visualization

Readings and Reflections

The Morgan Kaufmann Series in Interactive Technologies

SERIES EDITORS: STUART CARD, *PARC*
JONATHAN GRUDIN, *MICROSOFT*
JAKOB NIELSEN, *NIELSEN NORMAN GROUP*

The Craft of Information Visualization: Readings and Reflections
Written and edited by Benjamin B. Bederson and Ben Shneiderman

HCI Models, Theories, and Frameworks: Toward a Multidisciplinary Science
Edited by John M. Carroll

Designing Forms that Work: Creating Forms for Web-Based, Email, and Paper Applications
Caroline Jarrett and Gerry Gaffney

Getting the Work Right: Interaction Design for Complex Problem Solving
Barbara Mirel

Web Bloopers: 60 Common Web Design Mistakes and How to Avoid Them
Jeff Johnson

Observing the User Experience: A Practitioner's Guide to User Research
Mike Kuniavsky

Paper Prototyping: Fast and Simple Techniques for Designing and Refining the User Interface
Carolyn Snyder

Persuasive Technology: Using Computers to Change What We Think and Do
B.J. Fogg

Coordinating User Interfaces for Consistency
Edited by Jakob Nielsen

Usability for the Web: Designing Web Sites that Work
Tom Brinck, Darren Gergle, and Scott D.Wood

Usability Engineering: Scenario-Based Development of Human-Computer Interaction
Mary Beth Rosson and John M. Carroll

Your Wish is My Command: Programming by Example
Edited by Henry Lieberman

GUI Bloopers: Don'ts and Dos for Software Developers and Web Designers
Jeff Johnson

Information Visualization: Perception for Design
Colin Ware

Robots for Kids: Exploring New Technologies for Learning
Edited by Allison Druin and James Hendler

Information Appliances and Beyond: Interaction Design for Consumer Products
Edited by Eric Bergman

Readings in Information Visualization: Using Vision to Think
Written and edited by Stuart K. Card, Jock D. Mackinlay, and Ben Shneiderman

The Design of Children's Technology
Edited by Allison Druin

Web Site Usability: A Designer's Guide
Jared M. Spool, Tara Scanlon, Will Shroeder, Carolyn Snyder, and Terri DeAngelo

The Usability Engineering Lifecycle: A Practitioner's Handbook for User Interface Design
Deborah J. Mayhew

Contextual Design: Defining Customer-Centered Systems
Hugh Beyer and Karen Holtzblatt

Human-Computer Interface Design: Success Stories, Emerging Methods, and Real World Context
Edited by Marianne Rudisill, Clayton Lewis, Peter P. Polson, and Timothy D. McKay

The Craft of
Information Visualization
Readings and Reflections

WRITTEN AND EDITED BY

BENJAMIN B. BEDERSON
BEN SHNEIDERMAN
UNIVERSITY OF MARYLAND

MORGAN KAUFMANN PUBLISHERS

AN IMPRINT OF ELSEVIER SCIENCE

AMSTERDAM   BOSTON   LONDON   NEW YORK
OXFORD   PARIS   SAN DIEGO   SAN FRANCISCO
SINGAPORE   SYDNEY   TOKYO

Publishing Director:	*Diane D. Cerra*
Publishing Services Manager:	*Simon Crump*
Senior Developmental Editor:	*Marilyn Uffner Alan*
Production Editor:	*Brandy Palacios, George Morrison*
Text Design, Technical Illustration, and Composition:	*Susan M. Sheldrake/ShelDragon Graphic Design*
Editorial Coordinator:	*Mona Buehler*
Cover Design:	*Susan Shapiro*
Copyeditor:	*Robert Fiske*
Proofreader:	*Richard Camp*
Printer:	*Courier*
Cover images:	*Treemap with more than a million items. (Figure 1.1, Fekete, J.-D. and Plaisant, C. [2002]) Copyright © 2002, IEEE. Used with permission.*

Designations used by companies to distinguish their products are often claimed as trademarks or registered trademarks. In all instances in which Morgan Kaufmann Publishers is aware of a claim, the product names appear in initial capital or all capital letters. Readers, however, should contact the appropriate companies for more complete information regarding trademarks and registration.

Morgan Kaufmann Publishers
An imprint of Elsevier Science
340 Pine Street, Sixth Floor
San Francisco, CA 94104-3205
www.mkp.com

2007   2006   2005   2004   2003   5   4   3   2   1

Library of Congress Control Number: *2002116252*
ISBN: 1-55860-915-6

This book is printed on acid-free paper.

Contents

Preface

Information visualization has become a major theme during the past ten years for much of the work of the faculty, staff, and students at the University of Maryland's Human–Computer Interaction Lab (HCIL). Our roots are in human–computer interaction (HCI), but increasingly our attention has focused on information visualization. The reason is clear: The overall theme of our work is to improve the experience of people using computers, making that experience more effective and enjoyable. In order to reach that goal, we must create designs that enable users to develop control over the computer and, we hope, to attain a sense of mastery. For this to occur, users must have a fluid and efficient interaction with the computer—and the high bandwidth of visual interfaces is a compelling way to attain this goal.

A large component of human perception of the world is through sight. As we've said before, *the eyes have it*. There is simply more bandwidth and processing power for input through the human eyes than through any other sensory modality. Sound, touch, smell, and taste are important, but the HCIL's researchers have repeatedly returned to highly visual and dynamic displays as the best way to solve a surprisingly broad set of problems in an equally broad set of domains.

The HCIL is not alone in this belief. The field of information visualization has been maturing, along with its related discipline of scientific visualization. Both have strong ties to the broader field of human–computer interaction, as well as to graphics groups such as the ACM Special Interest Group on Graphics (SIGGRAPH) and many international graphics associations. Information visualization has grown rapidly since 1995, with annual conferences, organized in the United States by the IEEE and in the United Kingdom by the International Conference on Information Visualization.

An important distinction must be made between the more mature field of scientific visualization and the relative newcomer, information visualization. There are certainly overlaps, but scientific visualization researchers deal primarily with three-dimensional physical objects and processes such as blood flowing through heart valves, tornado formation, crystal growth, protein structures, and oil reservoir shapes. They focus on volumes and surfaces, studying formations and flows and asking questions about inside/outside, above/below, or left/right.

By contrast, information visualization researchers are concerned with abstract phenomena for which there may not be a natural physical reality, such as stock market movements, social relationships, gene expression levels, manufacturing production monitoring, survey data from political polls, or supermarket purchases. While both kinds of data sets come from the physical world, instead of dealing with three-dimensional aspects, the users of information visualization tools are interested in finding relationships among variables; discovering similar items; and identifying patterns such as clusters, outliers, and gaps.

Another important discriminator is that scientific visualization users are primarily interested in continuous variables such as density, temperature, or pressure, whereas information visualization users deal with continuous as well as categorical variables, such as gender, race, home ownership, date of birth, state name, and number of bedrooms. Another distinctive feature of information visualization is its attention to discrete structures such as trees and graphs. Of course, there are areas where ideas and applications cross over, but the distinctive aspects of information visualization are important to understand.

The interactive nature of information visualization stems from the use of powerful widgets that enable users to explore patterns, test hypotheses, discover exceptions, and explain what they find to others. Interacting with the data set gives users the chance to rapidly gain an overview, explore subsets, or probe for extreme values. Information visualization tools become telescopes and microscopes that allow users to see phenomena that were previously hidden.

A steadily growing set of books is helping to define the field and support graduate courses in many universities. The classic book by Bertin, *Semiology of Graphics* (1983), has inspired many researchers, while the more recent *Readings in Information Visualization: Using Vision to Think* (Card, Mackinlay, and Shneiderman, 1999) has stimulated numerous developers. The latter book includes 47 early papers from diverse sources with integrative commentaries and an extensive bibliography. Other books on visualization include the fine surveys by Robert Spence (2000), Colin Ware (2000), and Chaomei Chen (1999). Conference proceedings are important resources, and collections of papers on special topics are common in this discipline. Journals devoted to the topic such as *Information Visualization* (*www.palgrave-journals.com/ivs/*) serve to present current research. Guides for practitioners are beginning to emerge (Westphal and Blaxton, 1999).

The broader field of HCI is now also firmly established with major groups such as ACM's Special Interest Group on Computer Human Interaction (SIGCHI), Usability Professionals Association (UPA), British Computer Society Human Computer Interaction Group, and the Association Français pour l'Interaction Homme–Machine (AFIHM). These organizations have significant participation not only from academic researchers, but also from companies and governmental organizations. In fact, the premiere HCI conference (SIGCHI) typically has attendance split equally between researchers and practitioners.

THANKS TO THE HCIL COMMUNITY

On this 20th anniversary of the HCIL, we proudly bring together this collection of work from our colleagues—students, staff, visitors, and collaborators around the world. We hope that by offering this work, along with our reflections on what was important and why, and how the research unfolded as it did, we can shed some light on the often mysterious process of innovation and creation—and encourage others to further advance the field of information visualization.

We are deeply indebted to all of our colleagues at the University of Maryland and around the world. The rich intellectual atmosphere and warm, personable climate in which we work has made this book possible. Our close faculty colleagues, François Guimbretière in Computer Science, Kent Norman in Psychology, Allison Druin, and Doug Oard in Information Studies are true partners in the HCIL. Gary Marchionini was an important participant for many years before he moved to University of North Carolina. The HCIL's long-term research scientist, Catherine Plaisant, has been a key developer of many of the ideas in this book. Other contributors have been yearlong visitors and postdoctoral researchers such as Richard Biegel, Khoa Doan, Richard Salter, and Jean-Daniel Fekete.

Ten years ago, THE HCIL published a book called *Sparks of Innovation in Human–Computer Interaction* (1993), containing a selection of the lab's work from its first ten years. This decade, on the other hand, has been so fruitful that we have decided to focus on information visualization, leaving our colleagues to publish other specialized books, such as the collections on children's technology by Allison Druin (1999, 2000).

The work in this book could have been done only with the participation of a terrific staff. Research assistants, like Anne Rose, have stuck with us through thick and thin, contributing broadly to our research. Our newer staff, Aaron Clamage, Allison Farber, Jesse Grosjean, Trina Harris, and Sabrina Liao, have already made their marks, and we are excited about their joining us.

The rhythm of our work is tied to the seasons—fall, spring, and summer semesters. A new semester is a chance to learn from the past, and each affords an opportunity to start fresh. We have had extremely strong computer science doctoral students who have gone on to make notable accomplishments of their own. Master's students and undergraduates have also made important contributions and are co-authors on many papers. Our students, present and past, are what make the HCIL such a dynamic place.

Benjamin B. Bederson
bederson@cs.umd.edu

Ben Shneiderman
ben@cs.umd.edu

College Park, Maryland
January, 2003

Acknowledgments

CHAPTER OPENER QUOTES

Introduction Morris Kline, in Rosner, Stanley and Abt, Lawrence E. (eds.). *The Creative Experience.*
1970: Dell Publishers, p. 94.

Rosner, Stanley and Abt, Lawrence E. (eds.) (*ibid*). p. 381.

Chapter 1 John Tukey. "The Technical Tools of Statistics." *American Statistician*, 19 (1965).

Chapter 2 Leonardo da Vinci, 1452–1519.

Chapter 3 Eliel Saarinen, as quoted by his son Eero, in *Time*, June 2, 1977.

Chapter 4 Ralph Waldo Emerson. *Society and Solitude* (1870). 2001: Fredonia Books.

Chapter 5 Arthur Schopenhauer. *Parerga and Paralipomena.* Vol. 2, Ch. 22, Sct. 257 (1851).
2001: Oxford University Press.

Chapter 6 Mickey Hart, *Drumming at the Edge of Magic: A Journey into the Spirit of Percussion.*
1990: Harper SanFrancisco. p. 99.

Chapter 7 Don Norman, *Things That Make Us Smart: Defending Human Attributes in the Age of the Machine.*
1993: Perseus Publishing.

Chapter 8 Jennifer Preece, as quoted to Ben Shneiderman in a personal conversation, 2001.

FIGURES IN INTRODUCTORY MATERIAL

1.1   Shneiderman, B., Dynamic Queries for Visual Information Seeking. *IEEE Software*, vol. 11 (6)
(Nov. 1994) 70–77, Fig. 1. Copyright © 1994, IEEE. Used with permission.

1.2   Ibid, Fig. 3. Copyright © 1994, IEEE. Used with permission.

1.3   Courtesy of University of Maryland.

1.4   Courtesy of Christopher Ahlberg, Spotfire. *www.spotfire.com*

1.5   Courtesy of University of Maryland.

2.1   Copyright © International Center of Photography *www.icp.org*

3.2   Bederson, B. B., Hollan, J. D., Perlin, K., Meyer, J., Bacon, D., and Furnas, G. W. (1996).
Pad++: A Zoomable Graphical Sketchpad for Exploring Alternate Interface Physics.
Journal of Visual Languages and Computing, 7, pp. 3–31. Copyright © Elsevier, 1996.

4.2a–d Plaisant, C. Guide to Opportunities in Volunteer Archaeology: Case Study of the Use of a
Hypertext System in a Museum Exhibit. Berk E. and Devlin, J. (eds.), *Hypertext/Hypermedia Handbook.*
1991: McGraw-Hill.

4.4   Courtesy of Catherine Plaisant, Maya Venkatraman, Kawin Ngamkajornwiwat, Randy Barth,
Bob Harberts, and Wenlan Feng.

6.5   Fekete, J.-D. and Plaisant, C. Interactive Information Visualization of a Million Items.
INFOVIS 2002: IEEE Symposium on Information Visualization, 2002.

7.1   Courtesy of Catherine Plaisant and Anne Rose.

7.2   Courtesy of Catherine Plaisant and Jia Li.

PAPERS

Ahlberg, C. and Shneiderman, B. (1994). Visual Information Seeking: Tight Coupling of Dynamic Query Filters with Starfield Displays. ACM CHI '94 Conference Proc., 313–317. Copyright © 1994, Association for Computing Machinery, Inc. Reprinted with permission.

Shneiderman, B. (1994). Dynamic Queries for Visual Information Seeking. *IEEE Software*, 11(6), 70–77. Copyright © 1994, IEEE. Used with permission.

Fredrikson, A., North, C., Plaisant, C., and Shneiderman, B. (1999). Temporal, Geographical and Categorical Aggregations Viewed through Coordinated Displays: A Case Study with Highway Incident Data. *Proc. Workshop on New Paradigms in Information Visualization and Manipulation*, 26–34. Copyright © 1999, Association for Computing Machinery, Inc. Reprinted with permission.

Tanin, E., Plaisant, C., and Shneiderman, B. (2000). Broadening Access to Large Online Databases by Generalizing Query Previews. *Proc. Symposium on New Paradigms in Information Visualization and Manipulation—CIKM*, 80–85. Copyright © 2000, Association for Computing Machinery, Inc. Reprinted with permission.

Dang G., North C., and Shneiderman B. (2001). Dynamic Queries and Brushing on Choropleth Maps. Proc. International Conference on Information Visualization 2001, 757–764. Copyright © 2001, IEEE. Used with permission.

North, C., Shneiderman, B., and Plaisant, C. (1996). User Controlled Overviews of an Image Library: A Case Study of the Visible Human. *Proc. 1st ACM International Conference on Digital Libraries*, 74–82. Copyright © 1996, Association for Computing Machinery, Inc. Reprinted with permission.

Shneiderman, B. and Kang, H. (2000). Direct Annotation: A Drag-and-Drop Strategy for Labeling Photos. *Proc. International Conference Information Visualisation* (IV2000), 88–95. Copyright © 2000, IEEE. Used with permission.

Bederson, B. B. (2001). PhotoMesa: A Zoomable Image Browser Using Quantum Treemaps and Bubblemaps. *Proc. Conference on User Interface and Software Technology* (UIST 2001), 71–80. Copyright © 2001, Association for Computing Machinery, Inc. Reprinted with permission.

Shneiderman, B., Kang, H., Kules, B., Plaisant, C., Rose, A., and Rucheir, R. (2002). A Photo History of SIGCHI: Evolution of Design from Personal to Public. *ACM Interactions*, 9(3), 17–23. Copyright © 2002, Association for Computing Machinery, Inc. Reprinted with permission.

Bederson, B. B. and Boltman, A. (1999). Does Animation Help Users Build Mental Maps of Spatial Information? *Proc. InfoViz '99*, 28–35. Copyright © 1999, IEEE. Used with permission.

Bederson, B. B., Meyer, J., and Good, L. (2000). Jazz: An Extensible Zoomable User Interface Graphics ToolKit in Java. *Proc. UIST 2000*, 171–180. Copyright © 2000, Association for Computing Machinery, Inc. Reprinted with permission.

Good, L. and Bederson, B. B. (2002). Zoomable User Interfaces as a Medium for Slide Show Presentations. *Information Visualization* 1(1), 35–49. Copyright © 2002, Palgrave Macmillan Ltd. Reprinted with permission.

Hornbæk, K., Bederson, B. B. and Plaisant, C. (2002). Navigation Patterns and Usability of Zoomable User Interfaces with and without an Overview. *ACM Transactions on Computer–Human Interaction*, 9(4), 362–398. Copyright © 2002, Association for Computing Machinery, Inc. Reprinted with permission.

Plaisant, C., Marchionini, G., Bruns, T., Komlodi, A., and Campbell, L. (1997). Bringing Treasures to the Surface: Iterative Design for the Library of Congress National Digital Library Program. *Proc. CHI 97*, 518–525. Copyright © 1997, Association for Computing Machinery, Inc. Reprinted with permission.

Rose, A., Ding, W., Marchionini, G., Beale Jr., J., and Nolet, V. (1998). Building an Electronic Learning Community: From Design to Implementation. *Proc. CHI 98*, 203–210. Copyright © 1998, Association for Computing Machinery, Inc. Reprinted with permission.

Shneiderman, B., Feldman, D., Rose, A., and Ferré Grau, X. (2000). Visualizing Digital Library Search Results with Categorical and Hierarchial Axes. *Proc. 5th ACM International Conference on Digital Libraries*, 57–66. Copyright © 2000, Association for Computing Machinery, Inc. Reprinted with permission.

Druin A., Bederson B. B., Hourcade J. P., Sherman L., Revelle G., Platner M., and Weng S. (2001). Designing a Digital Library for Young Children: An Intergenerational Partnership. *Proc. ACM/IEEE Joint Conference on Digital Libraries*, 398–405. Copyright © 2001, Association for Computing Machinery, Inc. Reprinted with permission.

Hourcade, J., Bederson, B. B., Druin, A., Rose, A., Farber, A., and Takayama, Y. (2002), The International Children's Digital Library:

Viewing Digital Books Online. Forthcoming in *Interacting With Computers*, 14(6). Copyright © 2003, Elsevier.

Nation, D.A., Plaisant, C., Marchionini, G., and Komlodi, A. (1997). Visualizing Websites Using a Hierarchical Table of Contents Browser: WebTOC. *Proc. 3rd Conference on Human Factors and the Web*. Courtesy of Catherine Plaisant.

Kandogan, E. and Shneiderman, B. (1997). Elastic Windows: A Hierarchical Multi-Window World-Wide Web Browser *Proc. ACM UIST 97*, 169–177. Copyright © 1997, Association for Computing Machinery, Inc. Reprinted with permission.

Hightower, R., Ring, L., Helfman, J., Bederson, B. B., and Hollan, J. (1998). Graphical Multiscale Web Histories: A Study of PadPrints. *Proc. ACM Conference on Hypertext (Hypertext 98)*, 58–65. Copyright © 1998, Association for Computing Machinery, Inc. Reprinted with permission.

Asahi, T., Turo, D., and Shneiderman, B. (1995). Visual Decision-Making: Using Treemaps for the Analytic Hierarchy Process. *CHI 95 Video Program*, abstract in *ACM CHI 95 Conference Companion*, 405–406. Copyright © 1995, Association for Computing Machinery, Inc. Reprinted with permission.

Turo, D. (1994). Hierarchical Visualization with Treemaps: Making Sense of Pro Basketball Data. *CHI 94 Video Program*, abstract in *ACM CHI 94 Conference Companion*, 441–442. Copyright © 1994, Association for Computing Machinery, Inc. Reprinted with permission.

Kumar, H., Plaisant, C., Teittinen, M., and Shneiderman, B. (1994). Visual Information Management for Network Configuration. Technical Report CS-TR-3288, University of Maryland, Department of Computer Science. Courtesy of University of Maryland.

Bederson, B. B., Shneiderman, B., and Wattenberg, M. (2002). Ordered and Quantum Treemaps: Making Effective Use of 2D Space to Display Hierarchies. *ACM Transactions on Graphics*, 21(4), 833–854. Copyright © 2002, Association for Computing Machinery, Inc. Reprinted with permission.

Fekete, J.-D. and Plaisant, C. (2002). Interactive Information Visualization of a Million Items. *Proc. IEEE InfoVis 2002*, 117–124. Copyright © 2002 IEEE. Used with permission.

Plaisant, C., Grosjean, J., and Bederson, B. B. (2002). SpaceTree: Supporting Exploration in Large Node Link Tree, Design Evolution and Empirical Evaluation. *Proc. IEEE InfoVis 2002*, 57–64. Copyright © 2002, IEEE. Used with permission.

Bederson, B. B. (2000). Fisheye Menus. *Proc. UIST 2000*, 217–225. Copyright © 2000, Association for Computing Machinery, Inc. Reprinted with permission.

Plaisant, C., Mushlin, R., Snyder, A., Li, J., Heller, D., and Shneiderman, B. (1998). LifeLines: Using Visualization to Enhance Navigation and Analysis of Patient Records. *1998 American Medical Informatics Association Annual Fall Symposium*, 76–80. Copyright © 1998, American Medical Informatics Association. Used with permission.

Hochheiser, H. and Shneiderman, B. (2001), Interactive Exploration of Time Series Data. *Proc. Discovery Science 4th International Conference 2001*, 441–446. Copyright © 2001 Springer-Verlag. Used with permission.

Fekete, J.-D. and Plaisant, C. (1999). Excentric Labeling: Dynamic Neighborhood Labeling for Data Visualization. *Proceedings of CHI 99*, 512–519. Copyright © 1999, Association for Computing Machinery, Inc. Reprinted with permission.

Bederson, B. B. Czerwinski, M., and Robertson, G. A. (2002). Fisheye Calendar Interface for PDAs: Providing Overviews for Small Displays. Technical Report CS-TR-4368, University of Maryland, Department of Computer Science. Courtesy of University of Maryland.

Seo, J. and Shneiderman, B. (2002). Interactively Exploring Hierarchical Clustering Results. *IEEE Computer*, 35(7), 80–86. Copyright © 2002, IEEE. Used with permission.

North, C. and Shneiderman, B. (2000). Snap-Together Visualization: A User Interface for Coordinating Visualizations via Relational Schemata. *Proc. Advanced Visual Interfaces 2000*, 128–135. Copyright © 2000, Association for Computing Machinery, Inc. Reprinted with permission.

Plaisant, C., Carr, D., and Shneiderman, B. (1995). Image-Browser Taxonomy and Guidelines for Designers. *IEEE Software*, 12,(2), 21–32. Copyright © 1995, IEEE. Used with permission.

Shneiderman, B. (1996). The Eyes Have It: A Task by Data Type Taxonomy for Information Visualizations. *Proc. 1996 IEEE Conference on Visual Languages*, 336–343. Copyright © 1996, IEEE. Used with permission.

Shneiderman, B. (2001). Supporting Creativity with Advanced Information-Abundant User Interfaces. In Earnshaw, R., Guedj, R., Van Dam, A., and Vince, J. (eds.), *Human–Centred Computing, Online Communities, and Virtual Environments*, Springer-Verlag London, 469–480. Copyright © 2001, Springer-Verlag. Reprinted with permission.

Shneiderman, B. (2002). Inventing Discovery Tools: Combining Information Visualization with Data Mining. *Information Visualization*, 1(1), 5–12. Reprinted from *Proc. Discovery Science 4th International Conference 2001 (Lecture Notes in Computer Science*, Vol. 2226, Springer-Verlag Heidelberg). Copyright © 2001, Springer-Verlag. Reprinted with permission.

Introduction

*Visual images or visual understanding of what one is trying to do are
definitely helpful . . . I would say understanding is achieved and results come
more readily if one has a picture rather than by looking at a lot of formulas.*

Morris Kline,
The Creative Experience (1970)

Our goals in writing and editing this book were to give researchers and students an understanding of how ideas in information visualization evolve and spread. The dissemination of ideas is a fascinating and instructive process, especially if it involves your original ideas. It is a thrill to see someone adopt your ideas or software, often refining them substantially as they apply them to some novel domain. Fortunately, we have had very positive collaborative experiences. We have repeatedly found that by being open with our own ideas and honest about the source of others', a great harmony results—with innovation, excitement, and rapid improvement.

THE IMPORTANCE OF FLOW

Another important theme that has pervaded our work is something that has come to be called *flow* (Mihaly Csikszentmihalyi, 1990). Over the years we have developed an intuition about what makes information visualization (and other) interfaces work well, and we have discovered congruence between these ideas and the concept of flow, an idea from the psychology literature. Though we don't have a strict formula for a successful interface, we know that a few basic approaches do help. In general, we believe it is important that the users stay in control and that the computer offers choices with appropriate feedback for user actions. Conversely, computer-controlled interactions often lead to unpredictable, and therefore unacceptable, interfaces.

We also have learned that people are primarily interested in focusing on their tasks and not on operating the interface —and yet so much of a user's experience with a computer is manipulating widgets, resizing windows, and selecting from menus. It is crucial that computers give users prompt and informative feedback at every step along the way. Finally, users must stay engaged in the task for their experience to be effective in the long run. This means that the interface must not be too complex or confusing as to alienate users, nor so simplistic or condescending as to make them bored.

A computer interface that strikes the right balance can enable users to concentrate on the task at hand. The computer becomes a "tool" in the best sense of the word—an extension of the user's body. Time passes quickly, and the users develop a sense of control and confidence while making progress toward their goals.

When people experience this kind of focus, they sometimes refer to "being in the flow." Some psychologists refer to this as *optimal experience*, a shorthand that describes the best experience that one can hope for.* And though it may first seem far afield from computer work in information visualization, as researchers let us consider it our ideal: to create computer interfaces that enable users to forget they are using a computer and think only of the important work they are accomplishing.

This book is about that process in innovation during the last ten of the lab's twenty years as we concentrated on the field of information visualization, a subfield of HCI.

EVALUATING OUR WORK

How do we assess our progress? Are we any nearer to our goal of creating interfaces that support *flow*? Tough internal assessments—critiquing each other, challenging assumptions, and demanding evidence help prevent us from falling into traps of wishful thinking.

External reviews from colleagues add to our continuing assessments. We send drafts of papers to colleagues, invite visitors to see our work in progress, and engage potential users to try our software. We appreciate good feedback, taking to heart constructive comments that push us to refine our work.

The next level of assessment comes from anonymous reviewers of conference papers, journal articles, and grant proposals. We discuss rejections and try to learn from them. Even when we disagree with reviewers, we try to examine how we might have told the story more effectively. Some of our strongest papers have been shaped by tough reviewing processes.

Published papers are the clearest signs of our progress— they have been validated by peer review, and they are publicly available. Several members of our group appear high on the list of authors ordered by frequency of publication in HCI papers, conference presentations, and books (*www.hcibib.org/authors.html*).

Another imperfect but useful metric of success is the number of references to a paper. The NEC Citeseer

---

One popular book called Flow by Mihaly Csikszentmihalyi (1990) summarizes the body of work in understanding human optimal experience.

(*citeseer.nj.nec.com/directory.html*) index has a special section on human–computer interaction, and we are proud that the most cited paper for many years has been one of our works on information visualization. Similarly, when PARC researchers studied reference patterns in information visualization, they found that their group's papers were cited most frequently, but our lab came in second.

Citations in academic papers are one manifestation of our influence, but downloading our software is also quite validating. More than 30,000 individuals have downloaded PhotoMesa, one of our image browsers (Chapter 2).

Our software also influences commercial and government applications. Many of our ideas have become part of larger success stories, such as SmartMoney's MarketMap (*www.smartmoney.com/marketmap*), the Hive Group's treemaps (*www.hivegroup.com*) (Chapter 6), and Spotfire's (*www.spotfire.com*) visualization tools (Chapter 1). Contributions to important national and international projects include the Visible Human Explorer for the U.S. National Library of Medicine, NASA's Earth Science Information Partnerships, and the Library of Congress's American Memory Web site.

Finally, an important internal measure of the HCIL's success is the frequency with which our students graduate and join companies, universities, or government agencies where they make valuable contributions. It's especially satisfying to see young, often shy or quiet students become self-confident professionals who are valued by employers and respected by colleagues. As a community, we are gratified when former students return to tell us how much their time at the the HCIL influenced them both professionally and personally.

WORKING WITHIN A BROADER COMMUNITY OF SCIENTISTS

It is difficult to rank or even list all the people in our professional networks, so we must begin with an apology to anyone we have left out in this discussion. Those who want completeness can examine the hundreds of references in our papers. However, we cannot honestly review our work without reflecting on the influences of our colleagues. In several sections, we include more details related to that topic, but this opening mentions a few of the major groups whose influence cuts across many of the sections.

Our strongest and most enduring bonds have been with the community of researchers at the Xerox Palo Alto Research Center, now simply PARC (*www.parc.com*). Our contacts have been mostly with the user interface group and its related teams, especially the manager and long-term researcher, Stu Card. Stu is a leader in theory-driven thinking and research and is a remarkable innovator, as testified by his numerous patents and papers. The PARC group has also included key people such as Jock Mackinlay, George Robertson (now at Microsoft Research), Ramana Rao (now at Inxight), Peter Pirolli, Mark Stefik, and many others.

As Microsoft Research grew, we enlarged our contacts with George Robertson, Mary Czerwinski, and others. Other industry groups include those at AT&T-Bell Labs and spinoff groups, including Stephen Eick, Andreas Buja, and Stephen

North. We have also enjoyed long-running interactions with Clare-Marie Karat and John Karat at IBM. Special mention goes to Nahum Gershon of Mitre, who has been an effective champion and organizer for information visualization conferences and journals.

University colleagues include Steven Roth at Carnegie-Mellon University, Steve Feiner at Columbia University, George Furnas at University of Michigan, John Stasko and Jim Foley at Georgia Tech, Andries Van Dam at Brown University, Jim Hollan now at UCSD, Saul Greenberg at University of Calgary, Robert Spence at Imperial College, Keith Andrew at the University of Graz, and Alfred Inselberg at Tel Aviv University. Another special mention goes to Edward Tufte at Yale University, who is well known for his independently published books (1983, 1990, 1997) and for his annual public lecture tour—we regularly pay for students to attend when he swings through the Washington, D.C. area.

There are many others, but these people form the core of our community. We jointly write books and articles, organize conferences, and participate in workshops—all to promote information visualization to broader circles. Seeing each other for a beer or dinner once a year is important, and the continuity of contact is maintained by email. We tell our latest stories, probe for their new ideas, and seek each other's respect. These colleagues are who we turn to validate our innovations, to ask for reviews of our draft papers, and to be our partners in proposals.

THE MARYLAND WAY FOR INFORMATION VISUALIZATION

. . . feelings of excitement and pleasure accompany creative work. In many instances, this excitement is associated with arribing at insights, seeing new principles, and discovering relationships which were not fully expected.

Stanley Rosner and Lawrence E. Abt,
The Creative Experience (1970)

Occasionally, visitors and colleagues who appreciate our accomplishments will ask how we go about our work. In *Sparks of Innovation* (1993), Ben Shneiderman described what he called *the Maryland Way*. It has remained a useful guide. Of course, we've learned some new lessons, the field of HCI has matured, and the lab has grown. So we'd like to revisit those ideas in the narrower context of information visualization.

We begin by choosing motivated, strong researchers who will interact well with others. Then, the Maryland Way is to foster innovation through these seven steps.

1. Choose a good driving problem.
2. Become immersed in related work.
3. Clarify short-term and long-term goals.
4. Balance individual and group interests.
5. Work hard.
6. Communicate with internal and external stakeholders.
7. Get past failures. Celebrate success!

1. Choose a Good Driving Problem

Fred Brooks's advice to choose a good driving problem is especially relevant for information visualization, given its strong practical component. It helps enormously to have a clear goal; for example, design a video library that consumers can browse, or build a photo library program that three-year-olds can navigate. Finding good problems is like antique hunting: you are not quite sure what you want, but when you see it, you know it. In the early stages of choosing a problem, we brainstorm to come up with alternatives. Then, over a period of a few weeks, we discard the extreme ideas, refine the remaining possibilities, and focus on one.

Our favorite problems entail improving designs for a wide range of users in real-world contexts—building interfaces for museum users exploring historical topics; library patrons searching for a book or document; scientific researchers trying to understand gene expression levels; or business analysts seeking patterns in customer behavior.

2. Become Immersed in Related Work

We expect each of our students to become the "world's leading expert" on the problem he or she is investigating. Our students must acquaint themselves with related studies, sample similar commercial products, and personally contact active researchers. We expect our students to educate us about related work.

Our students must go to the library or the Internet and chase down every reference to their topic. This process has the dual benefits of compelling them to work on something narrow enough that they can become the leading experts and forcing them to clarify exactly what they are working on.

Trying out commercial products brings a sense of practical reality. The students come to understand the parts in the context of the whole and to see the tradeoffs that designers must make.

Getting in touch with current researchers or developers is a novel and threatening task for many students. Email helps facilitate the process, but phone calls, letters, and visits are also important. Shy students overcome their awkwardness and are often rewarded by a helping hand from a respected researcher or an invitation to present their work at a major company.

3. Clarify Short-Term and Long-Term Goals

After the brainstorming process (see Step 1), which sharpens our understanding of the project, we establish long- and short-term goals. Long-term goals provide a destination and a shared set of expectations that focuses effort. Short-term goals provide immediate feedback about progress and a chance to make inexpensive midcourse corrections.

4. Balance Individual and Group Interests

We give each student or staff person a clear role that serves his or her individual goals (*e.g.*, getting a master's degree within 18 months, doing an independent study summer project, or building a resume to get a desired job). Individual goals need to be in harmony with the overall goals and directions of the lab. A student who wants to do a master's thesis on a topic that is poorly related to our existing work will be encouraged to consider alternative topics.

When visitors tour the lab, students and staff show their work, get feedback, and promote their ideas. Our visitors often prefer chatting with the students who are doing the work to attending a private presentation by senior staff. When visitors are potential funders, direct student and staff involvement in the future of research projects increases motivation, participation, and work quality.

When individual and group goals are in harmony, fortuitous collaborations are likely. One of the ways we have been able to accomplish so much with limited resources is that individuals help each other. When one Ph.D. student needed a special routine on an unfamiliar hardware and software environment, another student stepped in and provided a few days of programming help. The favor was repaid by help in reviewing paper drafts and in preparing subjects for an experiment. Since our lab operates with a diverse hardware and software environment, hardly an hour goes by without someone calling out for help on some system.

5. Work Hard

Thomas Edison remarked that innovation requires 1 percent inspiration and 99 percent perspiration. An exciting and novel idea is just the starting point. Most ideas have a cascade of smaller ideas behind them and details to be worked out. Special cases, exceptions, and extreme conditions must be be investigated carefully to reveal the limitations of a new idea. Then converting an idea to a piece of functioning software, a set of screen designs of a prototype, or the materials, tasks, and statistics in an experiment takes devoted effort. Polishing, refining, and cleaning up can take ten or a hundred times more effort than the original innovation. Simply expecting things to take a great deal of effort removes some of the anxiety or expectation of perfection.

There is a definite improvement in quality when you can revise a project after reflection or comments from colleagues. The second time through almost any process or path is often smoother and faster. The "third-time charm" for experiments or designs suggests that persistence and repeated tries leads to excellence.

6. Communicate with Internal and External Stakeholders

Our group operates with a high degree of internal communication and external reporting. Internally, research teams working on related topics meet frequently. We also hold weekly seminars to discuss journal or conference papers or to hear formal presentations of results. Even more compelling than these traditional meetings, however, are the spontaneous demos, informal pre-experiment reviews, participation in pilot studies, pleas for help with statistics, and personal requests for reading draft papers.

While internal communication helps form and guide our work, external communications increase our intensity as we prepare for demonstrations to visitors; presentations at our annual Symposium & Open House; writing reports, theses, or journal articles; production of videotape reports; lectures at companies or universities; and papers and sessions at conferences.

Preparing a presentation for a friend, staff person, or professor may encourage some diligent effort, but it seems that preparation for a conference talk, a lecture to supporting companies, or important visitors raises the stakes considerably. Telling the story and listening for feedback are often unfamiliar skills to technically oriented people, so we try to practice often.

7. Get Past Failures. Celebrate Successes!

Many days seem filled with hundreds of responsibilities such as reviewing journal papers, showing visitors around, responding to requests for technical reports, writing proposals, or reading a draft of a thesis chapter. We are sometimes burdened with filling out travel vouchers, repairing computers, or preparing budgets; however, when it comes time to write annual reports or prepare for our Symposium & Open House, we are struck by how much we have accomplished during the previous year.

The good days are when students invite us to see a demonstration of their latest design, improvement, or experiment. As lab members gather around a computer display, we cheer, comment, and criticize. Other memorable days include working intensely to finish a paper, resolving a problem with statistics, brainstorming on designs, rehearsing for a videotape, fantasizing future user interfaces, and especially celebrating a student's successful dissertaiton defense or journal submission.

Even a successful research group must deal with disappointments. After many years of writing, it is still disappointing to be turned down by a conference program committee or journal editorial board. Requests from journal editors for major revisions are also unpleasant, but some of our most successful papers have had the longest gestation periods and endured the most revisions. We have had our share of rejected grant applications, students who choose to go elsewhere, and funders who decide not to renew.

However, careful acknowledgement of contributors, reviewers, and supporters of all kinds helps to keep such disappointing events to a minimum. In addition, we avoid much internal strife by discussing author credits early and often and seeking creative ways to resolve conflicts.

The HCIL's annual Symposium & Open House (Figure 0.1) is a major celebration in which students, staff, and faculty present their work to several hundred attending. In the morning, we make formal presentations and respond to questions. The afternoon is given over to tours, demonstrations, and personal discussions. At the end of the day, senior staff and faculty dine with the advisory board to reflect on the day and seek suggestions for future work.

In addition to the symposium, the HCIL holds an annual all-day retreat at some bucolic location within an hour's drive of the lab (Figure 0.2). We discuss our research directions, envision the big picture, and make resolutions in a safe and supportive environment. There is never enough time to discuss every project, but long lists are made for later contemplation.

CONCLUSION AND FUTURE DIRECTIONS

Through these processes the HCIL has continued for over 20 years to focus on topics that put humans at the center of technology. This book tells the story of the HCIL's work in information visualization over the past decade. The selected papers which exhibit our lab's most important outcomes, show our work process and evolution of ideas from one project to the next. Each chapter starts with our reflections on the people and problems that inspired the work, followed by the papers in chronological order (except Chapter 7). We've also included short lists of favorite papers from outside our lab that were the most relevant and influential. The listing of all technical reports published by the HCIL in the last 10 years is presented (in reverse chronological order) in Appendix D

As a research topic, the field of information visualization is still forming with a growing number of university courses, professional conferences, and scientific journals. The central research problems include perceptual psychology issues such as understanding change blindness, choosing color palettes, showing relationships between nonproximal items, and using retinal properties (color, size, shape, etc.) properly. Interface design research topics build on perceptual issues for presenting information, providing user control widgets, and using animation effectively. There is also a need for traditional computer science topics such as algorithms for rapid search, data structures for compact storage, software architectures for efficient implementation, and modular programs to facilitate collaborative development. New research methodologies are needed to improve user-needs assessments, controlled experimentation, and ethnographic observations.

Figure 0.1 *Picture of the HCIL cake from annual Open House.*

Figure 0.2 *HCIL members at the annual retreat.*

Central problems for commercial developers of information visualization tools include data integration to smoothly import data, data cleansing to remove or repair bad inputs, and data export to send result sets to other users in formats that will be acceptable. Once these basic problems are solved, commercial developers will succeed in *crossing the chasm* (to use Geoffrey Moore's term) if they can provide a whole product solution for a genuine need.

When developers solve problems for their customers, information visualization products will move from "nice-to-have" to "must-have." Industries likely to be the early adopters are those driven by continuous innovation and repeated discovery, including pharmaceutical drug research, oil–gas exploration, financial analysis, and manufacturing quality control. Other candidate adopters are transportation safety analysts, business fraud detectors, crime or terror investigators, and medical diagnosticians.

Researchers and product developers will have to cooperate in a massive educational process to teach potential users about suitable applications and appropriate visualizations. This process may take decades, just as it did for the move to graphical user interfaces. Collaboration with data mining enthusiasts, statisticians, information technology specialists, software engineers, business analysts, and other professionals will accelerate this adoption process.

BOOK REFERENCES

Bertin, Jacques, *Semiology of Graphics*, University of Wisconsin Press, Madison, Wis. (1983).

Card, S., Mackinlay, J., Shneiderman, B. (eds.), *Readings in Information Visualization: Using Vision to Think*, Morgan Kaufmann Publishers, San Francisco (1999).

Chen, Chaomei, *Information Visualization*, Springer Verlag (1999).

Csikszentmihalyi, Mihaly, *Flow: The Psychology of Optimal Experience*, HarperCollins, New York (1990).

Druin, Allison (ed.), *The Design of Children's Technology*, Morgan Kaufmann Publishers, San Francisco (1999).

Druin, Allison, Hendler, James (eds.), *Robots for Kids: Exploring New Technologies for Learning*, Morgan Kaufmann Publishers, San Francisco (2000).

Foley, James, van Dam, Andries, Feiner, Steven, Hughes, John, *Computer Graphics, Principles and Practice,*. 2nd ed., Addison-Wesley, Reading, Mass. (1990).

Marchionini, Gary, *Information Seeking in Electronic Environments*, Cambridge University Press, Cambridge (1995).

Shneiderman, B. (ed.), *Sparks of Innovation in human–computer Interaction*, Ablex Publishers, Norwood, N.J. (1993).

Spence, Robert, *Information Visualization*, Addison-Wesley, Essex, England (2001).

Tufte, Edward, *The Visual Display of Quantitative Information*, Graphics Press, Cheshire, Conn. (1983).

Tufte, Edward, *Envisioning Information*, Graphics Press, Cheshire, Conn. (1990).

Tufte, Edward, *Visual Explanations: Images and Quantities, Evidence and Narrative*, Graphics Press, Cheshire, Conn. (1997).

Ware, Colin, *Information Visualization*, Morgan Kaufmann Publishers, San Francisco (2000).

Chapter 1

Database Discovery with Dynamic Queries

▓   ▓   ▓   ▓   ▓

▓   ▓   ▓   ▓   ▓

*As yet I know of no person or group that is taking nearly adequate advantage
of the graphical potentialities of the computer . . . In exploration they are
going to be the data analyst's greatest single resource.*

John Tukey, "The Technical Tools of Statistics,"
American Statistician 19 (1965)

When users are confronted by a new and large database, they usually begin by trying to understand its schema, attributes, and attribute values, possibly by referring to data dictionaries. But understanding the extent of the data is often difficult— How many items are there? Which attribute values or patterns occur often or rarely? Where are the clusters, gaps, or outliers? Which attributes are correlated? These questions are very difficult to discover with existing tools. But the hardest task is to know which questions to ask in the first place.

The goal of designers of modern information visualization tools is to help users discover which questions to ask. These new tools enable users to gain an overview, explore rapidly, test hypotheses, and then share their results with colleagues.

One significant approach toward this end is called *dynamic queries*, a technique that enables interactive exploration. Dynamic queries allow users to update two-dimensional graphical displays in less than 100 milliseconds, even with databases of a million items. As users adjust sliders, buttons,

check boxes, and other control widgets, the continuously visible display of results updates rapidly. There is no Submit button because users can select rapidly from the set of permissible attribute values. There are no syntax errors, and users feel they are in control. They can explore quickly, testing their hypotheses, finding outliers, and identifying patterns.

The appropriate visual display depends on the data—world maps, tree diagrams, tree maps, body diagrams, timelines, scatter plots, and more innovative ideas have all been used. Two of our early applications of dynamic queries were a chemical table of elements (1992 video*), and HomeFinder, a regional map of the Washington, D.C. area (91-11). As query widgets were changed, the chemical symbols changed color to signify inclusion and dots indicating homes for sale lit up on the regional map (92-01) (free downloadable version at *www.cs.umd.edu/hcil/pubs/products.shtml*).

Christopher Ahlberg, a visiting student from Sweden during the summer of 1991, took up Ben Shneiderman's

---

*References to HCIL work are listed by tech report number without the term HCIL (e.g., 91-11), and if the paper is included in this book, it is also cited with the chapter and paper in which it appears (e.g., 2002-14 [2.4] means that tech report HCIL-2002-14 appears in this book as the fourth paper in Chapter 2). The HCIL videos are referenced by the anthology in which they appear (e.g., 1992 video). The complete HCIL video index can be found in Appendix A, and the complete HCIL tech report index is in Appendix D.

lunch-time challenge to work on dynamic query interfaces that applied the following direct manipulation principles (originally described in Shneiderman 1982):

- Continuous representation of the objects and actions of interest with meaningful visual metaphors
- Physical actions or presses of labeled buttons, instead of complex syntax
- Rapid, incremental, and reversible operations whose effect on the object of interest is visible immediately

When used appropriately, these principles can lead to designs that have these beneficial features.

- Novices learn quickly, usually through a demonstration by a more experienced user.
- Experts work rapidly to carry out a wide range of tasks, even defining new functions and features.
- Knowledgeable intermittent users can retain the operating concepts.
- Error messages are rarely needed because only permissible values are selectable.
- Reversible actions reduce anxiety.
- Users gain confidence and mastery because they are the initiators of action, they feel in control, and they can predict the system responses.

Christopher's first overnight success was making a modern slider-based version of a polynomial viewer first built in 1972 (Shneiderman 1974). As users move the sliders for each coefficient, the curve gracefully reshapes on the screen, creating dancing parabolas. Within a week, he had satisfied a second challenge of a dynamic query interface for the chemical table of elements. He put up the periodic table with chemical symbols in red with six sliders for attributes such as atomic radius, ionization energy, and electronegativity. As users move the sliders, the chemical symbols change to red showing the clusters, jumps, and gaps that chemists find fascinating. A study with 18 chemistry students showed faster performance with use of a visual display (versus a simple textual list) and a visual input device (versus a form fill-in box).

At about the same time, Christopher Williamson's

HomeFinder showed a map of Washington, D.C. and 1100 lights indicating homes for sale (Figure 1.1). Users could mark the workplace for both members of a couple and then adjust sliders to select circular areas of varying radii. Other sliders selected number of bedrooms and cost, with buttons for air conditioning, garage, and so on. Within seconds, users could see how many homes matched their query and adjust accordingly. Controlled experiments with benchmark tasks showed dramatic speedups in performance and high subjective satisfaction (93-01 [1.2], 94-16, 1993 video, 1994 video). This demo continues to be compelling and comprehensible even though it is more than ten years old.

Williamson earned a trip to the ACM SIGIR '92 conference in Copenhagen to present his work. Then he went on to the University of Colorado at Boulder to do a master's thesis that expanded the idea into a well-engineered and commercially viable version. One of the amusing stories about this project was the unwillingness of corporate or university sources of regional housing information to share their data. Each organization felt protective of its data and saw little benefit to cooperating with us. Undaunted, Chris Williamson and his friends took a Sunday *Washington Post* and typed in the data for the 1100 homes. The resistance of these same institutions to learning about or applying our approach is surprising. They were successful with their current interfaces and satisfied with doing training courses so that staff could serve clients. They had little motivation to change to an interface that enabled users to do searches on their own, until a serious competitor arose.

Soon after, we worked with the National Center for Health Statistics and built prototypes of Dynamaps (93-21, 1993 video). A thematic map of the United States showing cancer rates was animated by adjusting sliders (Figure 1.2). A time slider illustrated time trends, and states or counties could be filtered according to demographic criteria. Control panels gave users the choice of attributes to be used on the map and sliders.

The concept of a generic two-dimensional scatter plot with zooming, color coding, and filtering was first applied

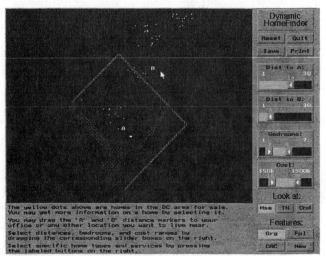

Figure 1.1 *The Dynamic Query HomeFinder showed 1100 homes for sale in the area of Washington, D.C. Users could set sliders to indicate distances from markers, number of bedrooms, and price.*

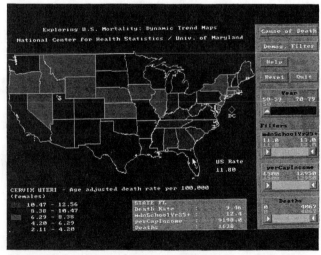

Figure 1.2 *Dynamaps of cancer mortality rates. A time slider shows trends over time, and demographic criteria filter the map.*

in FilmFinder (93-14, 1994 video, 1996 video). The HCIL was working on interactive TV applications for IBM during 1993, and we had a brainstorming session in the conference room with about eight attendees, including Christopher Ahlberg, who had joined us for a second summer. Each person described a possible interface for finding a film from a library of 10,000 videotapes. As the variants of traditional approaches with command lines and menus were rejected, it became more difficult for each speaker to come up with something fresh. Since every alternative was text based, Ben Shneiderman concluded the session by proposing a two-dimensional layout with years on the x-axis and popularity on the y-axis. The idea was quickly accepted and refined.

By the next morning, Ahlberg had a prototype showing 1500 films with color-coded spots (red for drama, white for action, etc.). As the weeks passed and other students built components, Ahlberg integrated them into FilmFinder (Figure 1.3). A range slider allowed filtering by the length of the film, and buttons allowed selection by ratings. A click on one of the spots produced a pop-up box with details of each film and a picture of one of the actors. The term *starfield*, a zoomable scatter plot with color-coded and size-coded markers, was used to convey the zooming experience of flying through a galaxy, as had been popularized in the *Star Trek* series.

The idea for an "alphaslider," selecting from a set of names, had been germinating at the HCIL for two years, but we were stuck with designs that had one item per pixel (93-08), limiting its use to a few hundred items. Ahlberg proposed the concept that many items could be tied to a single pixel, but I thought he misunderstood the technology when it was actually I who couldn't grasp his solution. It took me a few minutes to shake free from my assumptions, and then it was immediately clear that his approach would work. Ahlberg built four versions and ran a study with 24 subjects (93-15). FilmFinder used the alphasliders to select from thousands of actors and directors. The alphaslider idea spawned a variety of improvements and further empirical studies. FilmFinder videotape (1994 video) was also produced during Ahlberg's

intense 12-week summer visit, and it remains one of our most popular tapes.

The group became known as the Widget Carvers of College Park, commemorated by a hand-carved wooden sign that hangs at our lab's doorway. Later work on FilmFinder sought to improve the data structures (93-16) and make the zooming smoother (93-06). Our advanced research continued to increase the size of the database while keeping response times rapid (96-18, 97-14).

Christopher Ahlberg returned to Sweden to work on his Ph.D. titled *Dynamic Queries* at Chalmers University. He developed an enhanced Unix implementation, called IVEE (Information Visualization and Exploration Environment), that was flexible in reassigning the axes to other attributes and had a scroll bar to permit large numbers of sliders. It allowed importation of arbitrary flat files and therefore was applied in many projects, including one for the state of Maryland's Department of Juvenile Justice (96-15, 1995 video).

Ahlberg gathered his friends and found venture capital to start a company. The commercial version of the starfield display, now called Spotfire, allows increased user control and greater flexibility (Figure 1.4).

Spotfire was launched in mid-1996 by IVEE Development, which was renamed Spotfire Inc. (*www.spotfire.com*). Spotfire has become a leader in visual data mining and information visualization. It has become enormously successful in aiding pharmaceutical drug discovery, leading all 25 of the major pharmaceutical companies to become adopters. Easy import and export of data, rapid change to axes, color coding or size coding, and collaboration support have made Spotfire a leader in its class. Expansion to other application domains is proceeding.

The concept of dynamic queries became the basis for applications such as pruning of large tree structures based on sliders tied to attributes of nodes (95-12, 1995 video) and a youth services database for the Maryland Department of Juvenile Justice (96-07, 1995 video). Our later efforts have applied Spotfire to Web site log visualization, with the goal

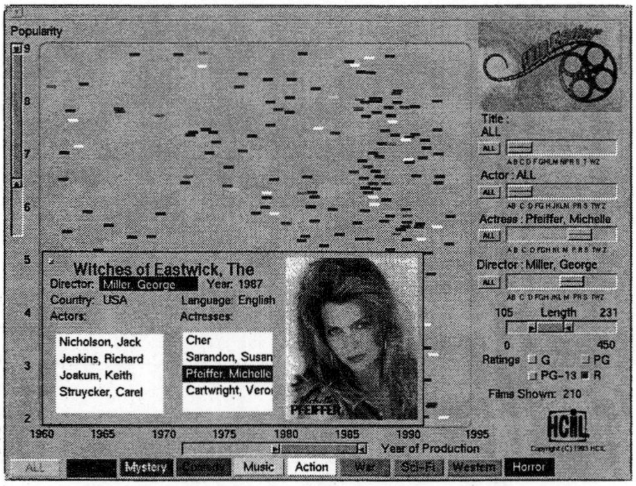

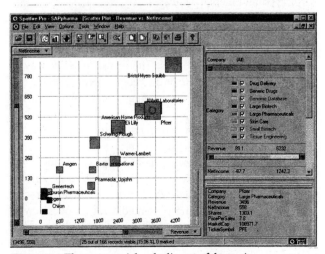

Figure 1.3 The FilmFinder prototype showed color-coded rectangles on a two-dimensional display (year on x-axis and popularity on y-axis) with range sliders and alphasliders.

Figure 1.4 The commercial embodiment of dynamic queries with starfield display became known as Spotfire (www.spotfire.com).

of understanding patterns of usage for e-commerce.

An important extension to the starfield model was to allow run-time aggregation by temporal, geographical, or categorical variables (99-31 [1.3]). For example, when users are overwhelmed by seeing a million markers indicating each store purchase during a year, they can aggregate by time, grouping all sales that occurred on the same day into one marker. Such an aggregation strategy reveals weekly cycles, seasonal patterns, and holiday events.

In developing the Baltimore Learning Community (*www.learn.umd.edu*), a Java-based visual tool for high school teachers to find educational resources, the HCIL's development team found that a simplified starfield display that had a discrete grid, rather than continuous axes, was easier to use (97-15 [4.2]). This graphical interface for digital libraries (GRIDL) is excellent for viewing databases or searching results with a few thousand items. The GRIDL interface uses color coding for media type, for example, red for videos, green for Web sites, blue for images, and yellow for texts. When 50 or more documents wind up in a grid box, GRIDL shifts to a color-coded bar graph showing the frequency counts for each type of document. The typical axes for this application are topics (Arts and Humanities, Careers, Conflicts, Geography, Religion, U.S. History, World History) and outcomes (Chronology, Civics, Cultures, Economics, Environment, Politics, Science and Technology). Other categorical axes used in this application were year (1991 to 1998) and source (Discovery Communications, National Geographic, Library of Congress, etc.). Users could control and quickly change the axes and the colorcoding.

Another extension of dynamic queries is to database searching. Users of dynamic queries are always impressed by the rapid update that comes from the use of special data structures running in local high-speed storage. But their natural question is how these ideas could be applied to search across distributed databases in a networked environment. We faced exactly that challenge in providing support for the National Aeronautics and Space Administration's (NASA) remote sensing environmental databases.

The problem they presented was that earth science researchers were frustrated by delays of several minutes for searches across NASA's networks, especially when the result set came back with zero hits. There was no easy way to determine the earliest date or the geographical coverage of a given data type or the time coverage of all polar data sets. Equally frustrating was a result set with thousands of hits, without any guidance on how to refine the query to narrow the result set.

Our solution was to use a two-step approach using query previews and query refinement (97-09, 97-20, 98-17, 2000-14 [1.4], 2001-22). Query previews use precomputed abstracted metadata tables. Users are presented with an overview of the data distribution over a small subset of attributes. They specify areas of interest by selecting rough ranges for the attributes, which updates the data distributions within 100 milliseconds. The reduced volume of the tables allows queries to be previewed and refined locally by the user before they are submitted over the network. A refinement phase follows, using a "normal" dynamic query interface with all attributes and values on a more manageable number of items.

Query previews reduce the wasted time and network delays with empty (zero hits) or overly large (megahits) result sets. The benefits to users are dramatic since they gain an overview of the data available and an understanding of its distribution, and the benefit to service providers is also substantial since server loads can be reduced. Allowing multivalued data sets (*e.g.*, some items cover multiple topics and areas) makes the implementation more difficult, which leads to the design of specialized techniques (98-17) limiting queries to ranges or limiting the review to a binary preview (merely showing if data is available or not). Finally, Egemen Tanin designed a generalized query preview architecture that eases the limitation of the number of attributes usable in query previews (2000-14 [1.4]).

Our solutions were implemented at NASA Web sites and have inspired some researchers and commercial developers to expand on this concept. The HCIL carried the concept further in the collection browser design for the Library of Congress, which influenced their American Memory Web site. Other examples of numeric counts for results sets include the Yahoo! Directory browser (*www.yahoo.com*), tools from i411 (*www.i411.com*), and the Epicurious (*www.epicurious.com*) recipe browser. Binary previews are also in use in the Global Land Cover Facilities (*glcf.umiacs.umd.edu*) and other NASA data repositories (Figure 1.5).

As we have learned in many projects, it is a long route from research innovation to successful product. Dynamic queries are showing up in research prototypes from other labs and beginning to appear in commercial tools, such as the SmartMoney Select stock market tool. Users can operate sliders to view only high-performing or low-performing stocks and select sliders for variables such as price–earnings ratios. The HCIL has worked with the U.S. Census Bureau to produce a powerful yet easy to learn tool for demographic

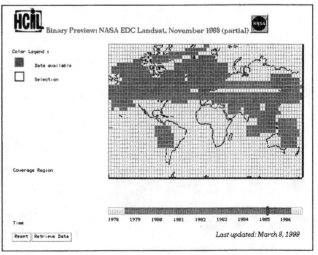

Figure 1.5 Binary previews show only if data is available or not, but are easy to implement even with multivalued attribute data.

data that could be distributed by this and other government agencies (2001-08 [1.5]). This tool is based on Dynamaps (93-21), but we had to change the name to YMaps to avoid trademark problems. Through usability testing at the U.S. Census Bureau and research studies at the HCIL, we have come to understand how novice users can be instructed and guided in their use of sliders, map selection, and starfield displays to uncover statistical patterns and outliers.

▨ ▨ ▨ ▨ ▨ ▨ ▨ ▨ ▨

FAVORITE PAPERS FROM OUR COLLEAGUES

Many researchers were creating innovative visualizations in the early 1990s. We liked the ones with dynamic aspects that gave user control to the visualizations, and we especially focused on data exploration for multidimensional data sets.

Buja, A., McDonald, J. A., Michalak, J., Stuetzle, W. Interactive Data Visualization Using Focusing and Linking, *Proc. IEEE Visualization '91* (1991), 156–163.

Chuah, Mei C., Roth, Steven F., Mattis, Joe, Kolojejchcik, John, SDM: Malleable Information Graphics, *Proc. IEEE Information Visualization '95*, IEEE Computer Press, Los Alamitos, Calif. (1995), 66–73.

Eick, Stephen G., Data Visualization Sliders, *Proc. ACM Symposium on User Interface Software and Technology* (1994), 119–120.

Feiner, S., Beshers, C., Worlds Within Worlds: Metaphors for Exploring n-Dimensional Virtual Worlds, *Proc. User Interface Software and Technology '90*, ACM, New York (1990), 76–83.

Fishkin, Ken, Stone, Maureen C., Enhanced Dynamic Queries via Movable Filters, *Proc. CHI 95 Conference: Human Factors in Computing Systems*, ACM, New York (1995), 415–420.

Goldstein, Jade, Roth, Steven F., Using Aggregation and Dynamic Queries for Exploring Large Data Sets, *Proc. CHI 95 Conference: Human Factors in Computing Systems*, ACM, New York (1995), 23–29.

Keim, D. A., Kriegal, H., VisDB: Database Exploration Using Multidimensional Visualization, *IEEE Computer Graphics and Applications* (1994), 40–49.

Korfhage, Robert, To See or Not to See—Is That the Query? *Communications of the ACM 34* (1991), 134–141.

BIBLIOGRAPHY

Shneiderman, B., The Future of Interactive Systems and the Emergence of Direct Manipulation, *Behaviour and Information Technology* 1, 3 (1982), 237–256

Shneiderman, B., A Computer Graphics System for Polynominals, *The Mathematics Teacher* 67, 2 (1974), 111–113.

Visual Information Seeking:
Tight Coupling of Dynamic Query Filters
with Starfield Displays

Christopher Ahlberg* and Ben Shneiderman
Department of Computer Science,
Human-Computer Interaction Laboratory & Institute for Systems Research
University of Maryland, College Park, MD 20742
email: ahlberg@cs.chalmers.se, ben @cs.umd.edu

ABSTRACT

This paper offers new principles for visual information seeking (VIS). A key concept is to support browsing, which is distinguished from familiar query composition and information retrieval because of its emphasis on rapid filtering to reduce result sets, progressive refinement of search parameters, continuous reformulation of goals, and visual scanning to identify results. VIS principles developed include: dynamic query filters (query parameters are rapidly adjusted with sliders, buttons, maps, etc.), starfield displays (two-dimensional scatterplots to structure result sets and zooming to reduce clutter), and tight coupling (interrelating query components to preserve display invariants and support progressive refinement combined with an emphasis on using search output to foster search input). A FilmFinder prototype using a movie database demonstrates these principles in a VIS environment.

KEYWORDS: database query, dynamic queries, information seeking, tight coupling, starfield displays

INTRODUCTION

In studying visual information seeking (VIS) systems for expert and first time users, we have found several user interface design principles that consistently lead to high levels of satisfaction. This paper defines these principles and presents a novel VIS system, the FilmFinder.

The exploration of large information spaces has remained a challenging task even as parallel hardware architectures, high-bandwidth network connections, large high-speed disks, and modern database management systems have proliferated. Indeed, these advances have left many users with the feeling that they are falling further behind and cannot cope with

the flood of information [3, 18]. Now, the user interface design principles for VIS have the potential to reduce our anxiety about the flood, find needles in haystacks, support exploratory browsing to develop intuition, find patterns and exceptions, and even make browsing fun.

The key to these principles is understanding the enormous capacity for human visual information processing. By presenting information visually and allowing dynamic user control through direct manipulation principles, it is possible to traverse large information spaces and facilitate comprehension with reduced anxiety [14,16]. In a few tenths of a second, humans can recognize features in mega-pixel displays, recall related images, and identify anomalies. Current displays of textual and numeric information can be extended to incorporate spatial displays in which related information is clustered in 2-dimensional or higher spaces. This use of proximity coding, plus color coding, size coding, animated presentations, and user-controlled selections enable users to explore large information spaces rapidly and reliably.

KEY CONCEPTS

The principles of direct manipulation were a good starting point for design of visual information seeking applications [16]:
- visual representation of the world of action including both the objects and actions
- rapid, incremental and reversible actions
- selection by pointing (not typing)
- immediate and continuous display of results

However, when designing systems especially for information seeking tasks [11], additional principles are needed. A key VIS principle is to support browsing, which is distinguished from familiar concepts of query composition and information retrieval because of its emphasis on rapid filtering to reduce result sets, progressive refinement of search parameters, continuous reformulation of goals, and visual scanning to identify results. These goals are supported by the VIS designs developed in this paper:
- dynamic query filters: query parameters are rapidly adjusted with sliders, buttons, etc.

---

* Current address: Dept. of Computer Science, Chalmers University of Technology, S-412 96 Göteborg, Sweden

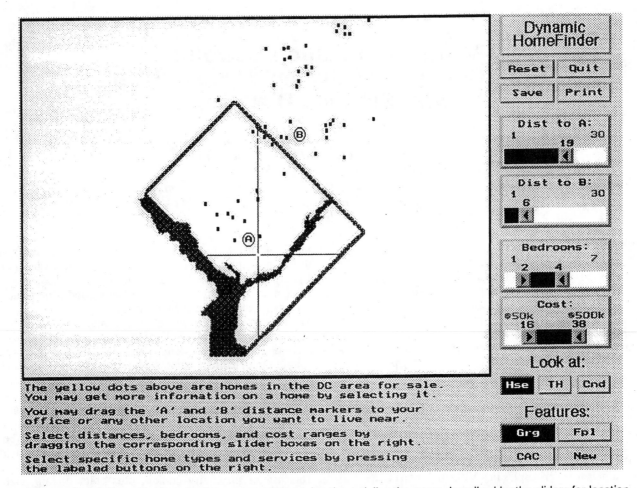

Figure 1: In the Dynamic HomeFinder query system each point satisfies the query described by the sliders for location, cost, number of bedrooms, home type (house, townhouse, or condominium), and buttons (Garage, Fireplace, Central Air Conditioning, or New construction). The points of light can be selected to generate a detailed description.

- starfield display: result sets are continuously available and support viewing of hundreds or thousands of items
- tight coupling: query components are interrelated in ways that preserve display invariants and support progressive refinement. Specifically, outputs of queries can be easily used as input to produce other queries.

Dynamic Query Filters
Our early work on dynamic queries [2, 6, 20] demonstrated dramatic performance improvements and high levels of user satisfaction. By allowing rapid, incremental and reversible changes to query parameters, often simply by dragging a slider, users were able to explore and gain feedback from displays in a few tenths of a second. For example, the Dynamic HomeFinder enabled users to adjust upper and lower bounds on home prices and see points of light on a map indicating available properties (Figure 1). This allowed users to immediately identify high or low cost communities, or find low cost homes in high-priced communities. Users could similarly adjust a slider to indicate number of bedrooms, and select toggles to indicate desire for garage, central air-conditioning, fireplace, etc.

Each of these query components (sliders, buttons, etc.) acted as a filter, reducing the number of items left in the result set. The effects were combined with simple AND logic, accounting for most naturally occurring queries. In situations where OR logic was required, users were usually quite satisfied, or actually preferred, generating a sequence of queries. This approach allowed users to see the size of the ORed components rather than merely the union of the result sets.

The work reported in this paper advances dynamic queries by demonstrating the efficacy of selection of items in alphanumeric lists with the Alphaslider [1, 12]. This query component allows users to select one item from a list of 10,000 or more, with a simple selection tool that takes little screen space, avoids use of the keyboard, and prevents typing errors.

Starfield Display
In our early work on dynamic queries the output was based on a naturally occurring spatial display. For example, the chemical table of elements was used with color highlighting of chemical names to indicate inclusion in the result set. In

the Dynamic HomeFinder, points of light on a map of Washington, DC indicated properties that matched the query components. One step in the direction of generality was to build a version of the HomeFinder that had textual output as might be found in the tuples of a relational database display. As the query components were adjusted, the display remained stable, but when the user let go of the mouse button, the screen was refreshed with the correct result set.

To further support the widespread application of dynamic queries it seemed necessary to find other approaches to visual information display [4, 5, 7, 17]. Points of light are convenient because they are small yet highly visible, could be color coded, are selectable objects, and can be displayed rapidly. But if a natural map did not exist for an application, such as a set of documents, photos, songs, etc., could we create one that would be suitable? While we need to try further examples, our initial answer is affirmative. For many situations we have been able to create meaningful two-dimensional displays by selecting ordinal attributes of the items and use them as the axes. This starfield approach is a scatterplot with additional features to support selection and zooming. Our intuitions about what choices are most effective is still rough, but there is hope that we can formalize our decisions.

For example, in a database of documents, the year the document was written might be the horizontal axis while length in words might be the vertical axis. Large old documents might be at the upper left while short new documents might be at the lower right. Other attributes such as an author assigned importance value, number of co-authors, or number of references could also be used. In a database of people, the axes might be the age, number of years of education, salary, number of children, or other demographic variables.

Tight Coupling

The principle of tight coupling of interface components began to emerge in some direct manipulation graphic user interfaces. For example, if a user saves a document, the SAVE menu item becomes grayed out until a change is made. Tight coupling helps reveal the software state, and often constrains the user from making erroneous or useless actions.

A more complex example of tight coupling is the interrelationship between the text in a word processor, the position of the thumb in the scroll bar, and the page number displayed on the window border. Moving the thumb causes the text to scroll and the page number to be updated. We could write a logical proposition describing the relationship among these three display components. Such a statement would begin by indicating that when the top of the document is displayed, the thumb is at the top of the scroll bar and the page indicator is set at 1. Good program design would ensure the preservation of the display invariants. However, some word processors may fail to preserve this invariant when sections of the document are deleted or when the document is reformatted with a larger font. To

compensate, some word processors may include a repaginate command, or update the thumb position only when it is moved. These errors violate the principle of tight coupling.

Tight coupling also applies to components of a query facility. In a well-designed facility, users should be able to see the impact of each selection while forming a query. For example, if a user specifies that they want films before 1935, then only certain actors or directors are selectable. This is to prevent users' from specifying null sets, e.g. films made before 1935 and directed by Francis Ford Coppola.

Another aspect of tight coupling is the linkage of *output-is-input* to support efficient use of screen space by eliminating the distinction between commands/queries/input and results/tables/output. In short, every output is also a candidate for input. This principle first emerged in our 1983 hypertext work [9] in which the notion of embedded menus replaced the earlier designs that had a paragraph of output followed by a menu to select further information. It seemed more logical to have highlighted words in the text and simply allow users to select those words with arrow keys, a mouse, or a touchscreen. The outputs-are-inputs principle reduced screen clutter by eliminating redundancy, and focused users' attention to a single location for gathering information and for applying an action to get more information.

This principle was applied in the chemical table of elements in which each element could be selected causing the sliders to be set to that element's values [2], in our health statistic map in which a state could be selected to retrieve its detailed data [13], and in the HomeFinder in which a point of light could be selected to retrieve detailed information or a photo, if it were available.

That database output can be used as input can be compared to functionality in spreadsheets where there is no such thing as input cells or output cells, or the Query by Example system [21] where input can be treated as output and vice versa. It has been referred to as a notion of Equal Opportunity [15]. In information retrieval systems this is useful as users can easily explore branches of a search and follow their associations as they come along -- associative database searching.

Tight coupling has several aspects:
- comprehensible and consistent affordances to guide users (highlighted words or areas, explicit handles, scrollbars, etc.).
- rapid, incremental, and reversible interactions among components.
- constraints on permissible operations to preserve *display invariants* (logical propositions relating the components, e.g. that the scroll bar thumb position constantly reflects the position in the document) and prevent errors.
- *continuous display* to always show the users some portion of the information space that they are

exploring. They begin by seeing a typical result set or item, which helps to orient them to what is possible in this information seeking environment. This seems more effective than starting with a blank screen or a form to fill in.

- *progressive refinement*, in which users can alter the parameters to get other results [18]. If the users see that there are too many items in the result set, they can reformulate their goal and seek a more restrictive value for one of the attributes.

- allow users to select *details on demand* [9]. This is the heart of hypermedia, but it applies to most designs. Instead of older query facilities which required alternation between query composition and result interpretation, our designs show results and invite further selections if details are needed. In the Dynamic HomeFinder, homes were shown as simple points of light until the user selected one of the points to get the details. This principle reduces clutter while the query is being shaped and allows users to get further information when they need it.

FILMFINDER DESIGN

To test these principles of visual information, we created a tool for exploring a film database, the FilmFinder. Watching a film is often a social activity so this tool was designed to encourage discussions and make the decision process easier for groups of viewers. Existing tools for learning about films include encyclopedias, such as *Leonard Maltin's Movie and Video Guide* [10]. They typically provide an alphabetic organization, with additional indexes, but these are difficult to use. Recently, computer-based encyclopedias such as Microsoft's Cinemania have appeared on the market. Although some of them employ novel approaches such as hypertext links they still do not provide users with an overview of the data. They employ a traditional approach to database queries with commands or form fill-in, and then provide a textual response in the form of scrolling lists. If the users are unhappy with the result, they compose a new query and wait for the new result. Progressive refinement can take dozens of steps and many minutes.

Before designing the tool, informal interviews were conducted with video store clerks and film aficionados. The FilmFinder [Color plate 1] tries to overcome search problems by applying dynamic queries, a starfield display, and tight coupling among components. Dynamic queries were applied by having a double box range selector to specify film length in minutes, by having buttons for ratings (G, PG, PG-13, R), large color coded buttons for film categories (drama, action, comedy, etc.), and our novel Alphasliders for film titles, actors, actresses, and directors.

The query result in the FilmFinder is continuously represented in a starfield display [Color plate 1]. The X-axis represents time and the Y-axis a measure of popularity. The FilmFinder allows users to zoom into a particular part of the time-popularity space [Color plate 2]. As users zoom in the colored spots representing films grow larger, giving the

impression of flying in closer to the films. The labels on the axes are also automatically updated as zooming occurs. When fewer than 25 films are visible, their titles are automatically displayed.

To obtain more information about a particular element of the query results, users click on that element, getting desired details-on-demand [Color plate 3]. An information card which provides more information about attributes such as actors, actresses, director and language, is displayed. In a traditional retrieval system users would obtain more information by starting a new query. In the FilmFinder users can select highlighted attributes on the information card and thereby set the value of the corresponding Alphaslider to the value of that attribute. This forms the starting point for the next query and allows graceful and rapid exploration with no fear of error messages.

Tight coupling is strongly supported in the FilmFinder. When users select categories of movies using the category toggles, the starfield display and the query ranges of the Alphasliders are immediately updated [Color plate 2]. This effectively eliminates empty and invalid query results. The same is possible when users zoom into a particular part in the search space -- only those films that appear during that range of years and are in the particular popularity range will be part of the Alphaslider query range. The Alphasliders can even affect each other, selecting Ingmar Bergman on the Director slider would set the Actor slider to only operate over those actors who appear in Ingmar Bergman's movies. This interaction between the query widgets, and the possibility to use query results as input, creates a tightly coupled environment where information can be explored in a rapid, safe, and comprehensible manner.

FILMFINDER SCENARIO

Tools like the FilmFinder might be found in video stores, libraries, and homes - they might even come as a part of standard television sets. Imagine the Johnson family sitting down at their TV Saturday night to watch a movie that they all like. They turn on the TV and are presented with a FilmFinder's starfield visualization and a number of controls [Color plate 1]. All controls are operable by a wireless mouse and no keyboard is needed.

The family members don't have a specific film in mind, but they know that they want to see something popular and recent. After some discussion they agree on the categories for a search: drama, mystery, comedy, or an action film. To cut down the number of films further they select an actor that they all like, in this case Sean Connery. Observe in [Color plate 2] how the category toggles have been manipulated - and the Alphaslider indexes updated to contain appropriate values, the visualization has zoomed into the correct part of the information space, and Sean Connery has been selected with the Actor slider.

Now the number of films in the starfield has been cut down from about 2000 to 25 and the Johnsons decide to look further at *The Murder on the Orient Express*. They select it with their remote control and are presented with an information card [Color plate 3]. The description and image remind the Johnsons that they have already seen this film, so the information card can now become the tool to further refine their search.

Mr. Johnson sees Anthony Perkins' name and decides he wants to see a movie starring Anthony Perkins, while Mrs. Johnson wants to see a movie with Ingrid Bergman. To resolve the disagreement they select both actors in the information card, and the selection is reflected in the Alphaslider settings. When the information card is closed, the query result is updated and the Johnsons are presented with one movie with both Anthony Perkins and Ingrid Bergman which they decide to watch [Color plate 4].

FUTURE WORK

The dynamic queries approach has much to recommend it, but it must be extended to deal with larger databases, more varied kinds of information, and a greater range of query types. Current dynamic queries do not satisfy the demands of relational completeness, but they offer other features that depend on spatial output that are not available in existing relational databases. It appears productive to combine the strengths of both approaches.

When searching films - as well as for other information - it would be desirable to incorporate fuzzy searching to find similar films. To include such functionality in the FilmFinder would probably be desirable - but first algorithms must be devised and more importantly, the issue of to what extent the mechanisms should be user controlled must be examined.

When browsing the information space by zooming, it is important that this is done smoothly so users get a feeling of flying through the data. New algorithms and data structures are necessary to support the smooth flying through the data. A natural extension would be to add a third dimension so that some films would appear closer than others.

The tight coupling among query components in the FilmFinder was helpful - but there may be cases when such interrelationships not are desirable. Formal specification of the logical propositions for display invariants is a useful direction, because it could lead to proofs of correctness and advanced tools to build such interfaces rapidly.

REFERENCES

1. Ahlberg, C. and Shneiderman, B., 1993. The Alphaslider: A rapid and compact selector, *Proc. ACM CHI'94 Conference*.
2. Ahlberg, C., Williamson, C., and Shneiderman, B., 1992. Dynamic queries for information exploration: An implementation and evaluation, *Proc. ACM CHI'92 Conference*, 619-626.
3. Borgman, C. L., 1986. Why are online catalogs hard to use? Lessons learned from information-retrieval studies, *Journal of the American Society for Information Science 37*, 6, 387-400.
4. Buja, A., McDonald, J. A., Michalak, J., Stuetzle, W., 1991. Interactive data visualization using focusing and linking, *Proc. IEEE Visualization '91*, 156-163.
5. Egenhofer, M.; 1990. Manipulating the graphical representation of query results in Geographic Information Systems, *1990 IEEE Workshop on Visual Languages*, IEEE Computer Society Press, Los Alamitos, CA, 119-124.
6. Eick, Steven, 1993. Data visualization sliders, AT&T Bell Laboratories Report, Napervillie, IL.
7. Feiner, S. and Beshers, C., 1990. Worlds within worlds: Metaphors for exploring n-dimensional virtual worlds, *Proc. User Interface Software and Technology '90*, ACM, New York, NY, 76-83.
8. Koved, L. and Shneiderman, B. 1986. Embedded menus: Selecting items in context, *Comm. of the ACM 29*, 4 (April 1986), 312-318.
9. Kreitzberg, Charles B., Details on Demand: Hypertext models for coping with information overload, in Dillon, Martin (Editor), *Interfaces for Information Retrieval and Online Systems*, Greenwood Press, New York, 1991, 169-176.
10. Maltin, L., 1993. *Leonard Maltin's Movie and Video Guide*, Penguin Books, New York.
11. Marchionini, G., 1993. *Information Seeking*, Cambridge Univ. Press, Cambridge, UK.
12. Osada, M., Liao, H., Shneiderman, B., Alphaslider: searching textual lists with sliders, *Proc. of the Ninth Annual Japanese Conf. on Human Interface*, Oct. 1993.
13. Plaisant, C., 1993. Dynamic queries on a health statistics atlas, Forthcoming Technical Report, Human-Computer Interaction Laboratory, University of Maryland, College Park, MD.
14. Robertson, G. G., Card, S. K., and Mackinlay, J. D., 1993. Information visualization using 3-D interactive animation, *Comm. of the ACM 36*, 4, 56-71.
15. Runciman, C. and Thimbleby, H., 1986. Equal opportunity interactive systems, *Int'l Journal of Man-Machine Studies 25* (4), 439-51.
16. Shneiderman, B., *Designing the User Interface: Strategies for Effective Human-Computer Interaction: Second Edition*, Addison-Wesley Publ. Co., Reading, MA (1992), 573 pages.
17. Singers, R., Endres, L., 1993, Metaphoric abstraction, the starfield and complex systems, in preparation, Johnson Controls, Milwaukee, WI.17. Welty, C., 1985. Correcting user errors in SQL, *Int'l Journal of Man-Machine Studies 22*, 463-477.
18. Welty, C., 1985. Correcting user errors in SQL, *Int' Journal of Man-Machine Studies 22*, 463-477.
19. Williams, M., 1984. What make RABBIT run? *Int'l Journal of Man-Machine Studies 21*, 333-352.
20. Williamson, C. and Shneiderman, B., 1992. The Dynamic HomeFinder: Evaluating dynamic queries in a real-estate information exploration system, *Proc. ACM SIGIR Conference*, 339-346.
21. Zloof M. Query-by-Example, *National Computer Conference*, AFIPS Press (1975), 431-437.

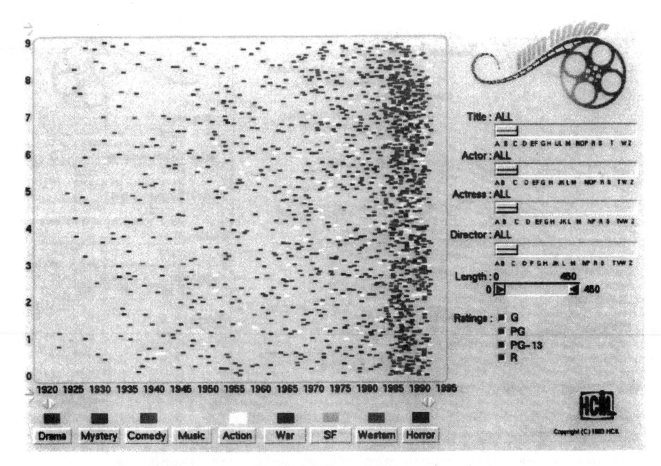

Ahlberg & Shneiderman, Color plate 1. The FilmFinder.

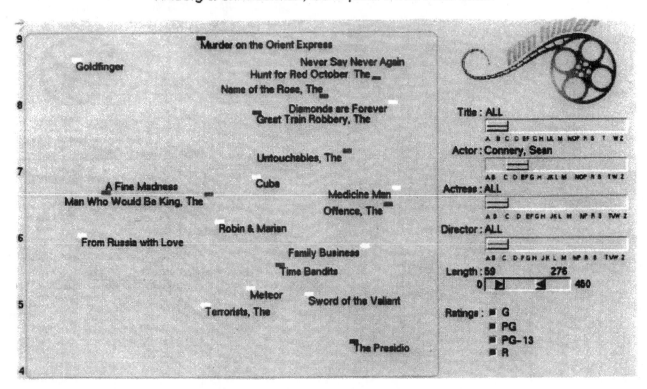

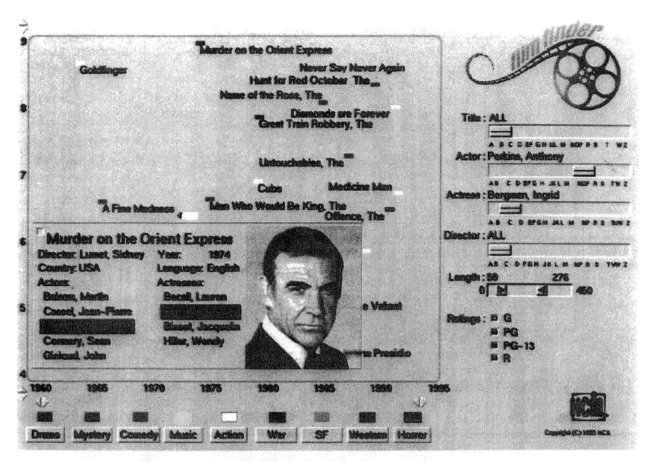

Ahlberg & Shneiderman, Color plate 3. Anthony Perkins and Ingrid Bergman has been selected in the information card - which is reflected in the Alphasliders.

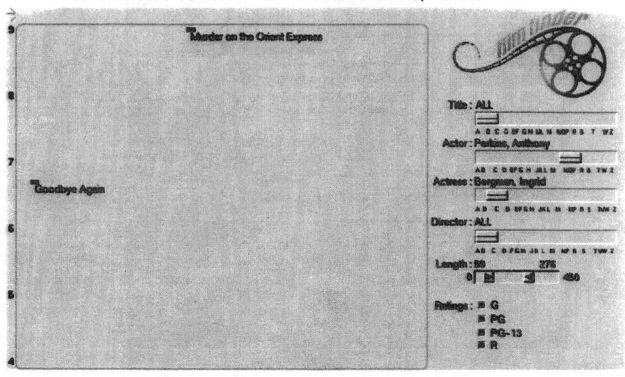

DYNAMIC QUERIES FOR VISUAL INFORMATION SEEKING

Dynamic queries let users "fly through" databases by adjusting widgets and viewing the animated results. In studies, users reacted to this approach with an enthusiasm more commonly associated with video games. Adoption requires research into retrieval and display algorithms and user-interface design.

The purpose of computing is insight, not numbers. — Richard Hamming, 1962

BEN SHNEIDERMAN
University of Maryland
at College Park

Some innovations restructure the way people think and work. My experience with dynamic-query interfaces suggests that they are dramatically different from existing database-query methods. Dynamic queries continuously update search results — within 100 milliseconds — as users adjust sliders or select buttons to ask simple questions of fact or to find patterns or exceptions. To accomplish this, the dynamic-query approach applies the principles of direct manipulation to the database environment:[1]

♦ visual presentation of the query's components;

♦ visual presentation of results;

♦ rapid, incremental, and reversible control of the query;

♦ selection by pointing, not typing; and

♦ immediate and continuous feedback.

In short, a dynamic query involves the interactive control by a user of visual query parameters that generate a rapid (100 ms update), animated, visual display of database search results. (This use of the term "dynamic queries" is not the same as a dynamic query in Structured Query Language, which is posted at runtime instead of compile time.)

Although languages like SQL have become standard and form-based interfaces widespread, dynamic queries can empower users to perform far more complex searches by using visual search strategies. The enthusiasm users have for dynamic queries emanates from the sense of control they gain over the database. They can quickly perceive patterns in data, "fly through" data by adjusting sliders,[2] and rapidly generate new queries based on what they discover through incidental learning.

By contrast, typing a command in a keyword-oriented language usually generates a tabular list of tuples containing alphanumeric fields. This traditional approach is appropriate for many tasks, but formulating queries by direct manipulation and displaying the results graphically has many advantages, for both novices and experts.

For novices, learning to formulate queries in a command language may take several hours, and even then they will still likely generate many errors in syntax and semantics. In contrast, visual information-seeking methods can help novices formulate queries, and presenting graphical results in context, such as on a map,[3] can aid comprehension.

Experts may benefit even more from visual interfaces because they will be able to formulate more complex queries and interpret intricate results. Air-traffic control could hardly be imagined without a graphical display, for example. Visual displays also help users deal with the extreme complexity inherent in applications like network management. And statisticians, demographers, and sociologists, who deal with large multidimensional databases, can explore and discover relationships more easily using dynamic queries.[4,5]

EXAMPLES

An abundance of applications would benefit from this approach: Those with geographic aspects include travel agencies, hotels and resorts, and college selection; science or engineering applications include electronic circuits, networks, satellite coverage, and astronomy guides. Another likely candidate is a calendar or time-line application that shows events (concerts, meetings, conferences) selected by cost, priority rankings, or distance from home.

Geographic. Geographic applications are natural candidates for dynamic queries. Figure 1 shows the interface of a system that lets real estate brokers and their clients find homes by using a slider to adjust for things like price, number of bedrooms, and distance from work.[6] Each of 1,100 homes appears as a point of light on a map of Washington, DC. Users can explore the database to find neighborhoods with high or low prices by moving a slider and watching where the points of light appear. They can mark where they and their spouse work and adjust the sliders on a distance bar to generate intersecting circles of acceptable homes.

We conducted an empirical study of the HomeFinder using 18 psychology undergraduates to compare dynamic queries to natural-language queries (Symantec's Q&A) of the same database and to a 10-page paper listing of the same real estate data. We found that dynamic queries offered statistically significant speed advantages over either alternative for the three most difficult tasks, as Figure 2 shows. Subjective ratings of satisfaction dramatically favored dynamic queries. One subject using dynamic queries said, "I don't want to stop, this is fun!"

Another geographic application we built highlights entire US states that have cancer rates above a specified value, as shown in Figure 3.[7] Users can explore the database by selecting a year or by adjusting sliders for per capita income, college education, and smoking habits. The rapid change in

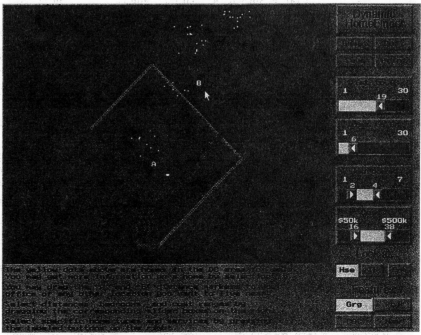

Figure 1. The DC HomeFinder dynamic-query system lets users adjust the sliders for location, cost, number of bedrooms, home type (house, townhouse, or condominium), and features. The results are shown as points of light that can be selected to generate a detailed description at the bottom of the screen.

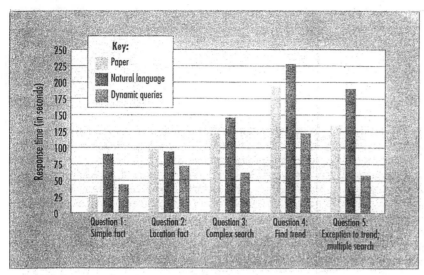

Figure 2. Means for response times of 18 subjects to five queries with paper, natural-language, and DC HomeFinder dynamic-queries interfaces. The results show an advantage for the dynamic-queries interface as query complexity increased.

colors, accomplished with color indexing on the palette, lets users detect changes in cancer rates over time and in correlation with demographic variables. The US National Center for Health Statistics is distributing an extended version of this system to its statisticians.

Education. One educational application is an element table, shown in Figure 4, that has sliders for atomic mass, atomic number, atomic radius, ionic radius, ionization energy, and electronegativity.[8] Students can refine their intuitions about the relationships among these properties and the atomic number or table position of the highlighted elements.

We evaluated this application against a form-based query interface with a graphical output and a form-based interface with a textual output. The results for several research tasks are shown in Figure 5. The 18 chemistry students achieved much faster performance using dynamic queries.

Alphanumeric. When there are no natural graphical displays for the output, dynamic queries can display result sets in a traditional alphanumeric tabular display. Figure 6 shows an example. In this application, the program creates the sliders and buttons semiautomatically, depending on the values in the imported ASCII database. As the users adjust the sliders with a mouse, the result bar on the bottom changes to indicate how many items remain in the result set, but the tabular display changes only when the user releases the mouse button. We adopted this policy to avoid the distraction of a frequently refreshed display.

Figure 7 shows another tabular display for a dynamic query system. This one lets users explore Unix directories.[9] Sliders for file size (in kilobytes) and age (in days) let users answer 10 questions, such as "How many files are younger than umcp_tai?" The results were displayed in standard long-directory display format.

We built three versions of the program and tested them on 18 users. The versions explored showing the results by

♦ highlighting matches with color,
♦ highlighting matches with asterisks on the same line, and
♦ displaying only the matching lines (that is, delete nonmatching files from the display).

The third approach, called expand/contract, was distracting if updates were made as the slider was being moved, so the displays were refreshed only when users stopped moving the sliders and released the mouse button. In five of the tasks there was a statistically significant speed advantage for the expand/contract interface. This result occurred only with medium-sized directories of

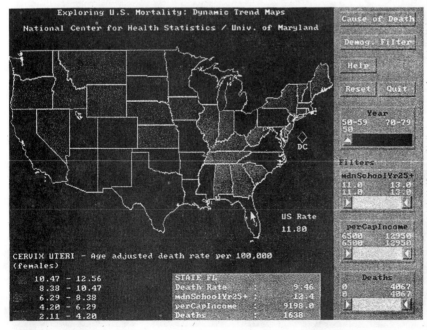

Figure 3. This dynamic query shows cervical cancer rates from 1950 to 1970 in each state. Adjustments can be made to the year and state demographic variables such as the percentage of college education, per capita income, and percent smokers.

approximately 60 entries (two screens), and not with smaller, one-screen directories. The benefits of expand/ contract seem likely to grow as the directory size increases. These results help us develop guidelines and theories about how to design displays for dynamic queries.

ADVANTAGES

The dynamic query approach lets users rapidly, safely, and even playfully explore a database. They can quickly discover which sections of a multidimensional search space are densely populated and which are sparsely populated, where there are clusters, exceptions, gaps, or outliers, and what trends ordinal data reveal. Overviews like these, the ability to explore, and the capacity to rapidly specify known-item queries makes dynamic queries very appealing for certain problems.

For data in which there is a known relationship among variables, the dynamic queries interface is useful for training and education by exploration. For situations in which there are understood correlations, but their complexity makes it difficult for non-experts to follow, dynamic queries can allow a wider range of people to explore the interactions (among health and demographic variables, a table of elements, and economic or market data, for example). Finally, where there is so much data that even experts have not sorted out the correlations, dynamic queries may help users discover patterns, form and test hypotheses, identify ex-ceptions, segment data, or prepare figures for reports.

DISADVANTAGES

The dynamic query approach is poorly matched with current hardware and software systems. First, current database-management tools cannot easily satisfy these requirements for rapid searches, and rapid graphical dis-

play methods are not widely available. Therefore, we are exploring which data structures and algorithms can accommodate large data sets and permit rapid access.[10]

Second, application-specific programming is necessary to take best advantage of dynamic query methods. We have developed some tools, but they still require data conversion and possibly some programming. Standardized input and output plus software toolkits would make dynamic queries easier to integrate into existing database and information systems.

Alternatively, dynamic queries could be generated by user-interface builders or user-interface management systems.

Third, current dynamic query approaches can implement only simple queries that are conjunctions of disjunctions, plus range queries on numeric values. Our filter/flow metaphor,[11] diagramed in Figure 8, offers one approach to providing full Boolean functionality. In Figure 8, users can select from the set of attributes and get an appropriate filter widget (type-in for interest areas, sliders for cost, and buttons for scholarships)

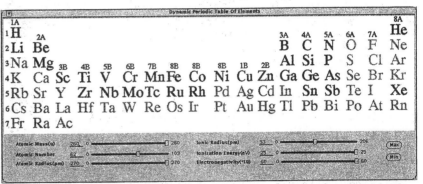

Figure 4. The chemical table of elements makes a natural visual display for information on chemical properties. Chemicals matching the query are shown in red. Runs and jumps are apparent.

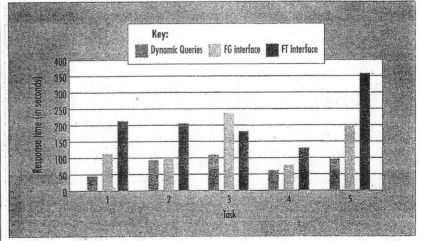

Figure 5. Mean response times for 18 subjects performing five tasks with the dynamic queries, form fill-in plus graphic output (FG), and form fill-in with tabular output (FT). The results strongly favor the dynamic-queries interface.

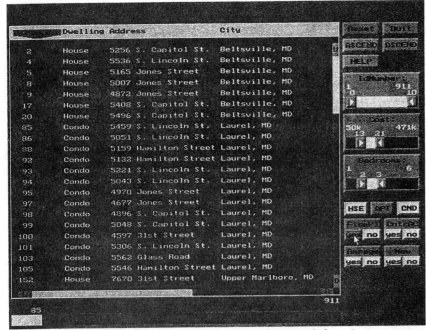

Figure 6. Even when there is no natural graphic framework for a dynamic query display, the method can be used with tabular alphanumeric output. As users adjust the sliders and buttons for the query, the result bar along the bottom indicates how many items match. When users stop moving the sliders and let go of the mouse button, the tabular display is rewritten.

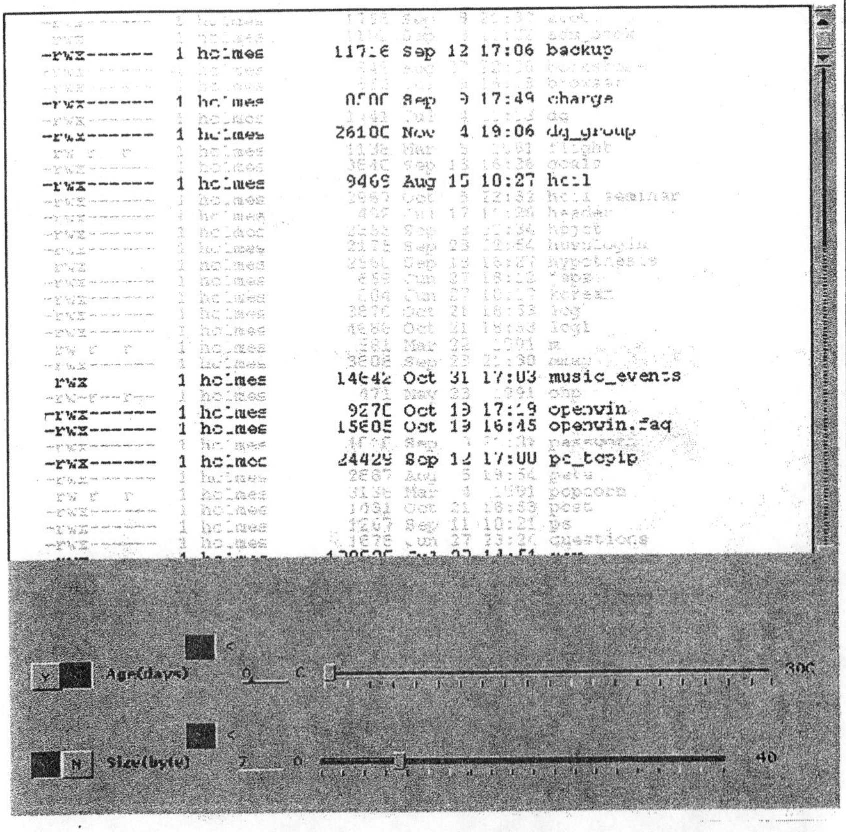

Figure 7. The standard long-format tabular display is the framework for Unix directory exploration. The sliders, built with Sun DevGuide, allow selections to be made on the age (in days) and size (in kilobytes) of files. We compare color high-lighting and expand/contract methods of display in an exploratory study.

which is placed on the screen with flow lines showing Ands (sequential flow) and Ors (parallel flows). The X in each filter widget could be selected to negate the filter values. Clustering of one-in-one-out segments to form a new and saveable filter is possible. This approach was shown to be statistically significantly more effective than SQL for composing and comprehending queries, but the prototype must still be refined and implemented within a database-management system. More elaborate queries (group by, set matching, universal quantification, transitive closure, string matching) are still research-and-development problems.

Fourth, visually handicapped and blind users will have a more difficult time with our widgets and outputs, but we are exploring audio feedback to accommodate these users as well.

RESEARCH DIRECTIONS

Our initial implementations have generated enthusiasm, but we are more aware of challenges than successes. There are rich research opportunities in database and display algorithms and user-interface design.

Database and display algorithms. Because rapid display updates are essential, algorithms to store and retrieve multidimensional information need refinement. For small databases that fit in main memory, we have experimented with array indexing, grid structures, quad trees, and k-d trees. We found linear array structures with pointers to be effective with small databases, but their inefficient use of storage limited the size of the databases they could handle. Grid file structures are efficient with uniform distributions, while the quad and k-d trees became more attractive as the distributions became more skewed.[10]

For larger databases, alternatives include R-trees, grid files, multiple B-trees, and reduced combined indices.

Treating inserts and deletes to stored information separately simplifies the design of efficient data structures.

The dynamic-query approach always displays the current query result. Each new query is a slightly enlarged or contracted version of the current query. In this case, special data structures kept largely in high-speed storage and algorithms might allow rapid updates. We believe an effective strategy is to organize data in "buckets" along each dimension. The size of the bucket is adjusted to the granularity of the slider mechanism. For example, if the slider has 100 positions for a field whose range is 1 to 50,000, the data should be organized into 100 buckets, each covering 500 points on the field. As the slider increases the selected set, buckets can be appended; as it decreases the selected set, buckets can be removed. With three dimensions of 100 buckets each, the database is conveniently broken into 1 million buckets, which can be stored and retrieved efficiently.

Also important are data-compression methods that will allow larger databases to fit in 32- Mbyte or smaller address spaces. Alternatively, dynamic queries could use parallel hardware and algorithms that search multiple storage spaces.

Screen-management algorithms also play an important role, and we expect that new algorithms will become an alternative to more expensive hardware. For example, it is often more effective to merely repaint the areas or points that have changed when a slider is moved or a button depressed, instead of repainting the entire display. Our early efforts suggest that in some cases manipulating the palette by color indexing may be an effective way to rapidly change irregularly shaped regions, even on popular personal computers.[7]

User-interface design. Humans can recognize the spatial configuration of elements in a picture and notice relationships among elements quickly.

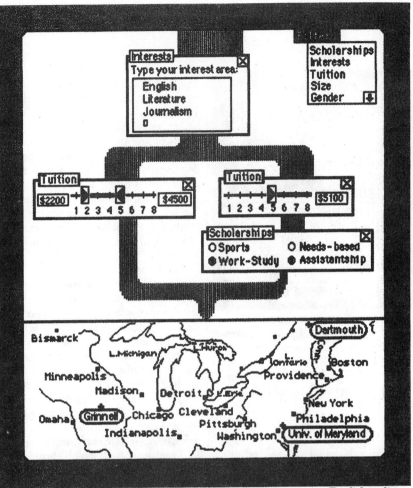

Figure 8. *A mock-up of a filter/flow Boolean query ((Interests = English or literature or journalism) and ((tuition greater than or equal to $2,200 or less than or equal to $4,500) or ((tuition greater than or equal to $5,100) and (scholarships are available by work-Study or assistantship)))) combined with map output to show the result (Dartmouth, Grinnell, and the University of Maryland).*

This highly developed visual system means people can grasp the content of a picture much faster than they can scan and understand text.

Interface designers can capitalize on this by shifting some of the cognitive load of information retrieval to the perceptual system. By appropriately coding properties by size, position, shape, and color, we can greatly reduce the need for explicit selection, sorting, and scanning operations. However, our understanding of when and how to apply these methods is poor; basic research is needed. Although our initial results are encouraging, there are many unanswered user-interface design questions. How can we

♦ design widgets to specify multiple ranges of values, such as 14 to 16 or 21 to 25?

♦ let users express Boolean combinations of slider settings?

♦ choose among highlighting by color, points of light, regions, and blinking?

♦ allow varying degrees of intensity in the visual feedback?

♦ cope with thousands of points or areas by zooming?

♦ weight criteria?

♦ select a set of sliders from a large set of attributes?

♦ provide "grand tours" to automatically view all dimensions?

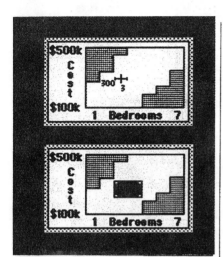

Figure 9. Two prototype two-dimensional widgets. (A) A point indicating the number of bedrooms (three) and cost of a home ($220,000) with a single selection. (B) A range of bedrooms (three to four) and cost ($130,000 to $260,000).

♦ include sound as a redundant or unique coding?

♦ support multidimensional input?

Display issues. We must reexamine basic research on color, sound, size, and shape coding in the context of dynamic queries. Of primary interest are the graphical display properties of color (hue, saturation, brightness), texture, shape, border, and blinking. Color is the most effective visual display property, and it can be an important aid to fast and accurate decision making.[12] Auditory properties may be useful in certain circumstances (for example, lower frequency sounds associated with large values; higher frequency with small values), especially as redundant reinforcement feedback.

We understand that rapid, smooth screen changes are essential for the perception of patterns, but we would like to develop more precise requirements to guide designers. In our experience, delays of more than two- to three-tenths of a second are distract-ing, but precise requirements with a range of situations and users would be helpful.

In geographic applications, sometimes points on a map are a natural choice, but other applications require overlapping areas. Points and areas can be on or off (in which case monochrome displays may be adequate), but we believe that color coding may convey more information. Texture, shape, and sound coding also have appeal.

Other issues emerge when we cannot identify a natural two-dimensional representation of the data. Of course we can always use a textual representation. Another possibility is a two-dimensional space, such as a scattergram. Instead of showing homes as points of light on a city map, they could be points of light on a graph whose axes are the age of the house and its price. We could still use sliders for number of bedrooms, quality of schools, real estate taxes, and so on.

Tree maps — two-dimensional mosaics of rectangular areas — are another way to visualize large amounts of hierarchical information. For example, we built a business application that visualized sales data for a complete product hierarchy, color-coded by profitability and size-coded by revenue.[13] Twelve professional users in our usability study could rapidly determine the state of financial affairs — large red regions indicate trouble and blue areas signal success. A slider let them observe quickly the changes to the tree map over time to spot trends or problems.

Input issues. Widget design is a central issue. Even in our early explorations we were surprised that none of the existing user-interface-management systems contained a double-boxed slider for the specification of a range (more than $70,000, less than $130,000). In creating such a slider we discovered how many design decisions and possibilities there were. In addition to dragging the boxes, we had to contend with jumps, limits, display of current values, what to do when the boxes were pushed against each other, choice of colors, possible use of sound, and so on.

We also came to realize that existing widgets are poorly matched with the needs of expert users, who are comfortable with multidimensional browsing. Two-dimensional input widgets to select two values at once are not part of any standard widget set that we have reviewed, so we created the one shown in Figure 9. Using a single widget means that only one selection is required to set two values and that correct selections can be guaranteed. In Figure 9, for example, the dotted areas indicate impossible selections (the cheapest seven-bedroom house is $310,000).

Input widgets that can handle three or more dimensions may facilitate the exploration of complex relationships. Current approaches for high-dimensional input and feedback are clumsy, but research with novel devices such as data gloves and a 3D mouse may uncover effective methods. With a 3D mouse, users lift the mouse off the desk and move it as a child moves a toy airplane.[14] The mouse system continuously outputs the six parameters (six degrees of freedom) that define its linear and angular position with respect to a fixed coordinate system in space.

Designers can decompose the rotation motion of the mouse into the combination of .

♦ a rotation around the handle of the mouse and

♦ a change in the direction the handle is pointing.

When the mouse is held as a pointer, the rotation around the handle is created by a twist of the arm, and it may be natural to users to make the same twisting motion to increase the level of a database parameter as they would to increase the volume of a car radio. Changing the pointing direction of the mouse handle is done by the same wrist flexion that a lecturer would use to change the orientation of a laser pointer to point at another part of the conference screen. It may then also feel natural to users to imagine the planar space of two database parameters as vertical in front of them and point at specific parts by flexing their wrist up, down, and sideways.

For example, sophisticated users could perform a dynamic query of the periodic table of elements using the 3D mouse. They would find elements of larger atomic mass by translating the mouse upward; for larger atomic numbers they would move to the right; for larger ionization energies they would move toward the display; for larger atomic radius they would bend their wrist up; for larger ionic radius they would bend their wrist to the right; for larger electronegativity they would twist their arm clockwise. Sliders should probably still be present on the screen, but would move by themselves and give feedback on parameter values.

Another input issue is how to specify alphanumeric fields. Although a simple type-in dialog box is possible, more fluid ways of roaming through the range of values is helpful. To this end we developed an *alphaslider* to let users quickly sweep through a set of items like the days of the week or the 6,000 actor names in a movie database.[15]

Dynamic queries are a lively new direction for database querying. Many problems that are difficult to deal with using a keyword-oriented command language become tractable with dynamic queries. Computers are now fast enough to apply a direct-manipulation approach on modest-sized problems and still ensure an update time of under 100 ms. The challenge now is to broaden the spectrum of applications by improving user-interface design, search speed, and data compression. ◆

ACKNOWLEDGMENTS

I thank Christopher Ahlberg, Christopher Williamson, Holmes Liao, Boon-Teck Kuah, and Vinit Jain for implementing these ideas in a way that was even better than I anticipated. Kent Norman and Catherine Plaisant made important contributions to the work and this article. This research is supported by Johnson Controls, the National Center for Health Statistics, NCR Corporation, Sun Microsystems, and Toshiba.

REFERENCES

1. B. Shneiderman, "Direct Manipulation: A Step Beyond Programming Languages," *Computer*, Aug. 1983, pp. 57-69.
2. S. Eick, "Data Visualization Sliders," tech. report, AT&T Bell Laboratories, Napervillie, Ill., 1993.
3. M. Egenhofer, "Manipulating the Graphical Representation of Query Results in Geographic Information Systems," *Proc. IEEE Workshop on Visual Languages*, IEEE CS Press, Los Alamitos, Calif., 1990, pp. 119-124.
4. R.A. Becker and W.S. Cleveland, "Brushing Scatterplots," *Technometrics*, No. 2, 1987, pp. 127-142.
5. A. Buja et al., "Interactive Data Visualization Using Focusing and Linking," *Proc. IEEE Visualization*, IEEE Press, New York, 1991, pp. 156-163.
6. C. Williamson and B. Shneiderman, "The Dynamic HomeFinder: Evaluating Dynamic Queries in a Real-Estate Information Exploration System," *Proc. SIGIR Conf.*, ACM Press, New York, 1983, pp. 339-346.
7. C. Plaisant, "Dynamic Queries on a Health Statistics Map," *Proc. Conf. American Statistical Assoc.*, American Statistical Assoc., Alexandria, Va., 1993, pp. 18-23.
8. C. Ahlberg, C. Williamson, and B. Shneiderman, "Dynamic Queries for Information Exploration: An Implementation and Evaluation," *Proc. CHI Conf.*, ACM Press, New York, 1992, pp. 619-626.
9. H. Liao, M. Osada, and B. Shneiderman, "Browsing Unix Directories with Dynamic Queries: An Analytical and Experimental Evaluation," *Proc. Ninth Japanese Symp. Human Interface*, Society of Instrument and Control Engineers, Japan, 1993, pp. 95-98.
10. V. Jain and B. Shneiderman, "Data Structures for Dynamic Queries: An Analytical and Experimental Evaluation," *Proc. Advanced Visual Interfaces Conf.*, ACM Press, New York, 1994, to appear.
11. D. Young and B. Shneiderman, "A Graphical Filter/Flow Model for Boolean Queries: An Implementation and Experiment," *J. American Society for Information Science*, July 1993, pp. 327-339.
12. A. Marcus, *Graphic Design for Electronic Documents and User Interfaces*, ACM Press, New York, 1991.
13. B. Johnson and B. Shneiderman, "Tree-Maps: A Space-Filling Approach to the Visualization of Hierarchical Information Structures," *Proc. IEEE Visualization*, IEEE Press, New York, 1991, pp. 284-291.
14. S. Feiner and C. Beshers, "Worlds Within Worlds: Metaphors for Exploring N-Dimensional Virtual Worlds," *Proc. UserInterface Software and Technology Conf.*, ACM Press, New York, 1990, pp. 76-83.
15. C. Ahlberg and B. Shneiderman, "Alphaslider: A Rapid and Compact Selector," *Proc. CHI Conf.*, ACM Press, New York, 1994.

Temporal, Geographical and Categorical Aggregations Viewed through Coordinated Displays: A Case Study with Highway Incident Data

Anna Fredrikson, Chris North, Catherine Plaisant; Ben Shneiderman

Human-Computer Interaction Laboratory, University of Maryland
UMIACS, A.V. Williams Bldg, College Park MD 20742
http://www.cs.umd.edu/hcil
(main contact: plaisant@cs.umd.edu)

ABSTRACT

Information visualization displays can hold a limited number of data points, typically a few thousand, before they get crowded. One way to solve this problem with larger data sets is to create aggregates. Aggregations were used together with the Snap-Together Visualization system to coordinate the visual displays of aggregates and their content. If two displays each hold one thousand items then rapid access and visibility can be maintained for a million points. This paper presents examples based on a database of highway incident data.

1- INTRODUCTION

An information visualization display can hold a limited amount of data points, typically a few thousand, before it gets crowded. One way to accommodate larger data sets is to create aggregates. An aggregate is a single item that represents or summarizes a group of data points. Aggregates simplify the display because fewer markers are needed and users can understand overall patterns and select the details that are relevant to their tasks. Aggregations were used together with the Snap-Together Visualization system to coordinate the visual displays of aggregates and their details. This paper presents a case study with incident data from Maryland highways in which aggregation and coordinated displays were used.

2- SNAP TOGETHER VISUALIZATION

Snap-Together Visualization (Snap) [NS99] enables users to explore their data by rapidly constructing their own coordinated displays. Users choose the set of component visualizations they need and specify the coordination between them as appropriate for their tasks. This allows users to mix and match visualizations and coordinations to their liking, without programming. Then, these customized displays maximize users⌣ capability to explore, understand, and discover phenomena in their data.

Snap⌣s coordination model is based on the relational database model. First, users load and display individual relations in visualizations. Then, they coordinate the visualizations based on the join relationships between the relations.

With Snap, users can create many different types of coordinations between visualizations. For example, the *brushing-and-linking* coordination enables users to identify corresponding data items between views. When users select and highlight an item in one view, the corresponding item is also highlighted in the other view. The *synchronized-scrolling* coordination enables users to easily scroll through two corresponding lists of data items simultaneously.

This paper focuses on using Snap for the *drill-down* coordination. This enables users to navigate from aggregates in one view to aggregate details in another view (one-to-many joins).

3- AGGREGATIONS

Aggregates are groups of data points that are used as summarization. They can be formed as a result of decomposition or aggregation [GR94]. The aggregates are used in the visualization instead of all the data points to simplify the display. There are a variety of aggregates, but our experience has been that the most common are geographical, temporal, and categorical. The aggregates have data characterizations that are derived from the data characterization of the elements, and they can be defined in advance in the database or specified when needed (··on the fly″ or ··just-in-time″).

In traditional databases, aggregation is specified as a query with a group function that is submitted to the system. The system processes a large volume of data and delivers the answer. Online aggregation [HHW97] is a new interaction interface that lets users observe the progress of the aggregate query execution and to control it when needed. Another tool for aggregates is Aggregation Eye [Moc98], which is used for manipulating the extent of an aggregate dynamically. Visage [GR94] takes a completely different approach, allowing users to create an aggregate by manually collecting a set of items into a group, much like a shopping basket. This deals with only one aggregate at a time.

Several systems, including DEVise [LRB97] allow users to display data in a variety of plots and establish different types of coordinations between them. However, its coordinations focus on synchronizing the panning and zooming of plots that share common axes.

One of the interesting problems about aggregation is to select the granularity of the aggregate. Depending on the task and the application domain, different aggregates are needed. For example, in an application with highway incident data, it is interesting to look at both the number of incidents per year and the average number of incidents per hour on one day.

4- AGGREGATIONS AND COORDINATED DISPLAYS

The increasingly popular visualization strategies, such as starfield displays [AS94], are effective in dealing with thousands or even tens of thousand data values. However many databases are much larger. As the number of values grow, the display can become too crowded with data points and it becomes difficult to recognize trends, clusters, outliers, or gaps in the data (Figure 1).

Aggregation can be used to provide an overview, and together with other coordinated displays show the details of the aggregates. This allows users to maintain an overview and at the same time look at the details. The aggregates are displayed in the overview, and the contents of the selected aggregate are displayed in detail views. The visualization displays are tightly coupled, so that when users select an aggregate the details of the aggregate are immediately shown in the other display. This is the drill-down coordination.

This technique enables the exploration of very large-scale databases. For example, 1,000,000 traffic

incidents could be aggregated into 1000 aggregates, each with 1000 incidents. This could be displayed with two coordinated views, an overview of 1000 points, and a detail view of 1000. Furthermore, this approach can be repeated by chaining several views, adding an additional view for each level.

The drill-down technique is used in the Visage system [LR96], but users have to drag and drop the aggregate onto a new display to see the details. The Apple Dylan programming environment [DP95] lets users split and link frames for drilling down through file structures (similar to Windows Explorer).

5- EXPLORING INCIDENT DATA

Maryland State Highway Administration is responsible for responding to incidents and gathering data for planning purposes. When an incident occurs on the highway, a traffic operator at one of the centers fills in an incident report form. The form has information about the incident, including location, time and date, weather conditions, vehicles involved in the incident etc. The data in this study is based on a subset of incident report forms from the Maryland State Highway Administration. Today those forms exist only on paper and had to be transcribed for this study. The only incidents that are routinely analyzed are the ones resulting in personal injury, and the analysis is based on the police reports, not the incident report forms. One of our goal was to inform the redesign of the highway management information system and explore what information would be useful to collect in an improved incident report form.

This study included more than ten different prototypes of coordinated visualization displays with highway incident data using Snap. We first defined the aggregates in the database by writing SQL queries, and then created the views with the specification of the coordination between the different views. For each prototype we documented it by writing down advantages, disadvantages, and other details about the view or the aggregation.

Most of the examples presented below used Spotfire for the data visualization (www.spotfire.com). Spotfire can display a single data table as a scatter plot (2D or 3D), bar chart, or pie chart. It can display the same table in multiple views simultaneously, with brushing-and-linking between them. However, it does not support multiple tables, aggregation, or drill-down coordination. Hence, Snap is used to coordinate multiple instances of Spotfire.

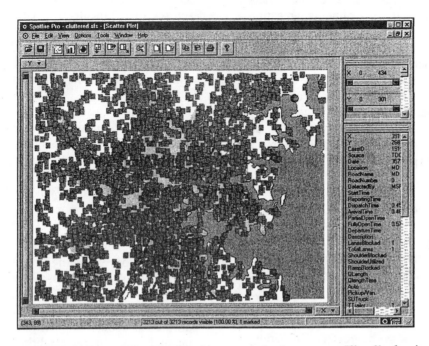

Figure 1: A Spotfire display with incidents around Baltimore marked on a map. The display is crowded with data points and it is difficult to identify any high hazard locations.

5.1 Geographical aggregations

The first prototype consisted of geographical displays coordinated with Snap. The first step (Figure 2) was to create aggregates for the exit numbers (geographical aggregation) and to use the incident database with the records from the Baltimore Beltway. We added data about the exits and calculated how many incidents occurred close to each of them. An estimated distance to a response unit for each exit number was used for color coding (Figure 2). When an exit was selected all the incidents were shown in a table grid at the bottom of the screen.

The map makes it easy to see where most of the incidents occurred, since the size of each exit marker indicates on the number of incidents close to that exit. The distance to a response unit is used as color-coding, with dark blue as the longest distance and white as the shortest. This view could serve as an aid in placing the response units where they are most needed. The exits with dark blue color and rather large size are probably in need of an extra unit!

To construct this coordinated display using Snap, we first open the incident database with Snap. The Snap Main Menu window (Figure 3a) displays the relations in the database and the available visualizations. We created an aggregate query to group the incidents by which exist they occurred near on the 695 Baltimore beltway. In SQL, this ··Exits·· query is:

> SELECT exit, count(*) FROM incidents695
> GROUP BY exit

Dragging the Exits aggregate query onto the Spotfire button displays the Spotfire chart of the exits, size-coded by the number of incidents near each exit. Likewise dragging a query for incidents at any given exit (aggregate contents) on the Table button displays the table at bottom.

Now we can coordinate the visualizations by dragging the Snap button from Spotfire to the table. These buttons are automatically added to each visualization by Snap. The Snap Specification dialog (Figure 3b) is displayed for specifying which actions to coordinate between the views. Choosing ··Select·· for Spotfire and ··Load·· for the table establishes a drill-down coordination. Now we can examine specific incidents near an exit by selecting the exit in Spotfire to display them in the table.

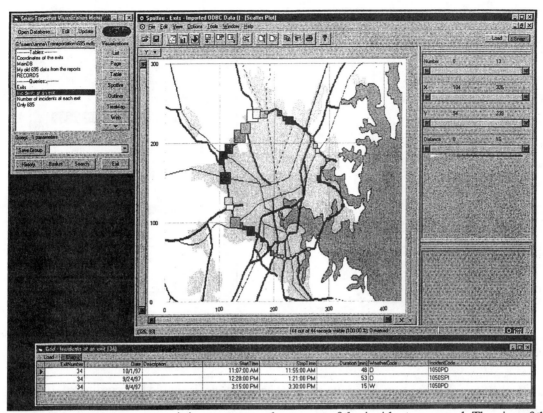

Figure 2a: With exit aggregates on a map it is easy to see where most of the incidents occurred. The size of the markers depends on the number of incidents and the color depends on the distance to a response unit.   When the users click on an intersection the incidents are shown on a table.

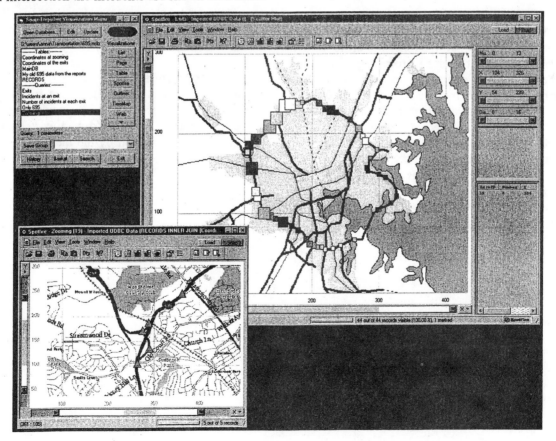

Figure 2b: Alternatively, users can view a detailed map with the location of each incident.

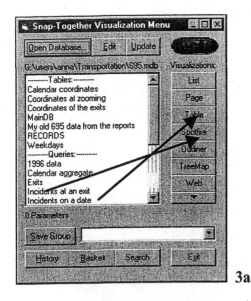

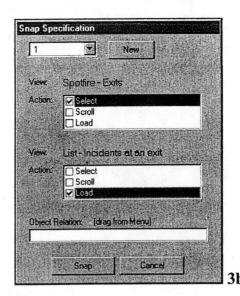

Figure 3a: The Snap-Together Visualization menu lists the tables and queries in the incident database and displays a menu of available visualizations.

Figure 3b: In the Snap Specification dialog, users select how two views should be coordinated. In this figure, selecting an exit in Spotfire will load the incidents that occurred near that exit in a textual list view.

5.2 Temporal aggregations

Since traffic during one week is similar to traffic during other weeks, it seemed promising to try and group the incidents by day of the week (Figure 4). The number of incidents each day was shown in a display with bar charts. Each bar represented one day of the week. When a bar was selected a map with markers of the incidents was loaded in the other display. The size of the markers in this display depended on the duration of the incident. In this sample, there were few incidents on the weekend compared to the weekdays. In Figure 5, instead of grouping the incidents by day, they were grouped by date in this prototype. A calendar was shown in one display and if a date was selected, information about the incidents was loaded into a table grid.

5.3 Categorical aggregates

Finally categorical aggregates were found useful: by vehicle type (cars, trucks,...), incident type (crash, fire,···), weather condition (dry, rainy,···), etc. Figure 6 shows an aggregation by the number of vehicles in the accident ‾ mostly 0, 1 or 2.

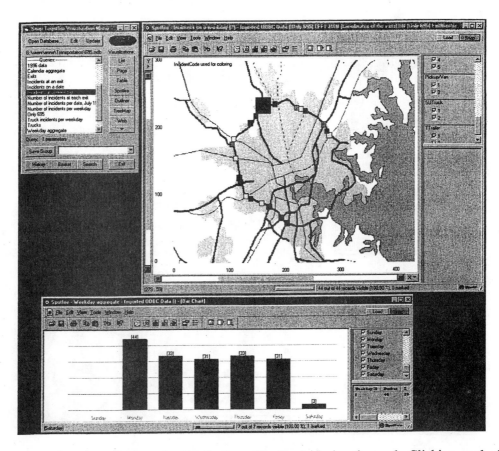

Figure 4: On the bottom a bar chart displays the distribution of incidents during the week. Clicking on the "Monday" aggregate shows the corresponding incident summaries by Exits on the map.

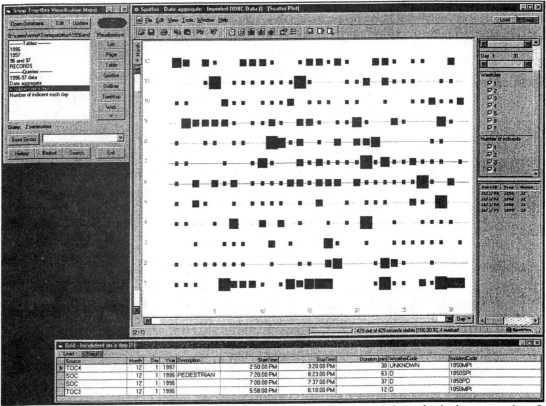

Figure 5: Using a yearly calendar Incident data from 1997 (blue markers) together with hypothetical average data from previous years (red markers).

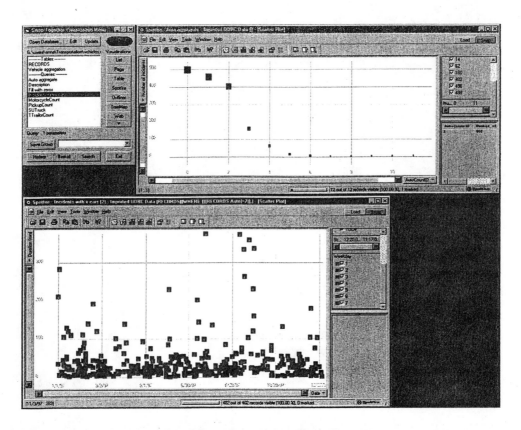

Figure 6: Aggregation by number of automobiles in the incident. The incidents with 2 cars are shown in the display at the bottom

6- COORDINATION ARCHITECTURE

Once a coordinated display is constructed, Snap maintains the specified coordination while users manipulate the display. When users invoke an action in one view, Snap automatically invokes actions coordinated to that action in other views (Figure 7).

In the case of the drill-down coordination, the Select action of the aggregates overview is coordinated to the Load action in the aggregate contents view. Figure 7 shows the structure of the example in Figure 2b. When users click on an Exit aggregate in the overview, the visualization reports the ID (primary key value) of the selected exit to Snap. According to the drill-down coordination specified by the user, Snap in turn invokes the Load action on the detail view. Snap binds the exit ID to the parameter of the aggregate-contents query, to retrieve all incidents at that exit from the database. Snap loads this data into the detail view.

6- CONCLUSIONS

More than ten different prototypes with different kinds of aggregates were developed and analyzed. Recommendations and advice regarding the use of aggregation were given to people working with transportation systems and the developers of Spotfire.

We encountered challenges in the development of the prototypes. Some were related to the limitation of the APIs of the visualizations we used. For example, we could not automatically load the maps into Spotfire. The calculation of the aggregates is also a challenge since it is unreasonable to calculate all the possible aggregates in advance but on-the-fly calculation may not always be practical.

We extended Snap to coordinate dynamic queries across multiple instances of Spotfire. For example, users could filter to show only the Truck-related incidents in both the aggregate and contents views in Figures 2 and 4.

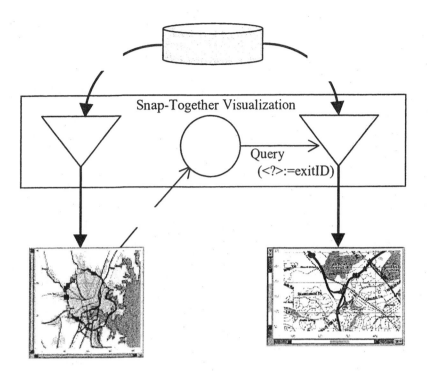

Figure 7: The Snap-Together Visualization architecture for drill-down coordination. Users select queries to load data into visualizations. Then, they snap visualizations together to coordinate actions between them. This example demonstrates how the actions propagate in the display in Figure 2b. When users select an exit aggregate in the left map, the query to the right map extracts the incidents in that aggregate from the database and loads them into the map.

visualization.

In future work on Snap, we would like to explore the use of multiple selection of aggregates to display unions and intersections of aggregates' contents:

- Selecting multiple aggregates in a **single overview** would display the **union** of their contents in the detail view. For example, in Figure 4 users could select both Monday and Tuesday to view all the incidents on both days in the map.
- Selecting multiple aggregates from **different overviews** would display the **intersection** of their contents in a detail view. For example, we might combine the geographical and temporal aggregations of Figures 2 and 4. Selecting an exit on the map and a day-of-year from the calendar would display only the incidents at that exit on that day in the detail table. This enables construction of simultaneous menus [HS99] applications with Snap.

To conclude, our experience confirms that Snap-Together Visualization is a valuable tool for rapidly prototyping interfaces, and indicates the importance of time, location and category as major attributes in the construction of aggregates.

ACKNOWLEDGEMENTS

Partial support for this work was provided by Spotfire the Maryland Department of Transportation and the U.S. Bureau of the Census.
This case study was mainly conducted during the visit of Anna Fredrikson from Chalmers University, Sweden, in the summer of 1999.

URL

A longer technical report on this work is accessible online in our project webpage
http://www.cs.umd.edu/hcil/highway
See also http://www.cs.umd.edu/hcil/snap

REFERENCES

[AS94] Ahlberg, C. and Shneiderman, B., "Visual Information Seeking: Tight coupling of dynamic query filters with starfield displays", *Proc. of ACM CHI94 Conference*, pp. 313-317 + color plates, ACM, New York (April 1994).

[DP95] Dumas, J., Parsons, P., "Discovering the way programmers think about new programming environments" ,*Communications of the ACM*, 38(6), pp. 45-56, (June 1995).

[GR94] Goldstein, J., Roth S. F., "Using aggregation and dynamic queries for exploring large data sets" , *Proc. ACM CHI' 94 Conference* , pp. 23-29, ACM, New York (April 1994).

[HHW97] Hellerstein, J. M., Haas, P.J., Wang H. J., "Online Aggregation", *Proceedings of the ACM SIGMOD International Conference on Management of Data*, pp. 171-182, ACM, New York (1997).

[HKVS99] Hochheiser, H., Kositsyna N., Ville, G., Shneiderman, B, ``Performance Benefits of Simultaneous over Sequential Menus as Task Complexity Increases," University of Maryland Computer Science Dept Technical Report CS-TR-4066, UMIACS-TR-99-60 , (September 1999).

[LRB97] Livny, M., Ramakrishnan, R., Beyer, K., Chen, G., Donjerkovic, D., Lawande, S., Myllymaki, J., Wenger, K., "DEVise: integrated querying and visual exploration of large datasets" , *Proc. ACM SIGMOD' 97*, pp. 301-312, ACM, New York (1997).

[LR96] Lucas, P., Roth, S., "Exploring Information with Visage" , *Conference Companion of ACM CHI' 96 Conference*, ACM, New York (April 1996).

[Moc98] Mockus, A., "Navigating Aggregation Spaces" , *Proc. IEEE Conference on Information Visualization '98*, IEEE, Los Alamitos, CA (1998).

[NS99] North, C., Shneiderman, B., "Snap-Together Visualization: Coordinating Multiple Views to Explore Information", University of Maryland Computer Science Dept. Technical Report CS-TR-4020, (1999).

Broadening Access to Large Online Databases by Generalizing Query Previews

Egemen Tanin
egemen@cs.umd.edu

Catherine Plaisant
plaisant@cs.umd.edu

Ben Shneiderman
ben@cs.umd.edu

Human-Computer Interaction Laboratory, Institute for Advanced Computer Studies,
Institute for Systems Research, and Department of Computer Science
University of Maryland at College Park, College Park, MD 20742

+1 301 405-2725

ABSTRACT

Companies, government agencies, and other types of organizations are making their large databases available to the world over the Internet. Current database front-ends do not give users information about the distribution of data. This leads many users to waste time and network resources posing queries that have either zero-hit or mega-hit result sets. Query previews form a novel visual approach for browsing large databases. Query previews supply data distribution information about the database that is being searched and give continuous feedback about the size of the result set for the query as it is being formed. On the other hand, query previews use only a few pre-selected attributes of the database. The distribution information is displayed only on these attributes. Unfortunately, many databases are formed of numerous relations and attributes. This paper introduces a generalization of query previews. We allow users to browse all of the relations and attributes of a database using a hierarchical browser. Any of the attributes can be used to display the distribution information, making query previews applicable to many public online databases.

Keywords

Query Previews, Visual Data Mining, Information Visualization, User Interfaces.

INTRODUCTION

Companies, government agencies, and other types of organizations are making their large databases available to the world over the Internet. IBM (e.g., www.patents.ibm.com), US Census Bureau (e.g., ferret.bls.census.gov), NASA (e.g., eos.nasa.gov/eosdis), and the World Health Organization (e.g., www.who.int/whosis/) are only a few of these organizations. The designers, engineers, and operators of these public online databases are facing various challenges. The users of the Internet form the most varied user pool in terms of their backgrounds, interests, ages, and genders. Hence, designing effective user interfaces to accommodate such a variety of users is one of the challenges.

Designers of user interfaces for traditional offline databases mostly use command languages or form fillin interfaces in their designs. They generally serve a homogeneous user domain. Recent advances in database and user interface research enabled designers to create visual user interfaces that are easier to use and learn than the traditional approaches. However, most of these advanced interfaces, even for online databases, still continue to target a narrower user domain than the general population. Employees of a bank accessing an Online Analytical Processing (OLAP) Server from their houses form a good example of such a restricted user pool. Customers of a bank accessing an Online Transaction Processing (OLTP) Server form another one. Thus, we need different approaches to serve the users of the public online databases.

Designers of user interfaces for many databases generally make the following assumptions during their design processes:

a) Users are informed about the data that they are working on or they will submit known-item queries rather than probing the database,
b) Users know or have the will to understand a specific querying environment,
c) Users will have the bandwidth or the time to access large databases.

Most of these assumptions are not valid for the user domain of user interfaces for public online databases. Many user interfaces do not give users an indication of the availability of data. However, this is essential for public online databases to guide the users in the query formulation process. Unguided novice users may waste time by submitting queries that have zero-hit or mega-hit result sets. Traditional user interfaces require users to fill lengthy forms or form complex queries. However, users of public online databases do not have the time or the will to learn a query language or they are annoyed when they have to fill a lengthy form. A more efficient, simple, and easy to learn approach for defining queries is needed. Finally, users of a public online database have to access large amounts of data using a low bandwidth congested network. Hence, strategies that introduce efficient means of communication are needed.

Query previews [3,12] form a novel approach for querying large online databases. Query previews supply data distribution information about the database that is being searched and give continuous feedback about the size of the result set for the query as it is being formed. Queries are incrementally and visually formed by selecting available items from a set of charts. Query previews take advantage of the fact that users are generally interested in a subset of the database. Once the scope has been narrowed, a second phase can start with local data. This second phase can be a simple list of hits or a sophisticated user interface that will allow users to visualize the hit set. The multi-phase approach will increase the network performance of the overall system. Figures 1 and 2 show a sample query preview panel [14] using the three commonly used attributes of a NASA database, the Global Change Master Directory (gcmd.nasa.gov). The distribution of data over these attributes is shown with bar charts and the result set size is displayed as a separate bar at the bottom.

Recent work by [6] shows that many users prefer query previews and perform better with them. Users

report that query previews are easy to use and understand. These results increase our hopes to serve a broad public user domain in a more satisfactory way.

Unfortunately, current applications of query previews use just a few pre-selected attributes of the data. The distribution information is displayed only on these attributes. These implementations of query previews work over a single table that has a relatively low number of attributes. The simplicity of the data structures and a user interface with only a few pre-selected attributes are the positive aspects of these implementations. However, databases are generally formed of numerous relations and attributes. Therefore, pre-selection of a few attributes is an important restriction of the query preview approach. Application of query previews to many public online databases requires this restriction to be relaxed.

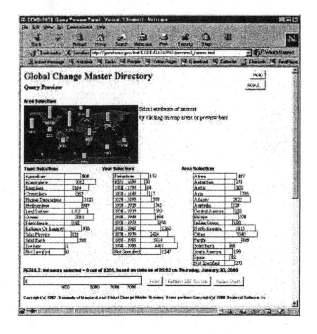

Figure 1: A sample query preview developed at the Human-Computer Interaction Laboratory, for NASA's Global Change Master Directory. Topic, Year, and Area are three most frequently used attributes of the data. These attributes are selected to show the data distribution information. The distribution is shown with bar charts. The result set size is displayed as a separate bar at the bottom.

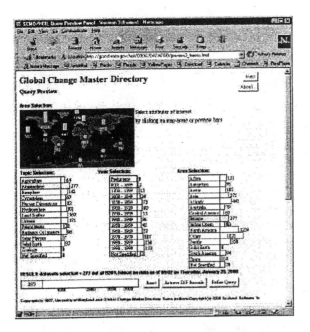

Figure 2: When users select attribute values (e.g. Atmosphere for Topic and Europe for Area in this snapshot), the bars are updated immediately to reflect the distribution of the data that satisfies the query. The result set size is also updated accordingly.

This paper introduces a generalization of the query preview approach. We allow users to browse all the relations and attributes of the database with a hierarchical browser. All the attributes of the database can be used to display the distribution information using bar charts and can be expanded, visualized, and manipulated. Thus, with this generalization, the query previews are made applicable to many public online databases. This will help us to serve a broader user domain with a simple novel user interface.

RELATED WORK

Many researchers are trying to devise methods for more successful querying. The Rabbit system, by Williams [16] and the work of Heppe, Edmondson, and Spence [9] were early demonstrations of the benefits of progressive querying. Other systems show relevance of results: for example Veerasamy and Navathe [15] used histograms, and Hearst [7] used TileBars to visually present relevance of results to the terms used in the query. WebTOC [11] uses a hierarchical outliner and a bar chart presentation to preview the size and type of items (e.g., image, sound, etc.) within each branch and serves a very wide user domain, the Internet. Eick [4] proposes to augment sliders of visualization systems with density plots or bar charts. Antis, Eick, and Pyrce [2]

introduce methods for visualizing the schemas of relational databases. Dynamic queries [1,5,13,17] use a direct manipulation approach to facilitate query formulation with a visual representation of query components and results. They allow rapid, incremental, and reversible control of the query. Results are presented visually. Continuous feedback guides users in the query formulation process. Marchionini and Greene [10] discuss the importance of user interface issues in public access and use of government statistical information. Hearst [8] lists many approaches to user interfaces for information retrieval systems.

QUERY PREVIEWS

The concept of query previews [3,12] was triggered by the need to extend the dynamic querying idea [1,5,13,17] to large networked databases. Query previews show the contents of a database during the query formulation process. In order to guide users in the query formulation process, query previews provide aggregate information on some pre-selected attributes of the data. Distribution of data over some attribute values is shown graphically using representations such as bar or pie charts. When users select a value on any of the attributes by just clicking on the related representations of a query preview panel, the rest of the user interface is updated immediately. This is called tight coupling. Actions are easily reversible, and error prevention instead of error correction is used. For every action users take, feedback is given continuously. As users see the potential size of their result set before submitting the query, they are less likely to create queries that return zero or mega hits. Users see the trends in the data and they learn where the data has gaps or clusters. (Figures 1 and 2 show a sample query preview panel.) The server load will be reduced if users do not waste their time with zero hit queries or consume network resources in downloading large sets of useless results.

Query previews only need aggregate information about the database. The data distribution information is represented with multidimensional histograms. Each cell of a histogram represents a count of the records from the database mapping to that cell. Hence, whatever the size of the data is, only the counts are needed to form a query preview panel. The size of this information is fixed regardless of the size of the data. Only the counts are incremented with each insertion to the database. This makes query previews a powerful tool for large online databases.

GENERALIZING QUERY PREVIEWS

Current applications of query previews use a few pre-selected attributes of the data. The distribution information is displayed only on these attributes. However, databases are generally formed of numerous relations and attributes. Therefore, pre-selection of a few attributes is a restriction of the query preview approach.

To relax this restriction, we combine a hierarchical browser and the query preview approach to let users browse all the relations and attributes of the database. With this generalization all the attributes of the database can be used to display the data distribution information.

Figure 3 presents a sample hierarchical browser. In this example, we use the Environmental Protection Agency (EPA) as our sample organization and a fragment of the Toxic Release Inventory from the EPA data collections as our sample database.

This sample database is formed of approximately 400,000 reports of toxic material releases to the environment from various facilities in United States. We put together four relations from this database, which are Contact Info, Release Info, Chemical Info, and Facility Info. Each relation contains a few sample attributes, e.g., Contact Info contains Contact Phone and Contact Name as its attributes.

The root of our browser is tagged with the name of the database. Each relation is represented by a separate branch. Each branch may also have leaves representing different attributes of that branch (relation). The result bar is visible on top of the panel showing the total number of hits (reports for our example with EPA data) to the current query. At any time, the users can fetch these hits by simply pressing the fetch button on the left of the result bar. We attach the distribution information next to the related branch of that attribute.

Figure 3: A hierarchical browser represents the schema for the database. The root is tagged with the name of the database. Each relation is represented by a separate branch. Each branch may contain a few leaves representing the attributes of that branch. In this example, Contact Info and Chemical Info branches are expanded to demonstrate this feature.

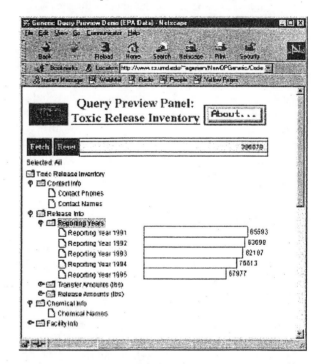

Figure 4: The Reporting Year attribute of the Reporting Info branch is expanded. A set of bars is attached to this presentation to show the distribution of data over this attribute.

Some of the attributes do not have the distribution information attached to them. For example, Contact Name of the Contact Info relation of Figure 3 does not have anything attached to it. The nature of the Contact Name attribute does not allow a useful representation. There are almost as many names in the database as the number of reports. Even if there were some overlaps, the total number of unique names would be so large that representing them with bars would simply clutter the display without adding much to the presentation. Finding a useful representation of such attributes will be beneficial to further generalization of the query previews. In this paper, we focus on other types of attributes, e.g., gender and age. These have useful representations. Figure 4 shows such an attribute. This attribute, the Reporting Year, is an attribute of the Release Info branch. It is represented as a folder. It can have other branches under it. Still, it is an attribute of the Release Info branch. This visual difference is used to show the expandability of this attribute. These types of attributes are expandable into buckets. Buckets show the possible values or ranges of values for that attribute. The distribution of data is shown over them.

In Figure 4, we see five bars showing the reports submitted in each of the five years of the EPA Data. The users can immediately see the number of reports has declined about 25% over the five years. Other attributes of the database can be expanded similarly. Figure 5 shows such a display that reveals high numbers of reports for the Southeast and Midwest, but relatively few for the Northwest.

Bars also form a mechanism for input to the user interface. Figure 6 shows such an example action. The reporting year 1994 is selected by just clicking on the bar.

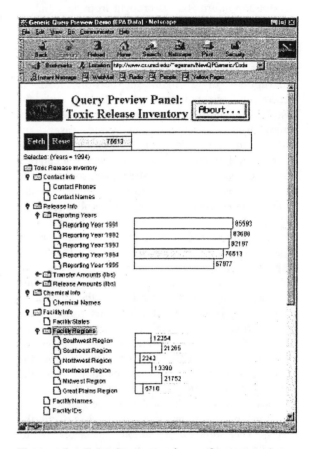

Figure 6: Selections on bars form an input mechanism. This panel shows that for 1994 there were 76,613 reports and shows the distribution by Facility Regions.

Upon any selection, the distribution information on all the other bars including the result bar is updated. A silhouette of the initial bar settings is kept to show the original sizes of the bars. The text field below the fetch button displays the selected values in text form. This is essential since the bars can also be collapsed to make room for other expansions. In this case, the visual feedback from the collapsed bars may be lost. Hence, the text field is a reminder for the previous

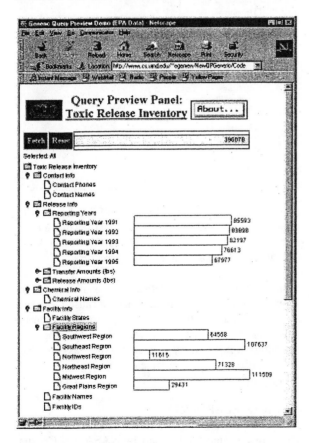

Figure 5: Facility Region attribute is expanded showing the data distribution on another set of bars. Each bar is used to show a different region.

selections. Another reminder for selections can be placed next to the attribute names. At any time, users can reset their selections by simply clicking on the reset button next to the fetch button. Figure 7 shows some further selections and updates on the bars. The session can continue as long as the users want to explore the database. When users want to see the hits to their query, they can fetch the desired reports from the EPA database matching their selections. They can view this hit set as a simple list or they can continue querying on it using various types of local tools.

As bars expand and collapse the desired data distribution information is brought from the database server. This creates short delays during the query formulation process. Despite these delays, the amount of data that is downloaded from the network is very small, and does not introduce large interruptions or a significant network load. In general, we do not fetch the hits, but only the distribution information about the hits at these intermediate connections. In some cases, the distribution information can already be cached to improve performance. In some other cases, it can be a subset of the previous distribution, so a second connection can be avoided. In our example, the size of the total distribution information is only 8 Kbytes.

One limitation on the distribution information is the number of attributes that can be simultaneously displayed. This number is equal to the number of dimensions of data representing the distribution information. As this number grows, the amount of data needed grows exponentially. Thus, manipulating many attributes of the database at the same time may not be feasible. A solution to this problem is downloading the actual attribute values for the matching hits after the first few selections. After the initial selections, the size of the hit set may be drastically reduced. This will relax the restriction of not downloading large amounts of data from the server. Therefore, this solution can allow us to continue working on a local minimized version of the database.

CONCLUSIONS

Query previews form a novel visual approach for querying large online databases. On the other hand, current applications of query previews use only a few pre-selected attributes of the data. Unfortunately, many databases are formed of numerous relations and attributes. Applicability of query previews to many public online databases requires this restriction to be relaxed. This paper introduces a generalization of query previews. We allow users to browse all the

relations and attributes of a database with a hierarchical browser. All appropriate attributes of the database can be used to display the distribution information using bar charts and can be expanded, visualized, and manipulated. Hence, with this generalization, we strongly believe that query previews will increase the accessibility to large online databases.

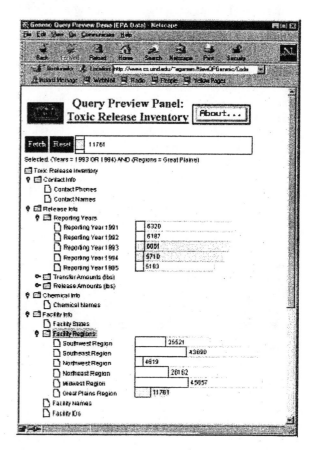

Figure 7: Further selections from the EPA data. Users continue to see updates on the bars as they make their selections. This panel shows "(1993 OR 1994) AND (Great Plains)" will produce 11,761 reports.

Some attributes of the database remain unused to show the data distribution. This is caused by the nature of these attributes (e.g., Social Security Number). As a future work, we believe relaxing this restriction on as many attribute types as possible forms a useful step in advancing the applicability of query previews.

ACKNOWLEDGEMENTS

This work is supported in part by NASA, US Census Bureau, and NSF Digital Government Programs. Thanks to Dr. Marchionini and Dr. Beigel for their comments on the previous versions of this paper.

REFERENCES

1. Ahlberg, C. and B. Shneiderman, Visual Information Seeking: Tight Coupling of Dynamic Query Filters with Starfield Displays, *Proceedings of the ACM CHI '94 Conference*, 1994, pp. 313-317.

2. Antis, J., S. Eick, and J. Pyrce, Visualizing the Structure of Relational Databases, *IEEE Software*, January 1996, pp. 72-79.

3. Doan, K., C. Plaisant, and B. Shneiderman, Query Previews in Networked Information Systems, *Proceedings of the Forum on Advances in Digital Libraries*, 1996, pp. 120-129.

4. Eick, S., Data Visualization Sliders, *Proceedings of ACM UIST '94 Conference*, 1994, pp. 119-120.

5. Goldstein, J. and S. Roth, Using Aggregation and Dynamic Queries for Exploring Large Data Sets, *Proceedings of the ACM CHI '94 Conference*, 1994, pp. 23-29.

6. Greene, S., E. Tanin, C. Plaisant, B. Shneiderman, L. Olsen, G. Major, S. Johns, The End of Zero-Hit Queries: Query Previews for NASA's Global Change Master Directory, *International Journal of Digital Libraries*, 2, 2, 1999, pp. 79-90.

7. Hearst, M., TileBars: Visualization of Term Distribution Information in Full Text Information Access, *Proceedings of the ACM CHI '95 Conference*, 1995, pp. 59-66.

8. Hearst, M., User Interfaces and Visualization, *Modern Information Retrieval*, 1999, ACM Press, Ricardo Baeza-Yates and Berthier Ribeiro-Neto, pp. 257-323.

9. Heppe, D., W. Edmondson, and R. Spence, Helping both the Novice and Advanced User in Menu-driven Information Retrieval Systems, *Proceedings of HCI '85 Conference*, 1985, pp. 92-101.

10. Marchionini, G. and S. Greene, Public Access and Use of Government Statistical Information, *Presented to the Federal Information Services*, ils.unc.edu/~march/, NSF Workshop, 1997.

11. Nation, D., C. Plaisant, G. Marchionini, and A. Komlodi, Visualizing Websites Using a Hierarchical Table of Contents Browser: WebTOC, *Proceedings of the 3rd Conference on Human Factors and the Web*, 1997.

12. Plaisant, C., T. Bruns, K. Doan, and B. Shneiderman, Interface and Data Architecture for Query Previews in Networked Information Systems, *ACM Transactions on Information Systems*, 17, 3, 1999, pp. 320-341.

13. Shneiderman, B., Dynamic Queries for Visual Information Seeking, *IEEE Software*, 11, 6, 1994, pp. 70-77.

14. Tanin, E., A. Lotem, I. Haddadin, B. Shneiderman, C. Plaisant, L. Slaughter, Facilitating Network Data Exploration with Query Previews: A Study of User Performance and Preference, CS-TR-3879, Department of Computer Science, University of Maryland, College Park, 1998.

15. Veerasamy, A. and S. Navathe, Querying, Navigating and Visualizing a Digital Library Catalog, *Proceedings of the Second International Conference on the Theory and Practice of Digital Libraries*, 1995.

16. Williams, M., What Makes RABBIT Run, *International Journal of Man-Machine Studies*, 21, 4, 1984, pp. 333-352.

17. Williamson, C., and B. Shneiderman, The Dynamic Home Finder: Evaluating Dynamic Queries in a Real-Estate Information Exploration System, *Proceedings of ACM SIGIR '92 Conference*, 1992, pp. 338-346.

Dynamic Queries and Brushing on Choropleth Maps

Gunjan Dang, Chris North*, Ben Shneiderman
Human-Computer Interaction Lab &
Department of Computer Science
University of Maryland, College Park MD 20742
{gunjan, north, ben}@cs.umd.edu
www.cs.umd.edu/hcil

Abstract

Users who must combine demographic, economic or other data in a geographic context are often hampered by the integration of tabular and map representations. Static, paper-based solutions limit the amount of data that can be placed on a single map or table. By providing an effective user interface, we believe that researchers, journalists, teachers, and students can explore complex data sets more rapidly and effectively. This paper presents Dynamaps, a generalized map-based information-visualization tool for dynamic queries and brushing on choropleth maps. Users can use color-coding to show a variable on each geographic region, and then filter out areas that do not meet the desired criteria. In addition, a scatterplot view and a details-on-demand window support overviews and specific fact-finding.

Keywords: choropleth maps, dynamic queries, sliders, brushing and linking, information visualization

Current address: Department of Computer Science, Virginia Tech, Blacksburg, VA 24061

1 Introduction

Organizations that publish increasingly large quantities of data face a major challenge in representing that data in a usable and helpful form. For example, the U.S. Census Bureau has the mandate to collect enormous amounts of data, and to disseminate this information to the public for the public good. It is necessary that this data be represented in a way that enables citizens to gain insight about the nation, to discover, decide, and explain.

The Census summary data is primarily represented in terms of geographic regions. Each region has a large number of attribute values for various demographic, economic, and geographic statistics. For example, there is data for each of the 3148 counties within the USA, such as population, area, per capita income, median rent, median property value, total sales, and distributions of ethnic groups, age groups, business sectors, etc.

This data is extremely useful for many users, tasks, and applications. Examples include: a senior citizen looking for a place to settle after she retires, a business considering relocation, lawmakers deciding on a new policy, and an elementary school student learning more about the country.

Typically, the user interfaces for such data dissemination systems force users to sift through vast detailed data or limit users to retrieve only a single data value at time. More advanced systems demand that the user possess the required skill set to formulate queries and presume the users' familiarity with the structure of the database and other details.

New user interfaces are needed that enable users to gain an overview of data available, discover exceptions or patterns and trends across regions, zoom in on relevant areas of interest, and quickly access desired details on demand. In the case of the census and other GIS (Geographic Information Systems) applications, it is critically important that users be able to relate the statistical data in the context of the geography.

The Census Bureau reports that they receive two general types of queries from patrons: (a) specific questions, such as "what is the population of my county?" and (b) open-ended questions, such as "where is a nice place to live?" Census data dissemination systems are minimally capable of answering the former type, but are completely unprepared to support the latter.

This wide range of tasks for GIS data is the motivating factor for the creation of *Dynamaps*, a generalized map-based information-visualization tool built for the Census Bureau.

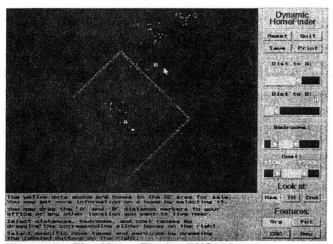

Figure 1: The HomeFinder [WS92]

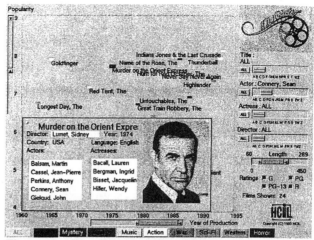

Figure 3: The FilmFinder [AS94]

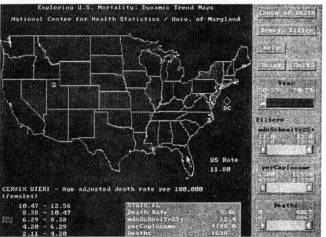

Figure 2: Dynamic Queries on a Health Statistics Map

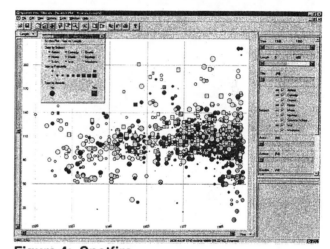

Figure 4: Spotfire

2   Related Work

2.1   Dynamic Queries

The inception of the dynamic query method started with the development the Dynamic HomeFinder [WS92] (see Figure 1). This tool consisted of a map of Washington DC, with homes displayed as dots on the map. Sliders were used to represent the query graphically, where each double-box slider represented the possible range of values for an attribute. Dragging a slider was equivalent to entering attribute values for a query, and updated the display in real time. The results of the query were displayed as the filtering out (or in) of dots representing houses. A real-time visual display of both the query formulation and results facilitated rapid exploration.

Soon thereafter, a variety of dynamic query prototypes were built. Figure 2 shows an early prototype for dynamic queries on a choropleth map of health statistics for the National Center for Health Statistics [PJ94][Pla93]. The FilmFinder [AS94] (Figure 3) demonstrated the use of dynamic queries on non-spatial databases, using a scatterplot to visualize a database of films.

Spotfire [AW95] (Figure 4) generalized the FilmFinder approach, enabling users to explore tabular data with dynamic queries and a variety of types of charts such as scatterplots, histograms, and pie charts. Spotfire also supports *brushing* [BC87], in which users select data items in one plot and the same items are highlighted in all other plots. This enables users to relate items across multiple plots, including maps with markers.

2.2   Geographic Information Systems (GIS)

ESRI ArcView (Figure 5) is a popular desktop GIS software package that provides a powerful map display engine and spatial analysis functions. One type of map ArcView can display is choropleth maps. Unfortunately, the user interface for interactive data exploration is limited. The Census Bureau web site (www.census.gov) also presents a number of data access tools, such as the American Fact Finder (Figure 6), which enables web users to view choropleth maps of selected attributes. The American Fact Finder uses the ArcView display engine.

Other work on data exploration in GIS includes [Mon89], [MK97], [SMC96], [AA99]. These prototypes and systems explore a variety of approaches for brushing with maps and dynamic queries.

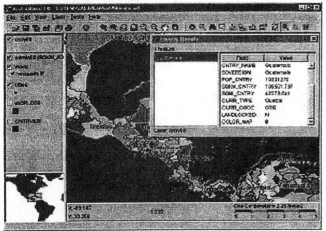

Figure 5: ESRI ArcView

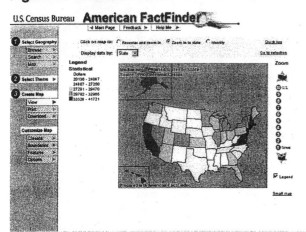

Figure 6: American Fact Finder on the Census Bureau web site.

3 Dynamaps

Dynamaps is a generalized map-based information-visualization tool, designed for map-related Census summary data that builds on these systems. It makes several contributions:

- Dynamic queries on choropleth maps as well as other types of geography. This enables a powerful

exploration capability for both specific and open-ended questions.
- Uniform-distribution sliders as well as standard sliders for dynamic queries. The new uniform-distribution sliders improve slider interaction for some census data, which is often overly non-uniformly distributed.
- Brushing across choropleth maps and scatterplots. Users execute a form of 2-dimensional dynamic query by selecting regions in a scatterplot to highlight the corresponding geographic elements in the map. Also, this enables reverse queries by selecting regions in the map to highlight the corresponding elements in the plot.
- Use of industry-standard commercial tool, ESRI ArcView components, for map display. This enables the use of standard data formats and files, and takes advantage of extensive existing GIS functionality in the ESRI software. In this sense, Dynamaps adds a powerful new information-visualization user interface to this existing commercial software.
- Algorithm for performing rapid dynamic queries with a commercial GIS display engine (ESRI) that was not originally designed for such dynamic interactivity.
- Generalized, distributable, GIS viewer tool with flexibility to load and display arbitrary geography and data types. Databases can be loaded with many attributes. Once a map is loaded, data with an appropriate join attribute can also be loaded and explored. Hence, Dynamaps could become the Adobe Acrobat viewer of GIS.

4 User Interface

4.1 Map

When using Dynamaps, users first load a geographic data file into the tool to display the map (Dynamaps displays US states and counties by default). Then, users can quickly display the map as a choropleth by simply selecting a data attribute from the drop-down list to color the map accordingly (see Figure 7). Map elements can be colored by any of the available attributes loaded in the data file. The color legend at top shows the minimum and maximum values.

For example, consider a situation in which a senior citizen, about to retire, is looking for a suitable location to move to. One of her primary concerns might be the cost of rent. She colors the Dynamap by the 'Median Rent' attribute (Figure 7) and notices that California and the northeast are clearly the high rent areas that she might choose to avoid. The darker regions indicate a low value of median rent and the lighter regions have higher values.

Dynamaps users can also zoom and pan the map to observe data patterns in smaller or denser regions (see Figure 8).

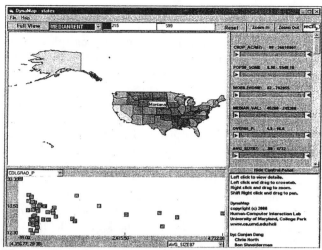

Figure 7: Dynamaps showing the US states colored by 'Median Rent' value. The west coast and east coast are most expensive.

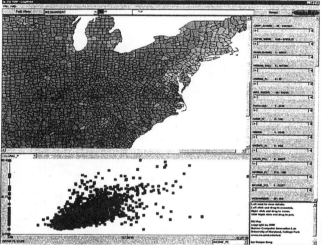

Figure 8: Dynamaps showing the US counties colored by 'Median Rent', and zoomed in on the northeast. The Washington DC to Boston corridor is most expensive.

4.2 Dynamic Queries

When a data file is loaded, the attributes related to each of the elements of the map also appear on the right in the form of adjustable dynamic-query sliders. Each slider represents the range of values (minimum to maximum) for its attribute. Adjusting sliders enables the formulation of a query and map elements are then filtered (in or out) accordingly (Figure 9). The real advantage lies in the presence of multiple sliders; the user can formulate conjunctive queries by adjusting more than one slider and view the results on the map. Map elements that have been filtered out by the query are colored dark gray. Elements that are not filtered remain colored according to the chosen

choropleth attribute. As users drag the sliders, the map animates to give immediate feedback in real time.

For example, in addition to rent considerations, our senior citizen might also want to live where there are more people of her age group. By adjusting the slider for the attribute 'percent of population over age 65', she filters out states with low values for this attribute to reveal that Florida and central US are good candidates. However, she finds that if she also insists on low levels of unemployment, then the central states are the best match (Figure 9). Now that she has narrowed her search, she can select a state of interest to view its attribute values in the detail view on lower right. Selecting multiple states shows their attribute values in a tabular form to facilitate comparison.

Each dynamic query slider can filter items according to one of two possible distributions of the items. In standard slider mode, the items are distributed along the slider like a histogram, ordered and located according to the corresponding attribute value. This enables users to quickly select desired value ranges for the attribute and view items meeting that criteria on the map. However, this approach is problematic when items are not uniformly distributed on the attribute. For example, California has a much higher population than all the other states. As a result, selecting among the low population states is difficult with a standard dynamic query slider because they are all tightly packed at the low end of the slider. Hence, Dynamaps' dynamic query sliders have an additional uniform-distribution mode. In this mode, items are uniformly distributed along the slider according to rank order for the attribute. This enables users to quickly select ranges of items by rank (e.g. the 5 least-populated states).

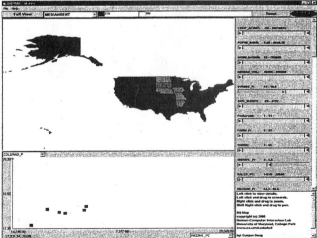

Figure 9: Dynamaps showing US states filtered for high 'Percent Over Age 65' and low 'Unemployment' using dynamic query sliders. Six states in the central US remain.

4.3   Scatterplot

Dynamaps displays a scatterplot of the map elements at the bottom of the screen. It plots a two-dimensional graph of the elements according to attributes selected from the drop-down menus on each axis as shown in Figure 10. Users can pick any two attributes to plot the elements by. All 4 sub-windows are tightly coupled: The dynamic query sliders filter both the map and the scatterplot. Selecting items in either the map or the scatterplot causes the corresponding items to be highlighted in the other ("brushing"), and also displays the items' attribute values in the detail view.

The scatterplot and the brushing capability enable more open-ended exploration of the data. Users can discover patterns, trends, outliers, and relationships from both a statistical and geographical perspective. For example, Figure 10 shows the US states plotted by 'Per Capital Income' (x axis) and 'Percent of Population with College Degrees' (y axis). Clearly there is a positive relationship between education and income. Selecting the highly educated and high-income states in the scatterplot reveals in the map that they are all located in the northeast (light color highlights in Figure 10). The outlier at the bottom center of the scatterplot is Nevada. These are forms of 2-dimensional dynamic queries that are not as obvious with the 1-dimensional sliders and sometimes not possible with sliders. Likewise, brushing also enables geographic dynamic queries. For example, selecting the southern states on the map reveals that they are all at the lower end of both scales in the scatterplot.

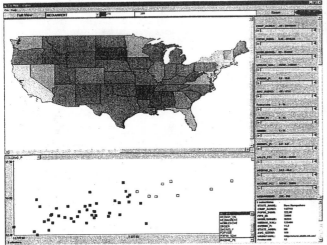

Figure 10: Brushing between scatterplot and map reveals that high income and highly educated states are in the northeast.

4.4   Geography and Data

In addition to handling polygonal geographic regions as in choropleth maps, Dynamaps also has the ability to handle map elements of different types, such as lines or points on a map, with the same dynamic query and brushing capabilities. For example, Figure 11 shows a map of US Highways. Exploring the 'length' attribute with Dynamaps reveals that the longer highways are in the Central and Western parts of the country. In Figure 12, Dynamaps displays data about the US state capital cities in the form of points on a map. The 'Load Geography' menu option allows users to load other map layers for visualization. The 'Load Geography Background' menu option supports the display of background layers. For example, the map of US highways and cities displays a background of the US states. Dynamaps uses geography data files in the standard ESRI Shape file format.

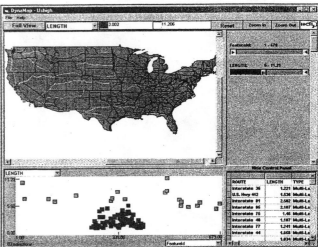

Figure 11: Dynamaps displaying highway data.

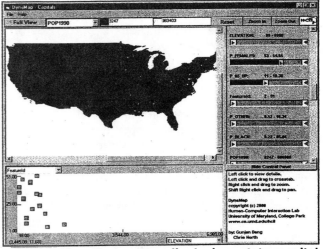

Figure 12: Dynamaps displaying state capital cities.

The 'Load Data Table' menu option allows users to load additional data attributes from a data table and join them to the currently loaded geography. This enables the use of many easily obtainable data tables from the Census Bureau or other sources without the need to reformat the data files into the more difficult geography format. Data table files can be in Microsoft Access database or dBase format.

5 Algorithms

Dynamaps is implemented on the PC/Windows platform. The map portion of the Dynamaps display uses ESRI MapObjects. The use of ESRI components is important because of its advanced GIS functionality, powerful display engine, industry standard file format, and continued ESRI-supported upgrade path. It is not our intention to attempt to compete with ESRI, but to build on and enhance ESRI's work.

A major challenge in developing Dynamaps was to extend the MapObjects components, which focus primarily on static presentation of map data, to efficiently support dynamic query interaction. We believe that this is an important general problem, as software engineering continues to evolve more towards component-based approaches. Many valuable software components simply are not designed with dynamic interaction in mind. User interface designers must then retrofit these components to build forward-looking systems using more advanced information visualization principles. Dynamic Queries on MapObjects is just one example of many, and we believe that our solution will be a helpful guide to other designers.

As query sliders are dragged, the display must update in real time. Previous work on dynamic query algorithms focused on linear and spatial data structures to efficiently compute the query result set [TBS97]. Dynamaps uses MapObject's database query functionality for such computation. In Dynamaps, the challenge is in the display of the result set. Since the objects being displayed are filled complex polygons, the bottleneck is in drawing the result set rather than computing it.

First, Dynamaps generates the SQL query string based on the current positions of the sliders, and then submits this query to the database engine. The SQL query contains a 'WHERE' statement with a minimum and maximum clause for each attribute that has been constrained by the user with a slider. To optimize construction of the SQL query while users drag a slider, Dynamaps first generates the SQL for all attributes except the slider currently being manipulated. Then, as the user manipulates the slider, only the updated clause for that slider needs to be inserted into the query string.

After submitting the SQL query to the database engine, the results must be updated on the display. To draw the results, we tried several algorithms each one improving upon the previous. The first algorithm simply drew the result set on a blank background. This approach was unacceptable because it completely eliminated the filtered items from display. Remaining items were out of context and disorienting for the user.

The second algorithm used two duplicate geographic layers. The background layer colored all the map items gray (as if filtered out). The foreground layer used the choropleth coloring. The SQL query was applied to the foreground layer only and then both layers were redrawn, background first then foreground. Actually the background only needed to be redrawn if the user had tightened the query (moved a slider box inwards) and filtered some items out. Unfortunately this resulted in a flashy display since MapObjects does not support double buffering, and slow performance because many elements are drawn twice (background + foreground).

The third algorithm eliminated the problematic overlap between background and foreground. The two map layers were used as a positive query and a negative query. The positive query layer represents the unfiltered (colored) map items, and the negative query represents the filtering (gray) items. Together, both layers combine to display all elements of the map. The SQL query is applied to the positive layer, and the complement of the SQL query applied to the negative layer. When users tighten the query (move sliders inwards) only the negative query layer needed to be re-queried and redrawn. When the query is loosened (sliders moved outwards) only the positive query layer is re-queried and redrawn. This algorithm led to a significant improvement (two-fold) in performance and aesthetics, but still lagged for larger maps.

The fourth algorithm attempts to query and redraw only those items that change state since the last update. As a slider thumb is dragged, at each incremental slider event received, a differential query computes the difference between the previous and current states. If the user's query is tightened, the SQL query retrieves all items that were just filtered out, by simply querying items with attribute value between the current and previous values of the slider thumb. This query is then applied to the foreground layer and drawn in gray. If loosened, the SQL query retrieves all items that were just filtered in, by querying items with attribute value between the current and previous values of the slider thumb but also meet current constrains of all other sliders. This query is then applied to the foreground and drawn in choropleth color. However, whenever the entire map must be refreshed, as in panning and zooming or resizing, Dynamaps must revert to the third algorithm. This fourth algorithm performs very well because it only needs to draw a few items on the map at each interaction increment. The update is real-time with approximately 1000 items (e.g. counties of the east coast; this measurement is taken on a Pentium 450 Mhz PC). At this point, the bottleneck now shifts to the database query performance. Implementing custom data structures (as in [TBS97]) would enable further speed up.

Highlighting selected map items is done with a third layer that is on top of all others and is drawn in translucent bright yellow.

6   Limitations and Future Work

Continued work on Dynamaps is underway. Future work includes:

- Automatically loading more detailed geography when users zoom in. For example, zooming onto a US state might automatically load and display the counties of that state. One approach to accomplish this is to integrate Dynamaps into the Census Bureau's meta-data database.

- Enabling simultaneous display and exploration of multiple geography layers. For example, users could load states, counties, and cities, and perform dynamic queries and brushing on each. This introduces a new problem of overlapping map elements. Our current display algorithms are optimized for non-overlapping elements, as is typically the case in choropleth maps.

- Displaying histograms of the data on each dynamic query slider similar to the Attribute Explorer [STD95] and Visage [RLS96]. This would enable users to see additional patterns, and also help users understand the difference between uniform-distribution sliders and standard sliders.

- Integrating dynamic query data structures to improve database query performance. A very useful project would be to construct a generalized dynamic query toolkit that enables many different data viewing components, such as ArcView, to be easily plugged into a dynamic query environment.

- Enable multiple views and flexibility in choice of views. Users could display any number of sub-windows as needed. For example, in Figure 13 a user is comparing spatially distant geographic locations, east coast and west coast. Figure 14 demonstrates the use of overview and detail. Selecting a state (Texas) in the overview map shows the counties of that state in the detail map. These examples were prototyped using the Snap-Together Visualization system [NS00].

- Usability studies and task performance data are needed to evaluate and improve the user interface design.

7   Conclusion

Dynamaps is a generalized map-based information-visualization tool for dynamic queries and brushing on choropleth maps and other GIS data. It supports both specific directed-search tasks as well as open-ended exploration tasks. It enables users to relate statistical and geographic data. Users can gain an overview, discover trends and outliers, zoom in on areas of interest, and access details on demand. It demonstrates the use of commercial GIS components in an advanced visualization user interface and algorithms to accomplish this efficiently. It also contributes the notion of uniform-distribution sliders for dynamic queries.

Dynamaps is an example of an application that was prototyped using the Snap-Together Visualization [NS00] technology to demonstrate the potential for the US Census Bureau. Dynamaps has created a wave of enthusiasm at the Bureau, and development is in progress to make Dynamaps the canonical viewer for census data. The Bureau hopes to distribute Dynamaps on their data CD-ROM products, and hopes to develop a web-based version in the future for convenient citizen access to census data. The Dynamaps information web page is at http://www.cs.umd.edu/hcil/census/.

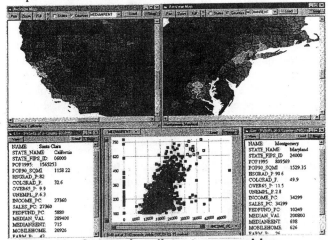

Figure 13: Comparing distant geographies

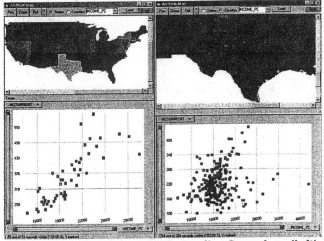

Figure 14: Overview and detail. Overview (left) shows US states. Detail (right) shows counties of the state selected in the overview.

8   Acknowledgements

This research is partially supported by the US Census Bureau. Thanks to Kent Marquis, David Desjardins, Rob Creecy, Tommy Wright, Sam Highsmith, Mark Wallace, Kathy Padget, and Tom Petkunas at the Census Bureau for their assistance and support. Thanks also to Danny Krouk at ESRI.

9   References

[AS94]   Ahlberg, C., Shneiderman, B., Visual Information Seeking: Tight coupling of dynamic query filters with starfield displays, *Proc. ACM CHI '94 Conference*, 313-317, (1994).

[AW95]   Ahlberg, C., Wistrand, E., IVEE: An Information Visualization and Exploration Environment, *Proc. IEEE Information Visualization '95*, 66-73, (1995).

[AA99]   Andrienko, G., Andrienko, N., Interactive maps for visual data exploration, *Intl Journal of Geographical Information Science, 13*(4), 355-374, (1999).

[BC87]   Becker, R., Cleveland, W., Brushing scatterplots, *Technometrics, 29*(2), 127-142, (1987).

[MK97]   MacEachren, A., Kraak, M., Exploratory cartographic visualization: advancing the agenda, *Computers and Geosciences, 23*, 335-344, (1997).

[Mon89]   Monmonier, M., Geographic brushing: Enhancing exploratory analysis of the scatterplot matrix, *Geographical Analysis, 21*(1), 81-84, (1989).

[Pla93]   Plaisant, C., Facilitating data exploration: Dynamic Queries on a health statistics map, *Proc. of the Annual Meeting of the American Statistical Association - Government Statistics Section*, 18-23, (Aug. 1993).

[PJ94]   Plaisant, C., Jain, V., Dynamaps: Dynamic queries on a health statistics atlas, Video in CHI '94 Video Program, *ACM CHI '94 Conference Companion*, 439-440, (1994).

[NS00]   North, C., Shneiderman, B., Snap-Together Visualization: A user interface for coordinating visualizations via relational schemata", *Proc. Advanced Visual Interfaces 2000*, 128-135, (May 2000).

[RLS96]   Roth, S., Lucas, P., Senn, J., Gomberg, C., Burks, M., Stroffolino, P., Kolojejchick, J., Dunmire, C., Visage: a user interface environment for exploring information, *Proc. Information Visualization*, IEEE, 3-12, (October 1996).

[STD95]   Spence, R., Tweedie, L., Dawkes, H., Su, H., Visualisation for Functional Design, *Proceedings Information Visualization '95*, 4-10, (1995).

[SMC96]   Symanzik, J., Majure, J., Cook, D., Dynamic graphics in a GIS: a biderectional link between ArcView 2.0 and Xgobi. *Computing Science and Statistics, 27*, 299-303, (1996).

[TBS97]   Tanin, E., Beigel, R. and Shneiderman, B., Design and evaluation of incremental data structures and algorithms for dynamic query interfaces, *Proc. IEEE Symposium on Information Visualization*, 81-86, (1997).

[WS92]   Williamson, C., Shneiderman, B., The dynamic HomeFinder: Evaluating dynamic queries in a real-estate information exploration system, *Proc. ACM SIGIR '92*, 338-346, (1992).

Chapter 2

Seeing the World Through Image Libraries

*The eye . . . the window of the soul, is the principal means by which
the central sense can most completely and abundantly appreciate
the infinite works of nature.*

Leonardo da Vinci, 1452–1519

Digital imagery has been receiving significant public attention in recent years with the emergence of high-quality and inexpensive digital cameras. Digital imagery also has a much broader reach as existing physical imagery is digitized by individuals as well as by institutions, such as Corbis and Getty Images, which are collecting hundreds of thousands of digital images of our world's culture.

The interface issues relating to digital imagery are numerous. People have to organize images for finding them later, and this organization can range from simple moving of images around on a hard disk to creating a database of metadata. However the images are organized, interfaces must help users find the images they want, which may be a very specific task (finding that image of President John Kennedy giving his inaugural speech on January 20, 1961) or a broader one (*i.e.*, pictures of grandma).

The HCIL's early work on photography systems was in connection with museum projects, such as the installations for New York's International Center of Photography about the photography of David Seymour (Figure 2.1).

Our efforts expanded in the mid-1990s when the National Institutes of Health made 60 gigabytes of groundbreaking anatomical images available by ftp to medical researchers and students. This was a tremendous new resource, but the images were extremely difficult to navigate given the standard

ftp interface. Graduate student Chris North applied the principles of dynamic queries to develop a simple interface that acted as a frontend to this great image repository (95-20 [2.1]). By presenting cross-sections of the bodies as the interfaces

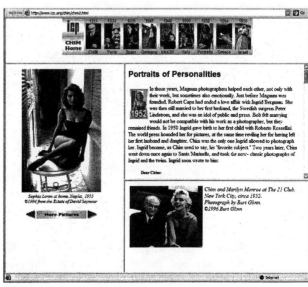

Figure 2.1 *This Web site built in 1996 for the International Center of Photography was related to an exhibit of the photos of David Seymour (1911–1956).*

themselves, with sliders to select images within those cross-sections, people were able to make sense of this data set, and it generated very positive feedback. In fact, the NIH now includes a Java version of this interface on the Visible Human project homepage (*vhp.nlm.nih.gov*). This project was interesting in another way as well because it motivated Chris to explore the importance of tight coupling between multiple views of data. This turned into Snap-Together Visualizations (97-18, 99-10, 99-26, 2000-05 [7.7]), which eventually resulted in Chris's very successful dissertation (2000-150).

Another important effort with photo databases was the HCIL's work for the Library of Congress's American Memory Project. Their millions of photos and accurate metadata is a great national, indeed international, resource that had been available only to those who could come to Washington, D.C. The advent of the World Wide Web enabled access from anywhere, permitting high school students to find images of Thomas Edison for their class report, or scholars to retrieve Mathew Brady's Civil War daguerreotypes. The metadata, carefully entered by the Library of Congress's catalogers, often enabled searchers to find exactly what they wanted. However, for those who were exploring, the browsing capability was weak. The HCIL developed strategies for finding images of different time periods, topics, and media. The HCIL's prototypes promoted broad and shallow organizations with numerous previews to lead users to the deeply buried treasures (96-16 [4.1], 98-01). The Library of Congress staff carried these ideas forward in their implementations (*www.loc.gov/ammem*).

As disk storage became cheaper and larger, we started developing interfaces to manage our own collections. Student Hyunmo Kang started building PhotoFinder in 1999 to support simple annotation and searching of images. We quickly realized that having good metadata was the key to effective searching, but there weren't any good interfaces that we found to support the simple and efficient annotation of photos; instead we found traditional form fill-in interfaces, which rapidly proved to be uninspiring to us as users. This motivated the invention of Direct Annotation, which allows users to simply drag someone's name from a database onto the photo to annotate not only the photo, but the spot on the photo that contains that person. This simple approach proved to be a crucial simplification that led to the current PhotoFinder, which is a fairly complete product that is broadly used (2000-07).

However, Ben Shneiderman's photo collection of CHI events over the past decades was still too vast to exhaustively annotate ourselves, and we realized that there was more to photos than just the names of the people in them. There were stories and anecdotes about the events depicted in those photos. So, the HCIL developed a networked kiosk version of PhotoFinder and deployed it to over 2000 attendees of the CHI 2001 conference (2001-23). This was an exciting time, since more than 800 people participated in annotating over 1000 pictures with 1700 labels and captions, which resulted in a permanent Web display of the photo collection with annotations hosted by SIGCHI at *turing.acm.org:18080/photolib* (Figure 2.2).

Around the same time, Ben Bederson started generating his own collection of digital family photos. He found that, like most home digital photo users, he tended to organize his photos by dumping unnamed photos into named directories. Furthermore, he was frustrated by commercial browsers, which required a significant amount of clicking, scrolling, and window management. He was inspired by this to build PhotoMesa, a tool to support browsing of images without metadata and with minimal organization (2001-10 [2.3]). One of his motivations was to support serendipitous photo finding, which implied the need to see many photos at once, but most photo browsers showed just a single directory or group of photos at a time. This led to the innovation of using treemaps (see Chapter 7) to show photos within each region of the tree. This work resulted in extensions to treemaps to support ordered layouts and layouts more suited to photo display (2001-18 [6.4]).

PhotoMesa has since been extended to run on the Pocket PC, to run as an applet on the Web, and to support search results of a database of metadata. PhotoMesa is currently being commercialized by Aurora Interactive, Inc., in Toronto for medical use, and by Ben Bederson's Windsor Interfaces, Inc., for general hobbyist and family use (*www.windsorinterfaces.com*).

▨ ▨ ▨ ▨ ▨ ▨ ▨ ▨ ▨ ▨

FAVORITE PAPERS FROM OUR COLLEAGUES

Balabanovic, M., Chu, L., Wolff, G., Storytelling with Digital Photographs, *Proc. ACM CHI 2000 Conference on Human Factors in Computing Systems*, ACM, New York (2000), 564–571.

Kuchinsky, A., Pering, C., Creech, M. L., Freeze, D., Serra, B., Gwizdka, J., FotoFile: A Consumer Multimedia Organization and Retrieval System, *Proc. ACM CHI 99 Conference on Human Factors in Computing Systems*, ACM, New York (1999), 496–503.

Robertson, G., Czerwinski, M., Larson, K., Robbins, D. C., Thiel, D., van Dantzich, M., Data Mountain: Using Spatial Memory for Document Management, *Proc. User Interface and Software Technology (UIST 98)* ACM, New York (1998), 153–162.

Rodden, K., Basalaj, W., Sinclair, D., Wood, K., Does Organisation by Similarity Assist Image Browsing?, *Proc. ACM CHI 2000 Conference on Human Factors in Computing Systems*, ACM, New York (2000), 190–197.

Figure 2.2 The PhotoFinder installation at the CHI 2001 conference of the Association for Computing Machinery (ACM) Special Interest Group on Computer Human Interaction (SIGCHI).

User Controlled Overviews of an Image Library:
A Case Study of the Visible Human

Chris North[†], Ben Shneiderman[†], and Catherine Plaisant*
Human-Computer Interaction Laboratory
[†]Department of Computer Science
[*]Institute for Systems Research
University of Maryland, College Park, MD 20742 USA
{north, ben, plaisant}@cs.umd.edu

ABSTRACT

This paper proposes a user interface for remote access of the National Library of Medicine's Visible Human digital image library. Users can visualize the library, browse contents, locate data of interest, and retrieve desired images. The interface presents a pair of tightly coupled views into the library data. The overview image provides a global view of the overall search space, and the preview image provides details about high resolution images available for retrieval. To explore, the user sweeps the views through the search space and receives smooth, rapid, visual feedback of contents. Desired images are automatically downloaded over the internet from the library. Library contents are indexed by meta-data consisting of automatically generated miniature visuals. The interface software is completely functional and freely available for public use, at: http://www.nlm.nih.gov/.

Keywords: Browsing, Digital Library, Image Database, Information Exploration, Information Retrieval, Internet, Medical Image, Remote Access, User Interface, Visualization, World-Wide Web.

INTRODUCTION
The Visible Human

The National Library of Medicine (NLM), for its Visible Human Project [NLM90], is in the process of creating a large digital library of anatomical images of the human body. It contains MRI and CT scans, as well as cryosection images (digital color photographs of cross-sections, Figure 1). Two cadavers, one male and one female, were carefully chosen as the subjects. The male dataset MRI and CT images were captured using the respective medical imaging scanners. The MRI images were captured at 4mm intervals throughout the body. Each is 256x256 pixels in resolution with 12-bit gray level encoding. The CT images were captured at 1mm intervals to correspond with the cryosections. Each is 512x512 pixels, also using 12-bit gray level. To capture the cryosection images, the cadaver was first frozen solid inside a large block of blue gel. Then, 1mm thick slices were successively cut away from an axial cross-section (planar cut perpendicular to the longitudinal axis of the body), and digital color images were taken of each newly exposed cross-section. A total of 1878 cryosection images were taken, spanning the body from head to toe. Each is 24-bit color and has a resolution of 2048x1216 pixels. The total result is a 15 Gigabyte image dataset of the male body. The female dataset will be captured at 1/3rd mm slices and, thus, is expected to require three times the storage space of the male dataset. In addition, 70mm film of cryosections may be scanned at higher resolutions for details of various anatomical structures.

The NLM provides public access to the Visible Human digital library via the internet. The entire dataset resides on a high capacity storage system with a high speed internet connection. A simple license agreement with NLM, intended for tracking data usage, allows any user with an internet capable computer to remotely access the full dataset. Each image is stored on the archive as a separate file with numerically indexed filenames ordered from head to toe. Using "ftp", a user remotely logs onto the archive machine with a special login ID and password provided with the license agreement, and downloads any number of image files by specifying the correct numerical filenames. The images can then be displayed locally using an appropriate image browsing software package. Also, several sample images are available to those without a license agreement on the Visible Human World Wide Web page at http://www.nlm.nih.gov/.

Because the library is available to the public, the user community is diverse. Users are of varying backgrounds and cover a wide range of expertise in human anatomy and computer skills. The most prominent user groups are medical professionals and students interested in using the images for education and modeling purposes, and computer science researchers and software developers creating medical imaging applications. Other users include elementary school teachers, curious internet surfers, and even martial arts experts! Some users wish to simply explore the dataset in an open-ended fashion, and download a sampling of images to browse. Other users, who desire a specific portion of the dataset, use a more directed search to locate and download images. Some desire only a single image or small set of images, perhaps to use as overheads while teaching an anatomy class. Others download an entire continuous block of images representing some portion of the body. In this case, the images are often used for 3D modeling of anatomical structures. For example, a medical expert might download all the cryosection images containing the heart, and load them into advanced software, such as Mayo Foundation's *ANALYZE*™, to visualize ventricle chambers. Very few attempt to download the entire library, since it would require weeks of continuous internet activity as well as overwhelming storage capacity.

Unfortunately, using the Visible Human digital library can be difficult. The ftp interface merely presents users with a long list of sequential image filenames. Browsing the data requires a trial-and-error process of guessing a file, downloading it (which could take several minutes), and

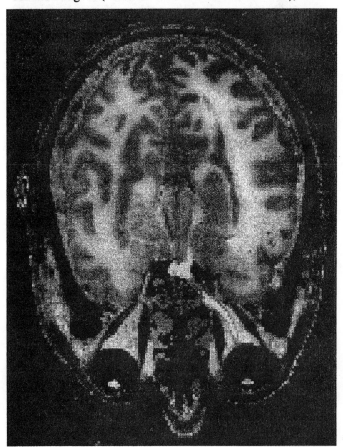

Figure 1: A Visible Human cryosection image of the male's head. Library cryosection images are full color and have 2048x1216 pixel resolution, larger than most CRTs.

displaying the image locally. A Web page interface that displays thumbnails of the library images would allow the user to visually browse the contents of the library, but would require paging through hundreds of thumbnails that must be downloaded for each access.

Whether a user wants to simply browse the library or retrieve images for some other use, it is important to avoid unnecessary downloads. Because the dataset is extremely large and would take weeks to download, and it is desired that users with smaller computers with limited storage capacity have access, the ability to remotely explore a visual representation of the dataset and download only desired images is a requirement. Hence, there is a great need for an effective user interface to assist users in browsing the library and retrieving images.

Related Work

As digital libraries quickly increase in number, researchers are continually developing improved public access methods for the many different types of library information. The primary user interface approach, especially for libraries containing unstructured collections of heterogeneous documents, is the keyword query method. In this case, Information Retrieval systems preprocess documents in the library, usually using automated algorithms, to generate comprehensive indices (meta-data). Then, when a user enters a query, the system can quickly generate a list of matching documents. Since many of these libraries contain textual documents only, such as computer science technical reports [Van94], and use strictly textual queries, interfaces are often text-based for simple WWW or teletype access. More advanced GUI interfaces afford additional capability to manipulate and visualize the textual query [VN95,YS92]. Image libraries may also provide for query by image content [FBF94]. In this case, images are indexed by content features and, if available, textual annotations. These interfaces allow users to specify example images, interactively sketch objects, or use an image content description language to create a query. KMeD [CCT95] is an example of a multimedia library in the medical domain which combines both textual and medical image elements. Digital video libraries expand the query method further, using speech recognition on the audio tracks of videos for textual indexing [GAE94]. While the query method may be an effective means for retrieving documents based on keywords or image features, it does not provide the capability to "explore" or build a mental model of the contents of a library.

However, if the documents within a library are organized using some consistent, natural, comprehensible, orderly structuring method, then interfaces using a browsing approach are also applicable. Advanced user interface techniques for information exploration can be used to explore the library structure, usually specified by meta-data, and its contents. This gives users a way to learn about the library and locate interesting documents without relying on keyword search. Several common structuring methods exist [Lev95]. For example, Hypertext systems such as the WWW organize documents in a hierarchy or other graph representation. With an interface for browsing graph structured information (see [Kor95] for a review of several), users can utilize the links, perhaps representing relationships between documents, to discover related documents that might not be found using a keyword query. Implementations include utilizing the Dewey Classification hierarchy to browse a library catalogue [All94] and reference citations to browse articles [RPH95]. MeSHbrowse [KS95] is an interface for browsing a medical terminology hierarchy containing arbitrary inter-relationships (meta-data) as an index to a medical image digital library. Another structuring method organizes information by defined textual and numerical attributes. Doan applies dynamic query interface techniques to arbitrary distributed information of this form, allowing users to quickly learn overall contents, find trends, and locate documents of interest [DPS95]. Browsing computer science literature has been handled by attribute structure as well, using author names, publication dates and sizes, etc. [HHN95]. Some interfaces use the map motif to browse spatial information, in which case attributes represent geographical locations [KJ95, Pla93]. All of these systems are examples of how advanced information-exploration user interface techniques can capitalize on the structure of an organized library to add a new dimension, namely the capability to browse, to the user's tool set for the task of information retrieval.

The Visible Human digital library exemplifies another organizational method for structuring libraries. The medical imagery, although un-annotated, is concretely structured. That is, the images have a strict sequential ordering defined by the physical objects (the human body) represented. Hence, because of the previously described successes, we expect that a user interface, which utilizes this structure to provide a browsing environment, would be an effective means for users to retrieve desired images.

Guiding principles for designing a user interface for the Visible Human library come from related research of browsing techniques. Firstly, direct manipulation, with compelling success in many exploration interfaces, provides these principles: [Shn92]

- Visual representation of the search space;
- Rapid, incremental, reversible exploratory actions;
- Pointing and selecting, instead of typing; and
- Immediate, continuous, visual feedback of results.

Research in digital medical atlases has developed reconstruction and visualization techniques for annotated, segmented, 3D medical image data [HPR95]. Interface elements and strategies for browsing individual 2D images are thoroughly identified [PCS95]. In particular, a

coordinated detail view and overview giving contextual feedback, as well as extraneous data download avoidance, are essential elements for remotely browsing very large images [CPH94]. Work on Query Previews [DPS95] shows the benefits of previewing downloadable data as a filtering process by issuing dynamic queries on meta-data. With this technique users drag sliders, click on options, and receive rapid visual feedback to identify desired data available for retrieval. With these principles as our motivation, we designed the interface described in the following section.

THE INTERFACE

We have developed a direct manipulation user interface, called the Visible Human Explorer (VHE), for remotely exploring the Visible Human digital library and retrieving images. It allows users to rapidly browse, on their own machine, a miniaturized version of the Visible Human dataset and, based on that exploration, download desired full resolution library images. The miniature dataset provides an overview of library content and acts as a preview mechanism for retrieval. The interface, along with the miniature dataset, is downloaded in advance and then used as an accessor to the archive. The payoff is quick, since downloading the VHE is equivalent to only about 3 image retrievals. With this paradigm, although implemented completely outside of any existing web browser, the interface can be thought of as an advanced, dynamic web-page application for browsing a medical image digital library.

The VHE direct manipulation interface (Figure 2) presents the user with a coordinated pair of orthogonal 2D cross-section views of the Visible Human body. The left view-window, or overview, displays a miniature coronal section, a front-view longitudinal cut of the body. It acts as an overview of the library, giving the user a general understanding of the contents of the body from head to toe. The images for this view were reconstructed directly from the cross-section images, taking advantage of the structural organization of the library, by sampling a single row of pixels from successive images to simulate a perpendicular cut. The resolution is decreased to approximately 150x470. The right view-window, or preview, displays a miniature axial section, the type of cut typically seen in medical atlas textbooks. The images for this view are reduced resolution thumbnail images (300x150) of the original library cross-sections and act as a preview of those higher resolution images. The magnification of this view is twice that of the overview, giving the user more detail of the library.

A horizontal indicator on the overview indicates the vertical position, on the body, of the axial section shown in the preview. The indicator is attached to a vertical slider widget spanning the height of the overview and can be dragged vertically across the body to sweep the cut, shown in the preview, through the body. As the user drags the indicator, the preview provides smooth, rapid feedback (<100msec) reflecting the axial cross-section at the sliding cut plane, resulting in a dynamic animated effect of motion through the body. This gives the user the ability to easily explore the contents of the entire body. Likewise, a sliding indicator in the preview controls the view shown in the overview. For example, the user can slide the overview to show a coronal section nearer to the front or back of the body. (See video report [NK96] for a demonstration of the dynamic interaction.)

While exploring, when the user locates an axial section in the preview for which high resolution data is desired, pressing the Full-Size Image button opens the Retrieval dialog box (Figure 3). This dialog handles the details of accessing the Visible Human library archive. After users

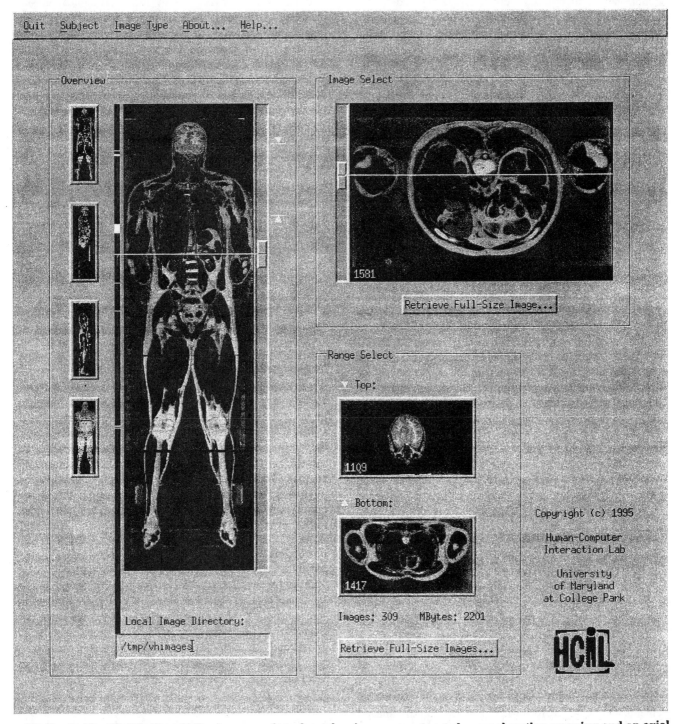

Figure 2: The Visible Human Explorer user interface, showing a reconstructed coronal section overview and an axial preview image of the upper abdominal region. Dragging sliders animates the cross-sections through the body.

type their Visible Human login ID and password into the corresponding textboxes and press the Retrieve button, the system begins to download the requested full resolution cryosection image from the NLM digital library over the internet to the user's computer. Since retrieval may take several minutes, depending on internet traffic, a status meter provides feedback on the progress of the retrieval. Users have the option to cancel the downloading at any time. Once the meter reaches 100%, the download is complete and the image is then displayed in a large detail view.

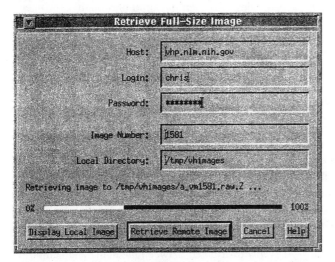

Figure 3: The VHE Retrieval dialog box meters downloading from the Visible Human digital library.

Since downloading over the internet can be a time consuming process, the system does have provisions for users with computers containing ample storage space. It can accumulate retrieved high resolution images on the user's computer, thereby allowing the user to browse not only the remote library but also a local cache as well. A vertical bar aligned next to the overview image shows tic marks indicating which axial cryosections are contained in the local cache. When one of these cross-sections is previewed by placing the cut plane slider over a tic mark, a flag in the preview window highlights to indicate that the corresponding full-size image is in the cache. Clicking on the Display button will then display the image from the cache, saving the download time. Below the overview, a text box shows the name of the user selectable directory containing the local image cache. This feature is particularly useful for users who acquire their own copy of the Visible Human digital library, since they can use the VHE to browse it as well.

The VHE also provides the capability to download any user specified range of cross-section images into this cache at once. The user simply places range indicators next to the overview slider, and selects a button to begin retrieval using the Retrieval dialog box. Two smaller axial cross-section views display images of the top and bottom slices of the

user specified range. Feedback on the number of images within the range and the total size, in megabytes, of those library images is also provided. This feature is useful for retrieving commonly examined portions of the body a priori, or for obtaining a continuous block of images for use in 3D modeling applications.

Also, using the icon buttons adjacent to the overview, the user can select amongst different overview image types, including the coronal section, sagital section (side view longitudinal section), and a simple front view of the body (no cut). This gives the user a variety of views of the overall search space. Menu options (Figure 4) enable selecting between the male or female subjects, and between the MRI, CT, and cryosection medical image types. Currently, only the male cryosection meta-data is loadable.

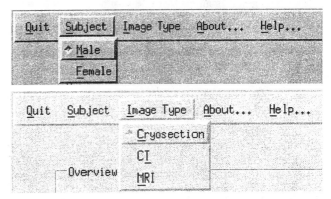

Figure 4: VHE menus for selecting amongst datasets.

Implementation and Performance

The VHE is implemented in the UNIX X/Motif environment on a Sun Sparcstation. The key to implementation is the use of meta-data, consisting of the miniature Visible Human thumbnail images, which acts as the library index. The benefit is two-fold: Firstly, the meta-data provides a manageable dataset for interactively browsing the library. Secondly, each axial section thumbnail provides a preview of and an index to the corresponding full size library image for automated retrieval purposes.

For optimal browsing performance, the meta-data is stored locally on the user's machine and is preformatted in 8 bit XImage [Nye90] format. Hence, as a slider is dragged, new thumbnail images can be moved directly from disk to screen using X Windows shared memory. On an older Sparcstation 1+, images are updated at approximately 20 per second. As a result, we expect that an implementation on a PC or Mac with reasonable I/O capabilities could also yield acceptable interactive performance.

The meta-data is pre-generated and comes packaged with the VHE software. To create the meta-data, we developed several tools to automatically generate it from the library images. The thumbnail meta-data preformatted for the axial preview window is cropped, spatially sampled, and color quantized directly from library images, and requires under 20 Megabytes of storage space. The overview meta-data formatted as coronal images is spatially sampled and reconstructed from the axial meta-data, and requires under 5 Megabytes of space. The total cryosection meta-data is 1/600th of the total size of the full resolution cryosection library data.

Benefits

The VHE interface design was chosen to be in harmony with user tasks. The tightly coupled 2D views of the dataset, combined with rapid, dynamic user control of movement through the third dimension, provides a highly interactive interface yet avoids unnecessary complexities. The result is an elegant interface affording convenient user exploration of the image data, for both novice and expert users. The need for learning time is essentially eliminated. Feedback is fast enough to engage the user. Users can quickly learn about the entire library by sweeping the views through the body, absorbing 20 MB of data in just a few seconds. Then, slower smaller movements to carefully examine interesting portions of the library help locate optimal images for downloading. Also, when dragging a slider, visualizing the resulting motion of the structural patterns in the cross-section thumbnails provides additional insight over, for example, simply viewing thumbnails side by side or in a click-and-wait incremental fashion.

As has been discovered in exploration interfaces for many other types of data, a visual overview of the data space is extremely helpful [Shn94]. When users search for specific data, the VHE overview quickly guides them to the desired location. It provides context for the axial preview thumbnails, some of which would otherwise be difficult to interpret exactly. It also promotes user exploration of the library, by eliminating the penalty of the possibility of getting lost or not being able to return to a desired location in a timely fashion. The preview allows users to select images, filtering out unwanted information, and download and zoom only on desired detailed data on demand.

DISCUSSION
Orthoviewer

While developing the VHE interface, we also implemented another prototype, dubbed the Orthoviewer (Figure 5), that generalizes the VHE motif. It presents the user with all three orthogonal views (sagital, coronal, and axial) of the Visible Human body simultaneously. Each view contains both a vertical and horizontal indicator line which reflects the position, with respect to the view, of the cut planes of the other two views. Each of these six indicators can be dragged, as in the VHE, to slide one of the views through the body. Pairs of corresponding indicators are tightly coupled. For example, dragging the vertical indicator in the

sagital section animates the coronal view and also slides the horizontal indicator in the axial section, which reflects the position of the same cutting plane. Interestingly, we discovered that the Orthoviewer interface confuses many users. The addition of a third view and four indicators makes it difficult to decipher which indicator manipulates which view. Users typically resort to a trial-and-error process to find the appropriate indicator to operate. Also, since each indicator is tightly coupled to 2 other components, when dragging an indicator, the user is distracted by the additional motion. The interface simply provides too much dynamic information for many users to process. Users' cognition is consumed by the Orthoviewer interface instead of the data itself. As a result, we designed the VHE interface with a distinct overview-preview pair, as used in many successful browsing interfaces in other domains [KPS95].

User Feedback

In July 1995, we publicly released the VHE system on our Web site, enabling users to download and use it to access the Visible Human library. Our access logs indicate that over 300 users, from all over the world, have downloaded the software, after just 2 months. As a result, we received some informal feedback about the interface and its usage from actual users. We received 34 responses. Of those who indicated their occupation or field of study, users were evenly distributed between medicine and computer science, and between professional and student. Others were simply curious internet users. The medical users identified their use of the library information being primarily for learning and teaching gross anatomy and as a reference for radiology. The computer scientists identified their primary usage as test data for image processing and computer graphics algorithms research. All of whom gave in-depth

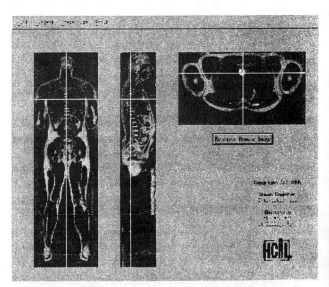

Figure 5: The Orthoviewer prototype interface shows three orthogonal views of the body. Dragging any of the six indicators animates corresponding views.

comments reported that the VHE interface was very helpful for visualizing the Visible Human library. One user stated: "Now I have a far better understanding of how the whole data-set looks." Users who need to download specific individual images were very pleased that, with the VHE interface, they were finally able to quickly locate and retrieve the proper library image. "Before using the VHE it was always a bit of a problem to get the right images." Short responses indicated the users' excitement with the interface's highly interactive nature, fast feedback, and quick learnability, trademarks of a direct manipulation interface. Also, some suggestions for improvement were offered. Multiple users suggested increasing the size of the preview image by a factor of 1.5 or 2, enabling visualization of most major organs. One user felt that simply displaying the existing preview images larger, without an increase in actual data resolution, would be sufficient. Several users were wary of the 25MB size of the meta-data. Another suggestion was to display MRI, CT, and cryosection previews simultaneously, enabling the user to browse all three portions of the library at once.

Generalizations and Limitations

The VHE interface demonstrates a browsing approach that could be generalized to other image sets in which images are sequenced in some meaningful progression. The Visible Human library contains spatially sequenced images, or volumetric data. While medical imaging is the most common form, the interface could be used to browse other cross-sectional or volumetric datasets, such as geological or atmospheric samplings, allowing users to visualize pattern changes in sedimentation layers or storm turbulence. Images could also be sequenced by time of capture, as in digital video. In this case, axial cross-sections would correspond to individual frames of the video sequence, and longitudinal sections would show motion patterns of video action across frames [ED94]. In fact, we originally encoded the VHE meta-data as an MPEG video, but opted for another representation for performance reasons. Also, the images themselves could be visual representations of more abstract scientific measurements. For example, astronomers could browse a library of spectrograms collected over a period of time to view changes in wave patterns. Applying the VHE interface to these different datasets would simply require creation of the miniature meta-data (we developed tools to automate this process for the Visible Human project), and alteration of interface dimensions to accommodate the appropriate image sizes.

Currently, the VHE interface approach is limited to libraries containing such sequenced images. For libraries containing heterogeneous collections of arbitrary, unrelated images or textual documents, the overview window would need to be redesigned to show a meaningful representation of the library. For example, chronological timelines or simple page numbers would provide additional understanding of library contents. In this case, the ability to quickly flip through many images or pages, like flipping through a book, would be very helpful when exploring large libraries.

Future Work

With respect to the VHE interface, improvements could be made, including those suggested in the User Feedback. Also, a helpful new capability might allow the user to browse higher resolution detailed data (retrieved from the Visible Human library) of a smaller portion of the body in the same fashion used to browse the initial miniature body. For example, if the user wishes to see the heart in higher detail, retrieving portions of all the library axial cross-sections containing the heart might be preferred over a single large axial image. A schema could allow the user to specify a small sub-region of the body to zoom on, then, after retrieval, the entire interface would be reused for exploring that sub-region in higher resolution. The overview and preview windows would display views of the zoomed sub-region, for example, a coronal and axial section (respectively) of the heart. Naturally, the user could return back to explore the initial miniature Visible Human body at any time. With this zooming method, users could browse high detailed data using the same interface techniques as described in this paper, instead of simply viewing high resolution data only as single large axial images.

In addition, investigation of other visual overview representation and browsing techniques for this type of digital library structure is needed. As computer hardware progresses, 3D representation techniques are becoming more tractable and attractive. Human factors research is required to determine usability measures of differences between 2D representations, of which the VHE is an example, and potential 3D representations.

In the broader picture, as the Visible Human digital library grows to include textual annotations, segmented images, attribute indexes, relationship graphs, video animations, and many other forms of information, additional user interface browsing techniques will apply. The graphical interface approach presented in this paper could be combined with Korn's textual browser intended for navigating a medical terminology hierarchy containing links to the Visible Human images [KS95]. If the two interfaces were tightly coupled, manipulating either the graphical or textual interface elements would immediately show effects in the other domain. Users could browse using a combined strategy, utilizing their knowledge of both medical terminology and visual appearance of human anatomy. We believe that integrating different interface approaches for various information types would provide a rich comprehensive browsing environment for an expanding Visible Human digital library.

ACKNOWLEDGMENTS
Chris North received a National Library of Medicine fellowship, administered by the Oak Ridge Institute for Science and Education. Additional funding was provided by a National Library of Medicine grant and National Science Foundation grant EEC 94-02384.

SOFTWARE
The VHE interface software is fully functional and freely available for public use. For more information, see http://www.cs.umd.edu/projects/hcil/Research/1995/vhe.html or anonymous ftp.cs.umd.edu in /pub/hcil/Demos/VHP.

REFERENCES

[All94]   R. Allen. Navigating and Searching in Hierarchical Digital Library Catalogs. *Proc. Digital Libraries '94 Conf*, pg 95-100, 1994.

[CCT95]   W. Chu, A. Cardenas, and R. Taira. KMeD: A Knowledge-Based Multimedia Medical Distributed Database System. *Information Systems*, vol 20, #2, pg 75-96, 1995.

[CPH94]   D. Carr, C. Plaisant, and H. Hasegawa. The Design of a Telepathology Workstation: Exploring Remote Images. University of Maryland, Dept. of Computer Science Technical Report, CS-TR-3270, 1994.

[DPS95]   K. Doan, C. Plaisant, and B. Shneiderman. Query Previews in Networked Information Systems. University of Maryland, Dept. of Computer Science Technical Report, 1995.

[ED94]   E. Elliott and G. Davenport. Video Streamer. *Conf. Companion of Human Factors in Computing Systems Conf*, pg 65-66, 1994.

[FBF94]   C. Faloutsos, R. Barber, M. Flickner, J. Hafner, W. Niblack, D. Petrovic, and W. Equitz. Efficient and Effective Querying by Image Content. *Journal of Intelligent Information Systems*, vol 3, pg 231-262, 1994.

[GAE94]   S. Gauch, R. Aust, J. Evans, J. Gauch, G. Minden, D. Niehaus, and J. Roberts. The Digital Video Library System: Vision and Design. *Proc. Digital Libraries '94 Conf*, pg 47-52, 1994.

[HHN95]   L. Heath, D. Hix, L. Nowell, W. Wake, G. Averboch, E. Labow, S. Guyer, D. Brueni, R. France, K. Dalal, and E. Fox. Envision: A User-Centered Database of Computer Science Literature. *Communications of the ACM*, vol 38, #4, pg 52-53, April 1995.

[HPR95]   K. Hohne, A. Pommert, M. Riemer, T. Schiemann, R. Schubert, and U. Tiede. Medical Volume Visualization Based on "Intelligent Volumes". *Scientific Visualization: Advances and Challenges*, Academic Press, pg 21-35, 1995.

[KJ95]   C. Kacmar and D. Jue. The Information Zone System. *Communications of the ACM*, vol 38, #4, pg 46-47, April 1995.

[Kor95]   F. Korn. A Taxonomy of Browsing Methods: Approaches to the 'Lost in Concept Space' Problem. University of Maryland, Dept. of Computer Science Technical Report, 1995.

[KPS95]   H. Kumar, C. Plaisant and B. Shneiderman. Browsing Hierarchical Data with Multi-Level Dynamic Queries and Pruning. University of Maryland, Dept. of Computer Science Technical Report, CS-TR-3474, 1995.

[KS95]   F. Korn and B. Shneiderman. Navigating Terminology Hierarchies to Access a Digital Library of Medical Images. University of Maryland, Dept. of Computer Science Technical Report, 1995.

[Lev95]   D. Levy. Cataloging in the Digital Order. *Proc. Digital Libraries '95 Conf*, 1995.

[NK96]   C. North and F. Korn. Browsing Anatomical Image Databases: A Case Study of the Visible Human. *Conf. Companion of Human Factors in Computing Systems Conf*, 1996.

[NLM90]   National Library of Medicine Long Range Plan: Electronic Imaging, *NIH Publication No. 90-2197*, U.S. Dept. of Health and Human Services, April 1990.

[Nye90]   A. Nye. *Xlib Reference Manual*, O'Reilly & Associates Inc, 1990.

[PCS95]   C. Plaisant, D. Carr, and B. Shneiderman. Image Browser Taxonomy and Guidelines for Designers. *IEEE Software*, vol 28, #3, pg 21-32, March 1995.

[Pla93]   C. Plaisant. Facilitating data exploration: Dynamic Queries on a Health Statistics Map. *Proc. of the Government Statistics Section, Annual Meeting of the American Statistical Assoc. Conf. Proc*, pg 18-23, 1993.

[RPH95]   R. Rao, J. Pedersen, M. Hearst, J. Mackinlay, S. Card, L. Masinter, P. Halvorsen, and G. Robertson. Rich Interaction in the Digital

Library. *Communications of the ACM*, vol 38, #4, pg 29-39, April 1995.

[Shn92]   B. Shneiderman. *Designing the User Interface: Strategies for Effective Human-Computer Interaction: Second Edition*, Addison-Wesley Publ. Co, 1992.

[Shn94]   B. Shneiderman. Dynamic Queries for Visual Information Seeking. *IEEE Software*, pg 70-77, Nov 1994.

[Van94]   M. VanHeyningen.   The Unified Computer Science Technical Report Index: Lessons in Indexing Diverse Resources.   *Proc. 2nd Intl*

WWW '94: Mosaic and the Web, pg 535-543, 1994.

[VN95]   A. Veerasamy and S. Navathe.   Querying, Navigating and Visualizing a Digital Library Catalog. *Proc. Digital Libraries '95 Conf*, 1995.

[YS92]   D. Young and B. Shneiderman. A Graphical Filter/Flow Representation of Boolean Queries: A Prototype Implementation and evaluation. *JASIS*, vol 44, #6, pg 327-339, 1992.

Direct Annotation:
A Drag-and-Drop Strategy for Labeling Photos

Ben Shneiderman, Hyunmo Kang
Dept. of Computer Science, Human-Computer Interaction Laboratory,
Institute for Advanced Computer Studies & Institute for Systems Research
University of Maryland, College Park, MD 20742 USA
{ben, kang}@cs.umd.edu

Abstract

Annotating photos is such a time-consuming, tedious and error-prone data entry task that it discourages most owners of personal photo libraries. By allowing users to drag labels such as personal names from a scrolling list and drop them on a photo, we believe we can make the task faster, easier and more appealing. Since the names are entered in a database, searching for all photos of a friend or family member is dramatically simplified. We describe the user interface design and the database schema to support direct annotation, as implemented in our PhotoFinder prototype.

Keywords: direct annotation, direct manipulation, graphical user interfaces, photo libraries, drag-and-drop, label placement

1. Introduction

Adding captions to photos is a time-consuming and error prone task for professional photographers, editors, librarians, curators, scholars, and amateur photographers. In many professional applications, photos are worthless unless they are accurately described by date, time, location, photographer, title, recognizable people, etc. Additional annotation may include details about the photo (for example, film type, print size, aperture, shutter speed, owner, copyright information) and its contents (keywords from controlled vocabularies, topics from a hierarchy, free text descriptions, etc.). For amateur photographers, annotations are rarely done, except for the occasional handwritten note on the back of a photo or an envelope containing a collection of photos.

For those who are serious about adding annotations, the common computer-based approach is to use database programs, such as Microsoft Access, that offer form fill-in or free text boxes and then store the information in a database. Data entry is typically done by typing, but selecting attribute values for some fields (for example, black&white or color film) is supported in many systems. Of course, simpler tools that provide free-form input, such as word processors, spreadsheets, and other tools are used in many situations. Captions and annotations are often displayed near a photo on screen displays, web pages, and printed versions. Software packages (Kodak PhotoEasy, MGI PhotoSuite, Aladdin Image AXS, etc.) and web sites (Kodak's photonet, Gatherround.com, shutterfly, etc.) offer modest facilities to typing in annotations and searching descriptions.

As photo library sizes increase the need and benefit of annotation and search capabilities grows. The need to rapidly locate photos of Bill Clinton meeting with Boris Yeltsin at a European summit held in 1998 is strong enough to justify substantial efforts in many news agencies. More difficult searches such as "agriculture in developing nations" are harder to satisfy, but many web and database search tools support such searches (Lycos, Corbis, etc.). Query-By-Image-Content from IBM, is one of many projects that uses automated techniques to analyze image (http://wwwqbic.almaden.ibm.com/). Computer vision techniques can be helpful in finding photos by color (sunsets are a typical example), identifying features (corporate logos or the Washington Monument), or textures (such as clouds or trees), but a blend of automated and manual techniques may be preferable. Face recognition research offers hope for automated annotation, but commercial progress is slow [1][2].

2. Related Work on Annotation

Annotation of photos is a variation on previously explored problems such as annotation on maps [3][4][5] in which the challenge is to place city, state, river, or lake labels close to the features. There is a long history of work on this problem, but new possibilities emerge because of the dynamics of the computer screen (Figure 1). However, annotation is usually seen as an authoring process conducted by specialists and users only chose whether to show or hide annotations. Variations on annotation also come from the placement of labels on markers in information visualization tasks such as in tree structures, such in the hyperbolic tree [6] (Figure 2) or in medical histories, such as LifeLines [7] (Figure 3).

Figure 1. US Map with City Names

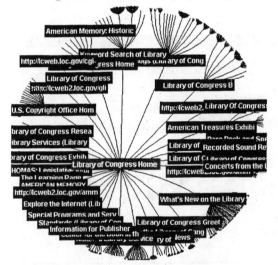

Figure 2. Hyperbolic Tree

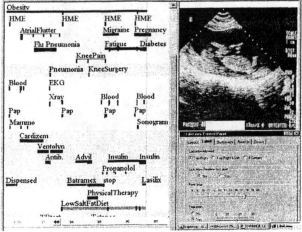

Figure 3. LifeLines Medical Patient History

Previous work on annotation focused on writing programs to make label placements that reduced overlaps [8], but there are many situations in which it is helpful for users to place labels manually, much like post-it notes, on documents, photos, maps, diagrams, webpages, etc. Annotation of paper and electronic documents by hand is also a much-studied topic with continuing innovations [9]. While many systems allow notes to be placed on a document or object, the demands of annotating personal photo libraries are worthy of special study [10]. We believe that personal photo libraries are a special case because users are concentrating on the photos (and may have a low interested in the underlying technology), are concerned about the social aspects of sharing photos, and are intermittent users. They seek enjoyment and have little patience for form filling or data entry.

3. The PhotoFinder Project

In the initial stages of our project on storage and retrieval from personal photo libraries (http://www.cs.umd.edu/hcil/photolib/), we emphasize collection management and annotation to support searching for people. This decision was based on our user needs assessment, reports from other researchers, and our personal experience that indicate that people often want to find photos of a friend or relative at some event that occurred recently or years ago [2][11]. Personal photo libraries may have from hundreds to tens of thousands of photos, and organization is, to be generous, haphazard. Photos are sometimes in neat albums, but more often put in a drawer or a shoebox. While recent photos are often on top, shuffling through the photos often leaves them disorganized. Some users will keep photos in the envelopes they got from the photo store, and more organized types will label and order them.

As digital cameras become widespread, users have had to improvise organization strategies using hierarchical directory structures, and typing in descriptive file and directory names to replace the automatically generated photo file numbers. Some software packages (PhotoSuite, PhotoEasy, etc.) enable users to organize photos into albums and create web pages with photos, but annotation is often impossible or made difficult. Web sites such as Kodak's PhotoNet.com, Gatherround.com, etc. enable users to store collections of photos and have discussion groups about the collections, but annotation is limited to typing into a caption field. The pioneering effort of the FotoFile [2] offered an excellent prototype that inspired our work.

Our goal in the PhotoFinder project was to support personal photo library users. We developed a conceptual model of a library having a set of collections, with each collection having a set of photos. Photos can participate in multiple collections. Collections and individual photos can be annotated with free text fields plus date and location fields stored in a database (see Figure 6 for our Photo Library database schema). Our interface has three main windows:

- **Library viewer**: Shows a representative photo for each collection, with a stack representing the number of photos in each collection.

- **Collection viewer**: Shows thumbnails of all photos in the collection. Users can move the photos around, enlarge them all or individually, cluster them, or present them in a compact manner. A variety of thumbnail designs were prototyped and will be refined for inclusion in future versions.

- **Photo viewer**: Shows an individual photo in a resizable window. A group of photos can be selected in the Collection viewer and dragged to the Photo viewer to produce an animated slide show.

We also put a strong emphasis on recording and searching by the names of people in each photo. We believed that a personal photo library might contain repeated images of the same people at different events,

and estimated 100-200 identifiable people in 10,000 photos. Furthermore we expected a highly skewed distribution with immediate family members and close friends appearing very frequently. The many-to-many relationship between photos and people is mediated by the Appearance relation (Figure 6) that stores the identification of all the people who appear in each photo.

Such a database would support accurate storage of information, but we recognized that the tedious data entry problem would prevent most users from typing in names for each photo. Furthermore, the inconsistency in names is quickly a problem with misspellings or variant names (for example, Bill, Billy, William) undermining the success of search.

A second challenge we faced was that the list of names of people appearing in a photo could often be difficult to associate with individuals, especially in group shots. Textual captions often indicate left-to-right ordering in front and back rows, or give even more specific identification of who is where.

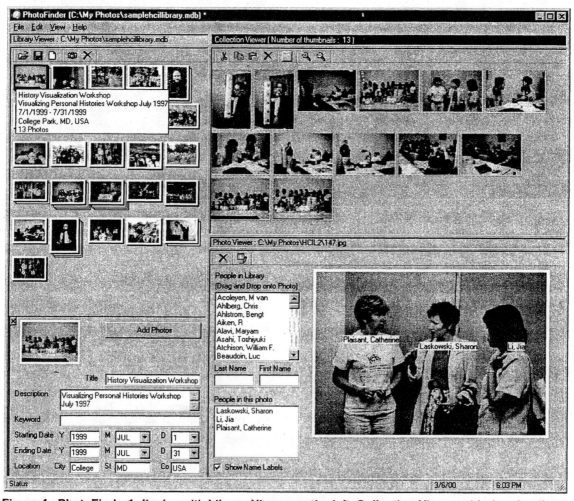

Figure 4. PhotoFinder1 display with Library Viewer on the left, Collection Viewer with thumbnails on the upper right, and Photo Viewer on the lower right.

4. Direct Annotation

To cope with these challenges we developed the concept of direct annotation: selectable, dragable labels that can be placed directly on the photo. Users can select from a scrolling or pop-up list and drag by mouse or touch screen. This applies direct manipulation principles [12] that avoid the use of a keyboard, except to enter a name the first time it appears. The name labels can be moved or hidden, and their presence is recorded in the database in the Appearance relation with an X-Y location, based on an origin in the upper left hand corner of the photo.

This simple rapid process also allows users to annotate at will. They can add annotations when they first see their photos on the screen, when they review them and make selections, or when they are showing them to others. This easy design and continuous annotation facility may encourage users to do more annotation. Figures 5 (a)-(f) show the process of annotation on a set of four people at a conference.

(a) Initial State

(b) Select Name

(c) Dragging

(d) Dropped

(e) Four Identified People

(f) Hide Annotations

Figure 5. The Process of Dragging and Dropping an Annotation on a Photo

The selection list is shown as being an alphabetically organized scrolling menu, but it could be implemented as a split menu [13]. This would entail having 3-5 of the most commonly occurring names in a box, followed by the alphabetical presentation of the full list. Thus the most frequent names would be always visible to allow rapid selection. Name completion strategies for rapid table navigation would be useful in this application. When users mouse down on a name, the dragging begins and a colored box surrounds the name. When users mouse up, the name label is fixed in place, a tone is sounded, and the database entry of the XY coordinates is stored. The tone gives further feedback and reinforces the sense of accomplishment. Further reinforcement for annotation is given by subtly changing the border of photos in the Collection viewer. When a photo gets an annotation, its thumbnail's white border changes to green. Users will then be able to see how much they have accomplished and which photos are still in need of annotation.

A Show/Hide checkbox gives users control over seeing the photo with and without the name labels. Since the photo viewer window is resizable, the position of the labels changes to make sure they remain over the same person. A small marker (ten pixels long) hangs down from the center of the label to allow precise placement when there are many people close together. The marker can be used to point at the head or body and it becomes especially useful in crowded group photos.

Future additions might include the capacity to resize the labels, change fonts, change colors, or add animations. Another interesting issue is collaborative annotation in which multiple users working side-by-side [14] or independently might annotate photos and then the results could be combined, with appropriate resolution of conflicts. Tools for finding variant spellings or switches between last and first names would help raise data quality. A valuable accelerator is bulk annotation [2], in which a group of photos is selected and then the same label is applied to every photo with one action, although individual placement might still be needed.

Of course, annotation by names of people in photos is only the first step. Drag and drop annotation for any kind of object in a photo (car, house, bicycle), map (cities, states, lakes), or painting (brushstroke, signature, feature) is possible. Annotation about the overall image, such as type of photo (portrait, group, landscape), map (highway, topographic, urban), or painting (impressionist, abstract, portrait) is possible. Colored ribbons or multiple star icons could be used to indicate the importance or quality of photos.

Searching and browsing become more effective once annotations are included in the photo database. The obvious task is to see all photos that include an individual. This has been implemented by simply dragging the name from the list into the Collection viewer or to a designated label area. The PhotoFinder finds and displays all photos in which that name appears in a label.

5. Database Design and Implementation

5.1 Schema of the Photo Library database

The PhotoFinder operates using a Photo Library database (Microsoft Access), which contains five linked tables (Figure 6). The basic concept is that a Photo Library contains Collections of Photos, and that Photos contain images of People.

In the Photo Library schema, the Collections table represents the collections of photos with attributes such as Collection Title, Description, Keywords, Starting Date, Ending Date, Location, Representative PhotoID and unique Collection ID. The Photos table is where references (full path and file name) of photos and their thumbnails are stored with important attributes such as the date of photo, event, keywords, location, rating, color, locale, and so on. Each photo should have a unique reference and photos with the same references are not allowed to be stored in this table even though they have different attribute values. The Linkage table is the connection between the Collections table and Photos table. It stores the links between collections and photos.

The People table stores all the information about the people who appear in the Photo Library. In our initial implementation, attributes include only the Given (First) name and Family (Last) name of the person, and the unique PersonID (people with the same first and last name are not allowed to be stored in People table). Eventually, the People table will be extended to include personal information such as e-mail address for exporting the Photo Library, homepage address, occupation and so on. The Appearance table stores the information about which Person is in which Photo. It serves as the linkage between the Photos table and the People table. Attributes include AppearanceID, PersonID, PhotoID, and relative (X, Y) coordinates (upper left corner is (0,0), lower right is (100,100)) of people in the photos.

In designing the Photo Library, we made three major assumptions concerning the Library, Collections, and Photos. These assumptions can be classified as follows:

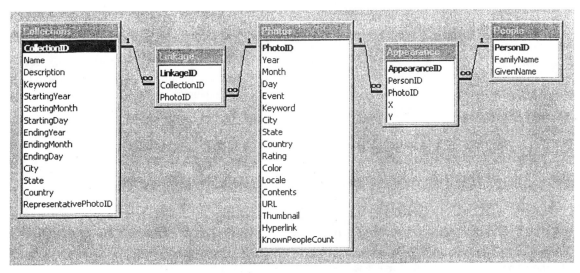

Figure 6. The schema of Photo Library database

- *Relationship between Collections and Photos*

A 1-to-many relationship between the Collections table and the Linkage table has been set so that a collection can contain multiple photos, and a 1-to-many relationship between the Photos table and the Linkage table has been set so that same photo can be included in multiple collections. It is also possible that a collection contains the same photo multiple times to permit reappearances in a slide presentation. Two different collections could have exactly same set of photos. If two photos have different path names, they are different photos even though they are copies of a photo.

- *Relationship between Photos and People*

A 1-to-many relationship between the Photos table and the Appearance table has been set so that a photo can contain multiple persons, and a 1-to-many relationship between People table and Appearance table has been set so that same person can be included in multiple photos. Multiple appearances of the same person in a photo are not allowed. A composite pair of Given name and Family name should be unique in the People table.

- *Relationship among Library, Collections, and Photos*

Within a library, the same photo could be contained in multiple collections multiple times, but their attributes and annotations must be the same.

In the first design of the Photo Library database, we only considered annotation by names of people in photos, but the Photo Library database can be easily extended by adding an Object table, Animal table, Keyword table, and so on, along with connection tables similar to the Appearance table. With such a Photo Library database design, more flexible annotation would be possible.

5.2 Updating the Photo Library Database by Direct Annotation

PhotoFinder keeps updating the Photo Library database whenever the direct annotation module causes any information changes. In this section, we classify the Photo Library database updating situations into five categories, and discuss corresponding algorithm and implementation issues.

- *Adding a New Name Label / Creating a New Person:*

When users drag a name from "People in Library" listbox and drop it onto a photo, PhotoFinder immediately checks whether there already exists an Appearance connection between the photo and the person since multiple appearances of the same person in a photo are not allowed. If a conflict occurs, PhotoFinder would highlight the existing name label on the photo and ignore the drag-and-drop event with a warning message. If there is no conflict, PhotoFinder finds the PersonID and PhotoID, calculates a relative (X, Y) position ($0 \le X, Y \le 100$) of the drag-and-drop point on the photo, and then creates a new Appearance record with this information. After adding a new record to the Appearance table, the PhotoFinder updates "People in this Photo" listbox and finally creates a name label on the photo. To show that the label has just been inserted, the newly added name in the "People in this Photo" listbox will be selected, and accordingly the new name label on the photo will be highlighted. If the added name label is the first one on the photo, PhotoFinder sends an event to the Collection Viewer to change the border color of the corresponding thumbnail to green, in order to show that the photo now has an annotation. The algorithm for creating a new person is simple. As soon as users type in the first name and last name of a person in the editbox and press enter, PhotoFinder checks whether the name already exists in the People table. If so, a warning message will be displayed with the name in "People in Library" listbox being selected. If not, PhotoFinder creates and adds a new Person record to the People table, and then updates the "People in Library" listbox, selecting and highlighting the newly added name.

■ *Deleting Name Label / Deleting Person:*

When the delete button of the Photo Viewer toolbar is clicked or the delete key is pressed, PhotoFinder checks whether the selected name label already exists. If not, PhotoFinder ignores the deleting action. But if it exists, PhotoFinder automatically calculates the PersonID of the selected name label and the PhotoID, and it searches through the Appearance table to find and delete an Appearance record having those IDs. PhotoFinder updates "People in this Photo" listbox and deletes the name label on the photo. If the deleted name label was the last one on the photo, PhotoFinder sends an event to the Collection Viewer to change the border color of the corresponding thumbnail to white, to show that the photo has no annotation. If focus is on the "People in Library" listbox and the delete key is pressed, PhotoFinder finds the PersonID of the selected name in the listbox. PhotoFinder deletes the PersonID from the People table and also deletes all the Appearance records containing that PersonID, which results in the complete elimination of the name label from the other photos in the Photo Library. Again, Collection Viewer updates the border color of thumbnails that no longer have annotations.

■ *Editing a Name of Person:*

Users can edit a name of person in library by pressing the edit button of the Photo Viewer toolbar or by just double clicking over the selected name in the "People in Library" listbox. When the edited name is typed in, PhotoFinder finds and changes the corresponding person record from the People table only if there is no duplication of the name in the People table. It also refreshes both the "People in this Photo" and the "People in Library" listboxes, and all the name labels on the current photo. If duplication occurs, the whole editing process will be ignored with a warning message.

■ *Positioning Name Label:*

Drag-and-dropping the existing label over the photo can change position of the name label. As mentioned before, the relative (X, Y) position of the center point of a name label is stored in the corresponding Appearance record. PhotoFinder uses a small marker hanging down from the center of the label to allow precise placement. But since the size and direction (downward) of the marker is fixed, it is somewhat difficult to distinguish labels when many people appear in the photo close together. Using Excentric labels [15] or adding an additional (X, Y) field to the Appearance table to allow a longer and directional marker could solve this problem. Other features such as changing the font size of labels and avoiding occlusion among labels in resizing the photo will be handled in future versions of PhotoFinder.

■ *Importing People Table from other Libraries:*

Retyping the names that already exist in other libraries is very tedious and time-consuming job. Therefore, PhotoFinder supports a function to import the People table from other libraries. The internal process of importing the People table is similar to that of creating a new person repeatedly. The only thing PhotoFinder should handle is checking and eliminating the duplication of a person name.

6. Conclusion

Digital photography is growing rapidly, and with it the need to organize, manage, annotate, browse and search growing libraries of photos. While numerous tools offer collection or album management, we believe that the addition of easy to use and enjoyable annotation techniques is an important contribution. After a single demonstration, most users understand direct annotation and are eager to use it. We are adding features, integrating search functions, and conducting usability tests.

Acknowledgements: We appreciate the partial support of Intel and Microsoft, and the contributions of Ben Bederson, Todd Carlough, Manav Kher, Catherine Plaisant, and other members of the Human-Computer Interaction Laboratory at the University of Maryland.

7. REFERENCES

[1] R. Chellappa, C.L. Wilson and S. Sirohey, "Human and Machine Recognition of Faces: A Survey" *Proceedings of the IEEE*, Vol. 83, pp. 705-740, May 1995.

[2] Allan Kuchinsky, Celine Pering, Michael L. Creech, Dennis Freeze, Bill Serra, Jacek Gwizdka, "FotoFile: A Consumer Multimedia Organization and Retrieval System", *Proceedings of ACM CHI99 Conference on Human Factors in Computing Systems*, 496-503, 1999.

[3] E. Imhof, "Positioning Names on Maps", *The American Cartographer,* 2, 128-144, 1975.

[4] J. Christensen, J. Marks, and S. Shieber, "An Empirical Study Of Algorithms For Point-Feature

Label Placement", *ACM Transactions on Graphics 14*, 3, 203-232, 1995.

[5] J. S. Doerschler and H. Freeman, "A Rule-Based System For Dense-Map Name Placement", *Communications Of The ACM* 35, 1, 68-79, 1992.

[6] John Lamping, Ramana Rao, and Peter Pirolli, "A Focus + Context Technique Based On Hyperbolic Geometry For Visualizing Large Hierarchies", *Proceedings of ACM CHI95 Conference on Human Factors in Computing Systems*, New York, 401-408, 1995.

[7] Jia Li., Catherine Plaisant, Ben Shneiderman, "Data Object and Label Placement for Information Abundant Visualizations" *Workshop on New Paradigms in Information Visualization and Manipulation (NPIV'98)*, ACM, New York, 41-48, 1998.

[8] Mark D. Pritt, "Method and Apparatus for The Placement of Annotations on A Display without Overlap", US Patent 5689717, 1997.

[9] Bill N. Schilit, Gene Golovchinsky, and Morgan N. Price, "Beyond Paper: Supporting Active Reading with Free Form Digital Ink Annotations", *Proceedings of ACM CHI 98 Conference on Human Factors in Computing Systems,* v.1 249-256, 1998.

[10] J Kelly Lee and Dana Whitney Wolcott, "Method of Customer Photoprint Annotation", US Patent 5757466, 1998.

[11] Richard Chalfen, *Snapshot Versions of Life*, Bowling Green State University Popular Press, Ohio, 1987.

[12] Ben Shneiderman, *Designing the User Interface: Strategies for Effective Human-Computer Interaction, 3rd Edition*, Addison Wesley Longman, Reading, MA, 1998.

[13] Andrew Sears and Ben Shneiderman, "Split Menus: Effectively Using Selection Frequency To Organize Menus", *ACM Transactions on Computer-Human Interaction 1*, 1, 27-51, 1994.

[14] J. Stewart, B. B. Bederson, & A. Druin, "Single Display Groupware: A Model for Co-Present Collaboration.", *Proceedings of ACM CHI99 Conference on Human Factors in Computing Systems*, 286-293, 1999.

[15] Jean-Daniel Fekete Catherine Plaisant, "Excentric Labeling: Dynamic Neighborhood Labeling for Data Visualization.", *Proceedings of ACM CHI99 Conference on Human Factors in Computing Systems*, 512-519, 1999.

66

PhotoMesa: A Zoomable Image Browser Using Quantum Treemaps and Bubblemaps

Benjamin B. Bederson
Human-Computer Interaction Laboratory
Computer Science Department, Institute for Advanced Computer Studies
University of Maryland, College Park, MD 20742
+1 301 405-2764
bederson@cs.umd.edu
http://www.cs.umd.edu/hcil/photomesa

ABSTRACT

PhotoMesa is a zoomable image browser that uses a novel treemap algorithm to present large numbers of images grouped by directory, or other available metadata. It uses a new interaction technique for zoomable user interfaces designed for novices and family use that makes it straightforward to navigate through the space of images, and impossible to get lost.

PhotoMesa groups images using one of two new algorithms that lay out groups of objects in a 2D space-filling manner. *Quantum treemaps* are designed for laying out images or other objects of indivisible (quantum) size. They are a variation on existing treemap algorithms in that they guarantee that every generated rectangle will have a width and height that are an integral multiple of an input object size. *Bubblemaps* also fill space with groups of quantum-sized objects, but generate non-rectangular blobs, and utilize space more efficiently.

Keywords

Zoomable User Interfaces (ZUIs), Treemaps, Image Browsers, Animation, Graphics, Jazz.

INTRODUCTION

There has been much work in recent years on information retrieval systems for multimedia, including systems concentrating on images. However, these systems focus on specifying queries or presenting results in a manner that helps users quickly find an item of interest. For image searches, in particular, there has been relatively little work on new interfaces, visualizations, and interaction techniques that support users in browsing images.

Image browsing is important for a number of reasons. First of all, no matter what information retrieval system is being used, the user has to browse the results of the search. It is certainly important to build query systems that help users get results that are as close to what is wanted as possible. But there will always be images that need to be browsed visually to make the final pick.

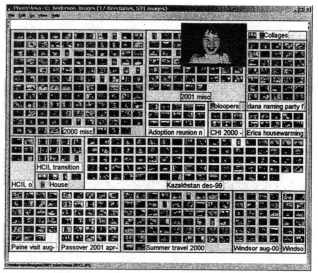

Figure 1: Screen snapshot of PhotoMesa with over 500 images in 17 groups.

Most image browsing systems present the images as a grid of thumbnails that the user can scroll through with a vertical scrollbar, and see a high resolution version of the image with some mouse interaction. There are also a few alternative designs, such as manually constructed digital photo albums, and one commercial zoomable image browser.

A second reason for needing new image browsers is more subtle, and was actually my primary motivation for doing the present work. Sometimes, people browse images just for the pleasure of looking at those images, and they often do it with other people. This is especially true for personal photos. As people take more digital family pictures, we need better tools to support users in home settings as they look at those pictures together on a computer screen. Looking at home photos has a lot of overlap with traditional retrieval systems. People still want to be able to find photos of particular people and events, etc. However, they are less likely to be time pressured to find a particular photo, and more likely to be interested in serendipity – that is, finding photos they weren't looking for [6].

I found I needed better tools to look at pictures with my two-year-old daughter. I did not want to spend the time to make custom "albums". In addition, I found using traditional software with a grid of thumbnails, scrollbars, and popup viewer windows unpleasant in this context. I wanted to concentrate on the images – and more importantly, as I was looking at the photos with my daughter, it was crucial that she be an active part of the interaction, and not just a passive bystander.

Motivated by the need of a tool that would support browsing of images with my family, I started to investigate techniques for presenting collections of images or other visual data. While much work has been done on visualizing complex datasets, surprisingly few techniques are available for presenting images. My goal was to come up with a mechanism that would be able to lay out groups of images automatically in a way that would offer a simple interface to browse while giving access to a large set of images and their context.

To this end, I developed PhotoMesa, a zoomable image browser that organizes images in a two-dimensional grid, where images with a shared attribute (such as directory location, nearness in time, or a shared word in their filename) are grouped together (Figure 1). It uses zooming and simple interaction techniques to make navigation straight-forward, and to eliminate the possibility of getting lost. In building PhotoMesa, I kept the following design goals in mind:

- Simple to use (interaction should focus on images, there should be no overhead to get started, and any layout should be entirely automatic)

- Work well for family-use settings, encouraging shared co-present use

- Support collections of photos, and use screen space efficiently

To lay out the groups of images automatically, I ended up developing two new algorithms, called *quantum treemaps* and *bubblemaps*. Quantum treemaps are a variation on existing treemap algorithms [21]. Treemaps are a family of algorithms that partition two-dimensional space into regions that have an area proportional to a list of requested areas. The problem with existing treemap algorithms is that they return areas of arbitrary aspect ratios. A requirement of photo display is that the regions that show groups of photos must have dimensions that are integer multiples of the dimensions of the photos – that is, they must be sized to contain *quantum*, or indivisible contents. The use of treemaps to display images is the first known use of treemaps to display visual content, such as images, rather then just using the size and color of the rectangles to visualize two numerical attributes of a dataset.

The bubblemap algorithm generates non-rectangular groups. The groups are generated with a grid-based recursive fill algorithm. They fill all the cells in a grid leaving almost no unused space, and generate groups of images that are approximately rectangular or circular.

This paper describes PhotoMesa and the quantum treemap and bubblemap layout algorithms. All the software described in this paper is written in Java 2, is fully functioning as described, and is available at http://www.cs.umd.edu/hcil/photomesa.

RELATED WORK

As mentioned previously, the standard way to let users browse a set of images is with a grid of thumbnails with a vertical scrollbar. Clicking on an image thumbnail usually brings up a window with the high-resolution version of the image. The user then has to manage the open windows manually, and close them when they are no longer needed. One good commercial example of this approach is ACDSee which offers a clean interface and fast interaction [1].

This approach has been extended by a research group at the University of Maryland developing PhotoFinder [16, 22]. It lets users organize photos into "collections" which are displayed with a representative image that the user selects. The interface first shows collections, and selecting a collection displays a traditional grid of thumbnails. PhotoFinder avoids the problem of window management, by displaying high-resolution photos in a pane within the interface. The PhotoFinder project concentrates on interfaces for managing and searching a database of meta information, but the browsing interface is essentially a polished traditional approach.

Document Lens is a technique that uses 2D fisheye distortion to present a grid of thumbnails of documents with a mechanism to zoom one document up to a readable size in place [18]. Document Lens, however, presents just a single collection of objects at a time.

Others have looked into automated algorithms for clustering semantically related information, and presenting the results visually. Hascoët-Zizi and Pediotakis built such a system for a digital library retrieval system, showing the available thesaurus as well as results of searches [14]. Platt has built a system for automatically clustering photos, and extracting representative photos for each cluster [17].

Several groups have investigated applications of images for story telling or sharing in the home. The Personal Digital Historian project at MERL is building a circular display on a tabletop intended for several people to interact with images together. The design includes search by several kinds of metadata, but the mechanism for interacting with many images was not described in detail [20]. This is an example of support for co-present use which is a theme described in some of the author's prior work [23].

A group at Ricoh is building a dedicated portable story-telling device based on the construction of sequences of images. It has a dedicated hardware interface for selecting sequences of images which can then be annotated with audio, and played back when telling the story associated with those images [6].

For a pure software approach, we and others have built Zoomable User Interfaces (ZUIs) for image browsing. ZUIs are interfaces that present information on a large flat space where the user can smoothly zoom into the space to see information in more detail, or zoom out to get an overview. ZUIs have the potential advantages that they are easy to comprehend, and they give a consistent and easy to use interface for getting an overview of the information, and seeing more detail.

An earlier ZUI-based image browser was ZIB (Zoomable Image Browser) [11]. ZIB combined a zoomable presentation of a grid of images with a search engine (that searched metadata), and a history mechanism to access previous searches. However, ZIB provided access to only a single group of images, and used manual zooming which was difficult to use.

The approach started in ZIB was continued in a new project that is creating an interface for elementary school-aged children to find multimedia information in a digital library [12]. This project, called SearchKids, presents visual results in a zoomable interface with a simpler interaction mechanism that PhotoMesa is based on.

Another ZUI-based image browser is currently available commercially by Canon, and is called ZoomBrowser EX [2]. The Canon browser presents a hierarchy of images (either manually constructed, or imported from a disk hierarchy) with containment. The top level shows a grid of squares, each of which contain a grid of image thumbnails and/or smaller squares that show more thumbnails, etc. It uses a layout very similar to what we used earlier in the Pad++ directory browser [8]. This layout has the disadvantage that all directories are the same size, and the contents are scaled to fit so that images in large directories are scaled small so as to be unreadable.

The interaction is to click on a square, and the contents of the square are smoothly zoomed into. Clicking on an image brings up a traditional high-resolution image viewer in a separate window. Clicking on a special zoom-out button zooms out to the next level in the hierarchy. There is also a magnification mode which zooms in a fixed amount each click, rather than zooming into the next level of the hierarchy.

PHOTOMESA

PhotoMesa allows the user to view multiple directories of images in a zoomable environment, and uses a set of simple navigation mechanisms to move through the space of images. It also supports clustering of images by metadata available from the file system. It requires only a set of images on disk, and does not require the user to add any metadata, or manipulate the images at all before browsing, thus making it easy to get started with existing images.

PhotoMesa is written entirely in Java 2, and is built using the Jazz framework for Zoomable User Interfaces [9]. The name *PhotoMesa* derives from the Spanish word *mesa* which means table, but is commonly used in the US

southwestern states to describe the natural volcanic plateaus which are high and have flat tops. Standing atop a mesa, you can see the entire valley below, much as you can see an overview of many photos in PhotoMesa.

To start using PhotoMesa, a user opens a directory, or a set of directories, and PhotoMesa lays out the directories of images in a space-filling manner as shown in Figure 1, using a quantum treemap to create one rectangular group for each directory. Even though a hierarchical directory structure is read in, the images are displayed in a flattened, non-hierarchical manner. The rationale for this is that users looking at images are primarily interested in groups of photos, not at the structure of the groups. In addition, the interface for presenting and managing hierarchies of groups would become more complicated, and simplicity was one of the goals of the PhotoMesa. However, this is a design characteristic of PhotoMesa, not of the of the treemap algorithms which can be applied hierarchically.

As the user moves the mouse, the group the mouse is over is highlighted, and the label is shown in full (it may have been clipped if there wasn't room for it). Then when the user clicks, the view is smoothly zoomed in to that group. Now, a highlight showing a set of images under the mouse lets the user know which images will be focused on when the mouse is clicked again. The number of images highlighted is chosen to be enough to fill about half of the screen so that the user will be able to drill down quickly to a full-resolution single image. At any point, the user can press the right button (or Enter key) to zoom out to the previous magnification. In addition, the user can double-click on an image to zoom all the way into that image and avoid intermediate zoom levels, or the user can double-right click to zoom all the way out to the top level.

The user can also press alt-left/right arrows to move back and forth in their history of views. Or, they can press the arrow keys to pan up, down, left or right. When zoomed all the way into a full-resolution image, the arrow keys stay within the current group of images, wrapping as necessary. When zoomed out so more than one image is visible, the arrow keys move across groups to let the user explore the entire space.

At all times, if the cursor is left to dwell over an image thumbnail for a short time, that thumbnail is zoomed up until it is 200 pixels wide overlaying the other, unchanged images (Figure 1). This preview is immediately removed whenever the mouse is moved.

While it is not necessary for users to do any authoring to browse images with PhotoMesa, they are allowed to change the color of image groups (although group background colors are assigned by default). This can make it easier to make sense of the large display of images since the colored areas can act as landmarks which are known to be effective navigation aids [15].

PhotoMesa supports drag-and-drop to let users directly export images to email, or other applications. Since emailing photos is a significant use, PhotoMesa automatically reduces the resolution and quality of images when they are dragged out of PhotoMesa. This resolution reduction is controllable through a preference panel. This eliminates the need to go through a special processing step when emailing images.

While the support of browsing is the primary goal of PhotoMesa, it is also sometimes desirable to find images in a specific group, and it can be difficult to scan labels in a 2D space. So, a search pane is available that shows all the directories in order. Mousing over a label highlights the corresponding group of images, and clicking on a label zooms into that group. In addition, the search pane has a search box where users can search for images by words in their filename.

After PhotoMesa was built, and we started using it to browse directories of images, I realized that another way of thinking about what PhotoMesa was doing was presenting a large set of images clustered by directory. So I then added support for clustering by other data. Since I didn't want to require users to add metadata, PhotoMesa uses whatever data is already available in the file system, which is just file date and name. If a user selects view by year, PhotoMesa uses the file date to group all the currently opened photos by year, and creates a layout with one region per year. It does the same thing for viewing by month.

Another clustering technique takes advantage of the fact that people sometimes give meaningful filenames to their images, often with several words per image to describe the contents of the image (Figure 2). If a user selects view by "filename words", it parses the filenames of all of the open images, and creates one cluster for each unique word in a filename (as tokenized with all the standard delimiters and where filename extensions and numeric tokens are ignored). Thus, if an image has 3 words in its filename (such as "ben-eats-cake"), then that image will appear in 3 clusters (one for "ben", one for "eats", and one for "cake").

PhotoMesa computes multiple sized thumbnails for each image, and dynamically loads the appropriate one. In this manner, it maintains good performance, even with large numbers of images. The thumbnails are created the first time an image is loaded, and cached in a special directory managed by PhotoMesa.

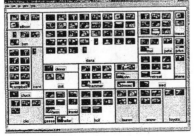

Figure 2: A directory of images (left), and the same images grouped by filename words (right).

The design of PhotoMesa presents an inherent difference compared to traditional scrolling thumbnail grids. The traditional approach has the advantage that it is searchable by navigating in one dimension (through vertical scrolling), while PhotoMesa requires navigation in two dimensions, which is typically harder for users. However, PhotoMesa has the advantage that the user can easily get an overview by zooming out. Through this interaction, the user can control the trade-off between the number of images shown and their resolution. This difference is a direct effect of the zooming nature of PhotoMesa. If a vertically oriented grid of thumbnails were zoomed out, the space would be mostly unused on either side of the linear list, and the display space would thus be largely wasted. Thus, it seems that a 2D zoomable interface and 1D displays of data are inherently incompatible.

USE OF PHOTOMESA

I have used PhotoMesa regularly with my two year old daughter for several months. We load in all of our family pictures (Figure 1) and sit together in front of a laptop computer. She will point at an area and I click and zoom in to it. I keep zooming in as she points at areas until we get all the way in to a single photo. I then zoom out one level, and if she asks to see another photo, I zoom into it. Otherwise, I zoom out another level until she sees something she is interested in. In this fashion, we look at the photos together, and she is able to stay in control and maintains a high level of interest. The zooming and smooth animation make it so that she is clearly able to follow what is going on, even though I operate the mouse.

In addition, over 9,000 people have downloaded PhotoMesa from the web. While this is obviously not a controlled study, it has been informative nevertheless. I have received very positive feedback, sometimes describing use scenarios I did not originally envision. One designer used it as a "disk mapper" to find out what was on her disk. Another put the software with photos on a CD and mailed it to family and friends. Others have envisioned embedding it in a range of applications, from supporting hobbyist aquarium logging to web-based photo sharing. Perhaps most importantly, several people reported they find it ideal to use with their families – supporting my original design goal.

QUANTUM TREEMAPS

In the course of developing PhotoMesa, I ran into a significant problem. I needed an automatic way to lay out groups of images in a visually simple manner that filled all the available space. I started to solve this by looking into treemap algorithms. Treemaps are a family of algorithms that are space-filling partitions of a two-dimensional area. Treemaps take as input, a list of *n* numbers and a rectangle. They partition the area into *n* rectangles, one per input number. The rectangles are guaranteed to fill the input rectangle, and each rectangle is proportional in area to a number on the input list. Treemaps are designed to be applied hierarchically, so any given resulting rectangle can itself contain a treemap, and so on, recursively.

In order to build PhotoMesa, I had to extend the treemap algorithms to accommodate fixed size images. To understand this, let us start by looking at existing treemap algorithms.

There are two desirable properties that treemap algorithms can have: generated rectangles with aspect ratios close to 1 (i.e., rectangles that are close to squares), and order.

Here, and for the rest of the paper, aspect ratio is defined as `max((width / height), (height / width))`, so that an aspect ratio of 1 is perfectly square, and aspect ratios larger than one are more rectangular. Rectangles with aspect ratios close to 1 are desirable because, generally speaking, they are more visually attractive. In addition, humans seem to be able to estimate the area of a square more accurately than a skinny rectangle, and one of the goals of treemaps is to use the area of each rectangle to present some useful attribute.

I define order here to mean that a treemap algorithm is ordered if the rectangles it generates are laid out in a spatial sequence that corresponds to the input sequence. Not all treemap algorithms are ordered, and order is important since it is easier for users to find specific items in ordered displays. Rodden has showed the importance of order in image browsing [19]. In addition, ordered displays make it easier to track items if they change over time since in an ordered display, each item will stay in approximately the same place on the screen.

Until recently, there were no algorithms that provided both properties.

Treemap Related Work

The original treemap algorithm by Shneiderman [21] uses a simple "slice and dice" approach. It divides the input rectangle into a single horizontal or vertical list of rectangles – each one typically being quite skinny. If the algorithm is applied recursively, the sub-rectangle would be split in the opposite orientation as the parent. This algorithm generates ordered rectangles, but they typically have extreme aspect ratios.

An important ensuing treemap algorithm, called squarified treemaps, gave up on ordering, but created rectangles with smaller aspect ratios [10]. Squarified treemaps work by recursively dividing the space in two, and laying out some of the rectangle in one part, and the rest of the rectangles in the other part, where the list of rectangles is split based on optimizing the resulting aspect ratios. A variation of this algorithm was independently developed for SmartMoney's MarketMap applet [4]. Recently, Shneiderman and Wattenberg introduced ordered treemaps [5] which offer a compromise solution where the resulting rectangles are ordered, and somewhat squarified, but do not have as good aspect ratios as those generated by squarified treemaps. Other approaches to space-filling algorithms have been considered but they typically do not have all the nice properties of treemaps, such as that by Harel and Yashchin

[13] which does not assign the size of the rectangles to any independent variable.

Treemaps have been applied to a number of domains, from visualizing hard disk usage [3] to the stock market [4]. However, in every current usage of treemaps to date, they are used to visualize a two-dimensional dataset where typically, one dimension is mapped to the area of the rectangles (as computed by the treemap algorithm), and the other dimension is mapped to the color of the rectangle. Then, a label is placed in the rectangles which are large enough to accommodate them, and the user can interact with the treemap to get more information about the objects depicted by the rectangles.

Surprisingly enough, there are not any published uses of treemaps where other information is placed in the rectangles. PhotoMesa appears to be the first application to put images within the area of each treemap rectangle.

There is a good reason why treemaps have not been used in this manner before. This is because while treemaps guarantee that the area of each generated rectangle is proportional to an input number, they do not make any promise about the aspect ratio of the rectangles. Some treemap algorithms (such as squarified treemaps) do generate rectangles with better aspect ratios, but the rectangles can have any aspect ratio. While this is fine for general purpose visualizations, it is not appropriate for laying out images because images have fixed aspect ratios, and they do not fit well in rectangles with inappropriate aspect ratios.

Let us look at applying existing treemap algorithms to laying out fixed size objects, such as images. For now, let us assume without loss of generality that the images are all square. We will see later that this does not affect layout issues. Given a list of groups of images to lay out, the obvious input to the treemap algorithm is the number of images in each group. The treemap algorithm will generate a list of rectangles, that each need the corresponding images to be laid out within.

For each rectangle and group of images, the first step is to decide on the dimensions of a grid with which to lay out the images in the rectangle. Given the aspect ratio of the rectangle, we compute the number of rows and columns that best fit the images.

The resulting grid may have more cells than there are images, but will not have any empty rows or columns. This layout, however, is not guaranteed to fit in the rectangle. For example, consider a rectangle that was computed to hold a single image. It will have an area of 1.0, but could be long and skinny, perhaps with a width of 10.0 and a height of 0.1. The obvious solution is to scale down the images just enough to fit in the bounds of the rectangle.

Herein lies the problem. Since each group of images has to fit in to a separate rectangle, each group of images will have to potentially be scaled down. This will result in each group of images being a different size. Furthermore, since

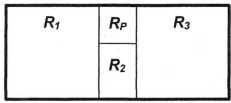

Figure 3: Basic layout strategy of the ordered treemap algorithm. The pivot is layed out in R_P, and $L_1...L_{P-1}$ are layed out in R_1 while $L_{P+1}...L_n$ are layed out in R_2 and R_3.

the rectangles are arbitrarily sized and positioned, and the images are scaled, the resulting groups of images will not align with each other in a visually attractive way.

It is standard graphic design practice to align content in a way that makes it easy for the eye to quickly scan different areas. If each group of images is a different size and they are not aligned, this will make the resulting layout less attractive, and may make it slower for a user to quickly scan. See Figure 4 for the result of laying out a simple sequence of images using the ordered treemap and quantum treemap algorithms to see the difference in overall layout. Note how with the ordered treemap, group #4 consisting of a single image is scaled much smaller than the other images. With the quantum treemap algorithm, all images are the same size, and all images are aligned on a single grid across all the groups.

Ordered Treemaps

To understand the quantum treemap algorithm, it is necessary to first understand the basics of the ordered treemap algorithm because the former is a direct modification of the latter.

The ordered treemap algorithm, as with all treemap algorithms, take as input and produces output:

Input	$L_1...L_n$	An ordered sequence of numbers.
	Box	A box to lay out the rectangles within.
Output	$R_1...R_n$	An ordered sequence of rectangles that completely fill Box, and where the area of R_i is proportional to L_i.

The algorithm is similar to QuickSort. It chooses a pivot, L_P, and places it in Box. It then recursively lays out $L_1...L_{P-1}$ on one side of the pivot, and $L_{P+1}...L_n$ on the other side of the pivot. Figure 3 shows the basic visual strategy for a horizontal layout. A corresponding approach is used for a vertical layout.

The ordered treemap algorithm is described in detail in [5], and is summarized here.

1. If $n == 1$, then return a rectangle $R = Box$ and stop.
2. Choose a pivot element, L_P. Pivot selection strategies include picking the middle element or the largest one.
3. Calculate R_1 so that its height fills Box, and so that its width is large enough to contain $L_A = L_1...L_{P-1}$.

4. Split $L_{P+1}...L_n$ into two sublists, L_B and L_C that will be laid out in R_2 and R_3. Calculate where the splitting point is so that R_P has an aspect ratio closest to 1.
5. Calculate R_P, R_2 and R_3. This is performed by using the ratio between the size of the corresponding lists, and breaking up the available space by the same ratios.
6. Recursively apply the ordered treemap algorithm to L_A in R_1, L_B in R_2, and L_C in R_3.

This algorithm results in rectangles that are fairly square, and are ordered approximately left to right (or top to bottom in a vertically oriented box).

Quantum Treemap Algorithm

The goal of the quantum treemap algorithm is similar to other treemap algorithms, but instead of generating rectangles of arbitrary aspect ratios, it generates rectangles with widths and heights that are integer multiples of a given elemental size. In this manner, it always generates rectangles in which a grid of elements of the same size can be laid out. Furthermore, all the grids of elements will align perfectly with rows and columns of elements running across the entire series of rectangles. It is this basic element size that can not be made any smaller that led to the name of *quantum treemaps*.

The quantum treemap (QT) algorithm is based directly on the ordered treemap (OT) algorithm. However, the basic approach could be applied to any other treemap algorithm. QT's input and output are similar to those of OT, but instead of returning a set of rectangles that precisely fill the specified input Box, it generates a set of rectangles that only approximate the input Box. Because there is some wasted space, the resulting set of rectangles are usually larger than Box, but have close to the same aspect ratio. In addition, QT takes an additional input parameter which is the aspect ratio of the elements to be laid out in Box.

QT starts in exactly the same manner as OT, picking a pivot, subdividing the space, and recursively applying the algorithm to each sub-space. It works in the same way until step 1 stops the recursion.

At this point (step 1), rather then just unwinding the recursive stack, it adjusts the computed rectangle by modifying its dimensions, making it big enough for precisely the specified number of elements.

Figure 4: The result of laying out a sequence of 4 groups of elements (of size 3, 20, 20, 1) using ordered treemap (left) and quantum treemap (right)

Then, as the recursion unwinds, the caller must accommodate the generated rectangles which may not fit precisely into the box that was asked for. This is the tricky part, and is captured in a modified version of step 6. Since the rectangles generated by the recursive call may be bigger or smaller in either dimension than was asked for, the rectangles from the other regions must be moved so they don't overlap, and possibly grown so they align nicely with neighboring rectangles. As an example, see Figure 4 (right). Rectangle #4 was originally computed to have dimensions (1x1), but since Rectangle #3 was much taller, Rectangle #4 was stretched to be 4 units tall to match the height of Rectangle #3. Similarly, Rectangle #1 was stretched to match the height of Rectangle #2. The new algorithmic steps are stated here:

new 1. If $n = 1$, then compute a rectangle R that contains exactly L quantums in a grid arrangement that has an aspect ratio as close as possible to that of *Box* and stop.

new 6. Recursively apply the ordered treemap algorithm to L_A in R_1, L_B in R_2, and L_C in R_3.

new 6a. Translate the rectangles in R_P, R_2, and R_3 to avoid overlapping R_1 or each other.

new 6b. Even out the rectangles in the sub-regions in the following manner. Make sure that R_P and R_2 have the same width. Make sure that R_P and R_2 together have the same height as R_1. Make sure that R_3 has the same height as R_1. Each of these evening steps can be accomplished similarly by finding if one of the regions is too small. Then if it is not wide enough, add the extra amount to the width of the rectangles in that region that touch the right boundary of the region. Do the analogous action to rectangles not tall enough.

Element Aspect Ratio Issues

QT assumes that all elements that will be laid out in the rectangles produced by QT are the same aspect ratio, and that aspect ratio is an input parameter to QT. It turns out, however, that it is not necessary to modify the internal structure of QT to accommodate the element's aspect ratio. Instead, the dimensions of the starting box can simply be stretched by the inverse of the element aspect ratio.

Growing Horizontally or Vertically

In step 1, the requested rectangle may be grown to accommodate the quantum element size. There is a basic question of whether to grow this rectangle horizontally or vertically. The simple answer is just to grow in the direction that results in a rectangle that most closely matches the aspect ratio of the original rectangle. However, the algorithm as a whole produces better layouts if it always grows horizontally (or vertically for layout boxes that are oriented vertically).

The issue here is somewhat subtle, but is related to step 6b where the rectangles are evened. If, for example, rectangles in R_3 are made taller, than all of R_1 and R_2 will

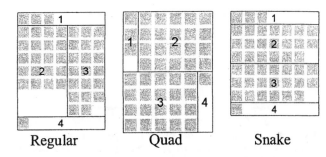

Regular   Quad   Snake

Figure 5: The result of applying the three stopping conditions to a sequence of 4 groups of elements (of size 3, 20, 20, 1).

have to made taller as well to match R_3. If instead, the rectangles in R_3 are made wider, than only the other rectangles in R_3 will need to be made wider, and the rectangles in R_1 and R_2 can be left alone.

In general, the evening aspect of the QT algorithm remains somewhat problematic. While it works well for most data sets, it occasionally yields undesirable layouts due to too much wasted space. This can happen when one region ends up growing a fair amount to accommodate data that doesn't happen to fit the starting rectangles, and then the other regions have to be grown to match. When these other regions are grown to match, the resulting rectangles are bigger than necessary, and there is wasted space. This doesn't seem to be a problem for datasets unless they contain many regions with a very small number of elements (< 10). In practice, it has not been a significant problem for the real image datasets I have viewed, although sometimes there is a little more wasted space than I would like.

Stopping Condition Improvements

Changing the stopping conditions and offering special layouts for a small number of special cases can produce substantially better total results. The new stopping conditions apply equally to QT as well as to OT.

The improvement is because the layout of rectangles depicted in Figure 5 (left) is not necessarily the one with the smallest aspect ratios. In addition, it generates a layout that is somewhat difficult to parse visually because the eye has to move in 3 directions to focus on the 4 rectangles (vertically from #1 to #2, horizontally from #2 to #3, and then vertically from #3 to #4).

The layout can be improved, and visual readability by offering two alternative layouts. The first produces a "*quad*" of (2x2) rectangles. The second produces a "*snake*" layout with all 4 rectangles laid out sequentially – either horizontally or vertically. The snake layout can be equally well applied to 2, 3, or more rectangles. PhotoMesa applied it up to 5 rectangles. Figure 5 shows the result of laying out a sequence of 4 groups of elements using the three strategies. The new algorithmic step is:

new 1a. If $n = 4$, then first try the regular layout by continuing and letting the recursion get down to the bottom level

new 1b. If $n == 4$, then layout the 4 groups in a quad. Split *Box* into two with either a horizontal or vertical split (depending on the orientation of *Box*) based on the number of elements in the 4 groups. Then, split each of the remaining boxes in two with the opposite orientation based on the number of elements in those 2 groups.

new 1c. If n $==$ 4, then layout the 4 groups in a snake by dividing *Box* into 4 sub boxes (horizontally or vertically, depending on the orientation of *Box*), based on the number of elements in the 4 groups.

new 1d. Compute the aspect ratios and wasted space of the 4 resulting rectangles from steps 1a, 1b, and 1c, and use the layout with the best overall results.

Since no one layout strategy always gives the best result for all input data, for 5 or fewer rectangles, PhotoMesa computes layouts using all strategies (original, quad, and snake) and picks the best one. In practice, this strategy produces layouts with substantially squarer aspect ratios. Running 100 randomized tests with 100 rectangles, and random numbers of elements per rectangle, ranging from 10 to 1000 produced an average aspect ratio of 3.92 with the original stopping conditions, and 2.68 for the new stopping conditions.

Pivot Selection Improvement

In addition to the two pivot selection strategies discussed in [5], a third strategy specifically targeted at the evening problem previously discussed offers improved results. The new strategy, called *"split size"* gives better results for some input data.

The basic approach is to pick the pivot that will split the lists of elements into equal sizes, or as close to equal as possible. With the sublists containing similar numbers of elements to lay out, there tends to be less evening, and therefore less wasted space. The new algorithmic step is:

new 2. Choose a pivot element, R_P. Pivot selection strategies include picking the middle element, the largest one, or the one that results in splitting the elements into lists that are as close to equal size as possible.

No single pivot selection strategy always works best, so in practice, PhotoMesa computes the layouts with all three pivot selection strategies, and picks the best one based on the average aspect ratios of the resulting rectangles, and the amount of wasted space.

Quantum Treemap Analysis

One of the basic characteristics of QT is that it works better when there are more elements per group. This is because it gives the algorithm more flexibility when computing rectangles. A rectangle of, say, 1000 elements, can be arranged in quantified grids of many different sizes such as (30x34), (31x33), (32x32), etc. – each of which use the space quite efficiently. Rectangles containing smaller numbers of elements, however, do not offer as many options, and often use space less efficiently. For example, a rectangle containing 5 elements can be laid out in (1x5), (2x3), (3x2), or (5x1). These four options do not give the algorithm as much flexibility as the dozens of grid options afforded by the larger number of elements.

In order to assess the effectiveness of QT, it was compared to OT with a series of trials using random input. Each algorithm was run 100 times generating 100 rectangles with the number of elements in each rectangle being randomly generated. This was done for 5 different ranges of the number of elements per rectangle. For each test, the average aspect ratio of all the rectangles was recorded as well as the space utilization, which was recorded as the percentage of space not used to display elements (wasted space). The same random numbers were used for each algorithm. Figures 6 and 7 show the results of these tests. Quantum treemaps did better in terms of aspect ratio, and ordered treemaps did better in terms of wasted space.

However, the crucial visual advantage of QT is that it always produces layouts where elements are the same size and are aligned on a single global grid.

BUBBLE MAPS

While quantum treemaps work well, they waste some space. While the use of some white space can be helpful to visually distinguish the groups, too much white space

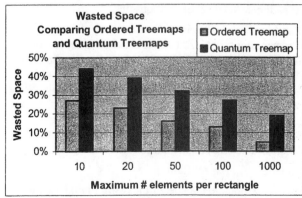

Figure 7: Average wasted space as a percentage of the entire layout space available. Tests run on both algorithms with 100 rectangles with random numbers of elements per rectangle.

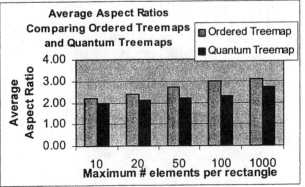

Figure 6: Average aspect ratio of all rectangles run on both algorithms with 100 rectangles with random numbers of elements per rectangle.

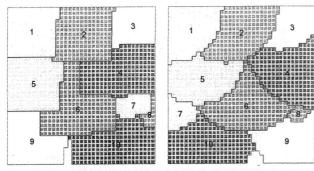

Figure 8: Bubblemap layouts of 10 groups of up to 200 rectangles. Rectangular (left) and circular (right).

becomes unattractive and wasteful. While it may be possible to improve the quantum treemap algorithm, it is impossible to lay out images in a rectangle without sometimes leaving unused space. An alternative approach is to give up on the idea that the space must be divided into rectangles, and instead allow more complex shapes.

Bubblemap is a new algorithm that lays out groups of quantum-sized objects in an ordered layout with no wasted space per group, although there is some wasted space for the entire area. The groups of objects can be created in different shapes, such as rectangular or circular, but the groups of objects only approximate those shapes, rather than define them exactly. Figure 8 shows a rectangular and a circular bubblemap layout of 10 groups of up to 200 rectangles per group. The bubblemap algorithm has also been integrated into PhotoMesa as a user-selectable layout option. Figure 9 shows the bubblemap algorithm applied to a set of images in PhotoMesa. There is no wasted space, but the regions have arbitrary shapes.

A more sophisticated approach to laying out related images in a grid has been pursued by Basalaj with his *Proximity Grid* algorithm [7]. It takes a set of objects with a high-dimensional set of relationships and generates a grid layout of those objects so that similar objects will be near each other on the grid. Bubblemaps, on the other hand, are much simpler and assumes the input is pre-clustered. They keep the clusters of images together, rather than optimizing an n-dimensional set of relationships.

The bubblemap algorithm is completely different than the treemap algorithm. Rather than subdividing rectangles, it is based on a standard pixel-based bucket fill algorithm. It works by filling cells in a grid, keeping track of which cells get assigned to images from which group. It fills the cells one group at a time. By using different algorithms to select the next cell to fill, the shape of the groups can be controlled. The basic algorithm runs in $O(n)$ time for n images. The basic algorithm follows:

Input: $L_1...L_n$, Aspect Ratio

1. Compute the size of the overall grid based on total number of images to layout, and the desired resulting aspect ratio.

2. Create a grid of size computed from step 1, and set each cell to the value UNASSIGNED.

3. For each group of images, L_i, call the fill algorithm, starting at step 4, and then stop.

4. Find the starting point to fill by looking for the first UNASSIGNED cell in the grid (in left-right, top-bottom order). Initialize a list of cells, called LIST, and add the starting point to LIST.

5. If LIST is empty than stop. Else, take the first element, P, off of LIST, and set the cell at P's location to the value ASSIGNED.

6. For each UNASSIGNED neighbor of P, Q, add Q to LIST, and set the cell at Q's location to the current group ID. GOTO 5. Note that the order in which the neighbors are added to LIST affect the shape of the resulting groups.

Bubblemaps are easy to implement, use space efficiently, and give ordered space-filling layouts like treemaps do. However, since they produce arbitrary-shaped regions rather than rectangles, it is likely that users will find them harder to parse visually. So, while they may be appropriate for applications where the goal is simply to have related items near each other, they may not be as appropriate for tasks where users need to distinguish clearly between groups.

FUTURE WORK

The PhotoMesa application has a long list of features to be added. An important one is to integrate it with PhotoFinder and other sources of metadata. Another area to look into is deploying PhotoMesa in different modalities, such as stand-alone CDs for sending to family and friends, running on a kiosk for museums or lobbies, and integration with the Web. The zoomable characteristics of PhotoMesa make it a good match with the Web, offering a potentially efficient manner to browse large image databases on the Web since only the resolution needed for the current view needs to be sent to the client. And of course, a detailed user study is needed to understand how the zoomable interaction of PhotoMesa compares to more traditional approaches, and which layout techniques are most effective.

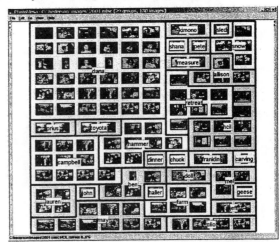

Figure 9: The same images as in Figure 3, but laid out with a rectangular bubblemap.

CONCLUSION

This paper presents PhotoMesa, a zoomable image browser, and two new algorithms for laying out groups of images or other fixed-size visual objects. The primary innovations are: 1) a simplified set of interactions for navigating through a set of objects in a zoomable user interface; and 2) algorithms to lay out fixed-size objects, such as images, in two-dimensional space, automatically creating groups for related objects.

By bringing together the aforementioned innovations with existing zoomable user interface technology, PhotoMesa offers a significant advance in the ability to comfortably browse large numbers of images. Based on its initial popularity and enthusiastic feedback, PhotoMesa appears to have satisfied its initial design goals of being simple to use in a family setting, requiring no setup time, and naturally supporting co-present use.

ACKNOWLEDGEMENTS

I appreciate the feedback on PhotoMesa by many HCIL members. In particular, thanks to Jesse Grosjean who suggested the approach taken in the bubblemap algorithm. In addition, I thank Ben Shneiderman for suggesting the interactive textual list of groups, to Allison Druin for suggesting the ability to color groups, to Jon Meyer and Catherine Plaisant for advise on the visual design of PhotoMesa, to Matthias Mayer for first suggesting I try to display several directories of images at once, and to Mark Stefik from Xerox PARC for suggesting the magnified preview images. Finally, I appreciate Susanne Jul's excellent editorial comments on this paper.

REFERENCES

[1] ACDSee (2001). http://www.acdsystems.com/english/products/acdsee/acdsee-node.htm.

[2] Canon ZoomBrowser (2001). http://www.powershot.com/powershot2/software/ps_pc_view.html.

[3] DiskMapper (2001). http://www.miclog.com/dmdesc.htm.

[4] SmartMoney MarketMap (2001). http://www.smartmoney.com/marketmap/.

[5] Baker, M. J., & Eick, S. G. (1995). Space-Filling Software Visualization. *Journal of Visual Languages and Computing, 6,* pp. 119-133.

[6] Balabanovic, M., Chu, L. L., & Wolff, G. J. (2000). Storytelling With Digital Photographs. *In Proceedings of Human Factors in Computing Systems (CHI 2000)* ACM Press, pp. 564-571.

[7] Basalaj, W. (2000). *Proximity Visualization of Abstract Data.* Doctoral dissertation, University of Cambridge, Cambridge, England.

[8] Bederson, B. B., Hollan, J. D., Perlin, K., Meyer, J., Bacon, D., & Furnas, G. W. (1996). Pad++: A Zoomable Graphical Sketchpad for Exploring Alternate Interface Physics. *Journal of Visual Languages and Computing, 7,* pp. 3-31.

[9] Bederson, B. B., Meyer, J., & Good, L. (2000). Jazz: An Extensible Zoomable User Interface Graphics Toolkit in Java. *In Proceedings of User Interface and Software Technology (UIST 2000)* ACM Press, pp. 171-180.

[10] Bruls, M., Huizing, K., & van Wijk, J. J. (2000). Squarified Treemaps. *In Proceedings of Joint Eurographics and IEEE TCVG Symposium on Visualization (TCVG 2000)* IEEE Press, pp. 33-42.

[11] Combs, T. T. A., & Bederson, B. B. (1999). Does Zooming Improve Image Browsing? *In Proceedings of Digital Library (DL 99)* New York: ACM, pp. 130-137.

[12] Druin, A., Bederson, B. B., Hourcade, J. P., Sherman, L., Revelle, G., Platner, M., & Weng, S. (2001). Designing a Digital Library for Young Children: An Intergenerational Partnership. *In Proceedings of Joint Conference on Digital Libraries (JCDL 2001)* ACM Press, pp. pp. 398-405.

[13] Harel, D., & Yashchin, G. (2000). An Algorithm for Blob Hierarchy Layout. *In Proceedings of Advanced Visual Interfaces (AVI 2000)* ACM Press, pp. 29-40.

[14] Hascoët-Zizi, M., & Pediotakis, N. (1996). Visual Relevance Analysis. *In Proceedings of International Conference on Digital Libraries (DL 96)* ACM Press, pp. 54-62.

[15] Jul, S., & Furnas, G. W. (1998). Critical Zones in Desert Fog: Aids to Multiscale Navigation. *In Proceedings of User Interface and Software Technology (UIST 98)* ACM Press, pp. 97-106.

[16] Kang, H., & Shneiderman, B. (2000). Visualization Methods for Personal Photo Collections Browsing and Searching in the PhotoFinder. *In Proceedings of IEEE International Conference on Multimedia and Expo (ICME2000)* New York: IEEE, pp. 1539-1542.

[17] Platt, J. (2000). AutoAlbum: Clustering Digital Photographs Using Probabalistic Model Merging. *In Proceedings of IEEE Workshop on Content-based Access of Image and Video Libraries (CBAIVL-2000)* IEEE Press,

[18] Robertson, G. G., & Mackinlay, J. D. (1993). The Document Lens. *In Proceedings of User Interface and Software Technology (UIST 93)* ACM Press, pp. 101-108.

[19] Rodden, K., Basalaj, W., Sinclair, D., & Wood, K. (2001). Does Organisation by Similarity Assist Image Browsing. *In Proceedings of Human Factors in Computing Systems (CHI 2001)* ACM Press, pp. 190-197.

[20] Shen, C., Moghaddam, B., Lesh, N., & Beardsley, P. (2001). Personal Digital Historian: User Interface Design. *In Proceedings of Extended Abstracts of Human Factors in Computing Systems (CHI 2001)* ACM Press,

[21] Shneiderman, B. (1992). Tree Visualization With Treemaps: A 2-D Space-Filling Approach. *ACM Transactions on Graphics, 11*(1), pp. 92-99.

[22] Shneiderman, B., & Kang, H. (2000). Direct Annotation: A Drag-and-Drop Strategy for Labeling Photos. *In Proceedings of IEEE Conference on Information Visualization (IV2000)* New York: IEEE, pp. 88-98.

[23] Stewart, J., Bederson, B. B., & Druin, A. (1999). Single Display Groupware: A Model for Co-Present Collaboration. *In Proceedings of Human Factors in Computing Systems (CHI 99)* ACM Press, pp. 286-293.

A Photo History of SIGCHI: Evolution of Design from Personal to Public

Ben Shneiderman,
with **Hyunmo Kang,**
Bill Kules, Catherine
Plaisant, Anne Rose,
and **Richesh Rucheir**
University of Maryland,
Human-Computer
Interaction Lab

For 20 years I have been photographing personalities and events in the emerging discipline of human–computer interaction. Until now, only a few of these photos were published in newsletters or were shown to visitors who sought them out. Now this photo history is going from a personal record to a public archive. This archive should be interesting for professional members of this community who want to reminisce, as well as for historians and journalists who want to understand what happened. Students and Web surfers may also want to look at the people who created better interfaces and more satisfying user experiences.

The vibrant personality of the serious researchers, the passion of the competent practitioners, and the eagerness of energetic students shine through the photos, revealing their enthusiasm and excitement. The leadership role of the Association for Computing Machinery's (ACM) Special Interest Group on Computer Human Interaction (SIGCHI) is apparent in the number and significance of events.

Since the famed 1982 conference in Gaithersburg, MD, that helped spawn SIGCHI, the events they arranged have been central to forming this new discipline and profession. The SIGCHI leadership, conference organizers, and speakers figure prominently in these photos, but notable outsiders such as Bill Gates or

Ralph Nader also appear. Heroes such as Doug Engelbart got my special attention when they attended, and key figures such as Stu Card or Don Norman often reappear. Important speakers include continuing contributors such as Judy Olson and Terry Winograd as well as those who, sadly, have died, such as Alan Newell, Ted White, and Michael Dertouzos.

Attendees at these events were often playfully suspicious of my motives, but my goals were simple: to record our emerging discipline, capture the process of communicating ideas, and remember the mature heroes as they communicated with the promising students.

It has long been my dream to digitize the SIGCHI photo archives, stored in chronologically organized paper folders, and make them available online. Fortunately, Marilyn Tremaine (former SIGCHI Chair) and the SIGCHI Executive Committee supported this vision with a grant to scan the thousands of photos during the summer of 2000. The photos were organized into directories, but we needed software to edit, annotate, caption, and search the photos.

Fortunately the PhotoFinder project at the University of Maryland Human-Computer Interaction Lab (HCIL) was well along in developing a personal photo library tool to organize, annotate, and search thousands of photos. The SIGCHI Photo Archive was somewhat different from personal photos, but the basic functions of PhotoFinder were well suited to the job [1, 2]. I spent many hours weeding out poor quality and redundant photos, then selecting some highlights and outrageous images. We greatly appreciated Intel's generous funding to the HCIL, and additional support from IBM, Microsoft, and Ricoh, which contributed to development of the PhotoFinder software (free download and description at www.cs.umd.edu/hcil/photolib) and which were sympathetic to our making the kiosk and later the Web version.

Personal photo collections are distinguished by having a small number of people who reappear frequently and a chronological sequence that covers five to 20 family events (weddings, birthdays, holiday parties) and

travel stories per year. Users seek photos of events to reminisce with the people whose photos appear and to tell stories to those who weren't. Finding all the photos at a known event is essential, identifying everyone who was there is desirable, and highlighting the memorable photos adds value (see PhotoFinder sidebar).

Dragging and dropping names onto the photos from a scrolling list of family members simplified annotation and made drag-and-drop search facilities a natural. This also gave us a distinctive and patentable feature that was a step ahead of good commercial packages such as ACDSee and PhotoSuite. Another important step was to add the StoryStarter feature to enable users to export a full collection including captions to the Web with just a few clicks.

Restructuring the PhotoFinder into the PhotoFinder Kiosk to support public access at the CHI 2001 conference pushed our team to make many innovations and improvements. We had to move from a trusting personal environment, in which users could delete or add photos, annotations, and captions, to a public environment that permits only additions or changes to annotations and captions made by the original author. We also had to strip out options in order to create a public access kiosk that was immediately usable without training or tutorials and add networking that supported a shared database for seven machines (see PhotoFinder Kiosk sidebar). The three-day conference was a great success—hundreds of users provided thousands of annotations—loudly demonstrating their strong interest and enjoyment in finding old pictures of familiar figures or recent photos of friends and colleagues. The roars of laughter and eagerness to show photos to friends made us feel that the enormous effort was worthwhile.

Restructuring again into PhotoFinder Web to support a Web interface required yet another re-design and implementation (see PhotoFinder Web sidebar). Our tools enabled automatic creation of a starter photo Web site from a PhotoFinder library. This Web interface was designed to accommodate slower modems and smaller screens and preserve a lively browsing environment. You can try it at www.acm.org/sigchi/photohistory.

You can choose among the three photo libraries in this Photo History of SIGCHI:

- **CHI 1982–2000:** 28 collections of my photos from CHI conferences and SIGCHI-sponsored conferences
- **CHI 2001:** 21 collections of photos taken by conference attendees using their own or borrowed digital cameras
- **Other HCI events:** 40 collections of my photos from non-SIGCHI events, including many of the same people from SIGCHI events.

You can browse the collections, each representing an event, and view all the thumbnails for a particular event. You can browse an index of the people and then view all the photos for each person. We've added a Send Comments function to let you make suggestions and help us fix mistaken name annotations.

My hope is that preserving the early history of SIGCHI will increase appreciation of what we have accomplished and provide a human perspective on the emergence of so many novel and influential technologies.

Acknowledgments

Graduate student Hyunmo Kang has been the key developer of PhotoFinder during the past three years, and Bill Kules has worked during the past year to coordinate and manage the project. Thoughtful comments were made by many members of the University of Maryland Human-Computer Interaction Laboratory, especially Catherine Plaisant and Anne Rose. Undergraduate and graduate student projects (whose reports are accessible from the PhotoFinder Web page) made important contributions, especially John Prebula, who programmed the StoryStarter, and Richesh Ruchir, who programmed the Java server pages for the Web version. Our colleague Ben Bederson became an active user with frequent long lists of fixes and suggestions. His experience of browsing his family photos with his two-year old daughter led him to develop the PhotoMesa browser with terrific overviews and a zooming user interface (http://www.cs.umd.edu/hcil/photomesa).

References

1. Kang, H. and Shneiderman, B. Visualization methods for personal photo collections: Browsing and searching in the PhotoFinder, *Proceedings of the IEEE Conference on Multimedia and Expo* (July 2000).
2. Shneiderman, B. and Kang, H. Direct annotation: A drag-and-drop strategy for labeling photos, *Proceedings of the International Conference on Information Visualization 2000*, July, pp. 88–95. Available from IEEE, Los Alamitos, CA.

k k k k k k k k k k k k k k k k k k k k k k k

PhotoFinder (www.cs.umd.edu/hcil/photolib)

The design goal of PhotoFinder was to allow users to manage a personal photo library containing multiple collections of photos. This led to the Library Viewer (see Figure 1), with a representative thumbnail photo for each collection. We had a modest goal to allow users to view 10 to 100 collections, which they could arrange in chronological or reverse chronological order. Users can readjust the space allocated to the library viewer, and thumbnails will resize to fit the available space. Each collection may have a description, keywords, date, and a geographic location.

When users select a collection, the thumbnails of each photo appear in the collection viewer. Most users choose the simple grid viewer; three others are also available. Users can resize the thumbnails and choose various orderings. Clicking a thumbnail enlarges the image in the photo viewer. Dragging a set of thumbnails to the photo viewer creates a full-screen slide show.

The photo viewer has a scrolling list of names and allows users to drag and drop the names onto the photos to produce an annotation. This simple operation creates the database entries that makes searches so easy. The thrill for PhotoFinder users is to be able to carry thousands of personal photos around in their laptops as they travel to family for friends. They can go back in time and find photos from a previous visit, or see photos of an individual over several years. The rapid browsing and search capabilities enable users to get what they want. Users can easily add name annotations while browsing with a friend who suddenly recalls the name of a person in the photo. This design evolved over two years with several usability and controlled studies that dealt with issues such as thumbnail sizes, annotation acceleration methods, and search strategies [1, 2]. As the design was further refined from user feedback, the need for new services grew. Printing and sending photos by e-mail were easy to add, but exporting a full Web page was more of a challenge. The StoryStarter module enables users to export the photos in a collection to a Web site. The users need only to choose titles, image sizes, and caption options, and StoryStarter produces Web pages with Next and Previous links to make a complete story. A nice example is a student's story of his winter trip to Florida (www.cs.umd.edu/hcil/photolib/Florida2000).

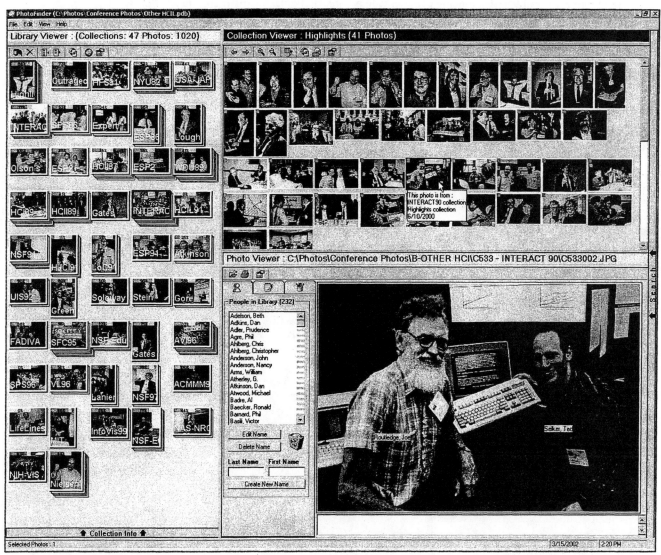

Figure 1. PhotoFinder display with Library Viewer on the left, Collection Viewer with thumbnails on the upper right, and Photo Viewer on the lower right. Library Viewer shows a representative photo for each collection, with collection information such as collection name, description, date range, location, number of photos, and percentage of annotations and captions. A stack represents the approximate number of photos in each collection. The Collection Viewer shows the photo thumbnails of the search result or the selected collection. The tool tip for each thumbnail shows which collection it comes from and the date the photo was taken. Photo Viewer shows the image of the selected thumbnail with annotations, captions and other individual photo information. The list of names, showing all the annotated people in the library, is used for search and direct annotation. Advanced search is possible by clicking Search on the right side of the PhotoFinder window.

PhotoFinder Kiosk

Redesigning the PhotoFinder to become the PhotoFinder Kiosk (see Figure 2) with network support and group annotation turned out to require a huge effort. We cut out many features such as multiple viewers, advanced search, and photo importing, then added highly visible instructions and logins for those who contributed captions or annotations. After our internal usability testing we installed three machines at the December 2000 Computer Supported Collaborative Work (CSCW) conference in Philadelphia. After CSCW2000, we streamlined the user interface further and went to a help overlay design.

For CHI 2001 (Seattle, April 3–5, 2001) we showed 3,300 photos from 65 events on a network of seven machines. People were very enthusiastic, making comments like "Great! Thanks for the memories!" "This is addictive," and "The PhotoFinder rocks!" CHI pioneers and newcomers spent hours browsing and annotating, returning to bring their friends. Visitors added 1,335 name annotations plus 400 captions, and attendees brought us 1,200 new photos.

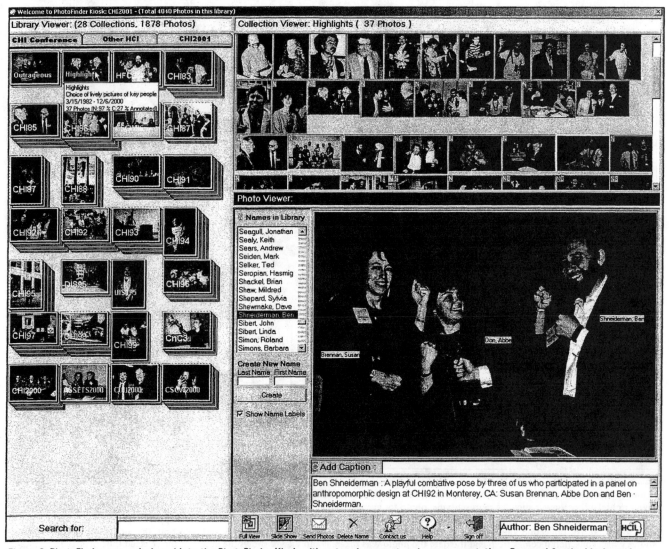

Figure 2. PhotoFinder was redesigned into the PhotoFinder Kiosk with network support and group annotation. Our goal for the kiosk version was to support zero-trial learning. Library Viewer was extended to support multiple libraries; it shows one of three different libraries at a time: CHI conferences, Other HCI, and CHI2001. Many hidden features have been removed, and the taskbar (bottom of the window) has been redesigned to accommodate only the essential features such as free text search, full view, slide show, send photos by e-mail, delete, annotation, help, and sign off. To protect the database from erroneous or malicious usage of the system, annotations and captions can be deleted or changed only by the original author. Only the administrator can update the database by adding a new photo collection or deleting photos from a collection.

To evaluate the use of the kiosk, we used trace logs, a survey, and informal observations of users. Because of the difficulty in detecting session endings, we could not record the exact number of users. Also, the trace log, which recorded 259 sessions, does not include users who browsed but made no annotations. Thus the total number of visitors cannot be estimated effectively, but was likely three to four times that number.

We received 61 completed surveys. More than half of these respondents had attended at least five CHI conferences and were more likely to contribute annotations. Heavy users were also more likely to answer the survey.

Of the 1,335 annotations added, 677 were for the new CHI 2001 pictures and 658 were for older photos. Of the 399 captions, 268 were for older photos and 131 were for the new CHI 2001 photos. A single user contributed 163 captions, all of which were for older photos. Thus the annotation activity of users was evenly divided between old and new collections, even though most of the users were long-time attendees.

We received 151 requests for a total of 2,591 photos (excluding one user who requested 399 photos), and 38 miscellaneous messages. These messages were often used to notify us of spelling and other minor errors, and a few people requested that several photos they had contributed be removed because of poor technical quality.

Analysis of trace logs showed that the two CHI libraries were each selected more often than the related HCI conferences library, showing a stronger interest in the more directly relevant material. We observed that long-time conference attendees spent more time on the historical photos, while newcomers appeared to divide their time more evenly between the libraries.

Visitors would often cluster around a display, sharing reminiscences. As we expected, many long-time attendees wanted to see pictures of themselves or their colleagues earlier in their careers. They found great satisfaction in adding a new name or contributing a caption and were pleased that they could send pictures to themselves or to friends who could not attend the conference. Smiles of amusement and appreciation accompanied finding youthful pictures of friends. Some were disappointed when they didn't find any pictures of themselves. Others volunteered to contribute pictures from their personal collections, and many offered useful suggestions for improvements and keen critiques of usability problems.

k k k k k k k k k k k k k k k k k k k k k k k

PhotoFinder Web

PhotoFinder Web helps PhotoFinder users export their collections or an entire library to the Internet. It produces a functional Web site using existing PhotoFinder data and allows users to make their images accessible and searchable on the Web. It still seems quite magical that the photos stored away in my file cabinets are now open to the world.

Each section of the site generated by PhotoFinder Web has the same navigational links as PhotoFinder on the left side (see Figure 3). The side navigation bar allows users to go to another library or its highlights section, go to search by name, or search the names, captions, and other metadata in the database. The site also has static top and bottom navigation, which allows users to visit different sections of the site. All sections allow users to retrace their previous selections.

The PhotoFinder Web library viewer allows users to see existing collections in the library by displaying the representative image from every collection as a thumbnail. This page provides the collection title, description, and total number of photos in each collection. Clicking a collection thumbnail in the library viewer takes users to the collection viewer, which shows thumbnails of all images in the collection.

The collection viewer includes detailed information such as the description, starting and ending date, and location of the collection. Clicking any thumbnail opens the image viewer in a new browser window, which shows the image and the names of the people in the photo, a caption, date, location, and at what conference event the photo was taken.

The name browser allows viewers to look for a particular person's images in the library. This page has links for all the names in the library and the number of photos of each person in the library. Clicking a name opens the collection viewer, which generates a collection of the person's photos. Clicking a thumbnail takes the users to the image viewer, which shows a larger image and all the information associated with the photo.

Take a look at the SIGCHI Photo History and let us know what you think. Does it help give you an idea of the history of this community? How might it be better?

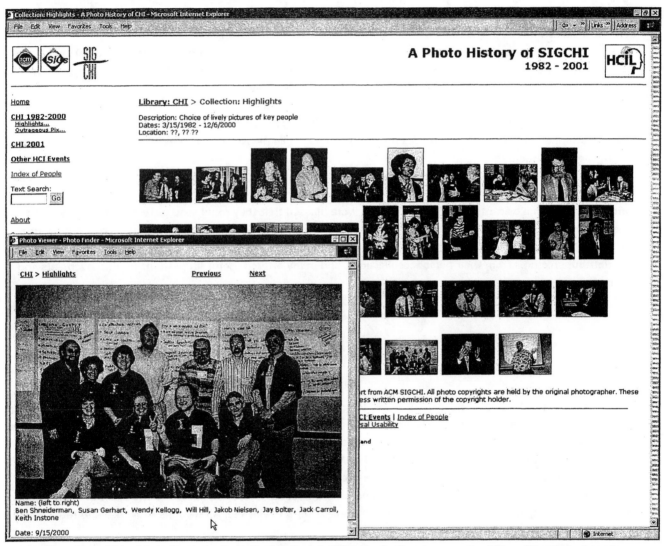

Figure 3. PhotoFinder Web with the navigation bar on the left, the hybrid library-collection viewer on the right, and the photo viewer in a separate window. The side navigation bar allows users to choose one of three libraries, go to the index of people in the database, or perform free text search. Once users choose a library, the right side of window becomes the library viewer, which shows the representative image of every collection in the library as the thumbnail. Clicking a collection thumbnail changes the library viewer into the collection viewer, which shows thumbnails of all images in the collection. Clicking any thumbnail in the collection viewer shows a larger image in a separate window with the photo information.

Chapter 3

Preserving Context with Zoomable User Interfaces

▨　▨　▨　▨　▨

▨　▨　▨　▨　▨

*Always design a thing by considering it in its next larger
context—a chair in a room, a room in a house, a house in an
environment, an environment in a city plan.*

Eliel Saarinen,
quoted by his son Eero, June 2, 1977

A basic and recurring problem that we as interface designers confront is that there is more information than fits on the screen, and users lose context as they navigate to specific pages of information. This book, of course, discusses a broad range of visualization approaches to creating dense and informative interactive displays of these large data sets. However, for more traditional content, such as documents, graphs, email, and calendars, the world of interface design has come to include several standard approaches to support users navigating through this information, including scrolling (*e.g.*, through long documents); linking (*e.g.*, with hyperlinks on the Web); abstraction (*e.g.*, Google search results, which also includes linking); and overview and detail (*e.g.*, Adobe Photoshop's overview window).

Another basic approach, though, is to put all the content on one very large surface and then enable users to look at individual documents by smoothly zooming in to see them. This approach naturally supports zooming out to see overviews, and also to position documents in space in such a way as to represent relationships among them. Objects can also be placed in this space at different sizes, and thus larger objects can represent others when zoomed out. We use the term *semantic zooming* to depict objects that change the way they are visually represented depending on their magnification. A simple example is a clock that shows only hours when zoomed out, but shows minutes and then seconds upon zooming in. This is an important concept because pure geometric scaling only goes so far, and it does not work well at all for text, which is readable only at a relatively small range of sizes.

This design approach has come to be called Zoomable User Interfaces (ZUIs), a term coined by Franklin Servan-Schreiber, a collaborator from Sony Research Labs. ZUIs were first described by Ken Perlin and David Fox at New York University in 1991 with the Pad system they had built, although such interfaces were then called Fractal User Interfaces. Pad used nonanimated jump zooming with black-and-white raster graphics, and supported only simple drawing and text. At that time, I (Ben Bederson) was a graduate student at NYU and watched with great interest as the tiny computer screen gave way to a great expanse of space. In 1992, having finished my dissertation on computer vision and robotics, I joined Bellcore and continued the work on ZUIs with Jim Hollan that I saw get started at NYU. We felt that the idea of zooming would best be understood by supporting a broad array of developers to build zoomable applications in domains of their interest. So, I started by building what turned out to be the first of a long sequence of toolkits to support ZUIs. The first one was Pa3D (with a silent "3") built in Lisp using 3D graphics running on SGIs (Figure 3.1). The goal here was to see how zoomable interfaces changed

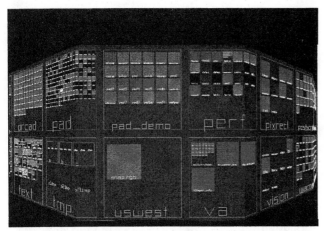

Figure 3.1 Pa3D showing how zoomable user interfaces can be positioned in three dimensions to create a "perspective wall."

when they supported color, vector graphics, and smoothly animated view transitions. This was followed by Pad++, a subsequent toolkit in C++ that I built with Jon Meyer when I moved to the University of New Mexico (Figure 3.2).

During those years, I concentrated on building toolkits and demos that showed what information looked like in ZUIs and what kind of interaction they supported. This was a difficult time because while we were convinced that ZUIs were a promising idea, coming up with compelling applications was difficult. It was only in 1997 that we built PadPrints (just before I moved to the.HCIL), a zoomable Web history mechanism that produced measurable performance improvements for specific tasks (98-06 [5.3]).

After moving to the University of Maryland, I quickly became immersed in the HCIL's domain-driven style of application development and focus on empirical quantitative evaluation. This shift in focus turned out to be very helpful. Graduate student Angela Boltman looked at the animation of ZUIs and showed that despite the concerns of critics, the time spent on animations didn't affect task performance time (98-11 [3.1]).

Since then, the HCIL has continued building toolkits to support ZUIs, which have become more general to support arbitrary 2D structured graphics. The first toolkit was Jazz (99-07,

2000-13 [3.2]), followed more recently by Piccolo. Although Jazz was powerful and flexible, it was hard to learn, leading us to design Piccolo, a much smaller and simpler toolkit (*www.cs.umd.edu/hcil/piccolo*). Current studies are comparing Piccolo to Jazz in terms of speed, memory usage, application size, and design characteristics.

A number of applications have been built that validate the idea that ZUIs offer a simple, flexible, and powerful approach to navigating large information spaces. One of our earliest observations about ZUIs was that we used our tools to make presentations—first about ZUIs themselves, and then about other topics as well (*www.cs.umd.edu/hcil/genex*). We then went on to build CounterPoint, a plug-in for Microsoft PowerPoint that supports organizing slides spatially for a presentation. This allows the audience to see connections among slides, and it enables the presenter to navigate without having to leave the presentation context (2001-03 [3.3]). As described in Chapter 2, another zooming interface, PhotoMesa, enables users to browse large numbers of images (2001-10 [2.3]).

The HCIL has also built a number of interfaces for children, applying ZUIs to several of those as well. KidPad is a children's authoring tool for creating pictures and stories (Figure 3.3), and we have found that children use zooming in simple but unexpected ways to create relationships among story elements (99-28). This work with children's authoring tools motivated us to explore how children search for information, and we have recently embarked on a major project called the International Children's Digital Library (ICDL), seeking to create interfaces for children to find, read, and communicate about children's books from around the world (Figure 3.4) (2000-18 [4.4], 2000-19, 2002-03 [4.5], 2002-07).

One of the crucial lessons we learned is that in order to tap the power of ZUIs, it must be very easy for users to navigate through the space. Our earlier interfaces had a kind of free-form flying where holding one button would cause the view to zoom in and holding another button would zoom out. This was very flexible but difficult to control, and it was very easy to get completely lost by zooming into white space. In fact, this problem was so severe that Susanne Jul and George Furnas at

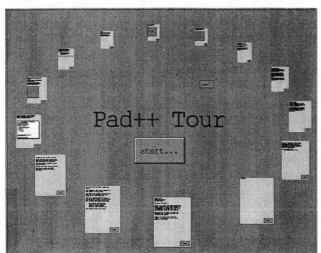

Figure 3.2 The Pad++ help system showing several documents in a zoomable space that could be navigated to directly or sequentially.

Figure 3.3 KidPad (built using Jazz) offers children access to collaborative storytelling tools in a zoomable environment.

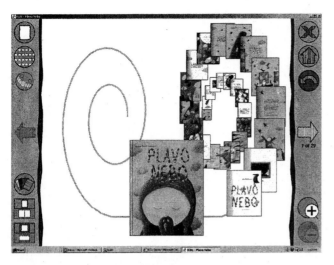

Figure 3.4 *The latest spiral book reader from the International Children's Digital Library (www.icdlbooks.org).*

the University of Michigan wrote a whole paper on what they called *desert fog* and ways to mitigate it. However, our current approach is to learn from the Web, making all navigation follow from a single click on the item of interest. We now use application- and content-specific navigation techniques that change the view appropriately depending on what the user clicks on. For example, in PhotoMesa, this means zooming in to a set of clearly depicted images. With SpaceTree (2002-05 [6.6]), a node-link tree browser, clicking means to expand and center the node that was clicked on. In general, this simpler but slightly less powerful approach makes ZUIs more broadly accessible.

A final point about ZUIs is that while the HCIL has been focusing on applications that use zooming as a primary navigation and organizational mechanism, many other commercial applications have been including zooming as an extra, but important, feature; for example, most Microsoft Office products now allow documents to be viewed at any magnification. Zooming here isn't animated or designed to be used as a navigational aid, but it nevertheless is quite helpful in understanding large documents. Similarly, zooming has long been a part of photo editing tools such as Adobe Photoshop, which also includes an overview window for navigation.

Overview windows are a feature of many applications, and they are generally thought of as a "sure thing" even though our ZUIs usually do not use overview windows. In fact, earlier studies from the HCIL demonstrated the benefit of overview windows (94-02 [8.1], 94-03). So, with some hesitation, we performed a study to try to understand overview windows more clearly, and the results were surprising (2001-11 [3.4]). We looked at how adding overview windows affected performance on map-based tasks. We found that although users definitely liked them, the overviews actually slowed down performance by about 20% for certain tasks. Furthermore, object recall was better without the overview window. As always, the devil is in the details, and this study showed that the details of how one navigates can affect the relative importance of other features—such as overview windows.

We have also pursued alternatives to pure geometric two-dimensional zooming. One-dimensional zooming was an effective feature in several information visualization projects, starting with FilmFinder (93-14), which allowed users to zoom in on recent films (right side of the x-axis) or popular films (top part of the y-axis). The importance of smooth zooming was readily apparent but difficult to attain in early implementations when data set sizes were large (94-06). One-dimensional zooming was a necessary feature for the patient histories in LifeLines (95-15, 97-19, 98-08), where the timeline was on the x-axis. This supported users in seeing an overview (by zooming out) or seeing recent treatments or an earlier hospitalization in detail (by zooming in).

A final variation on zooming is *fisheye distortion*—a technique that attempts to solve a limitation of more traditional ZUIs, which are good at showing context or detail but not both at the same time. Fisheye visualizations, on the other hand, show context and detail at once by distorting the information space. The item of focus is made large and central while less important data is made smaller and pushed off to the side. Even though this technique has been around for some time—initially created by Apperley and Spence in 1982 (they called it *bifocal* since they had two levels of detail) and then refined by Furnas in 1986 (who defined a variable *degree of interest* function)—it has not been fruitfully applied very broadly. We have recently pushed fisheye techniques by carefully applying them to specific domains, and designing for the needs of that domain to great affect. We created a one-dimensional menu system (2000-12 [7.1]) and a two-dimensional calendar system (2002-09 [7.5]), both of which are described in more detail in Chapter 6.

So, the final word on ZUIs is not out yet, but after ten years of building them, we are developing a deeper understanding of them; how to design them, where they provide benefits, and where they don't.

FAVORITE PAPERS FROM OUR COLLEAGUES

Perlin's original Pad system was a real inspiration for our work on ZUIs, and our early collaborations with Jim Hollan strongly helped shape the direction of our ZUI work. Furnas's fisheye concept and demos captivated attention for many years and influenced a large number of researchers. Marc Brown's ideas are always interesting—he is terrifically creative and a whiz at implementation. Here we cite his widely referenced paper, but be sure to see his videos as well. Saul Greenberg and his colleagues were also strong software builders who created innovative tools and made them available.

Furnas, G. W., Generalized Fisheye Views, *Proc. ACM CHI 86 Conference on Human Factors in Computing Systems* (1986), 16–23.

Mackinlay, J. D., Robertson, G. G., Card, S. K., The Perspective Wall: Detail and Context Smoothly Integrated, *Proc. ACM CHI 91 Conference on Human Factors in Computing Systems* (1991), 173–179.

Perlin, K., Fox, D., Pad: An Alternative Approach to the Computer Interface, *Proc. Computer Graphics (SIGGRAPH 93)*, ACM, New York, 57–64.

Sarkar, M., Brown, Marc H., Graphical Fisheye Views, *Communications of the ACM 37*, 12 (July 1994), 73–84.

Schaffer, D., Zuo, Z., Bartram, L., Dill, J., Dubs, S., Greenberg, S., Roseman, M. Comparing Fisheye and Full-Zoom Techniques for Navigation of Hierarchically Clustered Networks, *ACM Transactions on Information Systems 14*, 2 (1996).

Does Animation Help Users Build Mental Maps of Spatial Information?

Benjamin B. Bederson
Computer Science Department
bederson@cs.umd.edu
Human-Computer Interaction Lab
Institute for Advanced Computer Studies
University of Maryland, College Park, MD 20742

Angela Boltman
College of Education
aboltman@umiacs.umd.edu
Human-Computer Interaction Lab
Institute for Advanced Computer Studies
University of Maryland, College Park, MD 20742

Abstract

We examine how animating a viewpoint change in a spatial information system affects a user's ability to build a mental map of the information in the space. We found that animation improves users' ability to reconstruct the information space, with no penalty on task performance time. We believe that this study provides strong evidence for adding animated transitions in many applications with fixed spatial data where the user navigates around the data space.

1. Introduction

During the past decade, researchers have explored the use of animation in many aspects of user interfaces. In 1984, the Apple Macintosh used rudimentary animation when opening and closing icons. This kind of animation was used to provide a continuous transition from one state of the interface to another, and has become increasingly common, both in research and commercial user interfaces. Users commonly report that they prefer animation, and yet there has been very little research that attempts to understand how animation affects users' performance.

A commonly held belief is that animation helps users maintain object constancy and thus helps users to relate the two states of the system. This notion was described well by Robertson and his colleagues in their paper on "cone trees", a 3D visualization technique that they developed.

"Interactive animation is used to shift some of the user's cognitive load to the human perceptual system. ... The perceptual phenomenon of object constancy enables the user to track substructure relationships without thinking about it. When the animation is completed, no time is needed for reassimilation." [19 p. 191].

Researchers including Robertson have demonstrated through informal usability studies that animation can improve subjective user satisfaction. However, there have been few controlled studies looking specifically at how animation affects user performance. These studies are summarized below.

1.1. Animation takes time

One potential drawback of adding animation to an interface or visualization is that animation, by definition, takes time. This brings up a fundamental trade-off between the time spent animating and the time spent using the interface. At one extreme with no animation, system response can be instantaneous. Users spend all of their time using the system. However, the user may then spend some time after an abrupt transition adjusting to the new representation of information and relating it to the previous representation.

At the other extreme, each visual change in the interface is accompanied by a smooth transition that relates the old representation to the new one. While developers of animated systems hope that this animation makes it easier for users to relate the different states of the system, there is clearly a trade-off in how much time is actually spent on the transition. If the transition is too fast, users may not be able to make the connection, and if the transition is too long, the users' time will be wasted. The ideal animation time is likely to be dependent on a number of factors, including task type, and the user's experience with the interface and the data. In pilot studies and our experience building animated systems, we have found that animations of 0.5 – 1.0 second seem to strike a balance. Others have found one second animations to be appropriate [9 p. 185].

In the worse case, animations can be thought of as an increase in total system response time. Typically, system response time is defined to mean the time between when the user initiates an action, and when the computer *starts* to display the result. This definition comes from the days of slow displays on computer terminals. This metric was chosen because users could start planning their response as soon as the first data were displayed. With many animations, however, the user does not see the relevant data until the animation is nearly finished, and thus the animation time is an important part of system response. We thus define the *total system response time* to include the animation time (Figure 1).

In many application domains, the system may need some time to gather data (such as with the World Wide Web), or to process it. In these cases, inserting an animation where a delay is necessitated is not likely to harm productivity because users would have to wait anyway. However, since the delay associated with the Web is often hard to predict, matching animations to the Web retrieval time could be difficult. The bigger problem is when the computer could have responded instantly, and the animation slows down computer's response time.

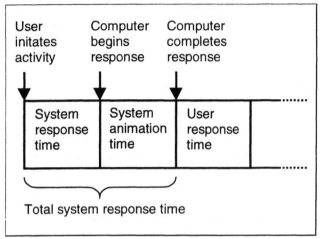

Figure 1:   Model of user interface timing with animation (adapted from [22 p. 353]).

Researchers have been studying system response time since the 1960s, and as it happens, users' responses to system delays are more complex than it may at first appear. There is much research showing that user satisfaction decreases as delays increase (see the recent report on the World-Wide Web for a typical example [21]). However, this satisfaction does not necessarily correlate with performance. One paper showed that users pick different interaction strategies depending on system response times [25]. This paper showed that users actual performance depends on a complex mix of the task, the delay, and the variability of the delay among other things. One typical study shows productivity increasing as delays decreased for data entry tasks [12]. However, another study found an increase in data entry productivity when delays *increased* to a point [3].

Thus, the fact that animations take time does not necessarily imply that they will hurt productivity. Since they may, in fact, reduce cognitive effort, as suggested by Robertson and others, we believe that animation may improve some kinds of task performance.

1.2. Types of computer animation

Animation in computer interfaces can actually mean many different things. Baecker and Small summarized many of the ways that objects can be animated on computer screens [1]. Animation can consist of moving a static object within a scene, or the object may change its appearance as it is moved. A scene may be larger than can fit on the screen, and the viewpoint can be changed with

animated movement by rendering "in-between frames" part way between the starting and ending state. There are numerous other types of animations as well.

In general, animation is often used to help users relate different states in the interface. These changes can be in the data within the interface or in the interface itself. Some systems that use animation of the data include the Information Visualizer [9], Cone Trees [19], the Continuous Zoom system [20], and WebBook and WebForager [10]. Chang and Ungar discussed the application of animation principles from the arts and cartoons to user interfaces, showing that more than just simple movement of interface objects is possible [11].

Some researchers have investigated the use of animated icons [2]. Others have used animation to try to improve teaching how algorithms work [8, 24]. There are also several user interface systems that include explicit support for creating animated interfaces. A good example of this is the Morphic system [18].

1.3. Zoomable User Interfaces

We are interested in understanding animation because for the past several years, we have been exploring Zoomable User Interfaces [4, 5, 6, 7, 15, 17]. Zoomable User Interfaces (ZUIs) are a visualization technique that provides access to spatially organized information. A ZUI lets users zoom in and out, or pan around to view much more information than can normally fit on a single screen. We have developed a system called Pad++ to explore ZUIs.

The ZUIs we have built typically provide three types of animated movement, as well as other kinds of animated transitions such as dissolves. The three types of animated movement are motion of objects within a scene, manual change of viewpoint (through various steering mechanisms), and automatic change of viewpoint (during hyperlinks).

We believe that animating changes of viewpoint during hyperlinks are the most important kind of animation in Pad++, since these animations appear to help users understand where they are in the information space. They are also easy to understand and use. As one child using KidPad (an authoring tool for children within Pad++) said, "With [traditional hypertext] it is like closing your eyes and when you open them you're in a new place. Zooming lets you keep your eyes open" [14].

We and others have also used Pad++ to make animated zooming presentations, and regularly receive very positive feedback from audiences. However, as HCI researchers, we want to develop an understanding of exactly where, if at all, animated ZUIs perform better than traditional approaches.

As we started to design a study that would help us to understand the benefits of ZUIs, we realized that the animation we employ is orthogonal to the use of zoom to organize data. It is possible to have an interface with or without animation, and with or without a multi-scale structure. In order to understand ZUIs better, we decided to attempt to understand the effects of animated movement, and multi-scale structure separately.

Thus, in this paper, we start by examining the most basic and fundamental kind of animation used in ZUIs. We examine how animated changes of viewpoint during hyperlink transitions affects users' ability to build a mental map of a flat information space. We specifically chose not to investigate zooming or multiscale structures in this work because we felt zooming would be a confounding variable to the animation effects we are investigating.

1.4. Previous Studies

There have been few studies that looked specifically at how animation affects user's abilities to use interfaces. One study looked at transition effects (such as a dissolve) and animation of an object within the view [16]. This study found that both a dissolve transition affect and animated motion of objects within a scene independently helped users to solve problems. This study is important because it motivates the common belief and intuition that animation can help user's maintain object constancy and thus improve task performance. However, this study did not address animation of viewpoint which is the primary focus of the current study.

Another study that is perhaps more relevant looked at animating the viewpoint of a spatial information visualization [13]. That study compared users' ability to find items where more items than could fit in a single display were used. Different navigation techniques were used to move through the items (scrollbars, zoom, and fisheye view), and each navigation technique was tested with and without animation. In this experiment, the use of animation did not have a significant affect on any of the navigation techniques. However, animation was implemented with just a single in-between frame. For animation to be perceived as smooth apparent movement, there must be several in-between frames, and they must be shown quickly (typically greater than 10 frames per second, and preferably 20 or 30 frames per second). Thus it does not appear that the results accurately describe the effects of animation. One interesting aspect of the study that does appear significant, but not relevant to animation, is that the zooming visualization technique performed significantly better than either the scrollbar or fisheye view visualization technique.

2. Experiment

We performed a study to test the effectiveness of animation of viewpoint on subjects' ability to build mental maps of spatial information spaces. Our hypothesis was that animation would improve subjects' ability to navigate through the information space, recall information, and to reconstruct the information space.   In addition, we hypothesized that subjects would prefer animation to the non-animated condition.

2.1. Equipment

The computer system used was a 166 MHz Pentium PC with 32 megabytes of RAM running Linux. The PC had 17" monitor and was running at a resolution of 1280x1024. Navigation was performed using only the left button of a standard 2-button mouse. The questions and tasks that were presented to the subjects were automated and recorded by a program that we wrote.

2.2. Stimuli

Subjects were asked to navigate family trees created in the Pad++ program. Subjects navigated these trees clicking on hyperlinks that were represented by yellow arrows. For each family member, subjects saw a single photograph. Above the photograph, subjects saw the family member's first name and yellow hyperlink arrows with the words "parent", "child", "sibling", and "spouse", where appropriate (Figure 2). In the non-animated condition, clicking on a link would result in the destination of the link immediately appearing on the screen. The animated condition would smoothly move the viewpoint to the destination, showing all of the places in-between the source and destination along the way. All animations took exactly one second, and they were animated at 20 frames per second with an average speed of 750 pixels per second. Animations used a "slow-in, slow-out" technique which means that the animation speed increases smoothly at the beginning, continues at a constant rate in the middle, and decreases smoothly at the end.

Figure 2:   Presentation of person in a family tree. Arrows are hyperlinks for navigation. Note that the actual faces that were used in the experiment were completely unfamiliar to the subjects.

Two different fictitious family trees were used in the test – the Goodman family and the Flemming family. We matched the two treatments by creating two family trees that were exactly alike in both the structure and the number of family members the tree contained, although the names and photographs of the family members varied (Figure 3). This design has the risk that users would remember the structure of the tree. However, we decided that this risk was better than the alternative of having different structures that may not be comparable. Each subject was presented with one family tree with animation, and the other family tree without animation.

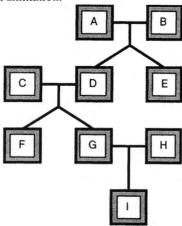

Figure 3:   The structure of the family tree. This view was never available to subjects. Lines represent marriage and child relationships (i.e., A & B are married, and D & E are their children).

We created family trees with nine individuals in each tree, and displayed only one or two nodes at a time. We used this size because the goal of our experiment was to understand how people navigated information spaces where each view showed a subset of the complete information. In addition, we wanted to test memory, and if we had hundreds of family members, it would be more difficult to test how well subjects could learn the whole tree. In a pilot test, subjects specifically stated that the nine-node tree was a reasonable amount of information to try and learn – a challenge, but not impossible.

2.3. Training

Prior to beginning the experiment, subjects were trained in the use of Pad++, and in the nature of a family tree and its relationships. The goals of the training exercise were to verify that our subjects understood family relationships, and to orient them to the interface used in the experiment. In the training section of the experiment, they were given a family tree with and without animation and asked to answer four questions about the family relationships and the photographs. We monitored our subjects during their training and only accepted subjects into the experiment who completed their training tasks with 100% accuracy. No subjects were turned away due to errors in training.

2.4. Method

We used a 2x2x2 incomplete block design for this study. Each subject was given matched tasks for the two family trees, one with animation, and one without. Half of the subjects were given an animated family tree first; and half of the subjects were given an animated family tree second. The independent variables were transition type (with or without animation), order (animation first or non-animated first), and family tree (Goodmans or Flemmings).

Within both of the family trees, subjects were given three kinds of tasks. First, the subject was presented with a series of nine statements and asked to navigate the family tree until the subject felt that he/she had the appropriate information to determine if the statement was true or false. The questions were presented one at a time in randomized order. These questions were solely about the family relationships. (E.g. "Victor's sister is Margaret".) This task was given to evaluate speed of navigation.

The second set of tasks evaluated recall memory. The subject was given 3 minutes of exploratory time, where he/she could navigate the family tree at leisure. After this 3 minutes of exploratory time, the family tree was hidden, and the subject was presented with 10 multiple choice questions in random order. These questions were about both the family relationships and the photographs of the family members. An example of a relationship question was "Who was Billy's mother?". An example of a photograph question was "Who was holding a puppy?".

The third set of tasks evaluated reconstruction ability. The subject was given the off-computer task of assembling the photos of all the family members into the organization of the family tree. The subjects were given a stack of the nine photographs of the family tree members, and were asked to duplicate the family tree that they had seen in the computer interface. They were given as much time as they needed. The position of each photo was recorded for future analysis. The subject was not given the opportunity to specify specific relationships. Subjects could only specify position. Thus, in this part of the experiment, we could not distinguish between a marriage and a sibling relationship.

The subject then repeated all three activities for a second family tree. Lastly, the subject was asked to complete two user satisfaction surveys – one about their experience with animation, and the other about their experience without animation.

Seven dependent variables were analyzed in the experiment. For each of the three task types, we measured accuracy and speed. The time to complete a question was measured from the time the subject initiated a request for a new question until they completed the task by providing an answer. Only questions a subject completed correctly were included in the time averages.

The seventh dependent variable was subjective satisfaction. We measured this using a subset of the

Questionnaire for User Interaction Satisfaction (QUIS) developed at the University of Maryland [23]. The satisfaction level of animation and non-animation was based on a series of questions: overall reaction, locating information, and remembering relationships. Subjects were also asked to give their opinions of the advantages and disadvantages of an interface with animation.

The task of reconstructing the family tree was performed away from a computer using printed photographs of each family member without the name of the person. For each subject, we recorded the time to complete the task and the number of errors. Because there were different kinds of errors, we measured them in two ways. Our goal was to try to understand if the kinds of errors that were made were different in the two conditions. First, we counted the number of faces placed in an incorrect position. Second, we weighted the errors by how far away from the correct position the faces were placed. For each incorrect placement, we assigned a weight of 1 if the face was simply swapped with another face, or if the face was away from its correct placement on the same row. We assigned a weight of 2 if the face was one row too high or low, and a weight of 3 if the face was two rows too high or low.

2.5. Subjects

Twenty subjects participated in the experiment. 55% of the subjects were male and 45% of the subjects were female. Subjects ranged in age from 20 to 44. Mean age was 27. All but one of the subjects were students at the University of Maryland at College Park.

Of the student subjects, 8 were computer science majors, 5 were library and information science majors, 2 were engineering majors, 1 was an animal science major, 1 was a math major, 1 was a journalism major, and 1 was a clinical psychology major. 15% of subjects reported spending under 10 hours per week using a computer, 20% reported averaging 11-20 hours, 35% reported averaging 21-30 hours, 30% reported over 31 hours. Subjects were paid $10 for their participation.

2.6. Results

We observed a statistically significant improvement in accuracy of the reconstruction task by navigation type with both the unweighted count ($F_{1,19} = 16.165$, p=.001) and the weighted count ($F_{1,19} = 16.816$, p=.001) as reported in Table 1. The animation treatment had fewer errors than the non-animated treatment. There was no statistically significant difference in any of the other tasks or subjective satisfaction by animation. For an effect to be considered significant, p had to be less than or equal to 0.01.

There was also a significant ordering effect in the reconstruction task accuracy by order ($F_{1,19} = 8.780$, p=.009). This ordering effect showed that if the animation was first, then there was little difference between animation

and no animation. If the animation treatment was second, however, then performance was significantly better with animation (Figure 4).

Measure	Animated	Non-Animated
Navigation Task Mean time/question	18.6 secs	18.9 secs
Navigation Task Mean errors	0.3 errs	0.1 errs
Exploratory Task Mean time/question	7.2 secs	7.3 secs
Exploratory Task Mean errors	2.4 errs	2.0 errs
Reconstruction Task Mean time	37.8 secs	50.9 secs
Reconstruction Task Mean errors, unweighted	0.4 errs	1.8 errs
Reconstruction Task Mean errors, weighted	0.4 errs	3.35 errs
Subjective Satisfaction	6.0 (max 9)	5.9

Table 1: Summary results for experiment. Significant effects are shaded

Finally, there were several significant secondary effects that are listed in Table 2. These five effects were not consistent in that they did not each show that one treatment performed better than another based on order.

After the entire experiment, subjects were asked to write down what they thought were the advantages and disadvantages of animation, and they were asked to give suggestions to improve the system. Each comment was categorized, and we report the totals of all of the comments in Table 3.

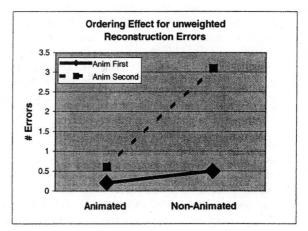

Figure 4:   Ordering effect for unweighted reconstruction errors.

	Measure	Effect
Animati on by Order	Navigation Time	$F_{1,19}=20.924$, $p<.001$
	Explore Errors	$F_{1,19}=11.845$, $p=.003$
	Explore Time	$F_{1,19}=13.411$, $p=.002$
	Reconstructio n Errors	$F_{1,19}=9.979$, $p=.006$
	Satisfaction	$F_{1,19}=8.450$, $p=.010$

Table 2: Secondary significant effects.

Question	Response	# of Responses
Advantages of animation	Improved understanding of relationships	12
	Easier to use	2
	Less strict	1
	More fun	1
	Prettier	1
Disadvantag es of animation	Slower	5
	Distracting	2
Suggestions	Add overall view	12

Table 3: Number of subjects per comment.

2.7. Analysis

This experiment shows that, for the spatial map of the family tree that we used, animation improved subjects' ability to learn the spatial position of family members within the tree without a speed penalty. Subjects did not perform navigation and recall tasks better with animation, although the animation did not change their response time either. Further, while subjects did not prefer the animated transitions to the non-animated transitions, 75% of them specifically stated that they thought the animations helped them learn the relationships between the data, and only 25% of them said that the animations slowed them down.

We find these data to support our hypothesis that animated transitions help users built mental maps of spatial information. While our dataset is small, the visual space that was navigated relative to the screen size was fairly large, and so while it would be useful to run another study with more data, we think this experiment's results can be generalized to other information systems where the space is larger than the display.

Subjects clearly performed better reconstructing the family tree in this experiment. It is interesting, however, that subjects did not perform better navigating the space, or

recalling relationships about family members. Let us examine these three task types more closely.

Animation had no significant effect on the first task of navigating the family tree in order to learn the relationships between family members. This task involved clicking on hyperlinks to explore the tree. Since this task involved many animated transitions, each of which took one second, it is not surprising that performance time was not improved. The fact that the animated transitions did not slow down performance implies that either subjects were able to find what they were looking for while following fewer links, or by following each link quicker. Unfortunately, we did not record the number of links followed, and so can not report on this. There was also no significant difference in correctness on this first task. This is also not surprising because nearly all of the questions were answered correctly in both cases.

The questions for the second task were answered from memory after the subjects had explored the family tree. This eliminated the time spent animating the viewpoint as a factor. It might be expected that if users really had built better mental maps of the information space, then performance would have been improved on this task. However, no performance improvement was seen for the animated condition.

Our explanation is that although animation directly aids in learning spatial relationships, it does not directly help learning more complex relationships among data. It could be that such a cross over takes more time. Or it could be that spatial memory and symbolic reasoning are independent enough that learning one does not necessarily improve the other – even if they are related, as they were in this study.

For the third task of reconstruction, animation did have a significant effect, reducing the errors that subjects made reconstructing the tree given pictures of the family members' faces. This effect was particularly strong because not only were the number of errors smaller, but the kinds of errors were less serious. All of the 8 errors in the animated treatment involved swapping of two faces, while errors in the non-animated treatment involved switching of 3 or 4 faces. Errors in the non-animated treatment included 14 swaps, 8 faces that were misplaced by sliding an entire row out of place, and 14 more errors that were the result of confusing 3 or 4 faces together. This effect appears to be strong because this task was heavily dependent on remembering the spatial position of family members.

This reconstruction task was the one that had an ordering effect (Figure 4). Subjects did significantly worse with the non-animated treatment if it was first. However, they performed only slightly worse with the non-animated treatment if it was preceded by the animated treatment. One explanation for this is that the subjects learned the structure better with the animated treatment, and because the family trees for each treatment had the identical structure, they could remember that structure from one treatment to the next. Since those subjects that had the non-animated treatment first did substantially better on the second animated treatment, this implies that the non-animated treatment did not help subjects learn the family tree structure as well as the animated treatment, because if it had, we would expect only a small improvement in the second animated treatment.

Finally, we were surprised that despite the positive comments about animation, subjects did not report a preference either way. This was especially puzzling because we have received positive informal feedback on previous occasions regarding animation [15, 17].

Our explanation here is twofold. The first issue is that subjects reported being quite frustrated doing this experiment. Most subjects wanted some way to see an overview of the entire family (see Table 3). The point of our experiment was to study how people navigated spaces where they could not see an overview. However, there were few enough people in the trees that subjects realized this was an unrealistic situation, and thus apparently felt that with or without animation, there were better alternatives for exploring family trees. Thus, subjects reported their dissatisfaction equally between treatments. A second issue is that we administered the satisfaction questionnaire separately for the animated and non-animated conditions, and we never specifically asked people to compare them. Since subjects did report positive effects of animation when asked specifically about animation (see Table 3), perhaps if we had asked subjects to directly compare the two conditions, we would have seen different results.

So, why does animation appear to improve people's ability to learn spatial position and relationships of data? We do not know the answer to this question, but think our initial intuition is part of the answer. We think that animation helps users to maintain object constancy, and that without animation, users must spend time rebuilding an understanding of which object is which. When an object does not appear in all the views, then animation may be even more important because users can see which direction it is going, and so they can build a mental map of where things are.

3. Conclusion

While the current study does provide interesting results, it does not answer all of our questions. For instance, we would like to run an animation experiment on a larger data set, and we would like to know what the factors are in determining an optimal time to be spent for the animated transitions. We also would like to study the issue of animation time more closely, making sure that the animation is responsible for the performance improvement, and not just the increased time of the transition. Animation has a strong visual impact, and not all users like it. So,

future studies should be careful to consider user satisfaction as well as performance. Finally, we also would like to understand animation well enough so that we can pursue our original question of how well multiscale presentations of data work.

Our positive results for animation lead us to some preliminary design guidelines. If a task requires subjects to know something about objects' spatial position, and the viewpoint is changed, then animating that change in viewpoint appears to helps users. While our experiment was for 2D data, our experience leads us to think that our results will generalize to other spatial formats such as 1D and 3D data (although we do not have any data to support this belief). This has direct implications for many applications that present linear data – including word processors, spreadsheets, and Web browsers.

Based on this study, we feel that we can make certain recommendations. We suggest that when a movement is made within a document, that movement should be animated. This applies to using the page-up and page-down keys, clicking in the trough of a scrollbar, and jumping to another page. There is no reason to think that a full one-second animation is necessary in all circumstances, but some animation does seem to help, and the time spent animating does not seem to hurt. Indeed, some current applications already do support some animation in this fashion. Microsoft Internet Explorer 4.0, for instance, animates page-up and page-down actions. However, this animation is not controllable by the user, and is not consistent across other interactions (such as Back). Most applications today still do not perform such animation.

4. Acknowledgements

We especially appreciate the efforts of Jim Beisaw at the University of Maryland and Susanne Jul at the University of Michigan who helped with the early design of this study. We thank Maya Venkatraman who helped us analyze the data, and Britt McAlister who helped write the automated data recording program. In addition, we thank all of the members of the HCIL at UMD who gave advice and help throughout this work. Finally, we wouldn't be doing this work in the first place if it weren't for the other members of the Pad++ team, especially Jim Hollan and Jon Meyer.

This work, and Pad++ in general has been largely funded by DARPA to whom we are grateful.

5. References

1. Baecker, R., & Small, I. (1990). Animation at the Interface. B. Laurel *The Art of Human-Computer Interface Design* (pp. 251-267). Addison-Wesley.

2. Baecker, R., Small, I., & Mander, R. (1991). Bringing Icons to Life. *In Proceedings of Human Factors in Computing Systems (CHI 91)* New York: ACM, pp. 1-6.

3. Barber, R. E., & Lucas, H. C. (1983). System Response Time, Operator Productivity and Job Satisfaction. *Communications of the ACM, 26*(11), 972-986.

4. Bederson, B. B., & Hollan, J. D. (1994). Pad++: A Zooming Graphical Interface for Exploring Alternate Interface Physics. *In Proceedings of User Interface and Software Technology (UIST 94)* New York: ACM, pp. 17-26.

5. Bederson, B. B., Hollan, J. D., Perlin, K., Meyer, J., Bacon, D., & Furnas, G. W. (1996). Pad++: A Zoomable Graphical Sketchpad for Exploring Alternate Interface Physics. *Journal of Visual Languages and Computing, 7,* 3-31.

6. Bederson, B. B., Hollan, J. D., Stewart, J., Rogers, D., Druin, A., Vick, D., Ring, L., Grose, E., & Forsythe, C. (1998). A Zooming Web Browser. C. Forsythe, J. Ratner, & E. Grose (eds.), *Human Factors and Web Development* (Chap. 19, pp. 255-266). New Jersey: Lawrence Erlbaum.

7. Bederson, B. B., & Meyer, J. (1998). Implementing a Zooming User Interface: Experience Building Pad++. *Software: Practice and Experience, 28*(10), 1101-1135.

8. Brown, M. H. (1988). Perspectives on Algorithm Animation Visualization. *In Proceedings of Human Factors in Computing Systems (CHI 88)* ACM Press, pp. 33-38.

9. Card, S. K., Robertson, G. G., & Mackinlay, J. D. (1991). The Information Visualizer, an Information Workspace. *In Proceedings of Human Factors in Computing Systems (CHI 91)* ACM Press, pp. 181-188.

10. Card, S. K., Robertson, G. G., & York, W. (1996). The Webbook and the Web Forager: An Information Workspace for the World Wide Web. *In Proceedings of Human Factors in Computing Systems (CHI 96)* ACM Press, pp. 111-117.

11. Chang, B.-W., & Ungar, D. (1993). Animation: From Cartoons to the User Interface. *In Proceedings of User Interface and Software Technology (UIST 93)* ACM Press, pp. 45-55.

12. Dannenbring, G. L. (1984). System Response Time and User Performance. *IEEE Transactions on Systems, Man, and Cybernetics, 14*(3), 473-478.

13. Donskoy, M., & Kaptelinin, V. (1997). Window Navigation With and Without Animation: A Comparison of Scroll Bars, Zoom, and Fisheye View. *In Proceedings of Extended Abstracts of Human Factors in Computing Systems (CHI 97)* ACM Press, pp. 279-280.

14. Druin, A. (1999). *The Design of Children's Technology.* San Francisco, CA: Morgan Kaufmann.

15. Druin, A., Stewart, J., Proft, D., Bederson, B. B., & Hollan, J. D. (1997). KidPad: A Design Collaboration Between Children, Technologists, and Educators. *In Proceedings of Human Factors in Computing Systems (CHI 97)* ACM Press, pp. 463-470.

16. Gonzalez, C. (1996). Does Animation in User Interfaces Improve Decision Making? *In Proceedings of Human Factors in Computing Systems (CHI 96)* ACM Press, pp. 27-34.

17. Hightower, R. R., Ring, L., Helfman, J., Bederson, B. B., & Hollan, J. D. (1998). Graphical Multiscale Web Histories: A Study of PadPrints. *In Proceedings of ACM Conference on Hypertext (Hypertext 98)* ACM Press, pp. 58-65.

18. Maloney, J. H., & Smith, R. B. (1995). Directness and Liveness in the Morphic User Interface Construction Environment. *In Proceedings of User Interface and Software Technology (UIST 95)* ACM Press, pp. 21-28.

19. Robertson, G. G., Mackinlay, J. D., & Card, S. K. (1991). Cone Trees: Animated 3D Visualizations of Hierarchical Information. *In Proceedings of Human Factors in Computing Systems (CHI 91)* ACM Press, pp. 189-194.

20. Schaffer, D., Zuo, Z., Bartram, L., Dill, J., Dubs, S., Greenberg, S., & Roseman, M. (1997). Comparing Fisheye and Full-Zoom Techniques for Navigation of Hierarchically Clustered Networks. *In Proceedings of Graphics Interface (GI 97)* Canadian Inforation Processing Society, pp. 87-96.

21. Sears, A., Jacko, J. A., & Borella, M. S. (1997). Internet Delay Effects: How Users Perceive Quality, Organization, and Ease of Use of Information. *In Proceedings of Extended Abstracts of Human Factors in Computing Systems (CHI 97)* ACM Press, pp. 353-354.

22. Shneiderman, B. (1997). *Designing the User Interface: Strategies for Effective Human-Computer Interaction.* Massachusetts: Addison-Wesley.

23. Slaughter, L. A., Harper, B. D., & Norman, K. L. (1994). Assessing the Equivalence of Paper and On-Line Versions of the QUIS 5.5. *In Proceedings of 2nd Annual Mid-Atlantic Human Factors Conference* pp. 87-91.

24. Stasko, J. T., Badre, A., & Lewis, C. (1993). Do Algorithm Animations Assist Learning? An Empirical Study and Analysis. *In Proceedings of Human Factors in Computing Systems (InterCHI 93)* ACM Press, pp. 61-66.

25. Teal, S. L., & Rudnicky, A. I. (1992). A Performance Model of System Delay and User Strategy Selection. *In Proceedings of Human Factors in Computing Systems (CHI 92)* ACM Press, pp. 295-305.

Jazz: An Extensible Zoomable User Interface Graphics Toolkit in Java

Benjamin B. Bederson, Jon Meyer, Lance Good
Human-Computer Interaction Lab
Institute for Advanced Computer Studies, Computer Science Department
University of Maryland, College Park, MD 20742
+1 301 405-2764
{bederson, meyer, goodness}@cs.umd.edu

ABSTRACT

In this paper we investigate the use of scene graphs as a general approach for implementing two-dimensional (2D) graphical applications, and in particular Zoomable User Interfaces (ZUIs). Scene graphs are typically found in three-dimensional (3D) graphics packages such as Sun's Java3D and SGI's OpenInventor. They have not been widely adopted by 2D graphical user interface toolkits.

To explore the effectiveness of scene graph techniques, we have developed Jazz, a general-purpose 2D scene graph toolkit. Jazz is implemented in Java using Java2D, and runs on all platforms that support Java 2. This paper describes Jazz and the lessons we learned using Jazz for ZUIs. It also discusses how 2D scene graphs can be applied to other application areas.

Keywords

Zoomable User Interfaces (ZUIs), Animation, Graphics, User Interface Management Systems (UIMS), Pad++, Jazz.

INTRODUCTION

Today's Graphical User Interface (GUI) toolkits contain a wide range of built-in user interface objects (also known as widgets, controls or components). These GUI toolkits are excellent for building hierarchical organizations of standard widgets such as buttons, scrollbars, and text areas. However, they fall short when the developer needs to create application-specific widgets. Developers typically write these application-specific widgets by subclassing an existing widget and overriding methods to define new functionality. However, GUIs have become more sophisticated, and the level of functionality needed to implement a new GUI widget has increased. Beyond writing the code to draw the widget, the developer must also write code to handle events, drag and drop, selection, layout, keyboard navigation, keyboard focus highlighting, tool tips, context sensitive help, popup menus, accessibility, internationalization, animated scrolling, and so on. Implementing a fully functional application-specific widget is a daunting task.

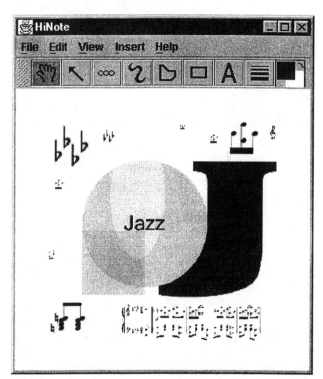

Figure 1: Screen snapshot of the HiNote application program, written using Jazz.

We believe that a significant problem with existing 2D user interface toolkits is that they follow a "monolithic" design philosophy. That is, they use a relatively small number of classes to provide a large amount of functionality. As a result, the classes tend to be complex and have large numbers of methods, and the functionality provided by each class is hard to reuse in new widgets.

To address code reuse, toolkit developers usually place generally useful code in a top-level class that is inherited by all of the widgets in the toolkit. There are several drawbacks to this approach. Firstly, it leads to a very complex hard-to-learn top-level class. (In Microsoft MFC, the top-level CWnd class has over 300 methods. The Java Component class has over 160 methods. Even Java Swing, a relatively new toolkit with a modern design, has a top level JComponent class with over 280 methods). Secondly, application developers are forced to accept the functionality provided by the toolkit's top-level class – they can not add their own reusable mechanisms to enhance the toolkit. Many researchers create their own custom toolkit so that they can have complete control over the capabilities of widgets in their application.

For several years, we have been investigating Zoomable User Interfaces (ZUIs), which use zooming as a principal method of navigation. ZUIs have a number of unique requirements, such as the need for "semantic zooming" where more detail is displayed as the scene is zoomed in, and the need for multiple views of the same scene at different magnifications. In practice, implementing a general purpose widget for supporting ZUI applications is very hard [7].

In this paper, we report on our experiences developing Jazz[1]. Jazz is a new toolkit for developing ZUI applications. It can also be used to build many other kinds of 2D widgets.

Unlike prior GUI toolkits, Jazz is based on a "minilithic" design philosophy. In Jazz, functionality is delivered not through class inheritance but rather by composing a number of simple objects within a scene graph hierarchy. These objects are frequently non-visual (e.g. layout nodes), or serve to "decorate" nodes beneath them in the scene graph with additional appearance or functionality (e.g. selection nodes). Jazz therefore tackles the complexity of a graphical application by dividing object functionality into small, easily understood and reused node types. Those nodes can be combined to create powerful applications. The base ZNode class in Jazz has under 60 public methods (16 are related to events, 16 are related to the scenegraph structure, 8 are related to coordinates, and the rest are for other functions such as painting, saving, properties, and debugging.)

We believe that minilithic scene graphs are an important mechanism for supporting custom 2D application widgets in general, and ZUIs in particular. While zooming has been one of our motivations for building Jazz, we think that its simple model will prove useful for non-zooming applications as well. In particular, we believe that Jazz's combination of extensibility, object orientation, hierarchical structure, and support for multiple representations will simplify the task of writing many application-specific 2D widgets.

In this paper, we first describe the unique requirements of ZUIs that led us to create Jazz. We outline related work and

---

[1] The name Jazz is not an acronym, but rather is motivated by the new music-related naming conventions that the Java Swing toolkit started. In addition, the letter 'J' signifies the Java connection, and the letter 'Z' signifies the zooming connection.
Jazz is open source software according to the Mozzilla Public License, and is available at:
http://www.cs.umd.edu/hcil/jazz

discuss the architecture of Jazz. We show how Jazz supports adding functionality by composition, and describe some applications we have built using Jazz. We conclude by describing some of our experiences building the Jazz toolkit, and outline future work.

REQUIREMENTS FOR ZUIS
Zoomable User Interfaces are a kind of information visualization application. They display graphical information on a virtual canvas that is very broad and has very high resolution. A portion of this huge canvas is seen on the display through a virtual "camera" that can pan and zoom over the surface.

ZUIs have unique requirements beyond those supported by standard 2D GUI toolkits. We list some of the requirements for the kinds of ZUIs we want to build below. Although these requirements reflect the complex nature of ZUIs, many non-zooming application-specific widgets have similar requirements:

1) The ZUI must provide support for custom application graphics that may be non-rectangular or transparent, as well as traditional interactive widgets such as buttons and sliders.

2) Large numbers of objects must be supported so that rendering and interaction performance doesn't degrade with complex scenes.

3) Objects must support arbitrary transforms and hierarchical grouping.

4) View navigations (pans and zooms) should be smooth and continuously animated.

5) Multiple representations of objects must be supported so that objects can be rendered differently in different contexts, for example, at different scales.

6) Multiple views onto the surface should be supported, both as different windows, and within the surface to be used as "portals" or "lenses".

7) Objects must be able to be made "sticky" so they stay fixed in one spot on the screen when the view changes. This is similar to a heads-up-display (HUD).

8) It must be possible to write interaction event handlers that provide for user manipulation of individual elements, and groups of objects.

The Jazz platform supports all of these requirements.

RELATED WORK
The influential InterViews framework [18] supports structured graphics and user interface components. Fresco [26] was derived from InterViews and unifies structured graphics and user interface widgets into a single hierarchy. Both Fresco and later versions of InterViews support lightweight glyphs and a class hierarchy structure similar to Jazz. However, these systems do not support large scene graphs well, or handle multiple views onto the scene graph.

They also do not support advanced visualization techniques such as fisheye views and context sensitive objects. Jazz adds new node types to the scene graph to support these additional features.

A number of 2D GUI toolkits provide higher-level support for creating custom application widgets, or provide support for structured graphics. The Tk Canvas [17] for example supports object-oriented 2D graphics, though it has no hierarchies or extensibility. Amulet [19] is a toolkit that supports widgets and custom graphics, but it has no support for arbitrary transformations (such as scaling), semantic zooming, and multiple views.

The GUI toolkit that perhaps comes closest to meeting the needs of ZUIs is SubArctic [16]. It is typical of other GUI toolkits in that it is oriented towards more traditional graphical user interfaces. While SubArctic is innovative in its use of constraints for widget layout and rich input model, it has a monolithic design. In addition, it does not support multiple cameras or arbitrary 2D transformations (including scale) on objects and views.

None of these 2D GUI toolkits adopt a scene graph structure that integrates structured graphics with user interface widgets. They are all implemented with a monolithic design. So, while it may have been possible to extend an existing toolkit to add support for zooming, it would not have been possible to pursue a minilithic design that we felt was also an important research goal.

It is possible to build ZUI applications using existing 3D scene graph tools, such as OpenInventor [5]. That may work from a structural standpoint. However, we would then be restricted to using a 3D renderer. That is problematic because 3D renderers do not support 2D business graphics or standard user interface widgets well.

```
import javax.swing.*;
import edu.umd.cs.jazz.*;
import edu.umd.cs.jazz.util.*;
import edu.umd.cs.jazz.component.*;

public class HelloWorld extends JFrame {

    public HelloWorld() {
                // Set up basic frame
        setBounds(100, 100, 400, 400);
        ZCanvas canvas = new ZCanvas();
        getContentPane().add(canvas);
        setVisible(true);

                // Add some sample text
        ZText text = new ZText("Hello World!");
        ZVisualLeaf leaf = new ZVisualLeaf(text);
        canvas.getLayer().addChild(leaf);
    }

    public static void main(String args[]) {
        HelloWorld app = new HelloWorld();
    }
}
```

Figure 2: Complete Jazz "Hello World!" program that supports panning and zooming.

Typical 3D renderers, such as OpenGL, support very efficient image and triangle rendering, but do not have direct support for high quality scalable fonts, 2D complex polygons, line styles, and other standard business graphics. We have discussed these issues in depth previously [7]. We are also interested in developing scene graph nodes that apply to 2D application domains. For this domain, many of the nodes found in 3D scene graph systems are not appropriate.

There are several prior implementations of Zoomable User Interfaces toolkits. These include the original Pad system [20], and more recently Pad++ [6, 7, 8], as well as other systems [13, 21][22], and a few commercial ZUIs that are not widely accessible [3, 4, 23; Chapter 6].

All of these previous ZUI systems are implemented in terms of a hierarchy of objects, and are therefore superficially similar to Jazz. However, like GUI toolkits, they all use a monolithic class structure that places a large amount of functionality in a single top-level "Node" class. For example, in Pad++, the top-level `Pad_Object` class has 235 methods, and supports fading, culling, spatial indexing, stickiness, layering, etc. We needed a cleaner and more flexible approach.

THE JAZZ TOOLKIT

Jazz is a new general-purpose toolkit for creating ZUI applications using zooming object-oriented 2D graphics. Jazz is built entirely in Java and runs on all platforms that support Java 2.

Jazz uses the Java2D renderer, and is organized to support efficient animation, rapid screen updates, and high quality stills. While we could have written Jazz using other rendering engines, such as OpenGL, we picked Java2D because of its clean design and focus on high-quality 2D graphics. As previously mentioned, OpenGL does not support business graphics well. In addition, using Java2D allows us to support embedded Swing widgets, which would be impossible with OpenGL.

Jazz borrows many of the structural elements common to 3D scene graph systems, such as Sun's Java3D [1] and SGI's OpenInventor [5]. By using a basic hierarchical scene graph model with cameras, Jazz is able to directly support a variety of common as well as forward-looking interface mechanisms. This includes hierarchical groups of objects with affine transforms (translation, scale, rotation and shear), layers, zooming, internal cameras (portals), lenses, semantic zooming, and multiple representations.

Figure 2 shows a complete standalone Jazz program that displays "Hello World!" where the user can pan and zoom the view. Default navigation event handlers let the user pan

with the left mouse button, and zoom with the right mouse button by dragging right or left to zoom in or out, respectively. Note that Jazz automatically updates the portion of the screen that has been changed, so no manual repaint calls are needed.

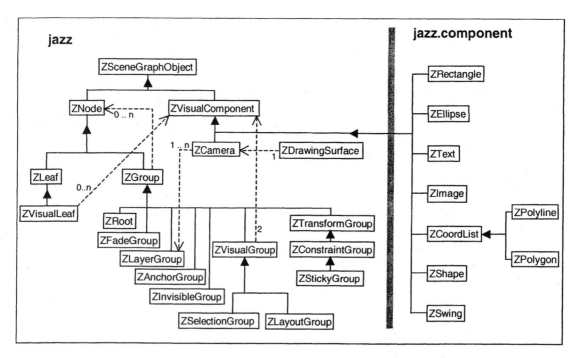

Figure 3: The Object hierarchy of Jazz.

The Jazz design follows standard 3D scene graph practices, segregating functionality into separate, non-visual grouping nodes. This approach leads to a modular scene graph design. Jazz has an extensible visual and interaction policy. It comes with a small set of visual objects and a well-defined mechanism for applications to define their own. Similarly, Jazz supports default selection, navigation, and other interaction mechanisms, but they are also designed to be modifiable by applications.

Why a 2D Scene graph?

Most application-specific widgets are built using custom data structures to support that particular application, rather than using a generic toolkit. While this approach works, it involves re-implementing many common operations from application to application. A scene graph architecture, on the other hand, provides a general-purpose reusable solution for many common operations. However this solution has costs as well. Let us look at some of the tradeoffs that come with the use of a scene graph in comparison to a custom application.

Advantages of a scene graph:

- **Handles Complexity:** Scene graphs scale nicely, and handle complex scenes well.

- **Abstraction:** Scene graphs decouple the components of the system, making it easier to improve the renderer, switch to different hardware, make platform-specific tweaks transparently, etc.

- **Reusability:** Scene graphs allow novice programmers to use professionally implemented algorithms, and to avoid implementing many common features.

- **Interactivity:** Scene graphs make it easier to implement things like selection and picking.

- **Reuse:** Scene graphs make it easy to reuse data in multiple places.

Disadvantages:

- **Footprint:** A general solution such as a scene graph will likely use more memory than a custom solution.

- **Efficiency:** It is typically more efficient to write a custom solution than to use a general-purpose scene graph. Bradley found that a toolkit-based solution to an Othello game ran 19 times slower than a handcrafted solution, and consumed 18 times more memory [27].

- **Restrictions:** Even with the most open-ended designs, a scene graph is likely to place some restrictions on the application, which may be avoidable with a custom solution.

ARCHITECTURE

Jazz is based on three primary concepts: nodes, visual components, and cameras. Figure 3 shows the object hierarchy of Jazz's public objects that applications use. Figure 4 shows the object structure of a typical application with several objects and a camera.

Nodes and Visual Components

The Jazz scene graph consists of a hierarchy of *nodes* that represent relationships between objects. The base node type (ZNode) is very simple. There are more complex node types, whose features are only paid for when used. Hierarchies of nodes can be used to implement "groups" and "layers" that are found in most drawing programs, and to facilitate moving a collection of objects together.

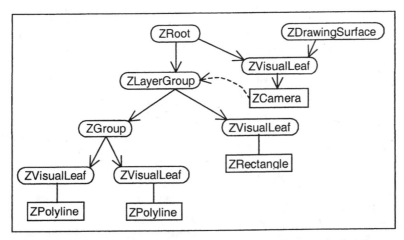

Figure 4: Run-time object structure in a typical application. This scene contains a single camera looking onto a layer that contains a rectangle and a group consisting of two polylines.

Scene graph nodes have no visual appearance on the screen. Rather, there are special objects, called *visual components*, which are attached to certain nodes in a scene graph (specifically to *visual leaf nodes* and *visual group nodes*), and which define geometry and color attributes.

In other words, nodes establish *where* something is in the scene graph hierarchy, whereas visual components specify *what* something looks like. All nodes have a single parent, and follow a strict tree hierarchy. Visual components can be reused – the same visual component can appear in multiple places in the scene graph, and thus have multiple parents.

There is a clear separation between what is implemented in a node and what is handled by a visual component. Nodes contain all object characteristics that are passed on to child nodes. For example, nodes are used to provide affine transforms (for translating, rotating, scaling, and shearing child nodes), culling sub-trees according to magnification, and defining transparency for groups of objects. Each of these characteristics modifies all of that node's descendants.

Visual components are purely visual. They do not have a hierarchical structure (they do not even specify a transformation). Each visual component simply specifies how to render itself, what its bounds are, and how to pick it (i.e. how to detect if the mouse is over the component).

This split between nodes and visual components clearly separates code that is aware of the scene graph hierarchy from code that operates independently of any hierarchy. It enables hierarchical structuring of scene graph nodes, and also reuse of visual components. It also separates the *structure* from the *content*. Visual components are interchangeable, making it possible to, say, replace all the circles w/ squares in a sub-tree of the scene graph without affecting the grouping or position of objects.

Cameras
A camera is a visual component that displays a view of a Jazz scene graph. It specifies which portion of the scene graph is visible using an affine transform. Multiple cameras

can be setup looking at a single scene graph, each defining its own view of the scene graph.

Drawing Surfaces vs. Internal Cameras
Cameras are usually mapped to a *drawing surface*. This encapsulates a Java `Graphics2D` class, which supports 2D rendering. The drawing surface is usually associated with a Jazz canvas, so that the user can see the surface on their display. The Jazz canvas is implemented as a Java Swing component, so ZUI interfaces can be embedded in any Swing application, wherever a Swing JComponent widget is expected. The `Graphics2D` of a drawing surface can also output to an off-screen buffer, or a printer. With this mechanism, a Jazz surface can be used to display, print, or to render into a buffer so an application can grab the pixels that were rendered.

In addition to being mapped to drawing surfaces, cameras can also be treated just like any other visual component – they can be embedded in a Jazz scene graph, so that nested views of a zoomable surface can be embedded recursively in a scene. Cameras used in this way are called *internal cameras*, and act like nested windows within the world that themselves look onto the world, or onto a different world (in previous ZUI implementations, we called these "portals" [25].)

Layers
Each camera contains a list of *layer nodes* specifying which layers in the scene graph it can see. A camera renders itself by first rendering its background, and then rendering all the layers in its layer list. This approach lets an application build a single very large scene graph and control which portion of the scene graph are visible in each camera.

Layers can be made temporarily invisible within a specific camera by removing it from the camera's layer list. Alternatively, a special node type called an "invisible group" node can be inserted into the scene graph to make all the children of a layer invisible. Changing the order of the layer nodes within a camera's layer list changes the drawing order of entire layers.

Rendering

Nodes are rendered in a top-to-bottom, left-to-right depth first fashion. Consequently, visual components are rendered in the order that their associated nodes appear in the scene graph. Changing the order of a node within a parent node will change the rendering order of the associated visual component.

Culling

All scene graph objects include a method to compute their bounding rectangle. Jazz uses this to decide which objects are visible, and thus avoid rendering or picking objects that are not visible in a given view. Bounds are cached at each node in the current relative coordinate system. Objects that regularly change their dimensions can specify that their bounds are *volatile*. This tells Jazz not to cache their bounds, and instead to query the object directly every time the bounds are needed to make a visibility decision.

Events

Jazz supports interaction through Java's standard event listener model. An event listener is an object that responds to events. They may be attached to any node in the Jazz scene graph. There are two categories of events – input events and object events. Input events result from user interaction with a graphical object, such as a mouse press. Object events result from a modification to the scene graph, such as a transformation change, or a node insertion. All events can be handled by attaching listeners to scene graph nodes. There can be multiple listeners per node. Unlike the standard Swing and AWT listener model, in Jazz by default each input event is passed up the tree to the listeners on ancestor nodes. However, if a listener consumes the event, the event is not passed on any further. With this mechanism, custom event listeners may be written for specific nodes that correspond to graphical items – or a listener may be attached higher in the scene graph tree, which then provides interaction support for the entire subtree below the listener. Event listeners can be written in either a specific or very general manner depending on the application's needs.

Jazz dispatches all mouse events to the node (and potentially its ancestors) returned by a *pick* operation at the location of the original mouse event on the Jazz drawing surface. Before dispatching the event, Jazz modifies the event records to reflect the local coordinates of the picked component. Visual component event handlers can therefore work in their local coordinate system.

Jazz comes with event handlers for several basic tasks, such as navigation, selection, and hyperlinks. Applications are free to use these or define their own.

COMPOSING FUNCTIONALITY USING NODE TYPES

A basic design goal of Jazz is to maintain a decoupled design so that different features do not depend on each other and so that applications only pay for features when they use them. This led us to keep the core ZNode very simple, and to add extra features by introducing new node types which are inserted into the scene graph as needed.

For instance, since not all nodes will be transformed, the core node type does not contain a transform. Instead, a transform node is created when needed and inserted above any node that should be transformed.

Developers are encouraged to achieve complex functionality by composing simple node types in a scene graph rather than by using subclassing and inheritance.

To validate the practicality of this idea for ZUIs, we have developed a number of Jazz node types, each implementing a specific functionality suitable for ZUI applications, and each remaining small and manageable. In this section we discuss some of the node types we have created.

Jazz includes nodes to support layers, selections, transparency, hyperlinks, fading, spatial indexing, layout, and constraints. In this section we discuss some of these node types.

Selection and Hyperlink Nodes

Some node types associate extra characteristics with a portion of the scene graph. These extra nodes act as "decorators" following a standard object oriented design pattern [15]. They wrap the core functions of the nodes below them, adding extra functionality. For example, we have written a Jazz selection decorator node that draws its children, and then draws a selection box with resize handles.

Similarly, Jazz defines a link node, which is used to create spatial hyperlinks. The link node associates the destination of a spatial hyperlink with a node, but does so without modifying the node and without the node's knowledge. When the user moves the mouse over a link node, it presents an arrow visual component to show what the link refers to. Clicking on the link navigates the camera to the linked object.

Position and Layout Nodes

The position and scale of objects is specified in Jazz by inserting transformation nodes into the hierarchy. Active layout managers can also be utilized by inserting a layout node into the hierarchy. We have developed a layout node that uses a layout manager analogous to the Java AWT and Swing layout managers. Layout managers can be inserted at different levels of the scene graph, yielding hierarchical layouts. Applications may define new layout managers, or use one of the built-in layouts. Currently, Jazz has two layout managers: a hierarchical tree layout manager, which will layout any subtree of the scene graph in a standard tree structure, and a path layout manager, which will position a set of nodes along any path. The hierarchical tree layout manager is interesting in that it shows lines indicating the linkages between nodes in the tree using a special visual component.

Constraint Nodes

We have developed nodes that use dynamic constraints to position their children. Currently we use these constraint nodes to implement "sticky objects" – portions of the scene graph that are associated with a particular camera and that do not move when the camera viewpoint is changed. Sticky nodes subclass a constraint node that contains a transform. They modify the transform by setting it to the inverse of a specified camera's view transform whenever the camera's view changes. The subtree rooted at the sticky constraint node then does not move as the viewpoint changes. It is as if they are stuck to the camera's lens.

Culling Nodes

A basic characteristic of zoomable applications is that there can be a large number of objects in a given scene graph, many of which are not visible in a given view of the graph. For example, in a zoomed-in view, only very small objects are visible, whereas in a zoomed-out view, only large objects need be shown. Thus, it is important to efficiently traverse the scene graph, culling invisible objects. Sometimes simple bounds-based culling is not sufficient. We have developed two additional mechanisms to support culling. First, "fade" groups can be inserted in the scene graph to cull a subtree when it appears larger or smaller than a specified magnification in a view (fade groups use alpha blending to smooth this transition - hence the name). Second, a "spatial index" node can be inserted in the scene graph to provide fast access to the visible children of that node. The spatial index node implements an RTree index [24] which is effective when there are many nodes, but only a small percentage of them is visible at a given time. This is quite common in ZUIs since this typically occurs whenever the view is zoomed in.

CUSTOM VISUAL COMPONENTS

To define new visual components, applications extend the visual component class and define two functions. The new object defines how to paint itself and how big it is. In addition, visual components may define picking methods if the object is not rectangular, so Jazz knows when the pointer is over the object.

Legacy Java Code

One of our motivations for splitting components and scene graph nodes in two was to make it easy to import non-zooming components and legacy applications into a zooming context. In Jazz, visual components can be easily defined to wrap legacy Java code that is written without awareness of Jazz. Those components can then be zoomed and interacted with by placing them in a scene graph. For example, it is possible to take some pre-existing code that draws a scatter plot and make it available as a Jazz visual component on a zooming surface.

This technique has been used to wrap existing code in two large systems. The first is a graphical simulation system from a research group at Los Alamos National Labs. We defined a new visual component that wrapped their core visual component, and were able to place their entire visualization inside of Jazz, complete with zooming and multiple views and interaction in about half of a day. The second was the LEIF system developed by DTAI [2]. This is a large information framework system with a major visualization component. With a similar technique, they were able to wrap their core object type with a Jazz visual component, and get their entire application to appear inside of Jazz.

Swing Visual Components

Any lightweight Java Swing component can be embedded into a Jazz scene graph by placing it in a Jazz ZSwing visual component in the scene graph. The Swing component can then be panned and zoomed like other Jazz components. This means that fully functioning existing Java Swing code with complete GUIs can be embedded into a zooming surface, and mixed and matched with custom graphics within Jazz. For example, a Swing interface with a table and buttons could be placed on a zooming surface and overlaid with an application-specific visualization. The Swing components can be manipulated in exactly the same way as other Jazz components, including applying rotation, scale, transparency, and multiple views. The embedded Swing integration occurs transparently to the Swing widget and to other nodes in the scene graph.

To implement embedded Swing widgets inside of Jazz, the widgets' input and output had to be remapped to accommodate their transformed rendering. Mouse input in Swing normally takes the pointer's screen location directly to the Swing component's local coordinate system. This mapping is not as straightforward since embedded Swing widgets may be arbitrarily transformed. So the ZSwing visual component registers listeners for mouse events, and forwards any events it receives to the underlying Swing component in its coordinate system.

Similarly, the ZSwing visual component must also alter repaint requests made by Swing components embedded in Jazz. These Swing repaint requests assume rendering in a traditional GUI rather than one arbitrarily transformed. The ZSwing visual component must reroute these repaints through the Jazz scene graph, including multiple views, to properly transform the Java Graphics2D object to be used by the Swing component for rendering. Fortunately, all of this remapping was done generically, and the Jazz code has no knowledge of specific Swing widgets.

CREATING APPLICATION SPECIFIC WIDGETS

To test Jazz, we developed a number of prototypes of application-specific widgets. These widgets explore various aspects of ZUIs and general graphical application design. In this section, we report briefly on these widgets.

Basic ZUI Application

To understand the requirements of ZUIs as well as the structure of Jazz, we created a simple zoomable application in Jazz. We built a graph editor (available as an applet on the Jazz website) that lets users draw a graph with many nodes that are connected by links. The links follow nodes that the user moves. The user can draw very large graphs and the view may be zoomed in or out on demand. Nodes can be grouped. When zoomed out, these node groups fade out and are replaced with a group node that represents an abstraction of the elements of the group. Finally, to support the user in understanding global context as well as detail, multiple views can be brought up simultaneously and the zoomed out views will show where the zoomed in views are.

It is difficult to build this application using existing GUI toolkits. GUI toolkits don't directly support zooming, multiple views, and multiple levels of information, so the application would have to manage all of these details. Building this application in Jazz was straightforward.

Since zooming, multiple levels of representation, and multiple views are all directly supported by Jazz, writing the graph drawing application was just a matter of adding appropriate nodes to the scene graph for each element of application. In addition, Jazz's support for interaction through event listeners makes it easy to add nodes and edit the graph. Object change events are generated when an object moves, so an event listener was attached to the nodes in order to update the connecting arrows so they always follow the nodes. Finally, Jazz takes care of screen updates, hierarchical transforms, etc. which simplifies application programming considerably.

Fisheye Views

The scene graph model in Jazz makes it easy to support advanced graphical features. For instance, while Jazz directly supports geometric zooming of entire scenes, it is also possible to create "fisheye" visualizations where each object is scaled according to some degree of interest function [14].

We implemented a simple fisheye view in Jazz by putting a special fisheye decorator node above every object that we wanted the fisheye effect applied to. The fisheye node is really just a special transform node that dynamically computes its scale according to a function. Admittedly, this is a simplified fisheye view, as entire objects are scaled whole rather than being distorted.

Context Sensitive Objects

By default, Jazz objects support a single presentation style. It is also desirable to be able to support *multiple* representations of a single data model. That is, to support different visual displays of objects in different contexts.

Applications can easily use Jazz to present different visual representations of data in different circumstances. Many different kinds of context can be used to influence how and what gets drawn, so we sometimes call this technique *context-sensitive rendering*. While an application can use any context whatsoever to control an object's rendering (such as author, or time), two especially common contexts are *magnification* (the size the object is rendered at) and *camera* (the camera the object is being rendered within). We sometimes use the more specific term *semantic zooming* to refer to objects that change the way they appear based on the current magnification. When an object appears differently when viewed with different cameras, we sometimes use the term *lens* or *filter* [6, 25].

Jazz's standard visual components render themselves the same way every time, except during interactions, when they may render themselves at lower resolution for efficiency. Applications can define new visual components and nodes whose paint methods are context sensitive.

Standard software engineering approaches call for decoupled representations. Each visual representation should exist independently of the others. This allows the application builder to design new representations, and modify old ones without affecting the other representations. A clean decoupled design would support different classes for each visual representation of the data. One design that accomplishes this is to make a special visual component that acts as a *Proxy* [15] for another visual component, and can delegate between them. A more elaborate delegation scheme is described by Fox [12].

Such a delegator is fairly straightforward to build. It maintains a list of ancillary visual components and exactly one of them is active at a time. It then defines its `paint`, and `pick` methods to call the active visual component.

We implemented a simple delegator as a proof-of-concept. Our sample delegator supports semantic zooming by selecting a specific visual component to render based on the current magnification level. This approach has the property of having decoupled visual representations while keeping those representations together on the screen. Because they are all controlled by a single node, moving that node (by changing its transformation) moves each zoom level's representation together. Figure 5 shows the basic structure of the scene graph for our delegator that supports semantic zooming.

NODE MANAGEMENT

A drawback of the "minilithic" approach adopted by Jazz is that it places a burden on the application programmer since they must manage a scene graph containing many nodes and node types. Adding a new element to a scene can take several steps.

In practice there is typically a primary node that the application cares about (usually the visual leaf node) and then there are several decorator nodes above it. We have implemented special support for managing these kinds of scene graph structures, using the notion of scene graph *editor* objects.

An editor instance can be created for any node on the scene graph. It has methods for obtaining parents of the node that

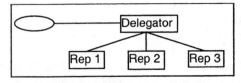

Figure 5: One way to implement semantic zooming in Jazz. The *Delegator* chooses which representation to use to paint itself depending on the current magnification.

are of a specific type. It uses lazy evaluation to create those parent nodes as they are required. Jazz maintains a special bit in each node specifying if it is created by an editor. With this structure, if an application wants to obtain a transform node for a given node in the scene graph, it can simply call:

```
node.editor().getTransformGroup().
```

If the node does not have a transform node associated with it, a new transform node is created and inserted above the node. Otherwise the existing transform node is returned. The `editor()` method actually calls a factory [10] to create the editor, so applications can define custom mechanisms for editing nodes.

CURRENT STATUS

Everything described in this paper is currently implemented in Java 2 and is publicly available as open source software. Jazz is being actively used by a number of research groups, has been used in university courses in and outside of the University of Maryland, and is being used within two commercial products currently being developed.

The Jazz distribution comes with a sample application called HiNote that demonstrates some of the basic features. In addition, we are currently building two other applications. The first is a new version of KidPad [9, 11] that provides collaborative storytelling tools for children, available at http://www.cs.umd.edu/hcil/kidpad. The second is an authoring tool for creating presentations. The authoring tool builds on our experience making zoomable presentations over the past several years. The authoring tool works as a plug-in for Microsoft PowerPoint allowing any existing presentation to be brought into a zoomable space. This tool is not yet publicly available.

CONCLUSION

This paper describes the architecture of Jazz, a new Java toolkit that supports the development of extensible 2D object-oriented graphics with zooming and multiple representations. It is a descendent from previous Zoomable User Interfaces that we have built in the past.

While Jazz does not introduce many substantially new individual ideas, it is novel in bringing together a variety of techniques from different domains. Jazz takes scene graphs from 3D graphics, screen and interaction techniques from 2D widgets, functionality from previous ZUI systems, and puts these elements together with clean decoupled object oriented design. Using Jazz, developers can write serious zoomable applications and advanced visualizations with a clarity and efficiency that has not been possible before.

The biggest contribution of Jazz is the creation of a graphics toolkit built using a "minilithic" design. By encouraging composition over inheritance, the Jazz feature-set is highly decoupled. This makes the code easier to maintain and extend compared with monolithic approaches. We and others have used Jazz to build a variety of applications. This proof by example demonstrates that the

approach has potential. There are, however, trade-offs with any design, and the minilithic approach also has costs.

Our experience with Jazz so far shows us that the biggest concerns with the Jazz design is ease-of-use and efficiency. The downside of a minilithic approach is that the application developer must manage many more objects than with a more traditional design. While you only pay for the features you use, you need a new node instance for each feature. While we have attempted to minimize this burden through the use of "editors", the developer still has to be aware of many node types.

Another basic issue is efficiency of a scenegraph-based solution compared to an entirely custom solution. An alternative to Jazz for some visualizations would be to build a custom data structure representing the model, and then to build a render method that simply walks through the model, rendering the entire scene. This approach is simple and very efficient. We believe that for simple applications, that kind of custom implementation may be best. The advantages of a scenegraph-based approach don't appear until the application requires features such as selection, layers, fading, or spatial indexing. Once a number of these features are required, the custom approach becomes very tedious, and difficult to maintain. So, while we do not yet have any quantitative data to inform a designer, it appears that there is a threshold of complexity above which Jazz provides more benefit than cost.

While we have not yet performed a rigorous quantitative performance analysis, we and others have used Jazz for a number of applications. We have consistently found that its performance is good. The primary bottleneck appears to be rendering large numbers of objects, and not the overhead incurred by traversing and maintaining the scenegraph.

We look forward to continuing the development of Jazz, and increasing our understanding of the trade-offs of the minilithic scenegraph design that we have chosen. As Jazz is used for more projects, we will gain enough experience to carefully analyze the construction of systems using Jazz, and compare them to alternative approaches.

ACKNOWLEDGMENTS

We enjoyed our collaborations with those involved with Pad++, especially Jim Hollan, Jason Stewart, Allison Druin, Britt McAlister, George Furnas and Ken Perlin.

We would like to thank our fellow members of the HCIL, especially the students in the seminar on ZUIs that had the patience to use early versions of Jazz and helped to identify its "features". Our thanks to Jim Mokwa and Maria Jump for their contributions to Jazz. We greatly appreciate the careful reading of earlier versions of this paper by Bay-Wei Chang, Jason Stewart, and Allison Druin.

Most importantly, the many users of Jazz have helped us design, debug, and understand the requirements of Jazz and have made Jazz much more broadly useful than would have been possible otherwise. Two important early users were David Thompson at LANL and Mike Behrens at DTAI.

Finally, Bob Hummel and Ward Page at DARPA have been instrumental in supporting this work, and Jazz wouldn't exist without their support. This work has been funded in part by DARPA, and an equipment grant from Sun Microsystems.

REFERENCES

1. Java [Web Page] (2000). URL http://www.javasoft.com.

2. LEIF [Web Page] (2000). URL http://leif.dtai.com.

3. MerzCom [Web Page] (2000). URL http://www.merzcom.com/.

4. Perspecta [Web Page] (2000). URL http://www.perspecta.com/.

5. SGI OpenInventor [Web Page] (2000). URL http://www.sgi.com/Technology/Inventor/.

6. Bederson, B. B., Hollan, J. D., Perlin, K., Meyer, J., Bacon, D., & Furnas, G. W. (1996). Pad++: A Zoomable Graphical Sketchpad for Exploring Alternate Interface Physics. *Journal of Visual Languages and Computing, 7*, pp. 3-31.

7. Bederson, B. B., & Meyer, J. (1998). Implementing a Zooming User Interface: Experience Building Pad++. *Software: Practice and Experience, 28*(10), pp. 1101-1135.

8. Bederson, B. B., Wallace, R. S., & Schwartz, E. L. (1993). Control & Design of the Spherical Pointing Motor. *In Proceedings of IEEE International Conference on Robotics and Automation (ICRA 93)* New York: IEEE,

9. Benford, S., Bederson, B. B., Åkesson, K.-P., Bayon, V., Druin, A., Hansson, P., Hourcade, J. P., Ingram, R., Neale, H., O'Malley, C., Simsarian, K. T., Stanton, D., Sundblad, Y., & Taxén, G. (2000). Designing Storytelling Technologies to Encourage Collaboration Between Young Children. *In Proceedings of Human Factors in Computing Systems (CHI 2000)* ACM Press, pp. 556-563.

10. Booch, G. (1994). *Object-Oriented Analysis and Design With Applications.* Addison-Wesley.

11. Druin, A., Stewart, J., Proft, D., Bederson, B. B., & Hollan, J. D. (1997). KidPad: A Design Collaboration Between Children, Technologists, and Educators. *In Proceedings of Human Factors in Computing Systems (CHI 97)* ACM Press, pp. 463-470.

12. Fox, D. (1998). Composing Magic Lenses. *In Proceedings of Human Factors in Computing Systems (CHI 98)* ACM Press, pp. 519-525.

13. Fox, D. (1998). *Tabula Rasa: A Multi-scale User Interface System.* Doctoral dissertation, New York University, New York, NY.

14. Furnas, G. W. (1986). Generalized Fisheye Views. *In Proceedings of Human Factors in Computing Systems (CHI 86)* ACM Press, pp. 16-23.

15. Gamma, E., Helm, R., Johnson, R., & Vlissides, J. (1995). *Design Patterns: Elements of Reusable Object-Oriented Software.* Addison-Wesley.

16. Hudson, S. E., & Stasko, J. T. (1993). Animation Support in a User Interface Toolkit. *In Proceedings of User Interface and Software Technology (UIST 93)* ACM Press, pp. 57-67.

17. John K. Ousterhout. (1994). *Tcl and the Tk Toolkit.* Addison-Wesley.

18. Linton, M. A., Vlissides, J. M., & Calder, P. R. (1989). Composing User Interfaces With InterViews. *IEEE Software, 22*(2), pp. 8-22.

19. Myers, B. A., McDaniel, R. G., Miller, R. C., Ferrency, A. S., Faulring, A., Kyle, B. D., Mickish, A., Klimovitski, A., & Doane, P. (1997). The Amulet Environment: New Models for Effective User Interface Software Development". *IEEE Transactions on Software Engineering, 23*(6), pp. 347-365.

20. Perlin, K., & Fox, D. (1993). Pad: An Alternative Approach to the Computer Interface. *In Proceedings of Computer Graphics (SIGGRAPH 93)* New York, NY: ACM Press, pp. 57-64.

21. Perlin, K., & Meyer, J. (1999). Nested User Interface Components. *In Proceedings of User Interface and Software Technology (UIST 99)* ACM Press, pp. 11-18.

22. Pook, S., Lecolinet, E., Vaysseix, G., & Barillot, E. (2000). Context and Interaction in Zoomable User Interfaces. *In Proceedings of Advanced Visual Interfaces (AVI 2000)* ACM Press, p. (in press).

23. Raskin, J. (2000). *The Humane Interface.* Reading, Massachusetts: Addison Wesley.

24. Samet, H. (1990). *The Design and Analysis of Spatial Data Structures.* Addison-Wesley.

25. Stone, M. C., Fishkin, K., & Bier, E. A. (1994). The Movable Filter As a User Interface Tool. *In Proceedings of Human Factors in Computing Systems (CHI 94)* ACM Press, pp. 306-312.

26. Tang, S. H., & Linton, M. A. (1994). Blending Structured Graphics and Layout. *In Proceedings of User Interface and Software Technology (UIST 94)* ACM Press, pp. 167-174.

27. Zanden, B. T. V. (1994). Optimizing Toolkit-Generated Graphical Interfaces. *In Proceedings of User Interface and Software Technology (UIST 94)* ACM Press, pp. 157-166.

Zoomable user interfaces as a medium for slide show presentations

Lance Good[1]
Benjamin B. Bederson[1]

[1]Human Computer Interaction Lab, University of Maryland, College Park, Maryland, USA

Abstract

In this paper, the authors propose Zoomable User Interfaces as an alternative presentation medium to address several common presentation problems. Zoomable User Interfaces offer new techniques for managing multiple versions of a presentation, providing interactive presentation navigation, and distinguishing levels of detail. These zoomable presentations may also offer several cognitive benefits over their commercial slide show counterparts. The authors also introduce CounterPoint, a tool to simplify the creation and delivery of zoomable presentations, discuss the techniques they have used to make authoring and navigation manageable in the multidimensional space. Lastly, some of the visualization principles compiled by the authors for designing these types of presentations are presented.
Information Visualization (2002) **1**, 35–49. DOI: 10.1057/palgrave/ivs/9500004

Keywords: Presentations; Jazz; PowerPoint; spatial hypertext; Zoomable User Interfaces (ZUIs)

Introduction

Zoomable User Interfaces (ZUIs) have recently emerged as an alternative to traditional techniques for visualizing information. ZUIs display information on a conceptually infinite two-dimensional plane. They allow users to change their view of this plane through panning and zooming to access more information than can typically be displayed on a single screen.

A fundamental characteristic of these types of zooming and panning operations in ZUIs is that they are animated. These types of animations give a sense of physical movement by mimicking such physical acts as sliding a paper on a table (panning), looking at a paper more closely for detail (zooming in), or holding a paper at a distance for more context (zooming out).[1] ZUIs have been used in such settings as visualizing histories,[2] authoring children's stories,[3] traversing file system hierarchies,[1] and image browsing.[4] Yet another application of ZUIs with which the authors have experimented and that is discussed here is the slide show presentation.

Most current commercial slide show presentation tools consist of a linearly ordered set of 'slides' that can be shown in sequence to an audience. There are also special mechanisms for moving back and forth in the sequence, jumping to a slide out of order (based on its title), and authoring hyperlinks in advance from any one slide to another.

Through the authors' experience, it has been found that zooming presentations naturally address several common problems with these presentation tools. These problems include: navigating to slides outside of a direct linear sequence during presentation delivery, maintaining multiple versions of very similar presentations, and differentiating levels of detail in presentation content. Although aware of workarounds in current tools to solve these problems, the authors believe that the zooming paradigm offers more elegant solutions (Figures 1 and 2).

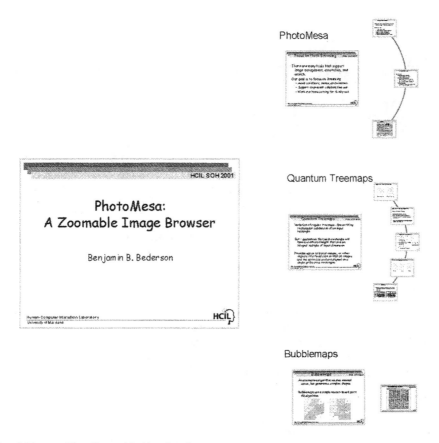

Figure 1 A presentation laid out with a Zoomable User Interface.

Zoomable User Interfaces address these problems in several ways. First, because it stores presentations in a single contiguous space, a ZUI can help make jumping out of a linear presentation sequence possible through animated spatial navigation. Second, ZUIs support multiple presentation versions by allowing multiple paths through a single zoomable space. These multiple paths are possible since navigation is not directly tied to the presentation content. Third, ZUIs intrinsically provide for differentiated levels of detail by allowing information to be displayed at varying zoom levels.

In addition to these concrete benefits, ZUIs may also facilitate more effective use of cognitive resources. Because they employ a metaphor based on physical space and navigation, ZUIs offer an additional avenue for exploring the utilization of human spatial abilities during a presentation. Likewise, the use of viewpoint animations in ZUIs offers similar opportunities for discovering more efficacious presentation techniques.

The benefits of ZUIs for presentations also have costs that are evident during both presentation authoring and delivery. ZUIs involve additional levels of complexity beyond traditional presentation tools since they require manipulating objects at multiple zoom levels and navigating a large zoomable space. As a result, a number of

papers have specifically addressed problems with authoring and navigation in zooming environments.[5–9]

The authors have created a tool called CounterPoint (available to download at: http://www.cs.umd.edu/hcil/counterpoint) (Figures 3 and 4) to simplify the authoring, management, and delivery of ZUI presentations. CounterPoint has facilities for hierarchically organizing presentation content to help automate spatial arrangement and assist in visually distinguishing levels of detail. CounterPoint also offers techniques for creating and managing paths through a populated presentation space. Lastly, CounterPoint augments standard controls for delivering a linear presentation by providing simplified navigations to support improvisation. Through use of CounterPoint and ZUIs for presentations the authors have found that these tools offer tremendous freedom for creativity. However, as with any creative medium, this flexibility introduces the possibility for bad design. Consequently, the authors have also begun to identify principles, from related work such as concept maps[10,11] and their own experience, for the design of ZUI presentations.

In this paper, the authors begin by discussing previous work in the areas of slide show presentations and other scripted presentations. Then described are the concrete advantages of ZUIs along with evidence for their cognitive benefits. This paper also describes CounterPoint's

Figure 2 A presentation laid out with a Zoomable User Interface.

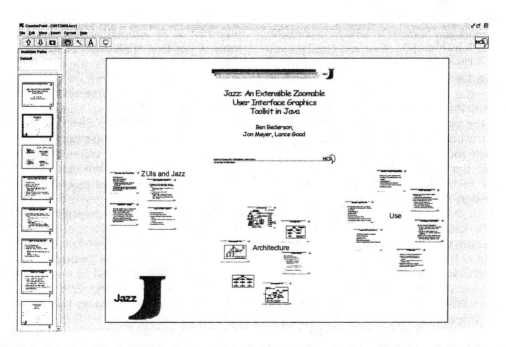

Figure 3 A screen shot of CounterPoint in spatial arrangement mode. The panel on the right, the 'Editing Canvas', is used to modify the positions and magnifications of pre-authored slides. The panel on the left is used to edit paths through the presentation.

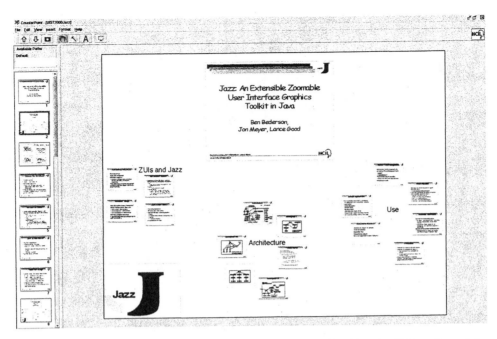

Figure 4 A screen shot of CounterPoint in spatial arrangement mode. The panel on the right, the 'Editing Canvas', is used to modify the positions and magnifications of pre-authored slides. The panel on the left is used to edit paths through the presentation.

implementation and its specific techniques for addressing the complexities of presentation authoring and delivery in ZUIs. The paper concludes with a discussion of principles for authoring ZUI presentations.

Previous work

This work came out of many years of ongoing research into ZUIs and the actual use of ZUIs for presentations. As such, it builds primarily on the results and experiences gained from both the Jazz[12] and Pad++[1] systems.

Naturally, this work also borrows heavily from concepts in Microsoft PowerPoint[13] and similar commercial presentation software. These commercial tools provide a software interface for mimicking physical presentation media such as 35-mm slides or overhead transparencies. A primary extension many of these tools add to this physical metaphor is the transition animation. Nevertheless, these animations usually provide little insight into the underlying content and are mainly used for visual effect.

Several systems have also addressed problems with, these commercial tools. The Palette system[14], for example, allows presenters to deliver a presentation using a barcode reader with paper copies of slides. This technique makes it possible to combine slides from multiple presentation files using only the paper representations and also to improvise slide orderings at presentation-time. While this type of a tangible interface has several desirable properties, it also requires users to manage both the physical and virtual representations of their slides. This technique only assists with slide management and does not help in content tasks such as distinguishing levels of detail.

Another tool suggested for improving slide show presentations is Hyper Mochi Sheet.[15] Hyper Mochi Sheet

employs a multi-focus distortion-oriented view to display a hypertext network. During a presentation, the system automatically resizes nodes in the network based on the presenter's current focus. While the multi-focus views allow it to show both an overview and detail, its dynamic nature makes it harder for the presenter to predict. Thus the authors feel it is less desirable for presentations where layouts and object sizes are often parameters of primary concern.

World Wide Web-style hypertext has also been proposed as an alternative to commercial presentation tools. A practical application of hypertext as a presentation media was Moore's use in teaching an undergraduate Computer Science course.[16] Moore found that this use of traditional hypertext facilitated better hierarchical organization than commercial tools and also allowed for better interconnection of related material. Nevertheless, the hyperlinks used by web-style hypertext (also found in several commercial tools) require an author to create them prior to giving the presentation. As a result, the presenter must anticipate all potential branches that might be required during a presentation. In addition, this type of hypertext may suffer from the traditional hypertext problem of audience disorientation.

Because a major component of the authors' work involves authoring paths through a zoomable space, it also builds on ideas found in several hypertext tools for authoring scripted presentation paths. One such tool was VIKI, a spatial hypertext tool for supporting emergent structure during authoring.[17] The particularly relevant application of VIKI was its use in gathering and organizing content for educational presentation on the web.[17] Here, preexisting web content and annotations were combined to create directed paths through collections of related information. Authoring ZUI presentations is similar to authoring in VIKI in that it involves spatially structuring information. However, because they are displayed to the audience, the structures created in ZUI presentations are an end in themselves rather than just a representation of the author's current understanding. Moreover, paths in ZUIs are animated traversals through the author's explicitly defined spatial layouts whereas in VIKI the spatial layout defined the path itself.[17]

Some of the earliest work in scripted hypertext paths was Zellweger's Scripted Documents.[18,19] Scripted Documents allowed the author to define timed traversals through a collection of documents with specifiable actions performed at each stop in the traversal. The 'Audio-visual presentation' application of scripts described in Zellweger's earlier work[18] closely resembles the authors' use of scripted paths in ZUI presentations.

Trigg's Guided Tours and Tabletops also defined a hypertext path authoring and navigation tool.[20] This system provided tools for creating a collection of 'tabletops', each of which contained a spatial arrangement of hypertext documents. An author could then define arbitrary paths through these tabletops with any number of available branches at each point in the path.

Paths in ZUIs resemble Trigg's paths in that they can combine both scripted and dynamic components. However, the dynamic changes available on a scripted path in a ZUI presentation do not have to be specified when the path is created. In addition, while both systems allow for navigation through collections of spatially arranged objects, ZUIs present data in a single continuous space whereas Guided Tours supports sets of disjoint spatial arrangements.

Concrete benefits of ZUI presentations

ZUIs offer a number of concrete advantages over traditional slide show presentations. Below, the novel affordances of ZUIs for some common presentation authoring and navigation challenges are discussed. The authors distinguish these concrete benefits from the later cognitive benefits because they offer motivation for the use of ZUIs in the presentation setting without requiring experimental validation.

Simple navigation for improvisation

One of the fundamental tradeoffs in the design of a presentation tool is providing support for rehearsed scripting *vs* presentation-time improvisation. Too much control can require needless attention from the presenter for interface adjustments. Too little control restricts the presenter from quickly returning to previous slides following audience feedback or smoothly jumping past less important content for time constraints.

Current presentation tools provide adequate support for controlling rehearsed scripts. However, the controls for improvisation, including linear forward and backward

controls and popup menus, are often inefficient or visually unappealing. The one additional control that some presentation tools offer for more dynamic presentations is web-style hyperlinking. Nonetheless, the author must predefine these links, requiring the author to predict all required presentation-time improvisations.

Instead, ZUIs can potentially balance the need for both scripting and improvisation by allowing spatial navigation in addition to the standard presentation controls for traversing a scripted path. These navigational controls allow a presenter to navigate between arbitrary points in the presentation via zooming and panning. Of course, unconstrained navigation in multidimensional environments can be extremely difficult so this is one of the actions addressed in the authors' implementation of CounterPoint.

Decoupled paths and content

The authors have also informally found that a common presentation authoring task is to modify existing presentations for new audiences or different time constraints. In this situation, current presentation tools encourage presenters to create different presentations for different situations because of the coupling between the presentation content and the presentation path (One should note that although PowerPoint[TM 10] technically allows for the decoupling of presentation content and path through the 'Slide Show → Custom Shows...' menu, the interface is very primitive. Moreover, these custom shows do not offer the same features, such as independently modifiable transitions, available in the primary slide show). This duplication of data across multiple presentations not only requires unnecessary storage space but also leads to data synchronization problems when the presentation content is modified. These same issues also arise when an author wants to duplicate a slide within a single presentation.

While storage space may seem insignificant in the age of multi-gigabyte disks, this space becomes more important in the presence of limited bandwidth networks. In fact, anecdotal evidence suggests that PowerPoint presentation files are a significant cause of congestion on Defense Department networks.[21] Alternately, from the use of ZUIs, the authors have found that the clear distinction between content and paths encourages a different presentation management strategy. The authors' early use suggests that presenters may find it useful to organize larger collections of related information in a single presentation space, authoring customized paths through the space as needed for a given audience. This strategy will also facilitate the repetition of slides on a presentation path without actually duplicating the content.

One drawback to this decoupling is that it can be confusing or misleading for the audience. If content appears in a presentation space but does not occur on the presentation path, the audience may construct incongruent interpretations of the presented structure. In the future, the authors intend to address this problem by fading out content that does not appear on the current presentation path.

A second drawback to this approach is that presentation files no longer correspond to a single presentation. This undermines the use of the presentation file as a historical archive. Instead, CounterPoint allows presentation authors to name the different paths within a presentation to serve this archival purpose.

Hierarchical support
One of the fundamental structures used in the presentation setting is the hierarchy. Hierarchies are a natural format for organizing data as they allow topics to be recursively subdivided into increasingly smaller units of information. In fact, current presentation tools often offer support for hierarchical bulleted outlines within slides, though they do not extend these hierarchical organizations to the slides themselves.

The authors have also found that though hierarchical language often metaphorically refers to spatial objects, trees for example, the depiction of these hierarchies often approaches linearity. These linear representations can be observed in the previously mentioned outline editors or in many other hierarchical authoring systems.

ZUIs facilitate a more spatial portrayal of hierarchies. Instead of depicting hierarchy levels through indentation, as is frequently done, ZUIs can present hierarchies in a format that more closely approximates a 2D representation of a tree (for example, see[2]). Alternately, ZUIs allow for visually distinguishing hierarchy levels by placing them at varying levels of scale or magnification. This change in magnification can naturally vary with the level of the hierarchy.

Creative control
Because they support the arrangement of presentation content in a two and half dimensional space, ZUIs offer an additional degree of creative freedom over current presentation tools. Additionally, unlike other novel user interface approaches such as Hyper Mochi Sheet,[15] ZUIs also support deterministic control over presentation layouts and transitions. This type of direct control ensures predictability, which authors are likely to expect for presentations.

Cognitive benefits of ZUI presentations
Although the authors have yet to empirically evaluate ZUI presentations, it is believed that these presentations will have several cognitive benefits over traditional presentations. Of course, since the authors have not experimentally verified the benefits of spatial layout and zooming specifically for slide show presentations, it is not known for certain that the evidence presented by the authors from other domains will apply to the presentation setting. Nevertheless, four people in the authors' laboratory have used ZUIs for about 10 public presentations, and a combination of their experience and informal audience reactions to actual zooming

presentations offer some validation of the authors' intuitions.

The authors are also aware that individual differences may affect the cognitive utility of zooming presentations. Indeed, animations[22] and spatial arrangements,[23] two elements of ZUIs, have been shown to support greater recall in users with low spatial abilities than in users with high spatial abilities. Fortunately these studies give some further evidence that animations and spatial arrangements do not negatively impact recall in users with high spatial abilities

Likewise, research into concept maps (see Figure 5), also called knowledge or node-link maps, suggests that subjects with low verbal ability may benefit more from a spatial display than from text.[24] Here again the type of display did not adversely affect the high verbal ability students. With these caveats in mind, listed below some potential cognitive benefits of ZUI presentations and supporting evidence from related tasks.

Dual encoding in memory
The most frequent use of a presentation tool occurs in combination with a presenter's oral discourse. Hence, the audience receives, usually simultaneously, visual input from the presentation tool and verbal input from the presenter. Therefore, an interesting question is whether humans learn differently from these two streams of data.

Psychological hypotheses suggest that human memory does encode spatial information distinctly from verbal information.[25,26,23,27] As a result, a presentation tool may exercise a larger portion of the memory resources of the audience if it employs a spatial, visual display in combination with the verbal discourse.

Robinson et al performed research into this phenomenon by comparing graphic organizers and concept maps with linear lists and outlines.[27] Graphic organizers and concept maps are simply graphical layouts of information, for example tables and flowcharts (see Figure 5). This research suggests that the information in the graphic organizers and content maps is encoded more spatially than the information in linear lists and outlines.

In an earlier study, Robinson et al also investigated the benefits of adjunct displays in a setting more comparable to that of presentations.[28] Here subjects were shown different visual displays while a related text was presented aurally. As in the other study, graphic organizers and concept maps facilitated a more spatial encoding of the information than the textual displays.

The spatial organization of data in ZUIs, though unconstrained, lends itself to structures similar to graphic organizers and concept maps. As a result, ZUI presentations are likely to allow for spatial memory encoding of the presentation data. Combining this spatial data with the conceptual encoding of the oral discourse may both reinforce this conceptual data and help reduce the audience's verbal load, ultimately increasing the retention of the presentation content.

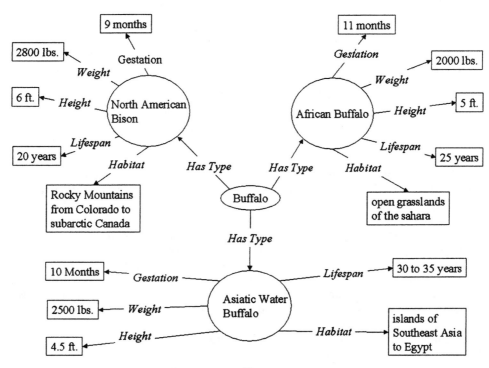

Figure 5 An example of a concept map taken from Robinson *et al.*[27]

The animated transitions in ZUI presentations may also benefit from another type of dual-encoding redundancy. Research has shown that animations accompanied by explanatory audio can improve understanding of abstract concepts over static graphics combined with explanatory audio.[29] This animation-audio combination also leads to better long-term retention than its static counterpart.[29] Because slide show style presentations almost always combine audio with the visual display, they may benefit significantly from animation.

Meaningful spatial structure
Research also suggests that, in certain situations, the memory for data and the spatial location of that data are correlated (summarized in[30]). For presentations, this implies that more meaningful spatial layouts may increase the retention of the underlying presentation content. As a result, one potential advantage of ZUIs over previous presentation tools is the ability to spatially organize data in two dimensions at different magnifications. This spatial layout may provide the audience with an additional attribute or memory pathway with which to recall the presentation content.

A related advantage of CounterPoint is that the structure or logical organization of the presentation can be incorporated into the spatial layout of the data. Then, because CounterPoint slide transitions animate through the space, this structure is itself revealed to the audience during the normal course of the presentation. Revealing the structure of a presentation in this manner exhibits a design principle similar to what Norman calls 'visibi-

lity'.[31] Likewise, Thüring *et al* suggest that presenting a hypertext document's structure to the audience is a necessary component 'for reducing the mental effort of comprehension'.[32] Rivlin *et al* offer a similar sentiment.[33]

This visual communication of structure has the potential to allow the audience to better understand the high-level concepts of a presentation and properly fit them into their own mental frameworks. Restated, the audience may be better able to incorporate the new knowledge with existing knowledge.

Landmarks
A well-known problem in traditional hypertext heard about anecdotally by the authors for slide show presentations is disorientation. Disorientation in traditional hypertext has been described as the point 'when readers do not know where they are, how they got there, or where to go next'.[32] For presentations, this generally corresponds to the point when the audience does not know how the current slide relates to higher-level points.

Needless to say, the development of orientation knowledge is a complex psychological phenomenon. However, one theory proposes landmarks as a fundamental component in this development.[30] That is, we know where we are in the larger space based on salient or memorable objects in our local surroundings.

One possible implementation of landmarks in the presentation setting is including such cues on every presentation slide. For instance, each slide could contain a thumbnail representation of important surrounding slides. This approach has several drawbacks, the most significant of which is reducing the amount of screen real estate available for actual data. As a result, the authors have not explored this solution in current ZUI presentations. Instead, the solution that the authors adopted is to rely on spatial slide transitions. Because ZUI transitions provide animated traversals in a 2D space they can naturally reveal neighboring information including memorable landmarks.

Improved overview support

Spatial, hierarchical overviews of hypermedia networks have been demonstrated to improve recall of overview titles when compared to both hypermedia with linear overviews and hypermedia without overviews.[34] This suggests that displaying a more overt and meaningful spatial overview during a presentation may increase the memorability and possibly the comprehensibility, of high-level presentation concepts. Similarly, overviews have been shown to improve the understanding of concept maps (see Figure 5) over several disconnected views in subjects with low spatial abilities.[11] Consequently, including these spatial overviews in the presentation may improve the comprehension of presentation material in certain individuals.

Overviews are intrinsic to ZUIs. One of the previously mentioned capabilities of ZUIs is the ability to zoom out to get more context. As a result, it is always possible in a ZUI to zoom out so that all presentation data, or localized subsets of that data, are in view. Whether these overviews convey meaningful information, of course, depends on the structure of the presentation. Nevertheless, this overview visualization capability exists at arbitrary magnifications in the presentation without any additional effort or input from the presenter.

Here again, the authors had the option of making the overview persistent, that is, visible on all slides at all times. However, this was not explored as a design alternative because of the screen real estate it would sacrifice. In addition, such an overview could be a continual distraction in the context of a presentation.

Incrementally revealing content

One problem mentioned in the use of concept maps (see Figure 5), a specific type of spatial display, is map shock.[35] Map shock occurs when map-readers feel overwhelmed, confused, or unmotivated by the size or complexity of a map. To solve this problem, map content can be incrementally revealed to help make information seem less intimidating.

An early technique used for incrementally revealing content is the stacked map.[11] Stacked maps divide a large or complex concept map into smaller cross-referenced maps. One study compared these stacked maps to unsegmented whole maps to determine if they improve comprehension of map content.[11] The results of this study suggest that the utility of different map formats may depend on subjects' individual differences. Subjects with low spatial abilities performed better with whole maps while subjects with high spatial abilities performed better with stacked maps.

A more recent technique, applicable to computer-based displays, that tries to address some of the limitations of stacked maps is using animation to incrementally reveal map content. Here, the map presents a subset of the map content and incrementally animates more details into the display. A recent study compared these animated maps against plain text, animated text, and static maps.[35] The results of this study indicate that animated maps may facilitate better recall of high-level points than the other three displays.

Because they use animations, ZUIs can similarly mediate between stacked and whole map displays by incrementally revealing content. Meaningful chunks of presentation content can be arranged at different spatial locations to achieve an effect similar to disjoint, stacked concept maps. Then, spatial animations can be used to navigate between these disjoint maps in the 2D space. And because they support zooming, ZUIs can display overviews of the collection of stacked maps to support whole-map displays.

Presentation progress

Another inadequacy of current presentation software tools is that they provide no inherent notion of presentation progress for the audience. One common technique presenters use to compensate for this deficiency is to add text specifying, 'Slide n of N'. However, such a display does not indicate more localized progress, such as the number of slides remaining in the current topic.

In contrast, if the various pieces of CounterPoint's spatial metaphor function properly, such as overviews and landmarks, a sense of presentation progress may naturally follow. However, ZUIs can also provide a more explicit indicator of progress by visually altering visited slides. This concept builds on the concept of visited hyperlinks in a web browser. In the authors' use of ZUIs, the combination of these implicit and explicit progress indicators was found to be generally effective at conveying progress.

Animated slide transitions

Although animated transitions are included in several current presentation tools, these transitions are mainly used for visual effect and usually do not attempt to give any insight into the underlying data. Moreover, the authors' experience is that the most commonly employed transition is the most basic, where one slide instantaneously replaces another. As a result, these transitions do not help an audience relate the source to its destination.

As already mentioned, ZUI presentations implement slide transitions as animated viewpoint navigations through a presentation space. As such, these animations are able to display the changing spatial context as the system transitions from one point in the 2D space to another. Although the actual benefits of viewpoint animation still require further investigation, initial research indicates that these animations are beneficial for learning spatial organizations and data relations.[36] This study further suggests that viewpoint animations allow for a more constant understanding of object positions and relationships than viewpoint transitions without animation. Research also indicates that animation may improve long-term understanding of various kinds of presented material.[22,29] This improvement was most profoundly observed in those with low spatial abilities.[22]

One of the biggest risks associated with animations is the time consumed by presenting extra intermediate frames during a transition. However, research also indicates that the extra time spent on animation does not result in longer task completion times,[36] which relates directly to comprehension time.

Of course, animated transitions also pose more subjective risks as well. For instance, some users may find these animations distracting or otherwise undesirable. However, there is some evidence to suggest a subjective preference for animated systems over non-animated systems.[37] Since user preference is a recognized quantitative measure of software usability,[38] these preferences require further study to determine their importance, both in general and specifically for presentations.

It is also important to note that there are a number of different types of animations (see [36] for a partial listing) that can make comparisons difficult across tasks. Similarly, whether a system's animation is automated or manually controlled can affect its cognitive utility. Therefore, these differences must be considered when comparing these results from other animated systems to our setting of animated slide show presentations.

Sense of semantic distance

A specific type of slide transition is one in which the presentation shifts from one topic to another. In this case, two adjacent slides may contain no semantic relationship though positioned in close proximity in presentation sequence. Here the presenter must bear the burden of orienting the audience to the context change. While this context switch seems a natural responsibility for the presenter, this switch is likely to be reinforced by a well-designed visual aid.

One type of visual depiction to which a ZUI's spatial layout lends itself is indicating the semantic difference between two slides by their separation in the virtual presentation space. Transitions between these two slides are able to portray this virtual separation through the distance traveled in the CounterPoint transition animations.

A similar example of this concept explored in hypermedia is the 'warp coefficient' suggested by Kaplan and Moulthrop.[39] Here a number is associated with each link on a hypermedia page to indicate the semantic difference between the content of the current page and the link's destination page.

Implementation of CounterPoint

The inspiration for CounterPoint came from designing a number of zoomable presentations in existing zoomable authoring tools. The use of these tools for creating zoomable presentations can be likened to using a drawing program to create standard slide presentations. A drawing program offers relatively unlimited creative freedom but is not optimized for common presentation authoring tasks. With that in mind, the authors have designed CounterPoint to simplify or automate many common presentation tasks in a zoomable environment. CounterPoint is built on top of Jazz,[12] a Java toolkit for building ZUIs, and is available for download.

In building CounterPoint, the authors also wanted to take advantage of existing presentation tools. Although there are currently a handful of commercial slide show presentation tools available, the tool that clearly dominates the market is Microsoft PowerPoint™.[13] Therefore, to have the greatest potential impact on presentation authors, it was decided to create CounterPoint as a plug-in to PowerPoint. This connection to PowerPoint not only allows for compatibility with existing PowerPoint content, but also reduces the functionality needed in CounterPoint.

CounterPoint uses Visual Basic's COM hooks into PowerPoint to add a toolbar button and manipulate slide content. Because the majority of CounterPoint is built on top of Jazz in Java, one of the Visual Basic application's primary responsibilities is to start a Java application when its toolbar button has been pressed. Its other major responsibility is to start a TCP/IP client by which it will communicate with this Java application.

Similarly, the first responsibility of the Java application is to create a TCP/IP server to communicate with the Visual Basic component. Once a connection has been established, the PowerPoint slide contents are transmitted to CounterPoint. For both efficiency and convenience reasons, the slide contents are not transmitted via the TCP/IP connection but are passed instead via the Windows clipboard.

This transfer of PowerPoint slide contents is possible because PowerPoint uses the Windows metafile format (i.e. files with a list of drawing commands) for posting to the clipboard, rather than something similar to their proprietary file format. However, this metafile format also has positive performance implications for our application since Windows provides native support for metafile rendering.

Consequently, a third component of this application is implemented in Windows native code for managing and rendering Windows metafiles. The authors' Java code uses the Java Native Interface (JNI) to communicate with the native code and to switch between native and Java rendering as appropriate.

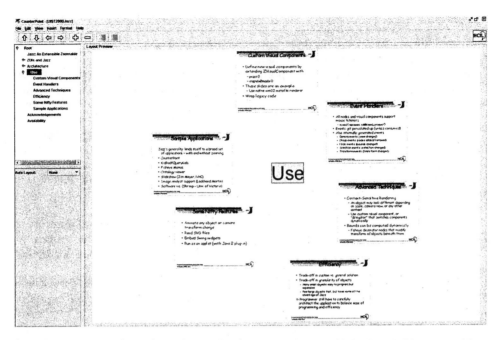

Figure 6 A screen shot of CounterPoint's layout hierarchy. The hierarchy is used to simplify both spatial layouts and interactive navigations.

The CounterPoint portion of the presentation data, such as slide border colorings, spatial layout parameters, and path orderings, are currently stored in a custom XML file residing in the same directory as the PowerPoint file. Because the format is XML, the file can be manually edited in a text editor in cases where the CounterPoint data has become out of sync with the PowerPoint presentation or for finer grain control over certain parameters.

Authoring in CounterPoint

Starting in PowerPoint
The model envisioned by the authors for using Counter-Point begins in PowerPoint. An author begins by creating slides in PowerPoint in much the same manner as if the slides were actually to be used in PowerPoint. The author can use almost any of the available PowerPoint tools for creating presentation content. One of the primary sets of PowerPoint features that is currently unsupported in CounterPoint is slide transitions. CounterPoint's animated navigation transitions are meant to replace any of the slide transitions in PowerPoint. Still, there are some transitions within slides, such as incrementally revealing slide content that we intend to support in future versions of CounterPoint.

An early decision was made not to try to replicate the functionality of PowerPoint in CounterPoint and to allow manipulations only at the slide level. While the authors feel that this was the best short-term solution, the long-term ideal for CounterPoint is to migrate the functionality of PowerPoint into CounterPoint (or vice-versa) for a finer granularity of control.

In the mean time, a single piece of the PowerPoint functionality that was found to be generally useful has been added to CounterPoint, namely simple text labels. Authors can use these labels to create landmarks in the CounterPoint space that highlight major points as indicated by collections of slides. For instance, the 'Architecture' label in Figures 3 and 4 was created in CounterPoint rather than PowerPoint.

Once the slides have been created in PowerPoint, pressing a custom toolbar button starts CounterPoint and transmits the slide contents from PowerPoint to Counter-Point. After the slides have been transmitted, the author begins working in CounterPoint to create spatial arrangements for the slides and author paths through the presentation space.

Creating spatial arrangements
When CounterPoint loads a presentation for the first time, the PowerPoint slides are arranged in a grid within CounterPoint's zoomable space. Hence, the typical first step in creating a presentation in CounterPoint is to modify the arrangements of the PowerPoint slides in the zooming space (see Figures 3 and 4). To arrange slides manually, one uses simple tools for manipulating objects in this space similar to those found in PowerPoint, drawing programs, and previous zoomable demo programs (e.g., PadDraw[1] and Jazz HiNote[12]).

A hierarchy editor (Figure 6) for automating these arrangements has also been provided. Using this editor, the author can organize the presentation contents into a semantically meaningful hierarchy. Then, for each parent in the hierarchy, the author can apply a modifiable layout template to spatially arrange the parent's children according to the template

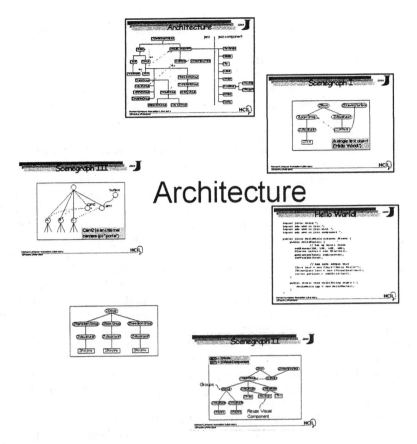

Figure 7 A screen shot of CounterPoint in presentation mode. Here, the presenter can alter pre-scripted traversals using various presentation-time interactions. Black borders indicate slides already visited during the presentation. This screen shot also represents a typical local overview in CounterPoint.

format. Currently, the authors provide layout templates corresponding to geometric shapes, such as lines, ellipses, arcs, and rectangles. For example, the slides that are children of the label 'Use' in Figure 6 can be automatically arranged using an ellipse layout to achieve this effect.

Creating scripted paths
The next step in the authoring process is to create paths through the presentation space. When CounterPoint loads a presentation for the first time, a single default path is automatically generated that visits each of the PowerPoint slides. In general, these paths are composed of two types of components. The first, more obvious type is the actual PowerPoint slide, which is inserted on a path to animate the slide to full screen size. These slides are inserted into the path using a simple scrolling list of thumbnails. Each slide can also be inserted multiple times in a single path.

The second type of path component is a view of a particular region of the zoomable space. These views are the more interesting path component as they allow the author to include views containing multiple slides and the structure of the presentation. Views are useful for

showing an overview of the entire presentation or focused overviews of particular subsections of the presentation.

The current mechanism used to create these types of views is similar to taking a picture or creating a screen snapshot. First, the author navigates to the particular region of space to be added to the path. The author then presses the camera toolbar button (Figures 3 and 4) and a new component, represented by a thumbnail image of the view, is added to the path. These thumbnails are actually implemented as live views onto the presentation space so that modifications to the zoomable space are reflected in the thumbnail.

While a one-dimensional representation of the current path is available in standard editing mode (see Figures 3 and 4), CounterPoint also provides a two-dimensional path editor that mimics the functionality of PowerPoint's slide sorter. The authors believe that this will allow for the transfer of pre-existing PowerPoint skills since the concepts of path editing and slide sorting are so similar.

Some indication of the current path is also available while spatially arranging slides. When the mouse is positioned over a slide on the editing canvas, the system displays arrows indicating the locations reachable from the slide in the current path. While this feedback is not intended as a primary path-editing interface, it does give some coupling between the two tasks.

Multiple paths are currently managed using the simple list component in the upper-left corner of Figures 3 and 4. Selecting a path's name in the list loads that path for editing or for starting a slide show. Currently, when a new path is added to this list, it is initialized with all the PowerPoint slides. However, the authors also plan to include more sophisticated algorithms for creating a new path such as a depth first search of the layout hierarchy (see Figure 6).

Delivering presentations in CounterPoint

Perhaps the most interesting and novel interactions occur in CounterPoint's presentation mode (Figure 7). The default behavior of sequentially stepping through one of the author's predefined paths is still available. This default behavior is achieved with the standard Power-Point controls of left mouse button, the space bar, the page down key, or right arrow key on the keyboard.

However, CounterPoint offers two modifications to this standard interaction for improvisation. First, the presenter can press the up arrow key to navigate up the previously defined hierarchy. This zooms out enough to get an overview of a semantically meaningful group of slides. If the layout hierarchy has not been defined, pressing the up arrow key zooms out to give an overview of the entire space.

A second interaction allows a presenter to dynamically navigate to various interesting locations in the presentation. However, before navigating to a target location, the presenter must navigate to an overview where the location is visible. This is typically achieved by zooming out using the up arrow key. For immediate access to a PowerPoint slide, right clicking on the slide animates the view to that location. The authors have found that other than slides, views of sub-trees in the layout hierarchy (such as that seen in Figure 6) and views explicitly added to the path during authoring are also targets for navigations. As a result, CounterPoint offers shortcuts for navigating to these locations. When the presenter moves the mouse within the bounds of either a sub tree or view, the bounds of the target view highlight. Right clicking within these highlighted bounds navigates to that location.

In cases where a presenter alters the presentation path using one of these dynamic navigations, the system attempts to pick an appropriate point in the path from which to resume. In cases where the target appears in multiple places on the path, CounterPoint picks the path entry closest to the point at which the presenter deviated from the path. If the slide does not appear at all in the current path, the system does not try to infer a new path entry but rather resumes from the point at which the presenter deviated from the path.

One other traditional hypertext element that the authors have added to CounterPoint to improve usability is visited colorings. CounterPoint provides modifiable slide border colorings to indicate which slides have been visited during a presentation. The authors have found these colorings to be useful both for the presenter and the audience for providing feedback as to which slides the presenter has visited and to give a sense of the overall progress of the presentation.

Principles for authoring ZUI presentations

Although CounterPoint's freeform 2D space essentially offers an unlimited variety of information layouts, the authors believe that some layouts are more desirable than others. During the authors' use of CounterPoint, a few common principles that generally result in effective presentations have been identified.

The authors have also found evidence for these intuited design principles in the research of spatial adjunct displays such as concept maps (see Figure 5). Spatial adjunct displays also include other diagrams, such as tables, flowcharts, or hierarchies, traditionally, used to supplement texts. The authors believe that these diagrams are comparable to ZUI presentations because they involve the arrangement of information 'chunks' or 'nodes' on a 2D surface. These displays further parallel CounterPoint presentations in that they are intended to supplement a verbal source.

Visual chunking

One of the problems mentioned in the design of concept maps is map shock. This occurs when the intended audience is overwhelmed by the size or complexity of a visual display. Based on common presentation guidelines (e.g. referenced in[21]) and the authors' own informal experience, this also seems to be a problem in presentations. Consequently, the first principle for CounterPoint layout is to create visual chunks.

Naturally, the corollary to this principle is determining the size of a chunk. In WWW page design, using larger chunks, or breadth, has frequently been emphasized over using smaller chunks, or depth (see[40] for example.) However, this is partly due to the latencies inherent on the WWW. Menu selection also tends to favor breadth over depth although Norman suggests that the optimal chunk size often lies in the range of three to twelve.[41] A common recommended chunk size among PowerPoint users seems to be seven.[21] This also coincides with the authors' human capability for perceiving seven plus or minus two items.[42] Since this also seems compatible with the authors' own experience in CounterPoint, it is expected seven plus or minus two will be a reasonable guideline for CounterPoint chunks as well.

Spatial configuration

Once the presentation has been segmented into meaningful chunks, the next step is to arrange these chunks in space. This issue has also been considered in the design of concept maps. Lambiotte *et al* proposed using 'gestalt' perceptual principles for the layout of concept maps to distinguish symmetry, similarity,

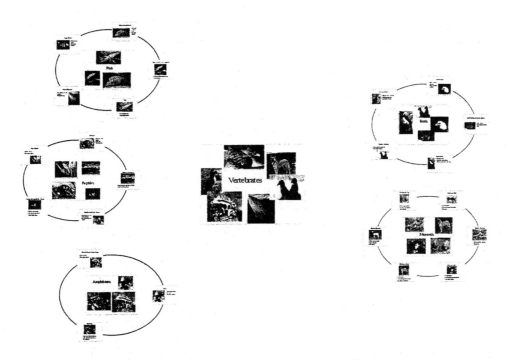

Figure 8 A presentation using hierarchy and clustering. This presentation depicts a sampling of the vertebrates, a sub-tree in the animal classification hierarchy. The sub-trees representing the different classes of vertebrates are then clustered according to whether the classes are warm or cold-blooded.

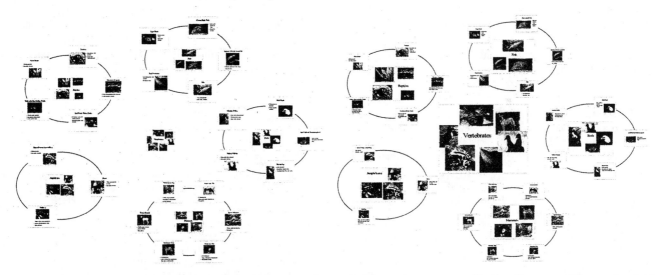

Figure 9 The presentation on the left uses only the 2D space and puts all slides at the same magnification. The presentation on the right also uses the zooming dimension by reducing the magnification of slides by 50% at each level in the hierarchy. This technique of combining area and scale often facilitates more meaningful overviews.

continuation, parallelism, and information gaps.[10] Wiegmann *et al* performed a study comparing concept maps designed with these gestalt principles to more randomly arranged concept maps.[11] The results of the study suggest that subjects using the gestalt maps had both better recall and understanding of the presented material.

The authors believe these gestalt principles can improve the design of ZUI presentations as well. Specifically, Lambiotte *et al* proposed several common layouts including hierarchies, chains, and clusters that the auhors have found useful in ZUI presentations. An example of hierarchy and clustering applied to a ZUI presentation can be seen in Figure 8. The authors recommend that authors of ZUI presentations use meaningful layouts that adhere to these gestalt principles whenever possible.

Balancing area and scale

A final consideration in the design of ZUI presentations is the extent to which the use of area and scale are balanced. For instance, the presentation on the left in Figure 9 shows a ZUI presentation that spans a large area but essentially ignores scale. In contrast, the presentation on the right in Figure 9 demonstrates a more balanced use of area and scale.

To some extent, this tradeoff between area and scale is one of aesthetics and depends largely on the presentation content. However, as studied by Hornbaek et al,[43] multi-scale representations of visual data leads to faster navigation.

Conclusion

In this paper, the authors present ZUIs as an alternative medium for slide show presentations. ZUI presentations enable spatial navigations, paths, and distinguished levels of detail with multi-scale 2D spatial arrangements. ZUIs also allow for the replacement of the slide transition with animated viewpoint traversals through the multi-scale 2D space.

The authors have also suggested several potential cognitive advantages of ZUI presentations over more traditional slide show presentations. However, future empirical studies are needed to verify these psychological advantages.

Based on experience with authoring zoomable presentations in freehand tools, the authors have designed and built a zooming presentation tool called CounterPoint. CounterPoint offers solutions to common presentation authoring and delivery challenges in ZUIs.

Lastly, the authors offer a set of principles for zooming presentations. These principles suggest dividing the content into visual chunks, arranging these chunks according to gestalt perceptual principles, and balancing area and scale.

Future work

Primary future work lies in empirically validating the cognitive advantages of zoomable 2D spaces for slide presentations. The authors also intend to evaluate CounterPoint's usability for various presentation authoring tasks.

Future development work by the authors will mainly focus on enhancing these tools for authoring spatial arrangements. It is also the intention of the authors to design a set of zoomable and projector-friendly layout templates to further automate the creation of zooming presentations. Finally, the authors plan to create improved tools for awareness and navigation in zoomable 2D workspace.

Acknowledgments

The authors would like to thank Allison Druin and Maria Jump for their early work on CounterPoint, and all the members of the Jazz team for helping with use of it. This work has been funded primarily by DARPA's Command Post of the Future project.

References

1 Bederson BB, Hollan JD, Perlin K, Meyer J, Bacon D, Furnas GW. *Pad++: a zoomable graphical sketchpad for exploring alternate interface physics. Journal of Visual Languages and Computing* 1996; **7**: 3–31.

2 Hightower RR, Ring L, Helfman J, Bederson BB, Hollan JD. *Graphical multiscale web histories: a study of PadPrints*. Proceedings of ACM Conference on Hypertext (Hypertext 98) (Pittsburgh, Pennysylvania, 1998), ACM Press: New York, 58–65.

3 Druin A, Stewart J, Proft D, Bederson BB, Hollan JD. *KidPad: a design collaboration between children, technologists, and educators*. Proceedings of Human Factors in Computing Systems (CHI 97) (Atlanta, Georgia, 1997), ACM Press: New York, 463–470.

4 Bederson BB. *Quantum Treemaps and Bubblemaps for a Zoomable Image Browser*. Proceedings of User Interface and Software Technology (UIST 2001) (Orlando, Florida, 2001), ACM Press: New York, 71–80.

5 Furnas G, Zhange X. *Illusions of infinity: feedback for infinite worlds*. Proceedings of User Interface and Software Technology (UIST 2000) (San Diego, California, 2000), ACM Press: New York, 237–238.

6 Furnas GW, Bederson BB. *Space-scale diagrams: understanding multiscale interfaces*. Proceedings of Human Factors in Computing Systems (CHI 95) (Denver, Colorado, 1995), ACM Press: New York, 234–241.

7 Furnas GW, Zhang X. *MuSE: a multiscale editor*. Proceedings of User Interface and Software Technology (UIST 98) (San Francisco, California, 1998), ACM Press: New York, 107–116.

8 Igarashi T, Hinckley K. *Speed-dependent automatic zooming for browsing large documents*. Proceedings of User Interface Software and Technology (UIST 2000) (San Diego, California, 2000), ACM Press: New York, 139–148.

9 Jul S, Furnas GW. *Critical zones in desert fog: aids to multiscale navigation*. Proceedings of User Interface and Software Technology (UIST 98) (San Francisco, California, 1998), ACM Press: New York, 97–106.

10 Lambiotte J, Dansereau D, Cross D, Reynolds S. Multirelational semantic maps. *Educational Psychology Review* 1989; **1**: 331–367.

11 Wiegman D, Dansereau D, McCagg E, Rewey K, Pitre U. Effects of knowledge map characteristics on information processing. *Contemporary Educational Psychology* 1992; **17**: 136–155.

12 Bederson BB, Meyer J, Good L. *Jazz: an extensible Zoomable User Interface graphics toolkit in Java*. Proceedings of User Interface and Software Technology (UIST 2000) (San Diego, California, 2000), ACM Press; New York, 171–180.

13 Microsoft PowerPoint. 2001. http://www.microsoft.com/office/powerpoint.

14 Nelson L, Ichimura S, Pedersen E, Adams L. *Palette: a paper interface for giving presentations*. Proceedings of Human Factors in Computing Systems (CHI 99) (Pittsburgh, Pennsylvania, 1999), ACM Press: New York, 354–361.

15 Toyoda M, Shibayama E. *Hyper Mochi Sheet: a predictive focusing interface for navigating and editing nested networks through a multi-focus distortion-oriented view.* Proceedings of Human Factors in Computing Systems (CHI 99) (Pittsburgh, Pennsylvania, 1999), ACM Press: New York, 504–511.

16 Moore T. *Active use of hypertext to aid learning and classroom instruction.* Proceedings of Technical Symposium on Computer Science Education (SIGCSE). (Nashville, Tennessee, 1995), ACM Press: New York, 297–301.

17 Shipman F, Furuta R, Marshall C. *Generating web-based presentations in spatial hypertext.* Proceedings of Intelligent User Interfaces (IUI 97) (Orlando Florida, 1997), ACM Press: New York, 71–78.

18 Zellweger P. *Active paths through multimedia documents.* Proceedings of International Conference on Electronic Publishing, Document Manipulation and Typography (Nice, France, 1988), ACM Press: New York, 19–34.

19 Zellweger P. *A hypermedia path mechanism.* Proceedings of Hypertext (Hypertext 89) (Pittsburgh, Pennsylvania, 1989), ACM Press: New York, 1–14.

20 Trigg R. Guided tours and tabletops: tools for communicating in a hypertext environment. *ACM Transactions on Office Information Systems* 1988; **6**: 398–414.

21 Parker I. Absolute PowerPoint: Can a software package edit our thoughts? *The New Yorker* 2001; **May**: 76–87.

22 Hays TA. Spatial abilities and the effects of computer animation on short-term and long-term comprehension. *Journal of Educational Computing Research* 1996; **14**: 139–155.

23 Allen B. *Information space representation in interactive systems: relationship to spatial abilities.* Proceedings of International Conference on Digital Libraries (DL 98) (Pittsburgh, Pennsylvania, 1998), ACM Press: New York, 1–10.

24 Patterson M, Dansereau D, Wiegmann D. Receiving information during a cooperative episode: effects of communication aids and verbal ability. *Learning and Individual Differences* 1993; **5**: 1–11.

25 Baddeley AD, Hitch GJ. Working memory. In: Bower G (Ed). *Recent Advances in Learning and Motivation*, Vol. 8. New York: Academic Press; 1974. 47–90.

26 Paivio A. *Mental Representation: A Dual Coding Approach.* New York: Oxford University Press, 1986.

27 Robinson D, Robinson S, Katayama A. When words are represented in memory like pictures: evidence for spatial encoding of study matierals. *Contemporary Educational Psychology* 1999; **24**: 38–54.

28 Robinson D, Katayama A, Fan A. Evidence for conjoint retention of information encoded from spatial adjunct displays. *Contemporary Educational Psychology* 1996; **21**: 221–239.

29 Lai S. Increasing associative learning of abstract concepts through audiovisual redundancy. *Journal of Educational Computing Research* 2000; **23**: 275–289.

30 Dillon A, McKnight C, Richardson J. Space – the final chapter or why physical representations are not semantic intentions. In: McKnight C, Dillon A, Richardson J (Eds). *Hypertext - A Psychological Perspective.* London: Ellis Horwood, 1993; 169–191.

31 Norman DA. *The Psychology of Everyday Things.* BasicBooks: New York, 1988; p4.

32 Thüring M, Hannemann J, Haake J. Hypermedia and cognition: designing for comprehension. *Communications of the ACM* 1995; **38**: 57–66.

33 Rivlin E, Botafogo R, Shneiderman B. Navigating in hyperspace: designing a structure-based toolbox. *Communications of the ACM* 1994; **37**: 87–96.

34 Dee-Lucas D. Effects of overview structure on study strategies and text representations for instructional hypertext. In: Rovet J, Levon J, Dillon A, Spiro R (Eds). *Hypertext and Cognition.* Erlbaum: Mahwah, New Jersey, 1996; 73–106.

35 Blankenship J, Dansereau D. The effect of animated node-link displays on information recall. *Journal of Experimental Education* 2000; **68**: 293–308.

36 Bederson BB, Boltman A. *Does animation help users build mental maps of spatial information?* Proceedings of Information Visualization Symposium (InfoVis '99) (San Francisco, California, 1999), IEEE Press: New York, 28–35.

37 Donskoy M, Kaptelinin V. *Window navigation with and without animation: a comparison of scroll bars, zoom, and fisheye view.* Proceedings of Extended Abstracts of Human Factors in Computing Systems (CHI 97) (Atlanta Georgia, 1997), ACM Press: New York, 279–280.

38 Shneiderman B. *Designing the User Interface: Strategies for Effective Human-Computer Interaction, 3rd Edn.* Massachusetts: Addison-Wesley, 1997; p15.

39 Kaplan N, Moulthrop S. *Where no mind has gone before: ontological design for virtual spaces.* Proceedings of ACM European Conference on Hypermedia Technology (Edinburgh, Scotland, 1994), ACM Press: New York, 206–216.

40 Zaphiris P, Mtei L. Depth vs. breadth in the arrangement of web links. 1997. http://otal.umd.edu/SHORE/bs04.

41 Norman K. *The Psychology of Menu Selection: Designing Cognitive Control at the Human/Computer Interface.* Ablex Publishing Corp: Norwood, New Jersey, 1991; 189–213.

42 Miller G. The magical number seven, plus or minus two: some limits on our capacity for processing information. *Psychological Review* 1956; **63**: 81–97.

43 Hornbaek K, Bederson BB, Plaisant C. *Navigation Patterns and Usability of Overview + Detail and Zoomable User Interfaces for Maps.* Tech Report HCIL-2001-11, University of Maryland, Human-Computer Interaction Lab, College Park, MD, USA.

Navigation Patterns and Usability of Zoomable User Interfaces with and without an Overview

KASPER HORNBÆK
University of Copenhagen
and
BENJAMIN B. BEDERSON and CATHERINE PLAISANT
University of Maryland

The literature on information visualization establishes the usability of interfaces with an overview of the information space, but for zoomable user interfaces, results are mixed. We compare zoomable user interfaces with and without an overview to understand the navigation patterns and usability of these interfaces. Thirty-two subjects solved navigation and browsing tasks on two maps. We found no difference between interfaces in subjects' ability to solve tasks correctly. Eighty percent of the subjects preferred the interface with an overview, stating that it supported navigation and helped keep track of their position on the map. However, subjects were faster with the interface without an overview when using one of the two maps. We conjecture that this difference was due to the organization of that map in multiple levels, which rendered the overview unnecessary by providing richer navigation cues through semantic zooming. The combination of that map and the interface without an overview also improved subjects' recall of objects on the map. Subjects who switched between the overview and the detail windows used more time, suggesting that integration of overview and detail windows adds complexity and requires additional mental and motor effort.

Categories and Subject Descriptors: H.5.2 [**Information Interfaces and Presentation**]: User Interfaces—*evaluation/methodology; interaction styles (e.g., commands, menus, forms, direct manipulation)*; I.3.6 [**Computer Graphics**]: Methodology and Techniques—*interaction techniques*

General Terms: Experimentation, Human Factors, Measurement, Performance

Additional Key Words and Phrases: Information visualization, zoomable user interfaces (ZUIs), overviews, overview+detail interfaces, navigation, usability, maps, levels of detail

1. INTRODUCTION

Information visualization [Card et al. 1999] has become a successful paradigm for human-computer interaction. Numerous interface techniques have been

This work was funded in part by DARPA's Command Post of the Future project, contract number F336159711018, and ChevronTexaco.

proposed and an increasing number of empirical studies describe the benefits and problems of information visualization, for example, Beard and Walker [1990], Schaffer et al. [1996], Hornbæk and Frøkjær [1999], Chen and Czerwinski [2000]. Interfaces with an overview and zoomable user interfaces have been extensively discussed in the literature on information visualization. Interfaces with an overview, often called *overview+detail interfaces* [Plaisant et al. 1995], show the details of an information space together with an overview of the entire information space. Such interfaces can improve subjective satisfaction (e.g., North and Shneiderman [2000]), and efficiency (e.g., Beard and Walker [1990]). Zoomable user interfaces organize information in space and scale, and use panning and zooming as their main interaction techniques [Perlin and Fox 1993; Bederson et al. 1996]. Research prototypes of zoomable user interfaces include interfaces for storytelling [Druin et al. 1997], Web browsing [Hightower et al. 1998], and browsing of images [Combs and Bederson 1999; Bederson 2001]. However, few empirical studies have investigated the usability of zoomable user interfaces, and the results of those studies have been inconclusive. In addition, the usability of overviews for zoomable user interfaces has not been studied.

In this article we present an empirical analysis of zoomable user interfaces with and without an overview. We investigate the following:

—how the presence or absence of an overview affects usability;

—how an overview influences the way users navigate information spaces; and

—how different organizations of information spaces may influence navigation patterns and usability.

With this work, we aim to strengthen the empirical literature on zoomable user interfaces, thereby identifying challenges for researchers and advising designers of user interfaces.

In Section 2, we review the literature on overviews and zoomable user interfaces. Then, we present our empirical investigation of differences in navigation patterns and usability in zoomable user interfaces with and without an overview. Finally, we discuss the trade-off between time and satisfaction in such interfaces and explain the interaction between usability and differently organized information spaces.

2. RELATED WORK

This section summarizes the research questions and empirical findings about interfaces with overviews and zoomable user interfaces. It explains the literature behind our design decisions and the motivation for the experiment, both described in subsequent sections.

2.1 Interfaces with Overviews

Interfaces with overviews present multiple views of an information space where some views show detailed information about the information space (called *detail windows*), while other views show an overview of the information space (called *overview windows* or *overviews*). Examples of such interfaces include editors for program code [Eick et al. 1992], interfaces for image collections [North et al. 1995], and commercial programs such as Adobe Photoshop.[1] Interfaces with an overview have been found to have three benefits. First, navigation is more efficient because users may navigate using the overview window rather than using the detail window [Beard and Walker 1990]. Second, the overview window aids users in keeping track of their current position in the information space [Plaisant et al. 1995]. The overview window itself might also give users task-relevant information, for example, by enabling users to read section titles from an overview of a document [Hornbæk and Frøkjær 2001]. Third, the overview gives users a feeling of control [Shneiderman 1998]. A drawback of interfaces with an overview is that the spatially indirect relation between overview and detail windows might strain memory and increase the time used for visual search [Card et al. 1999, p. 307]. In addition, such interfaces require more screen space than interfaces without overviews.

Taxonomies and design guidelines for overviews [Beard and Walker 1990; Plaisant et al. 1995; Carr et al. 1998; Baldonado et al. 2000] contain three main points. First, the overview and detail windows need to be tightly coupled [Ahlberg and Shneiderman 1994], so that navigation or selection of information objects in one window is immediately reflected in the other windows. Tight coupling of overview and detail views has been found useful in several studies (e.g., North and Shneiderman [2000]). Second, for any relation between overview and detail windows, the zoom factor is the ratio between the larger and smaller of the magnification of the two windows. For overview+detail interfaces, this factor is recommended to be below 25 [Plaisant et al. 1995] or below 30 [Shneiderman 1998]. It is unclear, however, if the sizes of the detail and overview windows influence the recommended zoom factor. Third, the size of the overview window influences how much information can be seen at the overview and how easy it is to navigate on the overview. However, a large overview window might take screen real estate from the detail window. Plaisant et al. [1995] argued that the most usable sizes of the overview and detail windows are task dependent. A large overview window, for example, is required for a monitoring task, while a diagnostic task might benefit from a large detail window.

A number of empirical studies have found that having an overview improves user satisfaction and efficiency over interfaces without an overview. Beard and Walker [1990] compared the effect of having an overview window to navigating with scrollbars. In a 280-word ordered tree, subjects used an overview window that allowed dragging a field-of-view and one that allowed both dragging and resizing the field-of-view. For tasks where subjects tried to locate a word in the tree and tasks where they repeatedly went from one side of the tree to the other, the overview window led to significantly faster task completion. North and Shneiderman [2000] compared 18 subjects' performance with a detail-only, an uncoordinated overview+detail, and a coordinated overview+detail interface for browsing textual population data. Compared to the detail-only interface, the coordinated interface was 30–80% faster and scored significantly higher on a satisfaction questionnaire. Hornbæk and Frøkjær [2001] compared an interface

---

[1]See http://www.adobe.com/photoshop/.

with an overview for electronic documents to a fisheye and a detail-only interface. Essays produced with aid of the interface with an overview scored significantly higher than essays produced with the detail-only interface. However, for tasks that required subjects to answer a specific question, the interface with an overview was 20% slower compared to the detail-only interface. All but one of the 21 subjects preferred having the overview.

2.2 Zoomable User Interfaces

While zoomable user interfaces have been discussed since at least 1993 [Perlin and Fox 1993], no definition of zoomable user interface has been generally agreed upon. In this article, we consider the two main characteristics of zoomable user interfaces to be (a) that information objects are organized in space and scale, and (b) that users interact directly with the information space, mainly through panning and zooming. In zoomable user interfaces, space and scale are the fundamental means of organizing information [Perlin and Fox 1993; Furnas and Bederson 1995]. The appearances of information objects are based on the scale at which they are shown. Most common is geometric zoom, where the scale linearly determines the apparent size of the object. Objects may also have a more complex relation between appearance and scale, as in so-called semantic zooming [Perlin and Fox 1993; Frank and Timpf 1994], which is supported in the zoomable user interface toolkit Jazz [Bederson et al. 2000]. Semantic zooming is commonly used with maps, where the same area on the map might be shown with different features and amounts of detail depending on the scale. Constant density zooming [Woodruff et al. 1998a] introduces a more complex relation between scale and appearance where the number of objects currently shown controls the appearance of objects, so that only a constant number of objects is visible simultaneously.

The second main characteristic of zoomable user interfaces is that the information space is directly visible and manipulable through panning and zooming. Panning changes the area of the information space that is visible, and zooming changes the scale at which the information space is viewed. Usually, panning and zooming are controlled with the mouse or the keyboard, so that a change in the input device is linearly related to how much is panned or zoomed. Nonlinear panning and zooming have been proposed in three forms: (a) goal-directed zoom, where direct zooming to an appropriate scale is supported [Woodruff et al. 1998b]; (b) combined zooming and panning, where extensive panning automatically leads to zooming [Igarishi and Hinckley 2000]; and (c) automatic zoom to objects, where a click with the mouse on a object automatically zooms to center on that object [Furnas and Zhang 1998; Ware 2000]. When zooming, two ways of changing scale are commonly used. In jump zooming, the change in scale occurs instantly, without a smooth transition. Jump zooming is used in Pad [Perlin and Fox 1993], Schaffer et al.'s [1996] experimental system, and commercial systems such as Adobe PhotoShop or MapQuest.[2] In animated zooming the transition from the old to the new scale is smooth [Bederson and Hollan 1994; Pook et al. 2000; Bederson et al. 2000]. An important issue in animated zooming is the

---

[2]See http://www.mapquest.com/.

duration of the transition and the user's control over the zooming speed, that is, the ratio between the zooming time and the zooming factor. Guo et al. [2000] provided preliminary evidence that a zoom speed around 8 factors/s is optimal. Card et al. [1991] argued that the zoom time should be approximately 1 s, although in some zoomable user interfaces, for example, Jazz, users can control both the zoom time and the zoom factor. Bederson and Boltman [1999] investigated whether an animated or jump zoom technique affected 20 subjects' ability to remember the topology of and answer questions about a nine-item family tree. Subjects were better at reconstructing the topology of the tree using animated zooming, but no difference in satisfaction or task completion time was found.

The empirical investigations of zoomable user interfaces are few and inconclusive. Páez et al. [1996] compared a zoomable user interface based on Pad++ [Bederson and Hollan 1994] to a hypertext interface. Both interfaces gave access to a 9-page scientific paper. In the zoomable user interface, the scale of the sections and subsections of the paper were manipulated, so that the entire paper fit on the initial screen. No significant difference was found between the two interfaces for the 36 subjects' satisfaction, memory for the text, or task completion time. Schaffer et al. [1996] compared 20 subjects' performance with a zoomable user interface and a fisheye interface. Subjects had to locate a broken link in a telephone network and reroute the network around the link. Subjects used 58% more time for completing the task in the zoomable user interface. Subjects seemed to prefer the fisheye interface, although this was not clearly described in the paper.

Hightower et al. [1998] presented two experiments that compared the history mechanism in Netscape Navigator with a graphical history in a zoomable user interface called *PadPrints*. In the first experiment, 37 subjects were required to answer questions about Web pages. No significant difference in task completion time was found, but subjects preferred the PadPrints interface. In the second experiment, subjects were required to return to already visited Web pages. Subjects were approximately 40% faster using the PadPrints interface and preferred PadPrints to Netscape Navigator. Combs and Bederson [1999] compared four image browsers: two commercial 3D interfaces, one commercial 2D interface, and an image browser based on Pad++. Thirty subjects searched for images in an image database that they had just browsed. Subjects were significantly faster using the 2D and the zoomable user interfaces, especially as the number of images in the database went from 25 to 225. The study presented some evidence that recall of images is improved in the zoomable user interface, but found no difference in subjective satisfaction between interfaces. Ghosh and Shneiderman [1999] compared 14 subjects' use of an overview+detail and a zoomable user interface to personal histories, LifeLines [Plaisant et al. 1996]. The zoomable user interface was marginally slower than the overview+detail interface. No difference in subjective satisfaction was found.

In general, the experimental results about zoomable user interfaces are mixed, reflecting differences in the interfaces that zoomable user interfaces are compared to, in the organization and size of the information spaces used, and in the implementation of zooming. In addition, the characteristics of zoomable user interfaces and interfaces with an overview are increasingly blended. For example, zoomable user interfaces have been combined with transparent overviews [Pook et al. 2000]; some interfaces with overviews have been extended with animated zooming [Ghosh and Shneiderman 1999]; and some effort has been put into extending zoomable user interfaces with navigation mechanisms that supplement zooming and panning (see, for example, Jul and Furnas [1998]). The main difference between research in zoomable user interfaces and in interfaces with an overview is that research in zoomable user interfaces has investigated the usefulness of zooming as a way of navigating, while other research has focused on the impact of a coupled overview. As interfaces with an overview begin to use panning and zooming as their main navigation technique and as zoomable user interfaces begin to provide overviews and other navigation aids, the central research questions become (1) what is the difference between different techniques for controlling and executing zooming, possibly taking into account the presence of an overview and other navigation aids; and (2) what is the effect of an overview (or other navigation aids), given that the interface provides pan and zoom techniques. In the experiment presented next, we address the latter question.

3. EXPERIMENT

To understand the differences in navigation patterns and usability between zoomable user interfaces with and without an overview, we conducted a controlled experiment. In the experiment, subjects used interfaces we will call the *overview interface* and *no-overview interface* to solve 10 tasks on each of two differently organized maps.

3.1 Hypotheses

In addition to the three aims mentioned in the introduction, three hypotheses guided the design of the experiment:

(1) Recall of objects on the map would be better in the no-overview interface. Zoomable user interfaces have been speculated to improve understanding of large information spaces, because of the integrated experience of the information space [Furnas and Bederson 1995]. As mentioned in Section 2, one experiment [Combs and Bederson 1999] found improved recall in zoomable user interfaces. In the interface with an overview, we expected subjects to occasionally use the overview window for navigation in the overview+detail interface, thereby losing the integrated experience of the information space. In addition, research has shown that users have difficulty in integrating multiple views [Card et al. 1999, p. 634]; lower recall with the overview interface may be one measurable implication of these observations.

(2) Subjects would prefer the overview interface, because of the information contained on the overview window and the additional navigation features. This hypothesis was based on the research on nonzoomable interfaces with overviews, summarized in Section 2.

(3) The overview interface would be faster for tasks that require comparison of information objects and scanning large areas (the latter we called *browsing tasks*). The literature suggests that comparison and scanning tasks are particularly well supported by an overview because the overview can be used for jumping between objects to be compared and because it can help subjects to keep track of which parts of the information space have already been explored.

3.2 Subjects

Thirty-two subjects participated in the experiment, 23 males and 9 females. Subjects were recruited at the University of Maryland and received 15 US dollars for participating in the experiment. The age of the subjects ranged from 18 to 38; the mean age was 23.4 years. Twenty-three subjects were computer science or engineering students, four had other majors, and five were research staff or loosely affiliated with the university. Thirty-one subjects used computers every day. Twenty-three of the subjects had never used zoomable user interfaces, while nine subjects had seen or used a zoomable user interface prior to participating in the experiment. We required that subjects had spent less than 2 weeks in the states of Washington and Montana, because the experiment used maps of those states.

3.3 Interfaces

For the experiment, we constructed an overview and a no-overview interface, both based on the zoomable user interface toolkit Jazz [Bederson et al. 2000]. When users held down the left mouse button, zooming in began after a delay of 400 ms. Users zoomed out by holding down the right mouse button. The maximum zoom factor was 20, meaning that subjects could view the map at scale 1 through scale 20. At scale 1, the initial unmagnified view of the map was shown; at scale 20 the initial view of the map was magnified 20 times. The zoom speed was 8 factors/s; that is, subjects could zoom from the initial view of the map to the maximum magnification in 2.5 s. Users panned by holding down the left mouse button and moving the mouse in the opposite direction of what they wished to see (i.e., the map followed the mouse). In the lower right corner of both interfaces was an icon showing the four compass points, which were referred to in some tasks. Next to this icon was a button labeled *zoom out*, which when pressed zoomed out to the initial view of the map. This button was expected to help subjects return to the initial view of the map if they were lost.

The no-overview interface is shown in Figure 1. Subjects could only interact with this interface using the zoom and pan techniques described above.

The overview interface is shown in Figure 2. In the top-right corner of the interface, an overview window shows the entire map at one-sixteenth the size of the detail window. This choice was arbitrary, lacking design guidelines on overview sizes (see Section 2.1). However, it was similar to the average size of the overviews we were familiar with. The current location of the detail window on the map was indicated in the overview window by a 70% transparent field-of-view box. The overview and detail windows were tightly coupled, so that

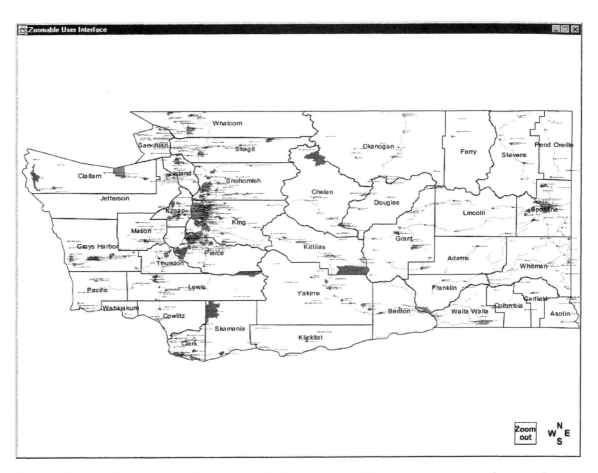

Fig. 1. *No-overview interface showing the Washington map*. The user may zoom and pan to change the area of the map shown. In the lower right corner of the window a button is shown that will zoom out to the initial view of the map. Next to this button is an indication of the four compass points. The colors of the map are reproduced here as different shades of gray. The map is shown at scale 1, that is, at the initial view of the map.

zooming or panning in the detail window immediately updated the overview window and dragging the field-of-view box changed which part of the map was shown in the detail window. The subjects could also click in the overview window outside of the field-of-view box, which centered the field-of-view box on the point clicked on. The field-of-view box could be resized by dragging the resize handle in the bottom right corner of the field-of-view box. The subjects could also draw a new field-of-view box by holding down the left button and moving the mouse until the desired rectangle was drawn. The field-of-view box always kept the same aspect ratio, which corresponded to the detail window and the overview window.

3.4 Maps

The motivation for using maps for the experiment was threefold. First, interfaces for maps constitute an important area of research. Second, maps include characteristics of other, commonly used information structures, for example, hierarchical information (nesting of information objects) and network information (connections between information objects). Therefore, results concerning maps may be generalized to other information structures. Third, the direct relation

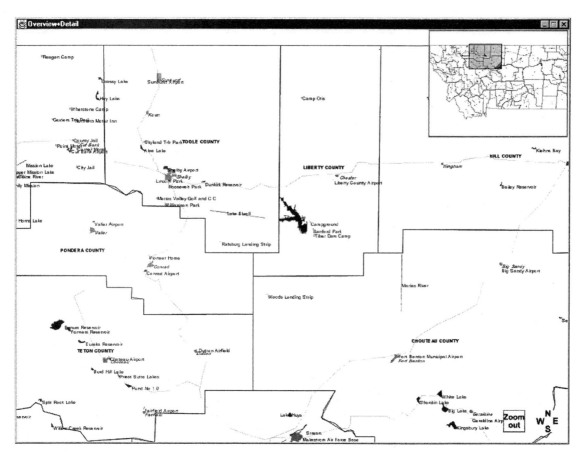

Fig. 2. *The overview interface showing the Montana map.* In the top right corner of the interface is the overview window, which shows an overview of the entire map. The gray area in the overview window is the field-of-view box that indicates which part of the map is currently shown in the detail window. In the bottom right corner of the field-of-view box is the resize handle that allows the user to make the field-of-view smaller or larger, that is, to zoom in or out. The two buttons in the lower right corner are similar to the buttons in the zoomable user interface. The map is shown at scale 4, meaning that the objects in the detail window are magnified 4 times.

between representation and physical reality aids interpretation of maps compared to the often difficult interpretation of abstract information spaces [Hornbæk and Frøkjær 1999].

We created two maps based on data from the 1995 United States Census.[3] The maps contained eight types of map objects: counties, cities, parks, airports, lakes, railroads, military installations, and other landmarks. Each map object, except railroads, consisted of a shape and a label. A distinct color identified each type of map object. In addition, county names were shown in bold type and city names in italic type. The maps were organized by placing labels for map objects at different scales, changing the apparent size of the labels as follows (also see Figure 3):

—The map of the state of Washington showed map objects at three levels of scale: county level (scale 1, 39 labels), city level (scale 5, 261 labels), and landmark level (scale 10, 533 labels). At the county level, labels were the same size as a 10-point font when the map was zoomed out (i.e., at scale 1)

---

[3]See http://www.census.gov/geo/www/tiger/ or http://www.esri.com/data/online/tiger/.

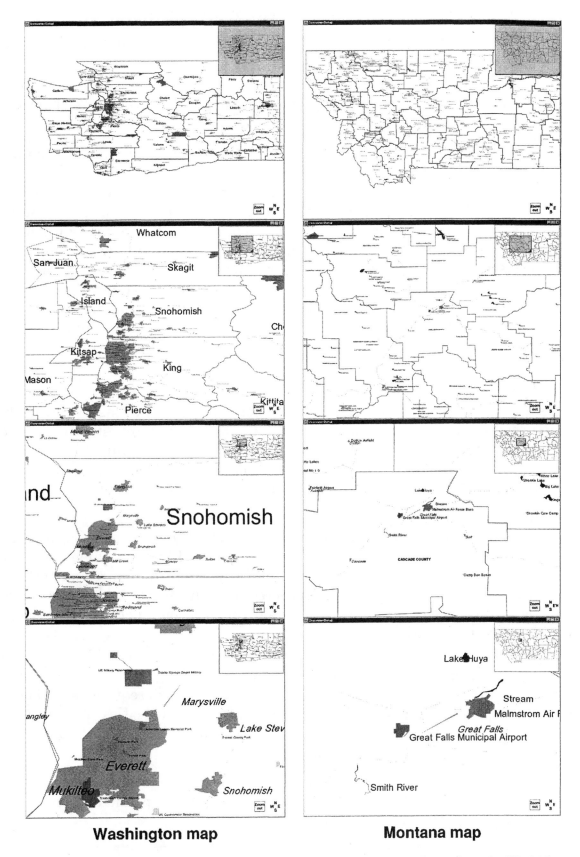

Washington map   **Montana map**

Fig. 3. *Eight screenshots of the maps.* The four screenshots in the left column show the Washington map; the right column shows the Montana map. From top to bottom the maps are shown at scales 1, 3, 7, and 20. On the Washington map, map objects are labeled at three different levels: county level (39 counties, for example, Snohomish in the left column, screenshot 2 from the top), city level

and larger when the map was magnified. When labels were shown at the city or landmark level, they had the size of a 10-point font when the user magnified the map 5 or 10 times, respectively.

—The map of Montana displayed all 806 labels at the scale 7, that is, similar in size to a 10-point font when the map was magnified 7 times. To aid visual search, county names were also shown in capital letters.

The Washington map was representative of information spaces that present the user with rich navigation cues everywhere in the information space (such as Yahoo style hierarchies or well-designed semantic zooming). The Montana map was intended to be representative of information spaces organized in a single level, with weak navigation cues at low zoom factors. We originally intended to formally compare single-level versus multilevel maps but only created two maps instead of the four maps necessary to properly separate the "number of levels" variable (single vs. multiple) from content "noise" variable (Washington vs. Montana). In Section 4, Results, we therefore only report differences attributed to the map used; in Section 5.2, we speculate on the origin of the difference of performance between maps, especially the role of map organization.

3.5 Tasks

Tasks were created to cover a large number of the types of tasks previously discussed in the literature [Plaisant et al. 1995] and to investigate specific hypotheses about when an overview would be especially useful (hypothesis 3, Section 3.1). We created 10 tasks for each map, five navigation tasks and five browsing tasks, which are described in the Appendix.

—Navigation tasks required subjects to find a well-described map object. All of the navigation tasks specified the names of the objects to be located. In addition, the counties the objects were to be found in were named, greatly limiting the area to be searched. Two navigation tasks required subjects to locate an object on the map, two tasks required subjects to find and compare objects, and one task required subjects to follow a route between two places specified in the task.

—Browsing tasks required subjects to scan a larger area, possibly the entire map, for objects fulfilling certain criteria. Two browsing tasks required a scan of the entire map for objects of a certain type; two tasks required subjects to scan an area of the map to find the county with the most cities or the largest cities in the area; and one task required subjects to find the first object of a certain type east of some county.

Between the maps, the tasks differed only in the map objects referred to. The answers to the tasks were evenly distributed over the map, and answers were also located at different scales.

(261 cities, for example, Everett in the lower left screenshot), and landmark level (533 landmarks, barely readable in the lower left screenshot). On the Montana map, all maps objects are labeled at the same scale, that is, all labels are same size but can appear very small at low scales. At scale 7 on this map, labels are as big as a 10-point font.

We also gave the subjects two recall tasks that test their memory of the structure and content of the map. The first recall task consisted of five small maps showing the outline of the state depicted on the map. For three of these small maps, a part of the map was darkened and the subjects were asked to write down as many objects within the dark area as they remembered. For two of the maps, subjects themselves could mark a county on the map with a cross, and write down any map objects they remembered within that county. The second recall task consisted of three county names, each associated with a list of 10 cities. Subjects were told to circle all cities within a county and cross out cities they were confident were not located in the county mentioned. The list of cities consisted of the three largest cities within the county mentioned, the three largest cities in counties just next to the county mentioned, and four cities in entirely different areas of the map.

3.6 Experimental Design and Dependent Variables

The experiment varied interface type (no-overview vs. overview), task type (navigation vs. browsing tasks), and map (Washington vs. Montana map), in a within-subjects balanced factorial design. The experiment consisted of two parts. In the first part, subjects used one interface giving access to one map and performed five navigation and five browsing tasks. In the second part, subjects used the other interface in combination with the not-yet explored map. Subjects were randomly assigned to one of the four possible combinations of interface and map. Within each of these four combinations, subjects were further randomly assigned to one of four permutations of task types in the two parts. Each of the resulting 16 groups contained two subjects. The order of the five tasks within a task type was the same for all subjects.

We used a range of dependent variables to capture information about navigation patterns and usability:

— *Accuracy in answering questions.*   Accuracy was calculated as the number of answers that were correct (all map objects given as answer to a task correct), partially correct (one correct and one wrong map object), and wrong (all map objects wrong).

— *Recall of map objects.*   For the recall task that required subjects to mark counties and cities on the map, we counted as correct the number of counties and cities within 1 cm of the actual location. For the recall task that required subjects to recognize the cities in a county after they had finished using the interface, we measured the number of correct indications, corrected with a penalty for guessing (the number of wrong guesses divided by the number of wrong answer possibilities for the question).

— *Task completion time.*   Task completion time was measured as the time subjects could see the map. The time subjects used for the initial reading of the task, as well as the time used for entering answers, was not included.

— *Preference.*   Preference was determined from subjects' indication of which interface they preferred using and from the reasons subjects gave for their indication.

—Satisfaction.   Satisfaction was measured using seven questions with 9-point semantic differentials. Five of the questions were taken from the Questionnaire for User Satisfaction [Chin et al. 1988] and two questions were custom made. The wording of the questions appears in Figure 6.

—Navigation actions.   We logged all interactions with the interfaces and measured the number of pan actions in the detail window and on the overview window (centering or dragging the field-of-view). We also measured zoom actions in the detail window and on the overview (resizing the field-of-view). An action was initiated when the mouse button signifying that action was pressed and was ended either when the button was released or when more than 1 s passed without any logged mouse movements. To compare these measures across interfaces, we combined them into a measure of total distance panned and the sum of scale changes, that is, the amount zoomed.

3.7 Procedure

The interfaces were run on a 650-MHz Pentium III laptop with an ordinary mouse. The screen was 13 in, with a resolution of 1024×768.

Upon arriving at the lab, subjects filled out a questionnaire about gender, occupation, and familiarity with computers. Then, subjects were introduced to the two interfaces and tried three practice tasks that lasted on average 11 min.

The main phase of the experiment consisted of two parts, each containing 10 tasks. For each task, subjects initially saw a window that covered the entire map. After reading a piece of paper that described the task, subjects clicked on a button to see a zoomed-out view of the map. When subjects had completed the task, they entered their answer using a tightly coupled text field and list box containing the labels of all objects on the map. For all tasks, subjects were asked to proceed to the next task when they had searched for 5 min. After solving all tasks in the first part of the experiment, subjects received the recall tasks and filled out a satisfaction questionnaire about the interface just used. After a 5-min break, subjects began the second part of the experiment, which used the same procedure as the first part.

After the second part of the experiment, subjects filled out a form about which interface they preferred. On average, the experiment lasted 1.5 h.

4. RESULTS

In Sections 4.1 through 4.4, we use univariate analyses of variance to investigate the accuracy of answers to tasks, recall of map objects, preference and satisfaction, and how subjects navigated. In the analyses, the four possible combinations of interface and map type are a between-subject factor (3° of freedoms, or df). This leaves 28 df for the error term. Within-subject factors are interface (1 df), map type (1 df), task type (1 df), and tasks nested within map type and task type (4 df). For each dependent variable, these factors and their interactions are used as the model for the analysis of variance. For the dependent variables satisfaction and recall, only interface and map type are used, as these variables were only measured once in each part of the experiment.

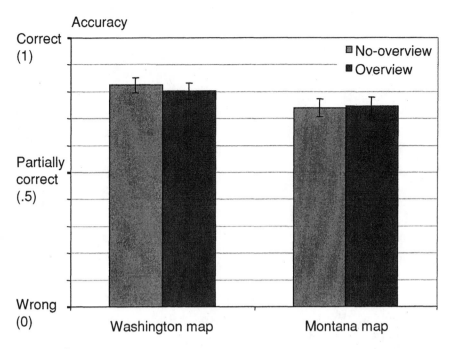

Fig. 4. *The average accuracy for the answers to the experimental tasks (for each bar N = 160). The figure shows the average accuracy for the two interfaces between maps. The answers to each task were scored as 1 for correct, .5 for partially correct, and 0 for wrong. A partially correct answer mentioned only one out of two map objects correctly. Error bars show the standard error of the mean [SD/SQRT(N)].*

4.1 Accuracy and Recall

Figure 4 summarizes the accuracy of the answers to the experimental tasks. We found no difference in the accuracy between interfaces, $F(1, 28) = .144$, $p > .5$. Between the two maps, a significant difference in the number of tasks correctly answered can be found, $F(1, 28) = 11.63$, $p < .001$. Tasks solved on the Washington map were more often answered correctly than tasks solved on the Montana map.

Figure 5 shows the measures of recall of map objects for the two interfaces. With the overview interface, subjects did better at the recall task with the Montana map compared to the Washington map. The no-overview interface showed the opposite pattern. These patterns were confirmed with a rank-based test of the number of marked cities and counties by a significant interaction between interface and map type, $F(1, 28) = 4.25$, $p < .05$. No such interaction was found for the number of recognized cities, $F(1, 28) = 1.69$, $p > .2$; only a marginally significant difference between interfaces for the Washington map was found, $F(1, 28) = 3.90$, $p < .06$.

Large individual differences existed in the accuracy and recall of cities and counties. One subject correctly answered 19 of the 20 questions; another subject answered only nine questions correctly. In the recall task, one subject marked on average 11 cities or counties on the map; another subject marked none.

4.2 Preference and Satisfaction

Twenty-six subjects stated that they preferred using the overview interface, while six subjects stated they preferred the no-overview interface. Thus,

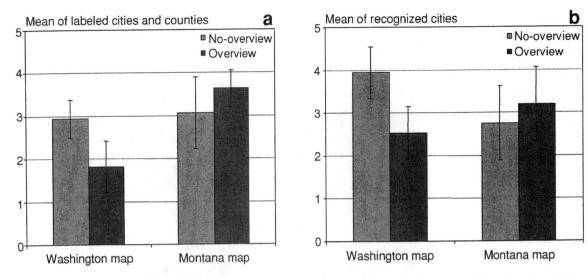

Fig. 5. *Mean number of correct answers to recall tasks (for each bar N = 16).* Panel a shows the mean number of correctly labeled cities and counties for each subject in one of the two parts of the experiment; panel b shows the mean number of correctly recognized cities, adjusted for guessing. Error bars show the standard error of the mean.

significantly more subjects preferred the overview interface, $\chi^2(1, N = 32) = 12.5$, $p < .001$. Subjects explained their preference for the overview interface as follows:

—The overview window provided information about the current position on the map; for example, one subject wrote: "It is easier to keep track of where I am." $N = 9$ subjects made similar comments.

—The overview window supported navigation ($N = 7$); for example, one subject wrote: "[It was] easier to navigate in the overview box while looking at the detail map for answers." Two subjects wrote similar comments at the end of the part of the experiment in which they had used the overview+detail interface.

—The overview window was helpful when scanning a large area ($N = 4$); for example, one subject wrote: "It made surveying a large map less disorienting especially when small landmarks had to be spotted."

—The overview window was useful for zooming ($N = 2$); for example, one subject wrote: "The zoom feature in the top right was extremely helpful."

—The overview window supported comparing objects ($N = 2$); for example, one subject worte: "Easier to move between counties while at the same zoom level -> easier to compare the size of objects".

The six subjects who preferred the no-overview interface mentioned the following:

—Locating objects felt faster using the no-overview interface ($N = 2$); for example, one subject wrote: "I found myself answering my tasks much quicker using the [no overview] interface."

—One subject preferred the no-overview interface because the overview window got in the way when using the overview interface: "Overview+detail

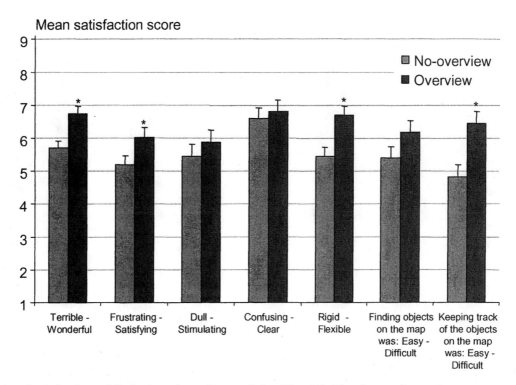

Fig. 6. *Satisfaction with the interfaces (for each bar N = 32)*. The figure shows the mean score for the seven satisfaction questions that each subject answered after using each of the two interfaces. Error bars indicate the standard error of the mean. The questions were answered on a 9-point semantic differential going from 1 (lowest score) to 9 (highest score). Significant differences at the .05 level are marked in the figure with an asterisk (*).

would seem to be more powerful, but the abundance of features got in the way to the effect of imposing on usability." Three subjects made similar comments at the end of the part of the experiment where they used the overview+detail interface. Nevertheless, these subjects preferred the overview interface.

In addition, four subjects commented that they found it hard to resize the field-of-view box; three subjects commented that the map seemed larger using the no-overview interface; two subjects commented that when using the no-overview interface it was sometimes unclear where they were on the map; and two subjects commented that it was useful that the overview window gave a visual indication of the current zoom factor.

Figure 6 shows the subjects' satisfaction with the overview and no-overview interfaces. The overview interface scored significantly higher than the no-overview interface on the dimensions Terrible-Wonderful, $F(1, 28) = 13.81$, $p < .001$; Frustrating-Satisfying, $F(1, 28) = 5.73$, $p < .05$; Rigid-Flexible, $F(1, 28) = 6.73$, $p < .05$; and Keeping track of objects was: Difficult-Easy, $F(1, 28) = 14.45$, $p < .001$. Between maps, we found a significant difference for four satisfaction questions, showing that subjects gave the interfaces higher satisfaction scores after using the Washington map.

4.3 Task Completion Time

Figure 7, panel a, shows the task completion time with the two interfaces and on the two maps. The Washington map was faster overall compared to the Montana

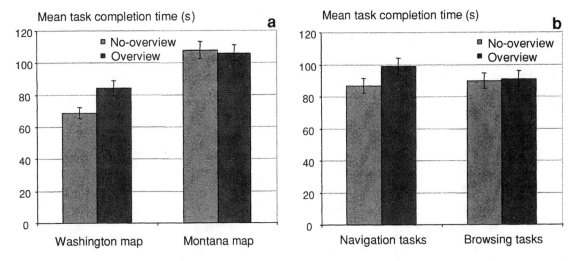

Fig. 7. *Task completion time in seconds (for each bar N = 160).* This figure shows the mean task completion time in seconds for each solution to a task. Error bars show the standard error of the mean. Panel a shows the task completion times for the Washington and Montana maps. Panel b shows the task completion times for navigation and browsing tasks.

map, $F(1, 28) = 48.94$, $p < .001$. We found a significant interaction between interface and map, $F(1, 28) = 4.50$, $p < .05$. Tasks solved with the no-overview interface on the Washington map were solved 22% faster ($M = 68.76, SD = 43.38$) than tasks solved with the overview ($M = 84.23, SD = 59.42$). Tasks solved on the Montana map were solved with comparable mean completion times (no-overview: $M = 107.81, SD = 68.05$; overview: $M = 105.85, SD = 59.42$).

Going into more detailed analysis using the same analysis of variance as above, we found no significant interaction between task types and interfaces, $F(1, 28) = 1.74$, $p > .1$. However, as can be seen in Figure 7, panel b, the no-overview interface was significantly faster for navigation tasks ($M = 86.9$, $SD = 60.4$), compared to the overview+detail interface ($M = 99.1$, $SD = 64.4$), $F(1, 28) = 5.27$, $p < .05$.

All navigation tasks solved on the Washington map with the no-overview interface had faster task completion times compared to the overview interface. Contradicting our task level hypothesis (hypothesis 3, Section 3.1), we found that one of the navigation tasks that required subjects to compare map objects was solved significantly faster with the no-overview interface (estimated marginal mean = 73.5, $SE = 11.12$) compared to the overview interface (estimated marginal mean = 113.9, $SE = 11.12$), $F(1, 28) = 7.46$, $p < .05$. On the Washington map, four of five browsing tasks were completed faster with the no-overview interface. One of these, a task that required finding the first airport east of some county, was solved significantly faster using the no-overview interface (estimated marginal mean = 81.81, $SE = 11.3$) compared to the overview interface (estimated marginal mean = 122.2, $SE = 11.2$), $F(1, 28) = 5.19$, $p < .05$. This also contradicted our hypothesis.

For the Montana map, no significant differences between interfaces for individual tasks were found. This contradicted our hypotheses that comparison tasks should be performed faster using the overview interface and that browsing tasks should be solved faster using the overview interface.

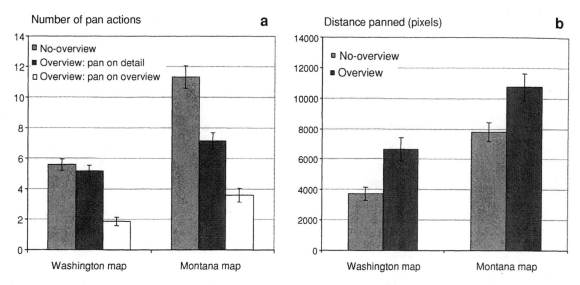

Fig. 8. *Panning in the two interfaces (for each bar N = 160).* Panel a shows the mean number of pan actions per task in the detail window without overview (left bar) and in the detail window with overview (middle bar), and the panning done by dragging or centering the field-of-view (right bar). Panel b shows the mean distance panned in screen pixels without the overview (left bar) and with the overview (right bar). In both panels, error bars show the standard error of the mean.

Large differences between subjects existed. The slowest subject used on average 169 s/task, or 3.4 times as much as the fastest subject. For individual tasks, differences between subjects were as large as 1:23.

4.4 Navigation Patterns

In the following, we investigate the differences between navigation in the two interfaces and try to provide detailed data about user actions that might explain the differences in task completion time, recall tasks, and satisfaction measures discussed on the preceding pages.

4.4.1 *Number of Pan and Zoom Actions.* Dragging the field-of-view box is the preferred way of panning on the overview. Subjects used this method of panning for half of the tasks solved with the overview. Figure 8, panel a, shows the mean number of panning actions made by panning in the detail view or by centering the field-of-view. We found an interaction effect between map type and interface type, meaning that more pan actions on the detail view happened on the Montana map with the no-overview compared to the overview interface, $F(1, 28) = 12.89, p < .05$. However, with the overview, subjects dragged or centered the field-of-view more frequently on the Montana map. Hence, as can be seen in Figure 8, panel b, the overall distance panned, that is, the sum of the distance panned both on the overview and on the detail view, was 51% higher with the overview ($M = 8690$ pixels, $SD = 10{,}554$), compared to no-overview interface ($M = 5{,}751$ pixels, $SD = 6{,}943$), $F(1, 28) = 10.90, p < .01$.

In 28% of the tasks solved with the overview, the field-of-view box was resized; in less than 4% of the tasks was the field-of-view box redrawn. Figure 9, panel a, summarizes the zoom actions made by resizing the field-of-view. We found a significant interaction between interface and map type, $F(1, 28) = 19.65, p < .001$, meaning that a comparable number of zoom actions were done in the

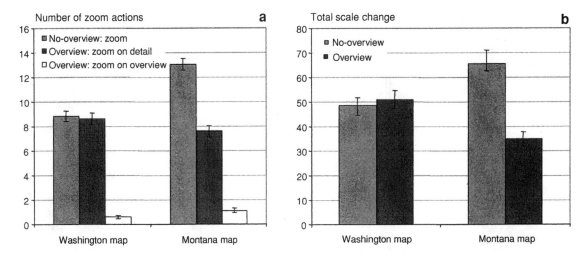

Fig. 9. *Zooming in the two interfaces (for each bar N = 160).* Panel a shows the mean number of zoom actions per task in the detail window without overview (left bar) and in the detail window with overview (middle bar), and the zooming done by resizing or redrawing the field-of-view (right bar). Panel b shows the mean scale change without the overview (left bar) and with the overview (right bar). In both panels, error bars show the standard error of the mean.

two interfaces on the Washington map, but that on the Montana map twice as much zooming happened with the no-overview interface as with the overview interface. Subjects seldom zoomed by changing the field-of-view box compared to how often they zoomed on the detail view. Looking at the sum of changes in scale (Figure 9, panel b), we found a significant interaction between interface and map type, $F(1, 28) = 12.70$, $p < .001$. On the Montana map, the no-overview interface ($M = 57$ scales, $SD = 58.9$) has a 33% higher number of scale changes than the overview interface ($M = 43$ scales, $SD = 43.2$), $F(1, 28) = 7.10$, $p < .05$.

4.4.2 *Use of the Overview Window.*   In 55% of the 320 tasks solved with the overview, subjects actively interacted with the overview window, that is, they moved or resized the field-of-view box. Tasks in which the overview window was used were frequently solved by first interacting with the detail view then switching to navigating using the overview and then possibly back to the detail view. To better understand the benefit of the overview window, we compared the tasks that were solved by actively using the overview window with the tasks solved without using the overview. Tasks solved with active use of the overview were solved 20% slower (estimated marginal mean = 103.93, $SE = 3.98$) than tasks where the overview window was not actively used (estimated marginal mean = 86.32, $SE = 4.57$), $t(319) = 2.91$, $p < .01$. Another way of understanding the use of the overview window is to look at the transitions between the overview and the detail window. We found that the number of transitions is strongly correlated with task completion time, Spearman's $r = .404$, $p < .001$. The more transitions between the overview and the detail window, the longer the task completion time.

Two subjects did not use the overview at all, while three subjects used the overview at least once for all 10 tasks solved with the overview+detail interface.

4.4.3 *Observations from the Experiment.*   We use our notes from observations during the experiment to make three points. First, many subjects experienced occasional problems with the combined zoom and pan button. Even though subjects practiced this combination button during the training tasks, 18 subjects zoomed at least one time when they verbally indicated that they were trying to pan. The delay before zooming began was sometimes too short. This appeared to happen when subjects began initiating a pan action without having made up their minds about which direction to pan.

Second, subjects' habit formation highlighted some limitations in the interfaces. At least eight subjects tried to use a way of navigating from the overview window in the detail window or vice versa. Some subjects tried to click on the detail window, probably with the intention of jumping to the place where they clicked. This way of navigating seemed to be taken from the overview window, where clicking on a point centers the field-of-view box on that point. Similarly, some subjects tried to zoom in and out while they had the mouse over the overview window. This way of interacting seemed to be mimicked after the interaction with the detail view.

Third, we observed that at least six subjects repeatedly experienced what has been called *desert fog* [Jul and Furnas 1998], that is, they zoomed or panned into an area of the map that contained no map objects. When we observed desert fog, two of these subjects were using the overview interface, four the no-overview interface.

5. DISCUSSION

5.1 Usability and Navigation Patterns

Subjects preferred the overview interface. Subjects also scored this interface significantly higher on the seven satisfaction questions, and commented that the overview helped them keep track of the current position and that the overview window was useful for navigation. This result confirmed our second hypotheses (see Section 3.1) and is coherent with previous empirical work on overviews [North and Shneiderman 2000; Hornbæk and Frøkjær 2001] and recommendations in the design literature [Plaisant et al. 1995, Shneiderman 1998]. For task completion times, we found that subjects who actively used the overview window were slower than subjects who only used the detail window. Our results are surprising considering previous studies, for example, Beard and Walker [1990] and North and Shneiderman [2000], which found that having an overview led to faster task completion times. However, in the studies by Beard and Walker [1990] and North and Shneiderman [2000], navigation in the detail-only interface was done with scrollbars. Our study shows that a direct manipulation zoomable user interface can in some cases (e.g., with the Washington map) reduce—or even eliminate—the need for a separate overview.

We did not find any support for our third hypothesis about an advantage for the overview interface for certain tasks. On the contrary, when considering the difference between browsing and navigation tasks, our results were similar to those of Hornbæk and Frøkjær [2001]. In both studies, it was demonstrated that a no-overview interface can be significantly faster for navigation tasks than an interface with an overview (here in the case of the Washington map).

In the context of our experiment, we consider four explanations of the difference in task completion time between the overview and the no-overview interfaces. First, the overview might be visually distracting, continuously catching subjects' attention and thus affecting task completion time. While we cannot definitively reject this explanation from the data collected, we note that subjects who did not actively use the overview window achieved task completion times comparable to tasks solved with the zoomable user interface (see Section 4.4.2). The straightforward explanation that, since the interface with an overview presented more information, it took more time to use, is also weakened by this observation. A second explanation of the task completion times suggests that switching between the detail and the overview window required mental effort and time moving the mouse. Our data modestly supports this explanation, since the number of transitions between overview and detail window were positively correlated with task completion time. A third explanation is that navigation on the overview window was coarse and that resizing the field-of-view box could be difficult at low zoom factors. Subjects commented that the overview was hard to resize. In support of those comments, we note that the overview window used in the experiment occupied 256×192 pixels. When a zoom factor of 20 was reached, the field-of-view box was only 13×10 pixels, which was probably hard for most users to resize and move using the mouse. Finally, it is conceivable that users never became competent in effectively using the added complexity of the overview. However, it should be noted that our experiment lasted longer than other experiments, for example, North and Shneiderman [2000], that did find an advantage for overviews.

We also investigated how subjects navigated with and without an overview. Interestingly, subjects only directly used the overview in half of the tasks where an overview was available. This rather low figure might indicate that adding zooming to an interface diminishes the value of the overview for navigation purposes compared to nonzoomable interfaces. Subjects panned 51% longer using the overview interface compared to the no-overview interface. One possible explanation for this large difference might be that the overview window did not support fine-grained navigation (as suggested above) and that subjects therefore had to do additional navigation on the detail view. Our data also shows that subjects made more scale changes in the no-overview interface when searching the single-level map. On the single-scale map, there was less information to help navigation. The difference observed might be one indication that the overview helped both navigation and keeping an overview: a function that subjects in the no-overview condition had to substitute for more zooming.

In summary, we found a trade-off between the two interfaces, with the no-overview interface being faster with the Washington map and the overview interface always leading to higher satisfaction. Our results challenge some of the common criticism of zoomable user interfaces without an overview, for example, that users lose their overview when zooming [Card et al. 1999, p. 634]. We found the two interfaces to be comparable with respect to accuracy; on the Washington map, the no-overview interface was faster than the overview interface. We do not know whether the speed difference observed might diminish when users learn to cope with the complexity of the overview interface.

5.2 Possible Influence of Map Organization on Usability

We found surprisingly large differences in usability and navigation patterns between the Washington and the Montana maps; the presence or absence of an overview also interacted with these differences. Because content (Washington vs. Montana) and number of level organization (single vs. multilevel) were confounded (see Section 3.4), this experiment does not allow us to make claims about the origin of those differences. However we believe that the maps (see Figure 3) were similar in most respects, except for the difference in the number of levels. The Washington and Montana maps were similar with respect to the number of map objects (1,591 vs. 1,540) and the area the state occupied (50% vs. 57% of the initial screen). The information density, measured as the mean distance in pixels from any map object to the nearest map object, was also similar (7.1 vs. 7.8). The similarity of the tasks conducted on the two maps was more difficult to measure precisely as browsing tasks require users to make many decisions and often sent them on sidetracks, but we did our best to choose similar tasks. Therefore we believe that the difference between the two maps consisted mostly of a difference in overall organization (single vs. multilevel). We recognize that a separate experiment is needed to verify this hypothesis.

When using the Washington map, subjects were faster and more accurate, and scored the interface higher on subjective satisfaction measures, irrespective of which interface they used. If the difference could be attributed to the use of multiple levels in the Washington map, the result would be consistent with the literature on landmarks [Vinson 1999], since the top-level landmarks—for example, the labels at the lowest scale on the multilevel map—were visible at all scales. Besides being faster with the Washington map, the no-overview interface also improved recall for map locations, partially confirming our first hypothesis. An explanation might be that the richer navigation cues on the Washington map helped the subjects to concentrate navigation and attention on the detail window, thereby relying less on the overview window. A multilevel map might also be more effective because it provides an implicit overview of the space that users memorize as they navigate the detail view. Only two users were seen experiencing desert fog with the Washington map, versus four with the Montana map. Feeling lost and having to reorient oneself, possibly by using the overview window, might be less common with a map like the Washington map.

5.3 Recommendations for Designers and Further Research

An interpretation of our study with the aim of providing advice for designers of information systems offers three main points:

(1) We recommend that designers closely consider the trade-off in subjective satisfaction and task completion time between providing an overview or not. We expect, in most cases, that an overview should be provided, but this depends on the critical usability parameters in the particular context designed for. A walk-up-and-use kiosk should perhaps aim for high satisfaction, while a navigation system for use in time-sensitive situations could

dispense with the overview if the information space contains rich cues for navigation and if the interface provides a flexible way of zooming.

(2) We believe that interfaces with an overview should eliminate navigation commands that are specific only to the overview window or to the detail window, that is, they should aim at unifying navigation [Raskin 2000]. All zoom and pan actions should therefore be similar across windows.

(3) To obtain the benefit of easy navigation provided by overviews (see Section 2.1), designers should use overviews at least one-sixteenth the size of the detail window (in area). For overviews coupled to a detail view less than the size of one screen or for screens on small devices, the overview might need to be larger to support navigation. For systems where much navigation is expected on the overview, for example, in support of monitoring tasks, a larger overview should be provided. For systems with zoom factors over 20 as used in our system, more usability problems will occur when using the overview, and consequently a larger overview will be necessary.

We propose five areas of further research:

(1) We believe that maps organized with multiple levels are likely to be preferable to single-level maps in terms of accuracy, task completion time, and satisfaction. More research needs to be conducted to confirm this hypothesis.

(2) The method for interacting used in the experiment occasionally caused subjects to zoom instead of pan. Research is needed to find a method for interacting with zoomable user interfaces using a two-dimensional input device that is intuitive and supports habit formation. We have used other interaction techniques ourselves, but picked the present interface because we believed it was easier to use for novices. Ideally, zooming and panning should be allowed to take place in parallel.

(3) Empirical research should explore integrating navigation cues within the detail view. Our observations and subjects' comments suggest that a detail-only interface could include cues about the current zoom factor (e.g., Furnas and Zhang [2000]), cues about the current position in the information space, and aids for avoiding desert fog (e.g., Jul and Furnas [1998]). If such cues are integrated into the detail view, the mental and motor effort associated with shifting to the overview might be reduced, as would the screen real estate lost due to the presence of an overview.

(4) Research should aim at improving the usability of the overview window. Usability might be improved by increasing the size of the overview window or by the use of distorted overview windows, which might give users better control over local navigation without losing the possibility of coarse global navigation. Optional overviews, or space multiplexed overviews, might also provide the navigation benefit without constantly taking up screen real estate. In our study the use of the overview for keeping track of ones position in the information space (as opposed to using the overview for navigation) was only addressed in so far as it influenced usability. The problems users encountered when shifting visual and mental attention to

the overview without interacting with it should be further explored, for example, by using eye tracking.

(5) Future research could investigate in more detail the effect on performance of expertise with the information space and the interface. It seems especially important to know how the satisfaction versus time tradeoff develops as users' expertise grows.

6. CONCLUSIONS

We compared the navigation patterns and usability of a zoomable user interface with and without an overview. Thirty-two subjects spent an average of 1.5 h solving tasks on two maps. Our results suggest a tradeoff between the two interfaces in subjective satisfaction and task completion time. Subjects scored the interface with an overview higher on seven subjective satisfaction questions, and 80% preferred this interface. In contrast, subjects were faster without the overview when using one of the two maps. Our results highlight the influence of the map design on usability. Subjects preferred using the Washington map independently of the interface used; they were also significantly faster at completing tasks on this map. We conjecture that this map was more effective because it was organized in multiple levels that might provide an implicit overview through the use of semantic zooming. We also found large individual differences in subjects' ability to navigate the map, in task completion times, and in accuracy. Based on our work, we recommend that the usability of overviews be improved, as should navigation aids for zoomable user interfaces. A better understanding of visual and mental attention in information visualization interfaces would help better explain the usability trade-off found. Common expectations about difficulties with zoomable user interfaces and the utility of an overview were not confirmed in this study. On the contrary, we found that zoomable interfaces without an overview offer certain benefits compared to interfaces with an overview.

APPENDIX: TASKS USED IN THE EXPERIMENT

Washington map, navigation tasks

1. Which city is closest to the city Colton in Whitman County?
2. Which state park is located north of the city Ione in Pend Oreille County?
3. Which of the following two cities is located most to the north: Shelton in Mason County or Warden in Grant County?
4. Which of the following cities covers the largest area: Sequim in Clallam County, Sumas in Whatcom County, or Deer Park in Spokane County?
5. Which are the two largest parks passed on the railroad going from Westport in Grays Harbor County to Vancouver in Clark County?

Washington map, browsing tasks

1. Which two national parks in Washington are biggest?
2. Find and name two counties in Washington that contain two or more military facilities.

3. Find and name the first airport east of the county Skamania.
4. Which two cities in the counties on the northern border of Washington cover the largest area?
5. Which of the counties on the southern border of Washington contains the most cities?

Montana map, navigation tasks

1. Which city is closest to Baker City in Fallon County (in the eastern part of Montana)?
2. Which city is located west of the city Eureka in Lincoln County (in the northwest part of Montana)?
3. Which of the following two cities is located most to the north: Darby in Ravalli County (western part of Montana) or Columbus in Stillwater County (southern part of Montana)?
4. Which of the following cities in the eastern part of Montana covers the largest area: Wolfpoint in Roosevelt County, Glendive in Dawson County, or Ekalaka in Carter County?
5. Which are the two largest cities on the railroad from the city Wibaux in Wibaux County (eastern part of Montana) to the city Red Lodge in Carbon County (southern part of Montana)?

Montana map, browsing tasks

1. Which two lakes in Montana are biggest?
2. Find and name two counties in Montana that contain at least three airports or airfields.
3. Find and name the first state park east of Furgus County (central Montana).
4. Which two cities in the counties on the northern border of Montana cover the largest area?
5. Which of the counties on the southern border of Montana contains the most cities?

ACKNOWLEDGMENTS

We thank all members of the Human-Computer Interaction Laboratory at the University of Maryland for valuable help and encouragement. Erik Frøkjær's and Ben Shneiderman's thoughtful comments improved the paper substantially. For thorough advice on statistics, we thank Per Settergren Sørensen. Constructive and concrete advice from the anonymous reviewers is also acknowledged. The work was done during a 6-month visit of the first author to the Human-Computer Interaction Laboratory at the University of Maryland.

REFERENCES

AHLBERG, C. AND SHNEIDERMAN, B. 1994. Visual information seeking: Tight coupling of dynamic query filters with starfield displays. In *Proceedings of ACM Conference on Human Factors in Computing Systems* (CHI '94, Boston MA, Apr. 24–28). C. Plaisant, Ed. ACM Press, New York, N.Y., 313–317.

BALDONADO, M. Q. W., WOODRUFF, A., AND KUCHINSKY, A. 2000. Guidelines for using multiple views in information visualization. In *Prooceedings of the 5th International Working Conference on Advanced Visual Interfaces* (AVI'2000, Palermo, Italy, May 24–26). L. Tarrantino, Ed. ACM Press, New York, N.Y., 110–119.

BEARD, D. B. AND WALKER, J. Q. 1990. Navigational techniques to improve the display of large two-dimensional spaces. *Behav. Inform. Techn. 9*, 6, 451–466.

BEDERSON, B. B. 2001. PhotoMesa: A zoomable image browser using quantum treemaps and bubblemaps. In *UIST 2001, ACM Symposium on User Interface Software and Technology, CHI Lett. 3*, 2, 71–80.

BEDERSON, B. B. AND BOLTMAN, A. 1999. Does animation help users build mental maps of spatial information. In *Proceedings of IEEE Symposium on Information Visualization* (INFOVIZ'99, San Francisco, Calif., Oct. 24–29). G. Wills and D. Keim, Eds. IEEE Press, New York, N.Y., 28–35.

BEDERSON, B. B. AND HOLLAN, J. D. 1994. Pad++: A zooming graphical interface system. In *Proceedings of the 7th ACM Symposium on User Interface Software and Technology* (UIST'94, Marina del Rey, Calif., Nov. 2–4). P. Szekely, Ed. ACM Press, New York, N.Y., 17–26.

BEDERSON, B. B., HOLLAN, J. D., PERLIN, K., MEYER, J., BACON, D., AND FURNAS, G. W. 1996. Pad++: A zoomable graphical sketchpad for exploring alternate interface physics. *J. Vis. Lang. Comput. 7*, 1, 3–31.

BEDERSON, B. B., MEYER, J., AND GOOD, L. 2000. Jazz: An extensible zoomable user interface graphics toolkit in Java. In *UIST'00, ACM Symposium on User Interface Software and Technology, CHI Lett. 2*, 2, 171–180.

CARD, S. K., MACKINLAY, J. D., AND SHNEIDERMAN, B. 1999. *Readings in Information Visualization.* Morgan Kaufmann, San Francisco, Calif.

CARD, S. K., ROBERTSON, G. G., AND MACKINLAY, J. D. 1991. The information visualizer, an information workspace. In *Proceedings of the ACM Conference on Human Factors in Computing Systems* (CHI'91, New Orleans, La, Apr. 27–May 2). S. P. Robertson, G. M. Olson, and J. S. Olson, Eds. ACM Press, New York, N.Y., 181–188.

CARR, D., PLAISANT, C., AND HASEGAWA, H. 1998. Designing a real-time telepathology workstation to mitigate communication delays. *Interac. Comput. 11*, 1, 33–52.

CHEN, C. AND CZERWINSKI, M. P. 2000. Special Issue on Empirical Evaluation of Information Visualizations. *Internat. J. Hum.-Comput. Studies 53*, 5.

CHIN, J. P., DIEHL, V. A., AND NORMAN, K. L. 1988. Development of an instrument for measuring user satisfaction of the human-computer interface. In *Proceeding of the ACM Conference on Human Factors in Computing Systems* (CHI '88, Washington, D.C., May 15–19). E. Soloway, D. Frye, and S. B. Sheppard, Eds. ACM Press, New York, N.Y., 213–218.

COMBS, T. AND BEDERSON, B. B. 1999. Does zooming improve image browsing? In *Proceedings of the ACM Conference on Digital Libraries* (DL '99, Berkeley, Calif., Aug. 11–14). N. Rowe and E. A. Fox, A., Eds. ACM Press, New York, N.Y., 130–137.

DRUIN, A., STEWART, J., PROFT, D., BEDERSON, B., AND HOLLAN, J. D. 1997. KidPad: A design Collaboration between children, technologists, and educators. In *Proceedings of the ACM Conference on Human Factors in Computing Systems* (CHI '97, Atlanta, Ga, Mar. 22–27). S. Pemperton, Ed. ACM Press, New York, N.Y., 463–470.

EICK, S. G., STEFFEN, J. L., AND SUMNER, E. E. 1992. Seesoft—a tool for visualizing line oriented software statistics. *IEEE Trans. Softw. Eng. 18*, 11, 957–968.

FRANK, A. U. AND TIMPF, S. 1994. Multiple representations for cartographic objects in a multi-scale tree—an intelligent graphical zoom. *Comput. Graph. 18*, 6, 823–829.

FURNAS, G. W. AND BEDERSON, B. B. 1995. Space-scale diagrams: Understanding multiscale interfaces. In *Proceedings of the ACM Conference on Human Factors in Computing Systems* (CHI '95, Denver, Colo., May 7–11). I. R. Katz, R. Mach, L. Marks, M. B. Rosson, and J. Nielsen, Eds. ACM Press, New York, N.Y., 234–241.

FURNAS, G. W. AND ZHANG, X. 1998. MuSE: A multiscale editor. In *Proceedings of the 11th Annual ACM Symposium on User Interface Software and Technology* (UIST '98, San Fransisco, Calif., Nov. 1–4). E. Mynatt and R. Jacob, Eds. ACM Press, New York, N.Y., 107–116.

FURNAS, G. W. AND ZHANG, X. 2000. Illusions of infinity: Feedback for infinite worlds. In *UIST 2000, ACM Symposium on User Interface Software and Technology, CHI Lett. 2*, 2, 237–238.

GHOSH, P. AND SHNEIDERMAN, B. 1999. Zoom-only vs. overview-detail pair: A study in browsing techniques as applied to patient histories. University of Maryland Technical Report CS-TR-4028. ftp://ftp.cs.umd.edu/pub/hcil/Reports-Abstracts-Bibliography/99-12html/99-12.html.

GUO, HUO, ZHANG, WEIWEI, AND WU, JING. 2000. The Effect of zooming speed in a zoomable user interface. *Report from Student HCI Online Research Experiments (SHORE)*, http://otal.umd.edu/SHORE2000/zoom/.

HIGHTOWER, R. R., RING, L. T., HELFMAN, J. I., BEDERSON, B. B., AND HOLLAN, J. D. 1998. Graphical multiscale Web histories: A study of PadPrints. In *Proceedings of the Ninth ACM Conference on Hypertext* (Hypertext '98, Pittsburgh, Pa., June 20–24). ACM Press, New York, N.Y., 58–65.

HORNBÆK, K. AND FRØKJÆR, E. 1999. Do thematic maps improve information retrieval? In *IFIP TC.13 International Conference on Human-Computer Interaction* (INTERACT '99, Edingburgh, Scotland, Aug. 30–Sep. 3). M. A. Sasse and C. Johnson, Eds. IOS Press, Amsterdam, The Netherlands, 179–186.

HORNBÆK, K. AND FRØKJÆR, E. 2001. Reading electronic documents: The usability of linear, fisheye, and overview+detail interfaces. In *CHI 2001, ACM Conference on Human Factors in Computing Systems, CHI Lett. 3*, 1, 293–300.

IGARISHI, T. AND HINCKLEY, K. 2000. Speed-dependent automatic zooming for browsing large documents. In *UIST 2000, ACM Symposium on User Interface Software and Technology, CHI Lett. 2*, 2, 139–148.

JUL, S. AND FURNAS, G. W. 1998. Critical zones in desert fog: Aids to multiscale navigation. In *Proceedings of the 11th Annual ACM Symposium on User Interface Software and Technology* (UIST '98, San Fransisco, Calif., Nov. 1–4). E. Mynatt and R. Jacob, Eds. ACM Press, New York, N.Y., 97–106.

NORTH, C. AND SHNEIDERMAN, B. 2000. Snap-together visualization: evaluating coordination usage and construction. *Internat. J. Hum.-Comput. Studies, 53*, 5, 715–739.

NORTH, C., SHNEIDERMAN, B., AND PLAISANT, C. 1995. User controlled overviews of an image library: A case study of the visible human. In *Proceedings of the 1st ACM International Conference on Digital Libraries* (DL '96, Bethesda, Md., Mar. 20–23). E. A. Fox and G. Marchionini, Eds. ACM Press, New York, N.Y., 74–82.

PÁEZ, L. B., DA SILVA-FH., J. B., AND MARCHIONINI, G. 1996. Disorientation in electronic environments: A study of hypertext and continuous zooming interfaces. In *Proceedings of the 59th Annual Meeting of the American Society for Information Science* (ASIS '96, Baltimore, Md, Oct. 19–24). S. Harding, Ed., 58–66.

PERLIN, K. AND FOX, D. 1993. Pad: An alternative approach to the computer interface. In *Proceedings of the 20th Annual ACM Conference on Computer Graphics* (SIGGRAPH '93, Anaheim, Calif., Aug. 2–6). J. T. Kajiya, Ed. ACM Press, New York, N.Y., 57–64.

PLAISANT, C., CARR, D., AND SHNEIDERMAN, B. 1995. Image browsers: Taxonomy, guidelines, and informal specifications. *IEEE Softw. 12*, 2, 21–32.

PLAISANT, C. M. B., ROSE, A., AND SHNEIDERMAN, B. 1996. Life lines: Visualizing personal histories. In *Proceedings of the ACM Conference on Human Factors in Computing Systems* (CHI '96, Vancouver, B. C., Canada, Apr. 13–18). B., Nardi and G. C., van der Veer, Eds. ACM Press, New York, N.Y., 221–227.

POOK, S., LECOLINET, E., VAYSSEIX, G., AND BARILLOT, E. 2000. Context and interaction in zoomable user interfaces. In *Proocedings of the 5th International Working Conference on Advanced Visual Interfaces* (AVI 2000, Palermo, Italy, May 23–26). L. Tarrantino, Ed. ACM Press, New York, N.Y., 227–231.

RASKIN, J. 2000. *The Humane Interface: New Directions for Designing Interactive Systems*. Addison-Wesley, Reading, Mass.

SCHAFFER, D., ZUO, Z., GREENBERG, S., BARTRAM, L., DILL, J., DUBS, S., AND ROSEMAN, M. 1996. Navigating hierarchically clustered networks through fisheye and full-zoom methods. *ACM Trans. Comput.-Hum. Interact. 3*, 2, 162–188.

SHNEIDERMAN, B. 1998. *Designing the User Interface*. Addison-Wesley, Reading, Mass.

VINSON, N. G. 1999. Design guidelines for landmarks to support navigation in virtual environments. In *Proceedings of the ACM Conference on Human Factors in Computing Systems* (CHI '99, Pittsburg, Pa, May 15–20). M. G., Williams, M. W., Altom, K., Ehrlich, and W. Newman, Eds. ACM Press, New York, N.Y., 278–285.

WARE, C. 2000. *Information Visualization: Perception for Design.* Morgan Kaufmann, San Fransisco, Calif.

WOODRUFF, A., LANDAY, J., AND STONEBREAKER, M. 1998a. Constant information density in zoomable interfaces. In *Proocedings of the 4th International Working Conference on Advanced Visual Interfaces* (AVI '98, L'Aquila, Italy, May 24–27). T. Catarci, M. F. Costabile, G. Santucci, and L. Tarantino, Eds. 110–119.

WOODRUFF, A., LANDAY, J., AND STONEBREAKER, M. 1998b. Goal-directed zoom. In *Summary of the ACM Conference on Human Factors in Computing Systems* (CHI '98, Los Angeles, Calif., Apr. 18–23). C.-M. Karat, A. Lund, J. Coutaz, and J. Karat, Eds. ACM Press, New York, N.Y., 305–306.

Chapter 4

The World's Information in Digital Libraries

In a library we are surrounded by many hundreds of dear friends, but they are imprisoned by an enchanter in these paper and leathern boxes; and though they know us, and have been waiting two, ten, or twenty centuries for us . . . it is the law of their limbo that they must not speak until spoken to. . . .

Ralph Waldo Emerson,
Society and Solitude (1870)

The vision of digital libraries is often traced to Vannevar Bush's (1945) description of Memex. He foresaw a microfilm technology device embedded in a desk that would provide professionals with access to patents, legal decisions, or scientific papers. He imagined documents that would be magically linked so that legal citations could be followed by merely typing a code number. J. C. R. Licklider refined this vision in his (1965) book that brought computing and networking technologies into the picture. Inspired by these futuristic conceptions, system designers began to build standalone and networked prototypes during the 1970s and 1980s. The technology of that era now seems primitive, but at the time the reality of a personal computer with a 640 × 480 pixel color display and a 10 megabyte hard disk opened the doors to innovations previously closed.

 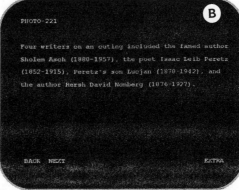

Figure 4.1 The transformation from numbered menus (a) to embedded menus (b) that were selectable by arrow key or mouse eventually contributed to the interface design for the World Wide Web.

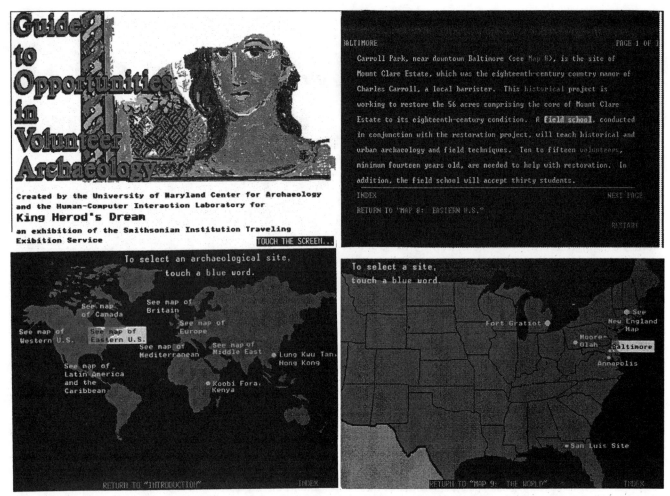

Figure 4.2 *Guide to Volunteer Opportunities in Archaeology (GOVA), a touch-screen kiosk installation for the Smithsonian Institution's traveling exhibit on King Herod's Dream.*

The HCIL's early contributions included working with the Library of Congress on their user interfaces and developing The Interactive Encyclopedia System (TIES) during 1983–1984. We had implemented Vannevar Bush's link idea by way of highlighted selectable text, which we called embedded menus, to contrast with the then currently common method of numbered menus (86–04, 87-01, 87-09, 89-01).

In 1984, the HCIL received funding from the U.S. Department of the Interior to develop computer applications for visitors to the U.S. Holocaust Memorial Museum and Education Center. The first museum prototype contained 106 articles written specially to emphasize the potential for links to related articles on key individuals, places, and events (89-01). Another influential example was the Guide to Volunteer Opportunities in Archaeology (GOVA), a touch-screen kiosk installation for the Smithsonian Institution's traveling exhibit on King Herod's Dream, which opened in March 1988 and toured 6 cities for 18 months (Figure 4.2) (89-08). In 1986, because of a trademark claim, we were forced to change the system name from TIES to HyperTies.

Another milestone was the HCIL's electronic version of the July 1988 special issue of *Communications of the ACM* devoted to hypertext (Figure 4.3). This first use of hypertext for a scientific journal was also a success in sales for the ACM.

Validation of the concept came when Tim Berners-Lee cited the ACM hypertext in his manifesto for the World Wide Web in early 1989. He also had the good sense to give embedded menus a more compelling name: *hot spots*. The World Wide Web invigorated the notion of digital libraries because the infrastructure naturally supported large collaborative projects to make sizable data sets available and also provided large enough audiences to justify substantial effort. Specialized collections gave way to broader resources, and by 1993 the National Science Foundation had launched a digital libraries funding initiative. A new field of research was born that continues to grow steadily with maturing conferences, journals, and academic programs.

The HCIL's work during the past decade emphasized information visualization and was supported by major projects from the Library of Congress, National Library of Medicine, National Aeronautics and Space Administration, National Science Foundation, and the U.S. Department of Education. For these large projects, we understood that users require powerful search capabilities, but we also knew that visual exploration is often the high payoff strategy for getting an overview and then browsing in a selected region to identify useful documents. An interface with dual visual overviews of the human body (head-to-toe and back-to-front) was the natural design for

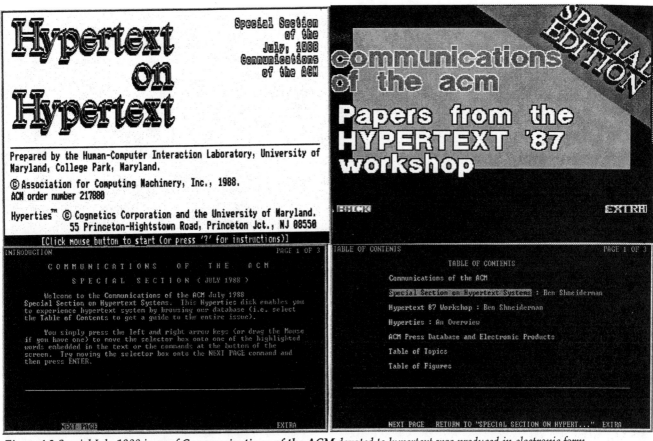

*Figure 4.3 Special July 1988 issue of **Communications of the ACM** devoted to hypertext was produced in electronic form using HyperTies and sold by ACM.*

the NLM's Visible Human Explorer (95-20 [2.1]), which nicely complements an index of organ and bone names. Similarly, enabling users to click on a world map provides an excellent index for NASA's remote sensing data in the Earth Sciences Information Partnerships (95-16, 97-02, 97-09, 97-16, 97-20). Then, users select their desired temporal choice on a timeline, narrowing the possibilities to a scrollable list of image types.

In addition to visual overviews, another key idea that we found useful was *query previews*, which indicate the cardinality of the result set (see Chapter 1). The main strategy is to show users how many data sets are available for a given geographic location and time period. Simply preventing zero-hit queries turns out to be highly beneficial, thereby avoiding user frustration. Equally important is preventing megahit result sets that overwhelm users, burden servers, and clog networks. In many applications, it is possible to present simple numeric counts of the result set size before the query is issued, thereby providing feedback for users so that they know whether further constraints are necessary to expand or narrow the result set.

These ideas were put to work for the Library of Congress's ambitious National Digital Library Program, which consisted of hundreds of collections containing millions of items (96-16 [4.1], 98-01). The HCIL's collection browser allowed users to select time periods, media types, and information categories; with each click, users would get immediate feedback by seeing the result set of collection descriptions shrink or grow.

In applying our emerging principles to the U.S. Department of Education's Baltimore Learning Communities project, we pushed further to accommodate hierarchical

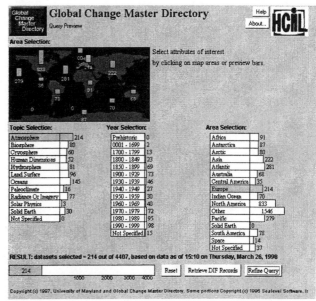

Figure 4.4 The interface for the NASA Global Change Master Directory (GCMD) provides a single-screen overview of the digital library. Here users have indicated their interest in atmosphere data covering Europe, and all counts have been updated in less than 100 ms using preview tables computed daily by GCMD.

categorizations (97-07, 97-15 [4.2], 99-03 [4.3], 2000-04). This project was to provide high school science teachers with tools to create rich multimedia lessons using high-quality videos from the Discovery Channel, NASA image resources, Web-based educational materials, and their own texts. Potential resources were first cataloged by the State of Maryland's curriculum and grade level, then made browsable with our two-dimensional information visualization tools based on hierarchical axes.

Each project brought us fresh challenges because of different user groups, varied tasks, diverse cataloging rules, and so on. The cross-fertilization enriched the work on every project. In addition to government-supported national efforts, we took on more commercial projects, such as West Publishing's enormous legal databases with their complex 81,000 node catalog. Intel and others supported the HCIL's work on photo libraries, and IBM requested prototypes based on patient and customer history databases. In recent years, the HCIL's engagement with design for and with children also produced innovative information visualization strategies (2000-18 [4.4], 2002-03 [4.5]). The intertwining of projects allowed us to try our ideas in new environments and to learn from new user communities.

More recently, the HCIL started an exciting project, led by Allison Druin, to create a digital library of books for children. Recently funded by major grants from the National Science Foundation and the Institute of Museum and Library Services, the International Children's Digital Library (ICDL) is already attracting attention (*www.icdlbooks.org*). The goal of the ICDL is to digitize 10,000 children's books—100 books from 100 cultures each. The Library of Congress joined as an early partner, and by digitizing rare children's books and introducing us to the national libraries of several other countries, this project received a great boost early on. The ICDL aims to provide children the ability to search, read, and communicate online about books. It is just getting started, but it has already applied the techniques of query previews, Zoomable User Interfaces, and specific methods for working with children (2002-03 [4.5], 2002-18).

FAVORITE PAPERS FROM OUR COLLEAGUES

The idea of overviews was strengthened especially by the visionary Spence and Apperley concepts and the early Beard and Walker study that neatly showed the benefits for tree browsing when an overview was available. Stasko reinforced the idea of overviews.

Beard, D. V., Walker, J. Q. II., Navigational techniques to improve the display of large two-dimensional spaces. *Behavior and Information Technology* 9, 6 (1990), 451–466.

Jerding, D. F., Stasko, J. T., The Information Mural: A Technique for Displaying and Navigating Large Information Spaces, *Proc. IEEE Information Visualization '95*, IEEE Computer Press, Los Alamitos, Calif. (1995), 43–50.

Spence, R., Apperley, M., Data Base Navigation: An Office Environment for the Professional, *Behaviour and Information Technology* 1, 1 (1982), 43–54.

BIBLIOGRAPHY

Berners-Lee, Tim, Information Management: A Proposal, *www.w3.org/History/1989/proposal.html*.

Bush, Vannevar, As We May Think, *Atlantic Monthly* 76, 1 (July 1945), 101–108.

Licklider, J. C. R., *Libraries of the Future*, MIT Press, Cambridge, Mass. (1965).

Bringing Treasures to the Surface:
Iterative Design for the Library of Congress
National Digital Library Program

Catherine Plaisant, Gary Marchionini, Tom Bruns, Anita Komlodi, Laura Campbell*

Human-Computer Interaction Laboratory
and Digital Library Research Group
University of Maryland, College Park MD 20742
(301) 405-2768, plaisant@cs.umd.edu
http://www.cs.umd.edu/projects/hcil

*Library of Congress
National Digital Library Program
Washington DC 20540

ABSTRACT

The Human-Computer Interaction Lab worked with a team for the Library of Congress (LC) to develop and test interface designs for LC's National Digital Library Program. Three iterations are described and illustrate the progression of the project toward a compact design that minimizes scrolling and jumping and anchors users in a screen space that tightly couples search and results. Issues and resolutions are discussed for each iteration and reflect the challenges of incomplete metadata, data visualization, and the rapidly changing web environment.

KEYWORDS

digital libraries, web design, browse, java, dynamic query, preview, design process, search.

INTRODUCTION

A team from the Human Computer Interaction Laboratory (HCIL) at the University of Maryland has been working with a team at the Library of Congress (LC) to develop and test interface designs for LC's National Digital Library Program (NDLP). The goals of the collaboration were to establish a user-centered design team for the NDLP, to create interface prototypes that serve a wide range of users, and to develop a variety of tools and widgets that LC may incorporate into future implementations. Beginning in the fall of 1995, HCIL team members met regularly with an LC team composed of librarians, managers, and technical staff to identify key interface challenges and brainstorm design approaches and features. As part of these efforts an extensive user needs assessment was conducted to determine characteristics of LC users and the types of information needs they bring to the Library. The needs assessment report presents a user typology with nine type/task components and identifies a series of interface challenges broken into content and user strategies categories [1]. During the January-August, 1996 period, a prototype interface evolved over several iterations. The

evolution of this prototype is the subject of this design briefing. It is important to note that the prototype is not meant as a design that will itself be fully implemented but rather a means to explore different design problems and suggest design techniques and widgets to the LC implementation team.

HCIL has collaborated successfully with LC in the past, most recently on the LC ACCESS interface--a graphical, touch-panel design that is used in the Library's Main Reading Room [2]. The current project goal was to foster a user-centered design team similar to the ACCESS team. HCIL has focused considerable effort on interfaces that allow users to browse and search collections of information and has been developing interface techniques such as dynamic queries [3], visual information seeking [4] and query previews [5-6]. Dynamic query interfaces extend direct manipulation to search tasks by closely coupling search specification with the display of results. These interfaces feature a visual representation of a database, (typically with a scatterplot or starfield display), a visual representation of a query using a collection of widgets (e.g. sliders), and tight coupling between these two components. Users browse the database by interacting with the interface widgets. Each change produces a new query, the results of which are immediately and continuously shown in the display, supporting a progressive refinement of the search, continuous reformulation of goals, and visual scanning to identify results. Query previews deal with large distributed databases, and use previews of the data to maintain real time feedback and limit access to the network.

A design objective for the LC project was to apply dynamic query and query preview techniques to make browsing and searching in the LC NDLP easy and effective. As the project progressed, the goal was sharpened to achieve a compact design that minimizes scrolling and jumping and anchors users in a screen space that tightly couples search and result services. Three major iterations (each included one or more revisions) are described here. The general procedure in each iteration was to sketch designs on paper during team meetings or in subgroups, HCIL would refine the skteches and use drawing tools to formalize the designs for team discussion. Finally, "mockups" were prepared using Netscape. The reviews were conducted with groups of 10 to 15 LC staff members including active members of the design team and others who mainly reacted to the designs. For early prototypes of specific widgets or mechanisms, specialized tools were used (e.g., the Information Visualization Exploration Environment (IVEE at http://www.ivee.com) for an early starfield display prototype, and Macromedia Director for an animation mockup). However, our aim was to use Netscape as much as possible to ensure adoptability by LC's implementation team and facilitate remote reviews. Each iteration is described below and the design rationale that led to the subsequent revision is discussed.

ITERATION 1: USERS' NEEDS DESIGN

After discussing various metaphors and critical features, a first prototype was sketched on paper and then mocked up in Netscape. Functionality for word search, browsing, help, and new topics was included in the prototype but much of the thinking in this iteration was shaped by the results of the user needs assessment. Having just observed the complexity of searching the vast and varied collections of the physical library (some collections even require a staff interview before use) the design tried to direct categories of users into customized ways to search the collections. It focused on "help" by defining a virtual information desk (VID) where users were strongly encouraged to begin their visit (it is the first link). The intention of the VID design was to provide customized help by asking users to classify their roles and information needs. Roles included:

> Tourist/surfer
> Novice researcher
> Casual researcher
> Expert researcher
> Teacher

Information needs included:
> Specific item
> General information on a topic
> Comprehensive information on a topic

Another aspect that we felt was important was to clearly indicate that only a very small portion of the entire LC collection is now available in digital form, to avoid users being frustrated by the narrow focus of the current system. An LC building icon was proposed with the tip of the building color coded to indicate this fraction (Figure 1.)

The first search function listed on the screen used filters. The needs assessment had shown that place, time, format and people were the most common characteristics of users' needs; sets of filters were "mocked up" to allow users to specify the scope of their searches (Figure 2). Filters included: geographic region (map), chronological period, and format (i.e. text, manuscript, photo, sound, movies

etc.) We did not include a name filter for two reasons. First, many of the objects are collections rather than authored items; furthermore, assigning attribution and/or who is depicted in a work remains a key metadata (i.e. data about data) challenge for digital libraries. Second, we wanted to avoid long, scrolling lists of names in this design. Word searching was also included for general queries.

Issues

As this iteration was discussed by the HCIL/LC team and revised, several implementation issues emerged. First, the team found it impossible to agree on written names for the user types and information needs and how to prompt users to understand what the expressions meant (e.g. Are "researchers" or "surfers" good categories and how do people identify themselves to categories.) More significantly, what to do with the user inputs was debated. Creating 15 different interfaces for the different combinations of user role and need seemed extreme and the subgroups working on specific versions were not making any progress. Another problem with this design is that it buried the browse and search functions under the user introductory services.

Resolution

The team decided to shift focus from user categories to tools for browsing and searching that would fit the needs of several categories at once. The 15 categories were collapsed into 5 more general user types and it was decided to provide specific introductory tours for each. Users would not be asked to identify themselves but would select a tour guide that matched the goal of their visit. To deal with the need to further assist certain categories of users a guided search was envisioned.

ITERATION 2: FOUR SERVICES DESIGN

The next version made the four main functions (browse, search, VID, and new arrivals/hot topics) more explicit by using the new HTML "tables" to visually separate the functions but compact them onto one screen to avoid scrolling. (see Figure 3). The first version of this design had one link for each box (e.g. the browse box had one link "browse" leading to a new page of browse options "by time", "by place" etc.). In later versions of this iteration items were moved up from lower levels of the hierarchy to the first page to minimize jumping (the browse box of Figure 3 includes a series of links).

In this design, the order of functions is revised as compared to Iteration 1. Browse and search actions are the first items: browsing was given prominence and a search box is available on the opening screen. Continuing our effort to deal with varied users, three types of search were included: quick (simple query), guided (a tutorial-like guided set of selections), and enhanced (Boolean queries with field limitations and other advanced features).

The Guided Search is available from the Virtual Informa-

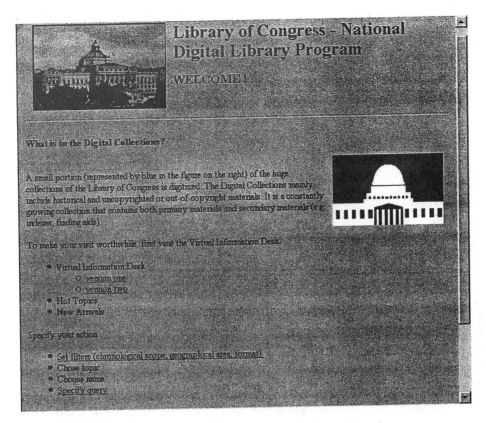

Figure 1: The home page in Iteraction 1 gives a short description of the collection and a graphic in the right to illustrate the proportion of the digitized materials to the whole collection at the Library of Congress. This screen uses a menu layout to present the options starting with user support services (Virtual Information Desk, Hot Topics, New Arrivals), and providing search and browse actions in the second part of the menu.

Figure 2: This figure shows a part of the "Set Filters" screen from Iteration 1. It provides customized graphical filters to the attributes found most important to users. After setting each filter a color coded result bar shows the amount of materials relevant to the attribute ranges selected.

tion Desk section of the homepage (Figure 4). Users are led through the process of setting filters screen by screen. An explanation of the actions is available in the middle of the screen, and setting the criteria is closely coupled with an estimate of the results size shown on the color coded result preview bar on the right. For example, when selecting a time period users can read that most materials are historical or out-of-copyright; they can see the distribution of volume of materials over the decades; and the bar on the right reflects the impact of their selection on the search scope, helping users learn about the content of the collection.

Results are presented in a framed list but it was envisionned that results could also be seen in a starfield display using metadata about the items such as date, size, type etc.

Issues

This design provided quick access to the tools but major concerns were now raised about feasibility. The lack of descriptive data (metadata) underlying different objects had become a central problem as a result of working with the two previous iterations. In the American Memory collections some objects are entire collections, some are finding aids that help users locate items in groups of items (e.g. a page in a manuscript collection), and some objects are individual items which ,in most cases, have no descriptive data. Those distinctions about object type are not always possible with a "search engine". Furthermore, most objects are not specific to a geographic region or time period or such metadata is not available in the underlying records, and many individual items are not catalogued at all. These challenges limited the usefulness of the general filters that could apply across all of the LC NDLP and make it difficult to construct adequate previews (e.g. the bars of figure 4). This led to the conclusion that additional metadata was necessary to design a good interface.

An additional concern was that the design focus on tools was still not bringing to the surface the treasures of the collections. Users still would have to navigate through several levels of the site hierarchy before being able to even see a sample of a collection and appreciate the value and coverage of the materials. Similarly, the rich "special presentations" written by domain experts about the materials were burried despite their great usefulness.

Resolution:

Samples of objects had to be brought forward, which implied a redistribution of the space for the tools on the front page.

Adding metadata is a necessity for comprehensive user access to individual items but doing so is prohibitively expensive for all items. A decision was made to add descriptive data only about collections. This was in harmony with the users' need assessment which showed that identi-

fying the best collections for searching was critical. The guided tour had to be abandoned because of lack of data and the visualization effort moved to the collection level.

To summarize, this iteration accomplished the goals of (1) decreasing the need for scrolling and (2) flattening the navigation hierarchy; however data visualization was limited by the lack of underlying metadata and user support remained an issue.

ITERATION 3: LEFT COLUMN TAB DESIGN

Whereas the first iteration focused on introducing users to the LC NDLP and the second focused on the tools for browsing and searching, the third iteration focused on bringing forward the materials of the LC NDLP. We aimed to aid users by bringing them quickly and visually to interesting materials that would serve as a springboard for defining their needs. The coupling of search and results was made tighter by anchoring users in a single dynamic screen rather than forcing them to jump to new screens.

Compact design

The main functions were arranged in "tabs" down the left side of the screen. Results for currently selected functions were displayed on the remainder of the screen (using HTML frames). The "tabs" are always present on the left side of the screen, and since real tabs could not be implemented in HTML color coding was use to match the tab and the right frame. This design (see Figure 5) is more compact than previous iterations and goes further in coupling search and results. The persistence of the titles and tabs gives the impression that it is possible to browse lists of collections, specify complex searches, and review results without ever leaving the first page.

Samples

On the introduction page an animated series of samples from collections and links to the special presentations written by experts aid users in familiarizing themselves with the digitized materials. The accent in this iteration was on providing immediate access to some of the treasures of the collections instead of users' categories or impersonal search tools. Users often have a vague idea of what they hope to find and browsing samples help them shape their query.

Collection browsing

Since the decision was made by LC to ensure that adequate metadata woul be available at the collections level, a major step was to use Java to implement a dynamic query application for browsing and selecting collections. The tab below Introduction is "Browse and Select Collections" (Figure 6) which update the right frame to a graphical overview of all collections, a few filters, and a list of collections which can be sorted on a variety of attributes, such as date, topic, and formats. Technically, this implied a visual representation of the available Collections, and widgets that allowed dynamic filtering of Collections on

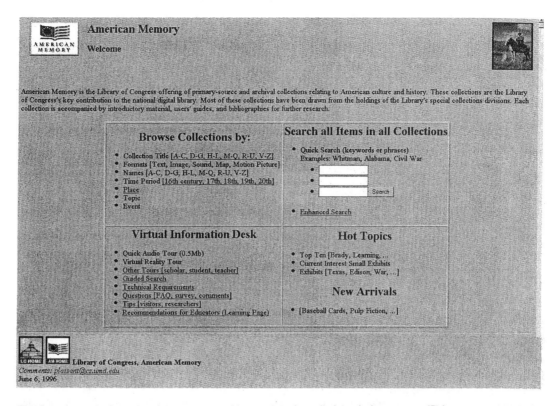

Figure 3: The homepage in Iteration 2 is compacted into a four-box design saving space. This page moves items up from lower levels of the hierarchy to the first page to minimize jumping. Here the order of services is revised as compared to Iteration 1, browse and search actions are the first items, and a search box is available right on the opening screen.

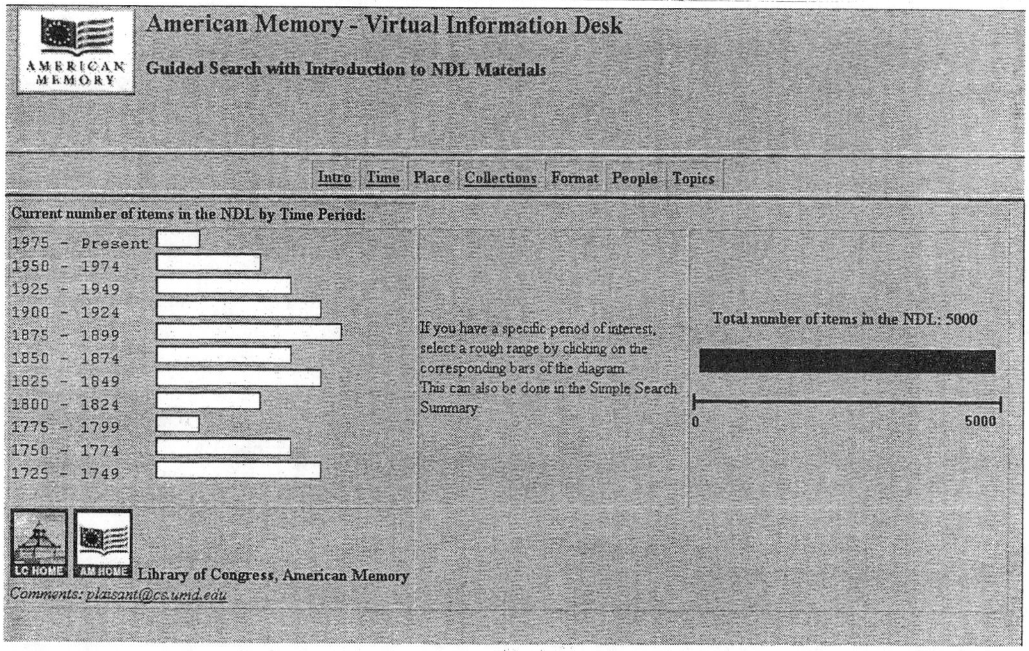

Figure 4: Guided search is available in Iteration 2 from the Virtual Information Desk section of the homepage. Users are led through the process of setting the filters screen by screen. An explanation of the actions is always available in the center, while setting the criteria is closely coupled with results shown on the color coded bar on the right. The bars on the left indicate the amount of materials relevant to a period and help users learn about the content of the collection.

various attributes. At the time this work began, web pages were generally static. Technologies such as server-push or CGI did not support the immediate response required for dynamic queries. JavaScript and dynamic GIFs were not yet available. The only client-side technologies that were sufficiently mature and available were Java and Shockwave/Director. HCIL chose Java because we had already started to work on a similar dynamic query interface for our NASA's EOSDIS project [5].

Graphic overview

Previously, starfield displays had been used to display "point" data, where database objects assume discrete values on each axis of the scatterplot. But few of the collection attributes could be represented as a single discrete value. Since the starting and ending dates defined an interval the starfield became an "interval" field, where each collection was represented by a horizontal bar, defining the x-axis as "time." The y-axis posed a problem. What other attribute could the intervals be plotted against? Size of the collection was considered but the LC team was reluctant to define a size for each collection (is size the number of items, byte size, time to read or review?). In the end it was decided that the y-axis would represent no other attribute. Instead, the intervals would simply be iterated in a non-overlapping manner down the vertical axis of the interval-field. Color-coding schemes for the intervals were also considered, and rejected. Most of the attributes for the collections can assume multiple values. For example, the Format attribute can be any combination of Text, Film, Sound, etc., so a single color code would not be appropriate. The interval field can be panned and zoomed by manipulating the double-box slider beneath the field, also implemented in Java.

Java Implementation

The Java prototype has three main components: the Collection Overview, the Collection Filters, and the Collection List. The use of Java allowed the Collection Overview and Collection List to dynamically change in response to collection filters, showing only those that satisfy the filter constraints. Furthermore, the Collection Overview itself acts as a filter. Panning or zooming on a particular interval of time specifies a temporal constraint, potentially filtering out more collections. The three interface components are linked via an active cursor. Passing the cursor over a collection interval or collection name highlights the other, as well as the appropriate attributes in the Collection Filters. Pressing the mouse button causes a jump to the collection homepage. The collection list can be sorted on any of the collection attributes. The use of Java allows interface objects to be created dynamically, based on the contents of a text file that defines the collections. Java facilitates the active linking between components, links to homepages, and collection sorting. Most importantly, Java facilitates dynamic queries by allowing each discrete user event, such as a mouse moving a slider, to be intercepted and processed, triggering a re-draw of the

visualization of results. This tight coupling of user events to graphical re-drawing is fundamental to dynamic queries.

Search and results

Quick Search is available from the first page and is meant to be run on all the collections or limited to the collections selected in the dynamic query interface presented above. Enhanced Search allows Boolean queries and gives access to the attributes common to the collections selected (e.g. restricting the search to photograph collections would add a new field to the Enhanced Search, allowing users to restrict the search to black and white or color photographs). Results are presented in tables which can be reordered according to any attribute. Glyphs could also be added to give information about type and approximate size of result items (e.g. a collection is distinguished from a photograph).

Issues

Feedback from the group shifted to implementation issues (how reliable is Java?) and graphical design (how to make those design prototypes more attractive?) which pushed us to sketch more polished graphic designs. As the project evolved it became clear that what was needed was not a self contained complete interface but a set of consistent interfaces for distinct collections and design directions for future interfaces. The team was encouraged to replace the planned usability testing with reviews by large audiences at LC and to explore the applicability of the design at other levels of the LC NDLP. In particular it was decided to apply the prototype design to the Coolidge Consumerism collection.

Design issues are now focusing on browsing the results list. Result lists are composed of heterogeneous materials (collections, items, finding aids, etc.) and the design needs to represent the different level of representation and provide overviews of the volume of material returned. Finally, once the results have been ordered and presorted it will remain a challenge for users to review large quantities of materials. For example if a search in photo collections returns 100 pictures, tools for rapidly browsing and using the most relevant images are needed.

CURRENT DIRECTIONS: MORE BROWSING TOOLS

As we continue our design process we are concentrating on tools to allow users to quickly scan scores of images and select some for more careful viewing or saving. For example a user preparing a photo report on Theodore Roosevelt needs to eliminate the many pictures of boats or bridges or family members, then flag the preferred views, and finally save them with annotations in a new page. See Figure 7 for an early prototype that allows users to quickly scan a set of thumbnails, examine full images and descriptive information, and flag those of interest for saving. Other tools are been built for other media (such as video or manuscripts) in order to provide fast access to preview materials, thus bringing the collection treasures to the

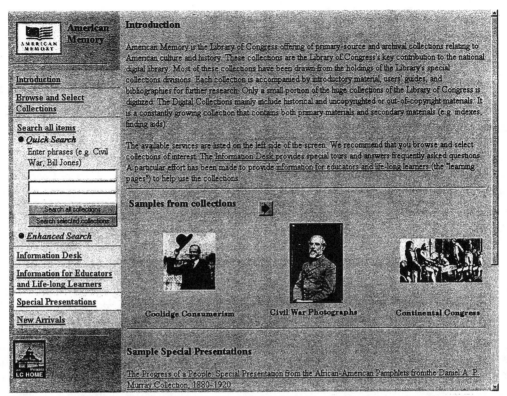

Figure 5: On the pages of the Iteration 3 the main choices are always present on the left of the screen, color coding between the tabs on the left and background on the right helps users to orient themselves in the site. On the introductory page animated samples from collections and links to the special presentations from different collections aid users in familiarizing themselves with the digitized materials.

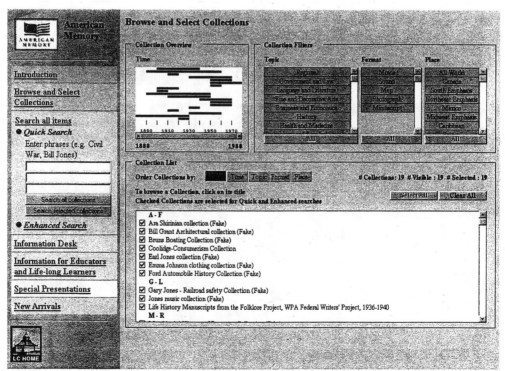

Figure 6: This figure shows the collection browser page with starfield display and closely coupled result lists. Filters here are represented by dynamic query interface widgets.

front. Results can be saved in an automatically generated page which will assist users with limited time and computer knowledge (e.g. teachers) to immediatly use the NDLP items in their own materials.

CONCLUSION

This project illustrates iterative design for a large-scale digital library that will serve the needs of a wide range of users. The iterations demonstrate ways to progressively more closely link query and results (the essence of dynamic queries), collapse hierarchy, compact design, and minimize scrolling and jumping. The project also provides an experience base for designers working on the problem of mapping metadata to browse/search and visualization widgets. Of course we are still far from a satisfying interface ready for extensive user testing and answering all the difficult digital library problems. Key challenges include: finding ways to show different levels of representation in results; providing search services for objects that have inconsistent or no descriptive data; developing guided tours and support through the VID; and integrating these designs with the larger LC site.

ACKNOWLEDGMENTS

This work is supported in part by the Library of Congress. Laura Campbell is the Director of the National Digital Library Program. In addition to the authors, the LC NDLP Team Members were: Martha Anderson, Maryle Ashley, Ardie Bausenbach, Mike Black, Jeff Bridgers, Beth Davis-Brown, Ernie Emrich, Floris Flam, Georgia Higley, Lois Korzendorfer, Sandy Lawson, Betsy Mangan, Gary Fitzpatrick, Barbara Natanson, Virginia Sorkin, Susan Veccia, Peter Yeager and Walter Zvonchenko. We also want to thank Ara Shirinian for his work on the image browsing tool and Teresa Cronnell for her participation.

REFERENCES

1. Marchionini, G., Plaisant, C., Komlodi, A., *User needs assessment for the Library of Congress National Digital Library*, Technical report CS-TR-3640 (also available from our project web pages at http://www.cs.umd.edu/projects/hcil/Research/1995/ndl.html.)

2. Marchionini, G., Ashley, M., Korzendorfer, L. (1993) ACCESS at the Library of Congress,*Sparks of Innovation in Human-Computer Interaction*, B. Shneiderman, Ed., Ablex Publ., Norwood, NJ (1993) 251-258.

3. Ahlberg, C., Williamson, C., & Shneiderman, B. Dynamic queries for information exploration: An implementation and evaluation. *ACM CHI '92 Proceedings* (Monterey, CA, May 3-7, 1992), 619-626.

4. Ahlberg, C., Shneiderman, B., Visual Information Seeking: tight coupling of dynamic query filters with starfield display, *ACM CHI'94 Proceedings* (Boston, MA, April 1994), 313-317.

5. Doan, K., Plaisant, C., Shneiderman, B., Query previews in networked information systems, Proc. *of the Third Forum on Research and Technology Advances in Digital Libraries* , ADL '96 (Washington, DC, May 13-15, 1996) IEEE CS Press,120-129. (Also a CHI 97 Video)

6. North, C., Shneiderman, B., Plaisant, C. User Controlled Overviews of an Image Library: A Case Study of the Visible Human, *Proc. of the 1st ACM International Conference on Digital Libraries* (Bethesda, MD, March 20-23, 1996) 74-82

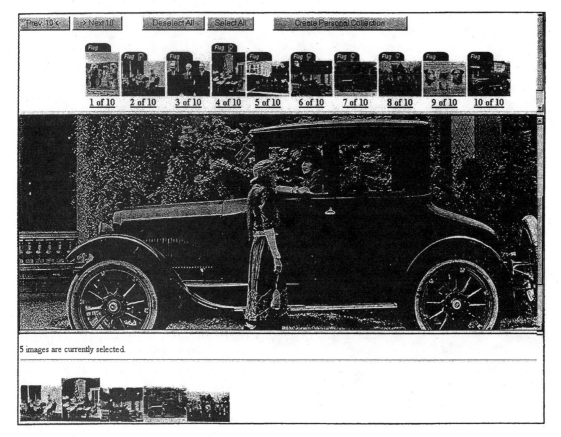

Figure 7:
One of the new tools developed to support image browsing. Here users can look at thumbnails and large images, select images and create their own collections of images.

Building an Electronic Learning Community: From Design to Implementation

Anne Rose*, Wei Ding, Gary Marchionini*, Josephus Beale, Jr., Victor Nolet

Digital Library Research Group
Human-Computer Interaction Laboratory*
University of Maryland, College Park, MD 20742
http://www.learn.umd.edu

{arose, weid, march, melc, vnolet}@learn.umd.edu

ABSTRACT
The University of Maryland at College Park in cooperation with the Baltimore City Public Schools and several partners is working to build an electronic learning community that provides teachers with multimedia resources that are linked to outcome-oriented curriculum guidelines. The resource library contains approximately 1500 videos, texts, images, web sites, and instructional modules. Using the current system, teachers can explore and search the resource library, create and present instructional modules in their classrooms, and communicate with other teachers in the community. This paper discusses the iterative design process and the results of informal usability testing. Lessons learned are also presented for developers.

Keywords
digital libraries, learning communities, dynamic query, java, video

INTRODUCTION
Educators have become increasingly interested in understanding the role technology can play in the classroom. One goal of the U.S. Department of Education's Technology Challenge Grant program is to demonstrate how public school-university-business consortia can cooperate to improve educational outcomes through enhanced technology. One of the projects funded, the Baltimore Learning Community (BLC), is a collaborative effort among the University of Maryland at College Park (UMCP), Johns Hopkins University (JHU), and the Baltimore City Public Schools (BCPS). The goal of this five year demonstration project is to create a learning community through the use of high quality educational resources and high-speed networking. The JHU component (The Baltimore Initiative) focuses on interactive video conferencing. The goal of the UMCP component (Maryland Electronic Learning Community) is to provide teachers with multimedia resources and link their use to outcome-oriented curriculum guidelines [4][5][6]. Constructivist learning theory is one of the educational philosophy that underlies this project [2]. This paper focuses on the technology component of the Maryland Electronic Learning Community.

For the past two years, the University of Maryland has been working with a team of middle school science and social studies teachers from three Baltimore City Public Schools and several partners including Discovery Communications, Inc., the U.S. Archives, the Space Telescope Institute and Apple Computer to build an electronic learning community. From a technology standpoint, this has thus far involved installing four or more computers in each of 12 classrooms; linking those machines and teachers at home to the Internet; creating a digital library of 1500 multimedia educational resources; and developing a prototype system that allows teachers to explore and search the resource library, build and present instructional modules, and exchange ideas with other teachers in the community (via email and video conferencing).

Classroom Setup
Apple Computer provided 40 Macintosh PowerPCs for use in the classrooms. Each classroom is equipped with 3-4 Macintosh 5200 computers capable of displaying MPEG video and a teacher machine, a Macintosh 5400 computer with a 4gb hard drive. Each classroom also has two 27 inch "s-video" monitors that can be used for classroom presentation. Currently, the machines in each school are networked via an ethernet LAN with a dial-up connection to an Internet service provider. High-speed networking solutions, such as fiber or hybrid wired/wireless solutions, are being investigated for the full implementation years of the project. Since teachers do much of their planning at home, they have also been provided with Internet access

at home and when necessary, with modems and computers.

Digital Library

The resource library is a collection of videos, texts, images, web sites, and instructional modules that cover a wide range of social studies and science topics. Each resource is digitized, indexed, and added to the project database. These resources have been collected from several sources including Discovery Communications, Inc. which is providing up to 100 hours of digitized video, the U.S. Archives, and the Space Telescope Institute. The selection of which resources to include in the community has been driven primarily by the teachers and their curricula. Teachers specifically requested several hundred images from the U.S. Archives and provided input to Discovery on what video programming to include. Discovery clears digitization rights and provides MPEG files based on segmentation (2-3 minute clips) done by UMCP staff. At the end of Fall 1997, six hours of video were included in the database and twelve additional hours had been segmented and indexed and were in the MPEG process. Selected websites are indexed after they are checked for student suitability and publisher stability.

The indexing process involves mapping a resource to one or more topic-outcome pairs. Currently, over 10,600 pairs are mapped to the 1500 resources. We chose to index by topic-outcome pairs because teachers currently select and organize materials by topic (e.g., space, ecology) but they organize their lesson plans according to the Maryland Statewide Performance Assessment Program (MSPAP) outcomes. A specific goal of this project is to help teachers develop more outcome-oriented lessons. Consider the science outcome "unifying concepts and processes". Anything that demonstrate the links/connections between a concept and the process that illustrates it is indexed by this outcome like a video clip that describes how humans need food to have energy (concept) and then explains how the food is converted to energy (process of digestion). We chose to use the outcomes proposed by the national science and social studies teacher organizations because this would allow our resource library to be shared with other states in the future.

Prototype System

For the past two years we have been working toward our goal of building an integrated system that supports resource exploration, module construction and presentation, and community exchange. Using the current prototype, teachers have created almost 100 modules on topics ranging from "Being a Space Explorer" to "Interpreting the Boston Massacre" to "The Bountiful Chesapeake". The rest of the paper discusses the iterative design process and the results of informal usability testing. Lessons learned are also presented for developers.

DESIGN PROCESS

Because the project is a longitudinal, demonstration project that aims to influence human behavior, a user-centered, iterative design process was adopted to "grow" a system according to the needs of an evolving community of users. We knew that we wanted to provide rich system support for a variety of resources and communication venues, but could not overload busy teachers who have a wide range of previous computer experience with a full-featured system. Moreover, we knew that over the five years of the project, the technological capabilities and costs (especially with respect to high-speed networking) would change dramatically. Thus, multiple phases were defined and this briefing focuses on interface developments in the first phase of the overall project. The first two years of work have involved three major iterations, which are detailed below.

Iteration 1: Concept Prototype

By the end of the project, the resource library is expected to grow to over 50,000 objects so the first prototype focused on the problem of how teachers could explore and search the available resources. In addition to the traditional keyword search strategy, we chose to use the dynamic query approach [1] because we thought it would encourage teachers to explore the library, not just search for specific resources. Dynamic query (DQ) applications support fast and easy exploration of data by allowing users to make queries by adjusting sliders and selecting buttons while the search results are continuously updated in a visual display (e.g., x/y scatterplot, map, etc.).

The aim of this prototype was to provide a tangible platform for discussing the pedagogical functionality for exploring the resource library and to introduce the dynamic query interface. We chose to develop the prototype using the PC-based Visual Basic because it allowed us to demonstrate our ideas to teachers very quickly. The data displayed was entirely mocked up for demonstration purposes.

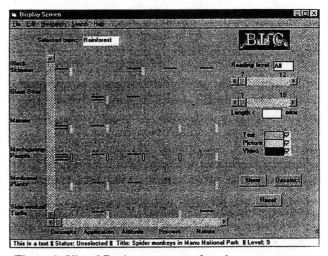

Figure 1. Visual Basic prototype of explorer component

To start, a subject (e.g., science, social studies) and a topic (e.g., chemistry, geography) were selected. Then the resulting resources were shown on an x/y display where the x axis showed outcomes and the y axis showed subtopics (Figure 1). Selecting a topic-outcome region displayed detailed bibliographic information for the selected resources. The axes were chosen to help teachers map their current practice of searching for materials by topic to outcomes of student learning which are the basis of assessment. A drawback of the x/y display was the number of resources mapped to the same point so we needed a strategy for handling this overlap (iteration 2). Controls also illustrated how users could filter the display by reading level (for text), resource type, and length.

Teachers' initial reactions to the explorer component were positive so we proceeded to build a WWW based system that teachers could actually use to create and present instructional modules.

Iteration 2: Web Prototype

Whereas the concept prototype focused solely on the search function, the web prototype considered three main functions: planning instructional modules (module construction component), searching for resources to use in modules (explorer component), and using the completed modules in class (presentation component). Thus, we created the first prototypes of the module construction and presentation components, and continued the development of the explorer component. Other components such as teleconferencing will be added in coming years.

The first module construction prototype used a simple HTML-based, form fill-in style interface with five main sections: a general heading section, a before instruction section, a during instruction section, an after instruction section, and a reflections section (Figure 2). The information contained in each of the sections was based on teacher input. A direct link to the MSPAP outcomes was provided so outcomes could easily be copied and pasted into teacher's modules. This approach also allows other states to plug in their outcomes very easily and with minimal change.

The first presentation prototype displayed a simple HTML module summary that allowed teachers to display resources by clicking on their URL links and to print out hard copies of their modules. After using the presentation component, teachers requested the addition of a simple slide show function that would make it easier to display the resources during class.

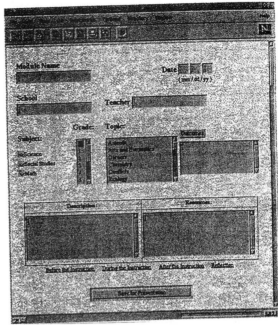

Figure 2. First module construction prototype

In continuing the explorer development, we moved from the conceptual Visual Basic prototype to a functional Code Warrior prototype that could run on Apple Macintoshs (Figure 3). Our intent was to integrate the explorer component with the other components by making it a Netscape plug-in. Major design changes included displaying overlapping resources as bar charts color coded by type, using real resource data, and providing image and video previews (four static key frames). We are using software that automatically detects scene changes to help automate the key frame selection process [3].

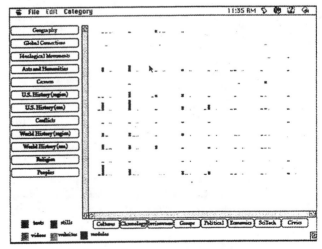

Figure 3. Code Warrior prototype of explorer component

Even though the display was very sparse initially, it allowed us to visualize which topics and outcomes had more resources and the quantity of various resource types (e.g., images, videos, etc.). Selecting a bar caused a popup window to appear with a list of titles and a preview specific to the given object (see Figure 4 for an example of a video object).

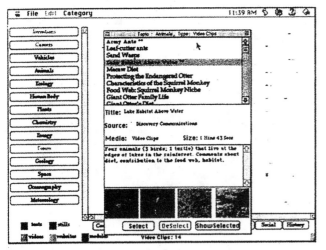

Figure 4. Popup details window showing static key frame video preview

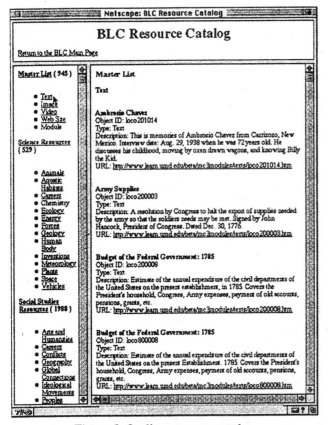

Figure 5. On-line resource catalog

Even though the Code Warrior version of the explorer was functional, it was still not integrated with the module construction component and had to be run as a standalone application. However, teachers were still able to begin creating their own modules by typing in the URLs for the resources they wanted to use. As an alternative to the paper catalogs some teachers were using to find resources

in the library, we created a simple HTML resource catalog that allowed them to search, print, and view resources on-line (Figure 5). This simple, interim solution enhanced the usability of the current system for many of the teachers during the 1996-97 academic year.

Iteration 3: Beta System

In the beta system, all the components were integrated to work from the main BLC web page and re-implemented in Java. Our original intention was to create a Netscape plug-in from the Code Warrior explorer but given the rapid development of Java tools and the difficulties of creating plug-ins for Netscape in a project where components would change each year, we decided to re-implement all the components in Java. This allowed us to build an integrated suite of tools available on the WWW with the added advantage that the tools would be platform independent (for the most part). This opportunity also allowed us to incorporate many significant design changes recommended by the teachers into the revised components. Overall, we tried to minimize the amount of scrolling and reduce popup windows whenever possible. Screen real estate was also an issue since teacher machines could only display 640x480 pixels.

In the module construction component, we added tabs for quick access to sections, multiple mechanisms for adding resources (e.g., explorer, resource catalog, personal resources (not in resource library)), and a section for controlling access level (read/write permissions) (Figure 6). This version not only added new functionality for the teachers but also greatly compacted the design.

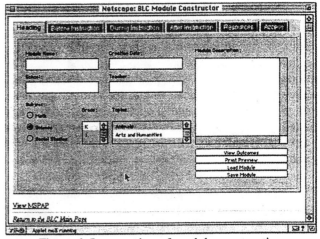

Figure 6. Java version of module construction

New functionality was also added to the explorer component (Figure 7) such as color coding by different attributes (e.g., type, source, etc.), changing axis attributes (e.g., topic, outcome, type, source, etc.), and "slide show" video previews that do not limit the number of key frames (Figure 8). In addition to bar charts, the explorer now supports jittered starfield displays (another alternative to

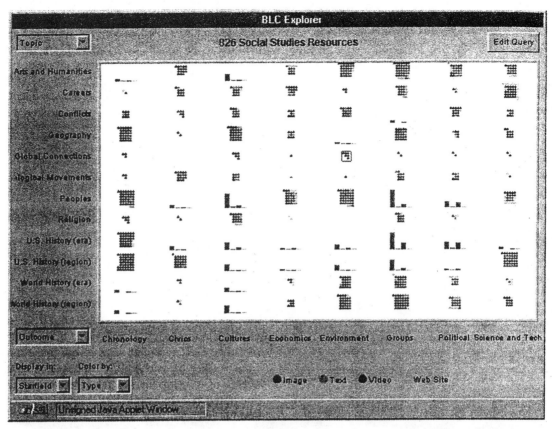

Figure 7. Java version of explorer showing available social studies resources in "jittered" display

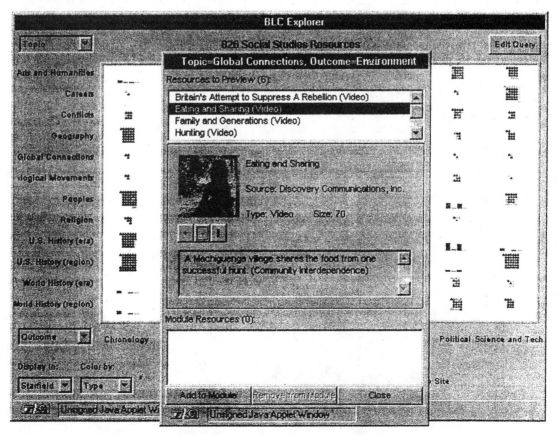

Figure 8. "Slide Show" video preview

the overlap problem) where all the resources mapped to the same point are shown by color coded dots circling the point. When too many resources are mapped to the same point (>50), a bar chart is shown.

Controls for querying by subject, type, source, and keyword are also provided (Figure 9). Initially the explorer supported dynamic querying (as a user manipulated a query control the display results on the starfield were updated simultaneously) but because of slow network speed users are now required to submit their queries (by pressing a button) before the results are displayed.

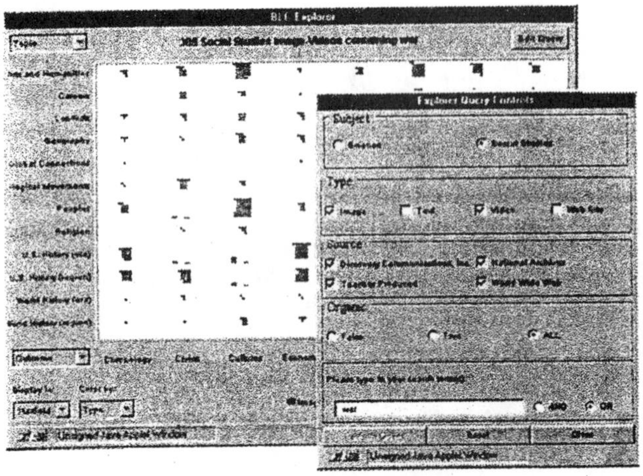

Figure 9. Query controls for filtering explorer display

Major changes to the presentation component included providing quick access to module sections and adding "slide show" controls to allow teachers to present their modules (Figure 10). For the 1997-98 school year, videos will be loaded from CD-ROM or local hard disk while we install video serving capabilities on the server and high-speed connectivity in the schools.

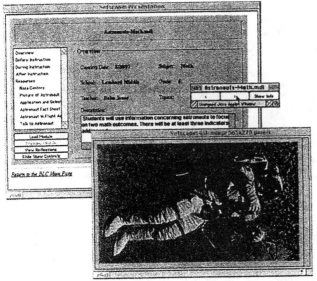

Figure 10. Java version of Presentation component

INFORMAL USABILITY TESTING

In addition to after school in-service meetings and periodic visits to the classrooms during the school year, the project brings all the teachers together each summer for a three day summer institute. At the 1996 institute, teachers used the web prototype components to construct sample modules and made suggestions for what became iteration 3. Since the explorer component was not functional, they used paper catalogs and web search engines to locate objects. During the 1996-97 school year, teachers mainly used web resources and some images in their modules while we worked on adding video to the library and developed the beta system.

Before the 1997 summer institute, teachers were asked to create a module using the old system (iteration 2). At that time, the resource library consisted of approximately 1000 resources with only 6 hours of indexed video. During the institute, the fourteen teachers who participated were introduced to the beta system and used it to enhance their existing modules by adding video and to construct new modules. The concept of what constituted a module varied from teacher to teacher. Some modules contained slide shows of several images or video clips, while others integrated non-computer tasks and were meant to span several days. The project leader for the teachers demonstrated how the system could be used to create a module very quickly. In 8 minutes, he created a module for discussing the patterns evident in a series of cities (images) by using the explorer to select resources. After he presented his module, we noticed more teachers trying the explorer rather than depending only on the resource catalog.

Overall, teachers thought the new components were more compact, intuitive, and easier to use. On a scale from 1 to 10 where 10 is worse, teachers rated planning time (9.4) and class time (8.5) as their biggest problems in implementing this project in their classrooms. The complexity of the system (1.9) and the software (3.3) were not considered obstacles. After using the new components for one day, teachers had the lowest comfort level with the explorer (3.9 out of 5) which was not surprising considering they had seen and reacted to prototypes but had never actually used a dynamic query application and were used to using the resource catalog.

One teacher noted that the improved module construction component (iteration 3) was "easier to use because you don't have to scroll up and down so much." Teachers also liked that the explorer was "compact, color coded" and the ability to explore/search by topic. Another teacher commented: "The dittered dots allowed me to know the general idea of how the resources are distributed." However, the explorer is very slow to load so some teachers preferred to copy and paste resource information from the resource catalog. Teachers also "surf the web" to find resources since the resource library is not very large yet. The slide show feature was definitely the most popular improvement to the presentation component.

During a discussion of when and how the modules will be used in September and October, one teacher noted: "I think the BLC project has taught me a great deal about how to use the technology in the classroom as a <u>tool</u> and not as a <u>play</u> toy for my students. They really get involved with learning." Another interesting observation echoed by several project staff was how teachers went to other teachers for help rather than always depending on a staff member -- a sign of an emerging community.

It was not surprising that teacher's reactions were very positive since they had been involved in the design of the system from the beginning. However, several usability issues did emerge during the institute that will be incorporated into future versions. Some of these are simple oversights or features not completed in time for the summer institute, but others require new functionality.

1. Allow users to edit personal resources - Initially, users could only add and delete personal resources so if they needed to make a change, like changing a URL that is out of date, they had to delete the resource then add it again with the new information. Teachers were constantly frustrated when they wanted to make minor adjustments to the personal resources that they included in their modules. Functionality to edit personal resources has been added in the latest version.

2. Move the save/load buttons in the module construction component to the bottom - At first the save/load buttons were only visible in the heading section so several teachers lost their work because they forgot to save their modules. The buttons have now been moved to the bottom of the tabbed panel and are visible from all sections. Messages to warn users of any unsaved changes will also be added in the future.

3. Add functionality to print hard copy of module - Teachers are required to turn in lesson plans that take a significant amount of time to prepare. This functionality was missing from the system initially but adding it has made using the system much more practical for the teachers.

4. Add a field to indicate the intended length of a module - Now that more modules are being created and teachers are sharing their creations with others, it would be useful to know the length of instruction, an hour or a few weeks.

5. Implement word wrap – Word wrap is not implemented in the module construction component and only primitively in the presentation component. This seemingly minor functionality causes the teachers a fair amount of frustration since they format their text in the module construction component then see it displayed very differently in the presentation component (due to inconsistent implementation and different sized text boxes). We realized this would be an issue before summer institute but did not have the time to add and coordinate word wrap.

6. Load the resource library more quickly in the explorer – One of the chief complaints when using the explorer is that it is too slow to load. Currently, the resource library is loaded from a flat file stored on the server. As the resource library grows, the problem will only worsen so we need a solution that will scale up. Some of the alternatives we are investigating include using more efficient data structures or a real database engine.

In addition to the summer institute, teachers have started having weekly professional education workshops that allow them to discuss how they are using the components in their classrooms with other teachers and get help with any problems they are having. The University is also using this forum as an opportunity to educate teachers about the indexing process so we can start migrating this task over to the teachers. We have also started looking at web server logs to understand when teachers are using the system and which components are used most often.

LESSONS LEARNED
After three iterations, we learned several important (and sometimes surprising) lessons that can benefit future developers.

Provide alternative search strategies - Providing different alternatives (e.g., explorer, resource catalog, keyword search) for teachers to search for resources enhanced the overall usability of the system by allowing users to choose the tool that best suits their work style, their computing environment, and the task at hand. The explorer's dynamic query interface provides an overview of all the available resources and allows users to search and explore using a variety of controls but its current implementation requires a fairly fast CPU with sufficient memory. Teachers working at home on slower machines through modem connections would more likely prefer to use the resource catalog or a simple keyword search. Using the resource catalog or keyword search is sufficient when searching for a specific resource. Some teachers may even prefer to work from a hard copy of the resource catalog that they can read at their leisure.

Provide "quick fixes" until functionality is available – There is always a tradeoff between waiting for a fully functional system and implementing interim solutions. Some developers may view interim solutions as a waste of time since they will be discarded when the final system is developed but in our case we were not only building a system but we were also building a community. Communities are defined by personal involvement so it is important for users start using the system early and contribute to its design on an ongoing basis. In the coming year, we plan on installing video streaming software on the server. In the mean time, the system has been configured to play videos from CD-ROMs given to the schools. The resource catalog was another interim solution that was built while the integrated explorer component was being developed. User reaction to the resource catalog was so positive that we decided to keep it in the current version even though the explorer was functional. These interim solutions have allowed teachers to use the system while development continues and in some cases have altered the system design.

1500 resources is very small – Collecting, cataloging, and indexing is a very time consuming process. Currently, it is being done by a few UMD graduate students. Even with 1500 resources it is still hit or miss whether teachers find what they need. For some topics, like space, there is a lot of material but for others there is very little. One benefit of using the explorer is that teachers can see how the resources are distributed. For example, there are currently more social studies resources than science resources and most of the videos are on science topics. Discussions regarding the process for contributing resources to the community library are ongoing.

Seemingly minor functionality can become a major usability roadblock – Most of the suggested changes were things we planned on fixing in the future but it was still surprising how much frustration they caused. Some of the problems were present in previous versions but had only come to the foreground in the beta prototype. This is most likely because teachers were now presented with an integrated system that they could really start using in their classrooms so they were more focused on usability.

Building a community takes time – It is no surprise that in many systems like ours the biggest challenges are social and political, not technical. While there are several technical challenges we still need to tackle, our ultimate goal is to build an electronic learning community. Early on we provided teachers with instructional tools and email in an effort to help "grow" our community. As the community grows and teachers become more comfortable with the technology, the system will continue to evolve and teachers will become even more active participants in the design process. By working with the early adopters, we hope to hasten the adoption of the system by others teachers.

CONCLUSION

In three iterations we went from a concept prototype that illustrated our ideas to a beta system that teachers actually use to create instructional modules. Involving teachers in the design process early on has enhanced the usability of the system and has helped "grow" the community. As designers we have learned the value of providing alternative strategies for performing tasks, the benefit of interim solutions, how time consuming it is to build a library, and that it is difficult to build a community. As teachers start using their modules more extensively in their classrooms, the system design will continue to evolve. Our current efforts are focused on collecting additional resources, implementing video streaming on the server, responding to teacher feedback, and assessing the impact of the project on teaching and learning. The system will continue to grow along with the community.

ACKNOWLEDGMENTS
We acknowledge the support of the U.S. Department of Education Technology Grant (#R303A50051) to the Baltimore City Public Schools. Thanks are due to the BCPS teachers and UMCP faculty and students who form the BLC community.

REFERENCES

1. Ahlberg, C., Williamson, C., & Shneiderman, B. Dynamic queries for information exploration: An implementation and evaluation. *Proceedings of CHI '92*, (Monterey, CA, May 3-7, 1992), ACM Press, 619-626.

2. Kafai, Y. & Resnick, M., *Constructivism in practice: designing, thinking, and learning in a digital world.* Lawrence Erlbaum, Mahwah, NJ, 1996.

3. Kobla, V., Doermann, D., & Rosenfield, A., Compressed domain video segmentation. *Technical Report CAR-TR-839*, University of Maryland, 1996.

4. Marchionini, G., Nolet, V., Williams, H., Ding, W., Beale, J., Rose, A., Gordon, A., Enomoto, E., & Harbinson, L. Content + Connectivity => Community: Digital Resources for a Learning Community. *Proceedings of Digital Libraries '97*, (Philadelphia, PA, July 23-26, 1997), ACM Press, 212-220.

5. Nolet, V., Marchionini, G., Enomoto, E. Full Motion Video and Dynamic Query in a Networked Learning Community. *Proceedings of EDMEDIA '97*, (Calgary, June 14-19, 1997), AACE, 777-78.

6. Pea, R., Computer support for knowledge building communities. In T. Koschmann (Ed.) *Computer support for collaborative learning: Theory and practice of an emerging paradigm.* Lawrence Erlbaum , Mahwah, NJ, 1996.

Visualizing Digital Library Search Results with Categorical and Hierarchical Axes

Ben Shneiderman*, David Feldman, Anne Rose, and Xavier Ferré Grau

Human-Computer Interaction Laboratory
Department of computer Science and *Institute for Systems Research
University of Maryland, College Park, MD 20742
http://www.cs.umd.edu/hcil
Email: ben@cs.umd.edu

ABSTRACT

Digital library search results are usually shown as a textual list, with 10-20 items per page. Viewing several thousand search results at once on a two-dimensional display with continuous variables is a promising alternative. Since these displays can overwhelm some users, we created a simplified two-dimensional display that uses categorical and hierarchical axes, called *hieraxes*. Users appreciate the meaningful and limited number of terms on each hieraxis. At each grid point of the display we show a cluster of color-coded dots or a bar chart. Users see the entire result set and can then click on labels to move down a level in the hierarchy. Handling broad hierarchies and arranging for imposed hierarchies led to additional design innovations. We applied hieraxes to a digital video library of science topics used by middle school teachers, a legal information system, and a technical library using the ACM Computing Classification System. Feedback from usability testing with 32 subjects revealed strengths and weaknesses.

KEYWORDS: Digital libraries, graphical user interfaces, information visualization, hierarchy, categorical axes, hieraxes

INTRODUCTION

Digital library researchers face numerous challenges in helping users find what they want. Among them are designing meaningful overviews so that patterns can be easily recognized, creating comprehensible interfaces to specify what they want, and providing effective displays of search results. The visual information seeking mantra: overview first, zoom and filter, then details on demand provides a good starting point, but interpreting the mantra has produced a remarkably diverse set of research and commercial interfaces (Shneiderman, 1998; Card, Mackinlay and Shneiderman, 1999;

http://otal.umd.edu/Olive). Within this body of work, two important strategies are (1) two-dimensional visualizations and (2) browsers for hierarchical data sets.

Two-dimensional visualizations with meaningful axes have been an effective visualization strategy because thousands of items can be shown at once. Typical axes make use of continuous variables (for example, relevance or publication date) or categorical variables (for example, language or name of journal). The labels on such axes are cues to searchers and may contain valuable information if they are ordinal variables. Two-dimensional visualizations with non-meaningful axes have been tried in systems such as BEAD (Chalmers and Chitson, 1992), BIRD (Kim and Korfhage, 1994), and ThemeScape (Wise, Thomas, Pennock, Lantrip, Pottier, Schur, and Crow, 1995) (commercial version is at http://www.cartia.com). Clusters of documents in a two-dimensional space can be meaningful, but users can make mistakes in assuming that distances between clusters have strong significance.

Hierarchical browsers are common and often successful, such as Yahoo! Hierarchies have the potential to reduce complexity by organizing related information into comprehensible structures. Some hierarchies, such as the Dewey Decimal System, are fairly straightforward trees. Others, such as the National Library of Medicine's Medical Subject Headings (MeSH), the Universal Medical Language System (UMLS) (Pratt, 1997), and the ACM Computing Classification System are partially hierarchical, multi-hierarchical (organized simultaneously into multiple hierarchies), or otherwise complicated. Hierarchies are typically shown by textual lists of one level at a time, by node-link diagrams, cóne trees (Hearst and Karadi, 1997) or by an outliner in which levels and branches can be expanded and contracted (Nation, Plaisant, Marchionini, and Komlodi, 1997).

In this paper we apply hierarchical axes, also referred to as *hieraxes*, to combine the power of a hierarchical browse tool with a two-dimensional visualization. This combination preserves visual overviews and enables users to rapidly comprehend search results. We focus on search results that may include 100 to 10,000 items, but we anticipate that hieraxes may be useful for viewing much larger sets of

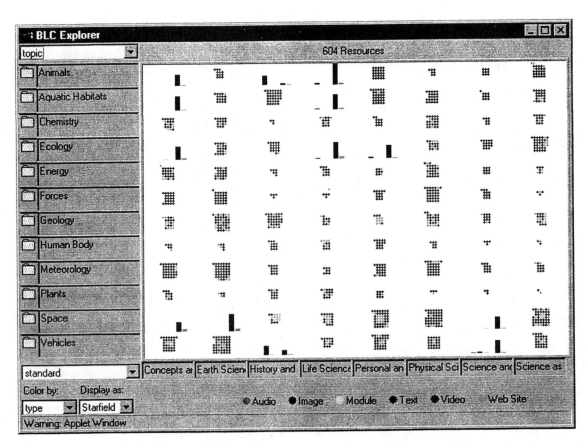

Figure 1: Early version of GRIDL, displaying a single hierarchical y-axis at the top level

items or entire digital libraries. We describe our initial work on a digital video library for middle school teachers, a legal information system, and a computer science library. Then we discuss design alternatives for hieraxes and report on a usability study. We call our interface GRIDL, a Graphical Interface for Digital Libraries, to convey its grid-like design.

PREVIOUS RESEARCH

Two-dimensional displays with meaningful axes have been used successfully to show document spaces, such as in Envision (Fox, Hix, Nowell, Brueni, Wake, Heath, Lenwood, and Rao, 1993; Nowell, France, Hix, Heath, Lenwood, and Fox, 1996) and FilmFinder (Ahlberg and Shneiderman, 1993). FilmFinder's x-axis was fixed as the year of a film's production, and its y-axis was the film's popularity (number of video rentals, on a scale of 1-9). Each spot on the graph was color-coded by film type (drama, action, musical, etc.). The commercial expansion of this tool (Ahlberg and Wistrand, 1995), Spotfire (http://www.spotfire.com) allows any spreadsheet data set to be visualized. Spotfire allows both continuous and categorical variables to be put on either axis or used for color and size coding (continuous variables are color-coded using a spectrum, categorical variables with a set of discrete colors). Shape and rotation are available options, but these codings are less easily perceived. Changes to the axes or codings can be made in a few seconds.

Our experience and Spotfire's commercial success shows

that it is powerful, but that some training is needed. Moreover, some users find the rich display and extensive controls (including control panels, sliders, and zooming) confusing. Additionally, the potential clutter of color-coded, size-coded, overlapping spots requires users to plan their visualizations carefully. Labels and lines connecting related items add further challenges for novice users.

Tree structures are commonly presented as indented outlines that can be scrolled and opened or closed to expose or hide levels – as in Microsoft's Windows Explorer, Allen's "Dewey GUI" (Allen, 1995a) or WebTOC (Nation et al., 1997). Trees represented as node-link diagrams are useful, but as they grow to include thousands of nodes and many levels, layout and navigation problems become serious. Treemaps ensure a fixed-size presentation, but are complex, and many users require 15-20 minutes of training (Johnson and Shneiderman, 1991). Allen (1995b) described two "facet space" browsers for exploring multi-hierarchical (multi-dimensionally hierarchical) data sets. However, these tools did not allow users to view their data along categorical axes. On an axis, a hierarchy must be represented one-dimensionally, so we chose the metaphor of opening and closing folders to move up and down the hierarchy, displaying one level at a time.

THE BALTIMORE LEARNING COMMUNITY

The need for hieraxes arose in designing user interfaces for the Baltimore Learning Community. This digital library consists of approximately 2000 educational resources, including digital video, websites, and images, for a community of thirty middle school teachers. In addition to several categorical and continuous fields, each resource was also indexed according to a three-level curriculum hierarchy (subject/topic/subtopic) to make searching easier. Teachers needed to be able to find resources of interest quickly, without the burden of complex controls. In response to usability testing with 14 teachers (Rose, Ding, Marchionini, Beale Jr., and Nolet, 1998) we created the first version of GRIDL (then called Dotfire, since it was a variant of Spotfire) that supports limited hierarchies (Figure 1).

GRIDL uses categorical variables to organize search results on a two-dimensional grid. Categorical axis variables reduce the number of XY regions and increase overlap (i.e., many data points are mapped to the same XY region). In GRIDL, displaying each region as a cluster of dots (one for each data point in the region) solves the overlap problem. If there are more than 49 items in a region, a bar chart showing the frequency of each type of object replaces the cluster. Users can click on a cluster or bar chart to reveal a list of resource titles. Selecting an item in this list provides a more detailed description. GRIDL supports basic hierarchical axes. In Figure 1, the y-axis shows science topics (the second level of the curriculum hierarchy). Users can refine their searches by clicking on the folder icon to the left of an axis value, which expands the selected category and filters the display. For example, clicking on the "Animals" folder changes the y-axis to display only Animal subtopics (Birds, Mammals, etc.) and filters the result set so only Animal resources are displayed (Figure 2). Users can click on the "up" icon at the top of the axis to return to the science topic level.

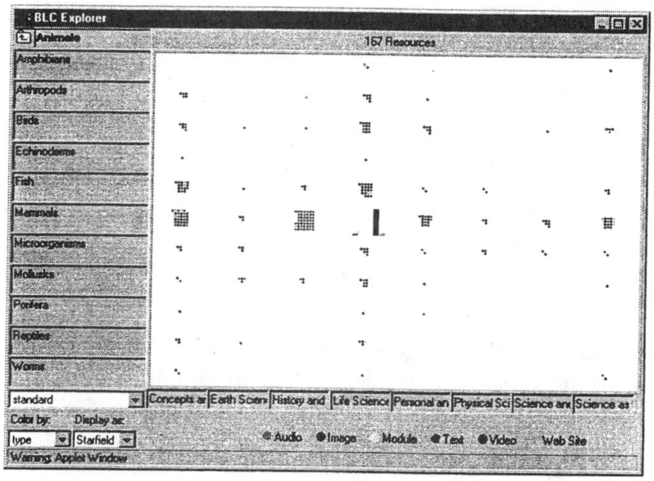

Figure 2: Expanding the "Animals" Category on the y-axis in the early version of GRIDL

However, the early version of GRIDL only handled the three-level curriculum hierarchy, and does not generalize to other hierarchies. It displays the immediate supercategory of the user's current location, but not the complete browse history. And it does not handle axis variables with large value sets (more than 15). Even with a relatively small set, all the values are added to the axis, thereby forcing the potential truncation of long names (Figure 3).

Concepts ar | Earth Scien | History and | Life Science | Personal an | Physical Sci | Science an | Science as

Figure 3: An Overcrowded Axis

LEGAL INFORMATION DIGITAL LIBRARY

Our interest in hieraxes grew in conducting research for WestGroup Publishers. Their digital library provides access to 12 million online cases, numerous statutes, and other valuable resources for the legal community. However, searching this digital library requires careful thought; a search result set could easily include tens of thousands of items, and users have pressing demands for comprehensiveness in their legal research. Finding a few relevant cases is rarely sufficient. Many search situations require review of every potentially relevant case and an understanding of the range of existing precedents.

WestGroup maintains an elaborate hierarchy of terms called the Key Number system. As this hierarchy is used as a topical index of cases and headnotes, its inclusion in our legal research system was crucial. The first three levels (473 items) are meaningful and familiar to many lawyers, but still complex. The entire 85,000-item hierarchy is many more levels deep, extremely complex, and specialists become familiar only with branches relevant to their work. A portion of the hierarchy is displayed below with the total number of branches for each item shown in parentheses:

- Persons (5)
- Natural Persons (16)
  - …
  - Drugs and Narcotics
  - Drugs and Druggists in General (31)
  - Narcotics and Dangerous Drugs (145)
    - …
    - Search under warrant
    - In general
    - Issuance, requisites, and validity of warrants in general (2)
    - Affidavits, complaints, and evidence for issuance of warrants (5)
      - In general
      - Probable cause in general
      - Error or ambiguity; omissions
      - Informants
      - In general
      - Personal knowledge
      - Reliability; corroboration
      - Confidential/unnamed informants
      - …
    - Execution and return of warrants in general (5)
    - Disposition of property

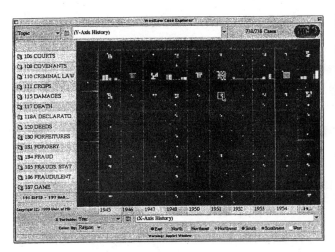

Figure 4a: GRIDL with hieraxis widgets for legal information, showing hierarchical data on the y-axis

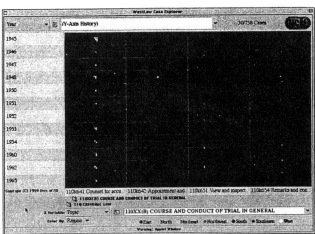

Figure 4b: GRIDL showing legal information after two category expansions on the x-axis, 110 Criminal Law and 110XX(B) Course and Conduct of Trial in General

- ■ …
  - o Food
  - o …
- Property (4)
- Contracts (4)
- Torts (0 at level 2,16 directly at level 3)
- Crimes (0 at level 2, 56 directly at level 3)
- Remedies (13)
- Government (6)

Both depth and breadth are variable: a particular item may have as few as 2 branches or over 100, and the tree is as shallow as 2 levels in some places and as deep as 7 in others. Items are not always ordered alphabetically or numerically.

Other hierarchies relevant to legal research are geographical region and court district. In addition, some ordinal non-hierarchical fields (such as dates, relevance, numbers of citations, and names) can have hierarchies imposed on them to improve ease of use (see Imposed Hierarchies below).

A scenario for a legal information seeker might deal with a case on "stolen furniture". The search might produce a 738 items in the result set. Displaying these on a grid with year along the x-axis and Key Number along the y-axis reveals that most of the cases found were under Criminal Law (Figure 4a). Another way to look at the result set would be to put the years on the y-axis and then move down the hierarchy on the x-axis (Figure 4b).

In trying to use GRIDL with this data set, we realized that more comprehensive hierarchy support would be necessary, and began development on the general purpose hieraxis widget. We made some modifications to GRIDL itself, and then wrote the hieraxis widgets in Java, including an API to allow them to work with diverse applications.

HIERARCHICAL AXES: HIERAXES
In response to the challenge of serving legal information searchers, we developed a general purpose hierarchical axis

widget for GRIDL and other applications, termed a hieraxis. Our goal was to support hieraxes on both x and y axes in a convenient manner that preserved screen space for viewing result sets, and to provide full-featured widgets for applications which meet the following criteria:

- Includes a two-dimensional visualization for which it is desirable that the user be able to change axis variables
- Data must include some categorical fields
- Data set must be large enough to necessitate some sort of management strategy

Categorical Zooming
Visualizations have been tried with both continuous and categorical/discrete axis variables. Though zooming on one or both axes has been a familiar concept for some time with continuous variables, it has not been used with categorical variables. Partly this is because "zooming" generally applies to continuous spaces. However, drilling down into a hierarchy is, in essence, categorical zooming. Such a process is already familiar to users in browse tools such as Yahoo, but not in conjunction with visualizations. We applied hieraxes to a two-dimensional visualization, explored design alternatives, and conducted a usability test (Figure 4a and b show the legal information system Key Topics and Figure 4c and 4d show the ACM Computing Classification System).

Browse History: Maintaining Context
As mentioned above, one shortcoming of GRIDL's original hierarchy support was the potential to get lost in a confusing hierarchy (Chimera and Shneiderman, 1994). To alleviate this, we added a simple browse history to the hieraxes. For each axis, users see their current location in the hierarchy in a drop-down list and as an indented series of labeled folder icons. Users can zoom out to any supercategory of their current location by selecting from the drop-down list or clicking on a folder (see Figure 4). Users can also zoom out one level by clicking on a standard "Up Level" icon near the browse history drop-down.

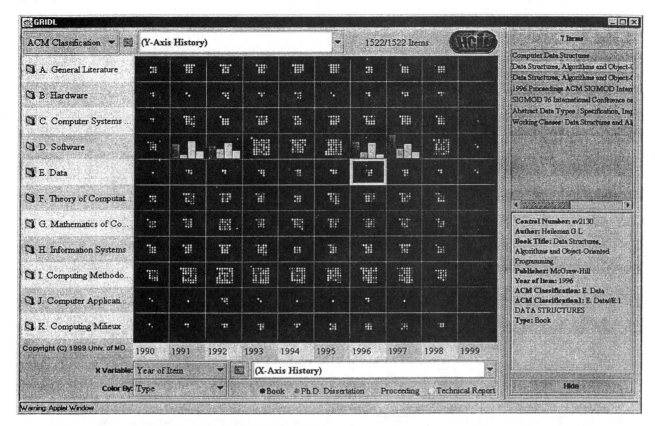

Figure 4c: GRIDL with the ACM Computing Classification System, after user clicks on a cluster

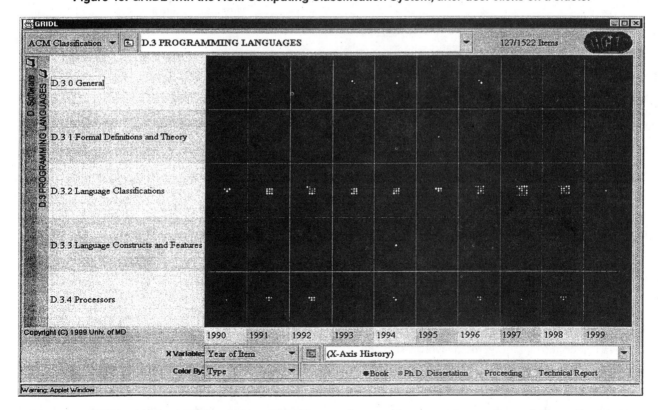

**Figure 4d: GRIDL with the ACM Computing Classification System after two category expansions on the x-axis,
D. Software and D.3 Programming Languages**

Any feature that allows users to view a subset of the entire visualization risks confusing them, causing users to lose their place. The browse history can help users remain aware of their location in the data set despite the fact that they may not be viewing the entire data set. By starting at the top, making all data exclusions user-driven, and providing an easy-to-use history we hope to reduce disorientation.

Hieraxes and Filtering

Some visualization tools have dynamic axes, for which the variable can be changed rapidly. With hieraxes, application developers can employ a powerful data filtering mechanism that allows a visualization to serve simultaneously as a search tool and results display.

If users filter such a display using categorical zooming, then select a new axis variable, the new variable's values will be displayed, but the displayed data will not increase; whatever data has been excluded by previous operations will continue to be excluded. Through successive category expansions (exclusions by zooming) and re-categorizations (changes of axis variable), users can graphically locate the information they desire. In this way we can continue to blur the unnecessary line between query and results. However, this approach might eventually need to be coupled with a more sophisticated search history, since the user's actions can no longer be represented accurately as a linear series of category expansions.

GRIDL does not employ this filtering mechanism, as such functionality is somewhat outside its scope: if users select a new axis variable, the axis returns to the entire data set.

Overcrowded Axes (Broad Hierarchies)

Often, categorical axis data is extensive: with hundreds or even thousands of discrete items. If the data is large enough, no labeling scheme can possibly enumerate all data items or distinguish among regions of the visualization (see Figure 3). We considered several solutions and implemented some of them (Figure 5).

Tool Tips (Figure 5a). For slightly crowded axes, a solution akin to Microsoft's tool tips is effective. Each axis label can be truncated to fit in the available space; moving the mouse pointer over a label reveals its full text, temporarily obscuring adjacent labels. However, if space becomes even more limited and no more than a few letters of a label can be displayed, users will not have adequate information to determine which labels interest them. If the axis becomes crowded enough, space may not be available for even a single letter.

A y-axis variant on the tool tip approach involves showing all tool tips at once when users mouse over the axis, or temporarily expanding the axis width to accommodate the labels. GRIDL implements standard tool tips on the x-axis, and temporary axis expansion on the y-axis.

Additional solutions exist when axes are only slightly overcrowded. Angling the axis labels, labeling in two or three staggered rows, and similar strategies can increase the number of readable labels significantly. But, as with tool tips, these techniques are ineffective when the number of items becomes too large, and users are once again faced with overcrowding.

Imposed Hierarchies (Figure 5b). There may be an appropriate hierarchical grouping – alphabetical, chronological, numerical, etc. – that can be imposed on the data before transfer to an axis, creating a hierarchy on the fly. If the grouping can be done in a meaningful manner, the groups will be comprehensible to users, who can then expand a group as they would a category in a semantic hierarchy. In particular, categorical but ordinal variables work well with this method: fields like date, age, rank, etc. which can easily be ordered, and therefore grouped, in a meaningful way (see Figure 5b).

Paging (Figure 5c). Another possibility is *paging*. If a display has room for 16 columns and the axis field has 80 items, the first 15 columns can be displayed as usual, with the 16th representing the remaining 65 items. The user will be able to see from the visualization how much data is contained in those 65 columns, and can move to the next "page" of data by clicking on a folder or arrow icon next to the 16th item in the x-axis. The distinction between the first 15 columns and the 16th column can be further highlighted by a different background color. If users are on a page other than the first or last, the first and last columns will contain the contents of all previous and remaining pages, respectively. This strategy has the advantage of maintaining a display of all data at all times, but a potential disadvantage of user disorientation due to too much paging. GRIDL implements paging.

Scroll/Zoom (Figure 5d). A fourth strategy is a combination scroll/zoom technique, using range (double-box) sliders as Spotfire does. All items are placed on the axis, but compressed together with labels minimized or removed when the entire display is visible. Users can zoom in on an area of the axis by decreasing the range of the slider and scroll along the axis by sliding the slider. At any time they can easily return to the full visualization by increasing the slider's range to its maximum. This strategy minimizes disorientation by maintaining users' connection with the full visualization and tightly linking the potentially confusing scrolling with zooming. However, with somewhat smaller data sets (16-100 items) this method is awkward as both scrolling and zooming become "chunky" and confusing.

Implementation Strategy. Our primary design for handling overcrowded axes is paging, supplemented by tool tips/axis expansion. However, paging through thousands of items is tedious. The other two strategies seem more compelling when the number of items is greater than a few hundred. Imposed hierarchies and scroll/zoom can speed the process of locating a known item (see Figure 5). Users could choose among imposed hierarchies, paging, and scroll/zoom by selecting from a pull-down menu.

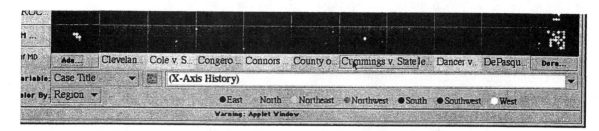

Figure 5a: Managing Overcrowded Axes: Tool Tips

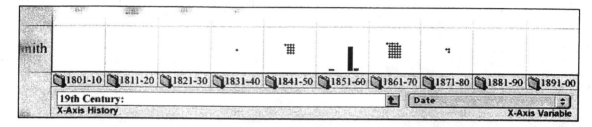

Figure 5b: Managing Overcrowded Axes: Imposed Hierarchies (Sketch)

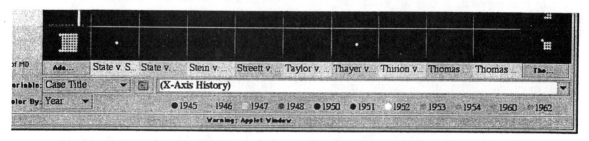

Figure 5c: Managing Overcrowded Axes: Paging

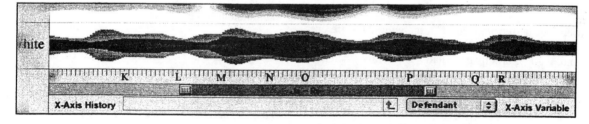

Figure 5d: Managing Overcrowded Axes: Scroll/Zoom (Sketch)

ACM COMPUTING CLASSIFICATION SYSTEM

Searching for articles related to a specific computing field can yield hundreds or thousands of records in big digital libraries, such as the ACM Digital Library, IEEE Computer Society Digital Library or INSPEC. GRIDL may be useful in this domain, by showing the data distributed according to the ACM Computing Classification System. This classification system contains 345 categories organized in a 3-level hierarchy, and it is widely known in the field.

The 11 first level links were easily accommodated, and all second and third levels can fit in the axis without paging.

We used GRIDL with bibliographic data taken from the database of the Computer Science Department Library at the University of Maryland. The library uses the ACM Computing Classification System for keyword searches.

The general-purpose design of the hieraxis widget allowed us to make the adaptation to this new domain in a short period of time, and with a low programming effort. Some new features were added, such as showing the database entry for the selected item in the description panel (lower right), and providing visual highlights about how data shown in the grid and the description panel are related (see Figure 4c).

USABILITY TEST

We tested GRIDL for the ACM Computing Classification System in two phases.

In the first set of tests we had 8 subjects, all of them computer science graduate students. After getting a 2-minute introduction to GRIDL, they were asked to perform 8 simple tasks using hieraxes.

Two tasks implied searching for a specific cluster in the grid, while the other 6 tasks implied comparison of clusters. Three tasks required distinguishing different color-coded items. Six tasks implied measuring the number of items in clusters.

Overall, test participants showed a good understanding of the concept of categorical zooming, and they were able to easily navigate through the hierarchy to find information. 7 participants accomplished 6 of the 8 tasks, and the remaining participant accomplished 5 of the 8 tasks.

Two participants suggested that more status information would be desirable, in order to reduce user disorientation. Two participants said it was helpful to get the number of items in a cell by clicking on them, they suggested using tool tips to give this information when moving the pointer to a cell. Two participants found temporary y-axis expansion annoying. Other improvements suggested by participants are:

- To make bar graph scale explicit.
- To provide more status information about the current position in the hierarchy.
- To order dots in a cell in a meaningful way.

We added vertical text labels with the categories (see figure 4d). This improvement was aimed at reducing user disorientation about their current position in the hierarchy.

We carried out a second set of tests with 24 different participants with greater diversity in their educational background: 10 participants had a library science background, 8 had a of computer science background, and 6 had other backgrounds.

After the 2-minute introduction, they were asked to perform 6 simple tasks, and to provide comments and suggestions about the tool. Two tasks required searching for a specific cluster in the grid, while the other 4 tasks required comparison of clusters and counting the number of items in clusters.

Seventy-one percent of the participants were able to complete the 6 tasks successfully, 8% completed 5 tasks, 13% completed 4 tasks, 4% completed 3 tasks, and 4% completed just 2 tasks.

The two main problems found by the participants were:

- "Clickability" of categories: 89% of participants clicked at least once on a category that could not be further expanded.
- Temporary-axis expansion: 49% of participants found it disturbing or annoying.

Participants with a library science background provided the following comments:

- 70% of them showed a high appreciation for the tool when asked about their impression.
- 50% of them compared the tool with other systems, stating that the kind of view that GRIDL offers cannot be obtained in other systems for exploring the contents of a library.

CONCLUSIONS AND FUTURE DIRECTIONS

Hieraxes, in combination with a grid display, offer a simple approach to browsing search result sets. Users can see an overview by color-coded dots or bar charts arranged in a grid and organized by familiar labeled categories. They can probe further by zooming in on desired categories or switching to another hierarchical variable. Our early success with middle school teachers has encouraged our development of a general-purpose tool. GRIDL was refined by applying it to the legal information Key Topics and the ACM Computing Classification System. Usability tests gave us insights for further developments and the encouragement to consider using GRIDL to visualize a complete library.

Although the basic idea of hieraxes is appealing to many users, not every user is visually oriented. For example, some legal researchers will prefer to see 20 titles of cases at a time, rather than 2000 color-coded dots. For digital libraries that do not have existing hierarchical categorizations, the imposed hierarchies may provide some benefit, but paging through long lists of authors or other unique (or relatively unique variables) could be tedious. Rapid visual exploration may be useful for some users and tasks, but it might undermine the willingness of users to reconsider their initial search terms. These and the following issues will be examined in future work:

Making Sure the User doesn't Get Lost

Though much of our effort has focused on avoiding user disorientation, it may continue to be a problem. Prominent indications of the user's location, carefully chosen icons, and animation may help with this, as well as a more extensive and intuitive search/browse history.

Multiple-Category Expansion

In many cases, users may want to expand several (adjacent) categories at once. This can be accomplished by allowing users to band-select several categories at once, expanding them onto the axis together. This could prove especially useful for ordinal axis fields and well-constructed hierarchies in which proximity is meaningful.

Category Expansion through Direct User-Visualization Interaction

Forcing the user to click on the axes in order to expand the visualization is comprehensible but a more direct alternative is to allow users to select portions of the visualization itself to expand, on one or both axes (depending on the shape of the selection).

Three-Dimensional Hieraxes

Our current work extends the early GRIDL functionality by including robust x- and y-hieraxes, with support for greater depth and breadth, allowing users to visualize complex, multi-hierarchical data sets. However, addition of a third dimension, through an additional hieraxis or another method, might yield an even more powerful tool.

ACKNOWLEDGMENTS

We appreciate the support of WestGroup Publishers and the U.S. Dept of Education Technology Grant (#R303A50051) to the Baltimore City Public Schools. We thank Robert B. Allen for his thoughtful comments on a draft of this paper.

REFERENCES

Ahlberg, Christopher and Shneiderman, Ben, Visual information seeking: Tight coupling of dynamic query filters with starfield displays, *Proc. CHI'94 Conference: Human Factors in Computing Systems*, ACM, New York, (1994), 313-321 + color plates.

Ahlberg, Christopher and Wistrand, Erik, IVEE: An information visualization & exploration environment, *Proc. IEEE Information Visualization '95*, IEEE Computer Press, Los Alamitos, CA (1995), 66-73.

Allen, Robert B., Two digital library interfaces that exploit hierarchical structure, *Proc. DAGS95: Electronic Publishing and the Information Superhighway* (1995).

Allen, R. B., Retrieval from facet spaces, *Electronic Publishing*, (1995), 247-257, 8.

Card, Stuart, Mackinlay, Jock, and Shneiderman, Ben, *Readings in Information Visualization: Using Vision to Think*, Morgan Kaufmann Publ., San Francisco (1999).

Chalmers, M. and Chitson, P, BEAD: Exploration in information visualization, *Proc. ACM SIGIR Conference*, ACM, New York (1992), 330-337.

Chimera, R. and Shneiderman, B., An exploratory evaluation of three interfaces for browsing large hierarchical tables of contents, *ACM Transactions on Information Systems 12*, 4 (October 1994), 383-406.

Fox, Edward A., Hix, Deborah, Nowell, Lucy T., Brueni, Dennis J., Wake, William C., Heath, S. Lenwood, and Rao, Durgesh, Users, user interfaces, and objects: Envision, a digital library, *Journal of the American Society for Information Science 44*, 8 (1993), 480-491.

Hearst, Marti and Karadi, Chandhu, Cat-a-Cone: An interactive interface for specifying searchers and viewing retrieval results using a large category hierarchy, *Proc. 20th Annual International ACM SIGIR Conference*, ACM, New York (1997), 246 - 255.

Johnson, Brian, and Shneiderman, Ben, Tree-maps: A space-filling approach to the visualization of hierarchical information structures, *Proc. IEEE Visualization'91*, IEEE, Piscataway, NJ (1991), 284–291.

Kim, H. and Korfhage, R., BIRD: Browsing Interface for the Retrieval of Documents, *Proc. of IEEE Symposium on Visual Language'94*, IEEE (1994), 176-177.

Nation, David A., Plaisant, Catherine, Marchionini, Gary, and Komlodi, Anita, Visualizing websites using a hierarchical table of contents browser: WebTOC, *Proc. 3rd Conference on Human Factors and the Web*, (June 1997). http://www.uswest.com/web-conference/proceedings/nation.html

Nowell, Lucy Terry, France, Robert K., Hix, Deborah, Heath, Lenwood S., and Fox, Edward A. Visualizing search results: Some alternatives to query-document similarity, *Proc. 19th Annual International ACM SIGIR Conference*, ACM, New York (August 1996), 67-75.

Pratt, Wanda, Dynamic organization of search results using the UMLS, *Proc. American Medical Informatics Association Symposium* (1997).

Rose, A., Ding, W., Marchionini, G., Beale Jr., J., Nolet, V., Building an electronic learning community: From design to implementation, *Proceedings of CHI'98: Human Factors in Computing Systems*, ACM, New York (1998), 203-210.

Shneiderman, Ben, *Designing the User Interface: Strategies for Effective Human-Computer Interaction*, Addison Wesley Longman Publishers, Reading, MA (1998), Chapter 15.

Wise, James A., Thomas, James, J., Pennock, Kelly, Lantrip, David, Pottier, Marc, Schur, Anne, and Crow, Vern, Visualizing the non-visual: Spatial analysis and interaction with information from text documents, *Proc. IEEE Information Visualization '95*, IEEE Computer Press, Los Alamitos, CA (1995), 51-58.

Designing a Digital Library for Young Children:
An Intergenerational Partnership

Allison Druin, Benjamin B. Bederson, Juan Pablo Hourcade,
Lisa Sherman, Glenda Revelle, Michele Platner, Stacy Weng
Human-Computer Interaction Lab
University of Maryland
College Park, MD 20742 USA
+1 301 405 7406

allisond@umiacs.umd.edu
http://www.cs.umd.edu/hcil/searchkids/

ABSTRACT

As more information resources become accessible using computers, our digital interfaces to those resources need to be appropriate for all people. However when it comes to digital libraries, the interfaces have typically been designed for older children or adults. Therefore, we have begun to develop a digital library interface developmentally appropriate for young children (ages 5-10 years old). Our prototype system we now call "SearchKids" offers a graphical interface for querying, browsing and reviewing search results. This paper describes our motivation for the research, the design partnership we established between children and adults, our design process, the technology outcomes of our current work, and the lessons we have learned.

Categories and Subject Descriptors

H.5.2 [**Information Interfaces and Presentation**]: User Interfaces – *graphical user interfaces, interaction styles, screen design, user-centered design*. H.3.7 [**Information Storage and Retrieval**]: Digital Libraries – *user issues*. H.3.3 [**Information Storage and Retrieval**]: Information Search and Retrieval – *query formulation*. D.2.1 [**Software Engineering**]: Requirements/Specifications – *elicitation methods*.

General Terms

Design, Human Factors.

Keywords

Children, digital libraries, information retrieval design techniques, education applications, participatory design, cooperative inquiry, intergenerational design team, zoomable user interfaces (ZUIs).

1. THE NEED FOR RESEARCH

A growing body of knowledge is becoming available digitally for adults and older students. Far less, however, has been developed with interfaces that are suitable for younger elementary school children (ages 5-10 years old). Children want access to pictures, videos, or sounds of their favorite animals, space ships, volcanoes, and more. However, young children are being forced to negotiate interfaces (many times labeled "Appropriate for K-12 Use") that require complex typing, proper spelling, reading skills, or necessitate an understanding of abstract concepts or content knowledge that are beyond young children's still-developing abilities [13, 18, 20]. In recent years, interfaces to digital libraries have begun to be developed with young children in mind (e.g., Nature: Virtual Serengeti by Grolier Electronic Publishing, A World of Animals by CounterTop Software). However, while these product interfaces may be more graphical, their digital collections tend to be far smaller than what is available for older children or adults.

A common trend over the past decade in children's digital libraries interfaces has been to use simulated books as metaphors for traversing hierarchies of information on the screen. One such well-known example in the library community was the Science Library Catalog (SDL) developed in the mid 1990s led by Professor Christine Borgman at UCLA [20]. While this system didn't necessitate keyboard input, it did require reading keywords on the sides of graphical books and reading lists of content results. This system exemplified technologies that were created for older elementary school children (ages 9-12) where reading skills are an important part of the interface. An early example of visual interfaces for accessing digital libraries is BookHouse [14]. This system used icons and a spatial metaphor for searching, but used text lists to show the results.

Novel work in the HCI community has also produced numerous alternative approaches to visualizing searches and their results. One such approach is the "Dynamic Queries" interface developed at the University of Maryland [1]. It enables the user to drag sliders to specify the range of each query element, select from check boxes or radio buttons, or type for string search. Colored and size coded markers for each item represent search results. This approach works well with ordered data that can be filtered by a linear range, for categorical values that can be selected one-by-one, and for nominal values that can be string searched. For young children however, this interface may be cognitively challenging. It is somewhat abstract to connect the idea that changes to the query criteria on the side of the screen result in changes to the visualization of the query results.

On the other hand, a somewhat more concrete approach is "NaviQue," developed at the University of Michigan as a part of their Digital Libraries initiative [10]. With this system, there is no separate space for query results; any object can be used to launch a query. A user simply selects one or more objects and that becomes the query. Then by dragging that data set over another collection of objects, a similarity-based search is launched. The results of the query are highlighted in the data set. While the interaction for this system is deceivingly simple, the abstraction used to query is surprisingly difficult for children to grasp. This system, while extremely flexible, needs more concrete labeling for young children to understand what question they are asking in the query.

Another approach is the idea of "Moveable Filters" based upon the work done at Xerox PARC on lenses [9]. With this graphical query interface, transparent boxes or filters are dragged over a scatter plot of data. Each filter contains buttons labeled for Boolean query operations (e.g., "and", "or"), and a slider that controls the threshold for numeric data. When two filters overlap each other, their operations combine. The results of the query are immediately highlighted. For children, the difficulty in this system lies in the need to understand Boolean query concepts.

Another approach to presenting Boolean searches is to use Venn-like diagrams [12]. Developed by the University of Waikato in New Zealand, "V-Query" is a system where users drag circles around query terms. A new term is created by typing it into the workspace. Depending on the placement of the circles, an "and", "or", "not" query can be created. Each time, a dynamic result of digital resources is displayed. This system while somewhat simple to manipulate, still asks users to type keyword terms and read lists of results, both difficult for young children.

While there are many more researchers focusing on graphical direct manipulation interfaces for querying, the handful of examples just discussed shows promising possibilities. However, there are definite limitations to these systems when young children are the users. To address these limitations, we have begun our own research in developing a graphical direct manipulation interface for searching, browsing, and viewing query results of digital libraries. Supported by a 3-year DLI-2 National Science Foundation grant, we began our research in September 1999. Content provided by the Discovery Channel and the U.S. Department of the Interior's Patuxent Wildlife Research Center, has enabled us to develop a digital library prototype devoted to multimedia information on animals. The technologies and teaching strategies we are developing are not limited to this content area, but that is our starting point.

2. THE ROLE OF CHILDREN AND TEACHERS IN THE DESIGN PROCESS

We believe children can play an important role in creating new technologies for children [6, 7]. Therefore, we have established an interdisciplinary, intergenerational team of researchers that include computer scientists, educational researchers, visual artists, biologists, elementary school children (ages 5-11) and classroom teachers. Throughout the research process, we have looked for methods that make use of our diverse points of view and enable each voice to be heard in the design process. During our research

activities, not only have we come to understand the impact children can have on the design of children's digital libraries, but we have also come to understand how these new technologies can impact children as users.

These understandings have developed as we have worked with children in two different ways in two different locations. In our HCI lab, we have collaborated with a team of seven children ages 7-11 years of age as "Design Partners." At the same time, we have worked in a local elementary school with almost 100 children 7-9 years old in 2nd and 3rd grades as informants. We saw the design partner children in our lab as having a critical role in the initial brainstorming experiences that would set directions for our digital libraries research. On the other hand, we saw the children in school as informants in helping us to understand if our ideas were generalizable among a diverse population of children. As a team, we have not previously made use of both roles for children in a large-scale research study. In addition, the integration of teachers as design partners in our lab was something new to our group. In the sections that follow, each role will be described in regards to methods, context, and challenges.

2.1 Design Partners

The role of *design partner* for children includes being part of the design process throughout the experience [6]. With this role, children are equal stakeholders in the design of new technologies. While children cannot do everything that adults can do, we believe they should have equal opportunity to contribute in any way they can to the design process. For the past three years, our research team has been developing new technology design methodologies to support children in their role as design partners (Figure 1).

This strategy of working with children as partners is something we have come to call *Cooperative Inquiry* [6]. It combines and adapts the low-tech prototyping of participatory design [11, 17], observation and note-taking techniques of contextual inquiry [5] and the time and resources of technology immersion [7]. Children and adults alike gather field data, initiate ideas, test, develop new prototypes, and reflect by writing in journals. Together we pursue

Figure 1: Children and adults collaborating as design partners in our HCI lab

projects, write papers, and create new technologies [2, 7]. In a subsequent section of this paper (The Design Process), we will discuss in more detail the specific design methods we used in brainstorming our digital libraries technologies.

The current design partner team includes two faculty members, one graduate student, two undergraduate students, two staff members, three teachers, and seven children (ages 7-11 years old). The disciplines of computer science, education, psychology, biology, and art are represented. Members of the team meet two afternoons a week in our lab or out in the field. Over the summer we meet for two intensive weeks, six hours a day.

When we began our digital libraries research in the fall of 1999, we added to our design team three elementary school teachers (one 2nd grade teacher, one 3rd grade teacher and one technology coordinator for the school). The children on our team did not come from the school of those teachers. In addition, the children had already been with the lab team working with University researchers on other projects for a minimum of six months. We did not meet at the teachers' school when we began, but rather in our HCI lab environment. Thanks to this process of introduction for the teachers, the children in some sense became mentors for the teachers who had never before considered developing new software. As one teacher pointed out, "At first I was bit worried that I wouldn't know how to contribute to the team. What did I know about research labs? But the children made it easy. They knew what they were doing. And since I'm not their teacher, I wasn't worried I'd look too foolish." (Teacher Journal, November, 1999).

One of the challenges of this kind of design partnership is that adults are not in charge, but neither are children. Design partners must negotiate team decisions. This is no easy task when children are accustomed to following what adults say, and adults are accustomed to being in charge. Children must learn to trust that adults will listen to their contributions, and adults must learn to elaborate on children's ideas, rather than merely listening passively or not listening at all [2]. This idea-elaboration process takes time to develop, but is something that we have found to be extremely important to work towards in a design partnership. We have found however, that it can take up to 6 months for an intergenerational design team to truly develop the ability to build upon each other's ideas (regardless of who originated the idea). Due to this challenge, the development process can take more time than expected.

On the other hand, a strength of the design partnering experience is that there is no waiting to find out what direction to pursue. A continuous relationship with children can offer a great deal of flexibility for design activities. If researchers know that children will always be available at certain times, then less formal schedules need to be made. Another strength of this partnership is that all members of the design team can feel quite empowered and challenged by the design partner process. Children for example have so few experiences in their lives where they can contribute their opinions and see that adults take them seriously. When a respect is fostered, we have found that it does change how children see themselves [2]. As one child shared with us, "My idea helped the team today. The adults saw we don't need books on the screen. I was cool" (8-year old Child Journal, December, 1999).

2.2 Informants

In our lab's previous research [19], we attempted to adapt the design partner experience to school settings in Europe. What we found is that the parameters of the school day and the existing power structures between teachers and students, made it quite difficult to develop a true design partnership. Very little time could be devoted to the necessary activities in building a partnership. Therefore, in looking to involve more children and teachers in the technology development process, we chose to integrate the role of *informant* in our research. This role became more clearly defined in the late 1990s by Scaife and Rogers from the University of Sussex [16]. They described the notion of "informant design" and questioned when children should be a part of the design process. Before this time, numerous researchers were including children in the design process, but not making a distinction of when. Were children testers at the end of the design process? Were children partners contributing throughout the process? Were children informants helping the design process at various critical times?

With this role of informant, children play some part in informing the design process. Before any technology is developed, children may be observed with existing technologies, or they may be asked for input on paper sketches. Once the technology is developed, children may again offer input and feedback. With this role, young people can play an important part in the design process at various stages, but not continuously as is the case in a design partner experience.

For our digital libraries research, we found this method of working with children much easier to negotiate in a school setting. We had the opportunity to work with an ethnically diverse population of children, yet we minimally disrupted their busy school day. We learned from these children how our digital libraries technologies should be changed to make them more useable by children with a wide variety of backgrounds and styles.

In all, 100 children have been working with our research team as informants. 50% of the children are males and 50% females. 52% are Caucasian, 36% African American, and 22% are either Asian or Hispanic. To work with our team, same-sex pairs of children were pulled out of their regular schedule for no more than one-hour at a time, for no more than three times over the school year. The children worked with one to two university researchers for a session. While this may seem quite minimal in time contribution, it did complement quite well the on-going research efforts of our design team back at the lab. Since the children we work with at the school are taught by the teachers who are also our design partners, we have run into much less resistance to changes in the school day than one might expect. The teachers have taken ownership of the technologies we are developing, since they too are designing them in partnership. Yet this partnership minimally impacts their busy school day. For details of the methods we used as informants and design partners, see the section that follows.

3. THE DESIGN PROCESS

We began our digital libraries research with what we call a "low-tech prototyping" session. Before the teachers or children looked at any other systems, we thought it was important for them to brainstorm without consideration to previous work. We felt that this would encourage a feeling that anything was possible. The team was split into three groups consisting of 2-3 children, 1 teacher, and 1-2 university researchers. Each group was asked to

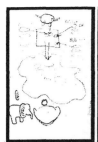 

Figure 2: Note from children's journals on what an animal digital library should look like

design a digital library of the future that contained all of the animal information they ever wanted know. To do this, each group used low-tech prototyping materials (the children call "bags of stuff") containing paper, clay, glue, string and more. From this brainstorming session, three low-tech prototypes were developed that generated ideas for digital libraries (e.g., the interface did not have to look like a book, the interface should be specific to the content area—in our case animals, the interface should use graphical representations as queries).

Following this experience, the team spent some time using and critiquing various children's digital libraries systems that contained animal content: *The Magic School Bus Explores the World of Animals* by Microsoft, *Amazing Animals Activity Center* by DK Multimedia, *Premier Pack: Wildlife Series* by Arc Software, The National Zoo (www.si.edu/natzoo), and Lincoln Park Zoo, Chicago (www.lpzoo.com).

We had two children use a particular technology and one teacher and one university researcher observe their use. While the children were using the technologies the adults were writing down what the children were saying and doing during the session. Meanwhile the children were also taking notes. They wrote on "sticky notes" three things they liked about what they were using and three things they did not. When the sessions were over we collated the sticky notes on the board and looked for frequency patterns in likes and dislikes. Two overwhelming conclusions that came out of these sessions were: (1) there needs to be a purpose for the search and something needs to be done with the information once it is collected; (2) the use of animated characters to tell a child what to do were extremely annoying to the children. At the beginning of our "sticky note session," the adults on the team were quite baffled by numerous sticky notes with comments such as, "It doesn't do anything" "I was bored at looking" "Nothing happens" (Researcher notes, November 1999). As it turned out the children were explaining that it just wasn't good enough to search for things, they wanted to use them to make something. The one application that did allow them to do something with their images, the children found particularly annoying due to the use of an animated character that kept telling the children what to do. After the session, the adults on the team compared their notes, and found that their observations were very much the same as the children's.

The team then spent a few sessions brainstorming and drawing in their journals (Figure 2). From this experience, a few critical ideas crystallized for the team. One idea the team particularly liked was the metaphor of going on a journey. One of our 8-year old design partners explained that "Finding things is like going on a trip, so you should go with friends" (Researcher notes,

December 1999). She thought that these friends shouldn't be "pushy" like the character we saw, but should give kids a reason for wanting to find things. Another idea that emerged was that the interface should be based on animals "the thing you're looking for." The notion of dragging animal parts that represented things you wanted to search for came out in a number of journals. So instead of a text question of "what do animals eat," a picture should be dragged into a "mixing space" that represents that question. Other ideas that emerged had to do with the questions that the children wanted answered about animals. These included: (1) what do they eat; (2) how do they move; (3) where they live; (4) what animal family are they part of. One additional area of information that an 11-year old design partner wanted to know more about was "what waste products do animals make?" Even though the children loved this idea, it was decided that the information would be so hard to find, that this would have to wait for version 2.

Other ideas that emerged from the teachers were also critical in structuring our approach to digital libraries. One teacher pointed out that in the youngest grades, the children learn about animals grouped by "pets at home" or "farm animals." While older children learn about animals by where they might come from geographically (e.g., Australia, Africa, etc.). Therefore, various ways to browse for animals were needed, so that children at different grade levels could take advantage of the library. As the teachers pointed out, there are big differences between what a 2nd grade teacher needs to cover as compared to a 3rd grade teacher, even though this represents only one year's difference in the children's ages.

Soon after this set of sessions, three members of our team began working with 50 elementary school children in our local school. We realized that as a team we knew very little about how young children actually searched for animals, and how complex their queries could actually be. To understand this, we conducted an empirical study at the school to develop an understanding of how children searched based on what we had already learned in the lab [15]. We developed a set of hierarchically nested envelopes based on the four categories of information our child design partners were interested in (e.g., habitat, food, movement, and animal taxonomy). The children in the school were asked to search within those envelopes for pictures of animals.

From observing the children's behavior in this situation, we learned that the children appear to search very differently depending on gender. For example, we found that boys tended to dump all the envelopes on the floor (with little thought of putting things back) in search of the animal they wanted. On the other hand, the girl teams tended to be quite careful in their search style, but at times seemed to be more interested in browsing the pictures rather than finding the exact animal in question. This led us to the notion that the application should fully support both structured searching and browsing as equally valid and efficient methods of accessing information.

Our next step back at the lab was to begin designing an "interactive sketch". By this we mean something that could begin to help us get a feel for some of the ideas that had emerged in our previous design sessions. For this we used KidPad, a zoomable authoring tool for children [4, 8]. The group's artist began sketching with this tool, and as she sketched, the team refined its ideas. The notion of how to use characters became clearer to the team. These were not characters that told you to do things, but

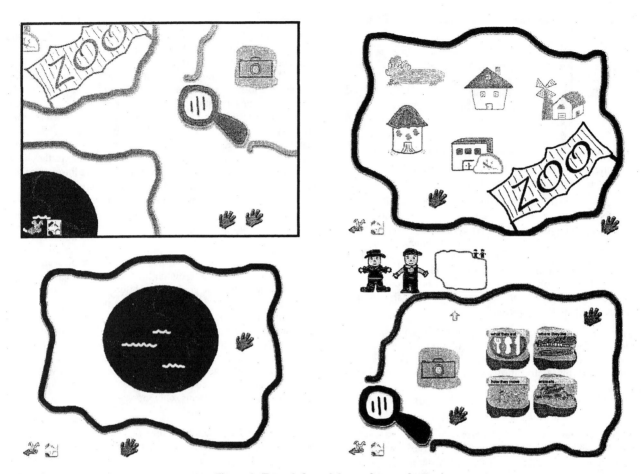

**Figure 3: From left to right, and top to bottom:
The prototype's initial screen, the zoo area, the world area, and the search area.**

rather, they represented the query as it was being formulated. The characters held onto the search criteria a child wanted to use. Also the notion of "doing something" with the search results began to take form. Since the team was already helping to develop KidPad (www.kidpad.org), it made sense to link the digital libraries application with an authoring tool. Ultimately this meant building our first interactive prototype on top of KidPad. In addition to these ideas, the concept of having three different areas to look for animals evolved. This took the form of the zoo (with a farm house, a pet house, a bird house, and more), the world, and the search area.

As our technical team was developing the first functional prototype, we continued to refine its interface by using paper chips to represent the search criteria and people to represent the kids. We also populated, in consultation with our team biologist, a Microsoft Access database with metadata on animal images contributed by our content partners. At one point, however, one of our child design partners insisted our biologist had "gotten it all wrong for gorillas" about what they ate, so this 8-year old spent the afternoon looking up on the web what gorillas ate to prove his point (he was quite correct and the metadata was fixed). When our first interactive prototype was far enough along to be usable by someone besides the design team, it was brought back into the school to be used with our informant children. Fifty of them who had not previously taken part in exploring the paper prototype

were asked to offer feedback on the computer prototype. This study is reported in detail in [15]. In the section that follows a full description of our current prototype is presented.

3.1 Today's Prototype
As previously discussed, our initial interactive prototype we now call SearchKids is built upon KidPad, a real-time continuous zooming application that our lab originally developed in partnership with researchers at the Royal Institute of Technology, Sweden, the Swedish Institute of Computer Science and the University of Nottingham for the purpose of children's collaborative storytelling [4, 8]. KidPad and SearchKids make extensive use of Jazz, a Java toolkit we developed for research in Zoomable User Interfaces (ZUIs) [3]. SearchKids accesses metadata about images of animals from the Microsoft Access database mentioned in the previous section.

The prototype follows a few interface design principles that we have learned through years of work with our design partners. We made the interface very visual, avoiding the use of text as much as possible and therefore reducing the cognitive load. We also made interactions with the mouse as simple as possible by using a one-click interface (i.e. no dragging, no double-clicking) with all mouse buttons having the same functionality. The fact that we are using a one-click interface makes SearchKids easy to use on touch screens therefore avoiding the problems many young children have controlling mice.

The current version of SearchKids consists of three areas through which users can look for media about animals. Figure 3 shows the prototype's initial screen and the three areas. Users may navigate between areas and within areas by clicking on their destination or making use of the "home" and "back" icons that are always at the bottom left of the screen.

The zoo area provides a way of browsing the contents of our animal database in a familiar setting. When entering the zoo area, users see the map of a virtual zoo. By zooming into parts of the zoo, children can find representations of animals and through them, access media. For example, to access media about lizards, children can zoom into the reptile house and click on a representation of a lizard.

The world area provides a way for children to browse the animal database by looking for animals geographically. It presents children with a globe they can spin and zoom into. By zooming into a region of the world they can find representations of the animals that live in that part of the world and though them, access media. For example, to access media about polar bears, children could zoom into the North Pole and click on a representation of a polar bear. The world area is currently not fully implemented.

The search area gives users the ability to visually specify and manipulate queries. It also provides previews of query results. The initial look of the search area is shown in the right-most picture of Figure 3. The query region makes up most of the search area. The chips in this region are the components from which queries can be formed. The chips on the left side of the region represent the types of media available through the database. Currently, only images are available and a camera represents them. The chips on the right side of the region represent the hierarchies under which the animals in our database have been classified. They enable children to look for media about animals based on what they eat, where they live, how they move, and a biological taxonomy.

To explore these hierarchies, users can click on the shadows under the chips. For example, clicking on the "what they eat" chip

brings into focus three chips representing animals that are carnivorous, herbivorous, and omnivorous. To move up in a hierarchy, users can click on the up arrow to the left of the hierarchical chips. Figure 4 shows the search area after the shadow under the biological taxonomy chip has been clicked on. The chips on the right side of the figure are the children of the biological taxonomy chip and represent the types of animals present in the database.

When a chip (media or hierarchical) is clicked on, it zooms towards one of the characters on the top-left corner of the screen (Kyle and Dana, the "search kids"), to hold around their neck. This chip becomes part of the query criteria. Media chips zoom to Kyle while hierarchical chips go to Dana. Clicking on a chip that is on Kyle or Dana makes it go back to its original location therefore removing it as one of the criteria for the current query.

The chips on Kyle and Dana visually represent the queries children formulate. Our prototype returns an intersection of the media items represented by chips selected from different categories and a union of the media items represented by chips selected from the same category. This approach, while somewhat limiting expressive power, successfully enables children to specify their desired queries and does so without requiring them to explicitly distinguish between unions and intersections. Figure 5 shows a series of screenshots that demonstrate how children may pose a query.

The red region to the right of Kyle and Dana shows the results of the current query. Children can zoom into the region by clicking on it. By seeing the results of their queries as they pose them, children can quickly tell whether the database has any items that correspond to their query criteria. The items shown in the results area can be zoomed into (this feature was not available during testing at the school). We are currently working on a mechanism that will allow children to transfer media of their choice into KidPad.

This prototype has been used with our child informants in school and the results have been encouraging. The differences by gender the children displayed in their searching disappeared when they used this prototype [15]. In addition, children were able to

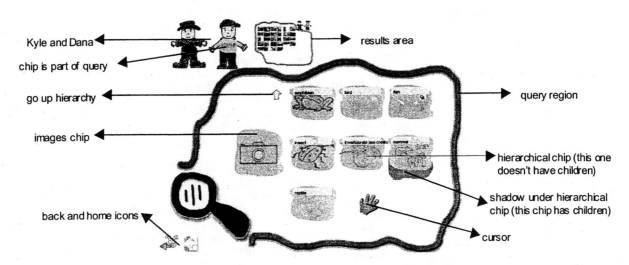

Figure 4: Components of the search area when exploring biological taxonomy.

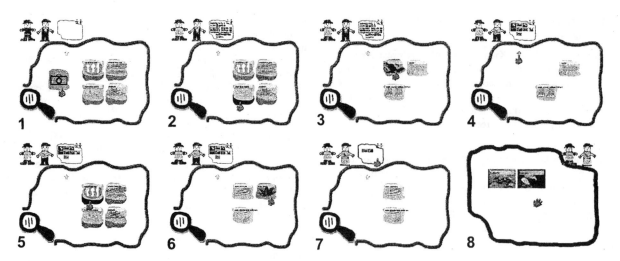

Figure 5: Process of querying for images of animals that fly and eat plants.

1. Child clicks on the item representing images.
2. Child clicks under "how they move" category (notice the thumbnails in the results area, and the camera on top of Kyle).
3. Child clicks on "fly" item.
4. Child clicks on up arrow to go up in the hierarchy. The query at this point is asking for images of animals that fly. Notice there are less thumbnails in the results area.
5. Child clicks under "what they eat" category.
6. Child clicks on "eats plants" item. This completes the specification of the query.
7. Child clicks on results area.
8. Child browses results in results area.

construct more complex queries with SearchKids than with the paper prototype. However, most of the children did encounter some difficulty with the size of the images in the results screen, and the size of the navigational controls for up and back, but that has already begun to be addressed in later versions of the prototype.

4. LESSONS LEARNED

While our project is only in its second year, we have learned a number of lessons in regards to design process as well as digital library technologies. In terms of the design process, the combination of children as design partners in the lab and children as informants in the school helped considerably. We were able to quickly brainstorm possibilities with children, yet minimally disrupt school schedules or renegotiate power-structures between children and teachers. What we did come to understand was that without a design partner experience, child informants in the school could merely offer feedback on ideas presented to them, as opposed to elaborate or build upon ideas as was the case in our lab.

Another lesson learned in our design process concerned the teachers. By introducing the teachers the way we did with a delay and with children they did not teach, we helped to equalize the footing between child and adult. We found the teachers learning from the children in the group and the children not treating the "teachers" as they might normally. Yet thanks to this partnership, the teachers quickly embraced the technology as their own, and

helped a great deal in contributing to the design and content structure of the digital library, as well as facilitating our work in the school.

In terms of lessons learned concerning the technology, one of the most interesting was that children don't want to just search for information, they want to use it too. They want a reason to search or browse for items (besides some adult saying to look for it). This led us to a firm belief that our work is also in developing a connection between our digital library and authoring tools.

In addition, the notion of a content specific interface also emerged quite strongly. Needless to say, if we were developing an interface for a digital library containing all forms of plants, it would not make sense to have a zoo browsing area. But it does make sense that a content specific metaphor is critical for children. To some degree they see the digital library as not a library with books, but as a place to wander about looking for different kinds of information.

5. FUTURE DIRECTIONS

In terms of future directions, we look forward to exploring the possibilities of multi-user navigation and searching. Since our application is built upon KidPad, we have the functionality built right in to have multiple mice work at the same time. We are exploring what can happen when children collaborate as they navigate information.

In addition, we are enhancing the database content by adding video, sound, and text items. We are also developing a direct connection from SearchKids to KidPad. With these major additions to our prototype interface, we expect further empirical studies will be needed, especially those with younger children (ages 5-6).

6. ACKNOWLEDGMENTS

This work could not have been accomplished without our child design partners in the lab Alex, Abby, Jack, Joe, Lauren, Rebecca and Thomas and our 100 informants in the second and third grade at Yorktown Elementary School. We are also indebted to our teachers led by Technology Coordinator Carol Poundstone and Principal Libby Thomas. On-going inspiration and intellectual discussion has come by way of Ben Shneiderman, Catherine Plaisant, Anne Rose, Joseph Ja'Ja', and the KidStory research project supported by the i3, ESE. Financial support has come from the National Science Foundation's DLI-2, Discovery Channel, Patuxent Wild Life Refuge, and the Baltimore Learning Community project.

REFERENCES

[1] Ahlberg, C., Williamson, C., & Shneiderman, B. (1992). Dynamic Queries for Information Exploration: An Implementation and Evaluation. *In Proceedings of Human Factors in Computing Systems (CHI 92)* ACM Press, pp. 619-626.

[2] Alborzi, H., Druin, A., Montemayor, J., Sherman, L., Taxén, G., Best, J., Hammer, J., Kruskal, A., Lal, A., Plaisant, S. T., Sumida, L., Wagner, R., & Hendler, J. (2000). Designing StoryRooms: Interactive Storytelling Spaces for Children. *In Proceedings of Designing Interactive Systems (DIS 2000)* ACM Press, pp. 95-104.

[3] Bederson, B. B., Meyer, J., & Good, L. (2000). Jazz: An Extensible Zoomable User Interface Graphics Toolkit in Java. *In Proceedings of User Interface and Software Technology (UIST 2000)* ACM Press, pp. 171-180.

[4] Benford, S., Bederson, B. B., Akesson, K., Bayon, V., Druin, A., Hansson, P., Hourcade, J. P., Ingram, R., Neale, H., O'Malley, C., Simsarian, K., Stanton, D., Sundblad, Y., & Taxén, G. (2000). Designing Storytelling Technologies to Encourage Collaboration Between Young Children. *In Proceedings of Human Factors in Computing Systems (CHI 2000)* ACM Press, pp. 556-563.

[5] Beyer, H., & Holtzblatt, K. (1998). *Contextual Design: Defining Customer-Centered Systems.* San Francisco, CA: Morgan Kaufmann.

[6] Druin, A. (1999). Cooperative Inquiry: Developing New Technologies for Children With Children. *In Proceedings of Human Factors in Computing Systems (CHI 99)* ACM Press, pp. 223-230.

[7] Druin, A., Bederson, B. B., Boltman, A., Muira, A., Knotts-Callahan, D., & Platt, M. (1999). Children As Our Technology Design Partners. A. Druin (Ed.), *The Design of Children's Technology* (pp. 51-72). San Francisco: Morgan Kaufman.

[8] Druin, A., Stewart, J., Proft, D., Bederson, B. B., & Hollan, J. D. (1997). KidPad: A Design Collaboration Between Children, Technologists, and Educators. *In Proceedings of Human Factors in Computing Systems (CHI 97)* ACM Press, pp. 463-470.

[9] Fishkin, K., & Stone, M. C. (1995). Enhanced Dynamic Queries Via Movable Filters Papers: Information Visualization. *In Proceedings of Human Factors in Computing Systems (CHI 95)* ACM Press, pp. 415-420.

[10] Furnas, G. W., & Rauch, S. J. (1998). Considerations for Information Environments and the NaviQue Workspace. *In Proceedings of International Conference on Digital Libraries (DL 98)* ACM Press, pp. 79-88.

[11] Greenbaum, J., & Kyng, M. (Eds.), (1991). *Design at Work: Cooperative Design of Computer Systems.* Hillsdale, NJ: Lawrence Erlbaum.

[12] Jones, S. (1998). Graphical Query Specification and Dynamic Result Previews for a Digital Library. *In Proceedings of User Interface and Software Technology (UIST 98)* ACM Press, pp. 143-151.

[13] Moore, P., & St. George, A. (1991). Children As Information Seekers: The Cognitive Demands of Books and Library Systems. *School Library Media Quarterly, 19*, pp. 161-168.

[14] Pejtersen, A. M. (1989). A Library System for Information Retrieval Based on a Cognitive Task Analysis and Supported by and Icon-Based Interface. *In Proceedings of Twelfth Annual International Conference on Research and Development in Information Retrieval (SIGIR 89)* New York: ACM, pp. 40-47.

[15] Revelle, G., & Druin, A. (2001). Young Children's Search Strategies and Construction of Search Queries. *In Proceedings of Human Factors in Computing Systems (CHI 2001)* ACM Press, p. (submitted).

[16] Scaife, M., & Rogers, Y. (1999). Kids As Informants: Telling Us What We Didn't Know or Confirming What We Knew Already. A. Druin (Ed.), *The Design of Children's Technology* (pp. 27-50). San Francisco: Morgan Kaufman.

[17] Schuler, D., & Namioka, A. (Eds.), (1993). *Participatory Design: Principles and Practices.* Hillsdale, NJ: Lawrence Erlbaum.

[18] Solomon, P. (1993). Children's Information Retrieval Behavior: A Case Analysis of an OPAC. *Journal of American Society for Information Science, 44*, pp. 245-264.

[19] Taxén, G., Druin, A., Fast, C., & Kjellin, M. (2000). KidStory: A Technology Design Partnership With Children. *Behaviour and Information Technology (BIT),* pp. (in press).

[20] Walter, V. A., Borgman, C. L., & Hirsh, S. G. (1996). The Science Library Catalog: A Springboard for Information Literacy. *School Library Media Quarterly, 24*, pp. 105-112.

The International Children's Digital Library: Viewing Digital Books Online

Juan Pablo Hourcade, Benjamin B. Bederson, Allison Druin, Anne Rose, Allison Farber,
Yoshifumi Takayama

Human-Computer Interaction Laboratory
A.V. Williams Building
University of Maryland
College Park, MD 20742 USA
+1 301 405 7445
jpablo@cs.umd.edu

ABSTRACT

Reading books plays an important role in children's cognitive and social development. However, many children do not have access to diverse collections of books due to the limited resources of their community libraries. We have begun to address this issue by creating a large-scale digital archive of children's books, the International Children's Digital Library (ICDL). In this paper we discuss our initial efforts in building the ICDL, concentrating on an informal evaluation of innovative digital book readers.

Keywords

Children, digital libraries, books, book readers, graphical user interfaces.

INTRODUCTION

The importance of children's books in young people's lives cannot be minimized. Books can help children to understand who they are, explore the world around them, and contribute to a child's ability to be literate in today's society [11] [21] [26] [31] [33]. Access to diverse multicultural literature can be limited despite the best efforts of librarians, teachers, and parents. The financial resources for collections, particularly in urban areas are limited and insufficient to provide diverse collections reflective of today's school populations. We are working on bridging this gap by developing a large-scale digital archive of children's books called the International Children's Digital Library (ICDL). In this paper, we discuss our initial efforts in designing user interfaces appropriate for young children (ages 5-11) to access such an archive. In the sections that follow we discuss the need for research, our previous work, the goals of the project, our design methodology, and the results of our initial efforts, including an informal evaluation of the innovative book readers we introduce here.

NEED FOR RESEARCH

When children's books play an important role in young people's lives, research has shown an increase in children's cognitive, social, and motivational development [9] [20] [26] [31] [46]. In addition, access to narratives from different cultures can offer children opportunities to better understand the world around them as well as who they are in relation to that world [5] [7] [21]. Unfortunately, getting access to books for children from the United States and abroad can still be a challenge. Children in many communities have limited access to a wide variety of multicultural literature. Poor physical library and school facilities and limitations on funding for materials can lead to frustrated children, parents, and educators. However, with computer technologies becoming more widely available in school/public libraries and community centers, tens of thousands of books can be made available through online digital collections.

Developing new technologies appropriate for children can be challenging, since young people can have difficulty reading, typing, spelling, and are continually changing in their interests and abilities [15] [35] [41] [45]. Novel work in the HCI community has produced numerous approaches to visualizing searches and their results that may offer new opportunities for children [2] [22] [23] [30]. However, there are definite limitations to these systems when children are the users. Many interfaces are cognitively challenging due to abstract representations of Boolean search methods and the need to read result lists or query labels [15]. While there is an emerging and significant research field devoted to digital libraries and information retrieval, we have found that the vast majority of content and interfaces are targeted for adults or older students. For example, at last year's JCDL'01 conference, there were 76 papers, of which only two were focused on children's interfaces/content [15] [42].

Of the online digital libraries appropriate for children, there is a disappointing number of large-scale collections to explore. In January of 2002, the largest online digital collection of children's books we were able to find included only 67 titles. Out of 24 sites we found, a majority of these digital collections showed only titles, sometimes with summaries, reviews or associated activities [6] [10] [38] [43]. Others offered only options to purchase books [18] [29] [44]. Still other collections depended on out-of-copyright materials [17] [19]. The site that currently includes the most digitized books online is "Children's Books Online for Free" [19]. This collection, as of January 2002, includes 67 fully digitized books online, with plans to increase the number to 1,200 out of copyright titles. In evaluating the user interfaces of these sites for accessibility, it is clear that most were not designed primarily for use by children, but rather for access by adult researchers, teachers, or parents.

There is also a need for research in developing interfaces for children to read books on computer screens. Many researchers have looked at the difficulty of reading on a computer screen. O'Hara and Sellen compared reading from paper to reading on a computer screen [36]. These comparisons dealt mostly with document reading and marking by adults. Dillon has also done comparisons between electronic documents and paper and has proposed ways of evaluating interfaces for electronic documents [12] [13]. Shneiderman provides a nice summary of the research in this area [40].

Most of the research on book readers has come from industry. However, little has been published. Graham created the *Reader Helper*, a document reader meant to make it easy for adults to find relevant information in documents [25]. The Reader Helper highlights relevant information in a document and shows annotated thumbnails of the document's pages on the left side of the screen. Ginsburg el al. developed a reader for PostScript documents that shows thumbnails on the left side of the screen [24].

Today's industry standard book readers come from Microsoft and Adobe. Their e-book readers for personal computers are *Microsoft Reader* [34] and *Adobe Acrobat eBook Reader* [1], shown in Figure 1. Both Microsoft and Adobe suggest that the main advantage of using their products is their text-related features. Both products offer solutions for more screen-readable text (e.g. *ClearType, CoolType*). Both products also contain features for searching and annotating books, looking for words in the dictionary, and reading words out loud. Both products were mainly designed for adults reading long books or documents consisting mostly of text. Neither product provides major alternatives to their default screen layouts or visualizations of the books.

With these text readers, navigation between pages is primarily accomplished by using keyboard shortcuts or small next and previous page buttons, which are too small for young children. In *Microsoft Reader 2.0*, the riffle control, a widget that shows up when right-clicking at the bottom of a page can also be used to change pages. It allows the user to move to the next and previous pages, the

next and previous section, and shows a bar that tells users their position in the book and allows them to jump to other parts of the book. The table of contents can be accessed through popup menus. Due to the fact that the riffle control is accessible by right-clicking, accessibility for children is limited. From our experience, many young children cannot distinguish between the left and right mouse buttons.

Adobe Acrobat eBook Reader 2.2 has similar navigation options, with small buttons to move to the next and the previous page, and a widget at the bottom of the screen that has similar capabilities to Microsoft's riffle control. The table of contents is also available through menus. While the right mouse button has the same functionality as the left mouse button in most cases, there is no full-screen option, so children can accidentally click on the operating system taskbar (on Windows).

Commercially available e-books for children generally use one of these two readers, although other options exist. For example, Antelope Publishing [3] offers its books in HTML format for children to read in a web browser.

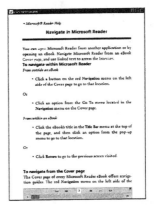

Figure 1: On the left, *Microsoft Reader 2.0* with the riffle control open at the bottom of the window. On the right, *Adobe Acrobat eBook Reader 2.2*, showing its navigation bar at the bottom of the window.

OUR PREVIOUS WORK

For the past three years, we have been developing *SearchKids*, a graphical direct manipulation collaborative interface for searching, browsing, and viewing query results of digital libraries. Our initial prototype is devoted to multimedia information on animals [15] [28] [39]. However, the technologies we developed are not limited to this content area and we are currently extending it to support books.

SearchKids consists of three areas, shown in Figure 2, through which users can look for media about animals. The zoo area provides a way of browsing the contents of our animal digital library in a familiar setting. When entering the zoo area, users see the map of a virtual zoo. By zooming into parts of the zoo, children can find representations of animals and through them, access media.

Figure 2: From left to right: *SearchKids'* initial screen, the zoo area, the world area, and the search area.

The world area provides a way of browsing our animal digital library by looking for animals geographically. It presents children with a globe they can spin and zoom into. By zooming into a region of the world they can find representations of the animals that live in that part of the world and through them, access media.

The search area gives users the ability to visually specify and manipulate queries. It also provides previews of and access to query results. Children can form queries by selecting icons that represent query terms and are organized hierarchically. The icons at the top of these hierarchies represent the different categories available for searching. Selecting icons from different categories returns an intersection of the items represented by the icons. Selecting icons from the same category returns a union of the items represented by the icons. We conducted a study of the effectiveness with which children could pose queries using the search area and obtained encouraging results [39].

SearchKids supports simultaneous multiple users through multiple mice by using MID [27]. Our team has experimented with two modes of collaboration. In one mode, independent collaboration, a user's click on an interactive item is enough to interact with that item. In another mode, confirmation collaboration, all users must click on an interactive item in order to interact with it. We are currently analyzing data from a study we conducted on how these collaboration modes affect collaboration between children.

PROJECT GOALS

Our book digital library research has five primary goals. The first is to develop interface technologies that support children in using large amounts of digital information (e.g., searching, browsing, reading, and sharing). This paper describes our initial efforts in pursuing this goal.

The remaining goals include:

- To give children around the world access to international children's literature.

- To evaluate the impact such a digital collection can have on collection development and program practices of librarians who work with children.

- To evaluate the impact such a digital collection can have on children.

- To better understand data acquisition and rights management by using the development of this large-scale digital library as a case study.

DESIGN METHODOLOGY

We believe that children should play an active role in the development of technology for children. Therefore, we have established an interdisciplinary, intergenerational team of researchers that include computer scientists, educational researchers, visual artists, library scientists, children and classroom teachers. To work together, we have used a combination of techniques known as *Cooperative Inquiry* [14] [16]. These techniques offer an approach to research that can be used to gather data, develop prototypes, and forge new research directions.

The group of children we work with consists of three boys and four girls aged 7 to 10 years old. They work as design partners with adult researchers in our lab on this and other projects. During the school year, they come to our lab twice a week, each visit for one and a half hours. In order for everyone to get ready for the school year activities, we run a two-week intensive design program every summer. During these two weeks, the children spend 8-hour days at our lab working with adult researchers on various design problems.

SUMMER SESSION

During the 2001 summer session we began modifying our existing *SearchKids* digital library interface to support books. We began the session with everyone bringing in their favorite children's books. These books varied widely, from short books with mainly pictures and very few words, to chapter books with a few hundred pages of words. Some of the books were in languages other than English.

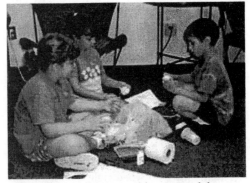

Figure 3: Children working at our lab.

We first reviewed *SearchKids* with the children, and then brainstormed how to adapt it to books. From this, we decided to concentrate on three areas: how to adapt the existing searching and browsing capabilities of *SearchKids* to the domain of children's books, how to create an online community of book readers (like book clubs at a neighborhood library), and how to support the reading of books on a computer. We found it necessary that books be read on computer screens, as it would be difficult for public libraries with little resources to own specialized book readers, or be able to print the books. We therefore broke up into three groups to address each of those areas, each with children and adults.

The browsing and searching group extended the world area from *SearchKids* (Figure 2) for the ICDL, where it could be used to find books based on where they are from, what part of the world they are about, and where they are popular. Our current design has one globe that when zoomed into a geographical area reveals three options representing books from that area, about that area, and popular in that area. Zooming into one of these shows the appropriate books.

The browsing and searching group also found that the search area in *SearchKids* could be adapted for the ICDL. The main issue with using the search area was to determine the different categories by which books could be searched for. While the group came up with metadata many adults would come up with, such as subject and popularity, it also decided books should be searched by the feelings they evoke, and the color and shape of their cover. The group then looked at how books should be categorized by subject. After doing some research, the group concluded that existing cataloguing methods used at libraries such as the *Dewey Decimal Classification* and the *Library of Congress Classification* are not easy to follow by children. After looking for alternatives, the group settled on the classifications used by amazon.com, which children found much easier to follow.

The online communities group looked at how to provide a community experience. The group focused on book clubs to connect children reading the same books. They would provide information about books, and enable children to read them, rate them, select the feelings the books evoke, and write reviews. Children would also be able to read other children's reviews, and see their ratings and feelings selections. In addition, book clubs would provide quizzes, games, discussion areas, links to websites, and activities related to each book. Figure 4 shows a design mockup of a book club.

The group dealing with how to read books on the computer screen felt that in addition to traditional book reader features, children needed extra support for navigation. Partly due to the visual nature of many children's books, and partly due to the children's desire to flip through pages in a manner more similar to paper books, we designed two alternate readers. These readers were designed assuming the

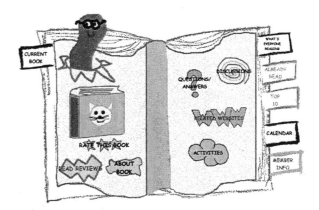

Figure 4: Book club design.

books were very visual, and had no more than approximately 50 pages. Our expectation was not that any one reader would be best in all circumstances, but that for some children, some books, and some tasks, different readers would be preferable.

In the comic strip reader (Figure 6), pages are laid out as if they were in a comic strip. The page of interest can be zoomed into to read it. The spiral reader (Figure 6) shows the current page in the middle of the screen, where the earlier pages get smaller in a spiral shape to the left and the following pages get smaller in a spiral shape to the right. Both readers are described in more detail below.

Following the reports by each group, we proceeded to adapt *SearchKids* to the needs specified by the searching and browsing group. By the end of our summer session, we managed to have a working prototype with a search area in which children could look for books based on subject, ratings, color and shape of the book cover, and feelings (see Figure 5). The search results showed the covers of the books that matched the search criteria. We also implemented a spinning globe through which books could be accessed based on where they were from. The children in our team created the art for the icons in the search area.

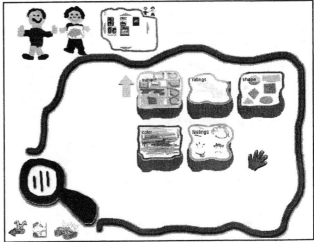

Figure 5: Screenshot of *SearchKids* search area adapted to book searching.

At the end of the session, the children demonstrated the prototype to their parents.

INFORMAL EVALUATION OF BOOK READERS

We have continued our work on the ICDL, concentrating on book readers. We implemented the comic strip and spiral readers using Jazz [4], a graphics toolkit, and performed a pilot study to understand if these types of readers are effective for children. While we thought that different users would prefer different readers under different circumstances, we needed to validate this. We therefore set out to build prototypes of these readers in order to informally evaluate them with children. We thought the best way to test them would be to compare them with a more traditional reader.

Description of Book Readers

Standard Reader

We built a reader with traditional interface mechanisms, which we will refer to as the standard reader. With this reader, a user can see one page at a time (Figure 6). The controls to read the book are at the bottom of the screen. The large left arrow takes the user to the previous page, while the large right arrow takes the user to the next page. Users can access the same functionality by using the left and right arrows and the "page up" and "page down" keys on the keyboard. No animation occurs when changing pages. We built this as the baseline because it provides the same basic functionality as the commercial readers.

Comic Strip Reader

The comic strip reader lays out book pages as if they were part of a comic strip (Figure 6). When the reader is started, the user sees all the pages in the book. The controls to read the book are at the bottom of the screen and are identical to those in the standard reader, with the exception of a "zoom out" button (not needed in the standard reader). The left and right arrows and the "page up" and "page down" keys have the same functionality as the arrows on the screen.

The user can also interact with the book by clicking on pages. When seeing the entire comic strip, clicking on a page smoothly zooms the user into that page. If the user is already zoomed into a page, clicking on that page zooms the user out, also accomplishable by clicking on the "zoom out" button. All zooming is animated over half a second. When zoomed into a page, the left and right arrows take the user to the previous and next page respectively. The transition between pages animates the view of the comic strip to the left or to the right as appropriate. If the end of a strip is reached, the view zooms out and then zooms in to the destination page.

Clicking on the left or right arrows when seeing the entire comic strip zooms the user to the previous or next page with respect to the last page the user visited. If the user clicks on the right arrow before visiting any pages (i.e. when starting the reader), then the view is zoomed into the first page of the book.

All pages in the comic strip reader have a border around them intended to give feedback to the user. Unvisited pages have a thick blue border, and pages that have been visited have a thinner magenta border (using standard web visitation colors). If the user's mouse cursor is over a page, the page's border changes to a thick red.

Spiral Reader

The spiral reader is the most novel of the readers we built. It shows the current page in the middle of the screen between two spirals (Figure 6). The spiral to the left shows the pages that come before the current page, while the spiral to the right shows the pages that come after the current page.

The spiral reader has the same screen and keyboard controls as the comic strip reader. Using the arrows changes the current page to the next or previous page and animates all pages accordingly around the spirals. Clicking on a page other than the current page makes that page the current page, animating all pages around the spirals in order to bring the new current page to the center of the screen. Clicking on the current page magnifies it so it occupies most of the screen in order to read its text more easily. Clicking on the current page again (or clicking on the "zoom out" button) takes the current page back to its

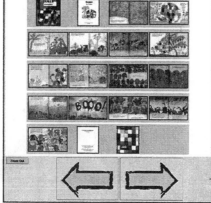
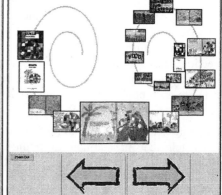

Figure 6: From left to right, standard reader, comic strip reader, and spiral reader. All readers are showing David McKee's Elmer [32].

normal size. Changes in size and zooming transitions are animated over half a second. When the current page is magnified, the arrows are still operational, animating the transition to the next and previous pages. However, we disabled the ability to click on another page to make it the current page, as very few other pages are visible, and clicks intended for the current page could end up on another page by accident.

The spiral reader uses colored borders around book pages in the same way as the comic strip reader. A page is considered visited if it was seen while magnified.

Description of Informal Evaluation

Research Participants
We used the last design session of the Fall 2001 semester as an opportunity to informally evaluate our book readers. We invited our research team to bring their parents, siblings, and friends and ended up having 16 children, aged 5 to 11 (see Table 1 for ages), from diverse backgrounds, including four children of color. Seven of the children were part of our design team, while the remaining were their siblings or friends, and the children of staff. Nine parents also joined. None of the children, including our design partners, had seen any of the readers working before although two of our design partners were involved with the original design. We wanted to independently observe the children using the readers, yet there were not enough adult researchers to do this. We therefore paired each child with one of their parents, having the parents observe their children. If that was not possible, we paired the children with an adult member of our staff.

Age (average 8.6)	Number of participants
5	1
6	1
7	2
8	4
9	1
10	5
11	2

Table 1: Ages of participating children

Conditions
We ran the study with a between subjects design so each child could try all three readers, each with a different book. For the evaluation, we changed the order of the readers, but kept the order of the books the same. The books we used, in the order they were shown, were: *Underground Train* by Mary Quattlebaum and Cat Bowman Smith (32 pages) [37], *The Very Busy Spider* by Eric Carle (26 pages) [8], and *Elmer* by David McKee (31 pages) [32]. Changing the order of the readers yielded six different conditions. Children were assigned evenly to conditions, with four

conditions assigned three children each, and two conditions assigned two children each.

Tasks and Data Gathering
The task assigned to the children was to read the books and answer two content-related questions about each book, such as: "What do the monkeys snack on at the zoo?" (for *Underground Train*), "Who talks to the spider after the cat?" (for *The Very Busy Spider*), and "What did Elmer do to look like the other elephants?" (for *Elmer*). These questions were given to them before reading the books as part of a questionnaire. The children then attempted to answer the questions as they read each book. All the questions were about parts of the books that were midway through the story. After they were done reading a book, the children had to answer two more questions, giving feedback on how they liked the book they just read and the book reader they used. They answered these questions by circling a sad face, a neutral face, or a happy face. After they were done with all three books, the children were asked to select which book they preferred, and which book reader they preferred.

We also gave the adults paired with children a questionnaire. For each book reader used, we asked the adults whether the children were confused or excited about the reader, and whether they thought the reader helped the children answer the questions. After the children were done with all three readers, we asked the adults which reader helped the children the most in understanding the story, and which reader they would prefer the children use.

Besides collecting data from questionnaires, we logged the use of each reader. The logs kept track of the pages that were visited, zoom in's and zoom out's for the comic strip and the spiral reader, and the amount of time spent in each page.

Setup
All research participants performed the study at roughly the same time in two large rooms. Since our participants arrived at different times, they started the evaluation at staggered times. There were enough computers in the two rooms so that there was at least one unused computer between two subjects. Once a child was paired with an adult, an adult researcher led them to a computer, gave them the questionnaires, and explained to them what they were going to do. The adult researchers (not the adults paired with the children) took care of starting and closing each reader. The children were asked to call them when they were done with a book. Questions about how to use the readers were answered if asked by the children or the adults. The adults were told to observe and not tell the children what to do, or operate the computer. A majority of participants completed the evaluation within 30 minutes, and all completed the evaluation within 45 minutes.

Results of Informal Evaluation

Given the informal nature of the evaluation and the small number of research participants, we decided not to use exhaustive statistical methods to analyze the data. Instead, we provide a frequency summary of our observations based on the data collected, together with some tables and charts to illustrate the suggestive results.

The questionnaires yielded information on the preferences of both children and the adults that were paired with them (Table 2). Children's preferences were similar when it came to book readers. While more children preferred the standard reader, if we only consider children under 10, the standard reader was the least popular. Adults, on the other hand, had a clear favorite: the comic strip reader. They also thought the comic strip reader helped children the most in understanding the stories they were reading. When it came to stories, children had a clear favorite: *Elmer*. However, this did not have an impact on the rating of the readers because the readers were rated evenly across all books (Table 3).

Reader	All children	children under 10	adults	adult's perception of help in understanding
comic strip	4	3	10	8
spiral	5	4	2	1
standard	7	2	4	5

Table 2: Preferred readers for all children, children under 10, adults, and reader adults thought helped children the most in understanding the story (two adults did not respond to this last question).

Book	children's preference	average rating of reader
Underground Train	4	1.4
The Very Busy Spider	1	1.5
Elmer	11	1.4

Table 3: Book preferences and average rating of readers by book. A sad face was assigned a rating of 0, a neutral face a rating of 1, and a happy face, a rating of 2.

Looking at the answers given to the questions at the story level, most children managed to answer all reading comprehension questions. Only three children answered questions incorrectly asked about three different stories using three different readers. There were no major differences in the ratings of the readers (Figure 7).

Adult observers suggested that the spiral and comic strip readers were the most confusing to the children, while at the same time they were the most exciting. This is not surprising, as it is common in visual design for the most

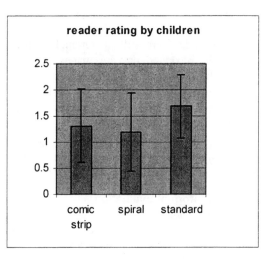

Figure 7: Reader ratings by children. A sad face was assigned a rating of 0, a neutral face a rating of 1, and a happy face, a rating of 2. Error bars are two standard deviations in length.

exciting visualizations to be the most confusing. Adult observers also thought the comic strip helped children the most in answering the content questions. Table 4 shows the results.

Reader	confusing	exciting	helpful
comic strip	4	8	11
spiral	6	7	4
standard	0	3	6

Table 4: Number of adult observers that thought each of the readers was confusing, exciting or helpful

Analyzing the logs did not yield major differences between the readers. As a matter of fact, when looking at time spent in each reader, the number of pages visited, and the number of changes of direction, there are no clear differences between the readers across the three books. Nonetheless, we did find two minor trends:

- On average, children spent more time reading all three books when using the spiral reader.
- The spiral reader had the most time spent, page changes and changes of direction when reading *Elmer*.

In both cases though, the differences with the other readers were small, within one and a quarter standard deviations. Figure 8 shows the corresponding charts.

There were also no major differences in the number of zoom in's and zoom out's between the comic strip and the spiral reader. However, the fact that children zoomed suggests that at some point they found it useful to get an overview of the books they were reading. Some children also jumped from one part of the book to another,

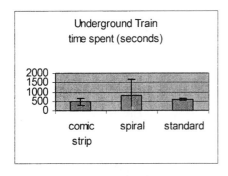

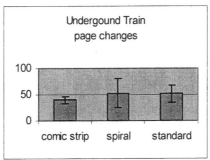

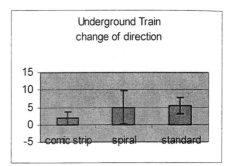

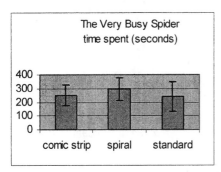

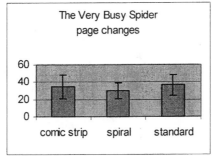

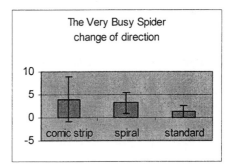

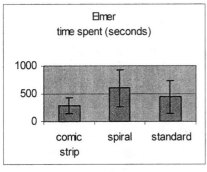

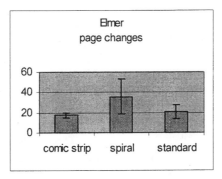

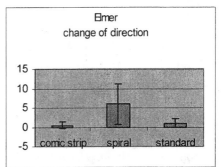

Figure 8: Charts showing log data for time spent (in seconds), number of page changes, and number of changes of direction for each book read under each type of reader. The error bars are two standard deviations in length.

suggesting again that this type of capability may be useful to some children under some tasks.

Overall, the results of the evaluation show that there is no clear winner. Different children prefer different readers. This suggests that pursuing multiple solutions for book readers may be a reasonable path. It also encourages us to find out more about why children prefer their favorite reader, and what tasks are better suited for each type of reader.

FUTURE WORK

We plan to further examine the possibilities of other book readers. In particular, we would like to investigate a book reader showing small thumbnails of all pages as a way to navigate the book while at the same time showing the current page large enough so it can be read. This would be a child-friendly version of the navigation bar in commercial products. Besides studying other types of readers, we need to further evaluate the readers we developed for this informal evaluation with more children. In particular, we

would like to determine what tasks the different readers are better suited for.

We also plan to make the interface components we developed for *SearchKids* highly configurable so they can be easily used with any digital library, including the ICDL. Developing the interface for the ICDL will also include working on the book club interface and ways of searching using text. We also plan to start building a large collection of books so we can learn how to deal with issues of scale.

CONCLUSION

This is just the beginning of our work in this area. We currently have a working prototype of a system with searching and browsing capabilities. We have also gained some initial insights into book readers. The main lesson is that different children prefer different types of readers. This means we need to learn more about what tasks are better suited for each reader, and why different children prefer different readers. It also means that current commercial book readers are likely not sufficient to satisfy children's diverse needs.

ACKNOWLEDGEMENTS

This work could not have been accomplished without our child design partners and the lab's staff members and students that helped with our informal evaluation. We would also like to thank Brewster Kahle and Jane White from the Internet Archive for their support and ideas. This project has been funded by the National Science Foundation's DLI-2.

REFERENCES

1. Adobe Acrobat eBook Reader Home Page. Available at http://www.adobe.com/products/ebookreader/main.html.

2. Ahlberg, C., Williamson, C., & Shneiderman, B. (1992). Dynamic queries for information exploration: an implementation and evaluation. In *Proceedings of Human Factors in Computing Systems (CHI 92)*, ACM Press, pp. 619-626.

3. Antelope Publishing Home Page. Available at http://www.antelope-ebooks.com.

4. Bederson, B.B., Meyer, J., Good, L. (2000). Jazz: An extensible zoomable user interface graphics toolkit in java. In *Proceedings of User Interface and Software Technology (UIST 2000)*, ACM Press, pp. 171-180.

5. Bettelheim, B. (1976). *The uses of enchantment: The meaning and importance of fairy tales.* New York: Knopf.

6. Book Adventure Home Page. Available at http://www.bookadventure.com.

7. Campbell, J. (1988). *The power of myth.* New York: Doubleday.

8. Carle, E. (1984). *The Very Busy Spider.* New York: Putnam Books for Young Readers.

9. Cass, J. (1967). *Literature and the young child.* London: Longmans, Green & Co.

10. CHILDE Project Home Page. Available at http://www.bookchilde.org.

11. DeHirsch, K., Jansky, J.J., & Langford, W.J. (1966). *Predicting reading failure.* New York: Harper & Row.

12. Dillon, A. (1994). *Designing Usable Electronic Text: Ergonomics Aspects of Human Information Usage.* London: Taylor and Francis.

13. Dillon, A. (1999). TIME - a multi-leveled framework for evaluating and designing digital libraries. *International Journal on Digital Libraries*, Volume 2, Issue 2/3, pp 170-177.

14. Druin, A. (1999) Cooperative inquiry: Developing new technologies for children with children. In *Proceedings of ACM CHI 99 Conference on Human Factors in Computing Systems,* ACM Press, pp. 223-230.

15. Druin, A., Bederson, B., Hourcade, J. P., Sherman, L., Revelle, G., Platner, M., & Weng, S. (2001) Designing a digital library for young children: an intergenerational partnership. In *Proceedings of ACM/IEEE Joint Conference on Digital Libraries (JCDL 2001)*, ACM Press, pp. 398-405

16. Druin, A. (in press) The role of children in the design of new technology. *Behaviour and Information Technology (BIT)*, (in press).

17. Ebook Library at the Electronic Text Center, University of Virginia Home Page. Available at http://etext.lib.virginia.edu/ebooks/.

18. eBooks.com Home Page. Available at http://www.ebooks.com.

19. Editec Communications Home Page. Available at http://www.editec.net.

20. Ellis, G. & Brewster, J. (1991). *The storytelling handbook for primary teachers.* England: Penguin Books

21. Erikson, E.H. (1950). *Childhood and society.* New York: Norton.

22. Fishkin, K., & Stone, M.C. (1995). Enhanced dynamic queries via movable filters papers. In *Proceedings of Human Factors in Computing Systems (CHI 95)*, ACM Press, pp. 415-420.

23. Furnas, G. W., & Rauch, S. J. (1998). Considerations for information environments and the navique workspace. In *Proceedings of International Conference on Digital Libraries (DL 98)*, ACM Press, pp. 79-88.

24. Ginsburg, A., Marks, J., Shieber, S. A reader for PostScript documents. In *Proceedings of the ACM symposium on User interface software and technology (UIST 96)*, ACM Press, pp. 31-32.

25. Graham, J. (1999). The Reader's Helper: A Personalized Document Reading Environment. *In Proceedings of Human Factors in Computing Systems (CHI 99)*, ACM Press, pp. 481-488.

26. Grugeon, E. & Gardner, P. (2000). *The art of storytelling for teachers and pupils.* London: David Fulton Publishers.

27. Hourcade, J.P., & Bederson, B.B. (1999). *Architecture and implementation of a java package for multiple input devices (MID).* Tech Report HCIL-99-08, CS-TR-4018, UMIACS-TR-99-26, Computer Science Department, University of Maryland, College Park, MD.

28. Hourcade, J.P., Druin, A., Sherman, L., Bederson, B.B., Revelle, G., Campbell, D., Ochs, S., Weinstein, B. (in press). SearchKids: a Digital Library Interface for Children. To appear in *Extended Abstracts of Human Factors in Computing Systems (CHI 2002).*

29. ipicturebooks Home Page. Available at http://www.ipicturebooks.com.

30. Jones, S. (1998). Graphical query specification and dynamic result previews for a digital library. In *Proceedings of User Interface and Software Technology (UIST 98)*, ACM Press, pp. 143-151.

31. Malkina, N. (1995). Storytelling in early language teaching. *Forum, 33*, 1, 38.

32. McKee, D. (2001). *Elmer*. New York: Lothrop, Lee & Shepard Books.

33. Meek, M. (1982). *Learning to read*. London: Bodley House.

34. Microsoft Reader Home Page. Available at http://www.microsoft.com/reader/default.asp.

35. Moore, P., & St. George, A. (1991). Children as information seekers: The cognitive demands of books and library systems. *School Library Media Quarterly, 19*, pp. 161-168.

36. O'Hara, K., Sellen, A. (1997). A comparison of reading paper and on-line documents. In *Proceedings of Human Factors in Computing Systems (CHI 97)*, ACM Press, pp. 335-342.

37. Quattlebaum, M., Bowman Smith, C. (1997). *Underground Train*. New York: Doubleday Books for Young Readers.

38. Reading Tree Home Page. Available at http://fusion.sims.berkeley.edu/ReadingTree.

39. Revelle, G., Druin, A., Platner, M., Weng, S., Bederson, B. Hourcade, J. P., & Sherman, L. (in press). A visual search tool for early elementary science students. *Journal of Science Education and Technology*.

40. Shneiderman, B. (1998). *Designing the User Interface: Strategies for Effective Human-Computer Interaction, Third Edition*. Reading, Massachusetts: Addison-Wesley.

41. Solomon, P. (1993). Children's information retrieval behavior: a case analysis of an OPAC. *Journal of American Society for Information Science, 44*, pp. 245-264.

42. Theng, Y.L., Mohd-Nasir, N., Buchanan, G., Fields, B., Thimbleby, H., & Cassidy, N. (2001). Dynamic digital libraries for children. In *Proceedings of ACM/IEEE Joint Conference on Digital Libraries (JCDL 2001)*, ACM Press, pp. 406-415.

43. Time Warner Bookmark/Little, Brown and Company Books for Children Home Page. Available at http://www.twbookmark.com/children.

44. Tundra Books Online. Available at http://www.tundrabooks.com.

45. Walter, V. A., Borgman, C. L., & Hirsh, S. G. (1996). The science library catalog: A springboard for information literacy. *School Library Media Quarterly, 24*, pp. 105-112.

46. Wright, A. (1995). *Creating stories with children*. England: Oxford University Press.

Making Sense of the World Wide Web

▦ ▦ ▦ ▦ ▦

▦ ▦ ▦ ▦ ▦

Just as the largest library, badly arranged, is not so useful as a very
moderate one that is well arranged, so the greatest amount of knowledge,
if not elaborated by our own thoughts, is worth much less than a far smaller
volume that has been abundantly and repeatedly thought over.

Arthur Schopenhauer (1788–1860),
Parerga and Paralipomena (1851)

Are users satisfied with existing text-oriented finding aids on the World Wide Web? Is browsing, searching, and navigation almost as good as it could be? Don't Google's rapid responses often provide just what users are looking for?

Techno-enthusiasts may answer "yes" to these questions, but critics complain that too often users get disoriented, can't find what they want, and give up in frustration. Whether you think the glass is half empty or half full, you still might give some thought on how to fill the glass higher.

Projects for improving the Web are common. Some scenarios include wishful thinking about mobile agents to find just what you need, or more mundane proposals for tagging fields with semantic information so searching can be more precise. These may yet prove effective, but the HCIL's approaches seek to enhance browsing tools by developing interfaces that support visual overviews, multiple windows, and history keeping.

When a search engine can deliver the single right result for a unique name or term search, it is hard to beat. However, many searches cover common terms that return a variety of Web sites that then must be scanned to understand what is available and what might be best. For example, a search for "Maryland parks hiking camping" produces thousands of results that must be carefully studied. Seeing these results on a map might facilitate decision making. Similarly, a search on "milk production" might be grouped by language or country of origin. Visual overviews might be in the form of scatter plots, as was done with legal information search results in the HCIL's SnapTogether Visualization (99-26, 2000-05 [7.7]).

Another visual overview interface built by the HCIL was in the form of a grid with hierarchical axes in GRIDL (99-03 [4.3]). Sometimes a visual overview of a single Web site can help users understand what is available and what is not much more easily than with textually supported navigation. The WebTOC system consists of a program that crawls a Web site and produces a hierarchical table of contents (97-10 [5.1]). Then the user can view the entire Web site with an expanding and contracting tree structure that shows depth through indented headings. In addition, WebTOC uses a simple but powerful visualization technique consisting of horizontal bar charts showing the volume of information and the media types for each entry in the table of contents. In a glance, users can spot which sections of the tree structure contain videos or music, or whether there is more information about, say, Buddhism than Shinto religions.

Most browsers operate within a single window so that when users click on a link the result comes up in the same or an overlapping window. This straightforward approach works well for many tasks and users, but most users could benefit from better window management. Often, users would like to open several windows at once; for example, after completing a search for a new home, you might like to compare all six of the real estate listings. With a large enough screen, you could open six tiled windows with one click and quickly see which had the best features (96-17, 97-08). Then you might like to close all six with another click and examine a map that shows the locations of all six at once. Strategies for managing multiple windows, such as the HCIL's *elastic windows*, require some additional training, but as user sophistication grows and large screens proliferate, they are likely to become increasingly attractive.

Since users very often need to return to Web pages they have previously visited, effective history-keeping interfaces are a necessity. Yet, current browsers have weak facilities that limit user views to textual lists when a visual representation with thumbnail views might be much more effective. The visual representation might be temporally sequenced, as was done in 1987 for the Apple Hypercard system that showed 42 thumbnails in its history page. Alternatively, a tree structure reflecting the traversal path of links and back buttons could provide a more meaningful representation that was in harmony with the Web site design. The HCIL's

multiple designs based on our first PadPrints browser were tested in experiments that provide valuable guidance for those seeking to improve history keeping in Web browsers (98-06 [5.3], 2000-03).

◼   ◼   ◼   ◼   ◼   ◼   ◼   ◼   ◼

FAVORITE PAPERS FROM OUR COLLEAGUES

Andrew, K., Visualising Cyberspace: Information Visualisation in the Harmony Internet Browser, *Proc. IEEE Information Visualization '95*, IEEE Computer Press, Los Alamitos, Calif. (1995), 97–104.

Card, S. K., Robertson, G. G., York, W., The WebBook and the Web Forager: An Information Workspace for the World Wide Web, *Proc. of ACM CHI 96 Conference on Human Factors in Computing Systems* (CHI 96), ACM Press, 111–117.

Tauscher, L., Greenberg, S., Revisitation Patterns in World Wide Web Navigation, *Proc. of ACM CHI 97 Conference on Human Factors in Computing Systems* (CHI 97), ACM Press, 399–406.

Georgia Tech's 10 WWW User Surveys: *www.cc.gatech.edu/gvu/user_surveys*.

Visualizing websites using a hierarchical table of contents browser: WebTOC

David A. Nation *
Department of Defense
dnation@acm.org
Catherine Plaisant, Gary Marchionini, and Anita Komlodi
Human-Computer Interaction Laboratory
University of Maryland
College Park, MD 20742
http://www.cs.umd.edu/hcil/webtoc/

Abstract

A method is described for visualizing the contents of a Web site with a hierarchical table of contents using a Java program and applet called WebTOC. The automatically generated expand/contract table of contents provides graphical information indicating the number of elements in branches of the hierarchy as well as individual and cumulative sizes. Color can be used to represent another attribute such as file type and provide a rich overview of the site for users and managers of the site. Early results from user studies suggest that WebTOC is easily learned and can assist users in navigating websites.

Keywords: Information Visualization, Exploratory Data Analysis, Graphical Representations, Hierarchical Table of Contents, Java applet, World Wide Web, Browsing.
* Mr. Nation was a visiting researcher at the University of Maryland when the work was performed. This paper represents the views of David Nation and not necessarily those of the DoD.

Introduction

One difficulty in information visualization on the World Wide Web is representing the quantity of information and its distribution within a set of linked documents. This information along with the type of document (text, image, audio, ...) can be helpful when deciding whether a web site may be interesting or useful without spending a great deal of time browsing the deep structure of the site.

A user might find a useful collection of audio or image files "hidden" down a series of links from the main page. Another site may be composed primarily of links without substantial content of its own. A way is needed to quickly get an overview of a site including overall size and composition and a way to look at a few sample pages without wading through the entire structure.

 Motivation: The initial motivation for WebTOC was to find a way to browse large numbers of documents in the growing Library of Congress American Memory collections. The Library of Congress (LoC) contracted with the University of Maryland to develop prototypes for future interfaces . The size and extent of such large collections makes them hard to understand. A method was needed to help the LoC staff develop and organize them.

Photographs, manuscripts, journals and other material are continually being digitized and added to the existing structure. Keeping up with the current configuration requires a dynamic system that can be updated automatically with minimal human intervention. The ability to get an overview of the whole collection and to rapidly "drill down" to get more details is essential to the management and use of the information.

WebTOC automatically generates a hierarchical table of contents of a site (or, in the case of our LoC application, a collection) using two different strategies: following existing links or using the underlying directory and file structure. Following links is appropriate for existing websites, while using the directory structure is appropriate for newly digitized "unprocessed" collections which have not yet been linked, indexed or annotated.

Related work: It is difficult for users to navigate large document spaces, since they often experience a disorientation problem. Hypertext readers must remember their location in the network, make decisions about where to go next, and keep track of pages previously visited. McKnight, Dillon, and Richardson [11] provided evidence of disorientation problems in a hypertext search task. One of the ways to improve hypertext design is to provide structural cues to the reader. Providing a structured overview of the hypertext contents facilitates users' orientation [13]. The Navigational View Builder [12] uses four strategies for web visualization: binding, clustering, filtering and hierarchization.

Tables of contents have been a common method of providing overview and navigation aid in books. Expand/contract tables of contents or outlines have been used for directory structures (e.g. Microsoft Explorer) and early Hypertext systems based on hierarchical structures (e.g. Superbook [6]). Versions of tables of contents that allow the user to expand and contract levels of the hierarchy have been shown to decrease browsing times in comparison to stable fully expanded versions [5]. WebTOC uses an expand/contract table of contents.

Earlier techniques have been used to browse or visualize directory structures. Previous work with Treemaps [8, 2] demonstrated the usefulness of presenting size and type information about directory structures compactly. It showed the importance of an overview and using visual cues to discover documents that seem out of place, are unusually large, or are duplicates. Parameters could be changed easily to represent a number of characteristics of the documents such as size, type and age. Treemaps have some drawbacks such as areas having different shapes which makes size comparison difficult. Finding space for labels on the treemap can also be difficult. WebTOC provides space for labels in a conventional indented list format and allows for comparisons of length with single dimensional lines.

WebBook[3] is a tool which helps users organize their Web activities. Pages in the "book" are Web pages and users can flip through the pages to find the ones they want. Users can also insert bookmarks among the pages. This application uses Furnas's [7] fisheye view paradigm to provide an overview for the contents of the "book". Fisheye view graphs [14] show the center of interest in a large scale and with great detail, while areas further from the center are successively smaller and in less detail. WebTOC allows the user to vary the amount of detail displayed using the expandable hierarchy, by removing text labels and by showing the results of a search while preserving the context of the hierarchy.

Docuverse[15] and Superbook[6] are applications that help users develop documents in an individual or group environment. Superbook uses an expand/contract table of contents, while Docuverse lays out the hierarchy of the content in a tree structure. Docuverse's developer realizes that the hierarchy may become unwieldy as the number of nodes increases. This is also a problem for WebTOC and many other systems.

Hyperbolic visualization [10] is a technique falling under the fisheye paradigm. The idea is to lay out the hierarchy in a uniform way on a hyperbolic plane and map this plane onto a circular display. Initial studies comparing hyperbolic browsers against conventional 2D scrolling browsers with a horizontal tree layout show that subjects preferred the hyperbolic browser, but there was no significant difference between the browsers in performance times for the task of finding specific node locations.

Web visualizations have used graphs to represent all the links or 3D "information landscapes" to visualize document sets [1] but those visualizations are typically more complex to learn and use than tables of contents.

Value bars [4] display quantifiable attribute values of items to help users visualize and navigate large information spaces. It is especially useful for multi-attribute listings. Among other features it gives an overview of attribute distribution, and makes it easier to locate outliers and exceptions. User studies showed that users liked the ability to quickly find extreme values of attributes (largest, youngest files, etc.). The ability to see multiple attributes for a single item was also a favored feature of value bars. The possibility of immediate navigation to the item selected in the context of the index of items was also mentioned as a "best feature". In a user test, subjects were asked to find files by different attributes (age, size, etc.) in a UNIX directory structure. Users of value bars were much more efficient in tasks looking for extreme values on attributes than users of UNIX commands. WebTOC uses a similar strategy except the bars are embedded in the table of contents and represent branches of the hierarchy instead of the whole document.

We believe that WebTOC will be helpful to browse websites and directory structures to quickly see where the bulk of files/pages are located, to compare relative sizes of directories and to see any outliers or unusually large branches of the hierarchy. This information can also be useful for space management and trouble-shooting functions.

Description

WebTOC consists of two parts: a parser program to generate a table of contents (TOC) file representing the site, and a user interface (Java applet) to display the TOC and allow interaction within a conventional web browser.

The interface: Figure 1 shows an example where WebTOC is used to provide an overview and browsing mechanism for one of the American Memory collections of the Library of Congress. On the right is the original home page, on the left the WebTOC table of contents.

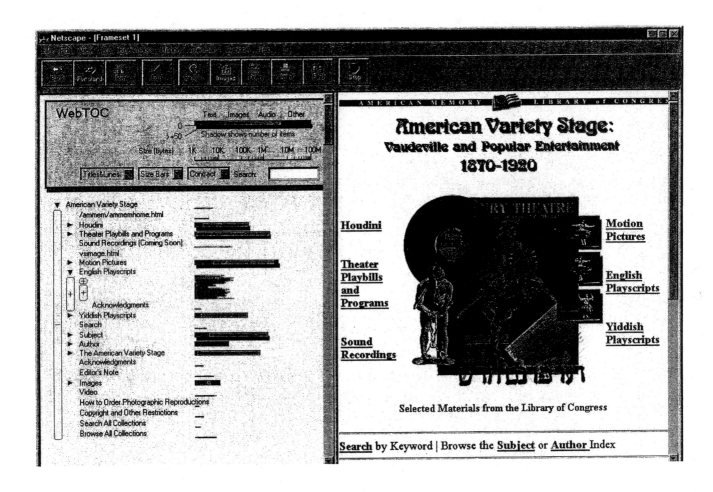

Figure 1. This figure shows WebTOC displayed in a frame to the left of the home page it represents: the American Memory collection entitled "American Variety Stage: Vaudeville and Popular Entertainment 1870-1920". The top portion is a legend and control panel for WebTOC. Links are listed with a bar that represent the volume of information available when following that link. Users can then expand the hierarchy (e.g. here "English Playscripts" has been expanded and the labels removed to compare file sizes).

The bottom left part of the display shows the Table of Contents with the first level links displayed. A line to the right of each text label shows the size and type of the file. A branch that hasn't been expanded is represented by a larger "size bar". Two levels of links have been opened up under "English Playscripts" but the display has been compressed in that area showing only the lines representing the files and not the labels. Clicking on any of the labels or individual lines causes that file to be displayed in the frame on the right. Clicking on the size bar or the triangular symbol to the left of the label opens or closes a level of the hierarchy. Clicking on the outlined area to the left of a level will add or subtract the display of text labels for the files. All links of the home page are shown on the table of contents but in addition users can estimate the volume of information available in a branch if they decided to follow the link.

As summarized in the WebTOC legend (top left of Figure 1) individual pages are shown with individual lines while bars aggregate groups of files behind a link or directory to represent the total size of the included documents. Color is used to represent file type, length the overall size and the shadow below the bar is proportional to the number of documents included. The number of documents and size represented are displayed in the browser status area when the user's cursor is over the bar. Figure 1's TOC shows that "Sound recording" is very small (close to empty) in comparison to the other categories like "motion pictures", while it would have been impossible to guess from the home page on the right. "Yiddish playscripts" is also smaller than "Motion pictures" but in addition the shadow is also very small suggesting that the number of pages is small there. "English playscripts" has been opened using the arrow button on the left of the name and the individual lines appear to show individual pages. Each line or label is a link to the corresponding page, making it possible to drill down the hierarchy quickly and access deep pages without loading the intermediate pages (either for sampling or quick access to known destinations).

The legend at the top shows the colors representing documents of types: Text, Images, Audio and Other. Those types were chosen for our Library of Congress application but other types might be useful in other situations. For example color could be used to show the type of link (outside link, within site link, within page link). The size of the shadow under the bar corresponds to the number or items in the branch. The shadow gets larger for more items to a maximum of the height of the bar for 50 or more items. This is arbitrary and will probably have to be changed for other sites. Below the bar is a scale for the size of files or collections of files. The left edge of the scale starts with 1000 bytes and is positioned to be in line with the lines and bars below. The reference bar and scale in the legend can be dragged to the left or right and can be compressed horizontally to dynamically modify the entire TOC display so as not to obscure the labels of items in the Table of Contents.

An alternative more compact representation of the table of contents is to display all the line segments without the text (Figure 2). This enables the user to get a visual overview of the site and the ability to directly compare file sizes. Due to extreme variability in file sizes, a log scale was used for representation of size. An alternative to the size bar is a linear scale bar representing the number of items in the hierarchy below a given item. The information about size, type and number of items behind a web page is missing from Web based link structures and conventional tables of contents.

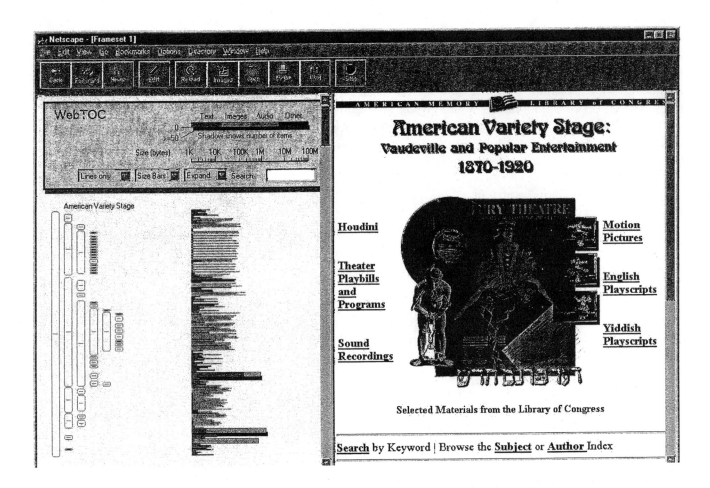

Figure 2. In this figure the "Expand" function has been used to open the entire table of contents and the labels have been removed using the "Lines only" option to show a compact representation of size and type of files. Some of the branches have been collapsed into bars to save space. Note the shadows under the bars indicating the number of items within the branch.

Figure 3 shows another alternative attribute visualization. Here the bars show the number of items in a branch of the tree (as opposed to the overall directory size). The example used is the HCIL web site, showing that most of the items in the site are in the student section of the site, making this section a

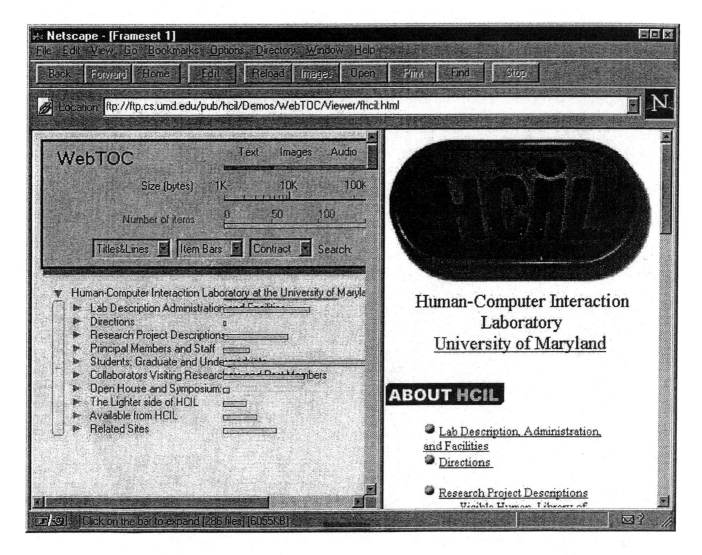

Figure 3. This figure shows the option of displaying the linear bars to indicate number of items in the branch instead of size. Lines indicating size are still used for individual files. This is a representation of the HCIL site which clearly indicates that the largest number of documents are included in the "Students: Graduate and Undergraduate" branch. The message in the status area at the bottom of the browser indicates the actual number of items and size for that branch.

Automatic generation of the table of contents: The implementation of WebTOC includes the automatic generation of the table of contents by following the links included in the documents and treating each new set of links as another level of the hierarchy.

Many choices had to be made in the selection of links to be included in the table of contents. Following all the links would normally lead to inclusion of the whole web. It was decided that the TOC file (WebTOC) would represent the size and links from the documents local to a web site. The server URL is used to limit following links only to documents local to the server. Another compile time option is set to use only the first occurrence of a link on the local site. A breadth first search is used to ensure that the link is displayed at the level of the hierarchy closest to the root. An option exists to display outside links in the WebTOC but without indicating the size or type of document. Therefore the total size indicated in the WebTOC corresponds to the size of the documents on the site.

It's not always possible to follow all paths in a site. For example when a search or other type of form is used to access parts of the site the parser would see only the form page. Other cgi-bin files generated on the fly in the normal structure are scanned as if they were static files.

The data file produced by the parser is in a format similar to HTML which contains information on the server and document base URL, an indicator of the start and end of a group of links, and information on each document or link including size, file name, type and label. It can be created automatically with the parser program or manually with a text editor. It has the extension ".hdir".

```
(dashes around names will be used to indicate types of field, e.g. -text-)

Format of data file:

&ltHDIR>-#items-                                          start of file
&ltSERVER>-server URL-                        line defining web server URL
&ltBASE>-starting directory-                  starting directory location
  &ltR>-size-,-URL (part/whole)-,-type-,-label- Header for level 0
&ltHL>-base directory for this level-         start of level
  &ltR>-size-,-URL (part/whole)-,-type-,-label- item at level 1
  &ltR>-size-,-URL (part/whole)-,-type-,-label- item at level 1
  &ltR>-size-,-URL (part/whole)-,-type-,-label- item at level 1
</HL>-base directory for this level-          end of level
</HDIR>                                       end of file


Values for the type field:
        h       html or text files
        i       image files
        a       audio files
        d       directory files (for directory structure)
        c       cgi-bins
        o       other types of file
```

An example file is shown below:

```
&ltHDIR&gt681
&ltSERVER&gthttp://www.cs.umd.edu
&ltBASE>/projects/hcil/
  &ltR&gt5457,"index.html",h,"Human-Computer Interaction Laboratory",39616
&ltHL>/projects/hcil/
  &ltR&gt7269,"lab.description.html",h,"Lab Description"
  &ltR&gt0,"http://inform.umd.edu/",h,"UNIVERSITY OF MARYLAND"
  &ltR&gt2967,"treeviz.html",h,"TreeViz (TM)"
&ltHL>/projects/hcil/Research/
  &ltR&gt2396,"treemaps.html",h,"Treemap"
  &ltR&gt95749,"DemoPics/treeviz.gif",i,
  &ltR&gt0,"ftp://ftp.cs.umd.edu/pub/hcil/Demos/Treeviz/",h,"Treevis Demos"
</HL>/projects/hcil/Research/
</HL>/projects/hcil/
</HDIR>
```

As mentioned earlier WebTOC can also generate the TOC file from the underlying directory structure of the site. This is useful when documents have been stored online but the link structure has not been created yet (e.g. unprocessed collections).

The parser program is controlled by a few simple parameters including the URL of the web site and whether to follow the links or scan a local directory. A scan over the web of several thousand links can take 4-6 hours to complete using a Pentium 166 or Sparc 20. A local scan on the same server can be done in less than an hour. A directory scan of a similar number of files can be done in 10 - 20 minutes because a system function can be used to find the length of the files.

User studies

Controlled experiment: A study was conducted by students in Dr. Shneiderman's Human Factors in Computer and Information Systems class at the University of Maryland to evaluate the usefulness of WebTOC for Web site navigation tasks during the Spring 1997 semester. Task completion time and subjective user satisfaction were measured on a set of simple and complex retrieval and navigation tasks for three groups of users. The first group used the full WebTOC version with size and number of items graphic displays as shown in Figure 3. The second group used a textual table of contents (a version of WebTOC without the size bars). The third group had no table of contents available and used only Netscape capabilities to browse the pages of the experimental site. The Web sites used in the study were selected collections within the Library of Congress American Memory collection. The Variety Stage collection and the Evolution of the Conservation Movement were used. Because of the large number of items in these collections the table of contents was limited to five levels of depth.

This experiment found no statistically significant differences between interfaces. This may be due to the limited number of subjects (only seven subjects were tested per treatment). The subjective satisfaction surveys showed a preference for WebTOC. Results on the five tasks showed that WebTOC is better suited for more complex tasks, when users have to traverse several levels of the hierarchy and for tasks where quantitative (size) comparisons are necessary between nodes in the hierarchy. In simpler tasks the textual table of contents and Netscape users performed better than users of WebTOC. This shows that the complexity WebTOC adds to the display makes simpler tasks more difficult but in the case of more complex tasks it helps users. This is confirmed by the fact that as tasks got more complex Netscape users gave increasingly higher difficulty ratings to tasks in the user satisfaction survey while the increase in difficulty ratings by WebTOC users was not so dramatic. Users found WebTOC easy to learn, and the subjects using WebTOC were the most satisfied with the tool they had available to solve the tasks. The presence of the WebTOC also increased the feeling of organization of the site. The full paper with detailed results is available at http://otal.umd.edu/SHORE. This paper presents a number of lessons learned and makes several recommendations for further study of WebTOC.

CHI 97 Browse-Off: Since WebTOC can also browse a directory structure WebTOC was used in an informal competition among browser products at the ACM Conference on Human Factors in Computer Systems (CHI 97). A directory structure representing an eleven level hierarchy of categories of world items was used as the source of data (Figure 4). Top level categories were People, Places, Things, Events, Qualities and Knowledge. The use of search functions was not permitted during the competition.

Six pairs of expert users competed in a limited time to find information in the hierarchy. The score indicated the number of items successfully found in the time period. Tasks were broken down into different levels of difficulty and complexity.

Although the WebTOC entry didn't win the competition, it came in second tied with the Windows Explorer entry from Microsoft. The winner was the HyperBolic browser [10] from Xerox PARC. There wasn't enough time in this panel session for a head to head competition between the teams with the highest scores but a set of novice users competed in a final round using the HyperBolic browser, WebTOC and a new manual "control" entry using a paper based system with a filing cabinet and file folders.

The novice users using WebTOC ended up with a higher score for this competition than the HyperBolic browser. The WebTOC users found the interface intuitive and easy to get used to. Although the HyperBolic browser users liked the interface, they had more trouble operating it than the expert user. While the paper based team didn't finish the entire event, they were in the lead at the end of three out of four sets of tasks.

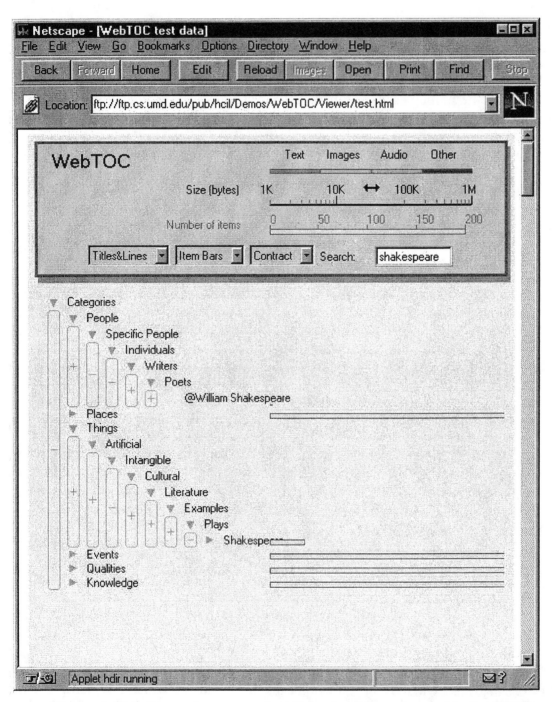

Figure 4. This figure shows a portion of the data hierarchy used in the CHI Browse-Off. It also illustrates how WebTOC can be used to display the search results within a site (although search was not permitted during the competition). The search function has been used to open up the hierarchy to items matching the search string, here "Shakespeare".

Clearly the CHI'97 Browse-off was a very informal test but it demonstrated the potential of WebTOC as a browsing tool.

Future Work

WebTOC could be used to display other characteristics of documents such as time since the last update to indicate the freshness of data on the site. The data from the parser could be used with other web visualization software.

Conclusion

WebTOC has been shown to combine the techniques demonstrated by previous work to provide a method of visualizing either directories of files or the contents of Web sites by providing an interactive hierarchical table of contents with additional information on size and composition that are useful for understanding the contents of a collection of documents.

Acknowledgments

We want to thank Ben Shneiderman for his feedback on the design, the Department of Defense for allowing Dave Nation to work with the Human-Computer Interaction Laboratory during nine months of training, the Library of Congress for partial support, and the other students in Dr. Shneiderman's class doing the experiment (Jeff Heflin, Nakul Pasricha and Theen-Theen Tan).

Availability

The WebTOC software and documentation is available from the HCIL FTP site (ftp://ftp.cs.umd.edu/pub/hcil/Demos/WebTOC/index.html).

References

1. Andrews, Keith, Browsing, Building, and Beholding Cyberspace, New Approaches to Navigation, Construction, and Visualisation of Hypermedia on the Internet, Doctoral dissertation, Graz University of Technology, September 1996.
2. Asahi, Toshiyuki, Turo, David, Shneiderman, Ben, Using Treemaps to Visualize the Analytic Hierarchy Process, Information Systems Research 6:4, December 1995, 357-375. [Postscript file] [Abstract file]
3. Card, Stuart K., Robertson, George G., York, William, The WebBook and the Web Forager: An Information Workspace for the World-Wide Web , CHI96 Electronic Proceedings.
4. Chimera, Richard, Value bars: An information visualization and navigation tool for multiattribute listings, Proc. CHI'92 Conference: Human Factors in Computing Systems, ACM, New York, NY (1992), 293-294. [*Postscript file*] [*Abstract file*]
5. Chimera, Richard, Shneiderman, Ben, An Exploratory Evaluation of Three Interfaces for Browsing Large Hierarchical Tables of Contents, ACM Transactions on Information Systems, 12, 4, October 1994, 383-406. [*Postscript file*] [*Abstract file*]
6. Egan, Dennis E., Remde, Joel R., Gomez, Louis M., Landauer, Thomas K., Eberhardt, Jennifer., Lochbaum, Carol C., Formative Design-Evaluation of SuperBook, ACM Transactions on Information Systems, 7, 1, January 1989, 30-57.
7. Furnas, G. Generalized Fisheye Views, in Proceedings ACM CHI'86 Human Factors in Computing Systems Conference, ACM Press, New York, 16-23.

8. Johnson, B. *Treemaps: Visualizing hierarchical and categorical data.* Doctoral dissertation. August 1993, UMI-94-25057.

9. Kumar, Harsha P., Plaisant, Catherine, Shneiderman, Ben, Browsing hierarchical data with multi-level dynamic queries and pruning, Int. J. Human-Computer Studies (1997) 46, 103-124. [*Postscript file*] [*Abstract file*] [*Text only*]

10. Lamping, John, Rao, Ramana, and Pirolli, Peter, A focus + context technique based on hyperbolic geometry for visualizing large hierarchies, Proc. of ACM CHI'95 Conference: Human Factors in Computing Systems, ACM, New York, NY (1995), 401-408.

11. McKnight, C., Dillon, A., & Richardson, J. A comparison of linear and hypertext formats in information retrieval. In R. McAleese & C. Green (Eds.), Hypertext: The state of art (p. 10-19). Oxford, England: Intellect Books, 1990.

12. Mukherjea, S. and Foley, J. D., Visualizing the World-Wide Web with the navigational view finder, Computer Networks and ISDN Systems 27, 1, (1995), 1075-1087.

13. Rouet, J., Lovonen J.. Studying and Learning with hypertext: empirical studies and their implications. In Rouet Jean-Francois, Lovonen Jarmo J., Dillon, Andrew, Spiro, Rand J.(Eds.): Hypertext and Cognition. Lawrence Earlbaum, New Jersey, 1996.

14. Sarkar, Manojit and Brown, Marc H., Graphical fisheye views. Communications of the ACM, 37 (12):73-84, December 1994. (Technical report) no. CS-93-40, Brown University, Dept. of Computer Science, Sept. 1993.

15. Spring, Michael B., Morse, Emile and Heo, Misook. Docuverse: Multi-level Navigation of a Document Space, Department of Information Science and Telecommunications, University of Pittsburgh, Pittsburgh, PA 15260 USA.

Elastic Windows: A Hierarchical Multi-Window World-Wide Web Browser

Eser Kandogan and Ben Shneiderman*
Department of Computer Science,
Human-Computer Interaction Laboratory
*Institute for Advanced Computer Studies
University of Maryland, College Park, MD 20742
kandogan@cs.umd.edu, ben@cs.umd.edu

ABSTRACT

The World-Wide Web is becoming an invaluable source for the information needs of many users. However, current browsers are still primitive, in that they do not support many of the navigation needs of users, as indicated by user studies. They do not provide an overview and a sense of location in the information structure being browsed. Also they do not facilitate organization and filtering of information nor aid users in accessing already visited pages without high cognitive demands. In this paper, a new browsing interface is proposed with multiple hierarchical windows and efficient multiple window operations. It provides a flexible environment where users can quickly organize, filter, and restructure the information on the screen as they reformulate their goals. Overviews can give the user a sense of location in the browsing history as well as provide fast access to a hierarchy of pages.

Keywords

World-Wide Web, Window Management, Information Visualization, User Interfaces.

INTRODUCTION

The World-Wide Web (WWW) is becoming an invaluable source for the information needs of many users. By clicking on a link, users can easily access related information. The ability to access more information in such a quick way fascinates most users, however, after a while users typically have difficulty in remembering where they are coming from and in accessing previously visited pages.

The one-window-one-click interface is appealing in its simplicity, but for many tasks and many users a more powerful browser with multiple windows and multiple selection of links may speed task completion.

Studies on users' navigation strategies, and browsing-task analyses provide interesting results [6, 21, 7, 19]. However, current interfaces for browsing on the WWW are still primitive, in that they do not support many of the navigation needs of users, as indicated by these studies. They do not provide an overview and a sense of location in the information structure being browsed, nor facilitate organization and filtering of information. They provide only rudimentary means to aid users in accessing already visited pages. Recent research offers varied solutions including 3-dimensional, zooming, and metaphorical web browser interfaces [1, 23, 3, 5, 4].

In this paper, a new browsing interface is proposed with multiple window operations and hierarchical windows. It provides a flexible organization in which users can easily organize, filter, and restructure the information on the screen as they reformulate their goals. Overviews can be created for visited pages that may give the user a sense of location as well as provide fast access to a hierarchy of pages.

This paper begins with a review of the observations and analyses made on the problems in hypertext browsers. Next, studies examining users' browsing strategies are briefly described with the lessons derived from these studies listed. Then, our browsing interface is presented with its design principles and examined based on its compliance with the results of these user studies. Technical information regarding the implementation of the Elastic Windows browser is also discussed with reference to a more detailed description.

PROBLEM MOTIVATION

Conklin [9] identified the problems with hypertext as:

- **Disorientation:** The tendency to lose one's sense of location and direction in a nonlinear document.
- **Cognitive overhead:** The additional effort and concentration necessary to maintain several tasks or trails at once.

Disorientation, as Conklin argued, stems from the lack of knowledge of the current position in the whole information structure, but also of the path(s) to the desired destination position. Utting and Yankelovich [22] identified these as spatial and temporal contexts, respectively.

Utting and Yankelovich's further examination provided more details on the problems in current browsers:

- Hard to remember which documents are open
- Following every link is tedious
- Amount of information is unpredictable
- Difficult to get back to a point in the history

The cognitive overhead problem is more related to the user's browsing strategy. It is about how users seek a balance between the gains of added knowledge and the losses from increased distraction by following a link. Marchionini and Shneiderman [16] argue that in browsing, goals are not well defined and change dynamically as new information is encountered by the user.

Cruz [10] observed that current web browsers give little flexibility to users both in filtering out unwanted information and in the specification of the spatial and temporal layout. This limits user's browsing and organization capabilities.

The fundamental mechanism for organization is composition. However, Halasz [13] argues that the hypertext model lacks a composition mechanism, i.e. a way of representing and dealing with groups of nodes and links as unique entities separate from their components.

Rosenberg [19] pointed out that current WWW browsers provide a single window on the document, and when users click to follow a link, the new document is opened in place, replacing the former. Some systems allow another window to be opened for the new document. Browsers simply rely on the window manager to organize these open documents. However, current window managers fail to provide an organization which reflects the semantic relationship that exists among documents browsed on the WWW.

LESSONS FROM USER STUDIES
Although several studies provide demographical information on users and web-sites, our interest is on studies that examine users' navigational access patterns. Studies done on users' navigational strategies by Catledge and Pitkow [6] and by Tauscher and Greenberg [21] are particularly interesting in that they are done in open systems for long durations.

Catledge and Pitkow captured client-side user events of the XMosaic browser from a population of 107 users in the Georgia Institute of Technology's College of Computing for a three week period.

They characterized users' navigation strategies according to the average frequency of following a path with a certain depth. Average frequency was found to be linearly dependent on the path length with a slope of -0.24. Users' browsing strategies are classified as *serendipitous browser*, *general purpose browser*, and *searcher* based on users' average slope.

Besides this classification of the navigation strategies, they also observed:

- Tendency to browse in a small area
- Frequent use of backtracking: Back button usage 41%
- Shallow browsing: Rarely more than two layers
- Infrequent save, print, hotlist addition and retrieval

Tauscher and Greenberg analyzed 6 weeks of detailed usage data from 23 users with at least a year experience of browsing on an instrumented XMosaic browser. They analyzed recurrence of page visits, growth of URL vocabulary, visit frequency as a function of distance, frequency of URL accesses according to page types, locality, and length of repeated sequences.

In summary, their observations are:

- High page recurrence rate: 58% of the pages revisited
- Continued growth of URL vocabulary
- High recency of revisits
- Frequent visits only to very few pages: Personal and organization pages, search engines, etc.
- Browse in small clusters of pages
- Short sequences of repeated URL paths

ELASTIC WINDOWS WEB BROWSER
Hierarchical Page Organization
The Elastic Windows browser is a multi-window browser, where pages are organized hierarchically [14, 15]. Hierarchical organization of pages allows the user to see the context, while exploring further details lower in the hierarchy. Although syntactic information structure on the WWW is an arbitrary graph, presenting the information in a hierarchy can help users in their information seeking activities. While hierarchical organization might facilitate navigation, it can also give users a sense of location in the information structure.

Figure 1 shows a user browsing the Human-Computer Interaction Lab (HCIL) web pages. Pages are hierarchically organized with the top level HCIL main page placed on the left. On the right, four pages (*Lab Description*, *Principal members*, *Students*, *Collaborators*, and *Research Project Description* pages) are opened as a group in the *About HCIL* window. Furthermore, five project pages are opened in the *Research Project Description* page. The hierarchy is created as a result of user actions, not prepared in advance.

Opening new pages In the Elastic Windows browser, a new page can be opened by clicking on the link. The window for the new page is opened "inside" the window of the parent page, placed on the right, using half of the space (Figure 2.a). Thus, when a link is followed, the context is preserved on the left, while the detail on a link is being examined on the right. By selecting a different link, the user might either replace the last selected link(s) or add the new link to the existing pages sharing the space.

Multiple links can be opened by the select operation with the left mouse button followed by a right mouse button click. All selected links are opened side by side, placed within their parents window on the right (Figure 2.b). Alternatively, vertical and tiled placement styles can be selected from the window menu. Links in a region can be selected by drawing a rectangle on the links with the left mouse button. Non-contiguous links can be added to the selection by pressing the control key with the left mouse pressed.

The conventional open-and-replace strategy is still available in the Elastic Windows browser by clicking the right mouse button with the Control key pressed. This way users can skip uninteresting intermediary pages when following a number of links to the desired information.

Multi-level context When browsing a large information structure, users might want to keep multiple levels of contexts on the screen at the same time. This might help users in their navigational strategy by greatly reducing the need to back up, and also lessens a possible disorientation.

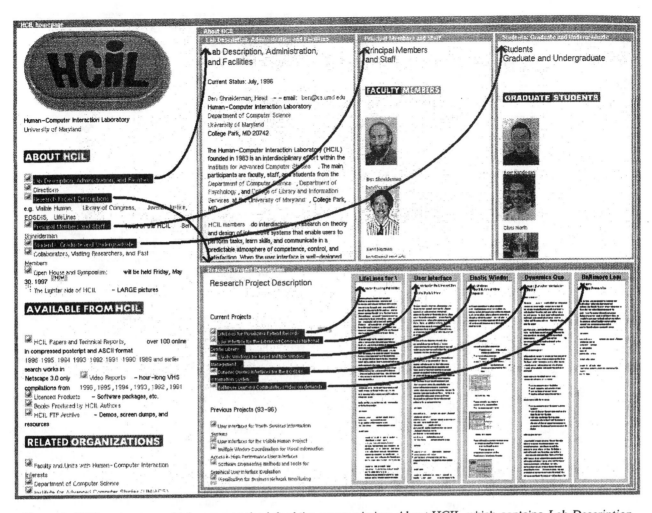

Figure 1: HCIL web pages: Main page on the left of the group window *About HCIL*, which contains *Lab Description*, *Principal members*, *Students*, *Collaborators*, and *Research Project Description* pages. Below, *Research Projects* page contains all five current project descriptions

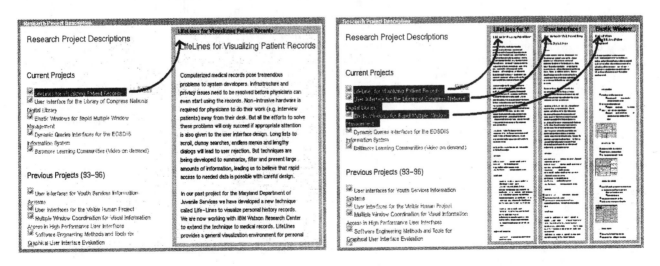

Figure 2: Opening new pages: a) Click to open a single page b) Select and click to open multiple pages

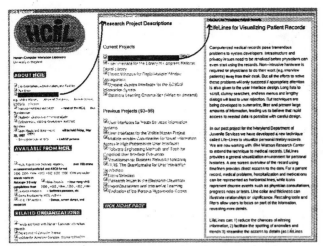

Figure 3: Keeping three levels of context in view: *HCIL Main page*, *Research Project Description*, and *Lifelines* project page

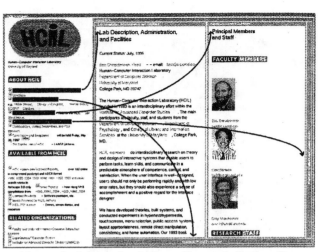

Figure 4: Information hiding: *Research Project Description* and *Students* pages are packed on the layout shown in Figure 1

In Figure 3, the user keeps both the HCIL main page and the *Research Project Description* page in view, while exploring the Lifelines project. Keeping the project description page allows the user to switch to other project pages easily. Keeping the HCIL main page gives users orientation as well as allows them to switch to other interesting links related to HCIL. In the Elastic Windows browser users can also follow more than one trail at the same time. Selecting another link from any page starts a new trail.

Multi-level focus   While keeping multiple levels of context helps preserve orientation, at times users may need to focus on a particular set of pages deeper in the hierarchy. In the Elastic Windows browser, users might maximize a subhierarchy of pages at any level to full screen, allowing more detail to be displayed. For example, a user might initially focus on all research projects in the HCIL page, then on a particular research page, and then on the participants' pages of that project. Users can also skip multiple levels and directly focus on a deeper subhierarchy. The maximize operation can be invoked from the window menu. Users can come back to the previous hierarchy by the return operation also selectable from the window menu. The return operation is more powerful than the conventional back operation in that users can skip levels and see breadth as well as depth.

Information Hiding   In the Elastic Windows browser, a hierarchy of pages can be packed into a small horizontal or vertical bar, giving more space to other pages. The pack operation can be selected from the window menu. This operation not only saves screen space but also facilitates information hiding. In Figure 4, the *Research Project Description* page containing five project pages and the *Students* page are packed into a horizontal bar at the bottom and into a vertical bar on the right, respectively, from the initial layout in Figure 1. Packed pages can be quickly restored to their previous sizes with a single click on the bar.

Overviews   In the Elastic Windows browser, a hierarchy of visited pages can be collapsed into a hierarchicon providing

an overview of those pages (Figure 5). A hierarchicon is an active thumbnail image of hierarchies of pages, which allows selection of any subhierarchy to be displayed on the screen. This facilitates fast access to a hierarchy of pages (Figure 6). Clicking on the same region more than once changes the depth of the selected subhierarchy.

At any time during exploration, a hierarchicon can be created for a hierarchy of pages by selecting from the window menu. As a result, a hierarchicon is created with the scaled image of the hierarchy of pages, added to the overview window. The selected subhierarchy is displayed in the same window as the top-level window of the hierarchicon replacing its contents. The overview window can hold more than one hierarchicon.

Hierarchicons best serve their purposes when the content of pages is rich with images or the text is well-structured. However, spatial characteristics (e.g. location, shape) of pages can also be used in the selection of the active group, though with more cognitive effort.

Since hierarchicons are only for visited pages, they do not serve as an overview of *all* the information in a site. The purpose of hierarchicons is to enable fast switching within a hierarchy of visited pages. However, sites might provide information in the form of images with URL addresses that allows the Elastic Windows browser to automatically build hierarchicons for accessing pages not yet visited.

Restructuring Pages

The structure of the information on the World-Wide Web is authored by individuals or groups of designers. Designers enforce a structure on the information by providing links between pages and pieces of information within a single page that indicate a certain relationship among information units. This structure guides the users in browsing the information and affects their navigational strategy directly.

However, the authored structure may not always match the structure desired by the users browsing the information for some tasks. Users with different backgrounds browse in-

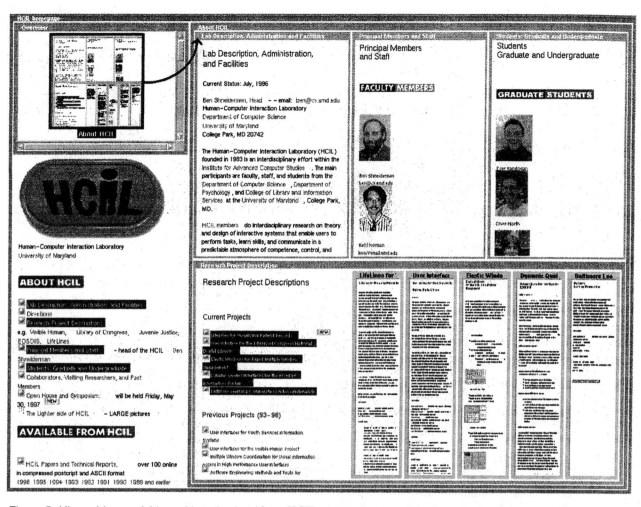

Figure 5: Hierarchicons: A hierarchicon for the *About HCIL* window is created as shown in the overview window

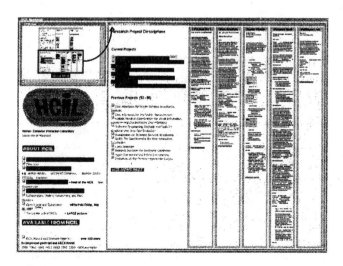

Figure 6: Hierarchicons: The hierarchicon for *About HCIL* window is used to switch the view to *Research Project Description* page and five projects

formation with a variety of goals and browsing strategies. Besides, in browsing goals are not well-defined and they may change based on the information collected. Changes in goals may necessitate changes to the structure of the information. Browsers should provide facilities that allow users to restructure the information to fit their needs.

The Elastic Windows browser allows users to restructure the information on the screen with efficient multiple window operations. Operations can be applied to a hierarchy of windows where effects of the operation are propagated down the hierarchy recursively. Thus, grouping, filtering, and restructuring of information can be done very efficiently.

Grouping   Users can create groupings of pages, that are originally in different locations in the authored information structure. This allows users to gather interesting related information and operate on them as a group.

The Elastic Windows browser allows users to open a container window at any point in the hierarchy. A container window can be opened by double-clicking on the border of a window. Selecting links, dragging and dropping them inside the container window opens the pages for the selected links

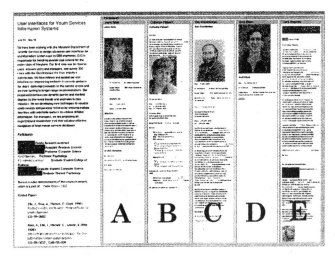

Figure 7: Grouping of participants pages (A, B, C, D, and E) in the HCIL working on the Youth Services project

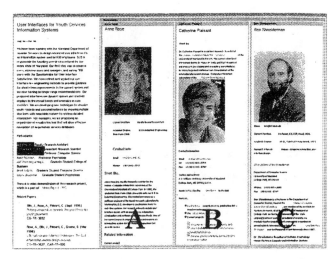

Figure 8: Filtering of the two programmers' pages (D and E) from the participants pages group of the Youth Services project from Figure 7

grouped in the container window. Pages can be added to or removed from an existing group at any time.

Figure 7 shows a grouping of pages of the participants that work on the Youth Services project in HCIL. Having opened them in a group allows the user to understand their responsibilities on the project, and compare their perspectives, backgrounds, educational levels, etc. Groupings can also be established from widely separated pages as well. One such example could be grouping of pages from projects related to Information Visualization.

Filtering   When presented with many pieces of information, users typically desire to filter out uninteresting ones. This allows users to have a better focus on the interesting pieces of information by giving them more screen space.

The Elastic Windows browser allows users to filter out multiple pages in a group quickl by unselecting the corresponding links from their parent page. Alternatively, pages can also be filtered out from their window menus one by one. When a window higher in the hierarchy is closed all its children are closed recursively as well. This way a hierarchy of pages can be filtered out with a single operation.

Figure 8 shows filtering of the two programmers' pages from the group that contains all the participants' pages in the Youth Services project by unselecting the corresponding links. This way users can easily focus on the researchers' pages, eliminating the programmers' pages.

Modifying Hierarchy   In browsing, goals are not well defined and may change as new information is received [16]. A change in goals might necessitate a change to the structure of the information. Facilities that allow users to change the information structure efficiently might help them perform their tasks by reorganizing the screen space.

In the Elastic Windows browser, a hierarchy of pages can be copied from and moved to different locations in the structure with efficient multiple window operations. Once the copy

(move) operation is selected from the window menu, the cursor shape changes to indicate the operation. Then, clicking on the new location copies (moves) the selected hierarchy of pages to their new location.

Figure 9 shows a restructuring scenario. While the user is initially focused on the participants pages (A, B, and C) for the Youth Services project and then on Catherine's page (B), other projects by Catherine (1 and 2) become interesting. Although these two projects pages are initially opened within Catherine's page context, they are moved to a higher level for further examination. The new location of these pages is at the same level with the Youth Services project page.

Personalization   Restructuring of visited pages and being able to save this structure allows users to use their personalized structure in later sessions. Users might find pages not only using the hierarchical structure but also recalling their spatial and visual characteristics. Thus, our approach might be superior to a hierarchical textual bookmark list.

Layout Dynamics

The Elastic Windows browser uses a space-filling tiled strategy for window placement. When a window is opened, closed, resized, or packed, the screen space is proportionally allocated for each window according to its previous size. Groups of windows stretch like an elastic material as they are being resized, and other windows shrink to make space. The extent of a window operation is the group window. The results of the operations are propagated to windows inside that group recursively.

Changes in the size of windows can cause automatic packing of windows which fall below a threshold size. Windows at any level might get packed, opening more space. Windows are packed into either horizontal or vertical bars appropriately. Packed windows are reopened as space becomes available. In Figure 10, initially the *Research Project Description* page is resized automatically packing the *Lab Description*, *Principal members*, and *Students* pages. Then, the Elastic Windows project page is resized, packing other research project pages.

Figure 9: Restructuring: Two project pages (1 and 2) within Catherine's page (B) moved to the same level as the Youth Services project page

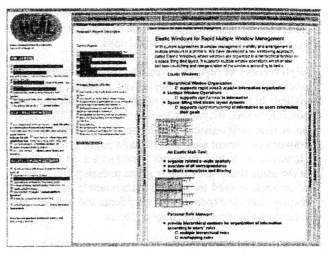

Figure 10: *Research Project Description* page and the Elastic Windows project page are resized automatically packing *Lab Description*, *Principal members*, and *Students* pages and the remaining research project pages on the layout in Figure 1.

Tiled approaches may have an advantage in that they avoid wasted space and disturbing overlaps. On the other hand, in space-filling tiled approaches, window contents may not always conform to different window sizes and small windows may not provide sufficient view of contents. To provide better visibility in the Elastic Windows browser, contents are scaled according to the width of the window. However, for windows above a threshold width, contents are reformatted rather than scaled to display more information. We believe that scaling of contents preserves visual attributes of information which can provide context to help orient the user, and also provide an overview of its contents. It also allows easier recall for later accesses. However, highly demagnified pages might not be very useful especially for text-only pages.

Scaling of contents coupled with the automatic packing feature makes the Elastic Windows browser spatially-scalable. Users can add more and more pages without degrading the screen space utilization. However, more training might be needed for effective usage.

In the current implementation of the Elastic Windows browser, when multiple links are opened, pages corresponding to these links are opened by default side by side and placed within their parent's window, sharing half of the space. Since the contents of these pages are scaled, it gives users an overview of possible interesting pages. Alternatively, vertical or tiled placements can be selected. Space can be partitioned in different proportions, giving more space to new pages.

USER STUDIES REVISITED

- **High page recurrence rate:** Since a considerable percentage of pages are revisited according to studies, browsers should support fast access and easy recall of visited pages. Current browsers use only temporal properties for intra-session revisits (e.g. Back button, History lists), and textual hierarchical listings (e.g. Bookmarks) for inter-session revisits. The Elastic Windows browser employs a hierarchical page organization which preserves spatial and visual properties of pages and the location in the hierarchy. Thus, each of these properties may improve recall of a visited page and thus facilitate faster access. However, in the Elastic Windows browser at high (de)magnification factors, the visual properties might not be very useful, especially for text-only pages.

- **Continued growth of URL vocabulary:** According to the user studies, users continually visit new web pages, thus browsers should provide fast open for new pages. While current browsers facilitate fast open for a page with a single click, they fail to provide facilities that enable fast retrieval of previously visited pages. Approaches should be scalable not only in terms of space allocation, but also retrieval. In the Elastic Windows browser only a single action (e.g. click) is needed to open a single page, and two actions (e.g. select and click) are needed to open multiple pages providing fast access. Hierarchical organization, scaling of contents, and automatic packing make the Elastic Windows browser scalable in terms of space allocation. While the Elastic Windows browser offers more powerful screen management facilities, it might require more user training than the current one-window-one-click style browsers. The

Elastic Windows browser is also more scalable in terms of retrieval, since not only the location of pages but also their visual and spatial properties can be used.

- **High recency of revisits / Frequent use of backtracking:** According to the studies people tend to revisit pages just visited. In Elastic Windows, when a link is followed, it is possible to keep the parent page on the screen. This can improve user performance since the need to go back and forth between the parent page and children pages is eliminated. However, since two (or more) windows are on the screen at the same time, less space is given to each page. Scaling of contents is used to increase the amount of information displayed at the expense of smaller fonts and images, thus it might be harder to read page contents.

- **Frequent visits only to very few pages:** Since the Elastic Windows browser is a multiple window browser, frequently accessed pages such as personal, organizational pages and search engines can simply be left open in windows, preferably packed. Thus, while allowing easy access, it does not occupy much of the screen space.

- **Browse in small clusters of pages:** While studies found that users only browse in small clusters of pages, Elastic Windows browser is capable of clustering any number of pages in a group, facilitating comparison. However, as the number of windows increase the readability can decrease. Pages can be resized, scaling page contents, making them more readable at the expense of more screen management. It is also possible that this result is due to with the one-window-one-click browser used in the observation.

- **Short sequences of URL paths / Shallow browsing:** Studies indicate that users generally do not traverse deep nestings, however, this result might also be related to the browser used in the observation. The Elastic Windows browser supports arbitrarily deep traversals and the maximize operation facilitates focus at any level. However, the maximize operation might lead to disorientation when traversing deep hierarchies, though users can reorient themselves by returning to the previous hierarchy.

- **Infrequent save, print, hotlist addition and retrieval:** Although hotlist addition (save) is rather infrequent, there is a high possibility that pages in the hotlist are used as an intermediate step to reach other pages. The low percentage of these operations does not imply their usefulness. The Elastic Windows browser allows users to save visited pages for later sessions with efficient hierarchical window save operation that recursively saves all pages in a hierarchy.

IMPLEMENTATION

We implemented Elastic Windows using the Galaxy C++ application environment by Visix Software Inc. It runs as an X Windows application under Solaris. Modified NCSA Mosaic 2.5 libraries were used for retrieving and formatting hypertext documents.

Spatial organization of hierarchical windows is kept in an ordered tree with variable number of children at each node. Each level of the tree corresponds to a division of the available space in alternating horizontal and vertical directions. In order to overcome this strict alternating division imposed by ordinary ordered trees, a special type of node is used which functions as a space holder in the structure avoiding the division at that level. Packed windows are marked to indicate that their subwindows will not be drawn on the screen.

In order to allow direct access to nodes at any level of the tree, an array with links to the nodes in the tree is maintained. When initiating operations on windows, references to the nodes are made from this array, thus avoiding unnecessary traversals. Changes in the upper levels of the tree are propagated down the subtree to lower level nodes recursively, also avoiding unnecessary node traversals. More details on the window operations and layout dynamics are described in [14].

Scaling of page contents is done based on the window widths. Windows wider than a threshold value are reformatted keeping the same scaling factor. Galaxy libraries used in the implementation yielded sufficiently rapid graphics performance.

RELATED WORK

Research on web browsers provided many approaches. While some are add-on visualizations to browsers, others are standalone browsers. These approaches can be classified as:

- **2-D Graph:** WebMap [11], Graphic History View [2], Navigational View Builder [18]
- **3-D:** Harmony [1], HyperSpace [23]
- **Hierarchical Windows:** IGD [12], VIKI [17], Elastic Windows [14]
- **Zooming:** Pad++ [3]
- **Metaphorical:** WebBook [5], DecScape [4]

The above list is not complete, but presented here to give an idea of alternative approaches in a classification. The Elastic Windows browser has an advantage over the other hierarchical approaches in that multiple window operations increase user performance and flexibility in arranging pages on the screen. 3-D approaches might have a disadvantage in that valuable information might be occluded, though it is possible to transform the structure in such a way that brings the occluded information into view. Although metaphorical approaches follow concepts familiar to users, they may be limiting in terms of interaction and screen utilization.

Although many solutions are provided, a taxonomy of the approaches is needed to have a better understanding of the relative advantages and disadvantages. Such a taxonomy should address issues related to navigation, presentation, interaction, querying, (re)structuring, composition, and tailorability.

We believe that approaches should be evaluated thoroughly by user studies based on observations examining users' browsing tasks and navigational strategies. Among the web browsers, only a few are evaluated by user experiments [3]. We have conducted a user study comparing the Elastic Windows approach to the independent overlapping windows approach. Results indicated faster user performance for the Elastic Windows interface among expert users in the context of personal role management tasks [15].

CONCLUSION AND FUTURE WORK

We presented a hierarchical multi-window WWW browser, which we believe supports users in their navigation strategies. Hierarchical window organization and multiple window operations allow users to organize web pages, and efficiently restructure the information on the screen. We are working to improve the implementation with smooth transitions on layout updates, leading to decreased user disorientation.

We are planning to observe users' navigational strategies. Although recording of every user action in a browser would yield important information on navigation strategies, observations might be dependent on the browser used. Besides, users might have made compromises on their strategies that can not be seen in the data collected. Thus, such a data collection should also be supplemented by a think-aloud observation, providing more information on users' goals, strategies, and the compromises they made due to the browser interface. These observations will allow us to devise more realistic task sets for effective comparisons among approaches.

ACKNOWLEDGMENTS

We are grateful to Chris North for his comments on this work at various times, and Gary Marchionini and Catherine Plaisant for their review of the draft of this paper. Special thanks go to Visix Software Inc. for their donation of the Galaxy Application Environment. This material is based upon work supported by the National Science Foundation under Grant No. NSF IRI 96-15534, and by IBM.

REFERENCES

1. Andrews, K., Visualizing Cyberspace: Information visualization in the Harmony Internet browser, *Proc. Information Visualization '95*, Computer Society Press, (1995), pp. 97-104.

2. Ayers, E. and Stasko, J., Using graphic history in browsing the World Wide Web, *Proc. Fourth International World Wide Web Conference*, http://www.w3.org/pub/Conferences/WWW4/Papers2/270/, (1995).

3. Bederson, B. B., Hollan, J. D., Stewart, J., Rogers, D., Vick, D., Ring, L., Grose, E. and Forsythe, C., A zooming Web browser, To appear in *Human Factors in Web Development*, Ratner, Grose, and Forsythe, (Editors), (1997).

4. Brown, M. H. and Shillner, R. A., DecScape; An experimental Web browser, *Computer Networks and ISDN Systems 27*, 1, (1995), pp. 1097-1104.

5. Card, S., Robertson, G. and York, W., The WebBook and the Web Forager: An information workspace for the World-Wide Web, *Proc. CHI '96 Conference - Human Factors in Computing Systems*, (1996), pp. 111-117.

6. Catledge, L. and Pitkow, J., Characterizing browsing strategies in the World-Wide Web, *Proc. Third International World Wide Web Conference*, http://www.igd.fhg.de/www/www95/papers/, (1995).

7. Carmel, E., Crawford, S. and Chen, H., Browsing in hypertext: A cognitive study, *IEEE Transactions on Systems, Man, and Cybernetics 22*, 5, (1992), pp. 865-883.

8. Cockburn, A. and Jones, S., Which way now ? Analysing and easing inadequacies in WWW navigation, *Int. Journal of Human-Computer Studies 45*, 1, (1996), pp. 105-129.

9. Conklin, J., Hypertext: An introduction and survey, *IEEE Computer 20*, 9, (1987), pp. 17-41.

10. Cruz, I., Talk in Multimedia User Interfaces panel at *Advanced Visual Interfaces '96 Conference*, (1996).

11. Doemel, P., WebMap - A graphical hypertext navigational tool, *Proc. Second International WWW Conference*, http://www.ncsa.uiuc.edu/SDG/IT94/IT94Info.html, (1994).

12. Feiner, S., Seeing the forest for the trees: Hierarchical display for hypertext structure, *Proc. Conference on Office Automation Systems*, (1988), pp. 205-212.

13. Halasz, Frank G., Reflections on NoteCards: Seven issues for the next generation of hypermedia systems, *Proc. ACM Hypertext '87*, (1987), pp. 345-365.

14. Kandogan, E. and Shneiderman, B., Elastic Windows: Improved spatial layout and rapid multiple window operations, *Proc. Advanced Visual Interfaces '96*, ACM, (1996), pp. 29-38.

15. Kandogan, E. and Shneiderman, B., Elastic Windows: Evaluation of Multi-Window Operations, *Proc. CHI'97 Conference - Human Factors in Computing Systems*, ACM, New York, (1997), pp. 250-257.

16. Marchionini, G. and Shneiderman, B., Finding facts vs. browsing knowledge in hypertext systems, *IEEE Computer 21*, 1, (1988), pp. 70-80.

17. Marshall, C., Shipman, F., and Colombus, J., VIKI: Spatial Hypertext supporting emergent structure, *Proc. ECHT'94, European Conference on Hypertext*, ACM, (1994), pp. 13-23.

18. Mukherjea, S. and Foley, J. D., Visualizing the World-Wide Web with the navigational view finder, *Computer Networks and ISDN Systems 27*, 1, (1995), pp. 1075-1087.

19. Rosenberg, J., The structure of hypertext activity, *Proc. Hypertext '96*, (1996), pp. 22-29.

20. Rivlin, E., Botafago, R. and Shneiderman, B., Navigating in Hyperspace: Designing a structure-based toolbox, *Communications of the ACM 37*, 2, (1994), pp. 87-96.

21. Tauscher, L. and Greenberg, S., How people revisit web pages: Empirical findings and implications for the design of history systems, To appear in *International Journal of Human Computer Studies*, Academic Press, (1997).

22. Utting, K. and Yankelovich, N., Context and orientation in hypermedia networks, *ACM Transactions on Information Systems 7*, 1, (1989), 58-84.

23. Wood, A., Drew, N., Beale, R., and Hendley, B. HyperSpace: Web browsing with Visualization, *3rd International World-Wide Web Conference*, (1995), pp 21-25.

Graphical Multiscale Web Histories: A Study of PadPrints

Ron R. Hightower, Laura T. Ring, Jonathan I. Helfman,
Benjamin B. Bederson[1], James D. Hollan[2]
Computer Science Department
University of New Mexico
Albuquerque, NM 87131
(505) 277-3112
www.cs.unm.edu/pad++
{high, lring, bederson, jon, hollan}@cs.unm.edu

ABSTRACT

We have implemented a browser companion called PadPrints that dynamically builds a graphical history-map of visited web pages. PadPrints relies on Pad++, a zooming user interface (ZUI) development substrate, to display the history-map using minimal screen space. PadPrints functions in conjunction with a traditional web browser but without requiring any browser modifications.

We performed two usability studies of PadPrints. The first addressed general navigation effectiveness. The second focused on history-related aspects of navigation. In tasks requiring returns to prior pages, users of PadPrints completed tasks in 61.2% of the time required by users of the same browser without PadPrints. We also observed significant decreases in the number of pages accessed when using PadPrints. Users found browsing with PadPrints more satisfying than using Netscape alone.

Keywords

World Wide Web, Web Navigation, Web Browser, Usability, Pad++, Zooming User Interface (ZUI), Hypertext, Multiscale Interfaces, Information Visualization.

INTRODUCTION

Navigating hypertext structures like the World Wide Web (WWW) is difficult for users. After following a number of links, people can have difficulty remembering where they have been and returning to previously visited pages. According to a WWW usability study, 13.4% of subjects report not being able to find pages recently visited [9].

The same usability study found that while only 0.1% of page accesses were through the history list, 42% of page accesses used the Back-Button. So, while pages are revisited with a high frequency, the history list is largely

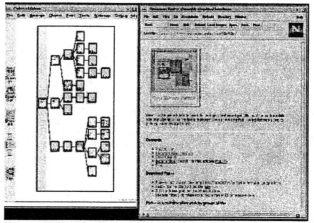

Figure 1: The PadPrints Browser Companion

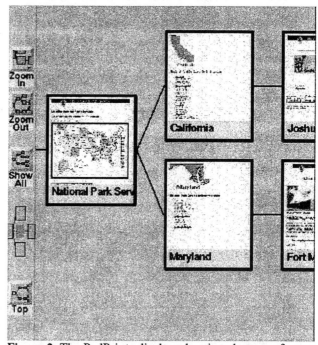

Figure 2. The PadPrints display, showing close-up of nodes in the graphical history hierarchy.

1. Current Address: Computer Science Department., Human-Computer Interaction Lab, University of Maryland, bederson@cs.umd.edu

2. Current Address: Cognitive Science Department, University of California, San Diego, hollan@cogsci.ucsd.edu

unused. This suggests a problem with the history mechanisms found in current browsers. Three shortcomings of the common history mechanism immediately suggest themselves. First, the history list is incomplete–large parts of the history disappear when users follow a branch point. Second, the history list is textual and page titles may lack the cues needed to find a particular page. Third, the history list is cumbersome to use. A user must pull down a menu before finding and following the desired entry.

Better history mechanisms could benefit millions of WWW users. There are a variety of human-factors issues to be considered [11]. Some issues are addressed by proposed alternatives and extensions to browsers. WebMap is a browser extension that shows a graphical relationship between web pages [6]. Each page is represented by a small circle that can be selected to display the actual page. Links between pages are colored to indicate information such as whether it is a link to a different server or whether the destination page has already been read. Webmap graphs may be saved and used by others. WebBook is a three-dimensional Web browser that allows multiple pages to be viewed simultaneously and supports collecting pages in books to replace bookmark files [4]. MosaicG is a modified version of the Mosaic browser that incorporates a graphical history mechanism [1]. In contrast to other systems that build maps for individual websites, MosaicG displays pages as users access them, resulting in personal maps of web usage.

WWW pages often have links to pages linking back to a starting point. It is difficult to visualize these cycles, so many web visualizations are based on hierarchies extracted from graphs of web structure. Some interesting work focuses on alternative visualizations of such structures. Furnas [8], for example, demonstrates how multi-trees can be used to represent a collection of hierarchies sharing parts of underlying structure. One application of multi-trees is visualization of bookmarks from multiple individuals [17].

In addition to problems associated with extracting hierarchies from general graph structures, layout and graphical display of large numbers of nodes is inherently difficult due to limited screen space. As we discuss below, zooming multiscale user interfaces [2][3][15][18] provide one viable approach to this problem.

A ZOOMING GRAPHICAL HISTORY
We have built a browser companion, called PadPrints, to aid web navigation. Figure 1 shows the PadPrints history-map to the left of a browser window. Figure 2 shows a detail of the history-map and some of the PadPrints controls. PadPrints is similar to the MosaicG graphical history (MGGH) [1] in depicting a left-to-right hierarchical history of web pages visited during a browsing session. Also in both systems a node in the hierarchy displays the title of the web page and a small picture associated with the

page. Finally, both systems construct the hierarchy as users traverse links from one page to another, as opposed to prebuilding a hierarchy for a single website as WebMap and other systems do [6].

As with MGGH, the PadPrints browser companion monitors and controls the web browser. When users access pages from the web browser those pages are added to the PadPrints display. Pages are added as children of the current node in the hierarchy, unless that page is already present in the hierarchy. A single click on a page in the PadPrints display sends the browser to the corresponding URL.

Three characteristics distinguish PadPrints from MGGH. First, PadPrints was implemented in Pad++, a substrate for building zooming user interfaces [2][3]. Pad++ allows users to zoom in and out to explicitly control how much context is viewed at any time. The multiscale nature of Pad++ allows geometric objects, text, and images to be displayed at arbitrary size on the screen. This permits the user to view the graphical history in its entirety or zoom in to focus on a particular part of the hierarchy. We conjecture that multiscale contextual display of the graphical history can provide important support for navigation. In addition, multiscale facilities of Pad++ allow natural ways to temporarily remove sub-hierarchies from view by shrinking them until they occupy minimal screen area. PadPrints was written as a Pad++ application using the Tcl scripting language [14].

The second difference between PadPrints and MGGH is the use of a proxy server to monitor browser behavior. Our proxy server notifies PadPrints when the browser (Netscape Navigator) retrieves a page. PadPrints then adds a new page to the graphical hierarchy or, if the URL is already present in the hierarchy, marks the existing page with a yellow outline to denote it as the current page. To achieve similar functionality in MGGH, Ayers and Stasko had to modify the Mosaic browser code to monitor page accesses. This has two drawbacks. Their graphical history is limited to use with one browser and their code changes must be reintegrated as the browser changes to support new HTML features. PadPrints was designed to work with any browser that supports a proxy server and should not require modification as browsers change to support new HTML additions.

Both systems display a small thumbnail sketch of a web page on each node in the hierarchy. The source of this small image represents the third difference between the two systems. Because they had direct access to the implementation of the Mosaic browser, Ayer and Stasko were able to re-render the web page into a hidden bitmap, subsample the resulting image, and display it in their graphical history. PadPrints, without direct access to the renderer, instead uses the X server to grab that portion of the screen associated with the browser. The resulting image data is subsampled and displayed with the node. We note that the multiscale nature of Pad++ supports displaying the full resolution view of a web page with each node, limited only by available memory.

USABILITY TESTING

We performed two usability studies to test the effectiveness of PadPrints. We hypothesized that a graphical hierarchical history mechanism would improve users' web browsing efficiency in terms of speed and number of pages accessed as compared to having only traditional history mechanisms as available in Netscape Navigator 3.0. We also hypothesized that users of PadPrints would find browsing more satisfying than using Netscape Navigator 3.0 alone.

Equipment

Experiments were performed personal computers, running Linux. All systems had 21-inch monitors. Questions and tasks were presented to the subjects by a program that recorded statistics such as the time subjects spent on each question, pages accessed, and questions answered correctly.

Stimuli

Two different sets of web pages were used in the testing. The first set was based on the database from the "browse off" at CHI'97 [13]. This is a hierarchical database of people, places, things, events, and facts. Each page contains a word or a list of words, possibly with links to other pages lower in the hierarchy. There are no images or graphics. This database was chosen because it provides a means to test simple navigation. Throughout the rest of the paper this database is referred to as the *CHI Database*.

Another web page collection was taken from the National Park Service (NPS) website. This website contains photographs and information about national parks in the United States. In contrast to the CHI database, the NPS database is a large real-life website containing images and has a complex structure that is not entirely hierarchical. A copy of the website was downloaded to a local server to avoid network problems during the experiments and to help minimize variability in access times.

EXPERIMENT 1

Method

Subjects were asked to find pages, answer questions about individual pages, and make comparisons between pages. Generally, all questions except the first required some backtracking. Example questions used with the CHI database include: *Go to the page that contains the Kangaroo. How many moons does the planet Uranus have? Are there more whales or more apes listed in this database?* Some example questions used with the National Parks website are: *How many National Parks are in California? Find a picture of the General Sherman Tree in*

Sequoia National Park in California. Which has more islands, Channel Islands National Park or Apostle Islands National Lakeshore? Subjects completed 14 questions using the CHI database and 12 questions using the National Parks website.

A 2x2x2 incomplete-block design was used. With this design we were able to collect more information from each subject than if we had used a between-subjects design and reduce some of the between-subject variability. The independent variables were, whether PadPrints was used, which website (CHI database or National Parks Site), and task order. Each subject was randomly assigned to one of four experimental groups. All subjects browsed both websites and did one set of questions with PadPrints and one set of questions without PadPrints. As a result of the incomplete-block design employed in the experiment, the PadPrints-by-Website interaction was confounded with the Subject-by-Block effect.

Three dependent variables of interest were average time to completion of each question, average number of pages accessed for each question, and user satisfaction ratings. User satisfaction was measured using selected questions from the Questionnaire for User Interaction Satisfaction (QUIS) developed at the University of Maryland [10], as well as some browsing specific questions written in the same format. The QUIS uses a 9 point rating scale.

Only questions a subject completed correctly were included in the time averages. Furthermore, the first question in each task was treated as a practice trial and not included. Questions that over 25% of subjects could not answer correctly were also not included. Two questions from the National Park's task were thrown out for this reason and one question from the CHI database task was thrown out.

Training

Prior to beginning the experiment subjects were trained in use of the Netscape browser and PadPrints. In the first experiment this training was done using the University of New Mexico website. Training for Netscape Navigator, consisted of having the subjects use the forward and back keys, the bookmark list, and the go list. Subjects were told they could make their own bookmarks if they felt it would help them with the task.

PadPrints training included telling subjects a little about PadPrints and how it could be used for navigation. It was explained that PadPrints was a visual history mechanism. Subjects were then instructed to visit a series of page on the UNM website and return to those pages using PadPrints. Subjects also practiced zooming and panning within the Pad++ environment.

Subjects

Thirty-seven subjects participated in Experiment 1. One subject's data was not used because of failure to complete over 70% of the questions correctly. Subjects ranged in age from 18 to 50 years old. Mean age was 26. All but two subjects were students at the University of New Mexico. 83% of subjects had previously used Netscape Navigator to browse the Web. 14% of subjects reported never browsing the World Wide Web. 50% of subjects reported browsing the web an average of two hours a week or less. All but two subjects used computers more than two hours a week. 56% of subjects used computers over 10 hours a week. Of the student subjects, 24% were computer science majors, 21% majored in other sciences or mathematics, 27% majored in health-related areas, 12% majored in education or educational technology, 9% majored in the arts, and 3% majored in business. 44% of subjects were female. All subjects were paid for their participation.

Results

In Experiment 1 we observed a statistically significant improvement in average number of pages accessed (i.e., fewer pages were accessed) when using PadPrints, increased user satisfaction ratings with PadPrints, but no difference in average time to complete each question

The subject effects were confounded with the Website-by-PadPrints-used interaction. Thus main effects only ANOVA models were fit, with effects estimated for Subjects, Website, Task-Order and PadPrints, for each dependent variable. The nine dependent variables were: average time on task, average number of pages accessed, total QUIS score, and 6 scores for the individual parts of the QUIS. Since 9 ANOVAs were run Bonferroni adjusted critical values were used. For an effect to be considered significant p had to be less than 0.006, but p > 0.09 for all tests so there were no significant effects due to task-order for any of the dependent variables.

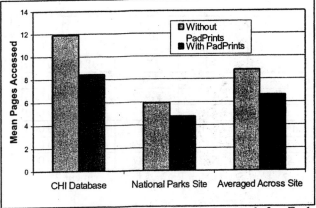

Figure 3. Mean Number of Pages Accessed for Each Question in Experiment 1.

Although we found using PadPrints resulted in significantly fewer page accesses ($F_{1,30} = 18.78$, p=.0002), this did not lead to faster task completion (with $F_{1,33} = .93$, p=.343). Mean pages accessed are displayed in Figure 3.

User satisfaction was measured using questions from the Questionnaire for User Interface Satisfaction (QUIS). Subjects indicated increased satisfaction when using PadPrints as is illustrated in Table 1.

QUIS Section	Average Satisfaction		$F_{1,33}$	p <
	Without PadPrints	With PadPrints		
Overall	5.748	7.506	29.49	0.0001
Screen	6.778	7.181	2.80	0.1038
Feedback	6.148	7.037	14.76	0.0005
Learnability	6.081	7.608	32.14	0.0001
Speed	7.602	8.120	3.50	0.0701
Browsing	6.053	7.681	29.97	0.0001
Total	6.402	7.522	29.58	0.0001

Table 1. User Satisfaction Ratings for Experiment 1

Using Bonferroni adjusted critical values, a significant effect was found for Overall User Satisfaction, Satisfaction with Feedback, Satisfaction with Learnablity, and Satisfaction with Browsing. The total User Satisfaction Score was also significantly higher when PadPrints was used.

EXPERIMENT 2

In Experiment 1 subjects using PadPrints expressed greater satisfaction and accessed fewer pages. However, we did not observe any savings in task completion times. We conjectured that although PadPrints did not save users time in finding information on pages not already visited that PadPrints would save time in returning to pages previously visited. In Experiment 2 we specifically tested this conjecture.

Method

In Experiment 2 subjects were instructed to visit a set of pages and to answer questions about certain pages. The CHI database and the National Parks Site were again used. For the National Parks website, subjects performed a pre-task with 16 questions. For the CHI database subjects were asked 23 questions. After the pre-tasks 10 questions were asked that required subjects to return to already visited pages. Half of these questions could be answered with information from one page, the other half required information from multiple pages. Subjects were instructed to try again if they answered a question incorrectly or failed to visit the correct page. After three tries if a subject could not complete the question they were allowed to move on.

For each subject, time to answer each question and number of pages accessed were recorded. Only questions subjects answered correctly within three attempts were included in computing averages. Only 1.4% of questions were not correctly answered within three attempts.

Training
The training in Experiment 2 was very similar to the training for Experiment 1. Prior to beginning the National Parks task, subjects were trained on the Olympic National Park website. Prior to beginning the CHI database task, subjects were trained using a portion of the CHI database. In each case, training involved portions of the databases not used in the experimental tasks.

Subjects
Thirty-six subjects participated in Experiment 2. Subjects ranged in age from 19 to 60 years old. The average age was 33. All but four subjects were students at the University of New Mexico. Five subjects had participated in Experiment 1. 92% of subjects had previous Netscape Navigator experience. 33% of subjects reported browsing the Web less than two hours a week. All subjects had some web browsing experience and reported using computers more than two hours a week. 72% of subjects used the computer more than 10 hours a week. Of the student subjects, 31% were computer science majors, 22% were education majors, 19% were social science majors, 16% were majoring in mathematics or engineering, 3% were art majors, 3% were business majors, and 6% were non-degree students. 53% of subjects were female. All subjects were paid for their participation.

Results
Data analyses for Experiment 2 were identical to Experiment 1, except we looked at ten dependent variables instead of nine. Bonferroni adjusted critical values were employed (p had to be less than .005 for an effect to be considered significant). The 10 dependent variables were: average time on the pretask questions, average time on the experimental questions, average number of pages accessed on the experimental questions, the total QUIS score and 6 scores for each individual part of the QUIS. There was one significant effect due to task order for the user satisfaction ratings, $F_{1,33} = 9.92$, p=.0035. A breakdown of means suggests this was due to users giving Netscape Navigator alone a lower rating after they had used PadPrints than if they had never used PadPrints. It is not possible to test this explicitly in the current model because of the confounding inherent in the design.

Consistent with Experiment 1 there was no significant difference in time to answer questions for the pre-tasks between subjects using PadPrints and those not using PadPrints, $F_{1,33}$=0.08, p=0.78. However, there was a significant decrease in time to answer questions using PadPrints for the experimental tasks requiring revisiting

pages, $F_{1,33} = 66.23$, p<0.0001. Mean times to complete questions are displayed in Figure 4.

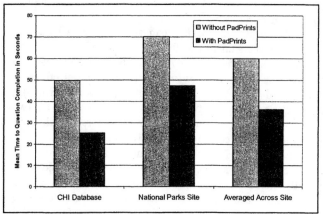

Figure 4. Mean Response Times in Experiment 2.

Fewer pages were accessed when PadPrints was used, $F_{1,33} = 133.61$, p < .0001. Means are shown in Figure 5.

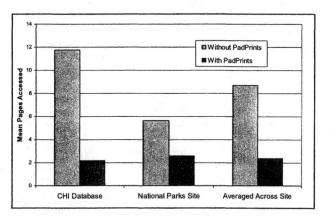

Figure 5. Mean Number Pages Accessed in Experiment 2.

Consistent with Experiment 1 subjects expressed greater satisfaction when using PadPrints. The User Satisfaction Ratings are given in Table 2.

QUIS Section	Average Satisfaction		$F_{1,33}$	p <
	Without PadPrints	With PadPrints		
Overall	5.106	7.977	101.82	0.0001
Screen	6.363	7.704	24.98	0.0001
Feedback	5.458	7.972	55.59	0.0001
Learnability	5.550	8.189	72.32	0.0001
Speed	7.592	8.611	21.25	0.0001
Browsing	5.229	8.069	83.44	0.0001
TOTAL	5.883	8.087	87.78	0.0001

Table 2. User Satsfaction Ratings for Experiment 2

The high satisfaction ratings were further supported by comments made by subjects. Examples of user comments are:

Navigating Without PadPrints

The [NPS] information was easy to read once I found it. It was frustrating that Go saved only my main link and not the pages I had been to.

[With Netscape Navigator] I have to rely on my own memory too much to find a way back to already visited pages.

Navigating With PadPrints

Enjoyed the ease of finding old pages.

It was so easy. There was no confusion whatsoever. It was simple to go where I needed to go and get back to my starting point. I never got lost and I loved the fact that everything was right in front of you without having to go and scroll down "book mark" or some other option. I would really enjoy using this system more often.

Very helpful I used it mostly for the big leaps - when I just needed to go back or forward just one page I used the netscape buttons - I like this global view and it is fun too.

This is a totally cool system, I'm going to miss not being able to have it on my desktop.

FUTURE DIRECTIONS

The development and testing of PadPrints raised a number of issues that should be resolved in future research. These issues fall into the three categories of system structure, interaction, and visualization issues.

The primary issue with system structure is the use of a proxy server as a way of monitoring user-browser interactions. The advantage of this technique is that the browser need not be modified to work with PadPrints. The disadvantage is that user actions must be deduced from the request stream passing through the proxy server. This makes it difficult to distinguish certain actions. For example, we could not distinguish between a user following a link and typing in a URL. Ideally browsers would supply this type of detailed information to external programs. However, we expect that we could deduce this with limited accuracy, based on parsing the HTML source.

Interaction issues are one of the most important parts of future work. One can imagine many different ways to interact with PadPrints and choosing among the variations will require additional usability studies. What information is most useful to the user? What history structures are most

appropriate? Is there a single history structure that is sufficient for all web tasks, or is there a handful of different tasks that each require a unique history structure? Should the history-map include only webpages from the current browsing session, all sessions of the last week, or all pages every visited by the user? The history-map could display all webpages visited by a group of users. How should the history-map be organized if a large number of pages are involved? Test subjects expressed a desire to delete nodes and modify the content of a history-map. What types of editing operations would be most useful?

Finally, there are many visualization issues. Are the thumbnail pictures essential to the success of the history-map, or are webpage titles sufficient? How should pages be arranged and connected in the history-map? Sometimes it is appropriate to display pages just once in the history-map, but other times multiple instances of the same page are appropriate. Also, the multiscale nature of Pad++ allows nodes in the history-map to be displayed at different sizes, but which nodes should be small and which should be enlarged? Is page size controlled automatically or should the user be responsible for controlling this feature of the display? Which of the many display options will be most beneficial to the user?

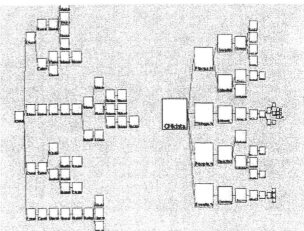

Figure 6. Using the multiscale capabilities of Pad to enhance the layout of the hierarchy.

The version of PadPrints used in the two experiments reported here was frozen for testing prior to adding a number of extensions. Among these are alternative tree layout algorithms and mechanisms for tree editing.

Figure 6 shows two views of a PadPrints graphical history hierarchy. The nodes in the left hierarchy are displayed at a constant scale factor while the nodes in the hierarchy on the right are scaled according to tree depth. This simple layout algorithm provides a fisheye view of the tree. Pad++ permits users to zoom into the tree and view the nodes at a legible size.

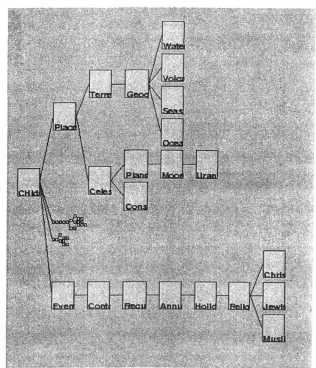

Figure 7. Manual editing of the tree layout. Two subtrees in the middle have been scaled very small to reduce their consumption of screen space.

Figure 7 shows a PadPrints graphical history after a user has edited the layout manually. Here two subtrees have been scaled very small in order to compress their space on the screen. Extensions like these need to be tested in order to discover which will make PadPrints more effective for the user's needs.

CONCLUSION

We have shown that the PadPrints graphical history-map is an effective way to support web navigation. In two usability studies, PadPrints reduced the number of page accesses during general navigation and significantly reduced access time for tasks requiring page revisitation. The results from questionnaire ratings showed subjects experienced higher degree of satisfaction navigating the web using PadPrints than without PadPrints.

In addition to these quantitative results, many subjects commented that they enjoyed using PadPrints. A number of our subjects expressed an interest in using the software for their own work. One subject was a teacher who suggested that PadPrints might be particularly useful in an educational setting. He indicated that while the web is becoming very useful in the classroom, teachers and students frequently experience problems navigating the web while trying to find specific information. He thought PadPrints might help reduce navigational problems. Furthermore, teachers could provide a condensed PadPrints history-map to students to summarize useful websites. In

the future it would be informative to bring PadPrints into the classroom and empirically evaluate these conjectures.

PadPrints is a promising graphical multicale history technique to aid web navigation. Providing users with a visual history-map allowed them to more effectively return to information found in previously visited webpages. By reducing the burden of navigation more cognitive resources can be spent on finding, integrating, and processing new information, potentially making the World Wide Web a more useful information source.

ACKNOWLEDGEMENTS

We acknowledge generous support from DARPA's Human Computer Interaction Initiative, Contract #N66001-94C-6039, and from the United States Department of Energy, Contract DE-AC04-96AL85000. This work was also supported by a gift from the Intel Corporation. In addition, we acknowledge our Pad++ collaborators at New York University Media Research Lab, especially Jon Meyer, and at the University of Michigan.

REFERENCES

1. Eric Ayers and John Stasko. "Using Graphic History in Browsing the World Wide Web", The 4th International World Wide Web Conference, www.w3.org/ Conferences/WWW4/Program_Full.html, December 11-14, 1996.

2. Benjamin B. Bederson and James D. Hollan. "Pad++: A Zooming Graphical Interface for Exploring Alternate Interface Physics", *Proceedings of UIST'94* ACM Press, 17-26.

3. Benjamin B. Bederson, James D. Hollan, Ken Perlin, Jon Meyer, David Bacon, and George Furnas. "Pad++: A Zoomable Graphical Sketchpad for Exploring Alternate Interface Physics", *Journal of Visual Languages and Computing* (7), 1996, 3-31.

4. Stuart K. Card, George G. Robertson, and William York, "The WebBook and the Web Forager: An Information Workspace for the World Wide Web", *Proceedings of CHI'96*, ACM Press, 111-117.

5. Andy Cockburn and Steve Jones. "Which way now? Analysing and easing inadequacies in WWW navigation", *International Journal of Human-Computer Studies* (45), 1996, 105-129.

6. Peter Doemel, "WebMap - A Graphical Hypertext Navigation Tool", *2nd International Conference on the World Wide Web*, Chicago, IL, 1994, 785-789.

7. William C. Donelson. "Spatial Management of Information", *Proceedings of SIGGRAPH'78*, ACM Press, 203-209.

8. George W. Furnas and Jeff Zacks. "Multitrees: Enriching and Reusing Hierarchical Structure", *Proceedings of SIGCHI'94*, ACM Press, 330-336.

9. GVU's WWW Surveying Team. "GVU's 6th WWW User Survey", www.cs.gatech.edu/gvu/user_surveys/ survey-10-1996, 1996.

10. B. Harper and K. Norman. "QUIS 5.56: Questionare for User Interaction Satisfaction", University of Maryland at College Park, 1994.

11. Wendy A. Kellogg and John T. Richards. "The Human Factors of Information on the Internet", *in Advances in Human Computer Interaction*, Ed. J. Nielsen, Ablex Press, (5), 1-36.

12. Sougata Mukherjea, James D. Foley, and Scott Hudson. "Visualizing Complex Hypermedia Networks through Multiple Hierarchical Views", *Proceedings of CHI'95*, ACM press, 331-337. .

13. Kevin Mullet, C. Fry, and Diane Schiano. "On Your Marks, Get Set, Browse!", *Proceedings of CHI'97*, Human Factors in Computing Systems, Extended Abstracts, 113-114.

14. John K. Ousterhout. *Tcl and the Tk Toolkit*, Addison-Wesley, 1994.

15. Ken Perlin and David Fox. "Pad: An Alternative Approach to the Computer Interface", *Proceedings of SIGGRAPH'93*, ACM Press, 57-64.

16. David Ungar and Randy B. Smith. "Self: The Power of Simplicity", *Proceedings of OOPSLA '87*, 227-241.

17. Kent Wittenburg, Duco Das, Will Hill, and Larry Stead. "Group Asynchronous Browsing on the World Wide Web", *Proceedings of the 4th International World Wide Web Conference*, Boston, MA, International WWW Conference

18. Benjamin B. Bederson and James D. Hollan. "Pad++: A Zoomable Graphical Interface System", Demonstration, SIGCHI'95 Companion, 1995, 23-24.

Chapter 6

Understanding
Hierarchical Data

. . . gradually I began to feel that we were growing something almost organic in
a new kind of reality, in cyberspace, growing it out of information . . .
a pulsing tree of data that I loved to climb around in, scanning for new growth.

Mickey Hart,
Drumming at the Edge of Magic: A Journey into the Spirit of Percussion (1990)

Before gigabyte-sized hard disks were common, most users had to carefully manage their disk space. While the operating system and most application programs were necessary, many downloaded software demonstrations, documents, multimedia, and various databases were candidates for deletion when the disk became too full. Unfortunately, it was difficult to get an overview with which to identify where disk space was being wasted or which files were no longer useful. There was no compact visualization of directory tree structures. During one memorable crisis in 1990, the shared 80-megabyte hard disk in the HCIL was filled by 14 users, making it still more difficult to determine how and where space could be freed. Finding large files that could be deleted, or even determining which users consumed the largest shares of disk space, was a difficult task.

File systems are representative of hierarchies in general in that they are large, arbitrarily shaped, and often used by people to make decisions. Recognizing the generality of the problem, and having the immediate problem at hand of a full disk, led to a range of activity in visualizing hierarchies.

Initial attempts to understand disk utilization with tree-structured node-link diagrams failed because they grew too large to be useful; however, it seemed possible to show a tree in a space-constrained layout that would fit on a single screen. Strategies that left blank spaces or those that dealt with only fixed levels or fixed branching factors were not acceptable. Showing file size by area coding seemed natural, but various rectangular, triangular, and circular strategies all had problems. Then, while puzzling about this in the faculty lounge, Ben Shneiderman had the "Aha!" experience of splitting the screen into rectangles in alternating horizontal and vertical directions while traversing down the levels. This recursive algorithm seemed attractive, but it took a few days to be sure that it would always work and to write the six-line algorithm. Choosing the right name probably took as long, but the term *treemap* described the notion of turning a tree into a planar space-filling map. This algorithm and the initial designs led to the first technical report (91-03) in March 1991, which was published in *ACM Transactions on Graphics* in January 1992.

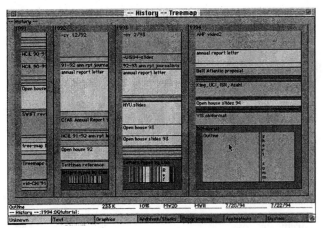

Figure 6.1 Four years of files in a Macintosh directory using TreeViz.

The initial design simply nested the rectangles, but a more comprehensible design used a border to show the nesting. Finding an effective visualization strategy took only a few months, but producing a working piece of software took over a year. Doctoral student Brian Johnson implemented the algorithms and refined the presentation strategies while preserving rapid performance even with 5000 node hierarchies. The TreeViz application (Figure 6.1) ran on color Macintosh models and led to the widely cited paper in the October 1991 proceedings of the IEEE Visualization Conference (91-06).

Treemaps are a convenient representation that have unmatched utility for certain tasks. The capacity to see tens of thousands of nodes in a fixed space and find large areas or duplicate directories is very powerful. It does take some learning for novices to grasp the tree structure layout in treemaps, but the benefits are great.

Brian Johnson's Macintosh implementation added many other interesting features as well, such as zooming, sound (as a redundant or independent code, for example, larger files had a lower pitched sound), hue and saturation control, many border variations, and labeling control. We struggled to deal with the problem of many small files in some directories, but wound up showing only a blackened area that invited closer examination by zooming. We knew that encoding a linear variable such as file size as an area was breaking a graphic design guideline, but the benefits of seeing a large range of file sizes seemed like a worthwhile compensation. We also knew that visually comparing long narrow rectangles to squarish ones was problematic, so cursoring over the boxes produced the exact file size on the bottom of the display.

We found that new users took some time to get acquainted with the treemap display, so we began to explore improvements and training methods. We had been excited about the possibility of examining complex hierarchies with thousands of nodes at five to seven levels, but novices found those displays challenging. We had to bring our training times up to about 15 minutes in order to demonstrate the strong benefits of treemaps. Brian Johnson's dissertation (94-04) reports on two studies, which were never published, that sort out the benefits of his treemap implementation.

Master's student David Turo also built a treemap system

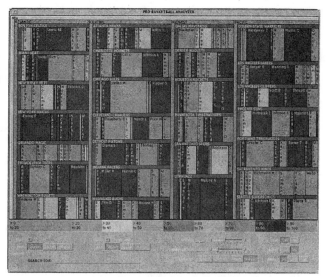

Figure 6.2 Data from the National Basketball Association shows 453 basketball players, organized into the 27 teams in 4 leagues.

on the Sun workstation. To make it more comprehensible in our demonstrations, we moved to examples with a fixed-level hierarchy. We used an appealing and familiar sports application: 453 basketball players, organized into the 27 teams in 4 leagues of the National Basketball Association (Figure 6.2) (94-15 [6.2]). With 48 statistics about each player for the 1991–1992 season, users could chose color and area coding from points scored, fouls, free throws, and the like. The 1993 HCIL video showed Turo's system with the basketball data. His unpublished master's thesis describes his implementations and an empirical study. Johnson and Turo also cooperated on a paper describing improvements they made to the visual presentation (92-06).

By now, we were pushing ahead on several application domains. A Swiss visitor, Alexander Jungmeiseter, worked with Dave Turo's implementation and built a stock portfolio visualization that showed clients, portfolios, industry groups, stocks, and trades (92-14). Size might indicate the worth of holdings, and color might indicate the degree of increase or decrease in value. A worthwhile application for

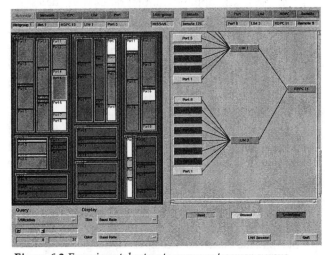

Figure 6.3 Experimental setup to compare treemap versus node-link tree diagram.

this might be a stock market monitor that showed the current daily trade activity. It could present the 30 Dow Jones Industrials, the Standard & Poor's 500, or all 3000+ companies on the New York Stock Exchange. They might be grouped by industry (airlines, chemicals, drugs, etc.), area coded by volume of trading, and color coded by price increase or decrease.

A Japanese visitor, Asahi Toshiyuki, built his own innovative treemap interface to implement the analytical hierarchy process used in decision making (94-08, 95-04 [6.1]). Users could express their opinions of the relative merits of a decision choice (such as which of three sites to chose for a factory) by pumping up areas for their preferred choices, and pumping up the areas for importance of costs, availability of labor, tax breaks, and so forth. The video demonstrates these processes (1994 video, 95-04 [6.1]), and an empirical study showed users could succeed with this tool (Figure 6.3).

Another success story for treemaps was their inclusion in a satellite management system for Hughes Network Systems (1994 video, 94-07 [6.3]). The three-level hierarchy showed each node of a network as a fixed size, and color was used to indicate available capacity. The engineering-oriented community of ground station operators grasped this simplified version quickly.

Treemaps were a major focus of the HCIL's work at that time. Sometimes Ben Shneiderman ran into resistance when showing still images of hard disk directories with thousands of nodes. Once, at the University of Washington, his talk produced a mixed reaction about treemaps, so he installed TreeViz and examined their hard disk directories. The local folks then saw for themselves that three copies of the same C compiler were installed on this machine. An x-ray vision metaphor had proved to be effective on this occasion. Similarly, at Apple Computers, several interested attendees tried out TreeViz, and the next day one of them reported finding many megabytes of useless information on their network servers.

TreeViz was appreciated for the Apple Macintosh, and we were getting requests for a Windows version. Graduate student Marko Teittinen took up the challenge and produced a Windows 3.1 implementation called *WinSurfer*. Marko's

video (1995) showed the features that were meant to match the Windows Explorer (Figure 6.4). WinSurfer allowed users to view, delete, copy, move, rename, and run files. It worked nicely, but novices struggled to understand the layout, which might show 5000 or more files at 7 or more levels. Plans to simplify the initial screen presentation to only two levels and to allow easier user control were never implemented.

Statisticians point out that the mosaic display, shown by Bertin and others (Bertin 1983), is similar to the treemap concept. For fixed-level hierarchies, there is a great similarity, but the gist of the treemap idea was intimately tied to the computerized implementation, interactive selections, and a user control panel for setting attributes. Mosaics are partitions of a rectangle, whereas the treemaps emphasize the nesting of levels and permit variable depth trees.

By 1995, treemap implementations were spreading, with interesting variations from researchers at Georgia Tech, the University of Southern California, Lucent, and Mitre. An early innovative commercial version gave Storyspace hypertext authors an overview of their work (*www.eastgate.com*).

Interest in treemaps was invigorated in 1999 when Martin Wattenberg of SmartMoney developed a polished implementation that showed 535 popularly held stocks, organized by industry groups, size coded by market capitalization, and color coded to show rise or fall (*www.smartmoney.com/marketmap*).

Wattenberg's clever variation, cluster treemaps, ensures low aspect ratio rectangles (most rectangles are squarish, and there are very few thin rectangles), but gives up the lexicographic ordering in slice-and-dice treemaps.

A visually intriguing treemap refinement was developed by the Visualization Group of the Technische Universiteit Eindhoven, headed by Jarke J. van Wijk. Their *cushion treemaps* show depth of nesting by shadows on cushionlike 3D mounds. They also created a new layout strategy called *squarified treemaps* that avoids high aspect ratio rectangles by using an alternative to Wattenberg's algorithm. They developed an excellent free program, SequoiaView, to show Windows PC file directories using cushion treemaps. This colorful representation shows nesting depth more clearly.

During the summer of 2000, the HCIL resumed work on treemaps, when Raghuveera Chalasani developed a Java version that included dynamic queries sliders. By early 2001, we polished his implementation into Treemap 3.0 (*www.cs.umd.edu/hcil/treemap3*), which is licensed by the University of Maryland's Office of Technology Commercialization. Treemap 3.0 includes dynamic queries to filter out unwanted items, squarified layout (as well as slice-and-dice), improved input, infotips, and color and font controls. A demo version with five data sets is available free. A useful feature of Treemap 3.0 is that it also allows you to visualize the contents of your Windows PC directory structure. The HCIL, under Catherine Plaisant's leadership, continues to refine this software in joint projects with companies such as Chevron.

The Smithsonian Institution developed a treemap exhibit during summer 2001, History Wired, with help from Martin

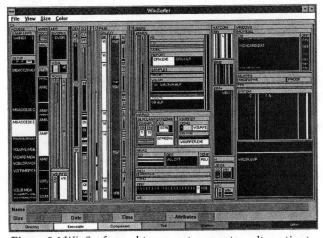

Figure 6.4 WinSurfer used treemaps to present an alternative to the Windows 3.1 Explorer.

Wattenberg. The 450 items are clustered into groups such as home, clothing, business, and computers, and linked to attributes such as politics, medicine, and science. Users can click to get more details, search by attributes, or filter by time period. This novel Web site invites users to record their level of interest for items, which grow in size as they get higher scores (*www.historywired.si.edu*).

The cluster and squarified treemap algorithms are visually appealing in part because the rectangles are more squarelike. They avoid the thin rectangles in the slice-and-dice algorithm, but sacrifice the alphabetic ordering of nodes. This creates an additional problem when leaf node sizes change because the position of rectangles can alter dramatically. The goal of ordered treemaps was achieved by a novel algorithm that nicely balanced squarelike nodes (aspect ratios close to one) while preserving order. This paper, "Ordered Treemap Layouts," was presented at the October 2001 IEEE Symposium on Information Visualization.

However, we found still more ways to improve the layout by organizing the screen space into horizontal (or vertical) strips. This idea helped keep the squarelike aspect ratio and made for an easier to follow ordering. We demonstrated this with a study of 20 users. Another innovation, *quantum treemaps*, satisfies the need to accommodate fixed-shape items like page thumbnails or photos. The paper, "Ordered and Quantum Treemaps: Making Effective Use of 2D Space to Display Hierarchies," appeared in *ACM Transactions on Graphics* in 2002 and provides a good summary of the evolution of treemaps (2001-18 [6.4]).

To support researchers and students, Ben Bederson and Martin Wattenberg wrote an open-source Java 1.1 library of five treemap algorithms (*www.cs.umd.edu/hcil/treemap-history*). Each takes a list of numbers and an input rectangle, generating a set of subrectangles that are proportional in area to the input numbers and the space of the input rectangle. This library includes animated deomonstrations that show the strengths and weaknesses of the algorithms.

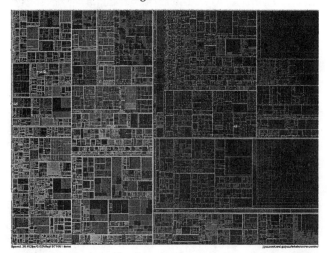

Figure 6.5 Jean-Daniel Fekete developed the latest HCIL treemap implementation to support large data sets of a million items and explore the uses of animation (www.cs.umd.edu/hcil/VisuMillion). This directory browser shows more than one million files.

The five treemap algorithms implemented are as follows:
- BinaryTree—Partially ordered, not very good aspect ratios, stable
- Ordered—Partially ordered, medium aspect ratios, medium stability
- SliceAndDice—Ordered, very bad aspect ratios, stable
- Squarified—Unordered, best aspect ratios, medium stability
- Strip—Ordered, medium aspect ratios, medium stability

Commercial treemap implementations are spreading. The Hive Group, a San Francisco Bay Area startup, promotes electronic product catalogs using treemaps with clever and appealing applications, such as the one for Peet's Coffee, presenting 32 coffees with area showing price, and color (from light to dark) showing flavor (*www.peets.com/tast/11/coffee_selector.asp*). The Hive Group puts treemaps to work for business analytics, thereby enabling executives to better manage their businesses. Others companies such as Chevron, Sun Microsystems, and Burlington Northern Santa Fe are already applying treemaps for business management.

Micro Logic Corp, a New Jersey company, sells a commercial product called *DiskMapper* (*www.miclog.com/dmdesc.htm*) for Windows machines based on the treemap idea. They have received great press attention and awards for their product. The University of Maryland receives a modest royalty on DiskMapper by way of a license agreement with the Office of Technology Commercialization.

Marc Smith's work at Microsoft Research applies treemaps in the Netscan project (*netscan.research.microsoft.com*) to data mine and visualize Usenet, one of the largest collections of social cyberspaces. Their initial goal is to provide an overview of the range of variation in Usenet activity and to highlight distinctive patterns of different groups.

Our most recent work with treemaps has been to look at issues of scale. It is usually easy to make sense of data when there is only a small quantity of it. The difficulty comes, and the value of visualization appears, when the data starts to grow. Yet most of the treemap visualizations that we and others had looked at are limited to a modest size of thousands or tens of thousands of items. Although this is quite valuable and has solved many important problems, the world of data grows much larger than that. And so we were pleased when Jean-Daniel Fekete joined us last year as a visiting professor to study how to improve our visualizations to support millions of items. Coming at this problem with a strong background in more traditional three-dimensional graphics enabled the development of new techniques that scale up scatter plot and treemap visualizations to support more than one million items (Figure 6.5) (2002-01 [6.5]).

The struggle to make treemaps comprehensible continues, but users increasingly recognize their uniquely powerful capabilities for exploring large hierarchical structures. Once they understand the idea, users often become devoted to the concept, sometimes suggesting additional features for their specific needs.

Despite, or perhaps because of, our long experience with treemaps, we have recently reopened our investigation into node-link diagrams to depict trees. The motivation here is that while treemaps are excellent for mapping arbitrary two-dimensional data to hierarchies and for seeing relationships between those data and the tree, they still have limitations. They require some training for new users, and they don't map well to most people's sense of a tree. Neither are they well suited for displaying arbitrary information within the nodes (imagine displaying an organizational chart with a treemap, with information about each person in a node). Such issues came up when we started a new project with Chevron (now ChevronTexaco), and they wanted to visualize organizational charts in a simple way for everyone in the company.

Ben Bederson and Catherine Plaisant had a debate over whether there was anything new to do in this area. On the one hand, there was a huge literature on tree visualization, including depictions using node-link diagrams. On the other hand, our understanding of zoomable and animated interfaces had increased to the point where we thought we still just might be able to contribute something. So, we embarked on creating a new tool, which came to be called SpaceTree (2002-05 [6.6]). It looks as though we made the right decision, because the result is quite promising and compares favorably to the existing standards. This history is also interesting because Stu Card, Dave Nation (a PARC visitor who had previously visited the HCIL for a year), and some of their colleagues at PARC also pursued building a new animated tree viewer, which they call DOI (Degree of Interest) Tree. Though visually different and developed completely independent, the core ideas for the two trees are quite similar.

The story of SpaceTree is interesting for another reason as well. We started building it using Jazz, our ZUI toolkit (2000-13 [3.2]). However, SpaceTree showed several performance problems that hadn't come up before. It forced us to revisit some basic design questions of Jazz, pushing us to create Piccolo, the new ZUI toolkit we are now developing. Piccolo solves the performance problems we had with Jazz, and since we were starting from scratch, enabled us to clean up a number of other problems we had found over the years.

FAVORITE PAPERS FROM OUR COLLEAGUES

Bruls, M., Huizing, K., Van Wijk, J. J., Squarified Treemaps, *Proc. Joint Eurographics and IEEE TCVG Symposium on Visualization,* IEEE Press (2000), 33–42.

Card, S., Nation, D., Degree-of-Interest Trees: A Component of an Attention-Reactive User Interface, *Proc. ACM Conference on Advanced Visual Interfaces (AVI 2002),* ACM, New York (2002), 231–245.

Lamping, J., Rao, R., Pirolli, P., A Focus + Context Technique Based on Hyperbolic Geometry for Visualizing Large Hierarchies, *Proc. ACM CHI 95 Conference: Human Factors in Computing Systems,* ACM, New York (1995), 401–408.

Van Wijk, J. J., Van de Weterhing, H., Cushion Treemaps: Visualization of Hierarchical Information, *Proc. IEEE Symposium on Information Visualization (Info Vis 1999),* IEEE, New York (1999), 73–78.

BIBLIOGRAPHY

Bertin, J., *Semiology of Graphics Design: Diagrams, Networks, Maps,* translated by Berg, W., University of Wisconsin Press (1983).

Visual decision-making:
Using treemaps for the Analytic Hierarchy Process

Toshiyuki Asahi*, David Turo and Ben Shneiderman

Human-Computer Interaction Laboratory,
Dept. of Computer Science &
Institute for Systems Research
University of Maryland, College Park, MD 20742 USA

ABSTRACT

The Analytic Hierarchy Process (AHP), a decision-making method based upon division of problem spaces into hierarchies, is visualized through the use of treemaps, which pack large amounts of hierarchical information into small screen spaces. Two direct manipulation tools, presented metaphorically as a "pump" and a "hook," were developed and applied to the treemap to support AHP sensitivity analysis. The problem of construction site selection is considered in this video. Apart from its traditional use for problem/ information space visualization, the treemap also serves as a potent visual tool for "what if" type analysis.

KEYWORDS

Visualization, treemap, analytic hierarchy process, AHP, decision support

* Current address: Kansai C&C Research Lab., NEC Corporation, 4-24, Shiromi 1-Chome, Chuo-Ku, Osaka 540, Japan, Tel: 81-6-945-3214, email: asahi@cobp.cl.nec.co.jp

INTRODUCTION

Treemaps graphically represent hierarchical information via a two-dimensional rectangular map, providing compact visual representations of complex data spaces through both area and color [2-5]. Their efficiency for particular data searching tasks has been tested through controlled studies [4,5] with primary benefits seen for two types of tasks: location of outliers in mass hierarchies and identification of cause-effect relationships within hierarchies. By extending the treemap into a "read/write" graphic through direct manipulation tools, the user is given the capability to massage the data and perform the outlier and cause-effect tasks much more effectively. Analytic Hierarchy Process (AHP) [1], given its decision tree hierarchy and inherent need for large-scale data visualization and user manipulation, is an appropriate choice for treemap visualization.

AHP was developed to promote improved decision-making for a specific class of problems that involve prioritization of potential alternate solutions through evaluation of a set of criteria elements. These elements may be divided into sub-elements and so on, thus forming a hierarchical decision tree. Once the hierarchical problem definition has been established, these criteria are weighted individually at every level relative to each other; prioritization of the alternate solutions can then be obtained via evaluation of these weights.

The treemap can represent both hierarchical structure and each elements' quantitative information simultaneously in a two-dimensional rectangular space; 100% of the designated screen area is utilized. Application arenas for treemaps have included computer directory browsing, stock market portfolio visualizations, an NBA player statistical browser, and a US budget viewer.

Treemaps are generated using a straightforward algorithm known as "slice-and-dice." The root node of a hierarchy is represented by the entire screen area. For the root node's children, the screen area is sliced (either horizontally or vertically) to create smaller rectangles with area dependent upon the value of a particular *weighting attribute*. Each node is then processed recursively, with the direction of the slicing switched by 90 degrees for each level.

Since the decision-making processes are represented by hierarchical trees in AHP, these trees translate directly to the treemap visualization method. Figure 1 is an example of a treemap generated with our prototype AHP application. A base rectangle representing the goal of decision-making is divided into small rectangular areas proportional to their relative importances. Users can identify any criterion by labels displayed in the offset areas (offset areas are also helpful for users to recognize the hierarchical structure). The hook and pump tools (upper right in Figure 1) enable users to adjust the size of areas by pulling on a boundary or by pumping up an area. Since areas represent preferences among the alternatives, the users can quickly grasp the relative impact of each component and understand which components most influence the outcome. On the bottom of the display, a horizontal histogram shows the aggregate result, and as users hook or pump areas the histogram changes within a few hundred milliseconds. This dynamic approach enables users to explore many alternatives in seconds as opposed the many minutes required to input a fresh set of preferences using the current keyboard entry approach. The treemap, which till now has been used as a way of displaying large amounts of data, now becomes a powerful input strategy.

A usability test was conducted with six business or management majors who were already familiar with the AHP. They performed five tasks and then rated the interface highly on all 12 criteria. Improvements were suggested, but the basic concept was strongly supported [6].

REFERENCES

1. Saaty, T.L. *The Analytic Hierarchy Process*. McGraw-Hill, New York, 1980.

2. Shneiderman, B. *Tree Visualization with Tree-maps: A 2-D space-filling approach*. ACM Transactions on Graphics 11, 1 (Jan. 1992), pp. 92-99.

3. Turo, D. and Johnson, B. *Improving the visualization with treemaps: Design issues and experimentation*. Proceedings of Visualization '92, IEEE Computer Society Press, 1992, pp. 124-131.

4. Turo, D. and Johnson, B. *Improving the visualization with treemaps: Design issues and experimentation*. Proceedings of Visualization '92, IEEE Computer Society Press, 1992, pp. 124-131.

5. Turo, D., *Enhancing treemap displays via distortion and animation: Algorithms and experimental evaluation*, Unpublished Masters Thesis, Department of Computer Science, University of Maryland, 1993.

6. Asahi, T., Turo, D., and Shneiderman, B., Using treemaps to visualize the Analytic Hierarchy Process, University of Maryland Department of Computer Science Technical Report CS-TR-3293 (June 1994).

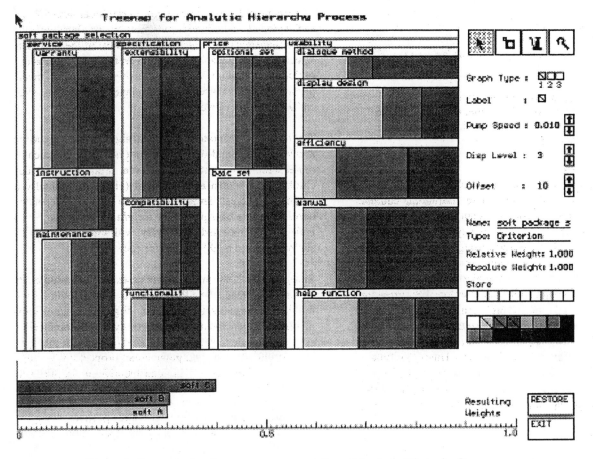

Figure 1: Screen design for treemap representation of Analytic Hierarchy Process with user interface tools for adjusting the treemap.

Hierarchical Visualization with Treemaps: Making Sense of Pro Basketball Data

David Turo
Human-Computer Interaction Laboratory
University of Maryland
A.V. Williams Bldg.
College Park, MD 20740
Tel: 1-301-405-2725
E-mail: turo@cs.umd.edu

ABSTRACT
Treemaps support visualization of large hierarchical information spaces. The treemap generation algorithm is straightforward and application prototypes have only minimal hardware requirements. Given primary graphical encodings of area, color and enclosure, treemaps are best suited for the tasks of outlier detection, cause-effect analysis and location of specific nodes—satisfying user-specified criteria—in their hierarchical context. Distortion effects extend treemap capabilities by emphasizing node relationships in the diagram.

KEYWORDS: Visualization, statistics, hierarchy, treemap

INTRODUCTION
The large information spaces of today can only be harnessed by new and innovative visualization tools that provide overview, exploration and dissection capabilities. Current software for data exploration of even moderately-sized spaces falls short in providing this data-harnessing functionality; users are asked to keep information in mind, use navigational tools such as scrollbars to view small chunks of data at a time, and piece together a data space bit by bit as a consequence.

Treemaps were developed to manage large hierarchical information spaces without requiring workstation-class hardware; prototypes have been implemented on a variety of platforms including 386 class DOS machines, Macintosh 68030 machines and Sun workstations. Treemaps are generated via a simple recursive slicing algorithm that partitions a rectangular screen area using a numeric weighting attribute; the direction of the slice is reversed at each tree level [2,3]. All nodes map to individual rectangles on the treemap; rectangular enclosure is used to convey parent-child relationships (Figure 1). As the algorithm uses all of the provided screen space, the treemap can display

about an order of magnitude more nodes compared to traditional methods such as tree diagrams; exact amounts depend on both screen resolutions and the statistical distribution of the weighting attribute used by the treemap algorithm.

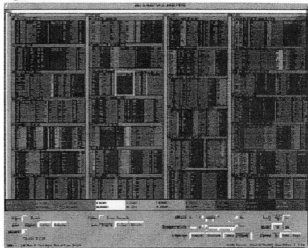

Figure 1: The four NBA divisions are displayed, sliced into teams and then players. The weighting attribute is points per season.

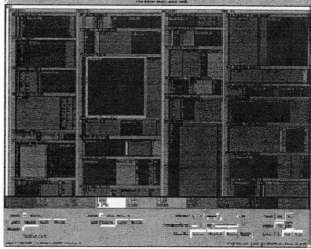

Figure 2: Chicago's Michael Jordan is emerging with the greatest area in this distorted view of Figure 1.

Many enhancements, outlined in the accompanying video and [5], have been added to the treemap since its inception. As the true benefits of the diagram can only be appreciated when the domain is familiar or of personal importance, the video explores the familiar domain of NBA basketball player statistics (1991-92 season data were used with 48 numeric attributes for over 450 players in the league).

Spreadsheets have traditionally been used to analyze this type of data with tables upon tables of different and intriguing statistics. Digesting a table of over 450 players is a difficult task, however; treemaps provide a solution to this problem through their visualization capabilities.

GRAPHICAL PROPERTIES AND TASKS
Area, color and enclosure are the inherent graphical properties of treemaps that directly convey information. Although an overall consensus has not been achieved as to the efficacy and general task applicability of these properties, some guidelines have emerged as to their usefulness when applied to particular task domains.

Area
Area is both an asset and a liability—treemaps use area to weight individual nodes, yet by the algorithm's nature, the aspect-ratios of the generated rectangles are different, making them ill-suited for simple comparison tasks [1,4]. Area, though, does have its benefits: because an overview of the entire information space is provided, the treemap allows the user to perform outlier identification tasks based upon the areas of individual rectangles. In the NBA example, a weighting attribute of "points per season" translates into large areas for players who have achieved high point totals over the entire season (this attribute can be inverted to identify low-scoring players as well).

Relative comparisons of siblings (teams within a division, players of a team) can also be accomplished as all children of a node are either the same height or width; viewed in the context of this task, the treemap becomes a meta-chart of relative bar charts.

Color
Color is also used to convey attributes, which may be continuous or categorical. For the NBA domain, color was applied to all of the numeric attributes used for area weighting—specific class intervals were established based on these attributes' maxima, minima and data distribution.

Careful consideration should be given to the use of color with treemaps given the potential for interaction effects. A more efficient use of color is as a filtering mechanism: the video demonstrates color as a highlighting tool for nodes that satisfy certain criteria. This accomplishes the task of pinpointing the location of specific nodes in the context of the complete hierarchy.

Enclosure
The concept of enclosure to indicate parentage has been well-studied and applied in many different domains. The enclosure provided by the treemaps triggers location-oriented tasks: are all high-scoring players located under a particular division or team? Enclosure also emphasizes cause-effect relationships. Child node weighting influences parent node weighting; sibling nodes compete for each other's space. Large child nodes, therefore, create a "ripple" effect up the hierarchy making cause-effect relationships obvious.

AREA DISTORTION
Difficulty arises when there is low variance in the underlying data points used as the weighting attribute. For this case, as well as enhancing the comparison capabilities of the diagram, distortion techniques have been introduced. Visually altering the rectangular areas through distortion clarifies node relationships in the diagram. Treemap distortion can be accomplished in three ways: altering the underlying weights that the treemap algorithm uses, applying geometric transformations to the diagram, or allowing the user to directly manipulate the treemap.

The first technique was used in the video. Each player's weight was altered using an exponential function. The visual impact of this function is that large areas grow even larger, overwhelming their smaller siblings and cousins; the effect is quite similar to a fisheye diagram with multiple foci. Figure 2 illustrates distortion on Figure 1; players with large season point totals have larger areas. Each of the four divisions is seen to have one or more standout players.

More advanced algorithms for providing distortion fluidity and efficiency are under research.

REFERENCES
1. Cleveland, W.S. and McGill, R. Graphical Perception: Theory, Experimentation and Application to the Development of Graphical Methods. *Journal of the American Statistical Association 79*, 387, 1984, pp. 531-554.

2. Johnson, B. and Shneiderman, B. Tree-Maps: A Space-Filling Approach to the Visualization of Hierarchical Information Structures. In *Proceedings of IEEE Visualization'91* (Oct. 22-25, San Diego, CA), IEEE Computer Society Press, 1991, pp. 284-291.

3. Shneiderman, B. Tree Visualization with Tree-maps: A 2-D space-filling approach. *ACM Transactions on Graphics 11*, 1 (Jan. 1992), pp. 92-99.

4. Simkin, D. and Hastie, R. An Information-Processing Analysis of Graph Perception. *Journal of the American Statistical Association 82*, 398, 1987, pp. 454-465.

5. Turo, D. and Johnson, B. Improving the Visualization of Hierarchies with Treemaps: Design Issues and Experimentation. In *Proceedings of IEEE Visualization'92* (Oct. 8-12, Boston, MA), IEEE Computer Society Press, 1992, pp. 124-131.

Visual Information Management
for Network Configuration

Harsha Kumar*, Catherine Plaisant,
Marko Teittinen*+, Ben Shneiderman*+

Human-Computer Interaction Laboratory
Center for Automation Research
*also Institute for Systems Research
+also Department of Computer Science
University of Maryland

Abstract

Current network management systems rely heavily on forms in their user interfaces. The interfaces reflect the intricacies of the network hardware components but provide little support for guiding users through tasks. There is a scarcity of useful graphical visualizations and decision-support tools.

We applied a task-oriented approach to design and implemented the user interface for a prototype network configuration management system. Our user interface provides multiple overviews of the network (with potentially thousands of nodes) and the relevant configuration tasks (queries and updates). We propose a unified interface for exploration, querying, data entry and verification. Compact color-coded treemaps with dynamic queries allowing user-controlled filtering and animation of the data display proved well-suited for representing the multiple containment hierarchies in networks. Our Tree-browser applied the conventional node-link visualization of trees to show hardware containment hierarchies. Improvements to conventional scrollbar-browsers included tightly coupled overviews and detailed views. This visual interface, implemented with Galaxy and the *University of Maryland Widget Library* ™, has received enthusiastic feedback from the network management community. This application-specific paper has design paradigms that should be useful to designers of varied systems.

1. Introduction

Today's networks are heterogeneous along several dimensions, for example, different transmission media (satellite, fiber optic), kind of data being transmitted (video, sound, images, data), and multivendor networks. This makes networks highly complex in their transmission, performance and communication characteristics. Tens of thousands of elements have to be controlled, each having dozens of parameters to be specified. Almost all of the control and monitoring functions of communication network systems are implemented as software. Therefore, such software systems themselves are of enormous size and complexity.

The ISO / ANSI standards committee has classified the functionality required of network management systems into the six categories of Configuration management, Fault management, Performance management, Security management, Accounting management and Directory management. We concentrated on configuration management, defined by ISO as "Defining, monitoring and controlling network resources and data".

Many network management systems take a database-centric approach, i.e., the network is represented in a database called the Management Information Base (MIB). Designing the user interface for a Network Configuration Management System (NCMS) is a very challenging problem because of the many configuration parameters that need to be entered into the MIB via the user interface, i.e. the task of configuring a network is data-intensive. NCMS users are network operators working under the pressure to keep the network running 24 hours a day under all circumstances. Current user interfaces typically consist of hundreds of forms that need to be filled in order to configure / update the network. Users get lost in piles of forms in the absence of effective organization and information visualization tools. "A fundamental feature of an advanced network management station is the capability to present to the human manager a comprehensible picture of the relevant scenarios" [Cons93].

We worked closely with *Hughes Network Systems* (HNS) who develops commercial network management systems and manages a large number of telecommunication networks. Researchers from the fields of human-computer interaction, databases and networking participated in the project. The work involved the development of a prototype network management system (henceforth referred to as *prototype*) with a graphical user interface, and an object-oriented database with embedded dynamic constraint-checking mechanisms.

Our group from the Human-Computer Interaction Laboratory designed and implemented the user interface. Our focus in the first stage of the project was on satellite networks. Satellite networks, in general, are less complex than heterogeneous networks, because of their *star* topology, as opposed to a *mesh* topology. However, starting with the satellite networks enabled us to design and develop initial prototypes rapidly and obtain immediate feedback from users.

2. Background

2.1. Literature Review

There is some literature that directly addresses the issue of user interfaces for network management. [Beck90] used color and size-coded nodes and links on an underlying geographical map to visualize network statistics. They used direct manipulation widgets like sliders to filter network data interactively. We believe that this approach has merits. [Mart93] applied several visualizations like Cone-trees, circle-diagrams and fisheye views for telecommunications network planning. They designed a language to describe the mapping between input data and visualization features. [Cons93] applied their Hy$^+$ visual database system to manipulate network visualizations through visually expressed queries.

[Moen90] gives algorithms for drawing dynamic trees. [Rada88] describes a system that graphically displays data structures, including trees. [Chig93, Robe91] describe 3D visualizations of hierarchies with their Info-TV and Cone-tree systems respectively. [Mess91] proposes a divide-and-conquer layout algorithm for graphs, [Henr91] presents a methodology for viewing large graphs, while [Ding90] provides a framework for automated drawing of data structures. [Bear90] compares navigational techniques to improve the display of large 2D spaces. [Gedy88] describes the design and implementation of a graphical browser for a large highly connected database. [Holl89, Scha92] present studies of fisheye views of graphs. [Shne92, Turo92] focus on treeemaps, a hierarchical visualization tool that uses a space-filling approach.

Thus, much of the related literature concentrates on the design, algorithmic and browsing aspects of graph and tree structures in general. Our work is different in that we address the specific application of telecommunications network configuration, and present design paradigms and visualization tools that we successfully applied to this application. The two visualization tools that we used were the *treemap* [John92, Shne92] and the *Tree-browser* (introduced in this paper).

2.2. Simplified description of the structure of the network

In the HNS architecture, the satellite networks consists of a centralized hub and many (thousands) of remotes. Each remote communicates with the hub via satellite (Figure 1). This communication is established by setting up a *session*. Any 2 remotes communicate via the hub.

The hub and each remote consist of a complex hierarchy of hardware (Figure 1) and software objects. A remote has many DPCs (Data Port Clusters), each DPC many LIMs (LAN Interface Modules), and each LIM many ports. Similarly, the hub hardware has a similar but larger containment hierarchy: many network groups, many networks, many DPCs, many LIMs and many ports. A hub typically has thousands of ports. A session is established between a port of the hub and a port of a remote.

Inroutes and outroutes are the satellite channels used by hub ports and remote ports to communicate. Each session is assigned an Inroute Group (group of Inroutes).

2.3. Problems with current interfaces for network management

Current network management systems rely heavily on forms in their user interfaces. Forms are easy the develop and customize. They are usually simple to understand and to start using. But complex systems require so many forms that screens quickly become cluttered with dozens of overlapping forms (windows), and window-management becomes a real burden (Figure 2). Operators need to learn the names of all the forms. The problem is often aggravated by the fact that unrelated forms look similar, while there is no visual connection between related forms. The design of forms could be substantially improved in terms of meaningful layout, consistency, and efficient utilization of screen space.

The user interfaces of current systems reflect the intricacies of the network hardware components but provide little support for guiding users through tasks. Each task typically consists of a sequence of forms that need to be filled. No feedback is given as to how much of the task has been completed and how much of the task remains to be done. This is important since operators often have to simultaneously work on several tasks and handle emergency calls as they come. There is a clear need for the ability to group windows together, iconize them and re-open them simultaneously.

Data remains mainly displayed in tables and lists; some of the data is even in incomprehensible hexadecimal format. Better visualization techniques are needed. Many network management systems provide area maps showing the location of the remotes and lines indicating the communication links. In one system that we saw, remotes were represented as dots on a map of the U.S., and the operator could zoom in and out. These maps were seldom used by operators because the drawing of the map was too slow and the information shown was not useful enough. The latter is especially true for satellite networks which have a star topology, i.e., each remote is linked to the hub and it communicates with other remotes through the hub only.

Operators are given written instructions (suggested ports and inroutes) which are the results of studies of performance data and planning information, always done off-line. The instructions are updated on an irregular basis and operators sometimes have to take decisions based on outdated information. Thus, the process of selection of hardware components is often one of trial and error: configurations are used as long as problems are not encountered. There is a need for the user interface to provide this information on-line so that decisions can be based on current information.

3. Design Methodology

3.1 "Know thy users' task"

The interface should be designed to match the tasks performed by network operators. In order to design a task-oriented user interface, we collaborated closely with operators and engineers at Hughes Network Systems. We took training classes that are taken by new operators, interviewed designers and engineers of the current systems, and observed operators during their shifts as they configured networks and responded to emergency calls from customer sites. Finally manuals and screen prints of the current system were perused to give us mastery of a representative subset of configuration tasks that our prototype would address.

The Task
As mentioned previously, an important task in network configuration is to set up a session between a hub port and a remote port (henceforth referred to as the session task). This translates into the following subtasks:

1. Find the correct remote. The customer usually provides the name of the remote or at least some information like the location and the LAN Group of the remote. Hence, this subtask is usually straightforward.
2. Choose a port on that remote on the basis of a number of parameters, e.g. LAN type, LAN group, and data rate. Configure the port by entering values - or confirming default values - for several attributes such as node addresses, data rates etc.
3. Choose a port on the hub, again on the basis of similar parameters. Configure the port by entering attribute values. Check for compatibility of the remote and hub ports.

4. Choose an inroute group for the session.
5. Establish (or commit) the session.

Essentially, the task is to link *two compatible leaf nodes* (remote port and hub port) from two different trees via a node (inroute group) from a third tree. Thus, the session task involves a combination of:

- *Data exploration* to find trends of use or availability of space,
- *Querying* to find optimum choices of elements,
- *Data entry* to modify the configuration, and
- *Verification* of correctness / monitoring of impact on the physical network.

3.2 Low fidelity paper prototypes

After the task analyses, we made some low fidelity paper prototypes. The use of post-it notes (windows) on paper (computer screen) worked well for us. This enabled us to get rapid feedback from intended users of the system at Hughes and refine our design.

4. A visual information management interface for network configuration

In the past year the Human-Computer Information Laboratory has been designing, developing and describing visual information seeking interfaces [Ahlb94]. We have identified the following features as key elements of successful interfaces:

- *Overview* of the entire search space,
- Ability to *zoom* into regions of interest,
- *Dynamic queries* for filtering the data interactively in real time, and
- *Tight-coupling* between related fields to avoid empty query results.

The term dynamic queries describes the interactive user control of visual query parameters that generates a rapid (100 ms update) animated visual display of database search results [Shne94]. This kind of real-time display maximizes the visual bandwidth of the users, enabling them to catch trends in the data and spot exceptions. Also, irrelevant information is filtered out. The concepts of dynamic querying and tight-coupling are similar to those of *Focusing and Linking* [Buja91]. We have developed prototypes of a HomeFinder [Will92], a FilmFinder [Ahlb94], a health-statistic atlas [Plai93] and other interfaces for searching people, documents and resources.

In our network configuration prototype, we provide several interchangeable overviews not only of the data, but <u>also of the task to be performed</u>, and we merge the environment for exploration and querying with that for data entry and verification.

4.1. Task overviews

After operators select a task they wish to accomplish, a list of subtasks (elements) is displayed at the top of the screen in order to guide operators through the task (Figure 3). The checklist provides guidance as to what subtasks remain to be completed, but does not enforce the order of completion.

For example, in the session task, the subtasks related to the hub are displayed on the left, those related to remotes are displayed on the right, and those related to the inroutes are displayed in the center. A subtask can be completed by typing in directly, e.g., the name of a remote can be typed in directly. Alternatively, each button brings up an overview (visualization) of the data from which a selection can be made. For example, when the DPC button on the hub side is clicked, an overview of the hub is displayed at the DPC level (using a treemap or Tree-browser). Selection of an element makes its name appear in the top check-list, correct configuration of all of its parameters makes the corresponding button turn green indicating that that subtask has been completed. Thus, when the complete line of buttons at the top becomes green, the operators know that they can commit the task (this usually corresponds to commitment of a database transaction).

4.2. Data overviews: General Hierarchy Visualization tools

There are a number of hierarchical structures in this application, e.g. hardware containment hierarchies of the hub and remotes. Therefore, we made use of the treemap and Tree-browser, which are general hierarchy visualization tools. These visualizations provide access to network nodes and links, from where operators can access forms if required. In Figure 3, the treemap was selected to visualize the hub hardware hierarchy while the Tree-browser was selected to visualize the remote hardware hierarchy. Operators can interchangeably use either tool.

The general screen layout is tailored to fit the task (Figure 3). For example, in the session task, all overviews and forms corresponding to the hub open by default on the left, remote overviews and forms open on the right, and inroute overviews and forms open in the center. This simple default positioning of windows has a definite advantage over the typical random window placement because the overhead task of window management is reduced. The operator retains the flexibility to reposition windows.

Treemap:
The treemap maps hierarchical information to a rectangular 2-D display space utilizing 100% of the designated space [John92, Shne92]. Treemaps use a slice-and-dice strategy to partition the display space into a collection of rectangular boxes representing the tree structure. The strengths of treemaps are that they provide access to detail while keeping the global context. Screen space utilization is maximized, and scrolling and panning are not required. The number of nodes that can be displayed by a treemap is an order of magnitude greater than that by a traditional node-link diagram [Turo92]. In this application we applied dynamic queries to the treemap.

Figure 3 shows the following 3 distinct components of the treemap visualization tool:

Treemap Display: The treemap display displays the visualization. For example, in figure 3, the hub hierarchy is displayed down to the port level. The operator can also see the hub at the Network, DPC or LIM levels by clicking on the corresponding buttons at the top. The treemap provides a mechanism to zoom into nodes. Thus, the operator can either choose a port directly (bottom-up approach) simply by clicking on it, or by choosing a network, then zooming into that network, selecting a DPC, and so on (top-down approach).

Display controls: The operator can use the display controls to set the size and color of each node to represent an attribute of that node.

Query controls: The operator can use the query controls to make queries on both numerical and textual attributes of nodes, e.g. baud rate and LAN Group respectively.

Getting back to the session task, a good strategy for selecting a port is to first find the LIMs which are not over-utilized and then within those LIMs to look for an available port with high baud rate. The following is a possible sequence of steps that the operator might take in order to find a good port:

1. Ask to see the hub at the LIM level by clicking on the LIM button at the top. In Figure 4a, the outer box corresponds to the network. That outer box is divided vertically into 3 DPCs. Then the space for each DPC is split horizontally, and each resulting rectangle represents one LIM that the DPC contains.
2. Query the LIMs on the basis of utilization using the double-box slider. Those LIMs not satisfying the query are grayed out (Figure 4b).
3. Ask to see the hub at the port level by clicking on the Port button at the top (Figure 4c). Note that the LIMs that did not satisfy the query in step 2 remain grayed out.
4. Set both size and color of the ports to represent port baud rate. The bigger the port, the higher the baud rate. Similarly, brighter reds represent higher baud rates and deeper blues lower baud rates (Figure 4d). It is also possible to set the size and color of nodes (i.e. LIMs, ports etc.) to represent different attributes.
5. Choose a big red port (Figure 4e).

When a port is clicked, a form pops up to show the attributes of that port. These can be modified. A port can be selected for the session with a different action (currently by shift-clicking on it, but the drag and drop metaphor seems more appropriate to drop a port into in the checklist). When a port is selected, the names of the corresponding Network Group, Network, DPC, LIM and Port appear in the checklist. If all attributes have been entered or confirmed, all the hub buttons in the checklist also turn to green, signifying completion of this subtask.

Tree-browser:
A node-link representation of trees is composed of nodes and links, where nodes represent individual nodes in the tree, and links represent interrelationships between nodes (is-child-of and is-parent-of).

Node-link diagrams make inefficient use of screen space, which means that even trees of medium size require large areas to be completely displayed. Scrolling and panning is usually needed, and global context is lost in the absence of an overview. Treemaps overcome these deficiencies of node-link diagrams by using a space-filling approach. On the other hand, node-link diagrams are well known, intuitive and clear. They allow better depiction of ordering amongst siblings and links can be used to display additional information when appropriate.

Figures 5a and 5b show node link diagrams of a remote hierarchy at the LIM and Port levels. The nodes are color-coded to represent the configuration status, i.e. whether a particular node (e.g. port) is used, unused, or undefined.

The Tree-browser is a visualization tool for tree structures which makes use of the node-link representation. It overcomes the problem of loss of global context by providing tightly-coupled detailed views and overviews, and is envisioned to provide dynamic querying and *semantics-based browsing* features (Section 5.1).

In figure 6, the Tree-browser shows a remote at the port level in two views. A detailed view shows the node-link diagram in full zoom with the node names displayed, and an overview shows a miniature version of the node-link diagram without the node names. A field-of-view (the black rectangle on the overview) indicates what part of the tree is seen in the detailed view and can be moved to pan the detailed view. Similarly, when the detailed view is scrolled by using the scrollbars, the field-of-view moves in the overview to provide global context feedback. This direct linkage between views is called *tight-coupling*.

In section 5, we discuss design issues for the Tree-browser.

4.3. Unified interface for exploration, querying, data entry and verification

Another design principle that we applied was to give a unified interface to the users for exploration, querying, data entry and verification. In other words, the Tree-browser and treemap act not only as means of output, but as means of input as well. The operators can click on any node, e.g. remote port, and get a form that gives the identity and attributes of that port. (Figure 7). Updates can then be made to the database via the forms. When an update is attempted, the embedded constraints in the database are checked and if they hold, the update is accepted and the buttons Remote, RCPC, LIM and Port all turn green, else an error message is displayed in a popup window. Our interface provides an easy mechanism for users to activate or deactivate constraints on objects at run-time.

Thus, when all three subtasks (selection and configuration of hub port, remote port and inroute) are completed, all the buttons at the top are green, and the operator is in a position to commit the session. When the "Commit" button at the lower right corner is clicked, a session is set up from the remote port to the hub port via the inroute.

4.4. Implementation of the prototype

Our prototype runs on Sun SPARCStations. C++ and ObjectStore, an Object-Oriented database, were used for the MIB. The user interface was developed using C and Galaxy, a platform-independent user interface builder.

5. Current directions

5.1. Enhancements to the Tree-Browser

Dynamic querying
As demonstrated in the case of treemaps, a majority of tasks in browsing information spaces can be facilitated by dynamic querying. We are currently implementing two types of dynamic queries on the Tree-browser:

Attributes-based: Queries on node attributes, for example, give me all high baud rate ports.

Topology-based: Queries based on tree topology, for example, give me the LIM that has maximum number of available ports.

Semantics-based browsing
Generic 2D browsers [Plai94] treat the information space being browsed as images only. We believe that browsing of trees can be facilitated by taking advantage of the underlying structure of the tree. We are exploring ways to enable fast navigation between siblings, up to parents and grand-parents etc., without having to manually scroll and pan. Traversal of the tree in preorder, postorder and inorder, and tours of nodes marked either manually or by a query are being investigated.

Coping with varying size and structure
As the size and complexity of a tree increases, the problem of visualizing it effectively becomes more and more challenging. This applies to all visualization methods. There is a clear need for guidelines on the design of overviews, as the size of the tree increases. As

the aspect ratio (fan-in / fan-out) of a tree varies, new layout strategies are needed. An intermediate view, which provides more detail than the overview, but less detail then the detailed view might be of help. With respect to dynamic queries, too many nodes might make the visualization cluttered and color-coding the results of queries might not be effective enough. Hierarchical clustering is a possible solution. The current implementation of the Tree-browser has uniform size for all nodes and uniform width for all links. Using the size, shape, color and texture of nodes and the width, color and texture of links would allow many attributes to be displayed simultaneously but might become difficult to interpret.

5.2. Hybrid (Mesh) networks

Our focus has now shifted to hybrid networks that include terrestrial links and ATM switches. From the user interface perspective, this means that the network topology is mesh, not star. Whereas in satellite networks, a communication link directly connects one remote port and one hub port, in the case of hybrid networks, a link between two nodes might be implemented as a dozen links through as many intermediate nodes.

Even in that case, the general hierarchy visualization tools described above can be used for many subtasks. But graph browsers are needed in order to see the overall structure of the network. We will extend dynamic queries and visual information management interfaces to browsing graphs.

6. Conclusions

We have received very encouraging feedback from Hughes Network Systems and other people from the network management community. This leads us to believe that a task-oriented approach to designing user interfaces, coupled with appropriate visualization tools is an effective strategy for successful user interfaces. Our proposed information management user interfaces should dramatically improve the time to learn, speed of use and error rate of next generation NCMS.

The combination of the treemap and dynamic queries was well received. We feel that expert operators will experience increased productivity in their tasks of configuring and managing networks. Formal usability evaluations are needed to quantify such productivity gains. The Tree-browser, when coupled with dynamic queries and semantics-based browsing features, promises to be a powerful, yet intuitive tool for visualizing hierarchies. Usability studies and experiments need to be conducted to access its strengths and weaknesses, and come up with more concrete design guidelines.

Acknowledgments:

We presented our work on the design of the user interface but the prototype was produced by a much larger team. We wish to thank Mulugu Srinivasarao, Shravan Goli and Konstantinos Stathatos, who worked closely with Harsha Kumar and Marko Teittinen to implement the prototype, Dave Whitefield of Hughes Network Systems who provided invaluable feedback, and George Atallah, Mike Ball, John Baras, Anindya Datta, Ramesh Karne, and Steve Kelley for their help managing the team and involvement in database issues. Thanks also to HCIL members who reviewed the paper and provided invaluable feedback.

Partial support for this project was provided by Hughes Network Systems, Maryland Industrial Partnerships, the Center for Satellite and Hybrid Communication Networks, and the NSF Engineering Research Center Program (NSFD CD 8803012).

References:

[Ahlb92]   Ahlberg, C., Williamson, C., Shneiderman, B., Dynamic Queries for Information Exploration: An Implementation and Evaluation. *ACM CHI '92 Conference Proc. (Monterey, CA, May 3-7, 1992)* . ACM, New York. (1992) 619-626

[Ahlb94]   Ahlberg, C., Shneiderman, B., Visual Information Seeking: Tight Coupling of Dynamic Queries with Starfield Displays. *Proc. of CHI '94*, ACM, New York (1994)

[Bear90]   Beard, D.V., Walker, J. Q. II., Navigational Techniques to Improve the Display of Large Two-Dimensional Spaces. *Behavior & Information Technology 9, 6*, (1990) 451-466

[Beck90]   Becker, R.A., Eick, S.G., Miller, E.O., Wilks, A.R., Dynamic Graphics for Network Visualization. *Proceedings of the first IEEE conference on Visualization*, San Francisco, California, October 1990, pp 93-96

[Buja91]   Buja, A., McDonald, J.A., Michalak, J., Stuetzle, W., Interactive Data Visualization using Focusing and Linking. *Proceedings of IEEE Visualization '91*, San Diego, California, October 1991, pp 156-163

[Chig93]   Chignell, M. H., Poblete, F., Zuberec, S., An Exploration in the Design Space of Three Dimensional Hierarchies. *Proceedings of the Human Factors Society*, 1993

[Cons93]   Consens, M., Hasan, M., Supporting network management through declaratively specified data visualizations. *Proceedings of the third {1FIP / IEEE} International Symposium on Integrated Network Management*, 1993, pp 725-738

[Ding90]   Ding, C., Mateti, P., A Framework for the Automated Drawing of Data Structure Diagrams. *IEEE Transactions on Software Engineering*. Vol. 16, No. 5, May 1990

[Gedy88]   Gedye, D., Browsing the tangled web, Master's thesis report, Division of Computer Science, University of California at Berkeley, May 1988

[Henr91]   Henry. T. R., Hudson, S. E., Interactive Graph Layout. *Proceedings of the ACM SIGGRAPH Symposium on User Interface Software and Technology*, November 1991

[Holl89]   Hollands, J.G., Carey, T.T., Matthews, M.L., McCann C.A., Presenting a Graphical Network: A Comparison of Performance Using Fisheye and Scrolling Views. *Designing and Using Human-Computer Interfaces and Knowledge Based Systems*, Elsevier Science publishers B.V., Amsterdam, 1989

[John92]   Johnson, B., Shneiderman, B., Tree maps: A space-filling approach to the visualization of hierarchical information structures. *Proc. of IEEE Visualization' 91*, San Diego, CA (Oct. 1992) 284-291.

[Mart93]   Martin, J.C., Visualization for Telecommunications Network Planning, *IFIP Transactions on Graphics, Design and Visualization*, Bombay, India, February 1993, pp 327-334

[Mess91]   Messinger. E. B., Rowe, L. A., Henry, R. R., A Divide-and-Conquer Algorithm for the Automatic Layout of Large Directed Graphs. *IEEE Transactions on Systems, Man, and Cybernetics 21*, 1, (1991)

[Moen90]   Moen, S., Drawing Dynamic Trees, *IEEE Software*, vol 7, num 4, July 1990, pp. 21-28.

[Plai93]   Plaisant, C., Facilitating Data Exploration: Dynamic Queries on a Health Statistics Map. *Proc. of the 1993 American Statistical Association conference - Section on Government Statistics, San Francisco, Aug. 1993.* A.S.A Alexandria, VA. (1993) 18-23

[Plai94]   Plaisant, C., Carr, D., and Shneiderman, B., Image browsers: Taxonomy, guidelines, and informal specifications, Department of Computer Science Technical Report CS-TR-3282, University of Maryland, College Park, MD, (March 1994)

[Rada88]   Radack, G., Desai, T., Akrti: A System for Drawing Data Structures, *IEEE Languages for Automation Workshop* (Aug 29, 1988, College Park, MD), IEEE Press, pp 116-120

[Robe91]   Robertson, G. G., Mackinlay, J. D., Card S. K., Cone Trees: Animated 3D Visualizations of Hierarchical Information. *CHI '91 Human Factors in Computing Systems*, ACM, 1991

[Scha92]   Schaffer, D., Zuo, Z., Bartrum, L., Dill, J., Dubs, S., Greenberg, S., Roseman, M., Comparing Fisheye and Full-Zoom Techniques for Navigation of Hierarchically Clustered Networks. *Research report No. 92/491/29*, Department of Computer Science, The University of Calgary

[Shne92]   Shneiderman, B., Tree Visualization with Treemaps: 2-d Space-Filling Approach. *ACM Transactions on Graphics*, Vol. 11, No. 1, January 1992, Pages 92-99

[Shne94]   Shneiderman, B., Dynamic queries for visual information seeking. *IEEE Software*, in press, 1994

[Turo92]   Turo, D., Johnson, B., Improving the visualization of hierarchies with treemaps: design issues and experimentation. *Proc. of IEEE Visualization '92*, Boston, MA, (Oct. 1992) 124-131

[Will92]   Williamson, C. and Shneiderman, B., The Dynamic HomeFinder: Evaluating Dynamic Queries in a Real-Estate Information Exploration System. *Proceedings of the ACM SIGIR T92*, Copenhagen, Denmark (June 21–24, 1992) 338–346.

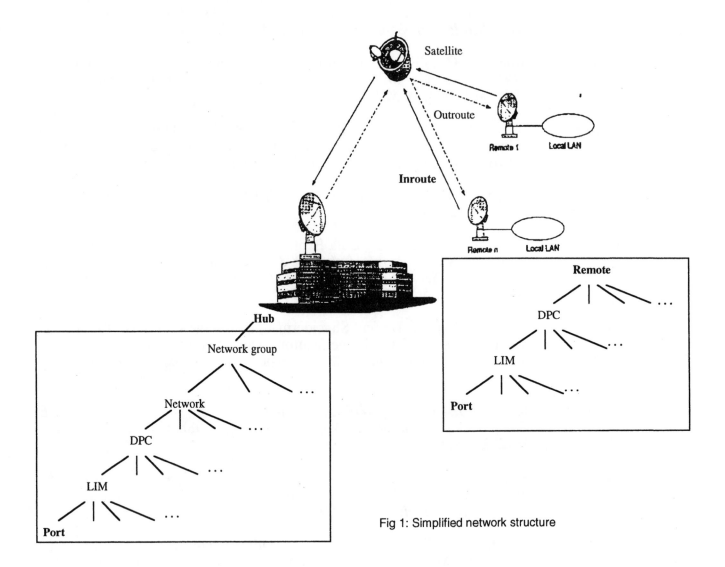

Fig 1: Simplified network structure

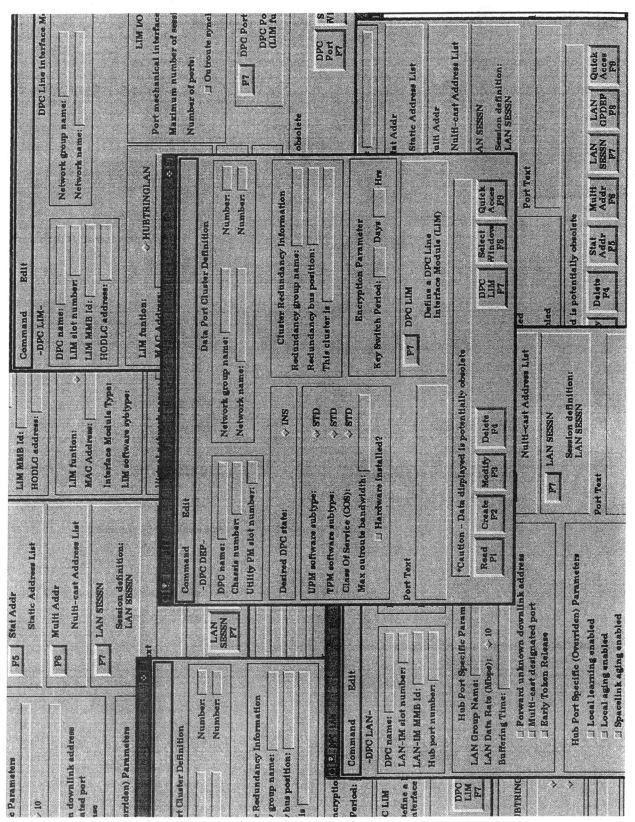

Fig 2: Example screen of a forms-based network configuration system

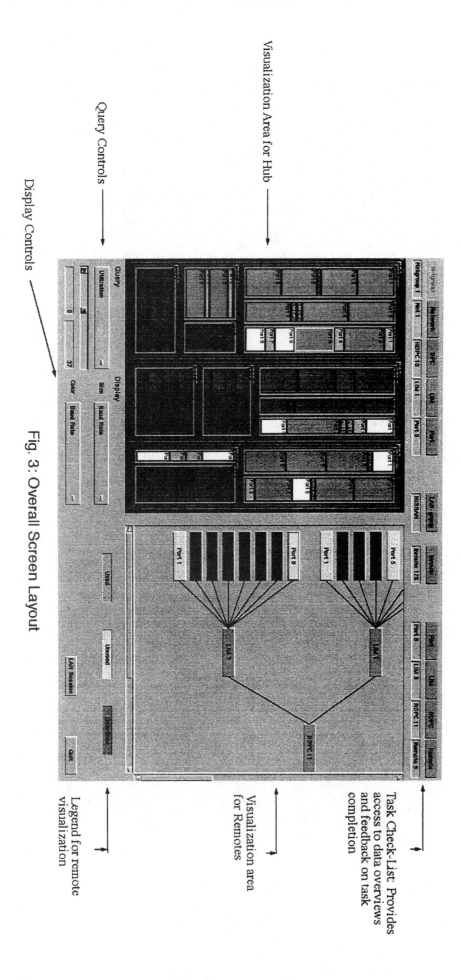

Fig. 3: Overall Screen Layout

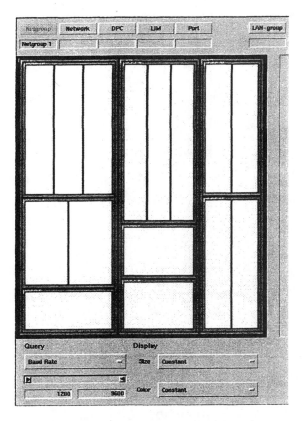

Fig 4a: Hub hierarchy at LIM level

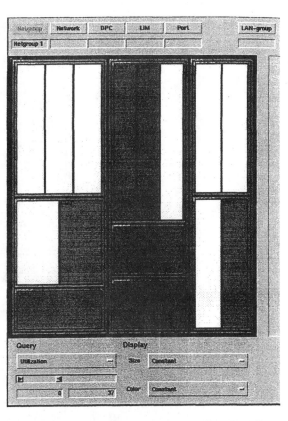

Fig 4b: Query LIMs on the basis of utilization

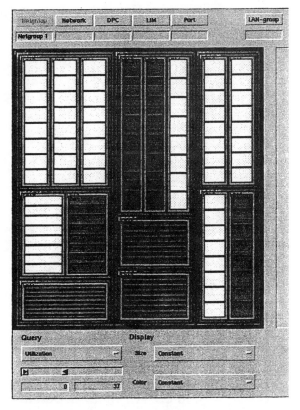

Fig 4c: Go to port level

Fig 4d: Set size and color of ports to port baud rate

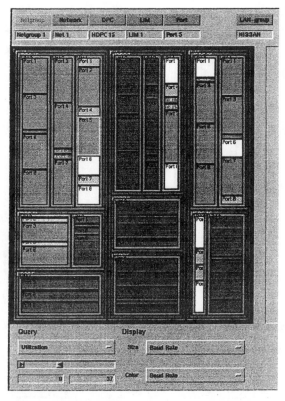

Fig 4e: Choose the "best port", i.e. one whose LIM has
low utilization, and which has high baud rate

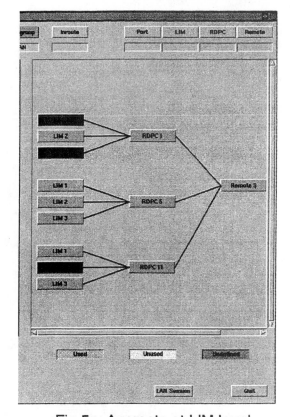

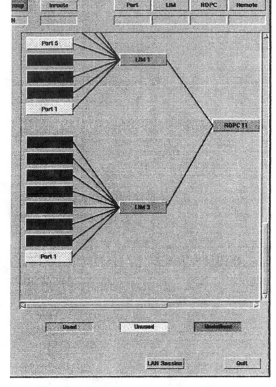

Fig 5a: A remote at LIM level   Fig 5b: A remote at port level

Red: Undefined   Yellow: Unused   Orange: Used

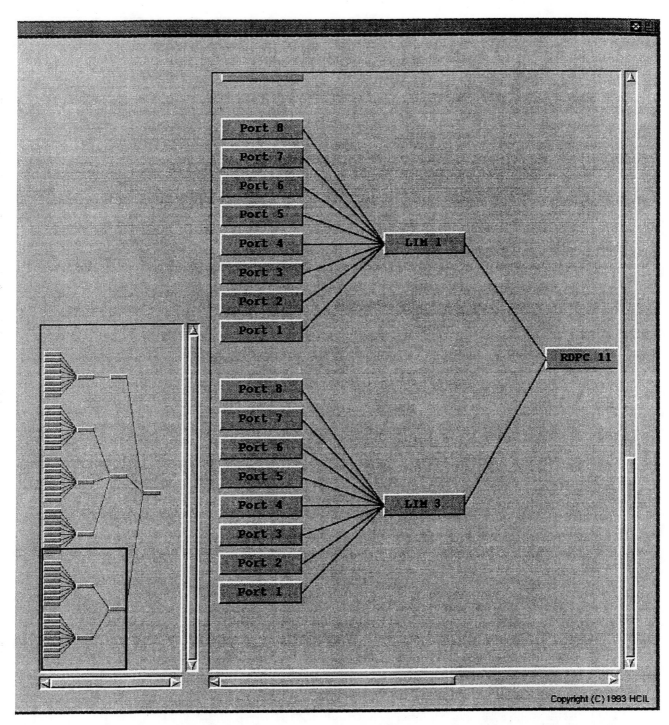

Fig 6: Tree-browser with overview and detailed view tightly-coupled

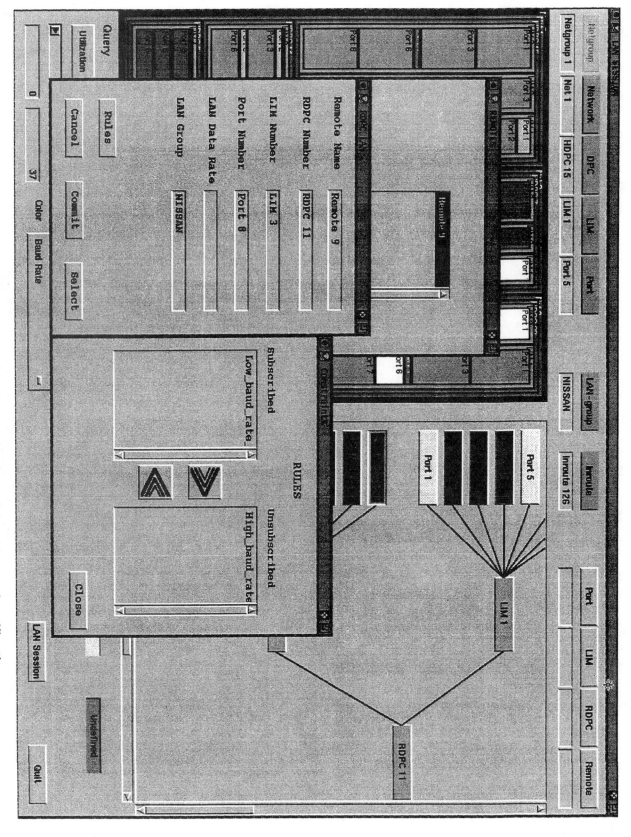

Fig 7: Unified Interface for exploration, querying, data entry and verification

Ordered and Quantum Treemaps: Making Effective Use of 2D Space to Display Hierarchies

BENJAMIN B. BEDERSON and BEN SHNEIDERMAN
University of Maryland
and
MARTIN WATTENBERG
IBM Research

Treemaps, a space-filling method for visualizing large hierarchical data sets, are receiving increasing attention. Several algorithms have been previously proposed to create more useful displays by controlling the aspect ratios of the rectangles that make up a treemap. While these algorithms do improve visibility of small items in a single layout, they introduce instability over time in the display of dynamically changing data, fail to preserve order of the underlying data, and create layouts that are difficult to visually search. In addition, continuous treemap algorithms are not suitable for displaying fixed-sized objects within them, such as images.

This paper introduces a new "strip" treemap algorithm which addresses these shortcomings, and analyzes other "pivot" algorithms we recently developed showing the trade-offs between them. These ordered treemap algorithms ensure that items near each other in the given order will be near each other in the treemap layout. Using experimental evidence from Monte Carlo trials and from actual stock market data, we show that, compared to other layout algorithms, ordered treemaps are more stable, while maintaining relatively favorable aspect ratios of the constituent rectangles. A user study with 20 participants clarifies the human performance benefits of the new algorithms. Finally, we present quantum treemap algorithms, which modify the layout of the continuous treemap algorithms to generate rectangles that are integral multiples of an input object size. The quantum treemap algorithm has been applied to PhotoMesa, an application that supports browsing of large numbers of images.

Categories and Subject Descriptors: I.3.6 [**Computer Graphics**]: Methodology and Techniques—*Graphic data structures and data types interaction techniques*; H.5.2 [**Information Interfeces and Presentation**]: User Interfaces—*Graphical user interfaces, screen design*; H.1.2 [**Models and Principles**]: User/Machine Systems—*Human factors*

General Terms: Algorithms, Design, Human Factors

Additional Key Words and Phrases: Hierarchies, human-computer interaction, image browsers, information visualization, jazz, ordered treemaps, treemaps, trees, zoomable user interfaces (ZUIs).

1. INTRODUCTION

Treemaps are a space-filling visualization method capable of representing large hierarchical collections of quantitative data in a compact display [Shneiderman 1992]. A treemap (Figure 1) works by dividing the display area into a nested sequence of rectangles whose areas correspond to an attribute of the data set, effectively combining aspects of a Venn diagram and a pie chart. Originally designed to visualize

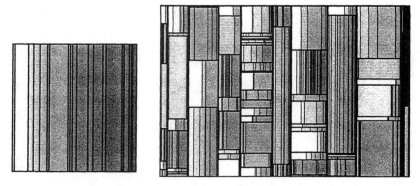

Fig. 1. The slice-and-dice treemap algorithm. Shading indicates order, which is preserved. The left image shows a single level treemap, and the right image shows a hierarchical application of the same algorithm.

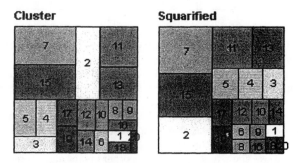

Fig. 2. Low aspect ratio layouts. Shading indicates order, which is not preserved.

files on a hard drive, treemaps have been applied to a wide variety of domains ranging from financial analysis [Jungmeister and Turo 1992; Smartmoney Marketmap 2002] to sports reporting [Jin and Banks 1997]. Treemaps scale up well, and are useful even for a million items on a single display [Fekete and Plaisant 2002].

A key ingredient of a treemap is the algorithm used to create the nested rectangles that make up the map. (We refer to this set of rectangles as the layout of the treemap.) The slice-and-dice algorithm of the original treemap paper [Shneiderman 1992] uses parallel lines to divide a rectangle representing an item into smaller rectangles representing its children. At each level of hierarchy the orientation of the lines—vertical or horizontal—is switched. Though simple to implement, the slice-and-dice layout often creates layouts that contain many rectangles with a high aspect ratio.[1] Such long skinny rectangles can be hard to see, select, compare in size, and label [Bruls et al. 2000; Turo and Johnson 1992]

Several alternative layout algorithms have recently been proposed to address these concerns. The SmartMoney Map of the Market [Smartmoney Marketmap 2002] is an example of the cluster treemap method described in Wattenberg [1999] which uses a simple recursive algorithm that reduces overall aspect ratios. Bruls, Huizing, and van Wijk [2000] introduced the squarified treemap, which uses a different algorithm to achieve the same goal. Figure 2 shows examples of these two layouts.

These methods suffer from several drawbacks. First, changes in the data set can cause dramatic discontinuous changes in the layouts produced by both cluster treemaps and squarified treemaps. (By contrast, the output of the slice and dice algorithm varies continuously with the input data.) These

---

[1]In this paper we define the aspect ratio of a rectangle to mean the maximum of width/height and height/width. Using this definition, the lower the aspect ratio of a rectangle, the more nearly square it is; a square has an aspect ratio of 1, which is the lowest possible value.

abrupt layout changes are readily apparent to the eye; below we also describe quantitative measurements of the phenomenon. Large layout changes are undesirable for several reasons. If the treemap data is updated on a second-by-second basis (e.g., in a stock portfolio monitor) then frequent layout changes make it hard to track or select an individual item. Rapid layout changes also cause an unattractive flickering that draws attention away from other aspects of the visualization. Moreover, even occasional abrupt changes mean that it is hard to find items on the treemap by memory, decreasing efficacy for long-term users.

A shortcoming of cluster and squarified treemap layouts is that many data sets contain ordering information that is helpful for seeing patterns or for locating particular objects in the map. For instance, the bond data described in Johnson [1994] is naturally ordered by date of maturity and interest rate. In many other cases the given order is alphabetical. The original slice-and-dice layout preserves the given ordering of the data, but cluster treemaps and squarified treemaps do not. Another recent algorithm [Vernier and Nigay 2000] offers some control over the aspect ratios but does not guarantee order. This paper includes a detailed description of a family of algorithms we call "pivot" treemaps (previously called "ordered" treemaps [Shneiderman and Wattenberg 2001]). Using a recursive technique motivated by the QuickSort sorting algorithm, these algorithms offer a trade-off, producing partially ordered layouts that are reasonably stable and have relatively low aspect ratios.

Since treemap algorithms generate visual layouts to be viewed by people, we also must consider the usability of the layouts by people for specific tasks. For someone to look for a particular item using existing algorithms (assuming they are labeled), their eye has to switch between horizontal and vertical scans many times, increasing cognitive load. A layout that has a consistent visual pattern would be easier to search. We propose a measure, which we call *readability*, that quantifies how easy it is to visually scan a treemap layout, and use it to demonstrate the benefit of ordered layouts. The readability metric counts the number of changes in direction a viewer's eye must make when scanning the rectangles in order.

We introduce a second ordered treemap algorithm, the "strip" treemap, that is specially designed to produce highly readable displays. A strip treemap layout has a consistently ordered set of rectangles while still maintaining good aspect ratios. Strip treemaps work by creating horizontal rows of rectangles, each with the same height. Implementations of the algorithms as well as an end-user visualization application using these algorithms are available at the University of Maryland's Human-Computer Interaction Lab web site.[2]

Another issue with treemap algorithms is what information is displayed in the generated rectangles. In every current usage to date, treemaps are used to visualize a two-dimensional dataset where one dimension is typically mapped to the area of the rectangles (as computed by the treemap algorithm), and the other dimension is mapped to the color of the rectangle. Then, a label is placed in the rectangles that are large enough to accommodate them, and the user can interact with the treemap to get more information about the objects depicted by the rectangles. Surprisingly enough, there are not any published uses of treemaps where other information is placed in the rectangles. We are interested in using treemaps to display large numbers of image thumbnails, clustered by metadata.

There is a good reason why treemaps have not been used in this manner before. This is because while treemaps guarantee that the area of each generated rectangle is proportional to an input number, they do not make any promise about the aspect ratio of the rectangles. Some treemap algorithms (such as squarified treemaps) do generate rectangles with better aspect ratios, but the specific aspect ratio is

---

[2]Java open source implementations of all the algorithms we describe here, dynamic demonstrations of these algorithms showing how their trade-offs, and Treemap 3.0—an end-user visualization application using treemaps are all available at http://www.cs.umd.edu/hcil/treemaps

not guaranteed. While this is fine for general purpose visualizations, it is not appropriate for laying out images because images have fixed aspect ratios, and they do not fit well in rectangles with inappropriate aspect ratios. This paper includes a detailed description and analysis of "quantum" treemaps [Bederson 2001], an approach suitable for laying out images within the generated rectangles.

In this paper, we describe the new ordered and quantum treemap algorithms in detail, along with some experiments that we performed which compare the new treemap algorithms to existing ones using natural metrics for smoothness of updates, overall aspect ratio, and readability. The results suggest that ordered treemaps steer a middle ground, producing layouts with aspect ratios that are far lower than slice-and-dice layouts, though not quite as low as cluster or squarified treemaps; they update significantly more smoothly than clustered or squarified treemaps, though not as smoothly as slice-and-dice layouts; one of the ordered treemaps offers layouts almost as readable as slice-and-dice, which is optimal. Thus ordered treemaps may be a good choice in situations where readability, usability and smooth updating all are important concerns.

Finally, we describe the application of quantum treemaps to a novel photo browser that shows many thumbnails of images, clustered by metadata (where each cluster appears visually within a treemap-generated rectangle). This application, called PhotoMesa, uses a zoomable user interface to enable simple interactions to quickly find the desired photos, while offering the user control over the trade-off between number and resolution of photos presented on the screen.[3]

2. ORDERED TREEMAP ALGORITHMS

We start by examining ordered treemap algorithms. These are treemap algorithms that create rectangles in a visual order that matches the input to the treemap algorithm. We describe two algorithms. The pivot treemap algorithm [Shneiderman and Wattenberg 2001] creates partially ordered and pretty square layouts while the new strip treemap algorithm creates completely ordered layouts with slightly better aspect ratios.

2.1 The Pivot Treemap Algorithm

The key insight that leads to algorithms for ordered treemaps is that it is possible to create a layout in which items that are next to each other in the input to the algorithm are adjacent in the treemap. The pivot treemap algorithm does not follow the simple linear order of the slice-and-dice layout, but it provides useful cues for locating objects, and turns out to provide constraints on the layout that discourage large discontinuous changes with dynamic data.

The pivot treemap algorithm follows a simple recursive process, inspired in part by the idea of finding a two-dimensional analogue of the well-known QuickSort algorithm. The inputs are a rectangle R to be subdivided and a list of items that are ordered by an index and have given areas. The first step is to choose a special item, the *pivot*, which is placed at the side of R. In the second step, the remaining items in the list are assigned to three large rectangles that make up the rest of the display area. Finally, the algorithm is applied recursively to each of these rectangles. The algorithm, as illustrated in Figure 3, can be described as follows. Note that although this assumes the input rectangle is wider than it is tall, the algorithm can be readily modified to accommodate input rectangles that are taller than they are wide, as described in step 3.

Pivot Treemap Algorithm
Input: Rectangle, R, to be subdivided
      List of items with area, $L_1 \cdots L_n$
Output: List of rectangles, $R_1 \cdots R_n$

---

[3]PhotoMesa is available for download at http://www.cs.umd.edu/hcil/photomesa

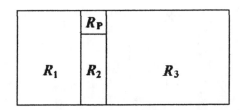

Fig. 3.   The pivot configuration.

1. If the number of items is <= 4, lay them out in either a pivot, quad, or snake layout as described in the next section, and pick the layout whose average aspect ratio is closest to 1. Stop.
2. Let P, the pivot, be the item with the largest area in the list of items.
3. If the width of R is greater than or equal to the height, divide R into four rectangles, R_1, R_P, R_2, and R_3 as shown in Figure 3. (If the height is greater than the width, use the same basic arrangement but flipped along the line $y = x$.)
4. Put P in the rectangle R_P, whose exact dimensions and position will be determined in Step 5.
5. Divide the items in the list, other than P, into three lists, L_1, L_2, and L_3, to be laid out in R_1, R_2, and R_3. L_1, L_2 and L_3 all may be empty lists. (Note that the contents of these three lists completely determine the placement of the rectangles in Figure 3.) Let L_1 consist of all items whose index is less than P in the ordering. Split the remaining items into L_2 and L_3 such that all items in L_2 have an index less than those in L_3, and the aspect ratio of R_P is as close to 1 as possible.
6. Recursively lay out L_1, L_2, and L_3 (if any are non-empty) in R_1, R_2, and R_3 according to this algorithm by starting at step 1.

2.1.1 Alternate Pivot Selection Strategies. The algorithm has some minor variations, depending on how the pivot is chosen. The algorithm described in section 2.1 chooses the pivot with the largest area (called *pivot-by-size)*. The motivation for this choice is that the largest item will be the most difficult to place, so it should be done first.

The alternate approaches to pivot selection are *pivot-by-middle* and *pivot-by-split-size*. *Pivot-by-middle* selects the pivot to be the middle item of the list—that is, if the list has n items, the pivot is item number $\lfloor n/2 \rfloor$. The motivation behind this choice is that it is likely to create a balanced layout. In addition, because the choice of pivot does not depend on the size of the items, the layouts created by this algorithm may not be as sensitive to changes in the data as pivot by size.

Pivot-by-split-size selects the pivot that will split L_1 and L_3 into approximately equal total areas. The selection works by examining each item and calculating the areas of L_1 and L_3 as if that item were the pivot. The pivot item that results in the most balanced area between L_1 and L_3 is chosen. With the sublists containing a similar area, we expect to get a balanced layout, even when the items in one part of the list are a substantially different size than items in the other part of the list. Figure 4 shows examples of the layouts created by these variations.

All pivot selection variations have the property that they create layouts that roughly preserve the ordering of the index of the items, which will fall in a left-to-right and top-to-bottom direction in the layout. The two algorithms are also reasonably efficient: pivot-by-size has performance characteristics similar to QuickSort (order $n\log n$ average case and n^2 worst case) while pivot-by-middle has order $n\log$ n performance in the worst case.

Although the variations produce layouts with relatively low aspect ratios (as described in the following sections) they are not optimal in this regard. The stipulations in step 5 of the algorithm avoid some, but not all, degenerate layouts with high aspect ratios, so we experimented with postprocessing strategies designed to improve the layout aspect ratio. For example, we tried adding a last step to the algorithm, in which any rectangle that is divided by a segment parallel to its longest side is changed so that it is divided by a segment parallel to its shortest side. Because this step gave only a small improvement

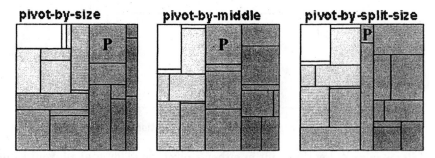

Fig. 4. Pivot layouts. Shading indicates order, which is roughly preserved. The "P" indicates the first pivot rectangle in each layout.

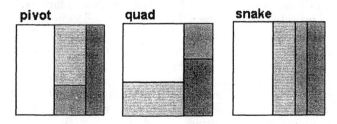

Fig. 5. Result of applying different layouts to the end of the recutsion with the same set of 4 rectangles.

in layout aspect ratio, while dramatically decreasing layout stability, we did not include it in the final algorithm.

2.1.2 *End-of-recursion Layout Actions.* Considering a few cases for laying out a small number of items can produce substantially better total results when applied to the layout at the end of the recursion of the pivot treemap algorithm.

The improvement comes from the realization that the layout of rectangles does not necessarily give layouts with the best aspect ratios for all sets of 4 rectangles. In addition, it generates a layout that is somewhat difficult to parse visually because the eye has to move in 3 directions to focus on the 4 rectangles of Figure 3 (horizontally from R_1 to R_P, vertically from R_P to R_2, and then horizontally from R_2 to R_3).

The layout and visual readability can be improved by offering two alternative layouts to the default "*pivot*" layout. The first alternative produces a "*quad*" of (2×2) rectangles. The second produces a "*snake*" layout with all 4 rectangles laid out sequentially—either horizontally or vertically. The snake layout can be equally well applied to 2, 3, or more rectangles. Figure 5 shows the result of laying out a sequence of 4 rectangles using the three stopping conditions.

Since no single layout strategy always gives the best result for all input data, the ordered treemap algorithm computes layouts using all strategies at the stopping condition (pivot, quad, and snake) and picks the best one. In practice, this strategy produces layouts with substantially squarer aspect ratios. We did a test to understand how these layout actions affect aspect ratio. We looked at the average aspect ratios of 100 tests with 100 rectangles each, and random area per rectangle ranging from 10 to 1000. This resulted in an average aspect ratio of 3.9 with the original layout actions, and 2.7 for the new layout actions.

2.2 The Strip Treemap Algorithm

An alternative and simpler strategy gives surprisingly good results. The *strip treemap* algorithm is a modification of the existing Squarified Treemap algorithm [Bruls et al. 2000]. It works by processing

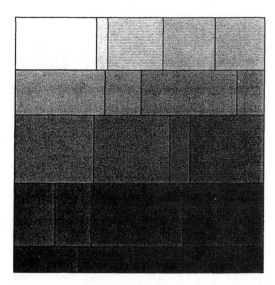

Fig. 6.   Strip treemap algorithm applied to 20 rectangles.

input rectangles in order, and laying them out in horizontal (or vertical) strips of varying thicknesses (Figure 6). It is efficient in that it only looks at rectangles within the strip currently being processed and produces a layout with significantly better readability than the pivot treemap algorithm, with comparable aspect ratios and stability.

As with all treemap algorithms, the inputs are a rectangle R to be subdivided and a list of items that are ordered by an index and have given areas. We describe here, the algorithm for a horizontal layout, but it can easily be altered to produce vertically oriented strips. We maintain a current strip, and then for each rectangle, we check whether adding the rectangle to the current strip will increase or decrease the average aspect ratio of all the rectangles in the strip. If the average aspect ratio decreases (or stays the same), the new rectangle is added. If it increases, a new strip is started with the rectangle.

The layout of any set of rectangles in a strip is completely determined by their order. We calculate the area of the set of rectangles, and from that, and the width of the layout box, we compute the height of the strip. Then, given the height of the strip, we calculate the width of each rectangle so that it has the appropriate area. The algorithm follows. Figure 7 shows the application of the algorithm to a simple input.

Strip Treemap Algorithm
Input: Rectangle, R, to be subdivided
       List of items with area, $L_1 \cdots L_n$
Output: List of rectangles, $R_1 \cdots R_n$

1. Scale the area of all the items on the input list so that the total area of the input equals that of the layout rectangle.
2. Create a new empty strip, the *current strip*.
3. Add the next rectangle to the current strip, recomputing the height of the strip based on the area of all the rectangles within the strip as a percentage of the total layout area, and then recomputing the width of each rectangle.
4. If the average aspect ratio of the current strip has increased as a result of adding the rectangle, in step 3, remove the rectangle, pushing it back onto the list of rectangles to process and go to step 2. When the rectangle is removed from a strip, restore that strip to its previous state.
5. If all the rectangles have been processed, stop. Else, go to step 3.

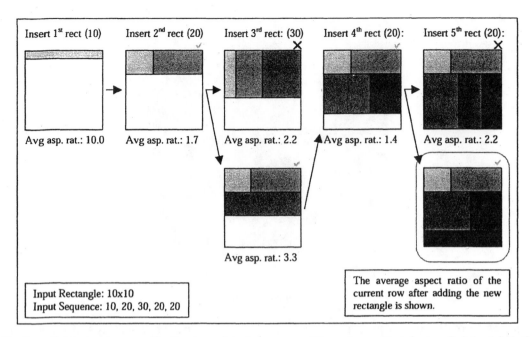

Fig. 7.   Application of strip treemap application to an input sequence of 5 numbers. At each step (left to right), the algorithm tries adding the new rectangle to the current strip, but creates a new strip if the average aspect ratio of the rectangles in the original strip increases as a result of adding the rectangle. A green checkmark indicates an accepted intermediate layout; a red X indicates one that is suboptimal. The bottom-right layout is the final result.

The strip treemap algorithm complexity is understood as follows. For each rectangle, the average aspect ratio of the current strip must be computed, and all the rectangles re-laid out (unless a new strip is started). Each strip is, on average, of length equal to the square root of the total number of rectangles. So, each rectangle on the current strip ($sqrt(n)$) must be touched for each rectangle in that strip ($sqrt(n)$) for each of the strips ($sqrt(n)$), resulting in $O(n\ sqrt(n))$ time on average.

As mentioned, this algorithm is similar to the squarified treemap algorithm [Bruls et al. 2000], but the squarified treemap algorithm is different in three ways. First, it sorts the input rectangles by size, which results in better aspect ratios, but (of course) loses the natural order of the rectangles. Second, rather than creating all the strips horizontally, it creates either horizontal or vertical strips in the remaining available space so as to produce the best aspect ratio. Finally, strip treemaps look at the average aspect ratio, while squarified treemaps look at the maximum aspect ratio, of the rectangles in a strip. In this sense, strip treemaps are a simplification of squarified treemaps, resulting in ordered layouts with aspect ratios that are only moderately worse.

The strip treemap algorithm also has some similarity to the space-filling treemap algorithm by Baker et al. [1995]. They designed a strip layout algorithm that does maintain order. But, instead of optimizing aspect ratios, they maintained near-constant strip heights to improve the ability of people to compare the areas of each rectangle. Their algorithm works by deciding in advance the number of strips, and then calculating the strip heights to be of constant height and laying the rectangles out within those strips. However, to avoid splitting rectangles across strips (which could be necessary since the strip heights are calculated independent of their content), they adjust the strip heights to accommodate moving the rectangles to one row or the other.

2.2.1 *Lookahead for Strip Treemaps.*   The strip treemap algorithm as defined above works well, but frequently has a problem in laying out the last strip. Since the decision to add a rectangle to a strip is made based only on the aspect ratio of the strip being added to, it is possible to be stuck with a few left over rectangles that get placed in a long skinny final strip.

This can be solved in a general way by adding lookahead to the layout. After a strip is constructed with the approach described previously, the next strip is laid out to decide if any rectangles would be better off moved from it to the current strip. The lookahead works as follows: The combined aspect ratio of the rectangles in the current strip, and the aspect ratio of the lookahead strip are compared to what would happen if the rectangles from the lookahead strip were moved to the current strip. If the average aspect ratio is lower when the rectangles are moved to the current strip, they are moved.

Adding lookahead to the strip treemap algorithm eliminates the final skinny strips that can significantly increase the total average aspect ratio. Adding the lookahead function does not change the complexity of the algorithm since the algorithm never processes more than one other strip, which will have, on average, *sqrt(n)* rectangles. However, the lookahead clearly increases the runtime of any implementation by at least a factor of 2.

2.3   Analysis of Ordered Treemaps

To evaluate the performance of ordered treemap layout algorithms, we compared them to squarified, cluster and slice-and-dice layouts with two experiments, and ran a user study. The first experiment consisted of a sequence of Monte Carlo trials to simulate continuously updating data. Our goal was to measure the average aspect ratio, average layout distance change, and readability produced by each of the algorithms. In the second experiment we measured the average aspect ratio, and readability produced by each of the algorithms for a static set of stock market data. Finally, the user study validated the readability metric by having users search for items in different treemap layouts.

2.3.1 *Metrics: Aspect Ratio, Change and Readability.*   In order to compare treemap algorithms we define three measures: 1) the average aspect ratio of a treemap layout; 2) a layout distance change function which quantifies how much rectangles move as data is updated; and 3) a readability function which is a measure of how easy it is to visually scan a layout to find a particular item. The ideal would be to have a low average aspect ratio, a low distance change as data is updated, and a high readability, though our experiments suggest that there may be no treemap algorithm that is optimal by all three measures.

We define the average aspect ratio of a treemap layout as the unweighted arithmetic average of the aspect ratios of all leaf-node rectangles, thus the lowest average aspect ratio would be 1.0, which would mean that all the rectangles were perfect squares. This is a natural measure, although certainly not the only possibility. One alternative would be a weighted average that places greater emphasis on larger items, since they contribute more to the overall visual impression. We choose an unweighted average since the chief problems with high aspect ratio rectangles—poor visibility and awkward labeling—are at least as acute for small rectangles as large ones.

The layout distance change function is a metric on the space of treemap layouts that allows us to measure how much two layouts differ, and thus how quickly or slowly the layout produced by a given algorithm changes in response to changes in the data. To define the distance change function, we begin by defining a simple metric on the space of rectangles. Let a rectangle R be defined by a 4-tuple (x,y,w,h) where x and y are the coordinates of the upper left corner and w and h are its width and height. We use the Euclidean metric on this space,—if rectangles R_1 and R_2 are given by (x_1, y_1, w_1, h_1) and (x_2, y_2, w_2, h_2) respectively, then the distance between R_1 and R_2 is given by

$$d(r_1, r_2) = \sqrt{(x_1 - x_2)^2 + (y_1 - y_2)^2 + (w_1 - w_2)^2 + (h_1 - h_2)^2}$$

We use this metric since it takes into account the visual importance of the shape of a rectangle. A change of 0 would mean that no rectangles moved at all, and the more the rectangles are changed, the higher will be this metric. There are several plausible alternatives to this definition. Two other natural metrics are the Hausdorff metric [Edgar et al. 1995] for compact sets in the plane or a Euclidean metric based on the coordinates of the lower right corner instead of height and width. These metrics differ from the one we chose by a small bounded factor, and hence would not lead to significantly different results.

We then define the layout distance change function as the average distance between each pair of corresponding rectangles in the layouts. We use an unweighted average for the same reasons as we use an unweighted average for aspect ratios.

Finally, the readability metric assigns a numeric value to how easy it is for a person to scan a layout to find a particular item. Scanning relies on an ordered layout since otherwise the entire layout would have to be scanned to find a particular item. We believe that this kind of readability is correlated with the consistency and predictability of a layout. Consistency allows the eye to quickly follow a pattern without having to jump. Predictability allows the eye to jump ahead to the region where the user thinks an item will appear.

We base our readability measure on the number of times that the motion of the reader's eye changes direction as the treemap layout is scanned in order. To be precise, we consider the sequence of vectors needed to move along the centers of the layout rectangles in order, and count the number of angle changes between successive vectors that are greater than .1 radians (about 6 degrees). To normalize the measure, we divide this count by the total number of rectangles and then subtract from 1. The resulting figure is equal to 1.0 in the most readable case, such as a slice-and-dice layout, and close to zero for a layout in which the order has been shuffled. For a hierarchical layout, we use an average of the readability of the leaf-node layouts, weighted by the number of nodes each contains.

We considered other measures such as counting the average angular difference between rectangles, but decided that once a rectangle sequence changed direction at all, it would force the eye to stop and the amount it had to change direction was not as important as the fact that it changed at all. Since the readability metric given above seems more subjective than the metrics for layout change and aspect ratio, we also performed a user study to validate it.

2.3.2 *Monte Carlo trials.*

We simulated the performance of the seven layout algorithms under a variety of conditions (slice-and-dice treemaps, pivot treemaps with all three pivot selection strategies, strip treemaps, clustered treemaps, and squarified treemaps). We performed experiments on three types of hierarchies. The first hierarchy ("20×1") was a collection of 20 items with one level of hierarchy. The second ("100×1") was a collection of 100 items with one level of hierarchy. The third ("8×3") was a balanced tree with three levels of hierarchy and eight items at each level for a total of 512 items.

For each experiment we ran 100 trials of 100 steps each. In each experiment we began with data drawn from a log-normal distribution created by exponentiating a normal distribution with mean 0 and variance 1. This distribution is common in naturally occurring positive-valued data [Sheldon 1997]. (Another common distribution, the Zipf distribution, has produced similar results in similar experiments [Shneiderman and Wattenberg 2001].) In each step of a trial the data was modified by multiplying each data item by a random variable e^x, where x was drawn from a normal distribution with variance 0.05 and mean 0, thus creating a log-normal random walk. All layouts were created for a square with side 100. The results are shown in Tables I through III.

The results strongly suggest a tradeoff between low aspect ratios and smooth updates. As expected, the slice-and-dice method produces layouts with high aspect ratios, but which change very little as the data changes. The squarified and cluster treemaps are at the opposite end of the spectrum, with low aspect ratios and large changes in layouts. The ordered and strip treemaps fall in the middle of the spectrum.

Table I. 20×1, Log-Normal Initial Distribution

Algorithm	Aspect Ratio	Change	Readability
Slice-and-dice	56.54	0.52	1.0
Pivot-by-middle	3.58	2.93	0.28
Pivot-by-size	3.09	7.12	0.19
Pivot-by-split	2.80	7.29	0.25
Strip	2.59	4.98	0.60
Cluster	1.72	11.00	0.11
Squarified	1.75	10.10	0.12

Table II. 100×1, Log-Normal Initial Distribution

Algorithm	Aspect Ratio	Change	Readability
Slice-and-dice	304.00	0.25	1.0
Pivot-by-middle	3.51	2.95	0.23
Pivot-by-size	3.05	7.84	0.11
Pivot-by-split	2.91	9.16	0.17
Strip	2.83	7.01	0.77
Cluster	1.63	14.34	0.03
Squarified	1.19	14.82	0.03

Table III. 8×3, Log-Normal Initial Distribution

Algorithm	Aspect Ratio	Change	Readability
Slice-and-dice	26.10	0.46	1.0
Pivot-by-middle	3.58	1.21	0.42
Pivot-by-size	3.31	4.14	0.33
Pivot-by-split	3.00	2.37	0.35
Strip	2.83	1.09	0.51
Cluster	1.79	7.67	0.26
Squarified	1.74	8.27	0.26

None produces the lowest aspect ratios, but they are a clear improvement over the slice-and-dice method, with the pivot-by-split-size and strip treemap algorithms producing slightly better aspect ratios. At the same time, they update more smoothly than cluster or squarified treemaps, with the pivot-by-middle algorithm having a slight advantage over the other pivot selection strategies, and the strip treemap doing especially well in the 8x3 case. Aside from the slice-and-dice layouts, strip treemap layouts are by far the most readable in all cases.

2.3.3 *Static Stock Market Data.*   Our second set of experiments consisted of applying each of the seven algorithms to a set of 535 publicly traded companies used in the SmartMoney Map of the Market [Microsoft PowerPoint 2001] with market capitalization as the size attribute. For each algorithm we measured the aspect ratio of the layout it produced. The results are shown in the first column of Table IV, and the layouts produced are shown in Figure 8. (The gray scale indicates ordering within each industry group that is the last level of hierarchy in this data set.) Although aspect ratios are higher than in the statistical trials, partly due to outliers in the data set, the broad pattern of results is similar.

2.3.4 *Performance Times.*   We compared the actual run-time performance of all of the algorithms discussed in this paper (including quantum strip treemaps from the next section). For this test, we generated flat trees with varying numbers of randomly sized elements (Figure 9). The tests were run on

Table IV. Stock Market Data for 535 Companies

Algorithm	Aspect Ratio	Readability
Slice-and-dice	369.83	1.0
Pivot-by-middle	19.90	0.43
Pivot-by-size	33.01	0.40
Pivot-by-split	17.65	0.38
Strip	7.95	0.61
Cluster	3.74	0.29
Squarified	3.21	0.29

a 700 MHz Pentium III computer running Windows XP. All algorithms were implemented in Java, and were executed with Sun's JVM, version 1.4. The results match our expectations. The pivot algorithms are the slowest, cluster, squarified, and slice-and-dice are the fastest, and the strip treemaps are in the middle. All algorithms except for the pivot treemaps run fast enough to be practical for even large trees. The strip treemap was able to lay out almost 2,000 rectangles in 0.1 seconds, the cluster and squarified treemaps were able to lay out over 5,000 rectangles in 0.1 seconds, and the slice-and-dice treemap laid out almost 20,000 rectangles in 0.03 seconds.

2.3.5 *User Study of Layout Readability.* To validate the readability metric, we performed a user study to see how long it took users to find specific rectangles laid out by different treemap algorithms. We compared the squarified, pivot, and strip treemap algorithms by having participants identify a specific rectangle by clicking on the rectangle with the requested numerical ID. Each algorithm was applied to 100 rectangles with random sizes from a uniform distribution. Each participant did 10 tasks for each of the three algorithms. Each task consisted of a random treemap where each rectangle contained the ID of the rectangle as specified in the input order to the algorithm (Figure 10).

The study was run with a completely automated Java application. The participants were first asked some demographic information. Then they were given training tasks followed by the experimental tasks where the participants were instructed to click on the rectangle containing the target number at the bottom of the window. As the participant moved the mouse around, the rectangle under the mouse was highlighted. The study was concluded with each participant rating the three algorithms. So, there was a single independent variable (the treemap algorithm), and two dependent variables (time and subjective preference).

We ran this experiment with 20 participants. The participants were 20% female and 80% male. They were 55% aged 30–39 and 45% aged 20–29. 50% were students. 95% reported using a computer 20 or more hours per week while 5% reported using a computer 10–19 hours per week. The participants reported their primary major or field as being computer science (65%), HCI (15%), informatics (5%), quality assurance (5%), marketing (5%), or unspecified (5%).

We analyzed the results of the experiment by running a single factor ANOVA for the two dependent variables. The measured time ($F_{2,57} = 92.3$) $p < 0.0001$ and subjective preference ($F_{2,57} = 85.6$) $p < 0.0001$ each had significant differences, so we performed a post-hoc analysis using Tukey HSD. For the measured time, there was a significant difference between the squarified treemap algorithm and the other two, but not between the pivot and strip treemap algorithms. For subjective preference, there was a significant difference between all three algorithms. Figure 11 shows the numeric results from the experiment.

The user study results suggest that the readability metric is predictive of real-world performance on simple search tasks. While the time measurement for the strip and pivot treemap were not significantly different, the trend was in the same direction as the readability metric (strip faster than pivot which is

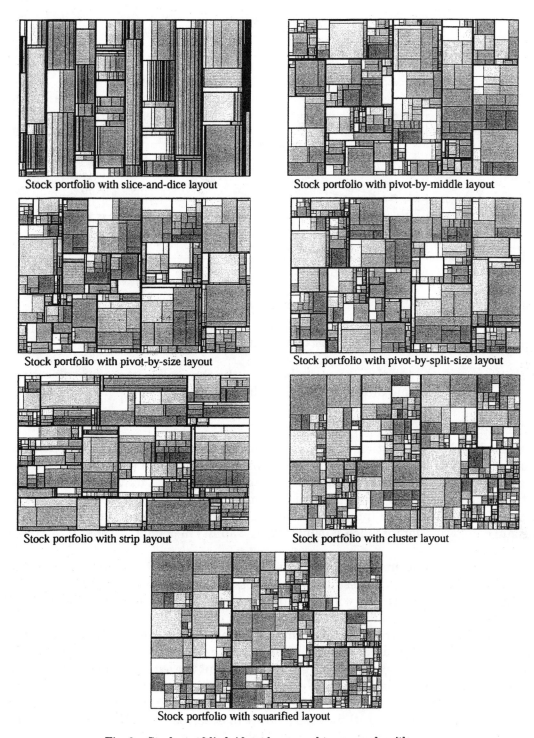

Stock portfolio with slice-and-dice layout

Stock portfolio with pivot-by-middle layout

Stock portfolio with pivot-by-size layout

Stock portfolio with pivot-by-split-size layout

Stock portfolio with strip layout

Stock portfolio with cluster layout

Stock portfolio with squarified layout

Fig. 8.   Stock portfolio laid out by several treemap algorithms.

Layout Algorithm Running Times

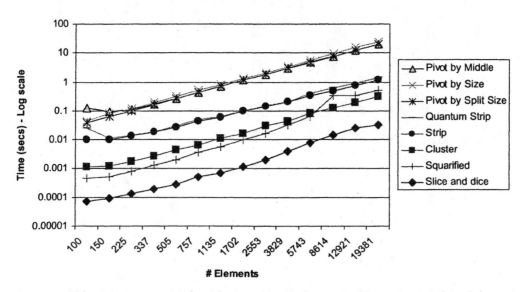

Fig. 9.   The performance of the various treemap algorithms running on flat trees with varying number of elements. The number of elements in each trial is increased by 50% from the trial before.

faster than squarified), and the difference between the three algorithms for subjective preference was significant, and in the same direction as the readability metric.

3.   QUANTUM TREEMAP ALGORITHMS

As mentioned in the introduction, we are also interested in using treemaps to present clusters of visual information, such as images (see Section 3.4). We would like to be able to lay out images within each rectangle generated by a treemap algorithm. That would enable us to create applications that allow users to see an overview of a large set of information, but grouped in some meaningful way. Some research in human-computer interaction shows that this kind of grouping of search results based on meaningful categories, for instance, can improve the ability of people to understand those search results [Hornof 2001].

Let us look at the problem of applying existing treemap algorithms to laying out fixed size objects, such as images. For now, let us assume without loss of generality that the images are all square (i.e., having an aspect ratio of 1). We will see later that this does not affect layout issues. Given a list of groups of images that we want to lay out, the obvious input to the treemap algorithm is the number of images in each group. The treemap algorithm will generate a list of rectangles, and then we just have to decide how to fit each group of images in the corresponding rectangle.

Since most treemap algorithms give no guarantees about the aspect ratios of the generated rectangles, the images would have to be laid out in arbitrary aspect ratio rectangles which can result in unattractive layouts. Figure 12 shows the result of laying out a simple sequence of images using the pivot treemap and the quantum treemap algorithm we are about to describe. With the quantum treemap algorithm, all images are the same size, and all images are aligned on a single grid across all the groups.

3.1   The Quantum Strip Treemap Algorithm (QST)

The quantum treemap algorithm generates rectangles with widths and heights that are integer multiples of a given elemental size. Thus, all the grids of elements will align perfectly with rows and columns

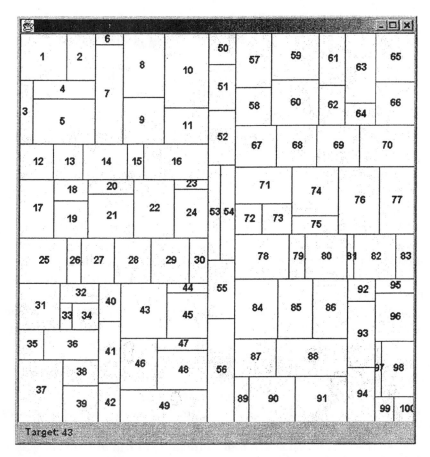

Fig. 10.   Screen snapshot from the user study showing what users were presented with when told to click on a specific rectangle. In this case, a pivot treemap was used and the user was told to click on rectangle #43.

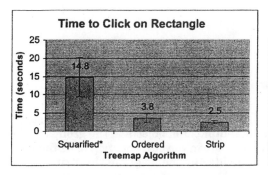
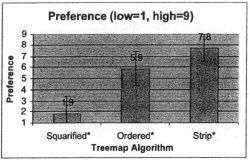

Fig. 11.   Results from user study validating readability metric. Error bars show standard deviation, and the algorithms marked with an * are statistically different than the others.

of elements running across the entire series of rectangles. It is this basic element size that can not be made any smaller that led to the name of *quantum treemaps*.

Any treemap algorithm can be quantized, so really quantum treemaps are a family of algorithms that parallel the other treemap algorithms. Quantum treemap's input and output are similar to those of other treemap algorithms, but instead of taking a list of areas as input, it takes an elemental object

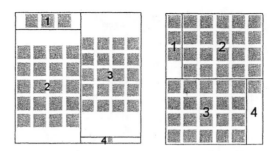

Fig. 12. The result of laying out a sequence of 4 groups of elements (of size 3, 20, 20, 1) using pivot treemap (left) and quantum treemap (right).

dimension, and a list of numbers of objects. The output is a sequence of rectangles where each rectangle is large enough (and possibly larger) to contain a grid of the number of objects requested. The basic idea is to start the regular treemap algorithm and then as rectangles are generated, they are *quantized*. That is, their dimensions are expanded or shrunk so that each dimension is an integral multiple of the input element size and the total area of the rectangle is no less than that needed to layout a grid of the requested number of objects.

An unusual property of quantum treemaps is that the area of the generated rectangles is typically *larger* than the object size multiplied by the number of objects to be laid out within that rectangle. The reason for this is that many layouts will not precisely fill up a grid, but will leave some empty cells in the last row. This is obviously true for numbers of objects that are prime (since they have no divisors), but is also true for non-prime numbers where their factors do not generate rectangles that have aspect ratios close to the aspect ratio of the rectangle generated by the treemap algorithm.

While a generic quantization program could be written that would apply to the result of any treemap algorithm, we have instead written custom quantum treemap variations of each ordered treemap algorithm. This is because the custom ones are more efficient (in the amount of wasted space) since they can adapt to the error that is generated by quantized rectangles. We describe here a quantized version of strip treemaps and then summarize the issues that affect quantization of other algorithms.

Quantum Strip Treemap Algorithm (QST)

Input: Rectangle, R, to be subdivided
      Elemental object dimensions, D
      List of groups with number of objects per group, $L_1 \ldots L_n$
Output: List of rectangles, $R_1 \ldots R_n$

1. Scale R so its area equals the total number of objects in the list $L_1 \ldots L_n$.
2. Create a new empty strip, the *current strip*.
3. Create a new rectangle to represent the next item on the list, and add it to the current strip. Compute the height of the strip to be the result of rounding up the total number of objects in the groups in the current strip divided by the width of R. Compute the width of each rectangle in the current strip to be the result of rounding up the number of objects in the associated list element divided by the height of the strip.
4. If the average aspect ratio of the current strip has increased as a result of adding the rectangle in step 3, remove the rectangle pushing it back onto the list of rectangles to process, and go to step 2. When the rectangle is removed from a strip, restore that strip to its previous state.
5. If all the rectangles have been processed, continue to step 6. Else, go to step 3.
6. "Justify" the ragged right edge: Compute W, the width of the widest strip. Distribute the extra space of each strip within the rectangles of that strip as follows: For each strip, S_i:
    a. Set W_C = the sum of the width of the rectangles in S_i
    b. Set E_C = W - W_C (the empty space to the right of the strip S_i)
    c. Distribute the empty space, E_C, through the rectangles in the strip S_i

Quantizing a treemap algorithm does not change the complexity of the algorithm since it only adds a constant cost to the processing of each rectangle (step 3), and then has a linear clean-up cost (step 6).

3.2 Implementation Details

Quantizing the strip treemap algorithm is somewhat simpler than others because the rectangles in each strip are known to all have the same height. Quantizing other treemap algorithms involves changes similar to the ones we made to the strip treemap, but the changes can sometimes be a bit more subtle since the layouts are not as straightforward as they are for the strip layout. We now look at a few issues that apply to quantization of any treemap algorithm.

3.2.1 *Element Aspect Ratio Issues.*

Quantum treemaps assume that all the elements to be laid out in the rectangles are the same aspect ratio, and that aspect ratio is an input parameter. It turns out, however, that it is not necessary to modify the internal structure of quantum treemaps to accommodate the element's aspect ratio. Instead, the dimensions of the starting box can simply be stretched by the inverse of the element aspect ratio. Simply put, laying out wide objects in a wide box is the same as laying out thin objects in a thin box. An example showing images of different aspect ratios is shown in Section 3.4.

3.2.2 *Evening Ragged Edges.*

For QST, the job of evening the right ragged edge was straightforward since all the rectangles are organized in strips and space could be readily distributed among the rectangles in each strip. For other treemap algorithms, with more complex layouts, handling ragged edges is a bit more subtle. Since the rectangles are not laid out in strips, it is harder to spread extra space among multiple rectangles. It requires working with the area as a whole, and evening the right-most and bottom-most edges.

3.2.3 *Growing Horizontally or Vertically.*

In the description of QST, we always grew the height of each rectangle, and then changed the width of the rectangle as needed. However, more generally, there is a basic question of which dimension to grow each rectangle. The simple answer is just to grow in the direction that results in a rectangle that most closely matches the aspect ratio of the original rectangle. However, for certain treemap algorithms, it may make more sense to grow in one direction, then another. As we saw for strip treemaps, for example, it makes most sense to have a constant height for each strip, and so we grow the height of each rectangle and then adapt the width.

We have found that the pivot treemap algorithms produce better layouts if they always grow horizontally (or vertically for layout boxes that are oriented vertically). The issue here is somewhat subtle, but is related to the evening of the rectangles. If (looking at Figure 3), for example, rectangles in R_3 are made taller, then all of R_1 and R_2 will have to be made taller as well, to match R_3. If instead, the rectangles in R_3 are made wider, then only the other rectangles in R_3 will need to be made wider, and the rectangles in R_1 and R_2 can be left alone.

3.3 Analysis of Quantum Treemaps

Quantum treemaps often waste some space, in that it is not always possible to create a rectangular grid that fits the precise number of requested elements. In general, quantum treemaps work better when there are more objects per group. This is because it gives the algorithm more flexibility when computing rectangles. For example, 1000 elements can be arranged in quantized grids of many different sizes such as 30×34 (holds 1020 elements), 31×33 (holds 1023 elements), or 32×32 (holds 1024 elements)—which each use the space quite efficiently, wasting between 20 and 24 elements, or about 2% each. Rectangles containing smaller numbers of elements, however, do not offer as many options, and often use space less efficiently. For example, a rectangle containing 5 elements can be laid out in grids of 1×5 or 5×1

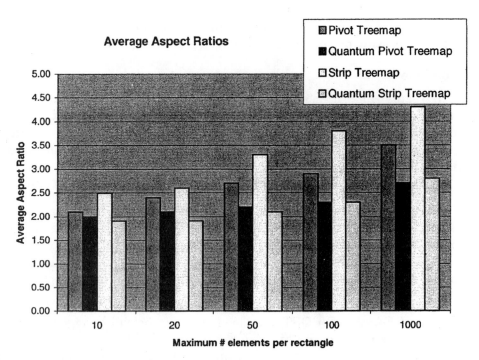

Fig. 13. Average aspect ratio of all rectangles run on both ordered treemap algorithms and their quantized counterparts with 100 rectangles with random numbers of elements per rectangle.

(holding 5 elements each), or 2×3 or 3×2 (holding 6 elements each). These four options do not give the algorithm as much flexibility as the dozens of grid options afforded by the larger number of elements. In addition, while the 1×5 layouts don't waste any space, the 2×3 layouts each waste 17% of the space (1 element out of 6).

In order to assess the effectiveness of quantum treemaps, the strip treemap and pivot treemap were compared to the quantized versions of the corresponding algorithm with a series of trials using random input. For each test, the average aspect ratio of all the rectangles was recorded as well as the space utilization, which was recorded as the percentage of space not used to display elements (wasted space). Inefficient use of space is an issue for quantum treemaps because rectangles can be expanded to match nearby rectangles resulting in rectangles larger than necessary to display the objects.

Each algorithm was run 100 times generating 100 rectangles with the number of elements in each rectangle being randomly generated with a uniform distribution. This was done for 5 different ranges of the number of elements per rectangle. The same random numbers were used for each algorithm. Figures 13 and 14 show the results of these tests. Quantum treemaps did better in terms of aspect ratio, and the non-quantized treemaps did better in terms of wasted space.

However, the crucial visual advantage of quantum treemap is that it always produces layouts where elements are the same size and are aligned on a single global grid. So, while understanding the characteristics of quantum treemaps is important, for applications that need them, the importance of their quantum characteristic will typically outweigh the others.

3.4 Application of Quantum Treemaps

We have written an application called PhotoMesa which is an image browser that makes use of quantum strip treemaps to layout groups of images. Figures 15 and 16 show screen snapshots of PhotoMesa which may help to illuminate our interest in this kind of algorithm.

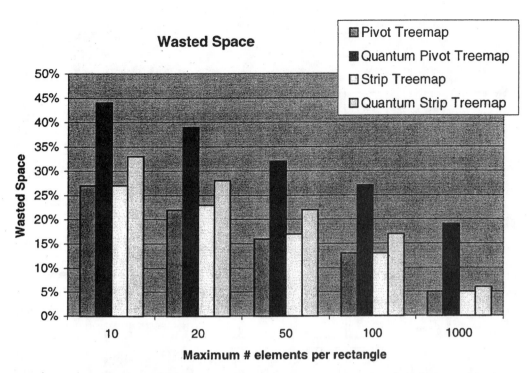

Fig. 14.   Average wasted space of all rectangles run on both ordered treemap algorithms and their quantized counterparts with 100 rectangles with random numbers of elements per rectangle.

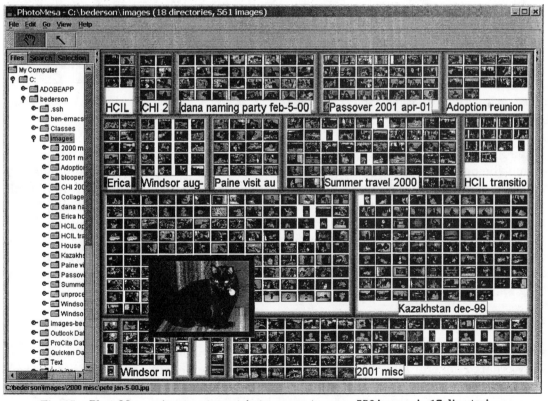

Fig. 15.   PhotoMesa using quantum strip treemaps to group 556 images in 17 directories.

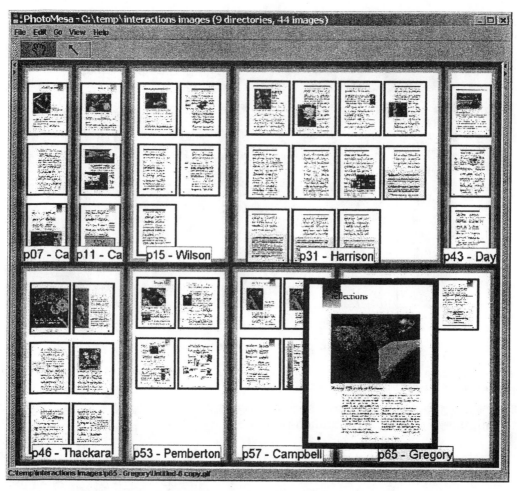

Fig. 16. PhotoMesa using strip treemaps to show the contents of an issue of ACM Interactions magazine. Note the aspect ratio of the images is different than Figure 15.

We designed PhotoMesa to support browsing of personal digital photos targeted for home users. Using metadata from the operating system (directory location, file change dates, and filenames), PhotoMesa groups the photos and lays out the groups using the quantum strip treemap algorithm. PhotoMesa uses a Zoomable User Interface (ZUI) to interact with the photos. Moving the mouse highlights a region of photos, and clicking results in the view smoothly zooming into the highlighted region. Right-clicking zooms out. In this way, users can easily get an overview of 1,000 photos at a time or more, and quickly zoom into photos of interest. Furthermore, this kind of interaction naturally supports serendipitous photo finding. Since so many photos are visible, users are likely to come across other photos of interest while looking for a specific one.

4. CONCLUSION AND FUTURE DIRECTIONS

Treemaps are a popular visualization method for large hierarchical data sets. Although researchers have recently created several algorithms that produce treemap layouts with low aspect ratios, these new algorithms have three drawbacks: they are unstable under updates to the data, they scramble any natural order on the items being mapped, and they are difficult to search for a specific item.

In this paper, we introduced strip treemaps, a new ordered treemap algorithm that generates fairly square aspect ratios. We also explained in detail, pivot treemaps and quantum treemaps, and compared the three algorithms. Through simulation experiments, we evaluated these and three other algorithms (slice-and-dice, cluster, and squarified) to understand the trade-offs between the issues of aspect ratio, order preservation, and stable updates under dynamically changing data. We found that strip treemaps offer the best combination, substantially improving readability while maintaining good aspect ratios and stability, and thus are likely to be preferred for a broad range of applications. However, when stability or aspect ratios are crucial, the slice-and-dice or squarified algorithms, respectively, may be more appropriate.

There are several directions for future research. First, there is room to optimize the ordered treemap algorithms discussed in this paper, especially to improve the overall aspect ratios they produce. It would also be useful to optimize the algorithms used by cluster treemaps and squarified treemaps to improve stability under dynamic updates. Another practical area to explore would be mixing different algorithms to combine their strengths: for instance, using a stable algorithm to lay out high-level nodes and an order-preserving algorithm to lay out leaf nodes might provide a useful combination of global stability and local readability. Or perhaps specific nodes could be anchored to a specific location with other nodes to be laid out around the anchored nodes. More speculatively, since experimental results suggest a tradeoff between aspect ratios and smoothness of layout changes, it would be worthwhile to look for a mathematical theorem that makes this tradeoff precise. It might also be fruitful to explore variants of treemap layouts that can update smoothly by using past layouts as a guide to current ones, or by using tiles that can have nonrectangular shapes [Bederson 2001].

More ambitious goals include accommodation of trees with millions of nodes. Rapid ways of aggregating data and drawing only visible features are necessary, especially to handle continuous updating. This is desirable for monitoring corporate computer networks with thousands of hard drives, stock market trading with millions of transactions, and oil production from thousands of wells and pumps.

Another challenge is to show more than two attribute values for each leaf node, possibly using texture, saturation, sound, or icons. Relationships between nodes might be shown by animation (e.g. blinking), connected lines, textures, or other perceptual methods.

ACKNOWLEDGMENTS

We appreciate the detailed comments of the anonymous reviewers of this paper who offered excellent advice.

REFERENCES

BAKER, M. J. AND EICK, S. G. 1995. Space-filling software visualization. *J. Vis. Lang. Comput., 6*, 119–133.

BEDERSON, B. B. 2001. PhotoMesa: A zoomable image browser using quantum treemaps and bubblemaps. *UIST 2001, ACM Symposium on User Interface Software and Technology, CHI Letters , 3*, 2, pp. 71–80.

BRULS, M., HUIZING, K., AND VAN WIJK, J. J. 2000. Squarified treemaps. *In Proceedings of Joint Eurographics and IEEE TCVG Symposium on Visualization (TCVG 2000)* IEEE Press, pp. 33–42.

EDGAR, G. A., EWING, J. H., AND GEHRING, F. W. 1995. *Measure, Topology, and Fractal Geometry*. Springer Verlag.

FEKETE, J.-D. AND PLAISANT, C. 2002. *Interactive Information Visualization to the Million*. Tech. Rep. CS-TR-4320, Computer Science Department, University of Maryland, College Park, MD.

HORNOF, A. J. 2001. Visual search and mouse pointing in labeled versus unlabeled two-dimensional visual hierarchies. *ACM Trans. Computer-Human Interaction*.

JIN, L. AND BANKS, D. C. 1997. TennisViewer: A browser for competition trees. *IEEE Comput. Graph. Appl. 17*, 4, 63–65.

JOHNSON, B. 1994. *Treemaps: Visualizing Hierarchical and Categorical Data*. Doctoral dissertation, Computer Science Department, University of Maryland, College Park, MD.

JUNGMEISTER, W.-A. AND TURO, D. 1992. *Adapting Treemaps to Stock Portfolio Visualization.* Tech. Rep. CS-TR-2996, Computer Science Department, University of Maryland, College Park, MD.

Smartmoney Marketmap 2002. http://www.smartmoney.com/marketmap.

SHELDON, R. A. 1997. *A First Course in Probability.* Englewood Cliffs, NJ: Prentice Hall.

SHNEIDERMAN, B. 1992. Tree visualization with treemaps: A 2-D space-filling approach. *ACM Trans. Graph. 11,* 1, 92–99.

SHNEIDERMAN, B. AND WATTENBERG, M. 2001. Ordered treemap layouts. *In Proceedings of IEEE Information Visualization (InfoVis 2001)* New York: IEEE, pp. 73–78.

TURO, D. AND JOHNSON, B. 1992. Improving the visualization of hierarchies with treemaps: Design issues and experimentation. *In Proceedings of IEEE Visualization (Visualization 1992)* IEEE Press, pp. 124–131.

VERNIER, F. AND NIGAY, L. 2000. Modifiable treemaps containing variable-shaped units. *In Proceedings of Extended Abstracts of IEEE Information Visualization (InfoVis 2000)* New York: IEEE, pp. 28–35.

WATTENBERG, M. 1999. Visualizing the stock market. *In Proceedings of Extended Abstracts of Human Factors in Computing Systems (CHI 99)* ACM Press, pp. 188–189.

Received July 2001; revised December 2001; accepted May 2002

Interactive Information Visualization of a Million Items

Jean-Daniel Fekete   Catherine Plaisant

Human Computer Interaction Laboratory
University of Maryland
http://www.cs.umd.edu/hcil
fekete@lri.fr   plaisant@cs.umd.edu

Abstract

Existing information visualization techniques are usually limited to the display of a few thousand items. This article describes new interactive techniques capable of handling a million items (effectively visible and manageable on screen). We evaluate the use of hardware-based techniques available with newer graphics cards, as well as new animation techniques and non-standard graphical features such as stereovision and overlap count.

These techniques have been applied to two popular information visualizations: treemaps and scatter plot diagrams; but are generic enough to be applied to other 2D representations as well.

1. Introduction

Information visualization is a research domain aiming at supporting discovery and analysis of data through visual exploration. Made popular by Edward R. Tufte's books [22], its principle is to map the attributes of an abstract data structure to visual attributes such as Cartesian position, color and size, and to display the mapping. This is in contrast with scientific visualization, which deals with data that usually has an intrinsic representation.

Popular mappings exist for a large range of data structures such as tables, trees, graphs as well as more specialized ones. During the last decade, dozens of new visualization techniques were invented, such as treemaps [13] or ConeTrees[18]. Most techniques have a strong interaction component allowing users to rapidly explore the data [1,15]. Commercial products are now available and successfully used in a wide array of applications domains such as oil production or drug discovery [7].

Yet, little is known about the limits of information visualization techniques in term of scalability. Current systems tend to avoid the problem by relying on aggregation or sampling techniques that limit the number of visible items to about 10^4 and occasionally 10^5 at the cost of interaction. Our goal is to display and manage a million items. By *item*, we mean *atomic object displayed as a distinguishable contiguous area using one visualization technique*. For systems displaying the same object several times according to different attributes, we count each instance as a different item. Management of the items involves maintaining continuous interaction and smooth animation.

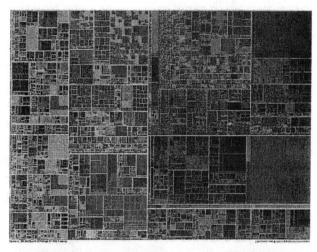

Figure 1: This treemap gives an overview of 970,000 files of a file system containing 1 million files (smaller files are smaller than one pixel and not counted), on a 1600x1200 display. The size of each rectangle is determined by the file's size; color represents file type. Deeply nested directories appear darker.

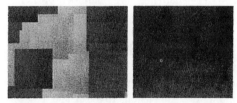

Figure 2: Smooth shaded rectangles help distinguish items in dense visualizations (details of scatter plots)

Figure 3: Scatter plot of 1 million items on the left and overlap counts on the right. The bright rectangle in the upper right corner reveal that many items are overlapping. They are aligned, and unnoticeable in the left view.

Scalability issues are important in information visualization because of the proliferation of large data sets requiring human-supervised analysis, but maximizing the number of items visible for a given display size is also a challenge for designers of visualizations on small devices like PDAs.

In this article, we describe new techniques to visualize a million items using standard displays. These techniques rely on:

- hardware acceleration to achieve the speed required for interaction and animation;

- non-standard visual attributes such as stereovision or synthetic overlap count to enhance visualization;

- animation and interaction while replaying recorded visualization configurations (views) using time multiplexing techniques to analyze the data across several views and mappings without losing context.

We have applied these techniques to treemaps (Figure 1) and scatter plots. Treemaps are representative of space filling visualizations whereas scatter plots are representative of visualizations with overlapping, but the techniques we describe here are general enough to be applied to other kinds of 2D visualizations.

2. Previous Work
Visualizing one million items is a problem of visualization, perception and interaction.

2.1 Visualization of Large Data Sets
Existing information visualization techniques are usually limited to the display of a few thousand items or avoid the problem of visualizing large number of items by using aggregation, sampling and extracting, or by not managing occlusion and overlapping.

Among the popular techniques is the use of scatter plots connected to interactive controls such as in Dynamic Queries [1]. Scatter plots visualize multidimensional data by mapping two dimensions to the X and Y coordinates and mapping other dimensions to visual attributes such as color, width, height, orientation, intensity or shape. When augmenting the number of visible data in scatter plots, overlapping cannot be avoided and is not managed at all by current systems.

Avoiding overlaps, space-filling techniques such as treemaps [13], VisDB [14] and SeeSoft [9], offer a high density of information. They use special layout algorithms to fill up all the screen pixels, thus requiring redrawing all these pixels when a visualization parameter changes. Current implementations of these systems are limited mostly by the redraw time and to a smaller extent by the time to compute the layout. VisDB handles 50,000 items; SeeSoft 50,000 lines of code and Microsoft NetScan project can render thousands of newsgroups in a treemap.

Treemaps are visualization techniques for trees. They were introduced by Shneiderman [13] and several variations have been created which improve their readability. The initial "slice and dice" algorithm is simple: it uses the entire screen to represent the tree root and its children. Each child of the root is given a horizontal or vertical strip of size proportional to the cumulative size of its descendents. The process is repeated recursively, flipping horizontal and vertical strips at each hierarchy level. Some variants try to avoid long thin rectangles and allocate strips containing sub-trees as square as possible [4].

Hybrid techniques such as Mihalisin Associates System can visualize data sets ranging from 10^4 to 10^8 data points [14] along with several dimensions and "measures"; however, they rely on sampling, limiting the number of visible items to numbers not specified by the author. Jerding et al. "Information Mural" technique [12] is a good example of system displaying hundreds of thousand items by relying on aggregation.

Current visualization systems are limited to about 10,000 items partly because control panels, labels and margins waste too many pixels, the data structures are not optimized for speed, and they use slow graphics libraries, which brings the interaction to a very slow motion when dealing with more than 10,000 items (for example Spotfire can load more than 10,000 items but the interaction suffers enormously). Addressing those three issues is necessary – but not sufficient – to handle a million items.

2.2 Perception
To be effective, visualization techniques should rely as much as possible on preattentive graphical features [11,21]. These features are processed by the low level visual system and can be recognized "at a glance" without effort. An example of preattentive processing consists in spotting red dots among several blue dots. It does not take any effort to see whether there are one or several red dots and it can be done in less than 200 milliseconds if the region is small enough to be seen in one glimpse (more experiments can be found at http://www.csc.ncsu.edu/faculty/healey/PP/PP.html). Without pre-attentive processing, spotting a feature requires time linear to the number of features and will not scale well to displays of millions of items. An example of non-preattentive feature is text reading. Finding a name in a non-sorted list requires a time proportional to the number of labels (or more when the user loses track or gives up.)

The list of visual features available to visualize abstract information is long, but only a small set can be used in a preattentive way. Healey lists them in [11] as: line (blob) orientation, length, width, size, curvature, number, terminators, intersection, closure, color (hue), intensity, flicker, direction of motion, binocular luster, stereoscopic depth, 3D depth cues and lighting direction. Furthermore, this list only means that in some controlled configuration, these features can be processed preattentively, not that they are always processed this way. For example, Healey has conducted experiments that show that only five to seven different well-chosen colors can be processed preattentively. When trying to use more colors, the error rate and time required to search colored items increased substantially and search time become linear. In addition, combining two or more preattentive features can create interferences so in practice only two or three features can be used together.

2.3 Interactive Techniques

In 1994, Ahlberg and Shneiderman [1] defined the steps of visual information seeking as: start with an overview of the data set, zoom in on items of interest and filter out uninteresting items, then details on demands. Increasing the number of visible items permits richer overviews to be presented. They also introduced the term "dynamic queries" to describe interactive methods for interactively specifying search queries in data sets. The definition is:

- visual presentation of the query's components (with buttons and range sliders);
- visual presentation of results;
- rapid [around 100ms], incremental, and reversible control of the query;
- selection by pointing, not typing; and immediate and continuous feedback.

Coupling visualization with dynamic queries has increased the effectiveness of visualization techniques by allowing user-controlled temporal research on the visualized data. Current systems dynamically filter visualized data through sliders and buttons up to 10,000 items. Above that, the refresh rate becomes unacceptable. An optimization technique developed by Tanin [20] demonstrates dynamic queries with 100,000 items by pre-computing the visible items for each reachable position of the slider bar but this technique was limited by the redisplay time.

To show more items or dimensions, all the visualization techniques can use space multiplexing, time multiplexing, overlapping, or space deformation techniques. Space multiplexing techniques display two or more visualization configurations on the same screen, using fewer pixels for each configuration. This is impractical when attempting to visualize a million items because space is already scarce to begin with. Time multiplexing techniques show each configuration successively, either at a regular pace (animation), or by using control panels, or by following interactive methods such as dynamic queries. Each configuration should appear in less than 100ms to maintain continuous interaction. Overlapping techniques such as Magic Lenses [5] and Excentric Labels [10] show transient information over the visualization and can be used

effectively on dense data. Several interactive techniques have been designed to enhance the interaction for visualization and sparing screen real estate. See-through tools [5] are interactive enhancements to Magic lenses; they filter the visualization in-place using transparency or overlapping. Extensions of Pie-Menus [6] such as Control Menus [19] can be used to overlay controls without using permanent screen real estate.

Space-deformation techniques such as [15] are sampling or aggregation techniques that try to show details in the zones of interest and only show "important features" or samples elsewhere.

Aggregations provide powerful summaries but can sometime hide phenomena only visible at finer grain. For example, a US map of mortality data at the state level will hide local outliers and even errors in the data. This article focuses on techniques that push back further the need for aggregation and sampling.

3. Technical Constraints

To display one million of items, we need to address screen resolution and speed issues.

Screen definition and resolution: Current high end screens display around 2 million pixels (1600x1200) at a resolution of 150dpi, with the newest screens capable of displaying around ten million pixels at 200dpi. So displaying 1 million of items should not be a problem if each item fits in 2 to 10 pixels in average, not counting the overlaps. Screens or video projections can be tiled to increase the number of pixels available, virtually removing any limitation, but increasing the physical size of the display requires more head movements and slows down perception. An alternative is to increase screen resolution. The limit would be human perception: theoretically around 24 million pixels, practically around 10 million, and head or body movements can still be used to get closer to or farther away from the display. The only alternative to these movements is time multiplexing, through constant animation or interactive control such as a scrollbars for panning and zooming, which are even less effective than movements.

We have focused our research on 1600x1200 displays because they are widespread and well managed by current accelerated graphics boards.

Redisplay time: when time multiplexing is used, the redisplay rate should be maintained around 10 frames per second. If one million items have to be displayed at this rate, using accelerated graphics cards is the only option and opens the door to visualization enhancements. Common graphics cards can display around 15 million triangles per second at best so maintaining an acceptable refresh rate for one million items demands special techniques and more expensive cards or waiting for the next generation of cards.

For our work, we have used NVidia GeForce3 and 3Dlab Wildcat hardware accelerated boards with 2GHz and 1.7GHz Pentium PCs and the OpenGL API [23] with code written in C++.

4. Reaching One Million Items

To address the technical issues involved in visualizing and interacting with one million items, we have designed novel techniques relying on accelerated graphics hardware to provide high-density interactive visualization. The accelerated graphics hardware reduces the load of the main CPU (e.g. all rendering is done there) and offers many non-standard graphics attributes that we used to enhance the visualization of dense data sets.

4.1 Appropriate Visual Attributes

We only use quadrilaterals to represent items because, in a dense configuration, the perception of shapes is subject to interference. As item density increases shapes overlap and appear to merge. Also, contrary to several existing systems, we don't outline items using a one-pixel black line, which wastes two lines and two columns of pixels and requires sending the coordinates twice. Instead, we use slightly shaded quadrilaterals so that they remain distinguishable when tiled or stacked (see figure 2). The other visual attributes we use are saturated colors (for categorical or numeral attributes), intensity (for numeral attributes), quadrilateral sizes and position in scatter plots.

We describe each quad vertex with four values: X, Y, Z and S. X and Y are positions. S is a texture coordinate index. The Z coordinate is mainly used for fog and stereovision: we tilt the quads so that the upper left corner is closer to the camera and the lower right corner farther away; the fog function changes their intensity and smooth shading interpolates it across the rectangle.

Instead of sending RGBA colors for each quad, we use one-dimensional texture indices. The texture can contain a set of colors for categorical attributes: one color per category. It can also contain starting and ending color for continuous valued attributes. We then rely on hardware linear filtering to generate in-between colors as shown in figure 2. We also use texture transforms to map from abstract attribute values to color values, avoiding all color computation on the CPU side.

More attributes can be used if required. For instance, for treemaps, we also use the fog function to fade the colors to black when items are deeper in the tree by assigning the tree depth attribute to the Z coordinate of the quadrilaterals (see Figure 1). More control could be obtained by using a two dimensional texture and assigning the U texture coordinate (also easily available via the accelerated graphics hardware) to one abstract attribute and the V coordinate to another one. However, the only coloring scheme we have found to

be effective using pre-attentive features with two attributes was assigning a saturated set of colors to one attribute and varying the brightness with the other.

4.1.1 Synthetic overlap attribute

When sending data to the graphics hardware, the count of overlapping items can be calculated using the stencil buffer. Displaying the content of the stencil buffer as intensity shows the overlapping counts (see figure 3.) This synthetic attribute is very important for visualization techniques that cannot avoid overlaps such as scatter plots and parallel coordinates. Even with hundreds of items, the distribution tends to be sparse with areas of high density that are hard to see. Transparency is useful when up to five items overlap, but with one million items, hundreds of overlapping items are common.

The overlap count can also be mapped to color, or used to filter the display and reveal a specific layer of items. This technique is similar to dynamic queries on standard attributes but instead relies on the stencil buffer for rejecting fragments above or below a specified number of overlaps.

4.1.2 Transparency and Stereovision

Using an accelerated graphics card provides graphic attributes not available or usable with traditional graphics APIs. We have experimented with transparency and stereovision. Transparency is beneficial with overlapped items but is not sufficient by itself to understand the number of overlaps. Furthermore, by blending colors, it interferes with its preattentive processing. Therefore, transparency is only useful when it can be varied interactively to reveal overlaps and density of overlapping items.

Stereovision hardware is now available for all the standard graphics cards for less than $100 through shutter glasses. Stereovision is preattentive, but there again, overlaps interfere with it and cannot be avoided at all, even with space-filling visualization techniques, since stereovision requires a perspective projection that introduces occlusion and therefore overlaps. Like transparency, we have found stereovision mostly useful for transient inspections.

4.2 Animation and Interaction

Exploring a large data set without a-priori knowledge typically requires trying several mappings of data attributes to visual attributes. A special problem happens when changing views using time multiplexing: the whole layout of the screen changes and the user cannot tell where sets of regions of interest in the original view have gone on the new one. A long time may be required to understand the relationship between items visualized in the new view and in the previous one. This problem is not addressed at all by current systems. When the number of items is small and space multiplexing possible, two or more views could be displayed together using "snap together" techniques [17] and brushing and linking techniques [8] can be used to explore the tightly coupled views by highlighting items in multiple views; but this is not an option in our case.

We first describe the simple case of non-geometrical changes and then the general case.

4.2.1 View Flipping

When the positions of the data items are preserved – i.e. when only changing colors or stacking order – flipping between views allows quick comparisons to be made using retina persistency. This technique is widely used in astronomy to track variations over time (called *blinking*.) By flipping back and forth and moving the focus of attention, two views can be compared in seconds.

More views can be flipped through, similar to flipping techniques of traditional animators, to help discover trends and outliers across multiple views. This technique only requires a redisplay time below 300ms and a refresh time below 50ms, only achievable with double buffering.

4.2.2 Interpolation of geometrical attributes

When the geometry is modified between two views, it becomes difficult to impossible to understand relationships between views with flipping [16].

We have implemented a set of interpolation techniques to animate the transformations from one view to the other so that the eye can follow sets of items and understand patterns of change between views. Because the changes could be complex, users can select a subset of items and we only animate those items. The animation lasts one or two second and can be replayed back and forth at will. A slider can also be used to manually control the interpolation between views to facilitate understanding of item movements.

The simplest technique for animation is linear interpolation. However, when several visual attributes change, linear interpolation is confusing [25] and only allow users to track position changes at best. To help users understanding changes, we found that animating in two stages was beneficial: changing positions, then changing dimensions.

For scatter-plot-like visualization, position and size are independent so the middle configuration is easy to compute. Linear interpolation of positions is used to reach the middle configuration from the initial and linear interpolation of sizes is used to reach the final configuration. Both show trends when they exist.

Space-filling visualizations compute positions according to the size of items. Most of them [3, 9, 12] can be animated by linearly changing the size attributes since they use a layout that remains stable. Only some treemaps described in [4] use layout algorithms that are not geometrically stable. However, we found a general way to stabilize all these layouts for stage 2 (i.e. size changes) by computing

the final layout using the final sizes values and linearly changing the sizes of all areas according to their initial values. This is shown in figure 4 where the final layout is computed by the "squarified treemap" algorithm, and used by previous frames with the sizes interpolated. The final layout tries to have items as "square" as possible but not the previous ones. Still, trends are visible.

For stage 1 (i.e. position changes), linear interpolation is usually the only option. Layout changes may be due to the underlying algorithm or to the change of an axis on a scatter plot, or the sorting order of a dimension linked to an axis. However, by only changing positions and not sizes, items are easier to track and trends are noticeable. For example, when changing the attribute to be mapped on the X axis of a scatter plot, items only move along the Y axis.

With treemaps, texture mapping [2] is very effective at speeding-up both stage 1 and 2. Most space-filling techniques use hierarchical containment, preserved by attribute change so one set of items is always inside a rectangle that can be warped and turned during the animation and there is no need to interpolate each item separately. With this technique, smooth interpolation can be achieved with one million item treemaps.

Logging/playback: Interactively specifying mappings from data attributes to visual attributes can become tedious and diverts the user from the visualization analysis. To avoid this distraction from occurring too often, we developed a tool allowing users to record sets of configurations and view them in turn using the left and right arrow keys, with animated transitions as described above. These views and configurations can also be saved to a file and applied to other data sets (e.g. to simplify routine examination of similar datasets.)

4.2.3 Dynamic Queries

Dynamic queries implies interactively filtering and redisplaying of the dataset through continuous interaction. Current systems use "range-sliders" to filter one attribute at a time, either changing the lower or upper value, or sweeping a given range of values between the smallest and the largest. The dataset needs to be loaded into main memory. To achieve the redisplay speed required for smooth interaction, we have designed a technique that relies on hardware acceleration. When the user activates a slider to perform the series of queries, all the items are sent to the graphics processor (GPU) and stored in a display list. The Z coordinate is calculated according to the attribute being filtered by the slider (e.g. if the user is filtering a film database on the size of the film, the size is assigned to the Z-axis.) Each time the slider moves, a new near or far plane value is computed and sent to the GPU and the list is redisplayed, leaving the visibility computation to the hardware.

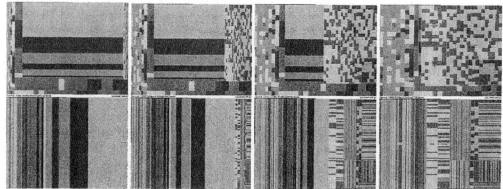

Figure 4: The animation of the treemap (with a squarified layout on the left or slice&dice layout on the right) allows users to follow specific items and observe patterns of change between two configurations using a different size attribute . A stabilized layout is used to avoid jumps.

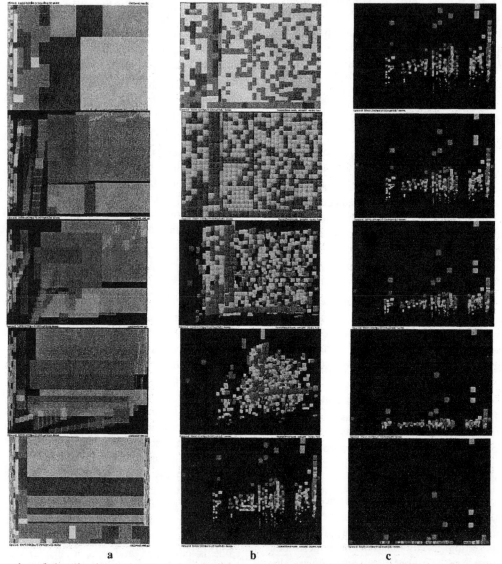

a   b   c

Figure 5: Animation of visualizations using linear interpolation: a) interpolation between squarified and slice and dicelayouts, b) interpolation between a treemap and a scatter plot, c) interpolation when changing the Y axis on a scatter plot.

This technique works very well as long as the GPU has enough memory to hold the items and the shape of the items doesn't change during the dynamic queries. Using quadrilaterals requires 64MB of free memory (4 vertices per item, 4 data per vertex with 4 bytes per data) for one million items and only fits on special machines such as SGI O2. When applying dynamic queries on scatter plots with PC graphics cards, we use points instead of quads. Currently, OpenGL doesn't allow sending one array of points with varying sizes, although it can be done with NVidia Vertex programs extension. We send arrays of points sorted by decreasing point-size, dividing by 4 the amount of data sent to the card and making dynamic queries possible with one million items on a PC.

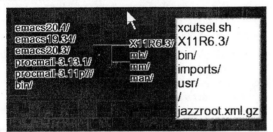

Figure 6: Dynamic Labeling of a Treemap (detail). When clicking on the treemap, labels are displayed dynamically on the outside of the region, which is grayed out. The popup menu allows users to adjust the depth of the region of interest.

4.2.4 Labeling

Text labels are not preattentive but are nevertheless important to understand the context in which visualized data appear. Labeling each item cannot be done statically on a dense visualization so we used the Excentric Labeling [10] dynamic technique for the scatter plot and extended its design for the Treemap, as shown in figure 6.

5. Performance

Our system reads data encoded in XML or a directory structure as input formats. It is made of 23,000 lines of C++, using high-performance techniques such as template metaprogramming [23] to achieve the required speed. We have used it with an NVidia GeForce3 board on a 2 GHz Pentium and a 3Dlab Wildcat 5110 on a dual 1.7GHz Pentium. To scale to a million items, the computation of layouts should be done in time linear with the number of items. This is the case with some treemaps and scatter plots but not with VisDB for example. Even using the fastest techniques, layout computation takes about 50% of the redisplay time.

Despite the high theoretical performance of the boards, we have not been able to go beyond 6 million quads per second on any of the boards we tried. The theoretical speed of 15 million triangles per second is only achievable for triangle strips, which is of no use for scatter plots and would require expensive computation for treemaps.

Combining software and hardware techniques provides a sustained performance around 2.5 million quads per second. By using texture mapping for animating treemaps, we achieve 10 frames per second for animating across any family of treemap. For scatter plots we have only reached 3 frames per second for animations on 1 million items, and 6 frames per second for dynamic queries. Finding techniques for improving that speed would be useful but the next generation of graphics cards and computers will solve the problem.

Our estimate is that these results correspond to a 20 to 100 time improvement on the available systems.

6. Conclusion and Future Work

Using a set of novel techniques we were able to visualize and explore for the first time 1 million items on a 1600x1200 display without aggregation. Our techniques rely heavily on commonly available accelerated hardware for displaying items in a dense yet manageable manner. We designed new animation techniques to help understand view changes and show trends and outliers when they exist. We developed a method to perform dynamic queries using the Z-buffer of a graphics card and achieved the speed required to interact with a million items. Finally, we experimented with non-standard visual attributes such as transparency and stereovision and found them effective for temporary inspections.

This work shows that the technical limits of information visualization are well beyond the typical 10^4 items handled by most existing systems, and opens the door to new possibilities for users: a library manager can use a treemap to review usage patterns of a million individual books organized with the Dewey decimal system; large databases of highway incidents or juvenile justice cases can be first examined without sampling or aggregation.

Our early user testing has been limited to collecting feedback from colleagues about the large treemap displaying our shared drives of one million files. It seems to confirm that users' experience analyzing data transfers to large visualizations, allowing them to make local and global comments on the data presented. Users appreciated the fine patterns, e.g. the distinctive pattern of web page directories that combine text and graphics, and seemed to actively engage their visual skills to compare and make sense of patterns. We have now identified two applications for user testing: 1) the visualization of the University of Maryland catalog and years of circulation data, and 2) fine grain analysis of Census Bureau data. The user testing will involve domain expert users, who are more apt to make sense of such large datasets and make suggestions for improvements.

More experiments are needed to understand how humans can cope with a large number of items and the possible limits of visualization, e.g. how can we best use visualization to gain an understanding of the organization and content of the 7 million items of the Library of Congress American Memory collection?

We are confident that human visual skills and the evolution of hardware will push information visualization much further than the million of items.

7. Acknowledgments
This work was supported in part by Chevron Texaco. We want to thank Ben Bederson and Ben Shneiderman for their helpful feedback on the paper.

For more information and demonstration of animations see:
http://www.cs.umd.edu/hcil/millionvis/

8. References
[1] Ahlberg, C. and Shneiderman, B. Visual Information Seeking: Tight Coupling of Dynamic Query Filters with Starfield Display. *Conference proceedings on Human factors in computing systems*, April 1994, 313–318, ACM New York.

[2] Aliaga, D. Visualization of Complex Models Using Dynamic Texture-Based Simplification, *Proceedings of IEEE Visualization'96*, Oct 27-Nov 1, pp. 101—106, 1996, IEEE, Piscataway, NJ.

[3] Baker, M. J. Eick, S. G. Space Filling Software Visualization. *Journal of Visual Languages and Computing*, Vol. 6, 119—133, 1995.

[4] Bederson, B., Shneiderman, B., Wattenberg, M. Ordered and Quantum Treemaps: Making Effective Use of 2D Space to Display Hierarchies, *To appear in ACM Transactions on Computer Graphics*.

[5] Bier. E. A. Stone, M. C. Fishkin, K. Buxton, W. Baudel, T. A Taxonomy of See-Through Tools, *Conference proceedings on Human factors in computing systems*, April 1994, 358–364, ACM New York.

[6] Callahan, J., Hopkins, D., Weiser, M. Shneiderman, B. An Empirical Comparison of Pie vs. Linear Menus, *Proceedings on Human factors in computing systems May 1988*. 95–100, ACM New York.

[7] Card, S. K., MacKinlay, J. D., Shneiderman, B., *Readings in Information Visualization: Using Vision to Think*, Morgan Kaufmann Publishers, 1998.

[8] Cleveland, W.S., McGill, M.E., Eds., *Dynamic Graphics for Statistics*. 1988

[9] Eick. S. G. Steffen, J. L. and Sumner, E. E. Jr. SeeSoft—A Tool for Visualizing Line Oriented Software Statistics. *IEEE Transactions on Software Engineering*, 18 (11) 957–968, November 1992

[10] Fekete, J.-D. Plaisant, C. Excentric Labeling: Dynamic Neighborhood Labeling for Data Visualization, *Proceeding of the CHI 99 conference on Human factors in computing systems*, May 1999, 79–90.

[11] Healey, C. G., Booth, K. S., and Enns, J, Visualizing Real-Time Multivariate Data Using Preattentive Processing, *ACM Transactions on Modeling and Computer Simulation* 5, 3, 1995, 190-221.

[12] Jerding D. F., Stasko J. T., The Information Mural: A Technique for Displaying and Navigating Large Information Spaces, *IEEE Transactions on Visualization and Computer Graphics*, 4(3), July/September 1998, 257—271.

[13] Johnson. B. and Shneiderman, B. Tree-maps: A space-filling approach to the visualization of hierarchical information structures, *Proc. IEEE Visualization' 91* (1991) 284 – 291, IEEE, Piscataway, NJ.

[14] Keim, D.A., Visual Exploration of Large Data Sets *Communications of the ACM*, August 2001, Volume 44, Issue 8, 38–44.

[15] Lamping J., Rao, R., Pirolli, P., A focus+context technique based on hyperbolic geometry for visualizing large hierarchies, In *Proceedings of the ACM SIGCHI Conference on Human Factors in Computing Systems*. ACM, May 1995, 401—408.

[16] Nowell, L., Hetzler, E., Tanasse, T., Change blindness in information visualization: a case study. *Proceeding of IEEE Symposium on Information Visualization 2001*, IEEE Press, 200, 11—15.

[17] North, C., Shneiderman, B., Snap-Together Visualization: Evaluating Coordination Usage and Construction, *Int'l Journal of Human-Computer Studies special issue on Empirical Studies of Information Visualization*, Volume 53, 5 (November 2000), 715-739.

[18] Robertson, G. G. Mackinlay, J. D. Card, S. K. Cone Trees: animated 3D visualizations of hierarchical information, *Proc. Human factors in computing systems conference*, March 1991, 189 – 194.

[19] Pook, S. Lecolinet. E. Vaysseix, G. Barillot, E. Context and Interaction in Zoomable User Interfaces, *Proceedings of the Working Conference on Advanced Visual Interfaces* May 2000, 227 – 231.

[20] Tanin, E., Beigel, R., and Shneiderman, B., Incremental Data Structures and Algorithms for Dynamic Query Interfaces, *SIGMOD Record* (25) 4, 21-24, December 1996.

[21] Triesman, A. Preattentive Processing in Vision. *Computer Vision, Graphics, and Image Processing*, 31 (1985) 156-177.

[22] Tufte, E. *The Visual Display of Quantitative Information*. Graphics Press, Cheshire, CT, 1983.

[23] Veldhuizen, T. "Using C++ template metaprograms," *C++ Report* (7) 4, May 1995, 36-43.

[24] Woo, M. Neider, J. Davis, T. and Shreiner, D. *OpenGL Programming Guide*, Third Edition, Addison-Wesley, 2001.

[25] Yee, K.-P., Fisher, D.; Dhamija, R.; Hearst, M., Animated exploration of dynamic graphs with radial layout. *Proceeding of IEEE Symposium on Information Visualization 2001*, IEEE Press, 2001, 43 – 50.

SpaceTree: Supporting Exploration in Large Node Link Tree, Design Evolution and Empirical Evaluation

Catherine Plaisant, Jesse Grosjean, Benjamin B. Bederson
Human-Computer Interaction Laboratory
University of Maryland
{plaisant, grosjean, bederson}@cs.umd.edu

Abstract

We present a novel tree browser that builds on the conventional node link tree diagrams. It adds dynamic rescaling of branches of the tree to best fit the available screen space, optimized camera movement, and the use of preview icons summarizing the topology of the branches that cannot be expanded. In addition, it includes integrated search and filter functions. This paper reflects on the evolution of the design and highlights the principles that emerged from it. A controlled experiment showed benefits for navigation to already previously visited nodes and estimation of overall tree topology.

1. Introduction

The browsing of hierarchies and trees has been investigated extensively [1]. Designers have demonstrated that many alternatives to the traditional node link representation (Figure 1) are possible, but the classic representation of trees remains the most familiar mapping for users and still is universally used to draw simple trees. Our goal was to take another look at this well-known tree representation and see how visualization advances in zoomable user interfaces and improved animation principles could lead to a better interactive tree browser while preserving the classic tree representation. Such a browser might encourage the adoption of visualization by a wider range of users (e.g. families browsing genealogy trees or biology students browsing taxonomies) or by more traditional work environments (organization charts for managers or personal office staff).

We present SpaceTree, a novel interface that combines the conventional layout of trees with a zooming environment that dynamically lays out branches of the tree to best fit the available screen space. It also uses preview icons to summarize the topology of the branches when there isn't enough space to show them in full. This paper reflects on the evolution of the design and highlights the principles that emerged from it. A controlled experiment compares SpaceTree to two other interfaces and analyzes the impact of interface features on the time to perform navigation tasks to new and already visited nodes, and topology evaluation tasks.

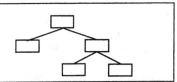

Figure 1: The "traditional" node link representation of a tree. It has a favored direction (here top down). Drawing every nodes makes very poor use of the available drawing space, and would fill up a screen before reaching 100 nodes.

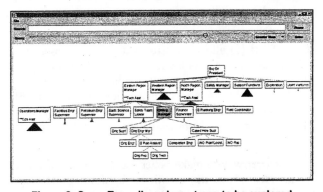

Figure 2: SpaceTree allows large trees to be explored dynamically. Branches that do not fit on the screen are summarized by a triangular preview. The number of levels opened is maximized. In this example, the 3 lower levels of the hierarchy were opened at once as users clicked on "Drilling Manager" (the colored node in the middle.)

2. Related work

Two large categories of solutions have been proposed to display and manipulate trees: space-filling techniques and node link techniques. Space filling techniques (e.g. treemaps [2], information slices [3]) have been successful at visualizing trees that have attributes values at the node level. In particular, treemaps are seeing a rapid expansion of their use for monitoring, from stock market applications (e. g. www.smartmoney .com), to inventory or network management, to production monitoring. Space filling techniques shine when users care mostly about leaf nodes and their attributes (e.g. outlier stocks) but do not need to focus on the topology of the tree, or the topology of the tree is trivial (e.g. 2 or 3 fixed levels). Treemap users also require training because of the unfamiliar layout.

Node link diagrams, on the other hand, have long been the plague of information visualization designers because they typically make inefficient use of screen space, leaving the root side of the tree completely empty – usually the top or left of the screen – and overcrowding the opposite side. Even trees of a hundred nodes often need multiple screens to be completely displayed, or require scrolling since only part of the diagram is visible at a given time. Specialized tools can help users manage the multiple pages needed to display those trees (e.g. www.nakisa.com for organizational chart). Optimized layout techniques can produce more compact displays by slightly shifting branches or nodes (e.g. [4], or [5]), but those techniques only partially alleviate the problem and are often not appropriate for interactive applications.

The coupling of overview + detail views with pan and zoom was proposed early by Beard & Walker [6] and found to be more effective than scrolling. Kumar et al. successfully combined the overview and detail technique with dynamic queries to facilitate the searching and pruning of large trees [7]. The technique allows ranges of depth dependant attribute values to be specified to prune the tree dynamically.

Another approach is to use 3D node link diagrams. Cone Trees [8] allow users to rotate a 3D representation of the tree to reveal its hidden parts. Info-TV [9] allows nodes and labels to be removed from sub trees (leaving the links) to show a more compact view of branches. 3D representations are attractive but only marginally improve the screen space problem while increasing the complexity of the interaction.

A clever way to make better use of screen space is to break loose from the traditional up-down or left-right orientation and use circular layouts [10]. The best known technique is the Hyperbolic tree browser [11] - now available as StarTree from Inxight (www.inxight.com) - which uses hyperbolic geometry to place nodes around the root and provides smooth and continuous animation of the tree as users click or drag nodes to readjust the focus point of the layout. The animation is striking but the constant redrawing of the tree can be distracting. Labels are hard to browse because they are not aligned and sometimes overlap. In addition, the unconventional layout may not match the expectations of users (e.g. it is not appropriate to present the organizational chart of a conventional business.)

Cheops [12] overlaps branches of the tree to provide a very compact overview of large trees. Labeling is an issue and interpreting the diagram requires training. Constrained by limited screen space, WebBrain (www.webbrain.com) chooses to prune the tree to show only a very local view of children and parent of the current selection – and some crosslinks. The nodes have to be reoriented at each selection. The benefits of pure zooming are illustrated by PadPrints [13], which automatically scales down a tree of visited pages as users

navigate the web. The use of fisheye effects to display branches at varying scales in the same display was also explored [14] [15]. The just published Degree-of-Interest Tree developed by Card and Nation [16] uses fisheye views and shares many features with SpaceTrees.

Expand and contract interfaces as exemplified by Microsoft Explorer allow the browsing of trees as well. Similarly, WebTOC [17] shows how information about size or type could be added to the expandable list of nodes.

3. Description of the interface

SpaceTree is our attempt to make the best possible use of the traditional node link tree representation for interactive visualization. Figures 3 to 6 show a series of screen captures of the main display area, showing the progressive opening of branches as users refine their focus of interest. Branches that cannot be fully opened because of lack of space are previewed with an icon. Here we describe an initial design using a preview icon in the shape of an isosceles rectangle. The shading of the triangle is proportional to the total number of nodes in the subtree. The height of the triangle represents the depth of the subtree and the base is proportional to the average width (i.e. number of items divided by the depth). The preview icons can be chosen to be relative to the root (for ease of comparison between levels) or to the parent (for ease of local comparison).

Users can navigate the tree by clicking on nodes to open branches, or by using the arrow keys to navigate among siblings, ancestors and descendants. Figure 6 illustrates how SpaceTree maximizes the number of lower levels to be opened.

Several layout options allow adjustments of the spacing between nodes, alignment, icon options etc. The choice of overall orientation of the tree layout, allows designers or users to match the layout to the natural orientation of the data. For example organizational charts are often oriented top down (suggesting power), while the evolution of species is more likely to be show left to right (suggesting time) or bottom up (suggesting progress). Figures 7 and 8 show examples of a left to right orientation. The choice of the most space efficient orientation depends on the tree topology and the aspect ratios of the labels and the window.

SpaceTree also includes integrated support for search and filter. As users type a string, the location of results is highlighted on the tree. Then users can navigate the tree, or click on the "prune" button to see a filtered view of the tree showing only the paths to the matching nodes.

We also implemented dynamic queries [18] to illustrate how dynamic queries allow the rapid pruning of the tree when attributes are available at the node level. As users manipulate a slider to limit the value of an attribute, leaves or branches of the tree are dynamically grayed out to show the effect of the query. (Note that the current version supports rudimentary dynamic queries with only one attribute, but the principle applies to any number of attributes such as income of employees, year in the company, or language spoken, etc. for our organizational chart example).

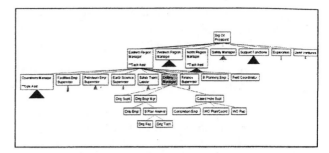

Figure 6: Upon each refocusing, the maximum number of levels that fit is opened (here 3 levels could fit so they were opened at once when user selected "drilling manager").

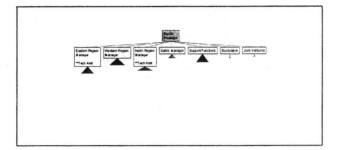

Figure 3: Top level overview. The triangular preview icons summarize the branches that cannot be opened. When room is available, two or more levels might be opened at once. Darker icons correspond to branches with more nodes. Taller icons (in this top-down layout) correspond to deeper branches, and wider icons correspond to a higher average branching factor.

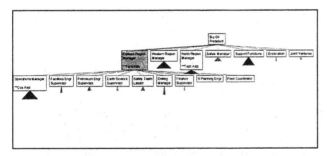

Figure 4: As users change the focus of the layout (i.e. click on a node – shown darker), more detail is revealed.

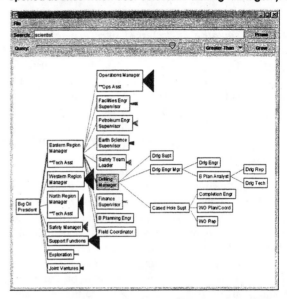

Figure 7: The tree shown in Figure 6 has been rotated to a different orientation, then a search for "scientist" was performed and the location of search results is shown in red. (not visible in a black and white prints

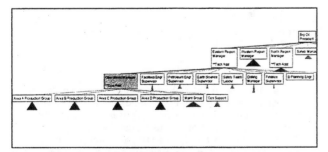

Figure 5: The tree is animated to its new layout in tree separate steps: trim, translate and expand (trim and translate is only done when needed).

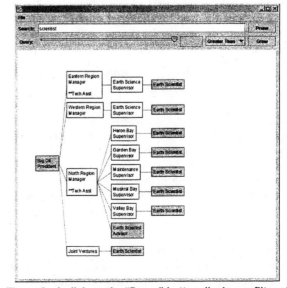

Figure 8: A click on the "Prune" button displays a filtered view of the tree, revealing only the branches that lead to scientists, opened as space permits.

SpaceTree was developed in Java using TinyJazz, a new toolkit that is an optimized subset of Jazz [19], and the tree layout is inspired from [20] and [21]

4. Review of the early versions and emerging design guidelines

The SpaceTree was designed with continuous feedback from our sponsors who had a particular need for hierarchy browsing at the time of the project. This included monthly discussions and exchange of prototypes. Through progressive refinement (about 10 versions were discussed) we learned lessons that we summarize here as guidelines for designers.

Semantic zooming is preferred over geometric scaling (i.e. "Make it readable or don't bother showing the nodes".) Our first designs attempted to use fixed progressive scaling down of the nodes – providing a nice overview of the tree (Figure 9) and continuous geometrical zooming to allow users to progressively reveal details of lower levels of the tree. The result was a smooth fly through of the tree (Figure 9 and 10) but was rejected bluntly by our users who rightly noted that only one level of the tree was even readable at a time (lower levels were "visible" but never readable). Readability and a good use of the screen space had not been optimized enough. The conclusion was that instead of continuous scaling, a step approach was needed: nodes should be either *readable* or not, and once they are not readable they could be seen as *individuals* or aggregated in an *abstract* representation. This was made possible by the semantic zooming afforded by Jazz. All scaling is therefore calculated on the fly. Figure 11 shows an example of alternative previews of a tree branches.

Maximize the number of levels opened at any time. Feedback from users made it clear that they resented having to open the tree "one level at a time" when there was room to open more levels at once. This is illustrated in Figure 6.

Decompose the tree animation. We experimented with several animations of the layout to reflect the change of focus and found that we received our most positive feedback with a decomposed animation following 3 main steps: trim, translate, and grow. When users select a new focus, SpaceTree evaluates how many levels of the new branch can be opened to fit in the window, then 1) trims the tree of the branches that would overlap the new branch to be opened; 2) centers the trimmed tree so that the new branch will fit on the window, 3) grows the branch out of the new focus point.

Maintain landmarks. As the tree is trimmed, expanded or translated it is crucial to maintain landmarks to help users remain oriented [22]. The obvious candidates for landmarks are the *focus points* users selected, i.e. the current focus and the path up the tree, which usually matches the history of focus points as users traverse the tree. The ancestor path of the current focus is highlighted

in blue. The node under the cursor is gold, and its ancestor path is shown in gold up until it meets the blue one. When users click on a node, their eyes are already on the gold node, which remains gold as the tree is animated to a new layout, and then turns blue to reflect the new focus.

The constant relative position of siblings and the overall shape of upper tree help maintain the larger context up the tree (Webbrain.com illustrates how changing the reorientation of siblings can be disorienting).

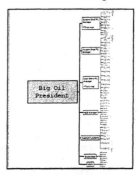

Figure 9: Early prototype: overview of the continuously scaled tree.

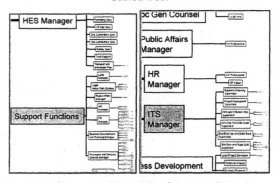

Figure 10: Early prototype: geometric zoom allowed users to fly through the tree but only made one new level readable at a time, and poorly used the screen space.

(a)   (b)   (c)

Figure 11: Current solution: semantic zooming on multiple representations of the tree. Previews can consist of a miniature of the branch (a) when the number of nodes is small or an abstract representation of the branch like the triangles of Figure 3 . Figure 11a(b) and 11(c) are alternatives to the triangle and provide more details on distribution of nodes in the next level branches.

Take advantage of overviews and dynamic filtering. Search and dynamic query techniques are not new, but SpaceTree offers a good demonstration of their application. One option we debated is whether to dynamically trim the tree of the nodes that would "fall off" with the query, or just gray them out and give "on demand pruning" after the query. We chose the later option that avoids constant and wild animation of the tree.

Use "data-aware" zooming controls. Another of the lessons we learned was the need to provide data-aware controls. Our initial browser permitted free zooming by clicking anywhere in the data space (on node or outside of nodes). This was the default control of Jazz but was only usable by expert zooming users, others being rapidly lost in the fog of empty information space. A second version gave users a preview of the area of the screen that would come to full view once they clicked (Figure 12). This helped users to avoid empty areas, but users complained that the area rarely matched the topology of the tree. Therefore, the best results were attained by only allowing users to zoom by clicking on nodes.

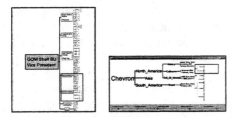

Figure 12: Early prototype: a rectangular cursor matching the window aspect ratio gave a preview of the area to be enlarged if users clicked, but didn't necessarily match a branch of the tree.

4. Controlled experiment

We conducted an experiment comparing 3 tree-browsing interfaces: Microsoft Explorer (Figure 13), a Hyperbolic tree browser[1] (Figure 14), and SpaceTree (Figure 15). Our goal was not to pit the interfaces against each other (as they are clearly at different stages of refinement and of different familiarity to users) but to understand what feature seemed to help users perform certain tasks. We used a 3x7 (3 interfaces by 7 tasks) repeated measure within subject design. To control learning effects, the order of presentation of the interfaces and the task sets were counterbalanced.

Eighteen subjects participated, and each session lasted a maximum of 40 minutes. Subjects each received $10 for their participation. To provide the motivation to perform the tasks quickly and accurately, an additional $5 was given to the fastest user within each interface (with no errors). We chose to use computer science students that could be assumed to have a homogeneous level of comfort with computers and tree structures.

---

[1] We attempted to use the downloadable version from inxight.com but could not transform the test data into the required format. Instead we used an older prototype, and asked three colleagues to compare the 2 versions. The old version was found similar to the current version in term of the features used in the experiment (e.g. we didn't use color, attribute values, graphics or database access in the test tree). Obviously the current commercial version has many more features that make it a useful product but that we were not comparing here.

Figure 13: Microsoft Explorer, a classic expand and contract interface. The same window size was used for all interfaces (1024x768 pixels of display area – excluding menus and control panels)

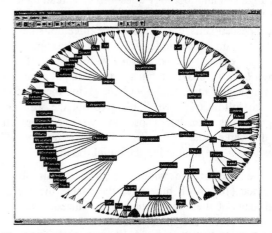

Figure 14: The hyperbolic viewer spreads the branches around the root making 2 or 3 levels of the tree visible. Users can click or drag a node to dynamically and continuously update the layout of the tree and quickly explore deeper levels of the tree.

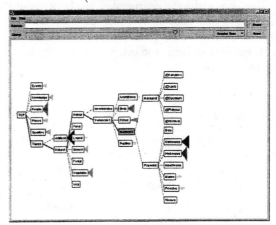

Figure 15: The SpaceTree opened to "mammals" and showing nodes seven levels down the tree.

Subjects were given a maximum of 2 minutes of training with each interface. In order to see what problems users would encounter without any training, the experimenter gave no initial demonstration, but after about 30 seconds of self-exploration, the experimenter made sure that users had discovered everything properly. Hyperbolic users were told that they could continuously drag nodes, and the meaning of the triangle icons was explained to SpaceTree users (misunderstanding were first recorded, and then clarified).

We used a tree of more than 7,000 nodes from the CHI'97 BrowseOff [23]. The three task sets used different branches of the tree and were carefully chosen to be equivalent in terms of number of levels traversed and semantic complexity of the data explored. Three types of tasks were used. Node searches (e.g. find kangaroo, find planaria), search of previously visited nodes (return to kangaroo) and topology questions (e.g. read the path up the tree, find in this branch 3 nodes with more than 10 direct descendants, and which of the three branches of this node contain more nodes). To avoid measuring users' knowledge about the nodes they were asked to find (e.g. kangaroos) we provided hints to users (e.g. kangaroos are mammals and marsupials) without giving them the entire path to follow (e.g. we didn't give out the well known steps such as animals). Those hints were also kept similar in the three sets of tasks. The terminology of the questions was explained in the initial training.

The size of the window was the same for each interface (1024x768 pixels for the usable display area). The focus of the tree layout was initialized at the top of the tree at the beginning of tasks but was not reset between tasks to match a normal work session. The entire explorer hierarchy was re-contracted in between users. After the short training, users were asked to conduct 7 tasks with each interface, after which they filled a questionnaire and gave open-ended feedback about the 3 interfaces. The dependant variables were the time to complete each task, the presence of errors (only relevant for 2 questions), and subjective ratings on a 9-point Likert-type scale.

5. Results

For each speed and preference dependant variable we performed a one-way ANOVA followed by a post hoc Bonferroni analysis. The confidence interval is set at 95% for all ANOVA and post-hoc analysis.

For conciseness our hypotheses are described for each type of task, followed by a brief summary of the results. We report mean times in seconds in the following order: (E) for Explorer, (H) for Hyperbolic and (S) for SpaceTree.

5.1 First-time node finding

For finding nodes that had never been seen before, we hypothesized that SpaceTree and Hyperbolic would be similar in term of speed and faster than Explorer because they both provide access to more than one level at a time, which enables users to select categories further down the tree. Explorer uses smaller fonts and the size of the targets is smaller than the 2 other interfaces, but the distances to travel are also smaller and users are extremely familiar with the interface. An advantage might be seen for the SpaceTree because of the alignment of the labels, allowing faster scanning of the items, but this advantage may not compensate for the advantage of the fast continuous update of the tree layout in Hyperbolic, which allows rapid exploration of neighborhoods.

Results: Only two of the 3 node finding tasks showed significant differences, Explorer being faster than Hyperbolic in the 1st task where learning may have been a factor (in seconds: E=10.5, H=13.2, S=11.1), and SpaceTree being faster than explorer in the third task (E=11.3, H=5.6, S=4.7). Observations confirmed that most users took advantage of the ability of Hyperbolic and SpaceTree to show multiple levels of the tree by clicking down often more than one level at a time. The faster users did continuously drag nodes to reveal details with Hyperbolic, while with SpaceTree they still had to select and animate the tree in steps when going deep in the tree. Explorer users showed their experience by avoiding using the small ⊞ icon and clicked on the labels to expand the hierarchy in the folder view.

5.2 Returning to previously visited nodes

We had predicted that the SpaceTree would be faster than the hyperbolic tree because the layout remains more consistent, allowing users to remember where the nodes they had already clicked on were going to appear, while in the hyperbolic browser, a node could appear anywhere, depending on the location of the focus point. Figure 16 shows 2 examples of different locations for kangaroo. We predicted that Explorer would be faster than both TreeBrowser and Hyperbolic when the start and end point were next to each other because Explorer allows multiple branches to remain open therefore making it very easy to go back and forth between 2 neighboring branches. On the other hand, if the start and end point are separated by many other branches that remained opened (resulting from other tasks), scrolling will be required and finding the beginning and end points will be much more difficult and frustrating, overweighing the advantage of seeing multiple open branches.

Results: One of the two tasks (the longer one involving a return trip between 2 known locations) showed significant differences. SpaceTree was significantly faster than Hyperbolic, and Explorer was significantly faster than the two other interfaces (E=6.5, H=22.7, S=15). Explorer was favorably helped by the ability to keep several branches opened. The other very short returning task did not show any significant differences. Explorer lost its advantage because other open branches now separated the target nodes.

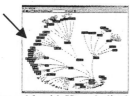 

Figure 16: with Hyperbolic the layout changes between visits. Kangaroo was on the right of screen (a), now on the left (b). With SpaceTree the relative location of nodes is more consistent.

For topology tasks:

5.3 Listing all the ancestors of a node

We had predicted that the SpaceTree would perform better than both Explorer and Hyperbolic as all ancestors are clearly visible and highlighted. Hyperbolic gives more screen real estate to the local lower levels therefore often hiding the ancestors, while Explorer keeps the path visible but the small offset makes it hard to separate siblings from parents.

Results: SpaceTree was significantly faster than Explorer (E=11.4, H=9.3; S=6.8). Two users made errors with Explorer (alignment problems) and one user made an error with Hyperbolic (skipped a level). Two users commented that they liked the clear highlight of SpaceTree along the path, in this path task as well as during other tasks.

5.4 Local topology (example: find 3 nodes that have more than 10 direct descendants):

We predicted that Hyperbolic would be faster that the SpaceTree, which would be itself faster than Explorer. With Hyperbolic users would be able to estimate the number of children by looking at the number of rods radiating from a node, and navigate through the leaf nodes by continuously fanning the tree at a varying depth level.

Results: Hyperbolic was significantly faster than the SpaceTree, but not significantly faster than Explorer (E=61.4, H=46.8, S=98.3). Hyperbolic users interpreted correctly the fans of lines, and Explorer users mostly chance. This task showed that SpaceTree users had not understood the width coding of the triangles (or didn't trust their understanding). Users could be seen intuitively following wider and darker triangles, but would give up after following 2 or 3 level down, even though the answer was often one click away because large fans were usually at leaf level. A wide base triangle only suggests that "somewhere" down the tree there are large fans. Obviously better coding is needed. The experiment was run with the icon size being relative to the parent, making

it more usable for local comparisons, but also more confusing as its meaning appeared to change with the depth in the tree. Icons relative to the root would probably be more easily understood.

5.5 Topology overview task (example: Which of the 3 branches of "measurements" contains a larger number of nodes).

We hypothesized that SpaceTree would lead to fewer errors in the estimation of size because of the icon representation of the branches. We had first measured the time to complete the task, but pilot test users spent so much time with Explorer and Hyperbolic trying to open every branch of the tree – without great success – that we gave a time limit and compared error rates.

Results: Users made 12 errors with Explorer (out of 18), 10 with Hyperbolic and only 2 with SpaceTree. Explorer users mostly made wild guesses or used "properties". Hyperbolic users were able to review the tree quickly but still made many errors, often deciding for a branch that was less than half the size of the correct answer (150 nodes versus 300). SpaceTree users seemed to have made errors when the small differences in the shading of the icons were confounded by size differences.

5.6 User preferences

Our hypotheses were that users would find the Hyperbolic Browser more "cool" than Explorer and SpaceTree, but would prefer to use the SpaceTree.

Results: Users significantly found Explorer less "cool" than the other interfaces, and no significant difference were found between SpaceTree and Hyperbolic (mean ratings on the 9 point scale with 9 being "very cool" were E=3.9. H=7.7, S=6.6.) There were no significant differences between interfaces in term of future use preference (E=5.9, H=5.1; S=6.2 with 9 being "much prefer to use").

5.7 Summary of results

Our hypotheses were only partly supported, but the careful observation of users during the experiment was very helpful to understand differences in user behavior. There were wide differences between subjects in terms of speed, leading to only a limited number of statistically significant results. There were also wide differences in preferences, confirming the general need for providing interface options to users. During training, we observed that users did not guess the 3-attribute-coding of the triangle that always had to be clarified. Users could guess that the icon represented the branch below and was linked to the number of nodes in the branch, but often misinterpreted the width of the triangle to be proportional to the number of direct descendants. This miscomprehension of the meaning of the icons had a particularly strong effect on the task that asked users to find nodes with more than ten descendants. Future research will focus on the design of a simpler preview for novice users, as well as a set of options for expert users who should be able to adapt the icon to their tasks.

6. Conclusions

SpaceTree illustrates that interactive visualization of node link diagrams can still be improved. It was found more attractive than Explorer, and performed relatively well for both navigation and topology tasks, even though no extreme performance differences were found between the interfaces. SpaceTree's consistent layout allowed users to quickly return to nodes they had visited before, making it more appropriate for trees that are used regularly. An example of this would be an organization chart used by a personal staff. SpaceTree preview icons are unique in helping users estimate the topology of the tree, and we will continue improving their design.

7. Acknowledgements

We appreciate the feedback and suggestions to improve SpaceTree from Cheryl Lukehart and Don Schiro from Chevron-Texaco and from Jean-Daniel Fekete and Ben Shneiderman from HCIL. Partial support for this research was provided by Chevron-Texaco and DARPA.

For more information see: www.cs.umd.edu/hcil/spacetree

8. References

[1] Card, S. K., MacKinlay, J. D., Shneiderman, B., (1999) *Readings in Information Visualization: Using Vision to Think*, Morgan Kaufmann Publishers.

[2] Bederson, B., Shneiderman, B., Wattenberg, M. (2002). Ordered and Quantum Treemaps: Making Effective Use of 2D Space to Display Hierarchies, *To appear in ACM Transactions on Computer Graphics.*

[3] Andrews, K., Heidegger, H. (1998) Information Slices: Visualising and exploring large hierarchies using cascading, semicircular disks. *Proc of IEEE Infovis'98 late breaking Hot Topics* IEEE, 9-11. ftp://ftp.iicm.edu/pub/papers/ivis98.pdf

[4] Ellson, J., Gansner, E., Koutsofios, E., Mocenigo, J., North, S., Woodhull, G., Graphviz, open source graph drawing software, http://www.research.att.com/sw/tools/graphviz/

[5] Herman, I., Delest, M., Melançon, G (1998) Tree Visualisation and Navigation Clues for Information Visualisation *Computer Graphics Forum*, **17**(2), 153-165.

[6] Beard, D. V., Walker II, J. Q. (1990). Navigational Techniques to Improve the Display of Large Two-Dimensional Spaces. *Behavior & Information Technology.* **9** (6), 451-466

[7] Kumar, H.P., Plaisant, C., Shneiderman, B. (1997) Browsing hierarchical data with multi-level dynamic queries and pruning *International Journal of Human-Computer Studies,* Volume 46, No. 1, 103-124

[8] Robertson, G. G. Mackinlay, J. D. Card, S. K. Cone Trees: animated 3D visualizations of hierarchical information, *Proc. Human factors in computing systems conference,* March 1991, 189-194

[9] Chignell, M, Poblete F., Zuberec, S. (1993) Exploration in the Design Space of Three-Dimensional Hierarchies *Proceedings of the Human Factors and Ergonomics Society 37th Annual Meeting,* v.1, 333-337

[10] Bertin, J. (1983) *Semiology of Graphics, Diagrams, Networks, Maps*, University of Wisconsin Press, Madison, WI.

[11] Lamping, J., Rao, R., Pirolli; P. (1995) A focus+context technique based on hyperbolic geometry for visualizing large hierarchies *Conference proceedings on Human factors in computing systems*, 1995, 401-408

[12] Beaudoin, L. , Parent, M-A, Vroomen, L. (1996) Cheops: a compact explorer for complex hierarchies, *Symposium on Volume Visualization - Proc. of the conference on Visualization '96*, 87-92 + color p. 471, ACM, New York

[13] . Hightower, R. R., Ring, L., Helfman, J., Bederson, B. B., & Hollan, J. D. (1998). Graphical Multiscale Web Histories: A Study of PadPrints. In *Proceedings of ACM Conference on Hypertext (Hypertext 98)* ACM Press, 58-65.

[14] Noik; E. (1993) Exploring large hyperdocuments: fisheye views of nested networks, *Proceedings of the fifth ACM conference on Hypertext*, 192-205

[15] Hopkins, D. (1989), The Shape of PSIBER Space: PostScript Interactive Bug Eradication Routines.. *Proc. 1989 Usenix Graphics Conference*, Monterey California. www.catalog.com/hopkins/psiber/psiber.html

[16] Card, S., Nation, D., Degree-of-Interest Trees: a component of attention-reactive user interface. Proc. of *Advanced Visual Interface '02*, May 22-24, 2002., ACM

[17] Nation, D.A., Plaisant, C., Marchionini, G., Komlodi, A. (1997) Visualizing websites using a hierarchical table of contents browser: WebTOC, *Proc. of 3rd Conference on Human Factors and the Web*, 1997, Denver, CO, June 12

[18] Shneiderman, B. (1994). Dynamic queries for visual information seeking. *IEEE Software*, **11**, (6), 70-77.

[19] Bederson, B. B., Meyer, J., & Good, L. (2000). Jazz: An Extensible Zoomable User Interface Graphics Toolkit in Java. *UIST 2000, ACM Symposium on User Interface Software and Technology, CHI Letters*, 2(2), 171-180.

[20] Walker II., J. Q. (1990) A node-positioning algorithm for general trees. *Softw. Pract. Exp.*, 20(7): 685-705

[21] Furnas, G. (1981) The FISHEYE view: a new look at structured files, *1981 Bell Lab. Tech. Report*, (also in [1])

[22] Jul, S., & Furnas, G. W. (1998). Critical Zones in Desert Fog: Aids to Multiscale Navigation. *In Proceedings of* User Interface and Software Technology *UIST 98*, 97-106, ACM

[23] Mullet, K., Fry, C., Schiano, D. (1997) On your marks, get set, browse! (the great CHI'97 Browse Off), Panel description in *ACM CHI'97 extended abstracts*, ACM, New York, 113-114

Chapter 7

Innovating the Interaction

> *Soft technology refers to compliant, yielding systems that informate,*
> *that provide a richer set of information and options than would*
> *otherwise be available, and most important of all, that acknowledge the*
> *initiative and flexibility of the person.*
>
> Don Norman, *Things That Make Us Smart* (1993)

At the HCIL, we frequently build on each other's work, and therefore follow certain themes. For example, Ben Bederson applied Ben Shneiderman's treemaps to photo browsing—resulting in PhotoMesa—and then extended the treemap algorithm itself, furthering the treemap work (see Chapter 6). Our focus on concentrated areas probably yields more fruitful results than a more scattered approach would.

Yet, of course, each of these themes starts with some initial work in a new area. Sometimes it is strategic, as with our new focus on bioinformatics (2002-10 [7.6]). Other times, it is based on satisfying a sponsor's request, such as Microsoft's suggestion that we investigate interfaces to support calendar management on PDAs (2002-09 [7.5]). And, occasionally, we just follow a hunch or try to improve an interface that is a pet peeve. But investigating a new area frequently leads to innovation as we tackle a problem with fresh eyes.

This chapter collects the lab's emerging work. As such, these papers don't build on each other in the same way that the papers from the previous chapters do. Nevertheless, the HCIL "signature" can often be found. These papers are domain specific and problem driven. They describe concrete solutions to real problems, include an evaluation to help understand their effectiveness, and attempt to generalize the results so that readers can see how this work may be applied in other domains.

To help make sense of this collection, we have grouped these papers by topic rather than chronologically as in the other chapters. The first five papers are grouped by the data type they support (1D, temporal, and 2D), and the last two papers describe mechanisms to support genomic data and integration of multiple visualizations.

This chapter starts with work that support one-dimensional data. **Fisheye Menus** investigates mechanisms to support selecting items from a long list (2000-12 [7.1]). This work was motivated by an apparent increase in the use of menus for data selection, as when one selects a product or location from a pop-up menu on an e-commerce Web page. This was an example where empirical evaluation has been quite important. Many people's first reaction to the fisheye menus was very positive (often generating audible "oohs" at demos), but when we tested it, we found they were not faster than hierarchical menus, and though they were preferred by some users, many did not like them at all. Some ideas end up being not as useful as they first appear. On the other

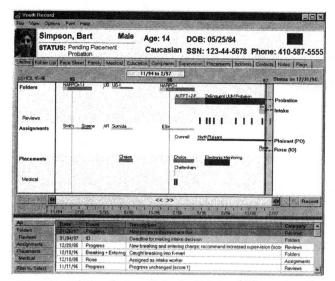

Figure 7.1 LifeLines for Juvenile Justice histories of delinquent youths.

hand, a more recent study showed that they are more effective than the standard Start menu on Pocket PC. Some ideas turn out to have merit in unexpected places if you look hard enough.

The next two papers deal with different kinds of time-varying data. LifeLines supports generic temporal data, where events occur at a specific time with a specific duration (98-08 [7.2]). This kind of data is common for personal histories and medical records, and LifeLines was designed to support those domains (Figure 7.1). This started with a collaboration with the Maryland Department of Juvenile Justice and continued with the work described in the paper on medical records.

This visualization had very positive results, and we remain optimistic about our approach. It was also prototyped for IBM to support customer histories so that customer service representatives could provide better assistance (Figure 7.2). We are looking forward to a collaboration with the right group to deploy it in a broader setting.

The other time-varying data paper supports time-series data. This is data that changes over time, and it is typically measured at intervals. TimeSearcher supports this kind of data, focusing on data from the stock market as well as gene expression data (2002-06 [7.3]). TimeSearcher is interesting because like many HCIL projects, it is based on an observation that in hindsight is quite simple, yet no one else had apparently

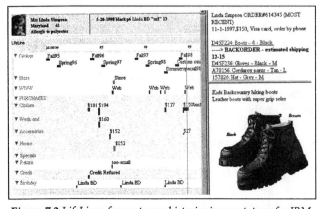

Figure 7.2 LifeLines for customer histories in a prototype for IBM.

done it before. It took us many months of looking at the problem to come up with the solution. Dynamically making sense of and finding specific items within a broad set of time-series data remained a problem until student Harry Hochheiser and Ben Shneiderman applied the dynamic queries of Chapter 1. By displaying all the time-series data on a single overlapping display and letting users create time-boxes that specify two dimensions (time duration and a range of values), a simple dynamic query could be performed on the data. Only the time-series with elements that fall inside the time-box are shown, and letting users dynamically manipulate those time-boxes afforded a simple and direct manipulation approach to browsing the data. This has proved to be an important technique, and it is the core of Harry's dissertation.

Moving into the domain of two-dimensional data, we have two papers. The first, **Excentric Labeling**, describes a technique for dynamically placing and drawing labels on dense information displays (98-09 [7.4]). It is a kind of dynamic query in that as the user moves the mouse pointer, information about the data elements the pointer is near are shown near to the pointer. Excentric Labeling is a good example of a straightforward technique that in itself is a modest contribution, but one likely to be incorporated as a basic technique in many visualizations in the future.

The other 2D paper is one that describes an interface for interacting with calendars on small displays (2002-09 [7.5]). This project (which has since been renamed DateLens) is interesting because of the long path from initial conception to the current prototype. Back in 1991, George Furnas, who was then at Bellcore, described a text-based two-dimensional fisheye distortion technique applied to calendars. It was a clever and novel idea, but didn't solve a pressing problem (existing calendar programs for the desktop were adequate) and was never pursued vigorously. Then, ten years later, John SanGiovanni at Microsoft Research suggested to Ben Bederson that he investigate calendar interfaces for PDAs because Microsoft was advancing their small Pocket PC devices, for which calendars were a notorious problem. Although these calendars were good at supporting simple tasks, such as finding what one was doing on a particular day, some users reported problems with planning and analysis tasks. Being aware of Furnas's earlier work, Bederson reapplied that approach to the calendar interface, adding a few new techniques, and showed that this approach is quite promising; it is now continuing to be pursued. This collection of projects shows how important an open research literature is. There are myriad examples both within the HCIL and among other institutions of projects cross-fertilizing each other—sometimes over great expanses of time.

Another new effort at the HCIL is to understand biological-based data. The Hierarchical Cluster Explorer (HCE) is an extension of an existing visualization approach to understanding gene arrays, a common analysis technique in the field of genetics (2002-10 [7.6]). As with TimeSearcher and other projects, the innovation here is the application of dynamic queries as well as tightly coupling multiple views to let users rapidly manipulate the data set in order to see patterns and outliers, and to quickly drill down to get to specific items. This approach, which we see repeatedly, is at the core of our visualizations. Even though it is impossible to state a specific formula for creating successful visualizations, we have found this basic approach works surprisingly well.

While developing the visualization techniques described in this book, we observed a recurring problem: that real solutions often require a combination of techniques. Our focus on any specific project was usually to concentrate on a specific new visualization, but we often wanted to link different visualizations. Because the visualizations were built separately, they were often hard to link since they used different file formats, data types, and technologies. This problem motivated student Chris North to create an architecture for linking several completely separate visualizations together. This approach, called Snap-Together Visualization, proved to be an important basic strategy and resulted in Chris's successful dissertation (2000-15). Chris has continued pursuing this at his new job as a professor at Virginia Tech, where he has developed a new round of Snap-Together interfaces.

So, at one level, this chapter presents a potpourri of work from different domains. And on another level, it shows how the same basic strategies looking at different problems can generate a range of related solutions. Finally, it is clear that having a critical mass of people working on related topics helps all the individual projects since we learn from and are inspired by one another.

FAVORITE PAPERS FROM OUR COLLEAGUES

Furnas, G. W., Generalized Fisheye Views, *Proc. Human Factors in Computing Systems (CHI 86)* ACM, New York (1986), 16–23.

Rao, R., Card, S. K., The Table Lens: Merging Graphical and Symbolic Representations in an Interactive Focus+Context Visualization for Tabular Information, *Proc. Human Factors in Computing Systems (CHI 94)* ACM, New York (1994), 318–322.

Fisheye Menus

Benjamin B. Bederson
Human-Computer Interaction Lab
Institute for Advanced Computer Studies
Computer Science Department
University of Maryland, College Park, MD 20742
+1 301 405-2764
bederson@cs.umd.edu

ABSTRACT

We introduce "fisheye menus" which apply traditional fisheye graphical visualization techniques to linear menus. This provides for an efficient mechanism to select items from long menus, which are becoming more common as menus are used to select data items in, for example, e-commerce applications. Fisheye menus dynamically change the size of menu items to provide a focus area around the mouse pointer. This makes it possible to present the entire menu on a single screen without requiring buttons, scrollbars, or hierarchies.

A pilot study with 10 users compared user preference of fisheye menus with traditional pull-down menus that use scrolling arrows, scrollbars, and hierarchies. Users preferred the fisheye menus for browsing tasks, and hierarchical menus for goal-directed tasks.

Keywords

Fisheye view, menu selection, widgets, information visualization.

INTRODUCTION

The concept of a "fisheye" distortion in a computer interface to present detailed information in context has been around a long time. Furnas first introduced the concept by discussing the cognitive aspects of how people remembered information [7]. Several researchers then applied fisheye distortion to a broad variety of applications [4, 15, 24, 25]. Several variations of the fisheye technique have been explored. They have been used in one dimension for word processing [9], access to time [12], and for long lists [13, 14]. They have been used in two dimensions for tables [17], graphical maps [20] and space-scale diagrams [8]. They have even been used in three dimensions for document browsing [19]. Some applications of fisheye distortion techniques have been carefully evaluated, often finding a significant advantage to fisheye views [5, 11, 21].

However, despite the careful investigation of fisheye view distortion techniques, and their application to a broad set of complex tasks, fisheye views have never been applied to

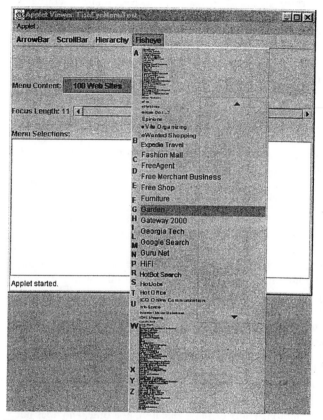

Figure 1: A screen shot of the fisheye menu in use. This shows 100 web sites taken from the most popular list of PC Magazine.

the mundane challenge of ordinary menus. This paper applies standard fisheye techniques to menus in Graphical User Interfaces with the goal of improving performance in user's ability to select one item from a long list.

Selecting items from menus is another well-studied area, and the trade-offs of menu design are well understood [10, 16]. Menu design has become quite standard with well-grouped menu items in consistent locations using common names. This is appropriate for carefully designed applications where every element of the menus can be chosen in advance.

However, with the introduction of the Web and e-commerce applications, it is becoming increasingly common to use menus for selecting data items, as opposed to selecting operations. For example, menus are used to select from a long list of fonts, to select one state out of 50, to select one country out of 250, or to select a web site from a list of favorites.

It was this last example that motivated the application of fisheye views to menus. Managing ones favorite locations on the web is an important application of web browsers, but one study showed that most web browser users don't put more than about 35 items in their favorite lists before resorting to using hierarchies [1]. While hierarchies certainly help to organize information, this study found that while some people used hierarchies, many stopped adding new favorites altogether. The user interface for managing favorites may contribute to this. Since web browsers use pull-down menus to store favorites, and since these menus don't work very well as the number of elements within the menu grows, it is not surprising that people don't put more than that many items in the menus before using hierarchies. Some researchers have looked at alternative interfaces for managing web favorites [18], but they have not yet made it into commercial products. Also, those approaches are fine-tuned to web favorite organization, and may not apply very well to other menu selection tasks.

Selecting data items from menus is different than selecting functions because the data items in the menu are likely to change from use to use, and there are typically many more data elements in a menu than there are in functional menus. In addition, since the user is not as familiar with the menu, it is more likely that they won't know the exact text of each item. Thus, supporting browsing as well as searching is important. The length of the menu is crucial in determining usability. It takes users a time proportional to the location of an item in a menu to access it [6, 22]. However, the real problem comes with menus that have more items than fit on the screen. AlphaSliders are one approach for selecting textual items from a long list in a small space [2]. However that approach only displays one item at a time, and does not fit into the pull-down menu metaphor.

The existing approaches to selecting from one of many displayed items in a long list are limited. There are three commonly used approaches which are to use scrolling arrows at the top and bottom of the list, to use hierarchical "cascading" menus to make the list smaller, or to use scrollbars. Let us look at each of these approaches in more detail.

Standard GUI toolkits today provide support for long pull-down menus by adding small scrolling arrows to the top and bottom of the list if the entire list doesn't fit on the display. When the user clicks on those arrows, the list is scrolled up or down. Each toolkit implements these arrows differently, some having fast scrolling if you hold the arrow down (Microsoft MFC), and some slow (Swing). Some automatically scroll when the mouse is just placed over the arrows without clicking (Internet Explorer). However, in any case, the user is required to first move the mouse to the arrow, and then scroll until the desired element becomes

visible. An additional, but uncommon problem is that if the menu is scrolled too far, the mouse must be moved to the arrow on the opposite side of the menu, and the user must then scroll in the other direction.

A common alternative to long lists is to use hierarchical "cascading" menus. This works by having the application developer, or sometimes the user, organize the menu elements into groups. Then, one entry that represents each group is placed in the menu. When the user selects that group element, the members of the group are displayed in a second menu off to the side. This approach solves the problem of physically navigating a long list, but replaces it with a new problem of requiring the user to know what group the desired element is in. If the user knows the hierarchy structure well, then this approach works. However, if the user does not know the hierarchy structure well, then the user must look in each group, which is potentially time consuming. Typical applications with stable menu structures regularly use hierarchical cascading menus because presumably the user will rapidly learn where each element belongs. However, it is uncommon in practice to find hierarchical menus that are used for organizing data driven menus.

Finally, the last common solution for managing long menus is to use a scrollbar that controls the portion of the menu that is visible. This seems like an excellent approach because it gives fixed time access to menus of any length unlike the more common scrolling arrows, which takes time proportional to the menu length. However, while scrollbars are commonly used in dialog boxes, they are rarely if ever used in pull-down menus. Perhaps this is because current toolkits do not provide this as a default behavior, although it is possible to implement it with some toolkits.

In addition to these visualization methods, nearly all toolkits support keyboard shortcuts for selecting menu items. There are often modeless shortcuts (such as Ctrl-C for "Copy") that select a menu element throughout the application, even when the menu is closed. In addition to those shortcuts, the keyboard can be used to select items in the menu when it is open. Developers can either specify which key should apply to each item by specifying a "mnemonic", or if it is left unspecified, the first character of the item is used. Thus, in an alphabetically sorted list, pressing any key will jump the cursor to the first item starting with that letter. Pressing it again will move to the next item starting with that letter, and so on.

These keyboard accelerators are very powerful as they bypass some of the shortcomings of the mouse-based interaction techniques just described. They give users direct access to either the target element, or at least to the general area if there is more than one element sharing the mnemonic. However, despite their power, many users do not use them at all. Some users are not aware of them, but others are aware of them and choose not to use them anyway. Perhaps this is because their hand is already on the mouse and takes too long to reacquire the keyboard, or perhaps they don't know the keyboard well enough to justify searching for the right key. Or they may not know the exact text and actually are browsing the menu. And finally, some users may just not like using the keyboard when interacting with menus. People that only use the mouse for selecting menu items are likely to be the largest beneficiaries of fisheye menus.

FISHEYE MENU DESIGN ISSUES

We offer a new solution to the problem of menus that have more items than fit on the screen by using a fisheye view to display the menu elements. In fisheye menus, all of the elements are always displayed in a single window that is completely visible, but the items near the cursor are displayed at full size, and items further away from the cursor are displayed at a smaller size. In addition, the interline spacing between items is also increased in the focus area, and decreased further away from the focus area. In this manner, the entire list of items fits on a single screen. The items are dynamically scaled so that as the cursor moves, a "bubble" of readable items moves with the cursor (Figure 1). A fisheye menu applet can be found at http://www.cs.umd.edu/hcil/fisheyemenu.

The fisheye menu uses all the available screen space, and will calculate a distortion function so that the menu items always just fill the menu. There are two principal parameters of the fisheye menu that the application developer can control: maximum font size, and focus length. As with traditional menus, the designer can specify the font size, which for the fisheye menu translates in to the maximum font size, since some elements are rendered smaller. However, the designer can also specify the desired focus length. This specifies the number of items that are rendered at maximum size near the cursor.

The focus length parameter is important because it controls the trade-off between the number of menu items at full size versus the size that is used to render the smallest items. The fisheye menu dynamically computes the distortion function based on the available space and these input parameters. So, if the focus length is set to a large number (i.e., 20), then this will push the peripheral items to be very small, and as the user moves the cursor, there will be a lot of distortion. If, however, the focus length is set to a small number (i.e., 5), then there will be more room for peripheral items and they will all be a bit larger. Figure 2 shows this trade-off.

Alphabetic Index

A fundamental characteristic of the fisheye menu is that many of the menu items are too small to read at any given position. However, since it is common to organize menu items alphabetically for data menus, we can encourage this organization for fisheye menus without undue burden. Then, users can use their alphabetic knowledge to move the cursor to the area they expect the item to be at, thus bringing that portion of the menu into focus at which point they can read the menu items and select the particular item

Figure 2: The same menu of 100 items displayed with varying focus lengths (7, 12, and 20). There is a fixed maximum font size.

they want. This is similar to how people use telephone directory books. Despite the fact that items are listed sequentially in the phone book, people use their alphabetic knowledge to jump to the portion of the phone book where they expect the item they are looking for to be. They then see where they actually are, and fine-tune their search.

This telephone book analogy guides the design. One of the reasons people can find items in telephone books so quickly is that telephone books have index information at the top of every page specifying in a large clear font what information is on that page. These indices allow users to just look at the indices while looking for the right page, and then look at the content when they have found the page they are looking for. It has been shown that indexes can decrease search time with lists [3].

We designed the fisheye menus to have an alphabetic index with the goal of making it easier for users to target the portion of the menu that contains the item they are looking for. The alphabetic index appears on the left side of the menu. Each letter of the alphabet for which there is room is displayed in the specified maximum font size.

The index letters are positioned so that when the pointer is moved to the same vertical position as an index letter, the first item starting with that letter will be just under the mouse pointer. This provides the user with the ability to rapidly move to the general area of the list they are targeting.

This is our second design of the index letters. The first design always positioned the letters at the current position of the first item starting with that letter. Thus, as the fisheye focus changed, the index letters would move around, following the items. This turned out to be

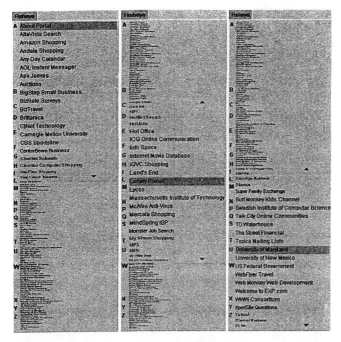

Figure 3: The same menu displayed with the cursor at three positions.

distracting and not useful. By the time a user moved the pointer to the position an index letter was at, that index letter would have moved (since the focus and thus item positioning would have changed.) We quickly realized the value of the index letters was to inform pointer motion, and shifted to the current stable design described above. Figure 3 shows the fisheye menu at different focus points.

High-Resolution Selection (Focus Lock Mode)

One difficulty with the fisheye menu mechanism as described so far is that small mouse movements result in a change of fisheye focus. With traditional menus, the mouse must move over the full height of a menu item to change the focus to the next item. However, with fisheye menus, the amount the mouse must move to go to the next item is equal to the *smallest* font size in the menu. This is a fundamental result of the fisheye algorithm since all of the menu items must be selectable by pointer movement in the fixed vertical space of the menu.

This is a significant liability because despite the fact that the focused elements are large and plainly readable, they are difficult to select.

We overcame this problem by offering a "focus lock" mode to the fisheye menu. Users operate the menu as described above until they get near the item of interest. They then move the pointer to the right side of the menu, which locks the focus on the item the cursor is over. Then, when users move the pointer up and down, the focus stays fixed, but individual menu elements can still be selected. The focus region on the right side of the menu gets highlighted to indicate that the menu is in focus lock mode.

Further, if the pointer is moved above or below the focus region (staying on the right side of the menu), the focus area is expanded. Eventually all of the menu items become

full-size and thus easy to select. But, of course, not all of the items are visible anymore as the ends get pushed off the screen as the focus area is expanded. Since the menu layout is quite different in focus lock mode, the index characters become inaccurate, and so they are faded out as the focus area is expanded in focus lock mode.

If users decide to continue looking in a different portion of the menu, moving the pointer back to the left side of the menu turns off focus lock mode, and the menu returns to regular behavior. This focus lock approach to high-resolution selection within a fisheye view solves the resolution problem at the cost of a small mouse movement.

We considered several alternative approaches to entering the focus lock mode. We first tried using the right button, but gave that up as it seemed too unlikely that users would discover it on their own – especially since it did not follow the standard Windows model of pressing the right button for a context-sensitive menu. And, of course, it would not work at all for systems without a second mouse button. We also considered using the speed of the mouse to determine the focus mode, but that seemed to be too unpredictable by users. Also, an earlier study of the AlphaSlider confirmed this intuition [2].

We ended up with the current design, which offers an affordance for the focus lock feature. There is a subtly shaded box on the right side of the menu that moves up and down with the focus. This was intended to draw user's attention to the right side of the menu. In addition, the two small arrows on the right side are intended to suggest to users that they can move the pointer up and down in focus lock mode. When the pointer is moved towards the arrows,

Figure 4: A fisheye menu in focus lock mode whose focus area is being extended upwards

the focus area is extended, and the arrows move accordingly. The users can thus discover that the focus can

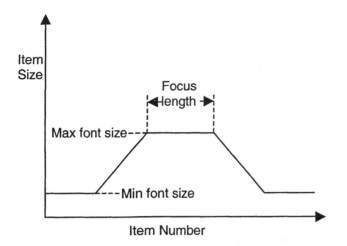

Figure 5: The basic Degree of Interest function used for the fisheye menu.

be extended. Figure 4 shows the focus lock mode with the focus area being extended upwards.

IMPLEMENTATION

The fisheye menu is a drop-in replacement for Java's standard "JMenu" component in the Swing GUI toolkit. This new widget, called FishEyeMenu, is written in Java 1, and works for applications and applets. This means that any Java code that currently uses traditional Swing menus can switch to using the fisheye menus with a one-word change by replacing "new JMenu()" with "new FishEyeMenu()"[1].

The standard approach to implementing fisheye distortion techniques is to compute a "Degree of Interest" (DOI) function for each element to be displayed. The DOI function calculates whether to display an item or not, and it calculates the item's size. Typical degree of interest functions include both the distance of an item from the focus point as well as the item's a priori importance [7]. Thus, certain landmark items may be shown at a large size even though they are far from the focus point.

The fisheye menu uses a very simple DOI function that only includes distance from the focus point, and does not use a priori importance. A simple function that captures the essence of the fisheye menu is shown in Figure 5. It keeps several menu items near the focus point at the maximum size, where the exact number is specifiable. Then, the menu items get smaller, one point in font size at a time until the minimum font size is reached at which time, all more distant items stay at the minimum font size.

Using this DOI function, the fisheye menu calculates the largest minimum size font that will result in a menu that fits on the screen. If there are so many items in the menu, or if there is so little available screen space that there is not enough room for the menu, then the DOI function parameters are adjusted so there is enough room. First, the focus length is reduced. If there is still not enough room

when the focus length is set to 1, then the maximum font size is reduced.

Complexities

In practice, the DOI function is actually a little more complex than just described for two reasons. The first reason is that we want the menu items to be visually stable outside of the focus area. That is, if the focus is on the first half of the menu, it is important that the second half of the menu doesn't move at all as the focus changes. The fisheye menu is stable using the above DOI function when the focus is not near one of the ends of the menu. However, when it is near the ends of the menu, there is a surprising side effect of the algorithm, which results in the entire menu shifting.

Since we render each item based on the position of the item before it, one item alone changing size will slide all other lower menu items up or down. Moving the focus in the middle of the menu doesn't cause a problem because for every item that gets bigger, another items gets smaller by the same amount. To understand the issue here, let us look at the simplest case where the focus is on the first item in the menu. In this case, there are no items before the focus item to get rendered, and the items after the focus item get smaller until the minimum size is reached. Compare this with the focus being on the second item in the menu. Now, one item before the focus is rendered at a large size while the items after the focus get smaller in the same way. Thus, more space is taken altogether, and the entire menu shifts down a little bit. The entire menu continues to grow as the focus moves down from the end until the distortion no longer goes to the end of the menu and the menu becomes stable.

Our solution is to increase the size of the focus area just enough to account for the smaller number of focus items when the focus point is near the menu end. This way, the total amount of space used by the focus area is always constant, and the entire menu remains visually stable.

The fisheye menu uses this modified DOI function to calculate the required size of the popup menu. This leads to the second reason that our DOI function is more complex in practice. We use integer calculations since text is only rendered in integer sizes, and so the popup menu size can end up being substantially smaller than the available space. We want to use as large a menu size as possible since the bigger the menu is, the more items we can render in a large enough font to read, and the more usable the fisheye menu will be.

Once the minimum size font is calculated, a menu that uses all the available screen space is created. Then the DOI function is modified using the same technique that we used to solve the first problem - the focus area is expanded until the text fills up the full menu space.

One remaining issue has to do with the alphabetic index. Since the index characters are always rendered at full size, they would overlap each other when they are far from the

---

[1] Note that the online applet uses Java 2 to decrease the portability problems associated with accessing Swing from Java 1.

focus area, since the associated menu items at that point are quite small. The fisheye menu avoids this overlapping problem by simply not rendering indices that would overlap with another. Thus, in the periphery, not every index character is shown.

The fisheye menu is implemented by pre-calculating the size of every item and the space between each item for each focus position, and storing that information in look-up-tables. This pre-calculation is necessary in order to calculate the position of the index letters. This also improves performance since there is very little calculation during rendering. One final, but important optimization is the use of region management. Since the fisheye menu is visually stable, only the changing focus portion of the menu changes as the pointer moves. Our implementation keeps track of the area on the screen that changes, and only renders that portion. Thus, for a menu of 200 items, typically less than 30 items need to be rendered for each mouse movement.

EVALUATION

We conducted a pilot study of fisheye menus comparing user preference of them against the three menu mechanisms commonly used today: arrow buttons to scroll up and down, scrollbars, and hierarchies. The intent of this study was to get a preliminary idea of whether fisheye menus had potential. We did not expect that the results of this study would provide a definitive understanding of whether fisheye menus were faster, more appropriate, or preferable for tasks. Rather, we hoped to get a rough idea of user's preferences that would let us know if our intuitions were realistic, and to inform future evaluations.

We picked 10 users that were not from our lab, and were not familiar with fisheye menus before the study. Five of the subjects were computer science students with programming experience, and five of the subjects were administrative staff that work in our building, and did not have programming experience. We felt that looking at programmers vs. non-programmers was important because fisheye menus are somewhat technical, and we sensed that people with less technical experience may not feel immediately comfortable with them. As it turned out, there was a difference between these two classes of users that will be reported in the *Results* section.

Seven of the subjects were female and three were male. Five were in there 20's, two were in their 30's, two were in their 40's, and one was over 50. All but one reported using computers more than 20 hours per week.

The test was entirely automated using a custom Java program. The program requested demographic information, and explained that the purpose of the test was to get feedback on the four types of menus for selecting an item from a list. The subjects were then instructed to try out each of the menu types, spending as much time as they liked. At that point, they were instructed to ask any questions about how the menus worked (the test was administered by the author of this paper.)

The four menu types were labeled ArrowBar, ScrollBar, Hierarchy, and Fisheye. All menu items were ordered alphabetically. The ArrowBar was implemented with arrows at the top and bottom of the screen. When the arrows were pressed, the list would scroll at a rate of 20 items per second. The ScrollBar was implemented with a standard scrollbar on the right side of the menu that could be used to scroll the menu. The Hierarchy was constructed with one menu item for each letter of the alphabet. Menu items were placed in cascading menus under the first letter of the text of that item. Finally, the Fisheye menu was that described in this paper. Each of these menus are available for trial at the fisheye menu website.

Then, the subject was instructed to select three different specific items from each menu. Each menu was populated with 100 websites that were selected from the list of most popular websites from PC magazine (with four well known universities that replaced four entries that did not have a short descriptive title.) The items that the subjects were told to select were chosen from near the beginning, middle, and end of each list. The subjects were also asked to browse the lists for a website they would like to visit. The selected item was displayed for the user to see, however, information was not logged as to whether to the subjects correctly selected the specified item.

The subjects were asked to rate the menus. They were asked to rate each menu using a 9-point Likert scale according to seven characteristics taken from QUIS – the Questionnaire for User Interface Satisfaction [23]. The seven characteristics were:

- terrible – wonderful
- frustrating – satisfying
- difficult – easy
- slow – fast
- hard to learn – easy to learn
- boring – fun
- annoying – pleasant

Finally, the subjects were asked to rank the four menu types in order of preference for goal-directed tasks and browsing tasks. They were also offered the option of typing in any comments they had about the four menu types.

Results

The average subjective satisfaction of the four menu types was recorded for all users, and separated by programmer vs. non-programmer. For all users, on a scale from 1 – 9 (with 9 being most positive), Hierarchy was the favorite (6.8), Fisheye (6.4) was rated slightly higher than Scrollbar (6.2), and ArrowBar (4.9) was the lowest.

When split by programmer, an interesting difference appears. The ratings of ArrowBar and ScrollBar did not change very much, but Fisheye and Hierarchy did. For programmers, Fisheye (7.0) and Hierarchy (6.9) were about the same. For non-programmers, the spread between Fisheye (5.8) and Hierarchy (6.8) substantially increased.

When looking at the individual questions, we see that the subjects had widely differing opinions about Hierarchy vs. Fisheye in different categories. Hierarchy was preferred over Fisheye in the three categories of 'frustrating – satisfying', 'hard – easy', and 'hard-to-learn – easy-to-learn'. However, Fisheye was preferred over Hierarchy in the four categories of 'terrible – wonderful', 'slow – fast', 'boring – fun', and 'annoying – pleasant'.

When asked to directly rank the four menu types in order of preference, there was a difference for goal-directed and browsing tasks (Figure 6). For goal-directed tasks, ArrowBar and ScrollBar were clear losers with Hierarchy just beating out Fisheye. For browsing tasks, ArrowBar was at the bottom, ScrollBar and Hierarchy were about tied in the middle, and Fisheye was the most preferred. However, the large standard deviation of Fisheye shows that there was a broader range of reaction. Some users ranked it about the same as ScrollBar and Hierarchy, and some users ranked it much higher.

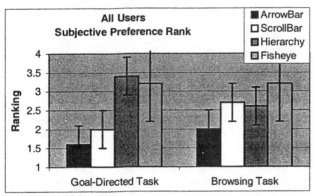

Figure 6: Rankings of four menu types by direct comparison for goal-directed and browsing tasks. Error bars mark 1 standard deviation.

When separated out by programmer vs. non-programmer, there was a similar effect as with the satisfaction ratings. Programmers preferred Fisheye to Hierarchy in all cases, with a small margin (0.2) for goal-directed tasks, and a big margin (1.0) for browsing tasks. Non-programmers preferred Hierarchy to Fisheye for goal-directed tasks by a margin of 0.6 and they were tied for browsing tasks.

The subjects' comments were informative and mirrored the rating and ranking results. Two non-programmers specifically said that they did not like fisheye at all. The other eight subjects all liked fisheye, but frequently had concerns about the difficulty of learning to use it. However, they also expressed optimism that with more training, it would become more enjoyable and perhaps preferable. A few typical comments were:

"Fisheye was the most difficult to learn yet with continued use may actually become the most useful."

"ArrowBar and ScrollBar are boring but very easy to use. I am used to it. Hierarchy and Fisheye are very interesting."

"Once one understands that one has to go to the colored area in Fisheye it becomes easier. But if one doesn't know that it's frustrating."

Analysis
While the study contained a small number of subjects and the results were not analyzed statistically, we noted some trends. These should be interpreted with caution, but do seem to make sense. The test was administered without a description of what fisheye menus were or how they worked. Instead, the subjects were told to play with them for as long as they wanted and only then could they ask questions.

By observing this initial exposure to fisheye menus, and by responding to the subjects' questions, it was clear that at least in the minute or two that they tried them, most subjects did not understand how to use the fisheye menu fully. All of the subjects quickly discovered that moving the mouse up and down on the left side of the menu operated the basic fisheye functionality. However, several were confused about the exact function of the alphabetic index on the left side. Several users tried clicking on them – which just selected the item that was currently highlighted. After one or two tries with this, they then realized that the index was just informative, and not interactive.

A more important problem was that only a single subject truly discovered how the "focus lock" mode on the right side of the menu worked. Despite the visual feedback, subjects were just not expecting to have different behavior when the mouse pointer was on different sides of the menu. Some subjects never moved the pointer to the right side and so never discovered that behavior at all. Other subjects moved the pointer to the right side of the menu accidentally or erratically. They just noticed that the menu would sometimes change behavior in an inconsistent manner. They did not correlate the change in menu behavior with the side of the menu that the pointer was over.

Once the subjects were done exploring the menus and asked questions, the focus-lock mode was explained. Interestingly enough, all 10 subjects completely understood how it worked in just a few seconds of explanation. Thus, the visual design of the menu clearly needs some work to make the focus-lock mode more discoverable.

Another major lesson learned from these studies is that subjects' response varied widely. Looking at the average results only tells part of the story. Two of the subjects did not like the fisheye menus at all. It had nothing to do with the difficulty they had to discover how they worked. Rather they just didn't like them. One of those users reported that the small menu items made her feel badly because she felt that her eyesight was poor.

On the other hand, several of the users were eager to start using fisheye menus in their regular work immediately. This bimodal preference suggests that fisheye menus, if deployed in an application, should be optional. Some users are likely to prefer them, and some are likely not to.

The last lesson we learned from this study is that application designers should consider the use of scrollbar and hierarchical menus instead of the traditional arrow menus used by default by current operating systems. Or better yet, let users set an option to specify how long menus will be presented.

The ArrowBar menu was the clear loser in all cases. Subjects felt it was boring, slow, and frustrating. Yet, this is the most common type of long menu in commercial systems. The ScrollBar menu, on the other hand, provided a nice compromise for goal-directed and browsing tasks, and was generally enjoyed by users. While the Hierarchy menu was often preferred for goal-directed tasks, the same menu will be used in different ways by different users. Some users will know exactly what they want while some will browse. So, the Hierarchy menu should be used cautiously if at all, and only when it is clear that users know exactly what they are looking for.

Expert Timing
We also performed a very simple test to see how fast an expert could use each of the menu types. The author of this paper selected an item from the middle of the menu from each of the menus 10 times working as quickly as possible. The fastest time was recorded. This was done for the 100 web sites, and also for a list of 266 countries.

For the 100 websites, the times were: ArrowBar (3.4 secs); ScrollBar (2.2 secs); Hierarchy (1.5 secs); Fisheye (1.7 secs). For the 266 countries, the times were: ArrowBar (8.8 secs); ScrollBar (2.6 secs); Hierarchy (2.1 secs); Fisheye (2.3 secs).

These timing results match closely with the subjective preferences for goal-directed tasks, and so suggest that these data may reflect a broader trend than would be indicated by so few subjects.

CONCLUSION
Selecting an item from a list is an important and frequent task. We have presented here fisheye menus, a new mechanism that supports this kind of selection. Based on our preliminary evaluation, we believe that this approach is promising. It clearly is not for all users, but just as clearly, many users prefer it, so at this point we recommend considering fisheye menus for optional use where selection from a long list is required.

We plan on continuing the investigation of fisheye menus by conducting a controlled empirical evaluation, including analysis of the speed users can select items with the different menu types. We also will consider other menu types such as matrix or multi-column layouts, and will look at other factors such as the number of items in the menu.

Finally, we have begun to look at putting content aside from text in fisheye menus, and using them for tasks other than menu selection. Putting in a horizontal bar indicating

a numerical value (similar to the strategy of Table Lens [17]) in the linear fisheye menu appears to be an interesting way to monitor time-varying data.

ACKNOWLEDGEMENTS
I appreciate the thoughtful comments of the members of the Human-Computer Interaction Lab who helped me fine-tune the details of the fisheye menus. In particular, I thank Harry Hochheiser who suggested the alphabetic index, and the subjects who volunteered their time to give me valuable feedback.

REFERENCES
1. Abrams, D., Baecker, R., & Chignell, M. (1998). Information Archiving With Bookmarks: Personal Web Space Construction and Organization. *In Proceedings of Human Factors in Computing Systems (CHI 98)* ACM Press, pp. 41-48.

2. Ahlberg, C., & Shneiderman, B. (1994). The AlphaSlider: A Compact and Rapid Selector. *In Proceedings of Human Factors in Computing Systems (CHI 94)* ACM Press, pp. 365-371.

3. Beck, D., & Elkerton, J. (1989). Development and Evaluation of Direct Manipulation Lists. *SIGCHI Bulletin, 20*(3), pp. 72-78.

4. Dill, J., Bartram, L., Ho, A., & Henigman, F. (1994). A Continuously Variable Zoom for Navigating Large Hierarchical Networks. *In Proceedings of IEEE International Conference on Systems, Man and Cybernetics* IEEE, pp. 386-390.

5. Donskoy, M., & Kaptelinin, V. (1997). Window Navigation With and Without Animation: A Comparison of Scroll Bars, Zoom, and Fisheye View. *In Proceedings of Extended Abstracts of Human Factors in Computing Systems (CHI 97)* ACM Press, pp. 279-280.

6. Fitts, P. M. (1954). The Information Capacity of the Human Motor System in Controlling the Amplitude of Movement. *Journal of Experimental Psychology, 47,* pp. 381-391.

7. Furnas, G. W. (1986). Generalized Fisheye Views. *In Proceedings of Human Factors in Computing Systems (CHI 86)* ACM Press, pp. 16-23.

8. Furnas, G. W., & Bederson, B. B. (1995). Space-Scale Diagrams: Understanding Multiscale Interfaces. *In Proceedings of Human Factors in Computing Systems (CHI 95)* ACM Press, pp. 234-241.

9. Greenberg, S., Gutwin, C., & Cockburn, A. (1995). Sharing Fisheye Views in Relaxed-WYSIWIG Groupware Applications. *In Proceedings of Graphics Interface (GI 95)* Morgan Kaufman, pp. 28-38.

10. Hochheiser, H., & Shneiderman, B. (2000). Performance Benefits of Simultaneous Over Sequential Menus As Task Complexity Increases. *International Journal of Human-Computer Interaction,*

pp. (in press).

11. Hollands, J. G., Carey, T. T., Matthews, M. L., & McCann, C. A. (1989). Presenting a Graphical Network: A Comparison of Performance Using Fisheye and Scrolling Views. *(Third International Conference on Human-Computer Interaction)* Elsevier Science Publishers, pp. 313-320.

12. Koike, Y., Sugiura, A., & Koseki, Y. (1997). TimeSlider: An Interface to Time Point. *In Proceedings of User Interface and Software Technology (UIST 97)* ACM Press, pp. 43-44.

13. Masui, T. (1998). LensBar - Visualization for Browsing and Filtering Large Lists of Data. *In Proceedings of Information Visualization Symposium (InfoVis 98)* New York: IEEE, pp. 113-120.

14. Masui, T., Minakuchi, M., Borden, G. R., & Kashiwagi, K. (1995). Multiple-View Approach for Smooth Information Retrieval. *In Proceedings of User Interface and Software Technology (UIST 95)* ACM Press, pp. 199-206.

15. Mitta, D., & Gunning, D. (1993). Simplifying Graphics-Based Data: Applying the Fisheye Lens Viewing Strategy. *Behaviour & Information Technology, 12*(1), pp. 1-16.

16. Norman, K. (1991). *The Psychology of Menu Selection: Designing Cognitive Control at the Human/Computer Interface.* Ablex Publishing Corp.

17. Rao, R., & Card, S. K. (1994). The Table Lens: Merging Graphical and Symbolic Representations in an Interactive Focus+Context Visualization for Tabular Information. *In Proceedings of Human Factors in Computing Systems (CHI 94)* ACM Press, pp. 318-322.

18. Robertson, G., Czerwinski, M., Larson, K., Robbins, D. C., Thiel, D., & van Dantzich, M. (1998). Data Mountain: Using Spatial Memory for Document Management. *In Proceedings of User Interface and Software Technology (UIST 98)* ACM Press, pp. 153-162.

19. Robertson, G. G., & Mackinlay, J. D. (1993). The Document Lens. *In Proceedings of User Interface and Software Technology (UIST 93)* ACM Press, pp. 101-108.

20. Sarkar, M., & Brown, M. H. (1992). Graphical Fisheye Views of Graphs. *In Proceedings of Human Factors in Computing Systems (CHI 92)* ACM Press, pp. 83-91.

21. Schaffer, D., Zuo, Z., Bartram, L., Dill, J., Dubs, S., Greenberg, S., & Roseman, M. (1997). Comparing Fisheye and Full-Zoom Techniques for Navigation of Hierarchically Clustered Networks. *In Proceedings of Graphics Interface (GI 97)* Canadian Information Processing Society, pp. 87-96.

22. Sears, A., & Shneiderman, B. (1994). Split Menus: Effectively Using Selection Frequency to Organize Menus. *ACM Transactions on Computer-Human Interaction, 1*(1), pp. 27-51.

23. Slaughter, L. A., Harper, B. D., & Norman, K. L. (1994). Assessing the Equivalence of Paper and On-Line Versions of the QUIS 5.5. *In Proceedings of 2nd Annual Mid-Atlantic Human Factors Conference* pp. 87-91.

24. Spence, R., & Apperley, M. (1992). Data Base Navigation: an Office Environment for the Professional. *Behaviour & Information Technology, 1*(1), pp. 43-54.

25. Spenke, M., Beilken, C., & Berlage, T. (1996). FOCUS: The Interactive Table for Product Comparison and Selection. *In Proceedings of User Interface and Software Technology (UIST 96)* ACM Press, pp. 41-50.

LifeLines: Using Visualization to Enhance Navigation and Analysis of Patient Records

Catherine Plaisant, PhD, Richard Mushlin[*], PhD, Aaron Snyder[**], MD,
Jia Li, Dan Heller, Ben Shneiderman, PhD

Human-Computer Interaction Laboratory,
University of Maryland Institute for Advanced Computer Studies
[*]IBM T.J. Watson Research Center
[**]Kaiser Permanente Colorado

LifeLines provide a general visualization environment for personal histories. We explore its use for clinical patient records. A Java user interface is described, which presents a one-screen overview of a computerized patient record using timelines. Problems, diagnoses, test results or medications can be represented as dots or horizontal lines. Zooming provides more details; line color and thickness illustrate relationships or significance. The visual display acts as a giant menu, giving direct access to the data.

INTRODUCTION

Computerized medical records pose tremendous problems to system developers. Infrastructure and privacy issues need to be resolved before physicians can even start using the records. Non-intrusive hardware might be required for physicians to do their work (i.e. interview patients) away from their desks and cumbersome workstations. But all the efforts to solve such problems will only succeed if appropriate attention is also given to the design of the user interface [1]. Long lists to scroll, endless menus to navigate and lengthy dialogs can lead to user rejection. But techniques are being developed to summarize, filter and present large amounts of information [2], leading us to believe that rapid access to needed data is possible with careful design.

While more attention is now put on developing standards for gathering medical records, still too little effort is devoted to designing appropriate visualization and navigation techniques for presenting and exploring personal history records. One possible, intuitive, approach to visualizing histories is to use graphical time series [3]. The consistent, linear time scale facilitates making comparisons and relationships between the quantities displayed. Data can be graphed on the timeline to show time evolution of quantitative data. Highly interactive interfaces turn the display into a meaningfully structured menu with direct access to whatever data is needed to review a patient record.

RELATED WORK

The use of overviews or summaries has been well studied: the Summary Time-Oriented Record, a pure text flowchart, was found helpful in an arthritis clinic [4]. Summary visualization software for intensive care data includes notions of filtering, severity scaling, and details on demand [5]. Tufte [6] describes timelines as a frequent and powerful form of graphic design, and presents many examples. A design using timelines for medical records was proposed by Powsner and Tufte [7], who developed a graphical summary using a table of individual plots of test results and treatment data. A few projects have proposed interactive personal histories. The TeleMed project [8] uses icons on a web timeline to summarize patient records. Cousin and Khan [9] have explored in depth the use of timelines and the problem of aggregation for drug data.

Our work on the visualization of personal histories started with a project with the Maryland Department of Juvenile Justice (DJJ). We developed LifeLines to represent youth records (including, cases, placements, worker assignments and reviews) [10]. LifeLines were designed to 1) present a personal history overview on a single screen, 2) provide direct access to all detailed information from the overview with one or two clicks of the mouse, and 3) make critical information or alerts visible at the overview level.

An experiment was conducted to study the benefits of such a graphical interface [11]. Thirty-six participants used a static version of either LifeLines or a tabular representation to answer questions about a database of personal history information. Results suggest that, overall, the LifeLines representation led to much faster response times (up to 50% faster), primarily for questions that involved interval comparisons and inter-categorical connections. A post-experimental memory test led to significantly ($p < .004$) higher recall with LifeLines. Finally, simple interaction techniques were proposed to enhance LifeLines' ability to deal with precise dates, attribute coding, and overlaps.

EXPLORING LIFELINES

Background

In our first exploration of LifeLines for medical records [3][10] we drew paper mockups of colorful series of timelines for consultations, medical conditions, documents, hospitalizations and medications. Each physician was assigned a different color, tying documents and medications to the originating physician. Icons were used for discrete events like consultation letters or tests; lines depicted continuous episodes such as conditions or hospital stays.

In 1997, collaboration was started between IBM Research and the University of Maryland to design and build a web prototype of LifeLines for computerized patient records. Our basis for modeling the record was a newly operational clinical information system at Kaiser Permanente Colorado [12]. We are now working closely with Kaiser's physicians to test our prototype using real data. This paper reports on our

progress, and demonstrates how LifeLines can be useful in presenting a structured patient chart, and how it can facilitate navigation and analysis of the computerized medical record.

Description of the LifeLines display

In LifeLines, the medical record is summarized as a set of lines and events on a zoom-able timeline. Figure 1 shows an example based on a real record. The display shows data spanning about 6 months. The current date (frozen as mid February for demonstration purposes) is on the right side of the display, indicated by a thin vertical line. Aspects of the record are grouped in facets: problems, allergies, diagnosis, labs, imaging, medications, immunizations, etc. At the top, problems are shown as lines. When a problem becomes inactive the line stops (e.g. "smoker"). Color can be used to indicate severity or type (e.g. the migraine and seizure problems are red[†] because their status is marked as "alert". Severe allergies are red as well.)

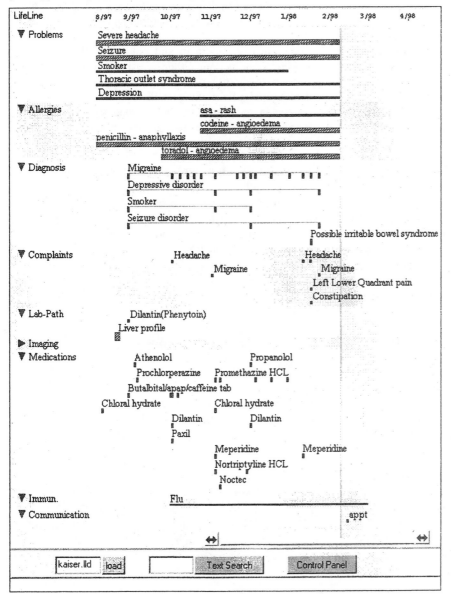

Figure 1: This patient has several problems and has been in the office about every two weeks. The elements seen as particularly significant, the severe headaches, the seizure disorder, and the multiple severe drug allergies are easily spotted because they are marked in red[†] in the interface. Temporal relationships and links across different sections of the record are made apparent (e.g., the temporal coincidence between the constipation and the closely preceding admin- istration of meperidine is suspicious.

[†] *To accommodate the black and white printing of this paper we made red events appear as thicker and patterned lines*

Similar diagnoses are grouped on common lines. The "migraine headache" lines show all dates where a migraine headache diagnosis was rendered. Two lab results are shown. One stands out in red since its status was abnormal. Series of similar labs would be grouped together on a line. Drug class has been used to group medications, with each mark representing a prescription date.

The first glance at the LifeLines display tells that this patient has several problems and has been in the office about every two weeks. It shows a series of concurrent problems and multiple medications. The elements seen as particularly significant, the severe headaches, the seizure disorder, and the multiple severe drug allergies are easily spotted because they are marked in red[†]. One can glance down from the headache line to the diagnosis section and see that the diagnosis of migraine headache was made soon after the problem presented, and review the evolution of its treatment. Correlation and its absence can be sought by scanning vertically and horizontally. For instance, it is suspicious that the constipation in 2/98 was closely preceded by a meperidine injection. After noticing that the Dilantin prescription has been continued, one can assess whether a blood level check that has not been done for several months is indicated at this time.

The patient whose record is shown in Figure 1 is quite sick and has had many clinical encounters. For comparison, imagine a healthy woman coming for a routine heath maintenance examination. A glance at her ten-year LifeLines display might reveal that this patient had a sparse record with only a few red events. The test facet might show that the last mammography was done five years ago, that Pap smears were done regularly, and that one of them was abnormal but was immediately followed by a normal Pap. Immunizations could be reviewed as well. This overall analysis could be done at a glance, while it might have taken several screens to gather this information across multiple sections of a traditional computerized record.

Dynamics and overall user interface description

Static visualizations such as the screen shown in Figure 1 can be enhanced by an interactive interface. The current prototype of Lifelines is implemented in Java and runs on the Internet.

Details on demand – All events visible on the display form a giant menu giving rapid access to detailed information (triggered by a double click on the event.) The detailed information appears in a separate page covering part of the display or optimally in tiled windows on the side (Figure 2.) In many cases, reviewing a long label containing simple text information might be sufficient (e.g. to read the ordering physician's name or the drug dosage). As users move their cursor over an event on a LifeLine, the long label of the event appears in the upper textbox next to the patient's general information (which gives age, gender, possibly a photo, etc.)

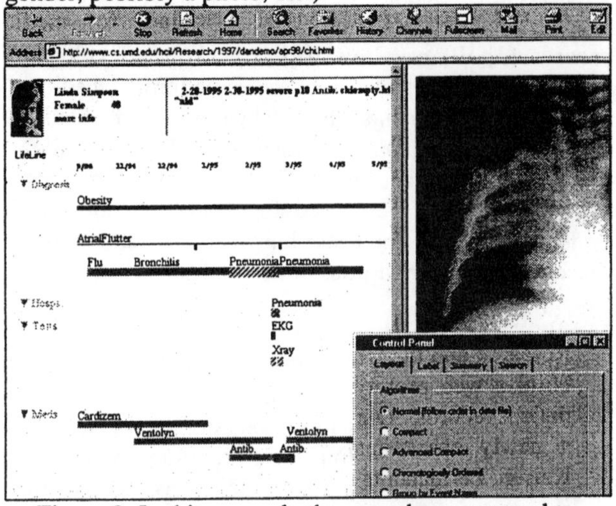

Figure 2: In this example the record was zoomed to reveal details of a long pneumonia episode. Details such as X-rays can be displayed in other windows. A control panel gives users access to layout and labeling options.

Zooming – Zooming in and out (or in this case "rescaling") can be done either by using the zoom-and-pan slider at the bottom of the display, or by clicking on the background of the image near the events that should end-up in the center of the zoomed image. A right-button click on the background zooms out again. Zooming in and out reveals different levels of detail.

Highlighting relationships – In addition to the implicit vertical and horizontal relationships, searches can be performed on the entire record, highlighting all parts of the record that match. In Figure 3, a simple text search for "migraine" was performed. Highlighted are all the drugs whose indication was migraine, all complaints explained by the diagnosis migraine, etc.

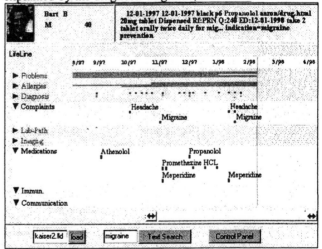

Figure 3: Here, a search for migraine selected all the events containing migraine in their description: complaints whose explanation were migraine, drugs whose indication was migraine, etc

Note the top facets, problems, allergies, and diagnosis have been closed, leaving only their "silhouettes". The silhouette of diagnosis shows that many visits were related to the migraine. More complex relationships could be computed and selected from menus or query forms (e.g. show all events linked to a given insurance claim.)

Coding attributes - Control panels are available to setup the mapping of the main display attributes (label, color and line thickness) to the data attributes. The most obvious choice is to map severity or status to color and use red to show alerts or severe events. Drugs can be color coded by indication or by class. On the other hand, an administrator might chose to map cost or payment status to the color attribute, and map severity to the size of the line.

In the example of Figure 1, color and size are not used very much, mainly because we explored in this example how an existing, "real-life", computerized record could be displayed with LifeLines. Although this particular patient did not exhibit large variations in the display-mapped data attributes, a variety of useful mappings can be configured. For example, many drugs have a predictable range of dosage, and this data attribute makes effective use of the line thickness. Problems may vary in severity and be shown by lines of varying size, reserving color for other attributes such as body system. Prescription management might benefit from information about a prescription's expected duration (derived from dosage and number of refills.) LifeLines could easily represent the expected end of the medication supply, or calculate the approximate refill request date if several refills are authorized. Figure 4 depicts the details of the dispense cycle for three prescriptions. Actual refills requested by the patient are shown in the past, while estimates are shown in the future following the "today" line. Using LifeLines it becomes possible to see when refills are being requested on time, too soon, or too late, using red to highlight possible overuse or under-use.

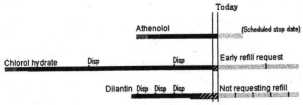

Figure 4: Details of three prescriptions' actual and expected duration. Estimated (i.e. calculated) refill dates can show possible overuse (chloral hydrate) or under-use (Dilantin) of the medication.

Outlining - Simple records of mostly healthy patients can fit easily in a small part of the display. But crowding problems arise when the time span, the number of facets, lines and events increases significantly. Zooming and summarization mostly takes care of the horizontal crowding, but vertical crowding remains a challenge to provide a global overview of the record. To address this problem, facets can be opened and closed in an outliner fashion. A closed facet only reveals the "silhouette" of the record (i.e. compacted lines with no labels, but color is preserved). Those silhouettes are useful to estimate the volume and type of information available and to guide users to the most important parts of the record. For example when the test facet is closed, one can still spot the presence and location of red dots. Bringing the cursor on a dot reveals its label, while a double click brings the detail in the detail window on the right. Opening and closing facets allows the user to dedicate screen space to the subjectively interesting topics, while maintaining access to, and more importantly, awareness of, the silhouetted information. For complex records, a hierarchy of facets may be needed, along with an optimization strategy for closing facets to get screen space. In all cases, offering users control panels to indicate their preferences is important.

Summarizing - Another way to deal with large records is to allow summarization of the events. Our architecture allows a set of events within a facet to be recursively aggregated and replaced with summary events. For example a series of athenolol prescriptions can be aggregated in a simple event, while series of athenolol and propanolol can be aggregated as beta-blockers (Figure 5).

Summary	Betablocker
	Phenothiazine
After zooming	Propanolol Propanolol Athenolol Propanolol Prochlorperazine Prochlorperazine Promethazine HCL

Figure 5: Example of summarization for four drugs in two classes

DATA ARCHITECTURE

We developed a general information architecture for personal history data [13]. Our focus was on medical patient records, but the design is applicable as well to other, simpler domains such as juvenile justice or personal resumes. Our model of personal history data groups events into aggregates that are contained in facets. Explicit and implicit links enable the representation of arbitrary relationships across events and aggregates. Data attributes such as severity, status, cost, dosage, etc., can be mapped to visual attributes such as label, color and line thickness. Data administrators set default profiles, while end-users have powerful controls over the display contents and personalized mapping of data attributes to display attributes to fit their tasks. For prototyping purposes the data is stored in an Access database, while the attribute mapping control panel generates the runtime data used by the LifeLines Java applet.

CONCLUSION

We have designed and implemented a visualization technique called LifeLines, and have begun testing it on real clinical data. Using the familiar metaphor of timelines, LifeLines takes advantage of our ability to visually analyze information-abundant displays, and facilitates access to the details in the record. We believe that such an interface can have a significant influence on the usability and overall impact of electronic medical records.

There are implications as well for the form of the medical record. The modern paper medical record revolves around progress notes. The progress note collects the details of the clinical situation at hand, coordinates those details temporally and causally, and gives commentary on both data and conclusions. If the computerized record increases access to details, then textual collections of data, such as review of systems, may become less useful. If LifeLines adds a clear and accessible view of temporal and causal relationships, then the main task left for the progress note might be to provide commentary. If so, then a computerized patient record using LifeLines may inspire, and perhaps require, a different role and format for progress notes.

Acknowledgements
We greatly appreciate the support provided by IBM through its Shared University Research program, and NSF (IRI 96-15534). We greatly thank Anne Rose for her contribution to the early designs of LifeLines, and John Karat for making the collaboration with IBM a reality.

Contact information
Catherine Plaisant, HCIL, UMIACS, A.V. Williams building, University of Maryland , College Park, MD 20742, plaisant@cs.umd.edu.
HCIL URL: www.cs.umd.edu/hcil.
Video demo available from HCIL

† *To accommodate the black and white printing of this paper we made red events appear as thicker and patterned lines*

References
1. Dewey, J.D., Manning, P., Brandt, S., (1993) Acceptance of direct physician access to a computer based patient record in a managed care setting. *Proc. 17th Symposium on Computer Applications in Medical Care.* 79-83, AMIA, Washington DC.

2. Stuart Card, Jock Mackinlay, & Ben Shneiderman, editors. (1998) *Readings in Information Visualization: Using Vision to Think*, Morgan Kaufmann Publishers.

3. Plaisant, P., Rose, A. (1996) Exploring LifeLines to Visualize Patient records. Poster summary in 1996 American Medical Informatics Association Annual Fall Symposium, pp. 884, AMIA, Bethesda MD.

4. Whiting-O'Keefe, Q.E., Simbork, D.W., Epstein, W.V., Warger, A. (1985) A Computerized summary medical record system can provide more information than the standard medical record. *JAMA*, 254, pp. 1185-1192

5. Factor, M., Gelernter, D.H., Kolb, C.E., Miller, P.L., Sittig, D.F. (1991)Real-time data fusion in the intensive care unit. *IEEE Computer*, November 24, pp. 45-54.

6. Tufte, E.R., (1983) *The Visual Display of Quantitative Information.* Graphics Press. Cheshire, Connecticut.

7. Powsner, S.M., Tufte, E.R., Graphical summary of patient status. *The Lancet*, 344 (Aug 6, 1994) 386-389

8. Kilman, D., Forslund, D. (1997) An international collaboratory based on virtual patient records, Comm. of the ACM, Vol. 40, 8 (Aug. 97), pp. 111-117.

9. Cousins, S., Kahn, M. (1991), The visual display of temporal information, *Artificial Intelligence in Medicine* 3 , 341-357

10. Plaisant, C., Milash, B., Rose, A., Widoff, S., Shneiderman, B. (1996) LifeLines: Visualizing Personal Histories. *Proc. of Human-Factors in Computing Systems, CHI' 96*, ACM, New York.

11. Lindwarm D., Rose, A., Plaisant, C., and Norman, K. (1998) Viewing personal history records: A comparison of tabular format and graphical presentation using LifeLines, *Behaviour & Information Technology* (to appear).

12. Rose, J.R., Gapinski, M., Lum, A., Pote et,J., Hushka,G. (1998) The Rocky Mountain Kaiser Permanente Clinical Information System, a computerized ambulatory electronic health record in large scale: strategy, vision, functionality, architecture, management, implementation, impact, and lessons learned, (accepted for presentation at TEPR, San Antonio, TX, May 9-16, 1998).

13. Plaisant, C., Shneiderman, B., Mushlin, R., (1998) An information architecture to support the visualization of personal histories. *International Journal of Information Processing and Management* (to appear, 1998)

Interactive Exploration of Time Series Data

Harry Hochheiser[1] and Ben Shneiderman[2]

[1] Department of Computer Science and Human-Computer Interaction Lab, University of Maryland, College Park MD 20742, +1 301 405 2725 hsh@cs.umd.edu
[2] Department of Computer Science, Human-Computer Interaction Lab, Institute for Advanced Computer Studies, and Institute for Systems Research, University of Maryland, College Park MD 20742, +1 301 405 2680 ben@cs.umd.edu

Abstract. Widespread interest in discovering features and trends in time- series data has generated a need for tools that support interactive exploration. This paper introduces timeboxes: a powerful direct-manipulation metaphor for the specification of queries over time series datasets. Our TimeSearcher implementation of timeboxes supports interactive formulation and modification of queries, thus speeding the process of exploring time series data sets and guiding data mining.

1 Introduction

Interest in time series data has prompted a substantial body of work in the development of algorithmic methods for searching temporal data [1, 5]. These methods would be more widely employed if the difficulty of query formulation was reduced. In order to build understanding of time series data users need tools that support data exploration via easy construction of queries and rapid feedback (100ms) [7].

Dynamic queries [2] and related information visualization techniques [4] have proven useful in meeting these goals. This paper introduces timeboxes: a dynamic query mechanism for specifying queries on temporal data sets.

2 Related Work

Data mining research has led to the development of useful techniques for analyzing time series data, including dynamic time warping [10] and Discrete Fourier Transforms (DFT) in combination with spatial queries [5]. To date, this work has paid little attention to query specification or interactive systems. One exception is Agrawal et al.'s Shape Definition Language, which specifies queries in terms of natural language descriptions of profiles [1]. Support for progressive refining of queries was addressed by Keogh and Pazzani, who suggested the use of relevance feedback for results of queries over time series data [6]. Our work with timeboxes is aimed at developing tools to address issues of user interaction with these data mining tools.

Existing time series visualizations tools generally focus on visualization and navigation, with relatively little emphasis on querying data sets. QuerySketch is an innovative query-by-example tool that uses an easily drawn sketch of a time series profile to retrieve similar profiles, with similarity defined by Euclidean distance [9]. Spotfire's Array Explorer 3 [8] supports graphically edit-able queries of temporal patterns, but the result set is generated by complex metrics in a multidimensional space.

3 Timeboxes: Interactive Temporal Queries

Timeboxes are rectangular query regions drawn directly on a two-dimensional display of temporal data. The extent of the timebox on the time (x) axis specifies the time period of interest, while the extent on the value (y) axis specifies a constraint on the range of values of interest in the given time period. More specifically, a timebox that goes between (x_{min}, y_{min}) and (x_{max}, y_{max}) indicates that for the time range $x_{min} \leq x \leq x_{max}$, the dynamic variable must have a value in the range $y_{min} \leq y \leq y_{max}$.

Timeboxes are created, moved, and resized using rectangle manipulation operations familiar to users of drawing and presentation software. Multiple timeboxes can be combined to specify conjunctive queries.

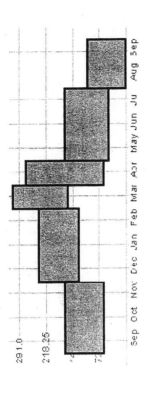

Fig. 1. Query containing multiple timeboxes

$\forall_{sep \leq x \leq nov}\ 57 \leq y \leq 160$	$\forall_{dec \leq x \leq feb}\ 124 \leq y \leq 230$	$\forall_{x=mar}\ 154 \leq y \leq 291$
$\forall_{x=apr}\ 58 \leq y \leq 266$	$\forall_{may \leq x \leq jul}\ 46 \leq y \leq 162$	$\forall_{aug \leq x \leq sep}\ 0 \leq y \leq 101$

Table 1. Constraints for query shown in Fig. 1

Fig. 1 provides an example query containing multiple timeboxes. In addition to being succinct and easy to create, the timebox version of this query provides a visual picture of the constraints that is not apparent in other notations. For example, the query in Fig. 1 is more easily interpreted than the mathematical expression of the same constraints (Table 1), which is cognitively more difficult for users to comprehend.

4 TimeSearcher

4.1 Overview

The main TimeSearcher window is shown in Fig. 2. Entities in the data set are displayed in a window in the upper left-hand corner of the application. This provides a scrollable list that can be used to browse through the data. Complete details about the entity (details-on-demand) can be retrieved by simply clicking on the graph for the desired entity; this will cause the relevant information to be displayed in the upper right-hand window (Fig. 2).

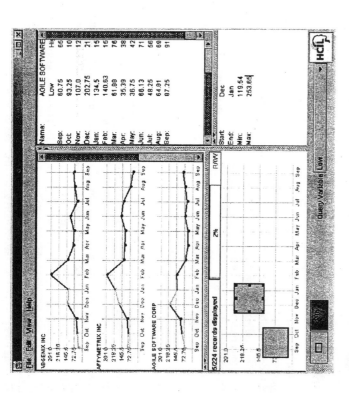

Fig. 2. TimeSearcher, displaying a query with two timeboxes and four of the five records in the result set

4.2 Query Creation and Modification

Queries are created in the query space in the bottom-left corner of the window. To specify a query, users draw a timebox in the desired location. Query processing begins as soon as users release the mouse, signifying the completion of the box. No "run" or "query" button is necessary because of the rapid update (a few hundred milliseconds). When query processing completes, the display in the top half of the application window is updated to show those entities that match the query constraints.

Rapid and dynamic update of the result set display provides prompt feedback regarding the results of the query. Once the initial query is created, query parameters can be changed by moving and resizing the timeboxes, either individually or simultaneously in groups.

4.3 Drag and Drop

Users might be interested in identifying entities that have profiles similar to a given template or example from the data set. TimeSearcher provides a drag-and-drop mechanism that can be used to identify items similar to a given example from the data set. The user can instantiate a query by dragging an item from the data display window and dropping it onto the query space. The resulting query has a separate timebox for each time point in the data set (Fig. 3). Once the query is created, the user can modify the timeboxes to modify the definition of "similar".

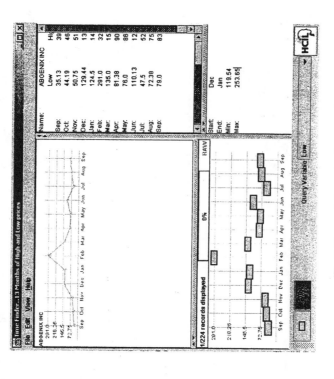

Fig. 3. Drag-and-drop query-by-example

4.4 Envelopes for Overviews

TimeSearcher uses envelopes to provide overview displays to help users make sense of large data sets [4, 7]. Optionally shown in the background of the query window, the data envelope is a contour that follows the extreme values of the query attribute at each point in time, thus displaying the range of values that may be queried. When the user executes a query, the data envelope is extended by a query envelope - an overlay that outlines extreme values of the entities in the result set (Fig. 4). This display provides users with a graphic summary of the relationship between the result set and the data set as a whole.

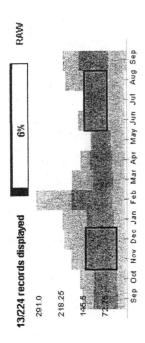

Fig. 4. Data and query envelopes for a query with two timeboxes

5 Software

TimeSearcher was implemented in Java 2, using the Swing toolkit. Drawing and scene-graph control in the data and query displays, along with functionality for moving and rescaling timeboxes, is provided by Jazz [3]. Timeboxes, graphs of each item, and query data envelopes are implemented as Jazz widgets.

Orthogonal range trees are used to index the data, with each timebox acting as an orthogonal range query. In this model, each timebox is an orthogonal range query of width w, and an entity from the data set must have w points that fall within the query range to be included in the result set for the query.

6 Discussion and Future Work

TimeSearcher users an "overview-first" [7] approach to the exploration of time series data. The data and query envelopes, together with the linear list of graphed elements, provide the necessary overview. Each timebox is a new filter that restricts the data set resulting from the query formed by the pre-existing timeboxes. Query processing on mouse release follows a model familiar to users of modern GUIs, whereby a mouse release is treated as completion of user input.

Several extensions to the timebox model might increase the range of queries that can be expressed. Queries involving events of fixed duration occurring at any point in time, events that are separated by minimum gaps in time, disjunctions and negations, trends involving relative changes ("increase of more than 50% within a given period") and multiple time-dependent attributes might be of interest.

Further gains in efficiency might be realized by using timeboxes to specify queries to be evaluated with existing data mining algorithms such as those described by Faloutsos, et al. [5]. In this model, TimeSearcher might be used to interactively search subsets of a larger data set, in order to refine queries that might be executed against the entire data set, using the more expensive data mining algorithms.

7 Conclusions

TimeSearcher uses dynamic queries, overviews, and other information visualization techniques that have proven useful in a variety of other domains [2, 4, 7] to support interactive examination of time series data. Timeboxes represent an extension of the dynamic query idea to include widgets that query multiple dimensions simultaneously, as each timebox specifies constraints over two dimensions.

The incorporation of data mining algorithms into systems that support exploration and interactive knowledge discovery is the next step in making data mining more accessible to a wider range of users and problem domains. A more diverse user population will also stimulate more research, as these users generate questions and problems involving further algorithmic challenges.

The utility of timeboxes will be a function of the usability of the interface, particularly in comparison with alternative approaches. Empirical studies and heuristic evaluations are needed to clarify the benefits and drawbacks of timeboxes, while suggesting additional interface improvements.

Acknowledgments Thanks to Martin Wattenberg for providing stock price datasets, and to Eric Baehrecke and Hyunmo Kang for valuable feedback. The first author was supported by a fellowship from America Online.

References

1. Agrawal, R., Psaila, G., Wimmers, E., and Zat, M. Querying Shapes of Histories. In Proceedings of 21st VLDB Conference (Zurich Switzerland, September 1995), 502–514.
2. Ahlberg, C., and Shneiderman, B. Visual Information Seeking: Tight bCoupling of Dynamic Query Filters with Starfield Displays. In Proceedings of CHI '94 (Boston MA, April 1994), ACM Press, 313–317.
3. Bederson, B. B., Meyer, J., and Good, L. Jazz: an Extensible Zoomable User Interface Graphics Toolkit in Java. In Proceedings of UIST 2000 (San Diego CA, November 2000), ACM Press, 171–180.
4. Card, S. K, Mackinlay, J. D. and Shneiderman, B. Readings in Information Visualization: Using Vision to Think. Morgan-Kaufmann Publishers, San Francisco, CA, 1999.
5. Faloutsos, C., Ranganathan, M., Manolopoulos, Y. Fast Subsequence Matching in Time Series Databases. In Proceedings of SIGMOD '94 (Minneapolis MN, May 1994), ACM Press, 419–429.
6. Keogh, E.J., and Pazzani, M. J. Relevance Feedback Retrieval of Time Series Data. In Proceedings SIGIR '99 (Berkeley, CA, August 1999), ACM Press, 183–190.
7. Shneiderman, B., Designing the User Interface. Addison-Wesley, Reading, MA, 1998.
8. Spotfire. http://www.spotfire.com. (Accessed July, 2001).
9. Wattenberg, M. Sketching a Graph to Query a Time Series Database. In Proceedings of CHI 2001, Extended Abstracts (Seattle WA, April 2001), ACM Press, 381–382.
10. Yi, B. K., Jagadish, H. V., and Faloutsos, C. Efficient Retrieval of Similar Time Sequences Under Time Warping. In Proceedings of the International Conference On Data Engineering (ICDE '98), IEEE Computer Society Press, 201–208.

Excentric Labeling:
Dynamic Neighborhood Labeling for Data Visualization

Jean-Daniel Fekete
Ecole des Mines de Nantes
4, rue Alfred Kastler, La Chantrerie
44307 Nantes, France
Jean-Daniel.Fekete@emn.fr
www.emn.fr/fekete

Catherine Plaisant
Human-Computer Interaction Laboratory
UMIACS, University of Maryland
College Park, MD 20742, USA
plaisant@cs.umd.edu
www.cs.umd.edu/hcil

ABSTRACT

The widespread use of information visualization is hampered by the lack of effective labeling techniques. An informal taxonomy of labeling methods is proposed. We then describe "excentric labeling", a new dynamic technique to label a neighborhood of objects located around the cursor. This technique does not intrude into the existing interaction, it is not computationally intensive, and was easily applied to several visualization applications. A pilot study with eight subjects indicates a strong speed benefit over a zoom interface for tasks that involve the exploration of large numbers of objects. Observations and comments from users are presented.

Keywords

Visualization, Label, Dynamic labeling, Evaluation

INTRODUCTION

A major limiting factor to the widespread use of information visualization is the difficulty of labeling information abundant displays. Information visualization uses the powerful human visual abilities to extract meaning from graphical information [1-2]. Color, size, shape position or orientation are mapped to data attributes. This visualization helps users find trends, and spot exceptions or relationships between elements on the display. Experimental studies have been able to show significant task completion time reduction and recall rate improvements when using graphical displays instead of tabular text displays (e.g., [3]) However textual information in the form of labels remains critical in identifying elements of the display. Unfortunately, information visualization systems often lack adequate labeling strategies. Often labels are entirely missing and users have to peck at graphical objects one at a time. Sometimes labels overlap each other to the point of obscuring the data and being less usable; or they are spread out in such a way that the relation between objects and labels becomes ambiguous. The problem becomes acute when the data density increases and the labels are very long.

To address this problem we propose "excentric labeling" as a new dynamic technique to label a neighborhood of objects (Figures 1-3). Because it does not interfere with normal interaction and has a low computational overhead, it can easily be applied to a variety of visualization applications.

The labeling problem is not new. It has been extensively studied for cartographic purposes [4] where printing or report generation is the main purpose of the application. Very few solutions have been proposed to automate the labeling process of interactive applications. In this paper, we propose an informal taxonomy of labeling methods, then describe our excentric labeling technique in detail, discuss its benefits and limitations, and illustrate how it can benefit a variety of applications.

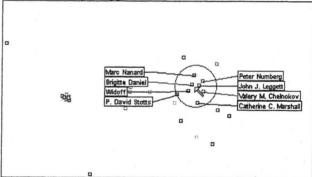

Figure 1: Excentric labeling provides labels for a neighborhood of objects. The focus of the labeling is centered on the cursor position. Labels are updated smoothly as the cursor moves over the display, allowing hundreds of labels to be reviewed in a few seconds. The color of the label border matches the object color.

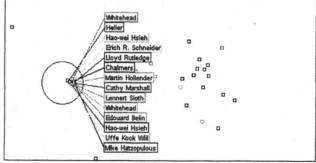

Figure 2: Labels are spread to avoid overlapping, possibly revealing objects clumped together on the display.

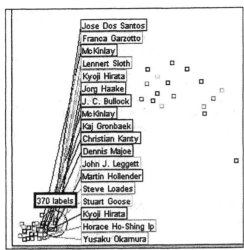

Figure 3: Special algorithms handle border effects (e.g., corners) When objects are too numerous, the total number of objects in the focus area is shown, along with a subset of the labels.

TAXONOMY OF LABELING TECHNIQUES

The labeling challenge can be stated as follows: given a set of graphical objects, find a layout to position all names so that each name (label) is:
1. Readable.
2. Non-ambiguously related to its graphical object.
3. Does not hide any other pertinent information.

Completeness (the labeling of all objects) is desired but not always possible.

Labeling techniques can be classified into two categories: static and dynamic. The goal of static labeling is to visually associate labels with a maximum of (all if possible) graphic objects in the best possible manner. But good static techniques are usually associated with delays not suitable for interactive exploration. Dynamic labeling began with interactive computer graphics and visualization. Two attributes account for the "dynamic" adjective: the set of objects to be labeled can change dynamically, and the number and layout of displayed labels can also change in real time, according to user actions.

Static Techniques

Static techniques have been used for a long time in cartography. Christensen et al., [4] wrote a recent summary of label placement algorithms. Cartography also needs to deal with path labeling and zone labeling, which is less widespread in visualization. We do not address those two issues in this article. But the same algorithms can be used for both cartography and general visualization. Since static techniques have to find "the" best labeling possible, the set of objects has to be carefully chosen to avoid a too high density in objects or labels. In cartography, this is achieved by aggregating some information and forgetting (sampling) others (this process is called "generalization"). This technique could be nicknamed the "label-at-all-cost"

technique since one of the constraints is to label all objects of the display.

For data visualization, a similar process of aggregation can be applied to achieve a reasonable result with static techniques (e.g., aggregation is used in the semantic zooming of Pad++ [5] or LifeLines [6,7]), but the logic of aggregation and sampling is mainly application dependent. Label sampling has been used occasionally [8].

The most common techniques (see Table 1) remain the "No Label" technique, and the "Rapid Label-all" technique which leads to overlaps and data occlusion (e.g., in the hyperbolic browser [9]). Also common is the "Label-What-You-Can" technique in which only labels that fit are displayed; other labels that would overlap or occlude data objects are not shown (e.g., in LifeLines),

Some visualizations avoid the problem completely by making the labels the primary objects. For example WebTOC [10] uses a textual table of contents and places color and size coded bars next to each label.

Dynamic techniques

Dynamic labeling techniques are more varied. The classic infotip or "cursor sensitive balloon label" consists of showing the label of an object right next to the object when the cursor passes over it. The label can also be shown on the side in a fixed window, which is appropriate when labels are very long and structured.

In the "All or Nothing" technique, labels appear when the number of objects on the screen falls below a fixed limit (e.g., 25 for the dynamic query and starfield display of the FilmFinder [11]). This is acceptable when the data can be easily and meaningfully filtered to such a small subset, which is not always the case. Another common strategy is to require zooming until enough space is available to reveal the labels; this requires extensive navigation to see all the labels. This technique can be combined elegantly with the static aggregation technique to progressively reveal more and more details - and refined labels - as the zoom ratio increases.

The overview and detail view combination is an alternative zooming solution [12]. The detail view can also be deformed to spread objects until all labels fit (i.e., in the way of a labeling magic lens [13]). Those last two techniques require either a tool selection or dedicated screen space.

Chalmers et al., proposed dynamic sampling where only one to three labels are displayed, depending on the user's activity. Cleveland [2] describes temporal brushing: labels appear as the cursor passes over the objects (similarly to the infotip), but those labels remain on the screen while new labels are displayed, possibly overlapping older ones.

Type	Technique	Comments/Problems
STATIC	No label	No labels!
	Label-only-when-you-can (i.e. after filtering objects)	Need effective filters. Labels are rarely visible.
	Rapid Label-All	High risk of overlaps or ambiguous linking to objects
	Optimized Label-All	Often slow - may not be possible
	Optimized Label-All with aggregation and sampling	Effective but application dependant- may not be possible
DYNAMIC		
One at a time	Cursor sensitive balloon label	Requires series of precise selection to explore space (slow), cannot reach overlapped objects.
	Cursor Sensitive label in side-window	Same as above. Constant eye movement can be a problem, but avoids occlusion of other objects.
	Temporal brushing (Cleveland)	More labels visible at a time, but overlapping problem.
Global display change	Zoom until labels appear	May require extensive navigation to see many labels (can be effectively combined with semantic zooming, e.g., Pad++)
	Filter until labels appear	May require several filtering to see labels (can be effectively combined with Zooming, e.g., starfields)
Sampling	Dynamic sampling (Chalmers et al.)	Few labels are visible.
Focus + context	Overview and detail view without deformation	Effective when objects are separated enough in the detail view to allow labels to fit (not guaranteed)
	Overview and detail with deformation/ transformation (i.e.fisheye or magic lenses)	Deformation might allow enough room for labels to fit. (not guaranteed). May require tool or mode to be selected.
	Global deformation of space (e.g., Hyperbolic Browser)	Requires intensive navigation and dexterity to rapidly deform the space and reveal all labels (e.g., by fanning the space).
	Labeling of objects in focus area (excentric labeling)	Spreads overlapping labels, and align them. Can be disorienting at first. Need to learn to stop cursor to better read labels.

Table 1: Taxonomy of labeling techniques

EXCENTRIC LABELING

Excentric labeling is a dynamic technique of neighborhood labeling for data visualization (Figures 1-3). When the cursor stays more than one second over an area where objects are available, all labels in the neighborhood of the cursor are shown without overlap, and aligned to facilitate reading. A circle centered on the position of the cursor defines the neighborhood or focus region. A line connects each label to the corresponding object. The style of the lines matches the object attributes (e.g., color). The text of the label always appears in black on a white background for better readability. Once the excentric labels are displayed, users can move the cursor around the window and the excentric labels are updated dynamically. Excentric labeling stops either when an interaction is started (e.g., a mouse click) or the user moves the cursor quickly to leave the focus region. This labeling technique does not require the use of a special interface tool. Labels are readable (non-overlapping and aligned), they are non-ambiguously related to their graphical objects and they don't hide any information inside the user's focus region.

Algorithm and Variations

To compute the layout of labels, we experimented with several variants of the following algorithm:
1. Extract each label and position for interesting graphic objects in the focus region.
2. Compute an initial position.
3. Compute an ordering.
4. Assign the labels to either a right or left set.
5. Stack the left and right labels according to their order.
6. Minimize the vertical distance of each set from the computed initial position.
7. Add lines to connect the labels to their related graphic object.

So far, we have used three main variations of this algorithm: non-crossing lines labeling, vertically coherent labeling and horizontally coherent labeling (the last two can be combined). Each uses a different method to compute the initial position, the ordering, to assign the labels to the stacks and to join the labels to their related graphic objects.

Non-Crossing Lines Labeling – Radial Labeling

The non-crossing lines labeling layout (Figure 4) avoids line crossings but does not maintain the vertical or horizontal ordering of labels. This technique facilitates the task of tracing the label back to the corresponding object. It can be used in cartography-like applications where ordering is unimportant. The initial position on the circle (step 2 of previous section) is computed with a radial projecting onto the circumference of the focus circle[1]. It is always possible to join the object to the circumference

---

[1] The name « excentric » comes from this technique which was the first implemented. The name is meant to evoke the center origin of the lines and the unconventional look of the widget. It is an accepted old spelling of eccentric, and close to the French spelling « excentrique ».

without crossing another radial spoke (but two radii - or spokes- may overlap). Then, we order spokes in counter-clockwise order starting at the top (step 3). The left set is filled with labels from the top to the bottom and the right set is filled with the rest.

Labels are left justified and regularly spaced vertically. We maintain a constant margin between the left and right label blocks and the focus circle to draw the connecting lines. For the left part, three lines are used to connect objects to their label: from the object to the position on the circumference, then to the left margin, and to the right side of the label box. This third segment is kept as small as possible for compactness, therefore barely visible in Figure 4, except for the bottom-left label. For the right labels, only two lines are used from the object to the initial position to the left of the label. The margins contain the lines between the circumference and the labels.

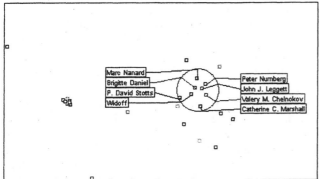

Figure 4: This figure shows the same data as in Figure 1 but using the non-crossing - or radial - algorithm.

Vertically Coherent Labeling

When the vertical ordering of graphic objects has a important meaning we use a variant algorithm that does not avoid line crossing but maintains the relative vertical order of labels. This will be appropriate for most data visualization, for example in the starfield application FilmFinder [11], films can be sorted by attributes like popularity or length, therefore labels should probably be ordered by the same attribute. Instead of computing the initial position in step 2 by projecting the labels radially to the circumference, we start at the actual Y position of the object. The rest of the algorithm is exactly the same. Figure 1 and 2 shows examples using the vertically coherent algorithm. We believe that the vertically coherent algorithm is the best default. Crossing can occur but we found that moving slightly the cursor position animates the label connecting lines and helps find the correspondence between objects and their labels.

Horizontally Coherent Labeling

When the horizontal ordering of graphic objects has a special meaning, we further modify the algorithm in step 5. Instead of left justifying the labels, we move them horizontally so that they follow the same ordering as the graphic objects, as in Figure 5. This algorithm should be

used with caution as it was found confusing by several of our reviewers.

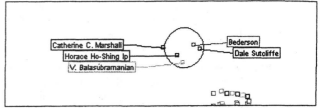

Figure 5: Here the labels order respect the Y ordering and the indentation of the labels reflects the X ordering of the objects, for example Catherine Marshall is the furthest left object in the focus circle so the label is also the furthest left.

Dealing with window boundaries

When the focus region is near the window boundaries, chances are that the label positions computed by the previous algorithms will fall outside of the window and the labels appear truncated (e.g., the first characters of the left stack labels would not be visible when the cursor is on the left side of the window).

To deal with window boundaries the following rules are applied. If some labels are cut on the left stack, then move them to the right stack (symmetric for the right side.) When labels become hidden on the upper part of the stack (i.e., near the upper boundary), move them down (symmetric for the bottom). Combining those rules takes care of the corners of the window (Figure 6).

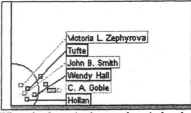

Figure 6: When the focus is close to the window boundaries, labels are moved so that they always fall inside the window.

DISCUSSION

Excentric labeling seem to fill a gap in information visualization techniques by allowing the exploration of hundreds of object labels in dense visualization screens in a matter of seconds. Many labels can be shown at once (probably around 20 at a time is optimum.) They are quite readable and can be ordered in a meaningful way. Links between objects and labels remain apparent, especially when matching color is used. The technique is simple and computationally inexpensive enough to allow for rapid exploration. Of course, these algorithms don't solve all the problems that may occur when labeling, and excentric labeling is most likely to be used in conjunction with other techniques (e.g., zooming).

Dealing with too many labels

We estimate that about 20-30 excentric labels are best displayed at a time, depending on the screen size. When more objects fall in the focus region, the screen becomes filled by labels and there is often no way to avoid that some labels fall outside the window. We implemented two "fallback" strategies: (1) showing the number of items in the focus region, and (2) showing a subset of those labels in addition to the number of objects (see Figure 3). The sample could be chosen randomly or by using the closest objects to the focus point. Although not entirely satisfactory, this method is a major improvement over the usual method of showing no labels at all, a pile of overlapping labels, or a subset of labels without mention of the missing ones.

The dynamic update of this object counts allow a rapid exploration of the data density on the screen. Of course, (this is data visualization after all) the number of objects should also been be represented graphically by changing the font or box size to reflect the magnitude of the number of objects. Showing the density and clustering of objects can also be shown using a glowing colored halo [14].

Dealing with long labels

Labels can be so long that they just don't fit on either side of the focus point. There is no generic way to deal with this problem but truncation is likely to be the most useful method. Depending on the application, labels may be truncated on the right, or on the left (e.g., when the labels are web addresses), or they may be truncated following special algorithms. Some applications may provide a long and a short label to use as a substitute when needed (e.g., Acronyms). Using smaller fonts for long labels might help in some cases. If long lines occur infrequently, breaking long labels in multiple lines is also possible.

Limiting discontinuities

One of the drawback of the dymamic aspect of excentric labeling is that the placement of an object's label will vary while the cursor is moving around the object. This is needed to allow new labels to be added when the focus area covers more objects, but leads to discontinuities in the placement of labels. For example, when the cursor moves from the left side of an object to its right side, the label will move from the right to the left stack. This effect is actually useful to confirm the exact position of a label but might be found confusing by first time users. We found that discontinuities were more common with the non-crossing algorithm than the Y coherent algorithm, which we therefore favor, despite the risk of lines crossing.

The evaluation section shows how users quickly learned to avoid this problem by hopping from place to place instead of continuously move the cursor.

Faciliting selection of objects

Excentric labeling does not interfere with the normal selection of objects but since it can reveal labels of objects that are hidden, it makes sense to use excentric labels as selection menus. Pressing a control key – or the right mouse "menu" button if it is not used in the application, can temporarily "freeze" the excentric labeling, free the cursor, and allow users to select any of the labels instead.

Furthermore, if objects are so numerous that only a subset is shown with the excentric labels, the temporary menu can become a scrolling list, guarantying access to all objects in the focus area.

OTHER OPTIONS TO CONSIDER

Depending on the application, several options might be considered:

- Changing the size and shape of the focus area can be allowed, either at the user's initiative, or dynamically as a function of the label density (with the condition that the automatic size change would be very noticeable);
- When too many items are in the focus area, excentric labels can show not only the number of objects but also a glyph or bar chart summarizing the contents of the area (e.g., showing the color distribution of the points in the focus).
- Labels can inherit more graphic attributes from the objects they reference, as is often done in cartography. We show examples where the color of the label border matches the object's color. But text font size, style or color can also be used if clear coding conventions exist and if adequate readability is preserved.

USE WITHIN EXISTING VISUALIZATION APPLICATIONS

We have implemented excentric labels within three different applications: a Java version of starfield display/dynamic query visualization [11] (Figure 7), a Java implementation of LifeLines [6-7] (Figure 9), and a map applet to be used for searching people in a building. The addition of excentric labeling to the first two applications was done in a few hours. The last program was built from scratch as an evaluation tool.

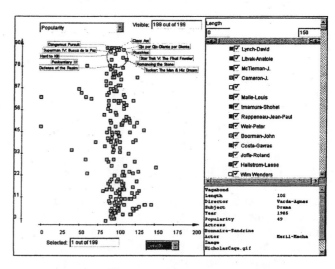

Figure 7: Excentric labeling seemed effective in a Java implementation of a starfield/dynamic query environment similar to the FilmFinder [11], or the Spotfire commercial product derived from it (www.spotfire.com). Excentric labeling provides a rapid way to review the names of the data objects and to fathom the density of the overlapping areas.

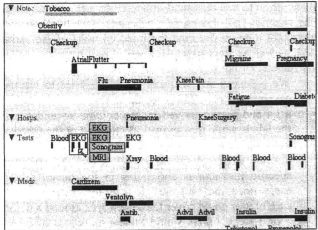

Figure 8: In LifeLines,[6-7] excentric labeling can be useful as it guarantees that all events in the focus area are labeled, even if events overlap. Chronological order is best for ordering labels, reinforced by color coding. In this example, the focus area is a small rectangle (i.e. a time range), only one column is used and there are no connecting lines. The label background is yellow to make them more visible.

EVALUATION

Excentric labeling is not meant to replace other labeling techniques but to complement them. Depending on the task, users may chose to use one or another technique. For example, to see the label of a single object, the infotip works well. To review in detail an area of the screen, zooming will be best to increase the resolution of the objects and also reveal more labels. But to quickly gain an understanding or the composition of one or several areas of interest, the infotip become tedious, the zoom may never reveal overlapping objects and the deformations are potentially disorienting as all objects have to move. In those conditions the excentric labels might become a useful addition. On the other hand it is a new feature that requires time to learn and may be found distractive.

Comparing labeling techniques is a challenge because of the many parameters involved. Screen size, zooming ratio, zooming speed, size of the excentric focus area, deformation rate, etc. would have a strong influence on the usefulness of the techniques. Making them all variables of a giant experiment would not be practical. Therefore we chose to focus our evaluation on a series of usability observations linked to an informal experiment in which we compare excentric labeling with a "virtual" instantaneous zoom. We choose to compare with a zoom because it is a very commonly used general technique.

We used the application shown in Figure 9. The map of a building is displayed with names assigned randomly to offices. Subjects have to determine if a given name appears next to one of three red dots shown on the map. This task simulates a situation where users have already identified areas of interest (e.g., areas close to both vending machines and printers, or close to the secretaries offices) and they are now looking for an empty space or someone

they know close to those points. A similar situation might be users looking at the names of objects in clusters revealed on visualization.

The questions asked were of the form: "is <the name> in the neighborhood of one of the red dots?" Subjects reply by selecting "yes" or "no". Subjects were told that the names either didn't exist at all, or were within one or two offices from the dots. The technique was quickly demo-ed, users could practice with four tasks and ask questions before the timed part of the experiment started. The time to perform each task and the number of errors were recorded. The total test lasted about 30 minutes per subject.

Subjects using excentric labels (Figure 9) had to move the cursor over and around each highlighted point and read the labels. Subjects using the zooming interface had to move the cursor over each highlighted point, left click to zoom until they can read the labels (2 or 3 zoom operations), right click to zoom back out and/or pan to the next point. The zoom was reset before the next task started.

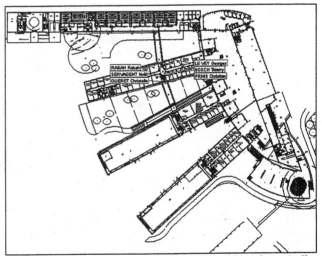

Figure 9: Map with a section of the building dynamically labeled. This application is being used to compare excentric labeling with a plain zooming interface when performing tasks that require the review of many labels.

In the Java application a zoom or pan takes about 3/4 seconds to redraw, this lead to a four time speed advantage for the excentric labels over the zoom in our first pilot test, and was dependant on the speed of the CPU. Our redraw time is representative of many zooming interfaces, but in order to avoid any obvious bias in favor of the excentric labeling, we chose to run the final test ignoring all redraw time, i.e. the clock was stopped during all redraws in the zooming interface version. We could have made the excentric labeling technique better for the task by making the focus area larger to "fit" the region users needed to search but we deliberately made it smaller, so that we could observe users browsing by having to move the cursor around the area. Overall we tried to simulate a fair and interesting situation to observe and verify the existence of speed improvements.

Eight subjects performed eight tasks for each interface. Task sets and order was counterbalanced. For six of the eight tasks the name could be found near the dots, while for the two other tasks, the name didn't exist.

Results

For the six "bounded" tasks where the name could be found there was about a 60% speed advantage for the excentric labels over the "virtual instantaneous zoom". The average time to complete the six tasks was significantly faster ($p<0,005$) with excentric labeling than with the virtual instantaneous zoom [Figure 10]. Of course the advantage would have been even much larger if we had counted the delays of the zooms and pans (an average of 10 per task, so 30 to 60 sec. additional time).

For the tasks where the searched name did not exist, there was so much variation among the eight subjects that a conclusion could not be made in this small study. Some users gave up rapidly while other searched for a long time. Both interfaces had a small number of errors (2 for zoom, 3 for excentric).

	Excentric Labels	Virtual Instantaneous Zoom	*Zoom with delays (estimated)*
Mean time to complete the six tasks (in sec.)	69.7	113.3	*140-170 function of CPU speed & application*
Standard Deviation	7.9	21.1	
Total # errors	3	2	

Figure 10a: Comparison of mean time for eight users to complete the tasks (see Figure 10b)

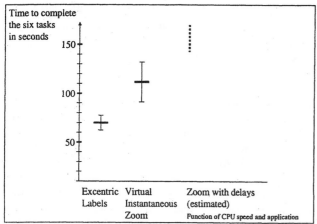

Figure 10b: Comparison of mean time for eight users to complete the 6 tasks where the names were found, for excentric labels, and for a virtual instantaneous zoom with all redraw delays removed. Any delay in zooming and panning would further increase the effect in favor of excentric labeling.

In addition to this measured effect, more was learned about the benefits and drawbacks of the interfaces by observing the eight users performing the hundred tasks of the entire test, as well as other users who helped polish the procedure by running earlier tests.

- We observed that all users quickly learned to use the excentric labels. Users would at first move the cursor a lot and seem annoyed by the continuous updates of the labels while they moved. By the end of the practice most had already stabilized their cursor, hopping in discrete steps around the red dots (we did not give specific instructions about this in the demo, letting users finds the best way to use the interface). A careful user could cover the search area around a dot in 2 or 3 steps, others would review more sets of labels by stopping in more places. Several users said that they realized they were looking at the same labels several times.

- Unsurprisingly, we observed that with the zoom interface users (who were all computer users) were already comfortable with the zoom technique. Many complained about the number of operations required to complete the tasks. Most users got lost at least once while panning and had to zoom out to find the red dots they had lost. They often over-zoomed and had to back up. On the other hand, when correctly zoomed and centered there were no problems.

Users were encouraged to "think-aloud" but generated comments only during the training phase and following the test. Comments tell the stories:

- Zoom: "I feel comfortable doing that, it's like yahoo's maps", "Where is that dot? I thought I would find it by panning there." "Oops, wrong way", "Once I am zoomed I feel confident I am looking at the right offices", "All that zooming is tiring".

- Excentric: "Ho, I like that", "It's hard to know what changed when I move the cursor". "It's better to stop moving". "I probably look at too many labels". "It would be nice if the neighborhood I am searching fit entirely in the circle". "I like the way it shows me that there are so many people here while I could not tell by just looking at the map".

- One user nicely compared the techniques by saying: "With the zoom I am confident that I read only the names in the right offices, but with the excentric label I can more easily go re-check the previous dots. We did observe that, in the tasks where the searched name did not exist, users went back to check the dots with excentric labels, while fewer did it with the zoom, or it took them a very long time.

CONCLUSION

Despite the numerous techniques found in visualization systems to label the graphical objects of the display, labeling remains a challenging problem for information visualization. We believe that excentric labeling provides a novel way for users to rapidly explore objects descriptions once patterns have been found in the display and effectively extract meaning from information visualization. Early evaluation results are promising. Users rapidly learn to use the excentric labels and stop the cursor to read the labels. A significant speed improvement was measured over a zoom interface for tasks requiring the rapid review of large numbers of labels. Finally we have demonstrated that the technique can easily be combined with a variety of applications, making excentric labels a promising new feature for information visualization environments.

ACKNOWLEDGEMENT

This work was started while Jean-Daniel Fekete visited the University of Maryland during the summer 1998. We thank all members of the HCIL lab for their constructive feedback, especially Julia Li for her initial research of the labeling problem and implementation in LifeLines, and Ben Shneiderman for suggesting the main-axis projection. David Doermann nicely allowed us to use his Java implementation of the starfield/dynamic query environment. This work was supported in part by IBM through the Shared University Research (SUR) program.

DEMONSTRATION

Excentric labeling is implemented in Java. A demo program can be found at **http://www.cs.umd.edu/hcil/excentric**

REFERENCES

1. Card, S, Mackinlay, J., and Shneiderman, Ben, *Readings in Information Visualization: Using Vision to Think*, Morgan Kaufmann Publishers, San Francisco, 1999

2. Cleveland, William, *Visualizing Data,* Hobart Press, Summit, NJ (1993).

3. Lindwarm-Alonso D., Rose, A., Plaisant, C., and Norman, K., Viewing personal history records: A comparison of tabular format and graphical presentation using LifeLines, *Behaviour & Information Technology*, *17*, 5, (1998) 249-262.

4. Christensen J., Marks J., Shieber S. Labeling point features on map and diagrams, to appear in ACM *Transactions on Graphics*.

5. Bederson, Ben B. and Hollan, James D., PAD++: A zooming graphical user interface for exploring alternate interface physics, *Proceedings of UIST '94* (1994), 17-27.

6. Plaisant, Catherine, Rose, Anne, Milash, Brett, Widoff, Seth, and Shneiderman, Ben, LifeLines: Visualizing personal histories, *Proc. of ACM CHI96 Conference: Human Factors in Computing Systems*, ACM, New York, NY (1996), 221-227, 518.

7. Plaisant, C., Mushlin, R., Snyder, A., Li, J., Heller, D., and Shneiderman, B.(1998), LifeLines: Using visualization to enhance navigation and analysis of patient records, *Proc. of 1998 American Medical Informatics Association Annual Fall Symposium* (1998), 76-80, AMIA, Bethesda, MD.

8. Chalmers M., Ingram R. & Pfranger C., Adding imageability features to information displays, *Proc. UIST'96*, 33-39, ACM.

9. Lamping, John, Rao, Ramana, and Pirolli, Peter, A focus + context technique based on hyperbolic geometry for visualizing large hierarchies, *Proc. of ACM CHI'95 Conference: Human Factors in Computing Systems*, ACM, New York, NY (1995), 401-408.

10. Nation, D. A., Plaisant, C., Marchionini, G., Komlodi, A., Visualizing websites using a hierarchical table of contents browser: WebTOC, *Proc. 3rd Conference on Human Factors and the Web*, Denver, CO (June 1997).

11. Ahlberg, Christopher and Shneiderman, Ben, Visual information seeking: Tight coupling of dynamic query filters with starfield displays, *Proc. CHI'94 Conference: Human Factors in Computing Systems*, ACM, New York, NY (1994), 313-321 + color plates.

12. Plaisant, C., Carr, D., and Shneiderman, B., Image-browser taxonomy and guidelines for designers, *IEEE Software 12*, 2 (March 1995), 21-32.

13. Stone, M., Fishkin, K., Bier, E., The moveable filter as a user interface, Proc. CHI'94, 306-312 (1994) ACM New York.

14. Hoffmann, C, Kim, Y, Winkler, R., Walrath, J, Emmerman, P., Visualization for situation awareness. Proc. of the Workshop on New Paradigms in Information Visualization and Manipulation (NPIV'98 in conjunction with ACM CIKM'98) also at http://www.cs.umbc.edu/cikm/npiv

A Fisheye Calendar Interface for PDAs: Providing Overviews for Small Displays

Benjamin B. Bederson
Human-Computer Interaction Laboratory
Computer Science Department,
Institute for Advanced Computer Studies
Univ. of Maryland, College Park, MD 20742
bederson@cs.umd.edu
+1 (301) 405-2764

Mary P. Czerwinski, George G. Robertson
Microsoft Research
One Microsoft Way, Redmond WA 98052
{marycz; ggr}@microsoft.com

ABSTRACT

Calendar applications for small handheld devices such as PDAs are growing in popularity. This led us to develop FishCal, a novel calendar interface for PDAs. It supports users in performing planning and analysis tasks by using a fisheye representation of dates coupled with compact overviews, user control over the visible time period, and integrated search. This enables users to see overviews and to easily navigate the calendar structure, and to discover patterns and outliers.

FishCal was evaluated in a benchmark usability study comparing it to Microsoft's Pocket PC 2002™ calendar. Eleven users performed complex tasks significantly faster and completed them more often with FishCal. Task by task user satisfaction data showed a significant advantage for FishCal as well. A number of usability issues were identified to aid in the iterative refinement of FishCal.

Keywords

Fisheye Views, Information Visualization, Calendar Interfaces, PDAs, Animation, Graphics.

INTRODUCTION

More and more people carry small Personal Digital Assistants (PDAs) with them to help manage day-to-day information. While these devices can be helpful for retrieving relevant information when it is needed, our informal polling of colleagues tells us that they are less helpful for planning and analysis tasks. In particular, we have heard many people complain about existing commercial calendar programs for PDAs.

This is not surprising since these devices have limited screen space, forcing users to jump around through multiple screens, making it harder to relate disparate pieces of information together.

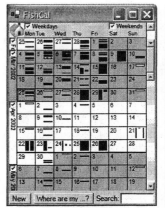

Figure 1: The FishCal interface with the view configured to show 12 weeks. The right view shows the result of tapping on March 6th which focuses on that day. All screenshots in this paper use the appointments that were used in the study described in this paper.

We designed a new calendar interface for PDAs that would support planning and analysis tasks such as "picking a good weekend this spring to go camping", "scheduling my next dentist appointment", or "finding all conflicting appointments in the next three months".

As a secondary goal, we hoped to design a calendar interface that would scale down to smaller devices such as mobile phones, and up to larger devices such as desktop displays. This second goal is important because individuals are likely to access their calendar information from these and other devices. Offering a single interface would give users a consistent user experience, and, eventually, the ability to more readily switch between devices using whichever one is readily accessible.

The FishCal design addresses these goals by using a fisheye distortion technique coupled with carefully designed visualizations and interactions appropriate for a pen-based device and small display (Figure 1). The fisheye visualization lets users see detail in context.

The basic approach starts with an overview of a large time period with a graphical representation of each day's activities. Tapping on any day expands the area representing that day, and reveals the list of appointments in context. Users may change focus days, zoom in further for a full day view, search for appointments, and reconfigure the viewable space.

This interface shows varying time span displays within the same framework using animated transitions between view changes, and thus, may improve users' ability to maintain a sense of where they are. This paper describes the interface along with the results of a user study comparing FishCal to the traditional Pocket PC calendar interface. Evidence from this study supports our hypothesis.

Related Work

Fisheye distortion techniques, initially called bifocal displays, were introduced by Spence and Apperly 20 years ago [14]. At that time, the basic concept was to distort the information space so focus items were enlarged while peripheral items were shrunk. A few years later, Furnas generalized this approach by suggesting a "degree-of-interest" function [5]. This calculates the relevance of each item in the information space, which is then used to calculate the size and visibility of that item.

Fisheye distortion techniques have been applied to a number of domains, from graphs [12] to trees [8] to menus [3], among others. Their effectiveness has been mixed, but in at least some cases, such as for hierarchically clustered networks [13], fisheye interfaces have been shown to be beneficial to users. The common theme has been that fisheye views are appropriate when users need to see details of some specific items in the context of a large information space.

The idea of using fisheye distortion to view calendars is not new. It was first suggested over ten years ago by Furnas [6] where he described a textual Lisp-based calendar program. We followed the basic approach Furnas created at that time. A tabular display shows days in the calendar, and clicking on individual days causes the amount of space allocated to that day to be increased. Furnas' calendar used varying amounts of space to show different days, so that the focus day was largest, and other days were sized in inverse proportion to the distance from the focus day (although days in the past were always tiny because the assumption was that users were more interested in the future.) This program, while impressive for its time, did not support graphical representations of appointments, searching, or full screen views, and did not have widgets to control which and how many weeks to display. It was not designed with small displays in mind. In addition, it was not evaluated with users, and was not pursued past the publication of the above-mentioned technical report.

While fisheye approaches have not otherwise been used to display calendars, fisheye visualizations have been used successfully to view and interact with tabular information – which is quite relevant, since calendars are typically viewed with tables. The best known example of this is Table Lens, which presents an interface for numerical and categorical tabular data [11]. This visualization approach was designed for tables with many rows, but a modest number of columns. It represents each row with a horizontal bar whose length is proportional to the value of the cell for numerical data, and whose position represents categorical data. The height of each row is scaled to fit the available space. Users may then focus on individual or multiple cells (or rows or columns) by clicking and other interactions. In addition, users can sort rows to help see relationships within the data. While this approach is somewhat similar to the present work in that it uses a fisheye distortion to view tabular data, it is not directly useful for calendar information as it really is designed for spreadsheet style information that has one item per cell, rather than the multiple and possibly conflicting appointments of calendars. In addition, it does not support searching or navigation that calendar users require. Nevertheless, the acceptance of this technique (as demonstrated by its successful commercialization [1]) gives hope that users will be able to understand and navigate calendar information in a tabular format using a fisheye view.

Researchers have also developed other techniques to visualize and interact with calendar information. Plaisant et al. were among the first to develop small visual representations of calendar information [10]. Mackinlay et al. developed a 3D "spiral calendar" visualization [9]. This approach, while not suitable for small devices since it displays several visual representations simultaneously, does have a fisheye-like quality in that it displays detailed appointment information with visual links back to larger scale calendars. So, users can see what week an appointment comes from, what month that week is in, what year that month is in, etc.

Perhaps surprisingly, fisheye techniques have been rarely used for interfaces for PDAs and other devices with small displays. One use was by Staffan et al. who used "flip zooming" to display web pages on a PDA [15]. This consisted of presenting one medium size focus page and several tiny pages that could be used for navigation.

FISHCAL

FishCal is the fisheye-based calendar interface we designed for use on a PDA (Figure 1). It was designed and built at the University of Maryland, and Microsoft Research then joined the project to run the experiment described below.

As described in the related work section, much of the groundwork for this design was laid by a range of earlier work. So, while the individual features of FishCal represent only variations of existing approaches, the primary contribution here is in the integration of a host of techniques to create a novel application that is both usable and useful in an important domain. In addition, we are benchmarking the design against existing calendar software for small devices. We hope that if FishCal is successful, it will illustrate how existing techniques can often be applied in new ways to new domains, and in doing so, advance the state of the art.

FishCal was built to target currently available devices running the Microsoft Pocket PC operating system. These devices are small enough to fit comfortably in a hand, have high quality 240 x 320 pixel screens, and fast enough processors to support modest animation.

Since FishCal was designed for a pen-based PDA, we have been careful to design the interaction so that it requires minimal text entry and simple interaction. The entire interface can be accessed with just single taps, although dragging offers some modest extra features – including access to tool-tips and fast scrollbar usage.

This rest of this section describes the FishCal interface in detail, including a description of its navigation capabilities, the visualizations that represent calendar information at different sizes, and how search capabilities are integrated into the interface.

Navigation

A fundamental characteristic of FishCal is its ability to support users in easily customizing their view of the calendar. Most commercial calendar applications provide mechanisms to directly switch between day, week, month, and year views, and to change which range of dates are visible with each view. However, the different views are disconnected. One goal of FishCal was to offer the same functionality in terms of a range of views, but to do so in an integrated fashion. Using animation and fisheye distortion, users can see the relationship between the range of dates they are viewing and the previous view. As such, users should not have to expend as much mental effort to manage context and figure out "where they are".

The basic organization of the display is tabular (Figure 1). Each row represents one week, with seven columns representing the days of the week. The number of visible rows can be changed from one (which represents a single week) to 52 (which represents an entire year).

The view can be changed through direct manipulation by interacting with the calendar itself, by manipulating widgets in the periphery of the display, or by using special hardware button shortcuts. One of the challenges was to make it extremely easy to configure the view. The final design only uses interaction mechanisms that most users are familiar with, including tapping on an item that they want more information about, and manipulating familiar buttons and widgets.

Direct Manipulation. FishCal was designed to take advantage of user familiarity with clicking on hyperlinks to find more detailed information about the thing they clicked on. It allows users to tap anywhere on a day to focus on that day, minimizing other days.

Within a focused day (Figure 1 right side), users can tap on the background, or tap on the maximize button to zoom in to a full day view. Or, users can tap on the minimize button to go back to original view with no days focused.

Within the full day view (Figure 2 left side), users can tap on the appointment background or the appointment's maximize button to view the appointment details. Tapping on the day's minimize button returns to the original view, and tapping on the overlapping-windows button returns to the focus day view.

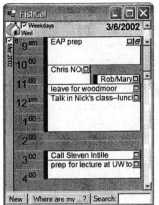

Figure 2: The FishCal interface zoomed in to a full day view (left) and then even further to see the details of a specific appointment (right).

Within the full appointment view (Figure 2 right side), scrolling shows the full contents of the appointment. Tapping on the minimize button returns to the full day view.

Peripheral Widgets. The custom double-headed scrollbar widget on the right side of the display controls how many weeks are visible at a time. It acts like a traditional scrollbar, but the thumb has two additional buttons that are used to manually set the low and high values of the current view. The view dynamically changes as the scrollbar is manipulated, but for efficiency, appointments within days are only shown when the scrollbar is released. Figure 3 shows a range of views as controlled by the scrollbar.

Another way to configure the space is to manipulate checkboxes on the top and left sides of the display. These checkboxes specify whether space gets allocated fully to the correlated set of items, or if those items are minimized. The left side of the display has one checkbox for each month. The top side of the display has one checkbox for weekdays and one checkbox for weekends. Figure 4 shows the result of two different configurations of checkboxes.

There is also a "home" button in the top-left corner of the display that resets all navigation settings to their default, so users can quickly return to the current day with a three month view.

Hardware Buttons. On desktop computers, graphical user interfaces typically offer keyboard shortcuts so that expert users can quickly access commonly used functions. On PDAs, there is no keyboard, but there are special hardware buttons that applications can use for a similar purpose.

When FishCal runs on actual Pocket PC device, the "calendar" button will be used to cycle between the preset views of one day, one week, one month, three months, and one year. The "joystick" (a small 4-way rocker switch) offers motion in four directions, and we plan on using that to move the "active" day which is indicated to the user by a dark blue highlight. Pressing the center of the joystick focuses on that day (or maximizes it if it was already focused). The joystick can be used even when a day is focused or maximized.

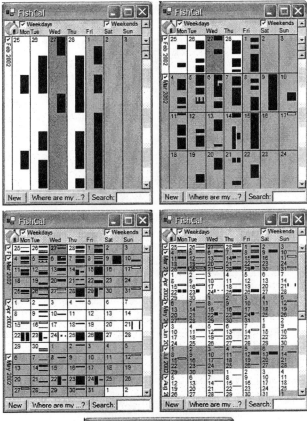

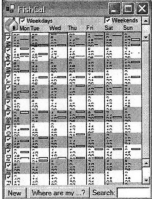

Figure 3: A series of views as the bottom of the scrollbar thumb is dragged downwards to shown in succession from left to right and top to bottom, 1 week, 1 month, 3 month, 6 month, and 1 year views.

For a desktop version of FishCal, we use the keyboard to offer these same shortcuts. The space bar changes between presets, the arrow and enter keys change the active day and zoom in. The escape key zooms out from focused and maximized viewpoints.

Visual Representations

A crucial aspect of the design of FishCal is the visual representation of the calendar for different configurations. We decided to use a "semantic zooming" approach that we developed from our prior work with Zoomable User Interfaces [4]. Semantic zooming means that objects are visually represented differently depending on how much space is available to display them. Using this technique, there are no explicit view modes. Rather, the fisheye

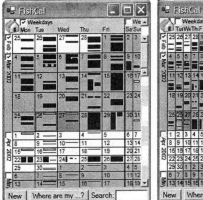

Figure 4: The views resulting from unchecking the April and May checkboxes, and on the left, the weekend checkbox is unchecked, and on the right, the weekday checkbox is unchecked.

distortion algorithms first allocate space, and then each cell renders itself using a view that is appropriate to the available space. The graphical views are scaled to fit the available space, while the textual views use a constant-sized font, and the text is clipped to fit in the available space.

The four views available are:

- *Tiny View.* This shows a graphical representation of the day's appointments. It includes depictions of all-day appointments with a white rectangle at the top of the rectangle. It uses color to represent different appointment types, and it depicts appointment conflicts using multiple columns. The pen can be dragged across appointments to show tool tips with textual information about the appointment under the pen. In large scale views, where each row is thinner than a threshold, the black lines separating rows are removed to make the display less "heavy" (Figure 3 bottom).

- *Agenda View.* This shows a textual list of appointments in order by time. There are actually two representations in this view. If there is a smaller amount of space available, a smaller font is used, and the appointment times are not listed. If there is more space available, a larger font is used, and the appointment times are listed (Figure 1 right).

- *Full Day View.* This shows a traditional full day view with a schedule of the entire day, and appointments positioned at the appropriate times. It shows all-day appointments and conflicting appointments, and uses color in the same way as the tiny view (Figure 2 left).

- *Appointment Detail.* A traditional textbox widget with scrollbars is used to show the detail of a particular appointment (Figure 2 right).

Search

The last primary component of FishCal is search. Search is important because it lets users identify patterns and outliers within a large time span. When users search in FishCal, the days that contain an appointment that match the search criteria are highlighted. The highlights are kept on while users continue to operate FishCal normally so the space can be explored to understand the results of the search.

In addition to highlighting the visible days within the current view, "attribute mapped scrollbars" [7] show which days are highlighted in both the past and the future (Figure 5). The scrollbar shows indicators representing which days are highlighted within and outside of the current view.

While it is natural to support searching for arbitrary user-entered text strings, that is somewhat problematic because it is notoriously difficult and slow to enter text at all on PDAs. So, while we support free text search, we also support two search mechanisms that do not require text entry: pre-built searches and searches based on existing appointments.

Free Text Search. To search manually, users enter text in the text box in the lower right corner of the display. Days that contain matching appointments along with the scrollbar marks are highlighted incrementally as users enter text.

If all matching dates are outside the current view, FishCal automatically scrolls to show the nearer hits. In addition, the view is automatically expanded (to a maximum of 4 months) to show multiple hits if they are far apart.

A somewhat trickier issue is how to deal with search strings that consist of multiple words. Should the search consist of the conjunction or disjunction of the words, or the actual search string? None of those approaches worked for each of the experimental tasks. Instead, FishCal operates like many current Web search engines, using a simulated "vector" based search.[2; pp. 27-30].

Vector searches work by using a number of characteristics of the search to rank the order in which the results are shown. This results in an ordering that usually matches user expectations. Exact string matches are typically listed first, conjunctions (where all the words match) are listed next, and disjunctions (where not all the words match) are listed last.

FishCal is a little different since it does not present an ordered list of search results, but instead highlights whichever days match. Rather than ordering search results, FishCal, just presents highly ranked search results. It works by first performing an exact string match, and if there are any results, they alone are shown. If there are no results, then it searches for days with appointments that match all the words in the search string, and highlights those days. If there are still no matches, it then searches for days with appointments that match any of the words in the search string and highlights those. This combination of search strategies mimics the main effect of vector searches, and works well in practice.

Predefined Searches. Since it seems likely that many searches by a particular user will be for the same thing, we added support for predefined searches. The goal is to make it even easier to search for commonly sought events, such as travel, meetings, doctor appointments, or holidays.

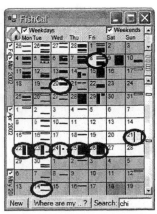

Figure 5: FishCal showing the results of searching for "CHI" (colored highlights are circled for black-and-white printing clarity). A few individual days with CHI-related meetings are highlighted, along with the week associated with the CHI conference. In addition, the scrollbar shows two days in the future that are highlighted, which have appointments for SIGCHI meetings.

A simple approach is to search on appointment metadata which is supported by Pocket PC as well as other calendar systems. The problem with this approach is that most users do not annotate each appointment with categories.

Rather than force users to do something they do not want to do, FishCal takes advantage of what information is already available – the appointment text itself. While there are no guarantees that a user will enter a similar event the same way every time, we have found through informal polling of our colleagues, that people often do represent similar events with similar textual descriptions – although they vary significantly from one user to another.

So we built support for predefined searches where each search would actually look for a match within any of a set of search strings. For example, searching "Doctor Appointments" actually searches for "doctor", "dr.", or "dr appt". While these predefined searches are currently hard-coded, our intention is for users to be able to modify them, or define their own.

This approach has been tested on the authors' calendar data, and it works quite well except for a few idiosyncrasies that we discovered. For instance, one of the authors uses textual graphics such as "->" to indicate travel. Some of these are searchable as a text string, but some are not because they span multiple lines.

Nevertheless, this approach still appears practical. Since having good quality predefined searches is so useful, some users are likely to adapt the way they write appointments to be more consistent. While the general idea of requiring users to adapt to system requirements is undesirable, this is better than the current solution which requires manual annotation of each appointment with categories.

Existing Appointment Search. Since it is quite common for people to create recurring appointments, where the same appointment happens at regular time intervals, it seems

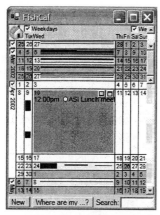

Figure 6: The results of clicking on the appointment "ASI Lunch Meeting". Every other Wednesday is highlighted in yellow which shows a recurring appointment. In addition, several days are highlighted in orange which match either "lunch" or "meeting".

natural to have a simple way to support finding and visualizing those recurrences.

We added one last search feature which is the ability to find all appointments matching an existing appointment. This works just by tapping on any appointment. All other days with exactly matching appointments are highlighted in yellow, just as if the text of the appointment subject had been typed into the search box.

We noticed, however, that sometimes users had similar appointments that were not exact matches. It would be natural to also support finding the relationships between those similar appointments. Based on the implementation of free text searching, we also search for days with appointments that partially match the specified appointment, and we highlight those in orange (Figure 6). This is a simple solution that can be readily ignored by users if they are only interested in the exact recurrence, but offers more information if desired.

Implementation

The implementation of FishCal consists of about 5,000 lines of C#. The most complex part of the implementation is the layout algorithm used to allocate space for each calendar day. The layout algorithm takes as input the number of days in a week, number of weeks displayed, the checkbox states, the focus day, and the size of the window.

The subtle part of the layout algorithm relates to the large set of configurations of the space for which it must work. Specifically, there must be a balance between the minimum size of unfocused cells and the maximum size of focused cells. That is, we have found it makes most sense for each day to stay within a range of sizes whenever possible. So, FishCal defines a preferred minimum and maximum size for unfocused and focused cells, and allocates space within those ranges whenever possible.

The other subtle part of the FishCal implementation is performance. To make FishCal respond to user interaction rapidly, and to animate transitions smoothly, the overall

structure had to be carefully designed. The primary things taken into account which contribute to its performance are:

- Custom rendering loop. Rather than use a toolkit, which might have been easier in some respects, FishCal uses a custom data structure, rendering loop, and "picking" implementation. This was particularly appropriate since the basic data structure is a table, and is easily handled as a two dimensional array.

- Space vs. time tradeoff. Things were always precomputed and stored, rather than being computed on the fly. The most obvious place this occurs is in the layout of the days.

- Render only what is needed during transitions. However, some visual aspects, such as highlighted days have to be shown during scrolling since users sometimes look for that while scrolling.

All transitions in FishCal are animated with simple linear interpolation that occurs over 250 milliseconds. We picked such a short animation time because the visual changes are quite small (usually not changing by more than a few centimeters).

FishCal is implemented entirely in C#, and runs on whatever platforms the Microsoft Common Language Runtime (CLR) is available on. Currently, the CLR is available on all desktop versions of Windows except Windows 95. Microsoft has an early version of the CLR available for Pocket PC (called the "Compact Framework"), but at the time of this writing, it is too slow to run FishCal well. While we were able to get FishCal running on Pocket PC, the animations were so slow as to make it unusable. Microsoft has promised a version of the Compact Framework that will be substantially faster, and should be available by the time this paper is published. When FishCal does run reliably on Pocket PC, we plan on making it available for download at http://www.cs.umd.edu/hcil/fishcal. Until that time, we have made a short video of FishCal available at that site.

All features described in this paper are fully implemented. FishCal loads calendar data from a simple text file that is exported from Microsoft Outlook. We also have an experimental version of FishCal that is integrated with Outlook through the Office Add-in architecture. It is launched from a toolbar button, and loads appointment data directly from Outlook.

BENCHMARK STUDY

We performed a benchmark usability study of FishCal compared to the current shipping user interface of Microsoft's Pocket PC 2002™ calendar (Figure 7). The goals of the study were to examine the initial design ideas behind the fisheye calendar, in order to see if the user interface design could be improved, and to compare its overall usability against an existing product.

We gathered eleven knowledge workers (five females) who were all experienced MS Windows and Office users, as confirmed through an in-house validated recruiting screener questionnaire. Participants were screened to be between 25-50 years of age (average age of 39.2). In addition, the participants fit some broad characteristics of being target end users of personal digital assistants (PDA), but were purposefully chosen to not own or use one at the current time. We thought this aspect of the user group would be especially interesting since for some reason these users had avoided buying a PDA, and perhaps the presentation of PDA information on a small screen was a primary issue for them.

Brief (approximately 5 minutes) tutorials were provided to participants prior to each set of tasks on each calendar. The tutorials consisted of a one page sheet of instructions on operating the interfaces, and the participants then tried each of the described mechanisms. The tutorial focused on the features and functions of each calendar that were necessary for completing the experimental tasks. However, 2 minutes were provided for the user to explore the calendar as he or she saw fit prior to starting. The participants performed an isomorphic set of 11 tasks using each calendar (example tasks are listed below). The order of calendar use and task set for the calendar were both counterbalanced in order to minimize the effects of training, or the possibility of one task set being slightly more difficult than the other. Participants completed a series of calendar viewing and planning tasks, introducing them to progressively more complex questions as they interacted with each calendar. The final task was the most complex, requiring the user to

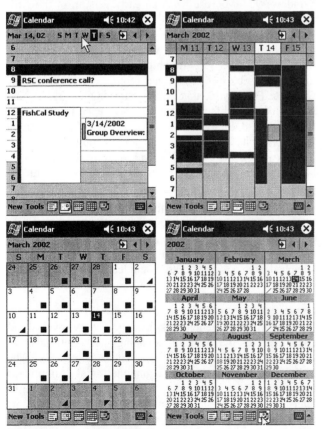

Figure 7: Screen shots of the Microsoft Pocket PC Calendar program that was used in the study showing day, week, month, and year views.

determine the number of conflicts in their calendars over a 3 month period. All tasks were given a deadline of two minutes to complete in order to keep the session under 1.5 hours (and because a two minute deadline seemed reasonable for being able to discover information from one's PDA calendar.) Task times and completion, verbal protocols, and user satisfaction and preference questionnaire data were collected throughout the session. Sessions lasted approximately one and one half hours.

One of the co-author's calendars, seeded with several artificial calendar events for the study, was utilized as the target calendar. Ideally, we would have run both FishCal and Pocket PC Calendar on a Pocket PC device. However, as mentioned previously, the CLR is not yet fast enough on the Pocket PC to run FishCal well. In order to minimize extraneous differences in the study, we ran both calendars on a PC using a mouse and keyboard. The Pocket PC Calendar was run on a Pocket PC emulator and synchronized using Microsoft ActiveSync prior to the study, so that both calendars had the same content.

Participants were asked to carry out a variety of tasks, from finding the dates of specific calendar events (such as visits or trips), to determining how many Mondays a month contained, to viewing all birthdays for the next 3 months. Several tasks focused on finding free time on the calendar in order to schedule events.

The user's display was a LCD set to 1024 x768 resolution with 16-bit color, and each calendar occupied a 240 x 320 pixel window centered on the display (standard Pocket PC resolution). All participants were run singly in a usability lab, on a Dell Pentium 450 MHz computer running Windows XP. A MS Natural keyboard and an MS IntelliMouse were used as input devices, though the "wheel" was not functional with the calendars.

Study Results

Task Times. Task times for one participant were unavailable, as his session expired before he was able to get to the 4th task using FishCal. A tape jam prevented us from obtaining the task times for one other participant for the Pocket PC, and both participants' data had to be ignored for the task time analysis. A 2 (calendar type) x 11 (Task) repeated measures Analysis of Variance (RM-ANOVA) was carried out on the completion times for the tasks. Tasks were performed faster using FishCal (49 seconds versus 55.8 seconds for the Pocket PC, on average), a borderline significant result, $F(1,8)=3.5$, $p=.08$. There was also a significant main effect of task, $F(10,80)=12.9$, $p<.01$, and a significant calendar x task interaction, $F(10,80)=2.05$, $p=.04$. Of particular interest was the fact that, as the tasks became more complex (tasks 3, 5, 8 and 11), the FishCal task time advantage grew. This result was primarily due to the fact that FishCal allowed flexible views across time in a user-defined manner. In addition, the integrated search mechanism and its resultant views made finding particular sets of events via keyword matching quite effective. These results can be seen in Figure 8.

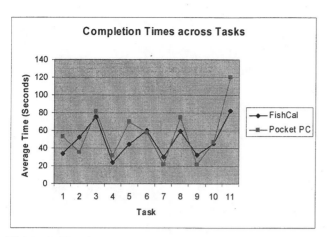

Figure 8: The time spent by study participants to complete each task using the FishCal and standard Pocket PC calendar interfaces.

Task Success. The participant who did not complete all of the FishCal tasks was also removed from the Task Success analysis. Tasks were completed successfully significantly more often using FishCal (on average, a 88.2% success rate, versus 76.3% for the Pocket PC), $F(1,9)=37.1$, $p<.001$. In addition, there was a significant main effect of task, $F(10,90)=12.9$, $p<.001$. The interaction was not significant. These data are shown in Figure 9, where it becomes clear that the more difficult and ambiguous tasks (3, 5, 8 and 11) were successfully completed more often with FishCal. This was primarily because the user had the ability to get all the information across a particular time span into one view in order to answer the question. The Pocket PC user was confined to "pre-determined" views (day, week, month and year views), making some of the questions more difficult to answer. In addition, the "find" capability is not integrated into the Calendar application on the Pocket PC, so that if a retrieved calendar event needed to be scrutinized in context more closely, this required additional effort and short-term memory of the date to navigate to in the calendar itself. For the most difficult task (#11), no participant using the Pocket PC completed the task successfully.

Satisfaction and Preference. Users completed "ease of use" ratings on a scale of 1 to 5 (1=very difficult, 5=very easy) after every task. FishCal was rated higher across a majority of the tasks, especially the most difficult task (task 11—how many conflicts are there for the next 3 months?). FishCal was rated higher than the Pocket PC in terms of task by task satisfaction, on average, $F(1, 9)=4.37$, $p=.06$, a borderline significant result. The average task by task ratings are shown in Figure 10.

Usability Issues. Many usability issues were observed with this initial version of FishCal, as well as the Pocket PC calendar, and good design feedback was received from the participants about how best to move toward redesign. For the purposes of this paper, the focus will remain primarily on those issues pertaining to FishCal.

Many users disliked the view of the calendar when more than 6 months were shown at once, claiming that the

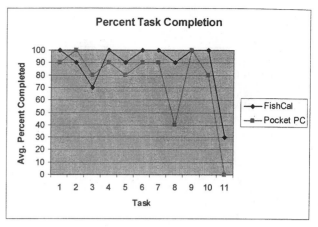

Figure 9: The percent of tasks completed by study participants for each task.

individual days were simply too small at that point to be useful. In addition, users wanted to see all 24 hours of a day's full view, but the prototype was limited in functionality to simply show a 9-5 view for this iteration of user testing. More importantly, a visualization of search results tried to show as many "hits" in the calendar as possible without making the view so crowded as to be useless. If the result a user was looking for was scrolled out of view (into the future), there was no visual indicator as such (the attribute mapped scrollbar that shows search results was added after the study was run.) Users voiced strong concerns about the readability of text, and being able to set their own default views according to their individual eyesight needs. Users also wanted more control about how their weeks were viewed (e.g., should the week start with Sunday or Monday?). Finally, users wanted better visual indicators of conflicts for both calendars, e.g., red highlights and/or a "conflicts" filter.

Participants completed an overall user satisfaction questionnaire after completing each set of tasks, and again at the end of the session. No significant differences emerged in this satisfaction data, though the Pocket PC was slightly more preferred overall (6 out of 11 participants chose the Pocket PC Calendar; one participant abstained and stated that she wanted features of both calendars in the ideal calendar; 4 participants chose FishCal). Most

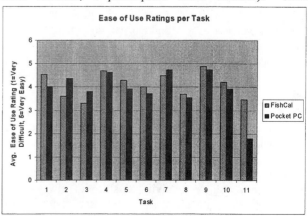

Figure 10: The ease of use rating for each task by study participants.

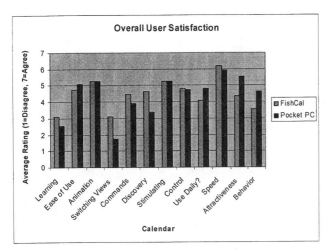

Figure 11: Overall user satisfaction.

participants said that they would prefer a combination of features from each of the two calendars during the post-session debriefing. The most often cited reason for choosing the Pocket PC calendar was the participants' familiarity with the Outlook XP calendar, which is similar in many ways. The overall satisfaction data is shown in Figure 11.

In summary, FishCal performed quite well despite its novelty and this being its first iteration of user testing. The responsivity to direct user manipulation, the ability to create custom views easily on the fly, its clear presentation of conflicts, and integrated search utility were all design innovations that participants thought would be valuable to any calendar used daily for planning and reviewing one's schedule. The Pocket PC calendar was seen by participants to be consistent with other MS calendar products, and this was seen as a plus. Several participants wanted to see a combination of the two calendars taking advantage of the good features of both in a final product.

MONDRIAN BACKGROUNDS

One last thing we did with FishCal was to experiment with making the display a little more fun. After visiting a modern art museum recently, the first author of this paper was inspired by several paintings he saw by Piet Mondrian (1872 – 1944).

We wrote a "Mondrian" mode for FishCal that takes a vectorized version of a Mondrian painting, maps it to the cells and edges of the current FishCal layout. The result is a fully functional Mondrian-style calendar interface. FishCal behaves normally, and the background painting moves and distorts as the user manipulates the calendar.

Admittedly, this is a distracting display that not many people are likely to use during most of their interactions. Nevertheless, we feel that as interface designers, it is important to move past pure function, and to also consider the form of our interfaces. While users are usually focused on efficiency and productivity, this is not always true. Sometimes, even the most serious of users have playful

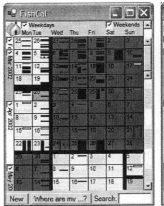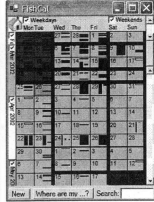

Figure 12: Two views of FishCal in "Mondrian" mode where paintings by Piet Mondrian are mapped to the FishCal display.

moments, and we want to encourage interface designers to support the full range of human activity and interests.

FUTURE WORK

There are several areas of future work for FishCal. From a technical standpoint, we have to integrate FishCal into the applications and devices that people are already using to make it easier for them to switch to an unusual tool for such an important task.

From a design standpoint, a number of usability issues that were found during the user study must be addressed. Naturally, there is also a long list of features that users have asked for that must be looked into as well, such as support for faster data entry. Understanding how these changes affect users, and keeping FishCal easy enough for novice users to feel comfortable with will be an ongoing and crucial challenge.

More studies must be run since it is likely that use of small hand-held devices with pens and touch-screens rather than mice and keyboards will affect usage patterns.

Finally, further design issues are likely to come up when the FishCal interface is applied to smaller devices (such as cell phones) and larger ones (such as desktop displays). While the basic paradigm scales nicely, there are likely to be specific details that need to be changed for different sized displays. Figure 13 shows what FishCal looks like on a large display. While FishCal currently runs as a standalone application on the desktop, we have started integrating it with Microsoft Outlook.

CONCLUSION

We are excited to have revived a useful application of fisheye technology. Given the encouraging results of our first user study, FishCal seems to be a viable competitor to traditional calendar interfaces. However, since managing one's calendar is so important, many users will be cautious about adopting non-traditional interfaces. Thus, one of the biggest remaining challenges is to refine FishCal so that it is appreciated by a broad spectrum of users.

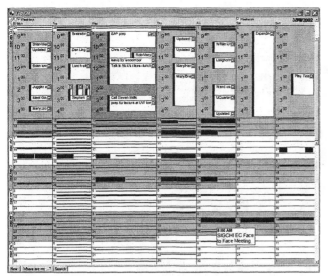

Figure 13: FishCal scaled up to 1024x768 pixels on a desktop computer. There is room to display an entire week with the full day representation, even while showing six months of the calendar.

ACKNOWLEDGEMENTS

We greatly appreciate the comments of our colleagues through the many revisions in the design of FishCal. We also appreciate the efforts of Neema Moraveji who has worked tirelessly to understand the intricacies of making FishCal work with Microsoft Outlook on the desktop. He has been among the first to create a complex .NET add-in for Outlook using MAPI and other undocumented APIs, running into a number of bugs along the way.

Finally, we thank Susan Wilhite for her help in running the user study, and her help along with Ben Shneiderman, Catherine Plaisant and Hilary Hutchinson for their comments on drafts of this paper.

The portion of this work performed at the University of Maryland was funded in part by a generous gift from Microsoft Research.

REFERENCES

[1] Inxight (2002). http://www.inxight.com.

[2] Baeza-Yates, R., & Ribeiro-Neto, B. (1999). *Modern Information Retrieval*. New York: ACM Press.

[3] Bederson, B. B. (2000). Fisheye Menus. *UIST 2000, ACM Symposium on User Interface Software and Technology, CHI Letters, 2*(2), pp. 217-225.

[4] Bederson, B. B., Meyer, J., & Good, L. (2000). Jazz: An Extensible Zoomable User Interface Graphics Toolkit in Java. *UIST 2000, ACM Symposium on User Interface Software and Technology, CHI Letters, 2*(2), pp. 171-180.

[5] Furnas, G. W. (1986). Generalized Fisheye Views. *In Proceedings of Human Factors in Computing Systems (CHI 86)* ACM Press, pp. 16-23.

[6] Furnas, G. W. (1991). *The Fisheye Calendar System.* Bellcore, Morristown, NJ.

[7] Hill, W., & Hollan, J. (1994). History-Enriched Digital Objects: Prototypes and Policy Issues. *The Information Society, 10*(2), pp. 139-145.

[8] Lamping, J., Rao, R., & Pirolli, P. (1995). A Focus+Context Technique Based on Hyperbolic Geometry for Visualizing Large Hierarchies. *In Proceedings of Human Factors in Computing Systems (CHI 95)* ACM Press, pp. 401-408.

[9] Mackinlay, J. D., Robertson, G. G., & DeLine, R. (1994). Developing Calendar Visualizers for the Information Visualizer. *In Proceedings of User Interface and Software Technology (UIST 94)* ACM Press, pp. 109-118.

[10] Plaisant, C., & Shneiderman, B. (1992). Scheduling Home Conrol Devices: Design Issues and Usability Evaluation of Four Touchscreen Interfaces. *International Journal for Man-Machine Studies, 36*, pp. 375-393.

[11] Rao, R., & Card, S. K. (1994). The Table Lens: Merging Graphical and Symbolic Representations in an Interactive Focus+Context Visualization for Tabular Information. *In Proceedings of Human Factors in Computing Systems (CHI 94)* ACM Press, pp. 318-322.

[12] Sarkar, M., & Brown, M. H. (1992). Graphical Fisheye Views of Graphs. *In Proceedings of Human Factors in Computing Systems (CHI 92)* ACM Press, pp. 83-91.

[13] Schaffer, D., Zuo, Z., Bartram, L., Dill, J., Dubs, S., Greenberg, S., & Roseman, M. (1997). Comparing Fisheye and Full-Zoom Techniques for Navigation of Hierarchically Clustered Networks. *In Proceedings of Graphics Interface (GI 97)* Canadian Information Processing Society, pp. 87-96.

[14] Spence, R., & Apperley, M. (1982). Data Base Navigation: an Office Environment for the Professional. *Behaviour & Information Technology, 1*(1), pp. 43-54.

[15] Staffan, B., Holmquist, L. E., Redström, J., Bretan, I., Danielsson, R., Karlgren, J., & Franzén, K. (1999). WEST: A Web Browser for Small Terminals. *UIST 99, ACM Symposium on User Interface Software and Technology, CHI Letters, 1*(1), pp. 187-196.

Interactively Exploring Hierarchical Clustering Results

The Hierarchical Clustering Explorer provides a dendrogram and color mosaic linked to two-dimensional scattergrams, a variety of visualization options, and dynamic query controls for use in genomic microarray data analysis.

Jinwook Seo
Ben Shneiderman
University
of Maryland,
College Park

Molecular biologists and geneticists seek to understand the function of genes, including the more than 6,000 genes in the yeast genome and the estimated 40,000 genes in the human genome. Recently developed for genome analysis, DNA microarrays—also known as gene arrays or gene chips—usually consist of glass or nylon substrates that measure 1 × 3 inches or smaller. These chips contain specific DNA gene samples spotted in an array by a robotic printing device. Researchers spread fluorescently labeled messenger RNA (mRNA) from an experimental condition onto the DNA gene samples in the array. This mRNA binds (hybridizes) strongly with some DNA gene samples and weakly with others. Finally, a laser scans the array and sensors detect the fluorescence levels, indicating the strength with which the sample expresses each gene.

Experimental conditions can include types of cancers, diseased organisms, or normal tissues. Microarray experiments typically have from 100 to 20,000 DNA gene samples and from two to 80 experimental conditions. These experiments produce data sets containing the profiles that include expression levels for each DNA gene sample under each experimental condition.

Researchers often use mathematical clustering methods to discover interesting patterns in these large data sets.[1-3] However, several limitations hinder biologists from recognizing important patterns, such as groups of genes with similar profiles, which might indicate similar function. The data volume makes it impossible to display a large microarray experiment—on one screen.

Researchers also struggle to understand the implications of a specific clustering result. Because the clusters occupy a high-dimensional space and involve so many experimental conditions, researchers find it difficult to view patterns on a 2D or even a 3D display. Further, data can contain hundreds of variously sized clusters, which makes spotting the meaningful clusters a challenge, especially when using a static display. Users need an efficient interactive visualization tool to facilitate pattern extraction from microarray data sets.

Hierarchical clustering has been shown to be effective in microarray data analysis for identifying genes with similar profiles and thus possibly with similar functions. This approach finds the pair of genes with the most similar expression profiles and iteratively builds a hierarchy by pairing genes (or existing clusters of genes) that are most similar.

This hierarchy is usually presented as a dendrogram—a branching diagram that represents the hierarchy of clusters based on degree of similarity. As Figure 1 shows, the binary trees lead down to the leaves, which typically appear at the bottom as a sequence of red and green tiles in a mosaic. Each tile represents an expression level for one of the experimental conditions. The distance of the binary tree's joining points from the root indicates the similarity of subtrees—highly similar nodes or subtrees have joining points farther from the root.

When viewing clusters, researchers use overviews to identify hot spots and understand the distribution of data. Hot spots are distinctive regions of interest that indicate high or low expression levels. However, screen resolution limitations hamper visualization of large data sets on commonly used displays, which measure only 1,600 pixels across. Even limiting each item to a single pixel means that for data sets larger than 1,600 points, the corresponding dendrogram and color mosaic do not fit onto a single screen.

HIERARCHICAL CLUSTERING EXPLORER

Adding interactive exploration features to hierarchical-clustering visualization tools is needed for the exploration of large data sets. To meet this need, we developed the Hierarchical Clustering Explorer (HCE), which integrates four interactive features:

- overview of the entire data set, coupled with a detail view so that high-level patterns and hot spots can be easily found and examined;
- dynamic query controls[4,5] that let users eliminate uninteresting clusters and show the interesting clusters more clearly;
- coordinated displays that forge a bidirectional link from the overview mosaic to two-dimensional scattergrams; and
- cluster comparisons to let researchers see how different algorithms cluster the genes.

Our work meshes with the current trend to take the substantial progress in data mining algorithms and give users more than just a printout. With novel information visualization techniques,[6] users can now control the processes and interact with the results. For example, recent decision tree packages let users manipulate incoming data and the rules generated, then examine the results with color- and size-coded visualizations. The capacity to interact and explore lets domain experts apply their knowledge by quickly testing hypotheses and performing exploratory data analysis. We hope to provide similar features to users of hierarchical clustering algorithms.

OVERVIEW IN A LIMITED SCREEN SPACE

To accommodate large data sets, HCE provides a compressed overview based on replacing dendrogram leaves with the average values of adjacent leaves. This view shows the entire hierarchy, at the cost of some lost detail at the leaves, as Figure 2 shows. A second overview allocates two pixels per item, but requires scrolling to view all items. In this scrolling overview, users can adjust the level of detail shown in the overview by moving the slider

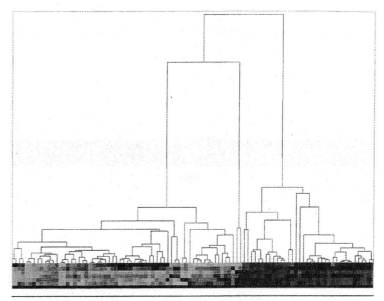

Figure 1. Sample dendrogram—a binary tree in which subtrees are each a cluster and the leaves are individual genes. The distance from the root to a subtree indicates the similarity of subtrees—highly similar nodes or subtrees have joining points farther from the root.

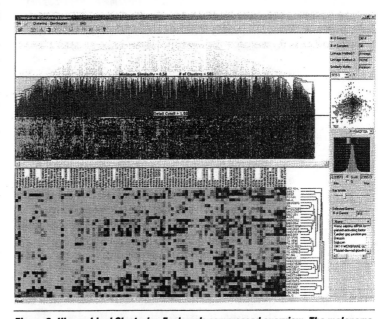

Figure 2. Hierarchical Clustering Explorer's compressed overview. The melanoma gene expression profile contains 3,614 genes and 38 experimental conditions. This view shows the entire hierarchy in one screen by replacing leaves with the average values of adjacent leaves. The detail information of a selected cluster, shown as a yellow highlight in the upper left, appears below the overview, together with the gene names and the other dendrogram at the lower right, by clustering the 38 experimental conditions.

to change item widths from two to 10 pixels. With either overview, users can click on a cluster and view the detailed information at the bottom of the display, which also includes the item names.

Researchers can examine the color mosaic to identify hot spots and understand the data distribution. In general, HCE displays a dendrogram with

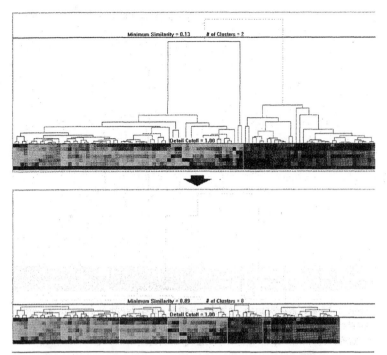

Figure 3. Using the minimum similarity bar. The bar's y coordinate determines the minimum similarity value. Users can drag the bar down to filter out items distant from a particular cluster. In this example, the minimum similarity values changed from 0.13 to 0.89 as the user separated two large clusters into eight small clusters.

a color mosaic at the leaves to show the underlying graphical pattern. The mosaic colors each tile on the basis of measured fluorescence ratio, which denotes the gene's expression level.[7]

The gene expression profile data consists of the ratio or relative amount of each specific gene in the two mRNA or DNA samples—corresponding to the normal and test conditions. Some data sets, including melanoma and yeast mutants, are more complicated. These data show expression levels for several mutants or cancer cell lines relative to a control condition. Researchers commonly use the log of ratio values and display the result using a 2D colored mosaic.

The HCE control panel, to the right of the dendrogram visualization in Figure 2, shows the data histogram by expression level. User controls help viewers see subtle differences in the ranges of interest. For skewed data distributions, this feature helps prevent large areas of all green or red, which would indicate all low or high gene expressions, respectively. Users can change the color mapping by adjusting the range of the color stripe displayed over the histogram. Because they can instantly see the result of a new color mapping on the display, users can identify the proper mapping for the data set.

DYNAMIC QUERY CONTROLS

Once users find a closely related group of genes, they can infer that an unknown gene clustered with a known gene may have a similar biological function to the known gene.[1] HCE users select a data set,

apply their desired clustering algorithm, then begin the process of understanding the output. First, they adjust the color mapping to get a clearer presentation of similarities and differences in expression levels. They can then study the main groupings—the two high-level clusters—which may not themselves be interesting but may combine interesting subclusters. For example, a set of 800 genes may be composed of 10 or 20 interesting subgroups, so looking at a simple two-group clustering does not reveal the relevant subgroups. Currently, static dendrogram users rely on their eyes and fingers to traverse the hierarchy and identify interesting clusters.

HCE provides a dynamic query on the dendrogram in the form of a filtering bar on which the y coordinate determines the minimum similarity value, as Figure 3 shows. As users pull down the minimum similarity bar, the mosaic display splits into two, three, four, or more groups. As the bar moves further down, the system removes the items far from a cluster, but users can still see the overall dendrogram structure. As the system removes more items, the tighter clusters can be seen more easily. Users' domain knowledge guides them in determining how far to go and how many clusters to examine.

To prevent users from losing global context during dynamic filtering, HCE maintains the entire dendrogram in the background. Users can see the position of a cluster in the original data set simply by clicking on the cluster, which causes it to highlight in yellow, as Figure 4 shows. Users can easily identify each cluster by the alternating blue and red lines in the dendrogram and by the one-pixel gaps placed between clusters. HCE highlights the selected cluster with a yellow rectangle, displays the corresponding gene names in the detailed color mosaic in the lower pane, and shows the other dendrogram that the clustering produces. When executed in a Windows 2000 environment run on at least a Pentium II, HCE processes all interactions and updates almost instantaneously for a moderate-sized data set of up to 4,000 genes in 40 experimental conditions.

Researchers need a sufficiently comprehensive overview as much as they need adequate detail. The overview reveals patterns across the entire data set, which guides users to the next step in their search. One generally accepted visualization scheme starts with an overview, then lets users dynamically access detail information.[6] Providing a data set overview while allowing detailed analysis of a selected part helps users place that part in a general context during their search.

However, too much detail can be a problem. If the set of 800 genes fits neatly into between six and

16 clusters, then seeing details of 800 genes below the cluster level can be confusing. To avoid this effect, HCE lets users represent highly similar items with the same coloring. Users can reduce the detail level by dragging the detail cutoff bar higher. The system renders all subtrees below the bar using the average of the leaf node values belonging to the subtree. Users can thus hide the detail below the bar to help them concentrate on more global structures.

Especially for a large dendrogram, the detail cutoff bar helps visually present cluster structures that satisfy the current minimum similarity level. Once users find an interesting cluster in the dendrogram, they can restore detail by dragging the detail cutoff bar downward.

COORDINATED DISPLAYS

The hierarchy shown in the dendrogram, and the linear presentation in the color mosaic, help reveal clusters that represent important patterns. However, they can hide some aspects of the data's high-dimensional nature. High-dimensional displays such as parallel coordinates[8] and other novel techniques[9] could be useful, but many users have difficulty comprehending these visualizations. Even three-dimensional displays can be problematic because of the disorientation brought on by the cognitive burden of navigation.[6]

The x and y axes of two-dimensional scattergrams limit them to two variables at a time, but most users can readily understand them. Further, without the distraction of operating 3D navigation controls, users can concentrate on finding patterns in the data.

HCE thus contains a scattergram view in which users first select any two dimensions for the x and y axes, representing two of the conditions. Then they use a rubber rectangle to sweep out an area on the scattergram, producing orange triangles that highlight the items in the scattergram and the related items in the overview color mosaic, as Figure 5 shows. Marking the selected items with similar shapes and orange color facilitates perceptual integration. Often, the neighboring items in the scattergram appear in the same cluster in the dendrogram, but items contained in other clusters can serve as important indicators to domain experts.

This coordination of displays is bidirectional. Users can click on the overview color mosaic to select a cluster, which highlights the related items in the scattergram. Seeing the distribution of items in the scattergram confirms the clustering and often produces intriguing patterns that invite further

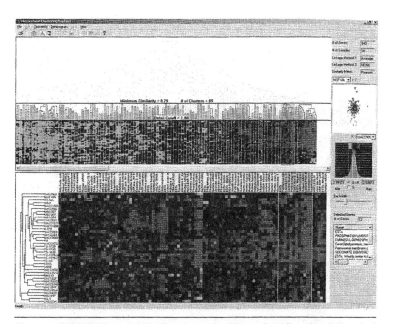

Figure 4. Highlighting a cluster. The alternating blue and red lines just below the minimum similarity bar and the one-pixel white gaps placed between clusters make it easy to identify each cluster. Users can select a cluster simply by clicking on it, which highlights it with a yellow rectangle. The system also highlights the corresponding gene names in the detailed color mosaic and displays the other dendrogram that clustering the data in the transposed dimension produces, as shown on the lower left side.

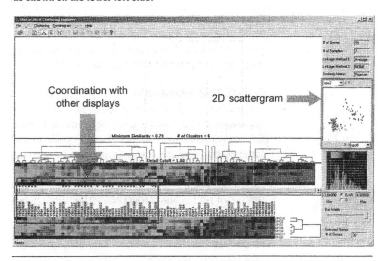

Figure 5. Two-dimensional scattergram and its coordination with other visualizations. Users can select a group of items by sweeping out a rectangular area on the scattergram. The Hierarchical Clustering Explorer simultaneously highlights the selected items in the scattergram, and the related items just below the overview color mosaic, with orange triangles.

investigation. Clusters are not always neatly circular—they often show up as odd-shaped bunches with some points embedded in nearby groups. These surprising patterns can be important to domain experts.

Coordinated windows have their problems, too. Scarce screen space must be allocated to two visualizations rather than one, and users must shift their attention back and forth rapidly. Minimizing the

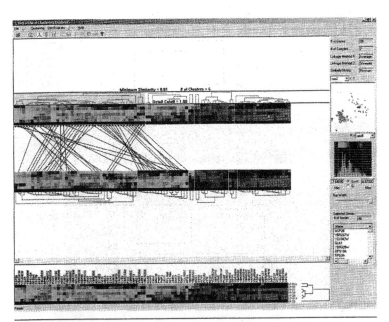

Figure 6. Cluster comparisons. Users can double-click on a specific cluster to see the mapping of each gene between the two different clustering results. The selected cluster will highlight in yellow, and lines from each item in that cluster will extend to their position in the second clustering result.

distance between visualizations, avoiding overlaps, and making rapid updates all contribute to improved human performance. After some exploration with a given scattergram, users often explore another pair of axes. Showing multiple scattergrams concurrently can help, but doing so exacerbates the screen-space management problem.

CLUSTER COMPARISONS

Often when performing a microarray data analysis, researchers know that groups of genes have similar functions. Similar genes should reside in the same cluster, and the researchers want to confirm that the hierarchical clustering algorithm finds these similar groups. They also want to see which unknown genes cluster together with known genes because this information may lead them to understand the unknown gene's function. Reviewing the clusters in the detail color mosaic helps uncover these relationships.

The lack of a perfect clustering algorithm complicates this process, however. Because molecular biologists and other researchers have different ways of computing distances between items in a multidimensional data set and the similarity values between groups of items, they need a mechanism to examine and compare two clustering results.

HCE users can view the results of two hierarchical clustering algorithms on the screen at once, as Figure 6 shows. Double-clicking on a specific cluster reveals the mapping of each gene between the two different clustering results. The selected cluster will highlight in yellow, and lines from each item in that cluster will extend to their position in the second clustering result. If some genes map to dif-

ferent clusters, users can examine the genes more carefully to understand what caused the difference.

Although crisscrossing lines can cause confusion, they enable users to compare competing clustering algorithms. Showing relationships between nonproximal items is a basic problem in information visualization research. Each of the three basic methods—color coding, blinking, and drawing lines—has problems. HCE already uses color coding heavily, and blinking would add distraction to an already complex display, so drawing lines provided our best alternative.

Our biology users, excited to have this capability, spent hours using an alternate clustering algorithm to probe the clusters to see which genes had switched into other clusters. Metrics for measuring similarity and tools to highlight important changes would further improve HCE.

Another possible verification method selects a subset of the experimental conditions and does the clustering on the reduced set. It is easier to verify the correctness of a clustering method in a low dimension that involves between two and four conditions than to do so in higher dimensions that involve between five and 80 conditions. HCE users can use a dialog box to select a subset of the conditions to take part in the clustering. The resulting color mosaic has a white space between the selected conditions and the others. Users can concentrate their inspection on the selected conditions and see the clusters more clearly in the scattergram. Using different conditions to redo the clustering helps users understand the relationships among conditions and identify which of them strongly affect the outcomes.

Microarrays, sequenced genomes, and the explosion of bioinformatics research have led to astonishing leaps in our understanding of molecular biology. To date, work in these fields has focused largely on algorithmic methods for processing and manipulating vast biological data sets. These efforts have made impressive gains, but additional help may be needed.

Future improvements will likely provide users with guidance in selecting the most appropriate algorithms and metrics for identifying meaningful clusters. Hybrid approaches that combine powerful algorithms with interactive visualization tools—such as those described in the "Visualization Software for Clustering in Bioinformatics" sidebar—will join the strengths of fast processors with the detailed understanding of domain experts. We

Visualization Software for Clustering in Bioinformatics

As computing became widespread, statistical analysts quickly developed the hierarchical clustering technique.[1] Extensions included alternative ways to compute

- distances between items in a multidimensional data set, such as Euclidean, correlation coefficient, and Manhattan distance; and
- the similarity values between groups of items—or linkage—such as average, complete, and single.

Meanwhile, presentation refinements focused on producing effective color printouts for publication.

TreeView

Software tools for hierarchical clustering have been developed in many disciplines and incorporated into a variety of software products. The widely used TreeView (http://www.pnas.org/cgi/content/full/95/25/14863), developed especially for genetic research, generates a dendrogram and color mosaic. Users can get an overview and detail view by selecting a contiguous region of the mosaic, which is magnified in a second view. Because TreeView's main purpose is to produce a good image in many formats for publications, the current version does not allow direct manipulation of the visualization.

GeneMaths

Developed by Applied Maths (http://www.applied-maths.com/ge/ge.htm), GeneMaths displays dendrograms for gene samples and experimental conditions on a single screen. Users can select a cluster by clicking a subtree's root. GeneMaths offers one of the fastest clustering algorithms and a visually appealing design. It shows only a few genes at a time, however, which makes it difficult to get an overview of the entire data set.

Spotfire DecisionSite

The Spotfire Array Explorer, now included in the DecisionSite product (http://www.spotfire.com/), does the hierarchical clustering, and users can view the entire green-black-red color mosaic or selected components. Users select a subtree in the dendrogram by clicking on the root of the subtree, or they can select a group of subtrees by selecting a similarity threshold. Users can coordinate scattergrams and bar charts with the dendrogram display to help understand the clustering results.

Expression Profiler

The European Bioinformatics Institute's Expression Profiler tool set does clustering, analysis, and visualization of gene expression and other genomic data (http://ep.ebi.ac.uk/). Among these tools, Epclust lets users do a hierarchical clustering with many different distance measures and linkage methods. When users select a dendrogram node, it shows detailed information about that node in a new window. Users can load their own data and try many kinds of hierarchical clustering algorithms. The institute's Web site also shows the great diversity in outcomes for different correlation-related distance metrics.

Clustering methods

In recent years, many clustering methods have been developed and implemented in software products. Popular methods include k-means clustering, which identifies starting points for a fixed number of clusters and then grows the region around the clusters. Recent work seeks to get beyond the limitation of spherical clusters[2] by using graph representations and developing clusters of arbitrary shapes, including interlocking geometries.[3] All clustering methods face validity challenges.[4] Does the clustering reflect known classifications? How many clusters are best? What should be done about outliers or intruders to clusters? What metrics could confirm or reject a perceived cluster?

References
1. S.C. Johnson, "Hierarchical Clustering Schemes," *Psychometrika 32*, 1967, pp. 241-254.
2. G. Karypis, E-H. Han, and V. Kumar, "Chameleon: A Hierarchical Clustering Algorithm Using Dynamic Modeling," *Computer*, Aug. 1999, pp. 68-75.
3. D. Harel and Y. Koren, "Clustering Spatial Data Using Random Walks," *Proc. 7th Int'l Conf. Knowledge Discovery and Data Mining* (KDD-2001), ACM Press, New York, 2001, pp. 281-286.
4. G.S. Davidson, B.N. Wylie, and K.W. Boyack, "Cluster Stability and the Use of Noise in Interpretation of Clustering," *Proc. IEEE Symp. Information Visualization* (InfoVis 01), IEEE CS Press, Los Alamitos, Calif., 2001, pp. 23-30.

need further research into bioinformatics visualization to develop the tools that will meet the upcoming genomic and proteomic challenges.

contributor to the software's development. Additional information about the HCE, more screen images, a user manual, and the software are available at http://www.cs.umd.edu/hcil/multi-cluster.

Acknowledgments
We thank Eric Baehrecke, Harry Hochheiser, Eser Kandogan, Yehuda Koren, Bill Ladd, and the anonymous reviewers for their thoughtful comments. Partial support for this project came from the University of Maryland Institute for Advanced Computer Studies. Bongshin Lee served as an early

References
1. M.B. Eisen et al., "Cluster Analysis and Display of Genome-Wide Expression Patterns," *Proc. Nat'l Academy of Sciences USA*, vol. 95, no. 25, 1998, pp. 14,863-14,868; http://www.pnas.org/cgi/content/full/95/25/14863.

2. M. Bitter et al., "Molecular Classification of Cutaneous Malignant Melanoma by Gene Expression Profiling," *Nature* vol. 406, 2000, pp. 536-540; http://www.nhgri.nih.gov/DIR/Microarray/selected _publications.html.

3. I. Hedenfalk et al., "Gene-Expression Profiles in Hereditary Breast Cancer," *The New Journal of Medicine*, vol. 344, no. 8, 2001, pp. 539-548; http://www. nhgri.nih.gov/DIR/Microarray/selected_publications. html.

4. B. Shneiderman, "Dynamic Queries for Visual Information Seeking," *IEEE Software*, Nov./Dec. 1994, pp. 70-77.

5. C. Williamson and B. Shneiderman, "The Dynamic HomeFinder: Evaluating Dynamic Queries in a Real-Estate Information Exploration System," *Proc. ACM Conf. on Research and Development in Information Retrieval* (SIGIR 92), ACM Press, New York, 1992, pp. 338-346.

6. S.K. Card, J.D. Mackinlay, and B. Shneiderman, *Readings in Information Visualization*, Morgan Kaufmann, San Francisco, 1999.

7. P.O. Brown and D. Botstein, "Exploring the New World of the Genome with DNA Microarrays," *Nature Genetics Supplement*, vol. 21, 1999, pp. 33-37; http://www.nature.com/ng/.

8. A. Inselberg and T. Avidan, "Classification and Visualization for High-Dimensional Data," *Proc. 6th Int'l Conf. Knowledge Discovery and Data Mining* (KDD 00), ACM Press, New York, 2000, pp. 370-374.

9. E. Kandogan, "Visualizing Multi-Dimensional Clusters, Trends, and Outliers Using Star Coordinates," *Proc. 7th Int'l Conf. Knowledge Discovery and Data Mining* (KDD 01), ACM Press, New York, 2001, pp. 107-116.

Jinwook Seo is a graduate research assistant in the Department of Computer Science & Human-Computer Interaction Laboratory, Institute for Advanced Computer Studies, University of Maryland, College Park. His research interests include information visualization and human-computer interaction. Seo received an MS in computer science from Seoul National University. Contact him at jinwook@cs.umd.edu.

Ben Shneiderman is a professor in the Department of Computer Science & Human-Computer Interaction Laboratory, Institute for Advanced Computer Studies, University of Maryland, College Park. His research interests include human-computer interaction and information visualization. Shneiderman received a PhD in computer science from the State University of New York, Stony Brook. Contact him at ben@cs.umd.edu.

Snap-Together Visualization:
A User Interface for Coordinating Visualizations via Relational Schemata

Chris North and Ben Shneiderman

Human-Computer Interaction Lab &
Department of Computer Science
University of Maryland, College Park, MD 20742 USA
http://www.cs.umd.edu/hcil

north@cs.umd.edu, ben@cs.umd.edu

ABSTRACT

Multiple coordinated visualizations enable users to rapidly explore complex information. However, users often need unforeseen combinations of coordinated visualizations that are appropriate for their data. Snap-Together Visualization enables data users to rapidly and dynamically mix and match visualizations and coordinations to construct custom exploration interfaces without programming. Snap's conceptual model is based on the relational database model. Users load relations into visualizations then coordinate them based on the relational joins between them. Users can create different types of coordinations such as: brushing, drill down, overview and detail view, and synchronized scrolling. Visualization developers can make their independent visualizations snap-able with a simple API.

Evaluation of Snap revealed benefits, cognitive issues, and usability concerns. Data savvy users were very capable and thrilled to rapidly construct powerful coordinated visualizations. A snapped overview and detail-view coordination improved user performance by 30-80%, depending on task.

Keywords

User interface, information visualization, multiple views, coordination, tight coupling, relational database, user study.

1. INTRODUCTION

In exploring information, two or more coordinated visualizations are often required to adequately display and browse the data [BWK00]. For example, Microsoft's Windows Explorer employs 3 visualizations to browse hierarchical file systems: an outliner view of the folders, a tabular view of the files in the selected folder, and a quick view of details of the selected file. In Spotfire [AW95], a commercial scatterplot visualization tool, selecting a record in the plot displays its attribute values in a web browser.

While these combinations of coordinated views are very helpful for some tasks, what about other combinations? What if, in Windows Explorer, users want to view their folders as a scatterplot instead of an outliner? Then they could quickly spot large old folders, and select them to see contents in the tabular view. If browsing a census database, why can't users click on a state in a Spotfire visualization to display its counties in a Treemap [Shn92] visualization? (See Figure 1)

These alternate combinations typically require custom development. In our lab, researchers stumble over this problem often, and must constantly re-implement coordinations between new unforeseen combinations of views. Unfortunately, this is a poor solution to the problem. Even with good component-based design, these hard-coded combinations are inflexible and difficult to construct.

A lightweight mechanism is needed to allow end-users to easily "snap" individual visualizations together into custom combinations. These combinations can exploit simple relationships in the data to support browsing. This must not be a toolkit that requires programming, but a user interface.

Specifically, users should be able to choose and coordinate visualizations so that: selecting or navigating to a data item in one view causes another view to select or navigate to corresponding items or load and display data related to that item. The "load" capability is particularly potent. For example, users can drill down through hierarchical levels in a database using different visualizations at each level, as in the states and counties example.

1.1 Related Work

Systems for information visualization via multiple coordinated views can be classified by their level of flexibility in data, views, and coordinations:

1. *Data*: users can load their own different data sets into the visualizations.
2. *Views*: users can choose different sets of visualizations as appropriate for the data.
3. *Coordinations*: users can choose different types of coordinations between pairs of views as needed for exploring or navigating relationships in the data.

Level 0 systems are not intended for flexibility. For example, Windows Explorer always displays the same data set (the hard drive file structure), with the same views and coordinations.

Most visualization tools are level 1, flexible for data but not views or coordinations. For example, the Treemap tool can load and display any hierarchical data set of users' choosing, but remains constant in its pair of views (the treemap view and the details pane) and the coordination between them (selecting a node in the treemap displays associated data in the details pane).

Level 2 systems include flexibility in choice of views. For example, systems such as Datadesk [Vel88], SAS JMP, EDV/

Advizor [EW95], and Spotfire, can display a single data table in many different types of views of users' choosing such as scatter plots or bar charts. All the views are coordinated for brushing-and-linking [BC87], allowing users to relate data points across views. When users paint points in one view, the system automatically paints the corresponding points in the other views in the same manner. This approach is useful for statistical data analysis.

In databases, Visage [RLS96] extends the brushing coordination to multiple tables by brushing across relational joins. However, users cannot establish a different type of coordination between two views with these systems.

Level 3 systems include flexibility in the coordinations between views. The Apple Dylan programming environment [DP95] lets users choose which pairs of views to coordinate. Users browse hierarchical object-oriented programs by splitting and linking frames so that selecting a folder in one frame displays its contents in the other frame (e.g. generalized Windows Explorer). Spreadsheet Visualization [CBR97] arranges many small 3D views as cells in a 2D grid. Then, users can select a whole row or column of views to synchronize their 3D navigation.

Devise [LRB97] allows users to select some different types of coordinations between views. Users can synchronize panning and zooming of plots with common axes, and establish set operations

between views so that data in one view can be combined with data in another.

In scientific visualization, data-flow systems such as ConMan [Hae88], AVS, and IBM Data Explorer, also employ a form of dynamic linking, but for a different purpose. Users link a variety of modules to create custom data processing and viewing pipelines, much like pipes on the Unix command line. Linkwinds [JBO94] extends the data-flow model for data filtering. Upstream widgets can filter the data that is displayed downstream.

Multiple coordinated visualization approaches have become an important and diverse topic. For a comprehensive review of many systems, see [Nor00].

2. SNAP TOGETHER VISUALIZATION

Snap-Together Visualization enables data users to rapidly and dynamically mix and match visualizations and coordinations to construct custom exploration interfaces without programming. Snap is flexible in data, views and coordinations. Snap focuses on (a) interconnecting the visualization tools created by researchers and developers in the field to (b) construct coordinated browsers for rapid exploration and navigation of data and relationships.

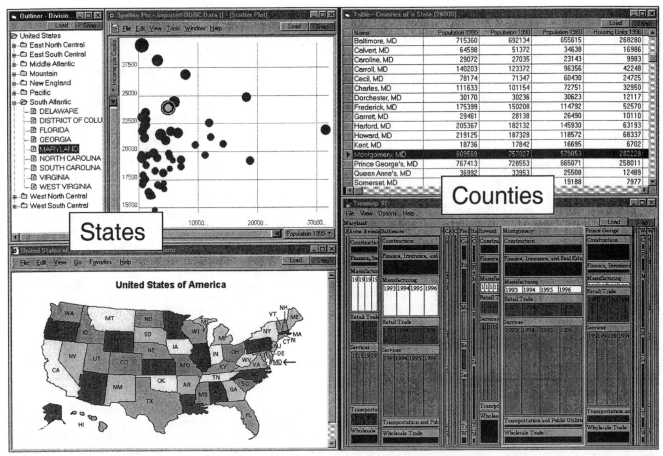

Figure 1: A coordinated visualization environment for exploring Census data of U.S. states and counties, dynamically constructed using Snap-Together Visualization. Users can explore states from nominal, geographic, and numeric perspectives using the outliner, map, and scatter plot. Selecting a state displays detailed county and industry information for that state in the table and Treemap on the right. Selecting Maryland on the map reveals a fairly high ranking in Per Capita Income in the plot, and immediately reveals in the Treemap that the Services industry in Montgomery County is responsible for a major portion of that income.

2.1 Model

Snap's conceptual model is based on the relational database model. To explore a database, users can construct interfaces composed of coordinated visualizations based on the database schema. Users load relations into visualizations then coordinate the visualizations based on the join relationships between their relations. There is a direct correspondence between relational concepts and Snap concepts: (see also Figure 2)

Relational Concept		Snap Concept
Relation	=	Visualization
Tuple	=	Item in a visualization
Primary key	=	Item ID
Join	=	Coordination

Hence, a graph of coordinations between visualizations corresponds to the graph of joins between the relations in the database schema diagram. This was inspired in part by RMM [ISB95], a system for constructing web site navigational structure from underlying relational databases. In RMM, database relationships correspond to hyperlinks, whereas, in Snap they correspond to coordinations.

2.2 Relations into Visualizations

When using Snap, users first load relations into visualizations. In Snap, a visualization displays a single relation. Generally, each tuple is depicted as an individual item in the visualization. For example, a scatter plot displays each tuple as a dot using 2 of its attributes as the coordinates. A table displays each tuple as a row.

Visualizations typically allow users to select a tuple, navigate to a tuple, or somehow indicate interest in a tuple. We will call these *primary-key actions*, because the tuples can be identified by their primary-key values. Users initiate the action via input, and the visualization responds with visual feedback. For example, users might *select* a tuple in a scatter plot by clicking on or mousing over the dot, and the system might respond by highlighting the dot in yellow. We extend this slightly to enable primary-key actions to be invoked programmatically. For example, the Snap system can also *select* a tuple in the scatter plot to cause the same yellow-highlight visual feedback as if the user had clicked on the dot. Hence, we can model primary-key actions as unary functions that take a tuple's primary-key value as argument: e.g. Viz.Select(<id>). Each visualization publishes the set of actions it supports to Snap.

Visualizations also have a *foreign-key* action that is managed by Snap: the *Load* action queries the visualization's original relation for tuples that are joined (by a foreign key) to the tuple given as the argument (primary key) and loads them into the visualization.

In the Snap user interface, users load relations into visualizations using the Snap Main Menu (Figure 3). It displays a menu of the tables and queries in the database and a menu of the available visualization tools.

2.3 Coordinating Visualizations

After loading relations into visualizations, users can then coordinate the visualizations ('snap them together'). When coordinating a pair of visualizations, users choose the actions in each view to coordinate. A Snap coordination tightly couples the actions between the two visualizations on tuples related by the join between the relations. Users coordinate the visualizations based on the join relationships between their relations. There are 4 cases:

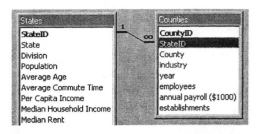

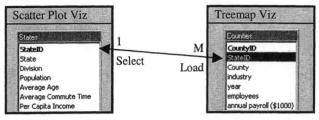

Figure 2: *Top*: A schema diagram for a database of Census information for U.S. states and counties (using Microsoft Access). *Bottom*: The data tables are loaded into visualizations and coordinated according to the join relationship between them. This example models a drill-down interface for States to Counties.

1. **One-to-One**: This is a primary-key to primary-key relationship. Users coordinate a primary-key action in one view to a primary-key action in the other. Then, when users invoke the former action on a tuple in the former view, the system automatically invokes the latter action on the corresponding tuple in the latter view, and vice versa.

This is often used to relate different perspectives on a single relation. For example, in Figure 1 different projections of the States table are displayed in a scatter plot and a map. Coordinating the select action in the plot to the select action in the map creates a brushing-and-linking coordination. When users click on Maryland in either view, it will also be highlighted in the other view.

2. **One-to-Many**: This is a primary-key to foreign-key relationship. Therefore, users can coordinate a primary-key action in the view on the *One* side of the relationship with a foreign-key action on the *Many* side. (See Figure 2)

This relationship indicates a hierarchical relationship between the relations. For example, in Figure 1 the States are displayed in a scatter plot and Counties in a Treemap. Coordinating the select

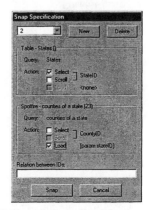

Figure 3: Snap's Main Menu (left) and Snap Specification dialog (right).

action in the plot to the Load action in the Treemap creates a drill-down coordination. Clicking on Maryland in the plot loads and displays only Maryland's counties in the Treemap.

3. **Many-to-Many**: This relationship is generally composed of 2 one-to-many relationships. Therefore, users employ the one-to-many case in the desired direction.

4. **No relationship**: If the schema has no relationship between the relations, then there is no coordination between the views. However, if users desire coordination based on more complex or indirect relationships, then it is probably possible to modify the schema with queries to specify the desired relationships with standard joins. Hence, with Snap, advanced coordination is simply a data-relationship representation problem rather than a custom user-interface programming problem.

Snap coordinations are bi-directional, so that either action triggers the other. Users can also chain coordinations end-to-end. For example, users can establish brushing across three views.

In the Snap user interface, users coordinate a pair of visualizations by dragging the Snap button from one to the other (similar to [JBO94] and [DP95]). This displays the Snap Specification dialog (Figure 3). Users select the primary-key or foreign-key actions for each visualization to coordinate. After construction, users can save a set of coordinated views as a group for later re-use or sharing.

2.4 Common Coordinations with Snap

With Snap, users can quickly construct common coordinations, such as:

- *Brushing-and-linking*: (Figure 1: outliner, plot, map)
Join relationship: one-to-one
Coordinated actions: select in Viz1 and select in Viz2
Usage: Selecting an item in one view highlights the corresponding item in another view. Typically used to identify like items when a set of items is displayed in different views for different contexts.

- *Overview and detail view*: (Figure 4)
Join relationship: one-to-one
Coordinated actions: select in Viz1 and scroll in Viz2
Usage: Selecting an item in the overview scrolls (or more generally navigates) the detail view to the details of that item. Items are represented visually smaller in the overview than in the detail view. Allows direct access to details, and provides context for details.

- *Drill-down*: (Figure 1, plot and table)
Join relationship: one-to-many
Coordinated actions: select in Viz1 and load in Viz2
Usage: Selecting an item in one view loads related items into another view. This enables exploring very large-scale data, by displaying aggregates in one view and the contents of a selected aggregate in another view [FNP99]. For example, 1 million 'stars' may be too much for single plot. Instead, break it down into 1000 'galaxies', each with 1000 stars. Then display one plot of galaxies and one of stars with a drill-down coordination between them.

- *Synchronized scrolling*:
Join relationship: one-to-one
Coordinated actions: scroll in Viz1 and scroll in Viz2
Usage: Scrolling through a list of tuples in one view also scrolls to corresponding items in another view.

- *Details on demand*:
Join relationship: one-to-one
Coordinated actions: select in Viz1 and load in Viz2
Usage: Selecting a tuple in a graphical view loads and displays additional details of that tuple in an adjacent textual view. This uses *load* as a primary-key action.

2.5 Snap API

Snap's model of a visualization is intentionally simple. Snap is designed to be *open* and easy for researchers and developers to make their independent visualizations snap-able. Therefore, Snap minimizes impact on visualization implementation. Snap uses a simple API (application programming interface) to communicate with visualizations. This is analogous to API's in modern window-management systems for utilities such as cut-and-paste or drag-and-drop. We propose the Snap API as a similar standard, that can be easily added to a visualization tool by its developers, enabling users to immediately snap it with many other visualizations. This greatly increases the value and usefulness of the tool for little cost.

To be snap-able, a visualization must support this API:

- Load method. When users load a relation into the visualization, Snap must be able to send the data to the visualization via file, memory, or ODBC, which ever is convenient for the tool. A translation routine may be needed to translate the relational structures to those used by the tool.

- Methods and events for each primary-key action: When users invoke actions, the visualization must fire an event to Snap. Likewise, Snap must be able to invoke actions in the visualization. The primary key value of the tuple acted on is passed. The visualization developer determines what actions it supports. *Select* is recommended as a minimum.

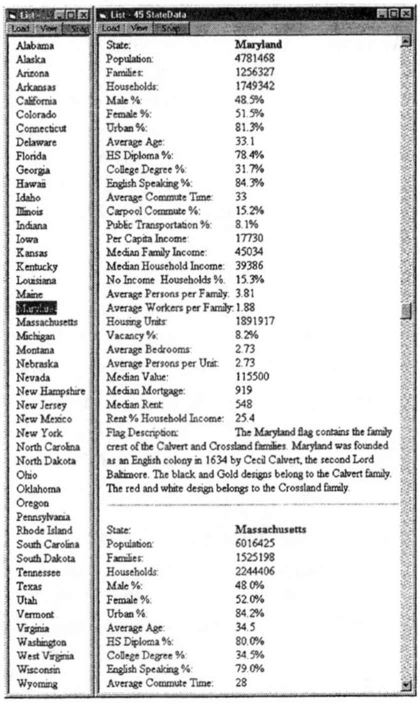

Figure 4: A textual interface for browsing Census information about the U.S. states. Using Snap, an overview is easily added to the scrolling report.

Other than these few hooks, visualizations remain independent software programs, maintaining their own data structures, etc. For example, Spotfire, a commercial software package, was integrated using its existing API and a 10-line VB wrapper to translate the communication calls.

Snap is currently implemented in the Windows platform. It uses COM for communication in the API and ODBC for database access. We have used Snap with MS Access and Oracle databases.

2.6 Scenarios

Snap is useful for rapidly constructing visualization interfaces for many different types of information. As the following examples illustrate, Snap makes information visualization capabilities immediately accessible and applicable for users.

2.6.1 Web-Site Logs

Recently, we have been interested in visualizing data from web logs [HS99], a database containing information about users' visits to a web site. In this scenario, we are interested in discovering what internet pages are referring many users, via hyperlinks, to specific pages on our lab's web site. A user interface to explore

this database can be quickly constructed with Snap (see Figure 5).

First, a user interface to explore specific pages on our site is needed. Opening a table of the pages and their URLs into an outliner displays a hierarchical view of the site. A web-browser visualization (MS Internet Explorer) can be used with URL data values to display the actual web pages. Snapping the outliner to a web-browser, by coordinating the outliner's select action to the browser's load action, creates a rapid site browser. Clicking on a page in the hierarchy displays the page in the browser (top of Figure 5).

Now, visualizations to discover referring pages are added. A table of hits to our site is aggregated by the referring and referenced pages and loaded into a scatter plot. There is a one-to-many relationship between the pages table and the hits table. The outliner is coordinated to the plot with select and load actions respectively. The plot displays the referrers as a histogram, with referrer name on the X-axis and number of hits referred on the Y-axis. Similar to the outliner, the plot is also coordinated to a web browser to view the actual referring pages (bottom of Figure 5).

Now, selecting our home page in the outliner displays that page in

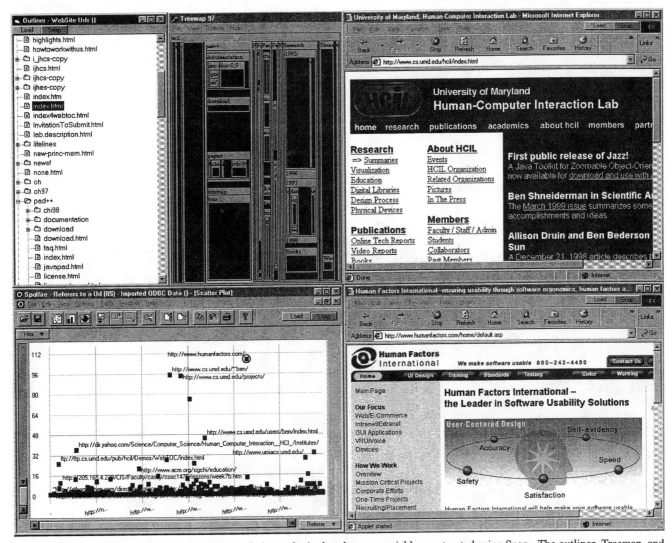

Figure 5: This visualization environment for exploring web-site log data was quickly constructed using Snap. The outliner, Treemap, and web browser at the top form a site browser for the HCIL web site. The scatter plot and browser at the bottom display pages that refer readers to the site. This example reveals that Human Factors International referred 110 readers to the HCIL home page that month.

the browser and the distribution of referrers to it in the plot. Selecting a high-ranking referrer in the plot reveals the Human Factors International page in the other browser. Exploring reveals other pages that send many users to our home page, including Ben Shneiderman's page, the Department page, and Yahoo's HCI institutes page. Selecting our Visible Human project page in the outliner shows nearly 1000 hits from the National Library of Medicine page. Selecting to open this page indeed reveals a prominent link to our page. Naturally, lab members explored to discover referrer patterns to their personal pages.

2.6.2 Photo Libraries

For a research project on user interfaces for browsing personal photo libraries, we have been using Snap to explore many interface variations. Our lab has accumulated a database of scanned photos of lab members and activities spanning 10 years. It includes annotations such as members' names, dates, locations, and other information.

In Figure 6, a thumbnail browser shows a collection of a few hundred photos. The scatter plot displays a time line of the photos, with date on the X-axis and members' names on the Y. Vertical stripes of dots represent group events, pictures of many members on the same date. The large stripe in the middle is many

photos from the 1992 Open House. Selecting a photo from winter '89 displays the full-size photo from a ski trip, a list of names of members in the photo, and details of photo attributes.

Other interface variations include locating photos by members' names or locations, selecting a person in a photo to find other pictures of that person, etc.

3. EMPIRICAL EVALUATION

To determine if Snap's model and user interface are usable and beneficial, it is important to empirically evaluate the two phases of using Snap:

1. **Construction**: First, can users successfully construct coordinated exploration interfaces by snapping visualizations together?
2. **Operation**: Second, can users then operate the coordinated interfaces constructed with Snap to explore information beneficially?

This section presents a summary of these two studies. For more details, see [Nor00]. Little work has been done to evaluate systems for coordination. [CS94] and [SSS86] indicate performance advantages at operation level for the drill-down type of coordination (e.g. level 1 systems). We are not aware of studies on coordination construction (level 3 systems).

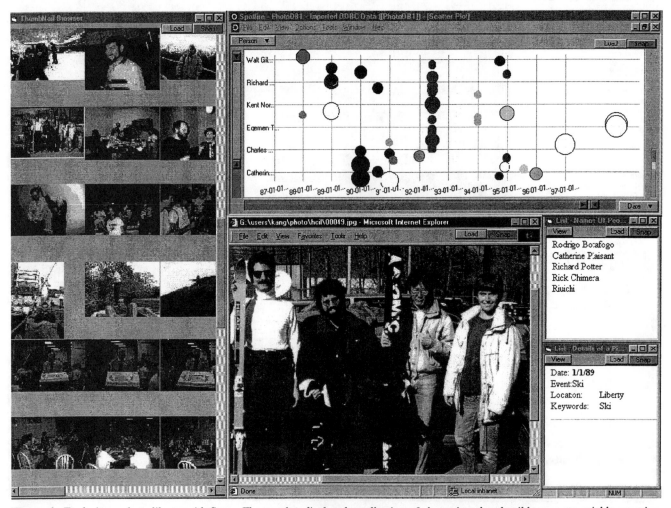

Figure 6: Exploring a photo library with Snap. The user has displayed a collection of photos in a thumbnail browser to quickly overview many photos and in a scatter plot to see trends on a time line. These are coordinated to a web browser to display the full-resolution picture of a photo when selected. Additional text views display names of people in the picture and other details.

3.1 Usability of Coordination Construction

The goal of the first study is to determine how difficult it is for relatively novice users to learn Snap and construct coordinated interfaces, in terms of success rate and time to completion. This study reveals cognitive trouble spots in the construction process and identifies potential Snap user interface improvements.

3.1.1 Procedure

We worked with 6 subjects on a one-on-one basis. Three of the subjects were data analysts or statisticians at the U.S. Bureau of the Census. The other three were programmers.

Subjects were first trained on using Snap-Together Visualization. At the time of this study, the Snap user interface did not have capability for users to easily create projections, join queries, etc. Hence, subjects were also trained on using Microsoft Access to manipulate the database, schema and queries.

Testing consisted of 3 exercises. Subjects were asked to construct coordinated exploration interfaces according to three provided specifications: two were printed screenshots (a simple one identical to Figure 4, and a more difficult one similar to Figure 1), and one a description of the task that the constructed interface should support. The database consisted of census data of the U.S. states and counties.

3.1.2 Results

Overall, subjects easily grasped the concept of coordinating views. All the subjects completed the training in 30-45 minutes, and were able to complete all three exercises. They accomplished each exercise in 2-15 minutes, depending on the difficulty. Much of this time was absorbed by window management (see [KS97] for a review of potential solutions) and Access. Subjects had very little previous experience with Access and database concepts.

As to subjects' general reaction to Snap-Together Visualization, we were impressed by their level of excitement. The subjects were quick to learn the concepts and usage, and were very capable to construct their own coordinated interfaces. Several stated that they had a gratifying sense of satisfaction and power in being able to both (a) so quickly snap powerful exploration environments together, and (b) with just a single click effect exploration across several visualizations and see the many parts operate as a whole. They commented that it made exploration seem effortless, especially in comparison to standard tools.

To our surprise, the data analysts performed better than the programmers did. During the training, they were already trying variations of snaps, exploring the data, and pointing out various anomalies in the data. After finishing the exercises, these subjects each stayed for an additional hour to play. All the Census subjects expressed desire to use Snap-Together tools in their work. In fact, a collaborative effort is underway.

An important result was the creativity and variation evident in the subjects' solutions to the 3rd exercise. Subjects designed interfaces that made sense to their perspective on the data. They used a mixture of visualizations and coordinations. For example, while one subject used scatterplots, another subject augmented this design with lists for state and county names. The subject stated that this would help to see which state and county was currently selected in the scatterplots, and allow for accessing states by name. Another subject who preferred to see the numerical values used tabular visualizations with sorting.

3.1.3 User Interface

Understanding the basic underlying model of Snap was critical. However, the Snap user interface apparently did not reflect this model well due to disparity between the schema management (Access), the Snap main menu, and the Snap Specification dialog. For example, to add a projection of a table as an overview visualization to an interface, users had to generate the query in Access, load it into a visualization using the Snap main menu, and coordinate it to other views using the Snap Specification dialog. In addition, users sometimes forgot which visualizations were currently coordinated. A 'debug' mode to show how coordination propagates between visualizations would have been helpful.

These problems might be solved by redesigning the Snap interface around a single direct-manipulation visual overview that merged the schema diagram with a visualization-coordination graph diagram. This diagram could be used for schema management, simple querying and loading into visualizations, and coordination specification and 'debugging'. In addition, the need to create queries by hand could be eliminated for common simple situations. For example, for projections users could simply select the desired attributes and drag them directly to a visualization. Snap could also generate queries for foreign-key loads automatically. These enhancements would likely reduce users' training and construction time significantly. We are already working on this.

3.2 Usability of Coordination Operation

The goal of the second study is to measure the magnitude of the benefit of using views coordinated with Snap over alternatives: independent views or a single view. Benefit is measured in terms of user task times and subjective satisfaction for browsing large information spaces. This study reveals whether the visual feedback across views is distracting or disorienting for users.

While there are many possibilities, this study examines an overview-and-detail-view coordination constructed with Snap. If there is a benefit over the single view, then what is the important factor causing improved performance? Is it (a) the information displayed in the overview, or (b) the coordination between the overview and detail view?

3.2.1 Procedure

18 subjects used 3 different interfaces for browsing Census state population statistics. They performed 9 different browsing tasks, ranging from easy to difficult. The 3 interfaces were: (similar to Figure 4)

1. *Detail-Only*: Scrolling view of all the states' data.
2. *Independent-Views*: Adds the overview not coordinated, to see if overview or coordination is more important.
3. *Snapped-Views*: Adds coordination using Snap. This is the same user interface from the 1st study, 1st exercise.

3.2.2 Results

On average, Snapped-Views achieves an 80% speedup over Detail-Only for easy tasks and 30-50% for difficult tasks, both significant. The Independent-Views interface results in a nearly binary pattern. For easy tasks, where only information in the overview is needed to accomplish the task, Independent-Views performs on par with Snapped-Views. Whereas, in difficult tasks, where subjects needed to access the details, Independent-Views is as bad as Detail-Only. Hence, when access to details is important, coordination is critical.

In fact, Snapped-View's performance times for lookup tasks are in the same extremely fast range as overview-only tasks. Whereas, Independent-View's times drop to Detail-Only level performance. When looking up details, perhaps the most common task, coordination especially excels.

In subjective satisfaction, Snapped-Views gains rankings twice as high (significant) as Detail-Only and Independent-Views. Independent-Views average 20% higher than Detail-Only. Users reported they were not distracted by the coordination, but in fact expected that functionality. We believe these results indicate that the Snap capability is indeed beneficial, wanted, and sorely needed.

3.3 Combined Analysis

Together, these studies indicate the breakpoint at which time savings during data exploration surpass interface construction time. The 2nd study used the same interface constructed in the 1st study. The time cost of constructing the interface was 2-5 minutes, while it saved 0.5-1.5 minutes over the Detail-Only interface for more difficult tasks. Hence, after a few tasks, users are already reaping savings with snapping their own interface. Of course, it is difficult to factor in learning time and effects of sharing snapped interfaces. Nevertheless, this simple analysis is revealing. Customized information visualization is within the grasp of novice users.

4. CONCLUSIONS and FUTURE WORK

Snap-Together Visualization introduces four novel contributions:

(a) *Conceptual model*: a relational model for visualization coordination, based on coupling actions across joins.

(b) *User interface*: a user interface that enables end users to construct custom coordinated visualization environments, based on the conceptual model, allowing flexibility in data, views, and coordinations.

(c) *Architecture*: an open architecture based on a simple API that enables visualization developers to easily snap-enable their visualizations.

(d) *Evaluation*: data savvy users were very capable at constructing coordinated visualization environments of their own using the model and interface. Users of a constructed interface obtained 30-80% performance speedup for many browsing tasks.

Snap has already proven useful in a variety of applications, including: West Group case law, Census Bureau and GIS data analysis, Maryland State Highway Administration accident data, research projects on personal photo libraries, web logs, mailing lists and technical-report databases.

Continued research is needed to explore alternate user interfaces for coordination overviews, strategies for aggregation and history keeping, multi-way coordination, window management, coordination guidelines, and more.

5. ACKNOWLEDGMENTS

This research was partially supported by funding from West Group and the U.S. Bureau of the Census.

6. REFERENCES

[AW95] Ahlberg, C., Wistrand, E., "IVEE: An Information Visualization and Exploration Environment", *Proc. IEEE Information Visualization '95*, pp. 66-73, (1995).

[BWK00] Baldonado, M., Woodruff, A., Kuchinsky, A., "Guidelines for using multiple views in information visualization", *Proc. ACM Advanced Visual Interfaces '00*, (May 2000).

[BC87] Becker, R., Cleveland, W., "Brushing scatterplots", *Technometrics*, 29(2), pp. 127-142, (1987).

[CBR97] Chi, E. H., Barry, P., Riedl, J., Konstan, J., "A spreadsheet approach to information visualization", *Proc. IEEE Information Visualization '97*, pp. 17-24, (1997).

[CS94] Chimera, R., Shneiderman B., "An exploratory evaluation of three interfaces for browsing large hierarchical tables of contents", *ACM Transactions on Information Systems*, 12(4), pp. 383-406, (Oct. 94).

[DP95] Dumas, J., Parsons, P., "Discovering the way programmers think about new programming environments", *Communications of the ACM*, 38(6), pp. 45-56, (June 1995).

[EW95] Eick, S., Wills, G., "High Interaction Graphics", *Euro. Journal of Operations Research*, #81, pp. 445-459, (1995).

[FNP99] Fredrikson, A., North, C., Plaisant, C., Shneiderman, B., "Temporal, geographical and categorical aggregations viewed through coordinated displays", *Proc. ACM CIKM '99 Workshop on New Paradigms in Info Vis and Manip.*, (1999).

[Hae88] Haeberli, P., "ConMan: a visual programming language for interactive graphics", *Proc. ACM SigGraph '88*, pp. 103-111, (1988).

[HS99] Hochheiser, H., Shneiderman, B., "Understanding patterns of user visits to web sites: interactive starfield visualizations of WWW log data", *Proceedings ASIS '99 Annual Conference*, (1999).

[ISB95] Isakowitz, T., Stohr, E., Balasubramanian, P., "RMM: a methodology for structured hypermedia design", *Communications of the ACM*, 38(8), pp. 34-44, (August 1995).

[JBO94] Jacobson, A., Berkin, A., Orton, M., "LinkWinds: interactive scientific data analysis and visualization", *Communications of the ACM*, 37(4), pp. 43-52, (April 1994).

[KS97] Kandogan, E., Shneiderman, B., "Elastic Windows: evaluation of multi-window operations", *Proc. ACM CHI'97*, pp. 250-257, (March 1997).

[LRB97] Livny, M., Ramakrishnan, R., Beyer, K., Chen, G., Donjerkovic, D., Lawande, S., Myllymaki, J., Wenger, K., "DEVise: integrated querying and visual exploration of large datasets", *Proc. ACM SIGMOD'97*, pp. 301-312, (1997).

[Nor00] North, C., "Snap-Together Visualization", University of Maryland, Computer Science Dept. Doctoral Dissertation, (Spring 2000, forthcoming).

[RLS96] Roth, S., Lucas, P., Senn, J., Gomberg, C., Burks, M., Stroffolino, P., Kolojejchick, J., Dunmire, C., "Visage: a user interface environment for exploring information", *Proc. Information Visualization*, IEEE, pp. 3-12, (October 1996).

[Shn92] Shneiderman, B. "Tree visualization with treemaps: a 2-d space-filling approach", *ACM Transactions on Graphics*, 11(1), pp. 92-99, (Jan. 1992).

[SSS86] Shneiderman, B., Shafer, P., Simon, R., Weldon, L., "Display strategies for program browsing: concepts and an experiment", *IEEE Software*, 3(3), pp. 7-15, (March 1986).

[Vel88] Velleman, P., *The Datadesk Handbook*, Odesta Corp., (1988).

Chapter 8

Theories for Understanding Information Visualization

Theories are the compass of the intellect.

Jennifer Preece (2001)

Developing theories is a crucial part of an academic's work. Researchers must call upon refined understandings and generalizations that come from careful observations, thoughtful analyses, and replicable controlled experiments. The typical goals of theories are to enable practitioners and researchers to:

- Describe objects and actions in a consistent and clear manner to enable cooperation
- Explain processes to support education and training
- Predict performance in normal and novel situations so as to increase the chances of success
- Prescribe guidelines, recommend best practices, and caution about dangers
- Generate novel ideas to improve research and practice

The researcher's understandings and generalizations range from informal concepts, themes, patterns, or ideas, to more formal frameworks, taxonomies, models, and principles. These may also be separated into qualitative and quantitative, as well as ordered by levels of granularity. Another spectrum is the degree of confidence, ranging from the uncertain hypotheses, conjectures, and assumptions to reliable laws, rules, and formulas.

Sometimes the broader understandings and generalizations may be described as frameworks, often presented in compact tables or charts that informally describe one, two, or more variables and their interactions. More formalized models may have process descriptions (as in Don Norman's (1993) seven stages model of interaction or in weather models) or executable simulations whose results are confirmable with reality (as in ACT-R, a unified theory of cognition that takes the form of a computer simulation, or in air-traffic simulations). Sometimes models may be mathematically precise and have predictive power that entitles them to be called laws (*e.g.*, Newton's laws of motion). A basic or fundamental insight might be honored by the term *theory*, as in the theory of relativity.

Mature scientific domains, such as physics and chemistry, are more likely to have rigorous quantitative laws and formulas, whereas newer disciplines, such as sociology or psychology, are more likely to have qualitative frameworks and models. Those who aspire to rigor prefer to use the language of theory and appreciate mathematical formulations. Those who appreciate the complexity of disciplines that study human performance are often more cautious and use the language of framework and model. They may make worthwhile contributions by providing taxonomies and guiding principles, as well as quantitative laws where possible.

In the emerging discipline of human–computer interaction research, the quest for understandings and generalizations has produced a broad range of theories that support explanation and prediction. The widely used framework for computer-supported collaborative work is a simple 2 × 2 table that separates collaborations that are same time or not (synchronous or asynchronous) from same place or not. This framework makes clear the similarity between online chat and telephones, as well as the distinctions between listservs and video-conferencing. It is clear, understandable, qualitative, and very helpful in sorting out the efficacy of proposed designs as well as guiding research and development.

More formal and quantitative laws have emerged to effectively guide human–computer interaction research, most notably Fitts's law, which predicts pointing times for objects based on the distance to be moved and the target object size (stopping distance). Hundreds of studies have tested variations on this law and influenced the design of input devices and strategies. Even a brief investigation of the language of theories reveals its confusion and inconsistent application across disciplines, countries, and cultures. Without going too deeply into a theory of theories, let's at least sort out some of the goals.

Theories may be primarily descriptive and explanatory, in that they clarify terminology about objects and actions, identify key concepts or variables, and thereby guide further inquiry and education. They may be predictive, in that they enable practitioners to make decisions about designs for products and services. They may be prescriptive, in that they convey guidance for decision making in design by recording best practices, common rules of thumb, or known dangers. Finally, they may be generative, in that they enable practitioners to create, invent, or discover something new. Of course, most theories have multiple roles. A familiar example of a generative theory is the periodic table of elements, which guided chemists to find new elements.

The HCIL has regularly contributed to developing these understandings and generalizations in human–computer interaction, starting with early work that characterized and validated the principles of direct manipulation. The HCIL's research is often theory driven and guided by hypothesis testing, with a healthy balance of qualitative ethnographic observation and quantitative controlled experimentation (95-07, 99-23, 2000-02). Other research methods such as interviews, surveys, and automated logging have been used regularly as well (95-09, 96-07, 98-04).

In the newer domain of information visualization, qualitative frameworks have already helped to sort out the remarkably rich variety of innovations from practitioners, and guide new developments. Sometimes the organizing framework helps by just stabilizing terminology and helping designers carry on meaningful discussions. These were the goals of our early paper on image browsers (94-02 [8.1]) that has broadly influenced design discussions by providing a clear set of concepts and terms, such as *overview, detail view, field of view box,* and *zoom factor*. That work cataloged a wide variety of existing implementations (descriptive), showing combinations that fail or succeed (explanatory), and suggesting novel possibilities (generative).

As the outpouring of novel information visualizations accelerated, the need to find order grew. Misleading comparisons were hampering research progress, and exaggerated claims were discouraging commercial adoption.

Some researchers had already made attempts at theories for information visualization. Pirolli and Card's writings on information foraging, Mackinlay's thesis on automatic design, and Casner's paper on task-analytic approaches are good early sources. However, we might see 1996 as a turning point. In April, at the CHI 96 conference in Vancouver, Lisa

Tweedie presented the work of Spence's group, which offered a provocative theoretical perspective. Then in May in Gubbio, Italy, at the Advanced Visual Interfaces conference (see Favorite Papers from Our Colleagues at the end of this chapter), Stu Card delivered the opening keynote. His elaboration of Bertin's retinal properties registered in a fresh way with me (Ben Shneiderman). The idea of describing the visualizations was important, but by the time I had to deliver my closing keynote two days later, I had formulated a descriptive framework based more on usage. I prepared a slide labeled "Gubbio Grid." This matrix had seven types down the side and five tasks across the top (the later versions had seven tasks).

By June, I had changed some of the terms to make a more coherent presentation and decided that this was a good organizing framework for my September keynote of the IEEE Visual Languages conference in Boulder, Colorado. As I formulated and built the case for this descriptive framework, I began to realize that this might make a good paper for the conference. I was in London at the time and emailed the conference organizers, Margaret Burnett and Wayne Citrin, to see if I could include such a paper in the proceedings. I reasoned that this paper would be a good conference keynote paper, but that it would be tough to get such a speculative piece accepted for a refereed journal or conference. Burnett informed me that the proceedings were already in production, but that if I got a clean version of the paper to the publisher within 36 hours, they would include it at the very end of the proceedings. This pushed me into an intense effort to clean things up, but the outcome was still in doubt because I was about to fly home to Washington, D.C. Just before boarding, I emailed the draft to Margaret for comments, and picked up her suggestions when I landed. The cleaned version was delivered in time and the resulting paper, "The Eyes Have It!" (96-13 [8.2]) has come to be widely referenced.

The task and data type taxonomies in that paper were meant to be descriptive and explanatory rather than predictive or prescriptive. However, "The Eyes Have It" also included a now well-known prescriptive principle for designers: *overview first, zoom and filter, then details-on-demand*.

The task and data type (one-, two-, three-, multi-dimensional, temporal, hierarchical, network) taxonomies were intended to help developers recognize what they were doing and enable fair comparisons among similar systems. Its immediate use was in arranging a reasonable course structure for a new seminar in information visualization so that students (and the instructor) would have a clear model of what topics were to be covered each week (*www.otal.umd.edu/Olive*). An unexpected payoff was the generative nature of these taxonomies because they revealed opportunities for new designs and improvements to existing systems.

The importance of generative theories has grown as the HCIL's work has moved more clearly into creativity support. The role of information visualization is strong in creative endeavors in many fields, presumably because visual presentations strongly support intuition, extrapolation, and discovery. The genex framework (97-21) and its refinements (99-01) suggested that creativity support tools had to support the iterative processes of collect-relate-create-donate.

Though it seems clear from the perspective of human–computer interaction researchers that advanced information visualization will play a key role in supporting creativity (99-16 [8.3]), some researchers are not convinced. There remain large numbers of respected researchers in areas such as data mining that give minimal attention to information visualization (2001-16 [8.4]). They believe that refined algorithms will be sufficient to discover interesting patterns in complex data sets. When pressed, they often acknowledge the role of visualization, but usually in presenting results rather than in discovering them. There are hopeful signs that the narrow bridge between data mining and information visualization will be expanded in the coming years.

The devotion of many computing researchers to purely algorithmic approaches to problem solving is a key issue for the future of human–computer interaction and information visualization research. These researchers are engrossed with novel ideas of statistical pattern discovery, genetic and neural net algorithms, and machine learning, so they are not drawn to the challenge of user interface design. This central distinction between machine-centered and user-centered thinking remains a vital topic that will determine research priorities for decades to come.

It is possible that improved theories will have a role in shaping this discussion, especially if accurate predictive theories can accelerate development of effective information visualizations and compelling generative theories can guide innovation. At the same time, meaningful prescriptive theories could facilitate development of improved interfaces, while comprehensible descriptive and explanatory theories could speed education and encourage rapid commercial product adoption.

FAVORITE PAPERS FROM OUR COLLEAGUES

Pirolli, P., Card, S., Information Foraging in Information Access Environments, *Proc. ACM CH '95 Conference on Human Factors in Computing Systems*, ACM, New York (1995), 51–58.

Casner, S. M., A Task-Analytic Approach to the Automated Design of Information Graphic Presentations, *ACM Transactions on Graphics* 10, 2 (1991), 111–151.

Mackinlay, J., *Automatic Design of Graphical Presentations*, PhD dissertation, Computer Science, Stanford University (1986).

Tweedie, L., Spence, R., Dawkes, H., Su, H., Externalising Abstract Mathematical Models, *Proc. ACM CHI '96 Conference: Human Factors in Computing Systems*, ACM, New York (1996), 406–412.

BIBLIOGRAPHY

Norman, D., *Things That Make Us Smart: Defending Human Attributes in the Age of the Machine*, Perseus Publishing (1993).

Image-Browser Taxonomy and Guidelines for Designers

CATHERINE PLAISANT, DAVID CARR, *and* BEN SHNEIDERMAN
University of Maryland

◆ *In many applications users must browse large images. Most designers merely use two one-dimensional scroll bars or ad hoc designs for two-dimensional scroll bars. However, the complexity of two-dimensional browsing suggests that more careful analysis, design, and evaluation might lead to significant improvements.*

The one-dimensional scroll bar is a well-established fixture in contemporary graphical user interfaces. For example, in word processors one-dimensional scroll bars help users navigate long documents. Without a scroll bar users must remember their position and use some command to jump within the document (for example, "173,193p" to display lines 173 through 193). Scroll bars let users move through the document incrementally and by jumps, and they indicate the current position of the screen. This visual feedback probably reduces memory and cognitive load.

Although all one-dimensional scroll bars have a common core functionality, their individual features and operation differ substantially. But because users

quickly accommodate these differences, research on scroll bars is limited.[1-2]

Building on user familiarity with one-dimensional scroll bars, many designers simply use two one-dimensional scroll bars when the application requires independent control over the horizontal and vertical directions, as in panning a map. This is effective if users frequently move in a single direction by small increments of less than one screen.

But in many cases this solution is inadequate:

♦ In painting and drawing programs, the image is often much larger than a screen, redisplay times are long, overviews are needed,[3] zooming is desirable, diagonal panning is required, or multiple detailed views are needed.

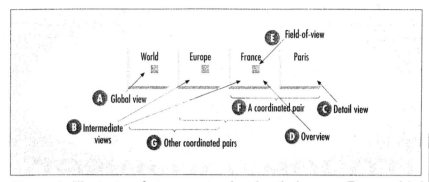

Figure 1. Illustration of some terms used to describe browsers. First, a global view (A) gives a view of the entire universe that can be explored. One purpose of the global view is to give a sense of what information will be in the image — and what is not. For example, a world atlas global view might show a map of the earth, telling the user that this "world" doesn't include the moon or the galaxy. An intermediate view (B) of the world map would include maps of Europe and France. The detailed view (C), also called the local view, shows a part of an overview (D), usually magnified. The level of detail required depends on the task to be performed. The zooming factor describes the level of magnification between two views. The field-of-view (E) indicates on the overview the location and shape of the coordinated detailed view. Taken together, an overview and detailed view are called a coordinated pair (F). In a coordinated pair, both the overview and detail are shown, letting users keep a sense of context while they view detail. Several coordinated pairs can provide a hierarchy of views, in which the detailed view of one pair becomes the overview of another pair (G). The global view is often used as an overview in a coordinated pair. But if the maximum zooming factor is too large, an intermediate view is called for.

(See Figure 1 for short definitions of some key terms we use in this article.)

♦ In geographic information systems, users browsing a world map may want to see detailed views of a country, county, or city. The world map provides a helpful — possibly necessary — overview, and the system must then support a zooming factor of 1 to 10, 1 to 10,000, or even 1 to 10,000,000. In addition, users may want to follow the route of a river, border, or highway (diagonal panning), compare two harbors (multiple detailed views), or simultaneously view highways and population-density maps (related views).

♦ In medicine, a doctor may need to see a full spinal X-ray and close-ups of vertebra pairs (an overview and multiple detailed views) or to examine a tissue boundary (pan a detailed view).

♦ In large applications such as power distribution, telephone networks, system administration, transportation systems, and chemical plants, managers typically use an overview diagram to monitor the system and detailed views to focus on anomalies. Some problems can be solved with local information only, but other problems require multiple detailed views or an understanding of the big picture.

All these situations call for browsing in two or more dimensions, and their requirements suggest that more careful analysis,[4] design, and evaluation might lead to significant improvements. Indeed, our exploration of existing 2D browsers has led us to identify many features and a wide variety of tasks performed with the browsers. Here we introduce an informal specification technique to describe 2D browsers and a task taxonomy, suggest design features and guidelines, and assess existing strategies. We focus here on the tools to explore a selected image and so do not cover techniques to browse a series of images (via, for example, a radiology workstation that shows dozens of images) or to browse large-image databases (via thumbnails or graphical searches, for example).

BROWSER SPECIFICATION

When we began to explore browsers, we found it difficult to even discuss our findings because there was no adequate method to describe browser fea-tures. This led us to expand a sketching technique, DMsketch (direct-manipulation sketch),[1] being developed in our laboratory. We had created DMsketch to help designers exchange and record ideas more quickly and clearly than a formal specification language.

Originally, DMsketch included icons to represent single clicking, double clicking, dragging, and so on. But this detail is too low-level for our purposes, so we extended DMsketch to show the major differentiating characteristics of browsers. With DMsketch, designers can informally specify

♦ a browser's most significant graphical elements,

♦ the interrelation among those elements, and

♦ the most important possible user actions.

DMsketch is based on a technique from both Scott Hudson and Shamin Mohamed's graphical specification of layout constraints in the Opus system.[5] Hudson and Mohamed introduced the idea of graphically representing a constraint on the layout of a user interface. They used an arrow to represent the presence of a constraint, which is a hidden equation. The layout designer views the equation by pointing at the constraint arrow.

However, we believe that equations do not convey meaning as clearly and quickly as a few specialized graphics. Moreover, equations cannot specify that an area in one window will be viewed in greater detail in another. In specifying browsers, we are not so much concerned with the details of interface operation at the keystroke level as we are with the relationships among windows.

Primitives. Figure 2 shows a few primitives used in our notation. As we describe browsers in this article, we will add new primitives and define composite objects as necessary.

♦ *Movement constraint.* The movement-constraint operator in Figure 2a specifies that the object at its tail is movable. If the arrow is horizontal, it is movable in the horizontal direction. If vertical, it is vertically moveable. An object without a movement-constraint operator attached is not moveable. The movement of the object at the tail is limited to be within the context of the object at the head of the arrow.

♦ *Proportional size constraint.* The proportional size-constraint-operator in Figure 2b joins two objects by its circle end points. The proportional size constraint forces the two joined objects to maintain the same relative size. For example, a line whose maximum length is four might be joined to a line whose maximum length is two. If the longer line is shortened to two, the smaller line is automatically shortened to one. This constraint operates both ways, so changing the shorter line changes the longer as well.

This operator is not confined to lines; 2D objects and movement-constraint operators may also be joined. We characterize the existence of such bidirectional links between user-interface elements by the concept of *tight coupling.*

♦ *Field of view.* The field of view encloses an area of an image and is displayed on the window that contains the image. They define a clipping rectangle for the image in its underlying representation. This means that images enclosed by a field of view do not automatically become coarser as they are magnified. This happens only when the maximum resolution of the underlying representation is reached.

The contents of the field of view are projected into a new window, which is identified by an arrow that points from the source field of view to the destination window.

Figure 2c shows the generic field of view; Figure 2d shows a generic field of view constructed by defining two points that represent its corners. This rectangle is typically defined by a "mouse down, drag, mouse up" operation. The field of view in Figure 2e is similar to one in Figure 2d, except that the point defines the center of the field of view instead of one corner. The field-of-view operator in Figure 2f represents a window that is always the same size and is defined by one point. The field of view in Figure 2g represents a view with several magnifications available, and Figure 2h shows a field of view with a shape that matches the destination window.

♦ *Fitted projection.* The symbol in Figure 2i shows that the image within the field of view is projected to a window that the arrow points to.

Composite objects. To simplify the specification, we defined composite objects, gave them their own symbol, and used them in subsequent specifications. For example, the object in Figure 3a specifies a standard coordination between an overview and detailed view of fixed sizes, as illustrated in Figure 3b.

In defining this composite object, we add the convention that unless otherwise specified all objects presented will be of fixed size. In Figure 3b, the left window is the source view of some image. As indicated by the movement-constraint operators, this field of view can move both horizontally and vertically. The image it encloses is projected on a second window, which has scroll bars. The horizontal and vertical scroll bars are linked to the field of view by the movement constraints. Thus, moving the field of view will not only change the image in the second window, it will change the scroll bar positions as well. And moving a scroll bar will change the position of the field of view and modify the projection dis-

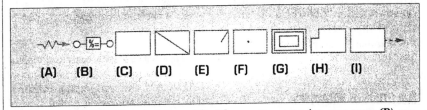

Figure 2. DMSketch primitives. (A) Movement-constraint operator; (B) proportional-size constraint operator; (C through H) six variations on the field-of-view operator; (I) fitted projection.

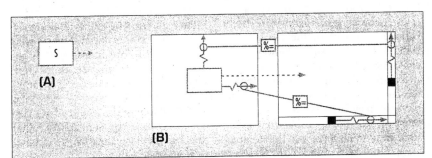

Figure 3. (A) Composite object for our recommended standard coordination between two fixed-size windows; (B) browser specification.

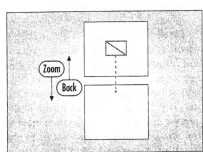

Figure 4. Zoom command specification.

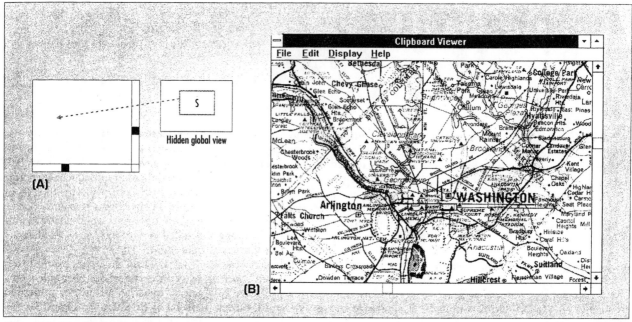

Figure 5. Single-view browser.

played in the second window.

This is our recommended standard coordination for fixed-window browsers and its symbol (the "S" in Figure 3a means "standard"). It is used frequently in specifying browsers. (Note that if the windows were resizeable, the shape of the field of view would have to be coupled to the shape of the detailed view.)

Commands. Currently, DMsketch provides only a rudimentary way of describing commands. As Figure 4 illustrates, the "before" and "after" state of the interface are shown with the command name associated with a directional arrow.

MULTITUDE OF BROWSERS

Our review of existing systems reveals great diversity in the design of 2D browsers. Here we review some classic techniques and their variations.

Detail-only browser. This method, which is used in X Windows, Microsoft Windows, and the Macintosh user interface, is the most common. The user is presented with a single window that can be panned both horizontally and vertically over the detailed view of the image. Figure 5a shows this in our notation; Figure 5b shows a common example.

This technique is easy to implement

but it is satisfactory only when the zooming factor is relatively small or if it is unnecessary to see the global view. For example, if the zooming factor is two, you can see a quarter of the image at once, so there is not much navigation required to see everything. However, if the zooming factor is much larger, navigation is difficult. Imagine looking at a map that details all of Europe at street level. With this technique, it could take you some time to realize that the view you are seeing is Brussels, when what you really wanted was to find your way around Paris.

Single window with zoom and replace. This technique, common to many CAD/CAM and geographic information systems, presents a global view of the entire image. The user marks a rectangular area which is magnified and replaces the original image. Again, this technique is easy to implement. Also, because it handles navigation separately, it uses the screen space efficiently because users work on the detailed view with all the screen space. However, the context switch can be disorienting.

Figure 6 illustrates three variations of this technique. Figure 6a shows the simplest; its major drawback is that users must return to the global view every time they want to adjust the zoomed view. The variation in Figure 6b solves this problem by letting the user scroll the detailed view, and the variation in

Figure 6c adds additional levels of magnification.

Of course the first two methods can be combined (global view, zoom, replace, scroll, as in Aldus PageMaker; or scroll, with option to zoom out to global view or in to more detail, as in MacPaint).

Single coordinated pair (overview-detail). Many 2D browsers are variations on our standard coordinated pair. These browsers combine displays of the overview and a local magnified view. The most common screen layout, shown in Figure 7a, reserves a small part of the screen for the global view, but others use windows of equal size, shown in Figure 7b, or reserve the large part of the screen for the global view, as shown in Figure 7c.

Tiled multilevel browser. These browsers combine global, intermediate, and detailed views, as the specification in Figure 8a shows. The global view is related to the intermediate view using our standard coordination, as is the intermediate to the detailed view. Figure 8b shows a sample application. In this technique, moving the global view or scrolling the intermediate view updates both views. Similarly, scrolling the intermediate view or the detailed view updates both.

Free zoom and multiple overlap. This is

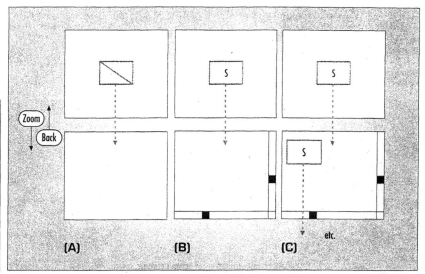

Figure 6. *Three variations of zoom-and-replace.* ***(A)*** *Zoom only;* ***(B)*** *zoom then scroll;* ***(C)*** *zoom with additional levels of magnification.*

a common design for applications running on fast platforms with large screens. Figure 9 shows the specification. Users are free (but required) to specify, move, reshape and delete every window as they wish. Any side-by-side comparison is possible.

The overview of the entire image is always presented first. The user must mark an area in the current view (top frame) and the boundaries for a new window (bottom frame). The system then creates the window and projects the marked area into the new window, which overlaps the source window. Both windows are linked to the undisplayed global view (not shown). Because there is no coordination between the views, the user has two independent browsers at different magnifications.

This design is flexible, but users must spend a significant amount of time managing the display because windows constantly obscure one another.

Bifocal view browser. A variant of the classic overview-detail browser is the bifocal browser,[6] specified in Figure 10. This browser uses a magnifying glass metaphor: It places a zoomed image on top of the area in which the

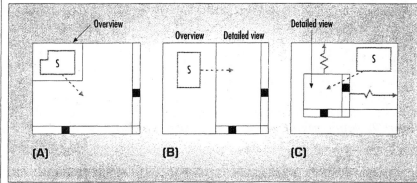

Figure 7. *Single coordinated pairs.* ***(A)*** *Fixed small overview;* ***(B)*** *Overview and detail of equal size;* ***(C)*** *Moveable small detailed view.*

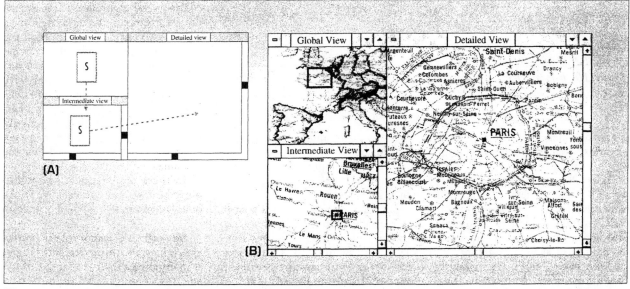

Figure 8. ***(A)*** *Specification of three-level browser with global, intermediate, and detailed views;* ***(B)*** *sample application.*

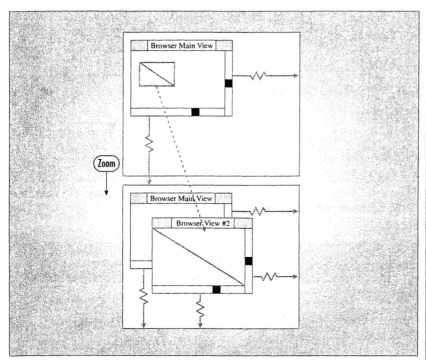

Figure 9. Specification of zooming in an overlapped window browser.

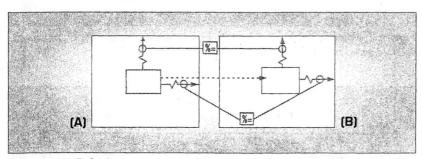

Figure 10. Bifocal view or magnifying-glass browser, with (A) areas hidden under detail view and (B) areas visible to users.

magnified object is located, thereby covering the neighboring objects.

Fish-eye view. An interesting extension of the bifocal view is the fish-eye view,[7] illustrated in Figures 11a and 11b. This browser distorts the magnified image so that the center of interest is displayed at high magnification, and the rest of the image is progressively compressed. In this way, it uses a single view to show a distorted glob-

al view, so no zooming or scrolling is required, but users must specify the focus of the magnification. However, distortion can be severe, especially with large images.

For example, Figure 11 is a small, hierarchically clustered telephone network with four levels of substations. The map in Figure 11b is a fish-eye view of San Francisco (the size of each color-coded area is made proportional to the 1980 white male population).

TASK TAXONOMY

We have identified five classes of tasks users accomplish with image browsers. Applications must often provide for different types of tasks, but usually one task is either performed repetitively or gets first priority because of safety requirements.

Image generation. When users draw or paint a large image or diagram, their attention is on a small part of the image but they often need to step back to look at the entire image. With a painting program a painter might concentrate on the drawing of a face, then return to view the entire scene. With a CAD/CAM program a boat designer might spend an hour drawing the bow of a boat then check the overall shape of the hull. Here units and sizes are often important. When a large document is automatically digitized by a scanner, progress is shown on a view of the whole document, but the refining work will be done in the few areas of the image that need retouching.

For image generation, an overview is important, but most of the time is spent at a detail level. Users tend to be experts.

Open-ended exploration. A tourist explores a remote city by navigating a map and accessing information on the local attractions. An adventure game player moves quickly around an imaginary space to become familiar with it. In both scenarios, the space is unknown to the user, so it's easy to get lost. The overview of the space being explored is not always complete or even available because it is explored for the first time.

In these applications, navigation must be fast and the user interface quickly mastered.

Diagnostic. An example of this special case of exploration is a pathologist who explores a digitized sample of tissue at low or high resolution, or a VLSI circuit specialist exploring a

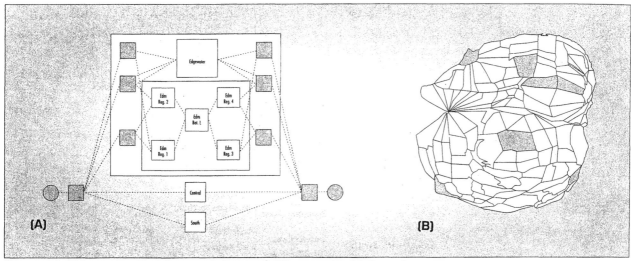

Figure 11. Fish-eye view for (A) network diagram;[8] (B) geographical information.

magnified view of a circuit. In these applications, panning speed and complete coverage is crucial because users spend most of the time panning the image and looking for patterns. The coverage must be complete or the wrong diagnosis can result. On the other hand, a complete automatic scan can also lead to boredom and errors, so the application must let the user save important locations for later review. Several browsers might be needed to compare cases.

Navigation. Here users more or less know the environment, but need to know how to get around. A delivery-truck driver uses a geographic information system to get directions. In this case, a global view must show the current position to provide context and point at the destination. Then the relevant information is presented at the minimum magnification level necessary to view the route. Zooming and panning occur only occasionally.

Monitoring. Here users must keep an eye on everything and always have information status on the entire system they are monitoring. Examples include the management of a large network, the central monitoring of the security or temperature of a large set of buildings, and the monitoring of a production plant. When a problem occurs, the user must be able to allocate some attention to local aspects while still watching the overview. Multiple views can be associated with a given problem that should be globally saved or retrieved, because the number of

windows can become very large. Window management is an important issue: an overlapping window can hide important changes in another window.

BROWSER TAXONOMY

Figures 12 and 13 present a taxonomy of the points of comparison we have identified among image browsers. Figure 12 shows presentation aspects; Figure 13 operation aspects. We separated static and dynamic presentation aspects and manual and automated operations.

Static presentation. Under this category, we classified single- and multiple-view techniques, but hybrid browsers are common. For example, a global view can be provided along a second window that functions as a zoom-and-replace, the field of view of the global view always providing feedback about the size and location of the zoomed area. Another nice hybrid is the free overlapping of multiple chained pairs of coordinated views.

Single-view browsers. These browsers dedicate all the screen space to a single view. They are very efficient when panning is limited and are the most commonly used browsers when display space is scarce. Appropriate when the task requires users to concentrate on the part of an image

that fits on the screen; they are inappropriate when users must compare several distant parts of an image.

We identified three variations of the single-view browser:

♦ *Detail-only:* Does not support zooming, only panning. The default for most windowing systems if the image is larger than the window, but seems to work well only when the entire image is not much larger (magnification of four or less) than the view. These are common for image generation because most work is done at the detail level. They are not appropriate for monitoring.

♦ *Zoom-and-replace:* More appropriate as the difference in size between the entire image and the detailed view increases and navigation becomes more difficult. Some do not offer panning, which can be annoying because

OUR BROWSER TAXONOMY SEPARATES STATIC AND DYNAMIC PRESENTATION ASPECTS.

users must zoom out and zoom in to adjust the detailed view. Some zoom-and-replace browsers do not update the hidden overview as the detailed view is panned, which causes confusion when zooming out. This large family of browsers is appropriate for image generation and diagnostics if the display-update speed is sufficient.

♦ *Fish-eye:* Gives detail and context in a single view but severely distorts the image and requires constant reorientation. Distortion is a severe problem in applications in which size and geometry are important. These

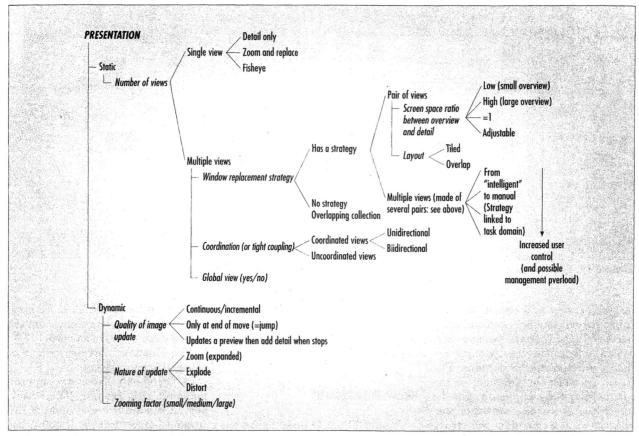

Figure 12. *Browser taxonomy for presentation aspects.*

browsers seem more appropriate for viewing abstract representations such as network diagrams, in which the view can be tailored for a user or a task but does not change constantly. Although transformations are complex and computationally demanding,[7] these browsers can be very effective (for hierarchically clustered networks,[8] for example). Designers should remember that fish-eye views can be inappropriate when fidelity to standard layout is important. The map in Figure 11b, for example, was rejected by epidemiologists because they could not compare it with the many other maps they are trained to memorize (such as maps of diseases).

Three techniques modify the fish-eye view: graphical distortion of the image, filtering to remove unwanted objects from the focus, and abstraction to replace blocks with symbols. Fish-eye views resemble domain-specific layout programs because they allow interactively generated custom layouts.

Multiple-view browsers. These browsers display several views. They are used when it is important to view details and context simultaneously, when fish-eye distortion is not appropriate, when parallel viewing is required for comparison, or when the display speed is insufficient to allow continuous zooming and panning.

We identified three important considerations when designing multiple-view browsers.

◆ *Window-placement strategy:* Too often, designers rely on window managers to handle the overlapping and resizing of windows. Although it is easier to implement a multiple-view browser without a window-placement strategy, we believe such browsers are more difficult to use. Research has shown that managing the overlapping windows can take considerable effort and time for the users.[9-10] We believe designers should provide an automatic window-management strategy that limits the need to move and resize windows incessantly. Many simple strategies (like the classic overview-detail pair) are available; researchers are investigating more complex strategies.[11] The more elaborate strategies are likely to be task-dependent, and designers would benefit from research

into guidelines and tools for the specifying and customizing of window-management strategies.

For now, the standard overview-detail pair described in Figure 3 is easy to implement and addresses many users' needs. We recommend it for all tasks. The paired views should have the same shape (boot-shaped in Figure 7a; rectangular in Figure 7b).

We compare systems using this technique by the ratio of the screen space devoted to the overview and detailed views (the SSROD — screen space ratio: overview, detail.). This ratio should be a function of the task. For example, drawing or open-ended exploration requires a large detailed view, monitoring requires a large overview, navigation requires an overview and a detailed view of similar size, and an application that includes different tasks requires an adjustable ratio.

In addition to the SSROD, these systems can be compared according to view layout. Tiling windows frees the user from managing the views. Overlapping windows gives more flexibility but forces the user to do more management. Some systems provide the specification in Figure 7a: overlapping windows that cannot be moved and that block access to part of the overlapped image (an early version of Publishers Paintbrush, for example). Of course, designers should avoid this.

♦ *Coordination:* The amount of coordination between views can be nonexistent (there is no overview), unidirectional (moving the overview updates the detailed view) or bidirectional (unidirectional, plus scrolling the detailed view updates the overview). We believe there are many opportunities for beneficial coordination. Indeed, our standard overview-detail pair in Figure 3a includes a bidirectional coordination: Moving the field of view in the overview updates the detailed view. Similarly, panning the detailed view should update the overview. This is an example of bidirectional tight coupling between two views.

♦ *Global view:* A global view shows the entire information space and allows quick access to any part. Just as a table of contents is required in print, a global view is required when browsing an image larger than one screen. This overview can be made simple and attractive for novice users or for public-access information systems. For experts, the global view should be as detailed as permitted by the display. Dense global views provide experts with direct access to details that would otherwise require several zooming operations (even if these global views appear unreadable to others!).

Dynamic aspects. Under this category, we classified the smoothness of the screen update when the image is panned or zoomed, the nature of the update, and the zooming factor.

♦ *Quality of the update:* A fast, smooth, and continuous image update makes navigation and exploration natural and simple, even over relatively long distances. It lets users concentrate on their tasks, not on the navigation tool. At one end of this spectrum

are the "fly-over" interfaces that are possible only on fast hardware. At the other end are the slow, jumpy updates that can be disorienting, if not dizzying. Smooth scrolling plus rapid and continuous zooming are the secrets of success for single-view browsers.

♦ *Nature of the update:* An area that is zoomed can be simply expanded (similar to the way a camera zooms in) or "exploded" to reveal an internal structure not apparent in the overview (such as zooming in on a network node to reveal the internal structure of a node that was represented as a sim-

ple rectangle). Explosion is regularly used for hierarchical or hierarchically clustered data sets.[8] It simplifies the overview, but it can cause disorientation because the image is always changing. When using an explode zoom, designers should consider what subset of information appears on the overview. This is especially important for monitoring applications, in which alarms should be visible on the overview. In addition to expansion and explosion, the zoomed image can be distorted, as is the case in fish-eye browsers.

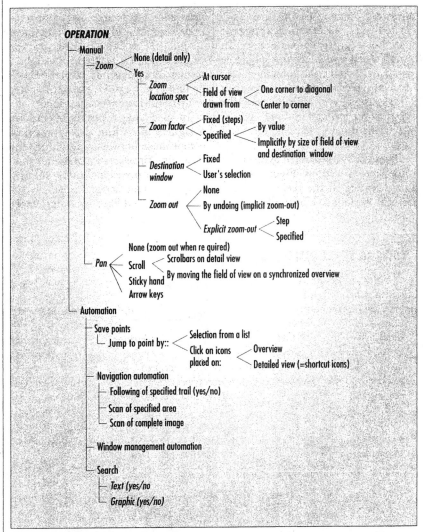

Figure 13. Browser taxonomy for operation aspects.

Again, designers can combine techniques. For example, when a user selects an object for zooming, the neighborhood around the object can be expanded and the object itself exploded to show its interior structure.

♦ *Zooming factor:* The zooming factor is the level of magnification between two views. Zooming factors can be fixed or specified. Fixed factors are set by the designer. This is a delicate task that requires designers to compromise between speed of access to details and the preservation of context information. No validated guidelines exist; designers must rely on usability testing with real users and tasks to adjust the zooming factors. For coordinated pairs, our experience suggests that the magnification between an overview and a detailed view should be less than 20. Once the zooming factor between screens gets to be more than 20 to 1, users have difficulty using the overview for navigation[12] and perhaps intermediate views are called for.

Operation. We separated manual and automated operations. Figure 13 lists and classifies all the techniques and features we found. Under the manual operations category, we classified zoom and pan techniques. Under the automated operations category, we classified saving, navigating, window-management, and searching techniques.

Manual operations. Browsers support two principal manual operations, zooming and panning. Panning and zoom can be readjusted simultaneously by redrawing the field of view or adjusting its size, placement, and even aspect ratio.

♦ *Zooming:* Users specify a zoom location by the cursor location or by drawing a field of view on the overview. Fixed-size rectangles specify a fixed zooming factor; user-controlled variable rectangles specify variable zooming. The new detailed view can be placed either by the user or by the system. Zooming out can be implicit by undo or it can be explicit, by step or by zoom-factor specification.

In specifying zooming operations, designers must find the appropriate compromise between complexity and flexibility. Browsers intended for public access or occasional users will benefit from simple designs (zooms at cursor location and fixed zooming factor),

while expert users will demand more control over zooming. It is unrealistic to implement every possibility in a single system. Instead, designers should carefully study the tasks to be accomplished. For example, if size is important or if measurements are to be done on the image, specifying the zooming factor by its value (200 percent, for example) is more important than giving control of the field of view.

♦ *Panning:* We observed three panning implementations. Scrolling is the most common, usually accomplished with vertical and horizontal scroll bars. When an overview is present, scrolling can be accomplished by moving the field-of-view indicator in the overview. The second way to implement panning is to use a "sticky hand," which grabs the picture when the mouse button is pressed (first used in MacPaint). The picture then follows the cursor until the mouse button is released. The sticky-hand metaphor is appropriate only when a real-time image update is possible, however. The third panning method is the use of arrow cursor keys.

We think most systems should provide some general panning. Only in

TOWARD THREE-DIMENSIONAL BROWSERS

So far, three-dimensional spaces generated and browsed on computer screens tend to be either small spaces (in which there is a limited need for navigation), exploratory adventure games (in which being lost is a feature), or based on some pseudonatural navigating interface (going somewhere or flying through).

These applications are not so much for drawing or constructing, but for viewing what was created with

other 2D tools. Many 3D applications are really 2D navigation (on the ground) or 2D with layers (in a building). There are more possible manual operations than just zoom and pan. More complex systems are like flight simulators, which use flight instruments and tools for navigation.

The basic browser in these cases is a zoom-and-replace browser (also resembling the fish-eye view with perspective). Three-dimensional browsing is based on

the "natural" navigation skills of the users (approaching, turning around). Overviews are sometimes provided, either as classic 2D overviews (a user in virtual reality, for example, can grab a virtual street map), or in three dimensions.

For monitoring applications that require the overview to be complete and always visible, three-dimensional overviews must either be automatically rotated so that all faces are periodically exposed or flat-

tened into multiple 2D slices.

In comparison, 2D image browsers provide much more functionality than the traditional "natural" browsing of 2D printed images because they can provide things like multiple windows, coordinated views, save points, and automations.

As 3D "spaces" become more widespread, we can expect the invention of better 3D navigation and exploration tools.

rare cases should designers have to disable detailed-view panning to avoid confusion between similar parts of an image. For example, it might make sense to restrict panning by moving the field of view when a user must closely examine a single vertebra of a spinal X-ray, because panning may lead to confusion as to which vertebra is currently on the screen.

Automated operations. It becomes difficult for users to concentrate on their task if there are too many potential browsing actions. We identified four categories of operations that designers should consider automating.

♦ *Save points*: Similar to setting bookmarks in text, marking points on an image can speed up image browsing. Locations of interest can be saved to allow rapid return to those saved points. Eventually, written or spoken comments can be saved with the location. This process of saving and retrieving points can greatly speed navigation and diagnostics (as when a second opinion is sought).

♦ *Navigation*: Direct-manipulation techniques can automate some navigation. An area can be marked on the overview to be systematically explored. A trail can be drawn on an overview and followed automatically, with the possibility to stop, explore locally, and resume the trail. Those techniques can be useful for diagnostics or even for simple exploration tasks. The areas already explored can also be shown on the overview to verify that all important parts of the image have been explored. Macro commands can be offered. For example, if users must analyze a series of similar images, they can mark the start point of a typical exploration sequence, which is then executed with a single command.

♦ *Window management*: When multiple views are used, designers can automate window placement. Fixed positioning of windows is, of course, an extreme example of such automation. The coordination of the field of view and the detailed view is another example. But more elaborate strategies can affect the sizing and placement of windows. For example, windows can become icons when unused for a certain time, or resized according to their estimated level of interest.[11] Synchro-nized windows can help users compare multiple images which they can pan simultaneously and then close simultaneously.[1]

♦ *Image search*: The automatic identification of image features is a growing field of interest based on the large body of work in computer vision on feature extraction and on similarity measures. A lot of work has recently been devoted to image retrieval, but similar techniques could be used to navigate within a large single image. For example, users may want to search a map for switching yards, a spinal X-ray for the location of each vertebra, and so on. Of course, a simpler search can be done on the text in the map. Such feature extraction might let designers adapt the browser to the task using content information. Multiple detailed views can be created automatically or panning speed can be adjusted according to the presence of features of interest (for example, the panning of a state map would be tailored to slow down when a switching yard is visible on the screen, or to jump from yard to yard).

Many automations are possible. Research is needed to determine the benefits of such automations (or even in some cases to prototype and implement them). In general, automated operations are likely to be task-dependent and found only in specialized browsers.

Research is also needed into how to let users specify the automated operations they need. This topic borders on the more general topic of programming the user interface.

As this taxonomy suggests, designing an image browser involves many choices. Improved design based on controlled experiments could improve speed, error rates, and subjective satisfaction. But we have only limited guidelines, and few of those have been validated. We must prototype and test new automations. Techniques allowing users to specify the needed automation should be investigated. The multiple-view browsers will indirectly benefit from an increased attention to the design of window managers and of coordinated window-placement strategies.

> DESIGNING AN IMAGE BROWSER INVOLVES MANY CHOICES, BUT WE HAVE ONLY VERY LIMITED GUIDELINES.

The many options, features, and parameters we have described show the complexity of image-browser interfaces. The goal is to design the simplest tools that fit the task. In some cases, this might mean avoiding a browser entirely! Browsing is rarely trivial. Before evaluating the details of an image browser, designers should consider larger screens (or even multiple screens) and denser representations that do not require zooming and panning. Pixels on the screen are precious and effort should be made to display as much information on the screen as the task and user population will permit. Elegance and readability are important for public access, while speed of use should be the goal for expert users who need less zooming, less panning, fewer automated functions, and dense screens.

Image-browser design is a lively topic. If zooming and panning cannot be avoided, the tasks and the user population should drive the selection of the browser characteristics. Usability testing remains a requirement because of the still small number of validated guidelines. Beyond flat-screen browsing, novel features for three-dimensional browsers have yet to be invented.   ♦

The Eyes Have It:
A Task by Data Type Taxonomy for Information Visualizations

Ben Shneiderman
Department of Computer Science,
Human-Computer Interaction Laboratory, and Institute for Systems Research
University of Maryland
College Park, Maryland 20742 USA
ben@cs.umd.edu

Abstract

A useful starting point for designing advanced graphical user interfaces is the Visual Information-Seeking Mantra: overview first, zoom and filter, then details on demand. But this is only a starting point in trying to understand the rich and varied set of information visualizations that have been proposed in recent years. This paper offers a task by data type taxonomy with seven data types (one-, two-, three-dimensional data, temporal and multi-dimensional data, and tree and network data) and seven tasks (overview, zoom, filter, details-on-demand, relate, history, and extracts).

Everything points to the conclusion that the phrase 'the language of art' is more than a loose metaphor, that even to describe the visible world in images we need a developed system of schemata.

E. H. Gombrich *Art and Illusion,* 1959 (p. 76)

1. Introduction

Information exploration should be a joyous experience, but many commentators talk of information overload and anxiety (Wurman, 1989). However, there is promising evidence that the next generation of digital libraries for structured databases, textual documents, and multimedia will enable convenient exploration of growing information spaces by a wider range of users. Visual language researchers and user-interface designers are inventing powerful information visualization methods, while offering smoother integration of technology with task.

The terminology swirl in this domain is especially colorful. The older terms of information retrieval (often applied to bibliographic and textual document systems) and database management (often applied to more structured relational database systems with orderly attributes and sort keys), are being pushed aside by newer notions of information gathering, seeking, or visualization and data mining, warehousing, or filtering. While distinctions are subtle, the common goals reach from finding a narrow set of items in a large collection that satisfy a well-understood information need (known-item search) to developing an understanding of unexpected patterns within the collection (browse) (Marchionini, 1995).

Exploring information collections becomes increasingly difficult as the volume grows. A page of information is easy to explore, but when the information becomes the size of a book, or library, or even larger, it may be difficult to locate known items or to browse to gain an overview.

Designers are just discovering how to use the rapid and high resolution color displays to present large amounts of information in orderly and user-controlled ways. Perceptual psychologists, statisticians, and graphic designers (Bertin, 1983; Cleveland, 1993; Tufte, 1983, 1990) offer valuable guidance about presenting static information, but the opportunity for dynamic displays takes user interface designers well beyond current wisdom.

2. Visual Information Seeking Mantra

The success of direct-manipulation interfaces is indicative of the power of using computers in a more visual or graphic manner. A picture is often cited to be worth a thousand words and, for some (but not all) tasks, it is clear that a visual presentation—such as a map or photograph—is dramatically easier to use than is a textual description or a spoken report. As computer speed and display resolution increase, information visualization and graphical interfaces are likely to have an expanding role. If a map of the United States is displayed, then it should be possible to point rapidly at one of 1000 cities to get tourist information. Of course, a foreigner who knows a city's name (for example, New Orleans), but not its location, may do better with a scrolling alphabetical list.

Visual displays become even more attractive to provide orientation or context, to enable selection of regions, and to provide dynamic feedback for identifying changes (for example, a weather map). Scientific visualization has the power to make atomic, cosmic, and common three-dimensional phenomena (such as heat conduction in engines, airflow over wings, or ozone holes) visible and comprehensible. Abstract information visualization has the power to reveal patterns, clusters, gaps, or outliers in statistical data, stock-market trades, computer directories, or document collections.

Overall, the bandwidth of information presentation is potentially higher in the visual domain than for media reaching any of the other senses. Humans have remarkable perceptual abilities that are greatly under-utilized in current designs. Users can scan, recognize, and recall images rapidly, and can detect changes in size, color, shape, movement, or texture. They can point to a single pixel, even in a megapixel display, and can drag one object to another to perform an action. User interfaces have been largely text-oriented, so as visual approaches are explored, appealing new opportunities are emerging.

There are many visual design guidelines but the basic principle might be summarized as the Visual Information Seeking Mantra:

> Overview first, zoom and filter, then details-on-demand
> Overview first, zoom and filter, then details-on-demand
> Overview first, zoom and filter, then details-on-demand
> Overview first, zoom and filter, then details-on-demand
> Overview first, zoom and filter, then details-on-demand
> Overview first, zoom and filter, then details-on-demand
> Overview first, zoom and filter, then details-on-demand
> Overview first, zoom and filter, then details-on-demand
> Overview first, zoom and filter, then details-on-demand
> Overview first, zoom and filter, then details-on-demand

Each line represents one project in which I found myself rediscovering this principle and therefore wrote it down it as a reminder. It proved to be only a starting point in trying to characterize the multiple information-visualization innovations occurring at university, government, and industry research labs.

3. Task by Data Type Taxonomy

To sort out the prototypes and guide researchers to new opportunities, I propose a type by task taxonomy (TTT) of information visualizations. I assume that users are viewing collections of items, where items have multiple attributes. In all seven data types (1-, 2-, 3-dimensional data, temporal and multi-dimensional data, and tree and network data) the items have attributes and a basic search task is to select all items that satisfy values of a set of attributes. An example task would be finding all divisions in an organization structure that have a budget greater than $500,000.

The data types are on the left side of the TTT characterize the task-domain information objects and are organized by the problems users are trying to solve. For example, in two-dimensional information such as maps, users are trying to grasp adjacency or navigate paths, whereas in tree-structured information users are trying to understand parent/child/sibling relationships. The tasks across the top of the TTT are task-domain information actions that users wish to perform.

The seven tasks are at a high level of abstraction. More tasks and refinements of these tasks would be natural next steps in expanding this table. The seven tasks are:

Overview: Gain an overview of the entire collection.
Zoom : Zoom in on items of interest
Filter: filter out uninteresting items.
Details-on-demand: Select an item or group and get details when needed.
Relate: View relationships among items.
History: Keep a history of actions to support undo, replay, and progressive refinement.
Extract: Allow extraction of sub-collections and of the query parameters.

Further discussion of the tasks follows the descriptions of the seven data types:

1-dimensional: linear data types include textual documents, program source code, and alphabetical lists of names which are all organized in a sequential manner. Each item in the collection is a line of text containing a string of characters. Additional line attributes might be the date of last update or author name. Interface design issues include what fonts, color, size to use and what overview, scrolling, or selection methods can be used. User problems might be to find the number of items, see items having certain attributes (show only lines of a document that are section titles, lines of a program that were changed from the previous version, or people in a list who are older than 21 years), or see an item with all its attributes.

Examples: An early approach to dealing with large 1-dimensional data sets was the bifocal display which provided detailed information in the focus area and less information in the surrounding context area (Spence and Apperley, 1982). In their example, the selected issue of a scientific journal had details about each article, the older and newer issues of the journal were to the left and right on the bookshelf with decreasing space. Another effort to visualize 1-dimensional data showed the attribute values of each thousands of item in a fixed-sized space using a scrollbar-like display called value bars (Chimera, 1992). Even greater compressions were accomplished in compact displays of tens of thousands of lines of program source code (SeeSoft, Eick et al., 1992) or textual documents (Document Lens, Robertson and Mackinlay, 1993; Information mural, Jerding and Stasko, 1995).

2-dimensional: planar or map data include geographic maps, floorplans, or newspaper layouts. Each item in the collection covers some part of the total area and may be rectangular or not. Each item has task-domain attributes such as name, owner, value, etc. and interface-domain features such as size, color, opacity, etc. While many systems adopt a multiple layer approach to dealing with map data, each layer is 2-dimensional. User problems are to find adjacent items, containment of one item by another, paths between items, and the basic tasks of counting, filtering, and details-on-demand.

Examples: Geographic Information Systems are a large research and commercial domain (Laurini and Thompson, 1992; Egenhofer and Richards, 1993) with numerous systems available. Information visualization researchers have used spatial displays of document collections (Korfhage, 1991; Hemmje et al., 1993; Wise et al., 1995) organized proximally by term co-occurrences.

3-dimensional: real-world objects such as molecules, the human body, and buildings have items with volume and some potentially complex relationship with other items. Computer-assisted design systems for architects, solid modelers, and mechanical engineers are built to handle complex 3-dimensional relationships. Users' tasks deal with adjacency plus above/below and inside/outside relationships, as well as the basic tasks. In 3-dimensional applications users must cope with understanding their position and orientation when viewing the objects, plus the serious problems of occlusion. Solutions to some of these problems are proposed in many prototypes with techniques such as overviews, landmarks, perspective, stereo display, transparency, and color coding.

Examples: Three-dimensional computer graphics and computer-assisted design are large topics, but information visualization efforts in three dimensions are still novel. Navigating high resolution images of the human body is the challenge in the National Library of Medicine's Visible Human project (North et al., 1996). Some applications have attempted to present 3-dimensional versions of trees (Robertson et al., 1993), networks (Fairchild et al., 1988), or elaborate desktops (Card et al., 1996).

Temporal: time lines are widely used and vital enough for medical records, project management, or historical presentations to create a data type that is separate from 1-dimensional data. The distinction in temporal data is that items have a start and finish time and that items may overlap. Frequent tasks include finding all events before, after, or during some time period or moment, plus the basic tasks.

Examples: Many project management tools exist, but novel visualizations of time include the perspective wall (Robertson et al., 1993) and LifeLines (Plaisant et al., 1996). LifeLines shows a youth history keyed to the needs of the Maryland Department of Juvenile Justice, but is intended to present medical patient histories as a compact overview with selectable items to get details-on-demand. Temporal data visualizations appear in systems for editing video data or composing animations such as Macromedia Director.

Multi-dimensional: most relational and statistical databases are conveniently manipulated as multi-dimensional data in which items with n attributes become points in a n-dimensional space. The interface representation can be 2-dimensional scattergrams with each additional dimension controlled by a slider (Ahlberg and Shneiderman, 1994). Buttons can used for attribute values when the cardinality is small, say less than ten. Tasks include finding patterns, clusters, correlations among pairs of variables, gaps, and outliers. Multi-dimensional data can be represented by a 3-dimensional scattergram but disorientation (especially if the users point of view is inside the cluster of points) and occlusion (especially if close points are represented as being larger) can be problems. The technique of parallel coordinates is a clever innovation which makes some tasks easier, but takes practice for users to comprehend (Inselberg, 1985).

Examples: The early HomeFinder developed dynamic queries and sliders for user-controlled visualization of multi-dimensional data (Williamson and Shneiderman, 1992). The successor FilmFinder refined the techniques (Ahlberg and Shneiderman, 1994) for starfield displays (zoomable, color coded, user-controlled scattergrams), and laid the basis for the commercial product Spotfire (Ahlberg and Wistrand, 1995). Extrapolations include the Aggregate Manipulator (Goldstein and Roth, 1994), movable filters (Fishkin and Stone, 1995), and Selective Dynamic Manipulation (Chuah et al., 1995). Related works include VisDB for multidimensional database visualization (Keim and Kreigal, 1994), the spreadsheet-like Table Lens (Rao and Card, 1994) and the multiple linked histograms in the Influence Explorer (Tweedie et al., 1996).

Tree: hierarchies or tree structures are collections of items with each item having a link to one parent item (except the root). Items and the links between parent and child can have multiple attributes. The basic tasks can be applied to items and links, and tasks related to structural properties become interesting, for example, how many levels in the tree? or how many children does an item have? While it is possible to have similar items at leaves and internal nodes, it is also common to find different items at each level in a tree. Fixed level trees with all leaves equidistant from the root and fixed fanout trees with the same number of children for every parent are easier to deal with. High fanout (broad) and small fanout (deep) trees are important special cases. Interface representations of trees can use an outline style of indented labels used in tables of contents (Chimera and Shneiderman, 1993), a node and link diagram, or a treemap, in which child items are rectangles nested inside parent rectangles.

Examples: Tree-structured data has long been displayed with indented outlines (Egan et al., 1989) or with connecting lines as in many computer-directory file managers. Attempts to show large tree structures as node and link diagrams in compact forms include the 3-dimensional cone and cam trees (Robertson et al., 1993; Carriere and Kazman, 1995), dynamic pruning in the TreeBrowser (Kumar et al., 1995), and the appealingly animated hyperbolic trees (Lamping et al., 1995). A novel space-filling mosaic approach shows an arbitrary sized tree in a fixed rectangular space (Shneiderman, 1992; Johnson and Shneiderman, 1991). The treemap approach was successfully applied to computer directories, sales data, business decision-making (Asahi et al., 1995), and web browsing (Mitchell et al., 1995; Mukherjea et al., 1995), but users take 10-20 minutes to accommodate to complex treemaps.

Network: sometimes relationships among items cannot be conveniently captured with a tree structure and it is useful to have items linked to an arbitrary number of other items. While many special cases of networks exist (acyclic, lattices, rooted vs. un-rooted, directed vs. undirected) it seems convenient to consider them all as one data type. In addition to the basic tasks applied to items and links, network users often want to know about shortest or least costly paths connecting two items or traversing the entire network. Interface representations include a node and link diagram, and a square matrix of the items with the value of a link attribute in the row and column representing a link.

Examples: Network visualization is an old but still imperfect art because of the complexity of relationships and user tasks. Commercial packages can handle small networks or simple strategies such as Netmap's layout of nodes on a circle with links criss-crossing the central area. An ambitious 3-dimensional approach was an impressive early accomplishment (Fairchild et al., 1988), and new

interest in this topic has been spawned by attempts to visualize the World Wide Web (Andrews, 1995; Hendley et al., 1995).

These seven data types reflect are an abstraction of the reality. There are many variations on these themes (2 1/2 or 4-dimensional data, multitrees,...) and many prototypes use combinations of these data types. This taxonomy is useful only if it facilitates discussion and leads to useful discoveries. Some idea of missed opportunities emerges in looking at the tasks and data types in depth:

Overview: Gain an overview of the entire collection. Overview strategies include zoomed out views of each data type to see the entire collection plus an adjoining detail view. The overview contains a movable field-of-view box to control the contents of the detail view, allowing zoom factors of 3 to 30. Replication of this strategy with intermediate views enables users to reach larger zoom factors. Another popular approach is the fisheye strategy (Furnas, 1986) which has been applied most commonly for network browsing (Sarkar and Brown, 1994; Bartram et al., 1995). The fisheye distortion magnifies one or more areas of the display, but zoom factors in prototypes are limited to about 5. Although query language facilities made it difficult to gain an overview of a collection, information visualization interfaces support some overview strategy, or should. Adequate overview strategies are a useful criteria to look for. Along with an overview plus detail (also called context plus focus) view there is a need for navigation tools to pan or scroll through the collection.

Zoom: Zoom in on items of interest. Users typically have an interest in some portion of a collection, and they need tools to enable them to control the zoom focus and the zoom factor. Smooth zooming helps users preserve their sense of position and context. Zooming could be on one dimension at a time by moving the zoombar controls or by adjusting the size of the field-of-view box. A very satisfying way to zoom in is by pointing to a location and issuing a zooming command, usually by clicking on a mouse button for as long as the user wishes (Bederson and Hollan, 1993). Zooming in one dimension has proven useful in starfield displays (Jog and Shneiderman, 1995).

Filter: filter out uninteresting items. Dynamic queries applied to the items in the collection is one of the key ideas in information visualization (Ahlberg et al., 1992; Williamson and Shneiderman, 1992). By allowing users to control the contents of the display, users can quickly focus on their interests by eliminating unwanted items. Sliders, buttons, or other control widgets coupled to rapid display update (less than 100 milliseconds) is the goal, even when there are tens of thousands of displayed items.

Details-on-demand: Select an item or group and get details when needed. Once a collection has been trimmed to a few dozen items it should be easy to browse the details about the group or individual items. The usual approach is to simply click on an item to get a pop-up window with values of each of the attributes. In Spotfire, the details-on-demand window can contain HTML text with links to further information.

Relate: View relationships among items. In the FilmFinder (Ahlberg and Shneiderman, 1994) users could select an attribute, such as the film's director, in the details-on-demand window and cause the director alphaslider to be reset to the director's name, thereby displaying only films by that director. Similarly, in SDM (Chuah et al., 1995), users can select an item and then highlight items with similar attributes or in LifeLines (Plaisant et al., 1996) users can click on a medication and see the related visit report, prescription, and lab test. Designing user interface actions to specify which relationship is to be manifested is still a challenge. The Influence Explorer (Tweedie et al., 1996) emphasizes exploration of relationships among attributes. and the Table Lens emphasizes finding correlations among pairs of numerical attributes (Rao and Card, 1994).

History : Keep a history of actions to support undo, replay, and progressive refinement. It is rare that a single user action produces the desired outcome. Information exploration is inherently a process with many steps, so keeping the history of actions and allowing users to retrace their steps is important. However, most prototypes fail to deal with this requirement. Maybe they are reflecting the current state of graphic user interfaces, but designers would be better to follow information retrieval systems which typically preserve the sequence of searches so that they can be combined or refined.

Extract: Allow extraction of sub-collections and of the query parameters. Once users have obtained the item or set of items they desire, it would be useful to be able to extract that set and save it to a file in a format that would facilitate other uses such as sending by email, printing, graphing, or insertion into a statistical or presentation package. An alternative to saving the set, they might want to save, send, or print the settings for the control widgets. Very few prototypes support this action, although Roth's recent work on Visage provides an elegant capability to extract sets of items and simply drag-and-drop them into the next application window.

The attraction of visual displays, when compared to textual displays, is that they make use of the remarkable human perceptual ability for visual information. Within visual displays, there are opportunities for showing relationships by proximity, by containment, by connected lines, or by color coding. Highlighting techniques (for example, bold-face text or brightening, inverse video, blinking, underscoring, or boxing) can be used to draw attention to certain items in a field of thousands of items. Pointing to a visual display can allow rapid selection, and feedback is apparent. The eye, the hand, and the mind seem to work smoothly and rapidly as users perform actions on visual displays.

4. Advanced Filtering

Users have highly varied needs for filtering features. The dynamic queries approach of adjusting numeric range sliders, alphasliders for names or categories, or buttons for small sets of categories is appealing to many users for many tasks (Shneiderman, 1994). Dynamic queries might be called *direct-manipulation queries*, since they share the same concepts of visual display of actions (the sliders or buttons) and objects (the query results in the task-domain display); the use of rapid, incremental, and reversible actions; and the immediate display of feedback (less than 100 msec). Additional benefits are no error messages and the encouragement of exploration.

Dynamic queries can reveal global properties as well as assist users in answering specific questions. As the database grows, it is more difficult to update the display fast enough, and specialized data structures or parallel computation are required.

The dynamic-query approach to the chemical table of elements was tested in an empirical comparison with a form-fill-in query interface. The counterbalanced-ordering within-subjects design with 18 chemistry students showed strong advantages for the dynamic queries in terms of faster performance and lower error rates (Ahlberg et al., 1991).

Dynamic queries usually permit OR combinations within an attribute with AND combination of attributes across attributes (conjunct of disjuncts). This is adequate for many situations since rapid multiple sequential queries allow users to satisfy their information needs. Commercial information-retrieval systems, such as DIALOG or Lexis/Nexis, permit complex *Boolean expressions* with parentheses, but widespread adoption has been inhibited by the difficulty of using them. Numerous proposals have been put forward to reduce the burden of specifying complex Boolean expressions (Reisner, 1988). Part of the confusion stems from informal English usage where a query such as List all employees who live in New York and Boston would result in an empty list because the "and" would be interpreted as an intersection; only employees who live in *both* cities would qualify! In English, "and" usually expands the options; in Boolean expressions, AND is used to narrow a set to the intersection of two others. Similarly, in the English "I'd like Russian or Italian salad dressing," the "or" is exclusive, indicating that you want one or the other but not both; in Boolean expressions, an OR is inclusive, and is used to expand a set.

The desire for *full Boolean expressions*, including nested parentheses and NOT operators, led us toward novel metaphors for query specification. *Venn diagrams* (Michard, 1982), *decision tables* (Greene et al., 1990), and the innovative InfoCrystal (Spoerri, 1993) have been used, but these both become confusing as query complexity increases. We sought to support arbitrarily complex Boolean expressions with a graphical specification. Our approach was to apply the metaphor of water flowing from left to right through a series of pipes and filters, where each filter lets through only the appropriate documents, and the pipe layout indicates relationships of AND or OR. (Young and Shneiderman, 1993)

In this filter–flow model, ANDs are shown as a linear sequence of filters, suggesting the successive application of required criteria. As the flow passes through each filter, it is reduced, and the visual feedback shows a narrower bluish stream of water. ORs are shown two ways: within an attribute, multiple values can be selected in a single filter; and across multiple attributes, filters are arranged in parallel paths. When the parallel paths converge, the width of the flow reflects the size of the union of the document sets.

Negation was handled by a NOT operator that, when selected, inverts all currently selected items in a filter. For example, if California and Georgia were selected and then the NOT operator was chosen, those two states would become deselected and all the other states would become selected. Finally, clusters of filters and pipes can be made into a single labeled filter. This facility ensures that the full query can be shown on the display at once, and allows clusters to be saved in a library for later reuse.

We believe that this approach can help novices and intermittent users to specify complex Boolean expressions and to learn Boolean concepts. A usability study was conducted with 20 subjects with little experience using Boolean algebra. The prototype filter–flow interface showed statistically significant improved performance against a textual interface for comprehension and composition tasks. The filter-flow interface was preferred by all 20 subjects.

5. Summary

Novel graphical and direct-manipulation approaches to query formulation and information visualization are now possible. While research prototypes have typically dealt with only one data type (1-, 2-, 3-dimensional data, temporal and multi-dimensional data, and tree and network data), successful commercial products will have to accommodate several. These products will need to provide smooth integration with existing software and support the full task list: Overview, zoom, filter, details-on-demand, relate, history, and extract. These ideas are attractive because they present information rapidly and allow for rapid user-controlled exploration. If they are to be fully effective, some of these approaches require novel data structures, high-resolution color displays, fast data retrieval, specialized data structures, parallel computation, and some user training.

Although the computer contributes to the information explosion, it is potentially the magic lens for finding, sorting, filtering, and presenting the relevant items. Search in complex structured documents, graphics, images, sound, or video presents grand opportunities for the design of user interfaces and search engines to find the needle in the haystack. The novel-information exploration tools—such as dynamic queries, treemaps, fisheye views, parallel coordinates, starfields, and perspective walls—are but a few of the inventions that will have to be tamed and validated.

References

Ahlberg, Christopher and Shneiderman, Ben, Visual information seeking: Tight coupling of dynamic query filters with starfield displays, *Proc. ACM CHI94 Conference: Human Factors in Computing Systems*, (1994), 313-321 + color plates.

Ahlberg, Christopher and Shneiderman, Ben, AlphaSlider: A compact and rapid selector, *Proc. ACM CHI94 Conference Human Factors in Computing Systems*, (1994), 365-371.

Ahlberg, Christopher, Williamson, Christopher, and Shneiderman, Ben, Dynamic queries for information exploration: An implementation and evaluation, *Proc. ACM CHI'92: Human Factors in Computing Systems*, (1992), 619-626.

Ahlberg, Christopher and Wistrand, Erik, IVEE: An information visualization & exploration environment, *Proc. IEEE Information Visualization '95*, (1995), 66-73.

Andrew, Keith, Visualising cyberspace: Information visualisation in the Harmony internet browser, *Proc. IEEE Information Visualization '95*, (1995), 97-104.

Asahi, T., Turo, D., and Shneiderman, B., Using treemaps to visualize the analytic hierarchy process, *Information Systems Research 6,* 4 (December 1995), 357-375.

Bartram, Lyn, Ho, Albert, Dill, John, and Henigman, Frank, The continuous zoom: A constrained fisheye technique for viewing and navigating large information spaces, *Proc. ACM User Interface Software and Technology '95,* (1995), 207-215.

Becker, Richard A., Eick , Stephen G., and Wilks, Allan R. Visualizing Network Data, *IEEE Transactions on Visualization and Computer Graphics 1,* 1 (March 1995), 16-28.

Bederson, Ben B. and Hollan, James D., PAD++: A zooming graphical user interface for exploring alternate interface physics, *Proc. ACM User Interfaces Software and Technology '94* (1994), 17-27.

Bertin, Jacques, *Semiology of Graphics,* University of Wisconsin Press, Madison, WI (1983)

Card, Stuart K., Robertson, George G., and York, William, The WebBook and the WebForager: An information workspace for the World-Wide Web, *Proc. ACM CHI96 Conference: Human Factors in Computing Systems,* (1996), 111-117.

Carriere, Jeremy and Kazman, Rick, Interacting with huge hierarchies: Beyond cone trees, *Proc. IEEE Information Visualization '95,* (1995), 74-81.

Chimera, Richard, Value bars: An information visualization and navigation tool for multiattribute listings, *Proc. ACM CHI92 Conference: Human Factors in Computing Systems,* (1992), 293-294.

Chimera, Richard and Shneiderman, Ben, Evaluating three user interfaces for browsing tables of contents, *ACM Transactions on Information Systems 12,* 4 (October 1994).

Chuah, Mei C., Roth, Steven F., Mattis, Joe, and Kolojejchcik, John, SDM: Malleable Information Graphics, *Proc. IEEE Information Visualization '95,* (1995), 66-73.

Cleveland, William, *Visualizing Data,* Hobart Press, Summit, NJ (1993).

Egan, Dennis E., Remde, Joel R., Gomez, Louis M., Landauer, Thomas K., Eberhardt, Jennifer, and Lochbum, Carol C., Formative design-evaluation of SuperBook, *ACM Transactions on Information Systems 7,* 1 (January 1989), 30–57.

Egenhofer, Max and Richards, J., Exploratory access to geographic data based on the map-overlay metaphor, *Journal of Visual Languages and Computing 4,* 2 (1993), 105-125.

Eick, Stephen G. , Steffen, Jospeh L., and Sumner, Jr., Eric E., SeeSoft- A tool for visualizing line-oriented software statistics, *IEEE Transactions on Software Engineering 18,* 11 (1992) 957-968.

Eick, Stephen G. and Wills, Graham J., Navigating Large Networks with Hierarchies, *Proc. IEEE Visualization '93 Conference,* (1993), 204--210.

Fairchild, Kim M., Poltrock, Steven E., and Furnas, George W., SemNet: Three-dimensional representations of large knowledge bases, In Guindon, Raymonde (Editor), *Cognitive Science and its Applications for Human-Computer Interaction,* Lawrence Erlbaum, Hillsdale, NJ (1988), 201-233.

Fishkin, Ken and Stone, Maureen C., Enhanced dynamic queries via movable filters, *Proc. ACM CHI95 Conference: Human Factors in Computing Systems,* (1995), 415-420.

Furnas, George W., Generalized fisheye views, *Proc. ACM CHI86 Conference: Human Factors in Computing Systems,* (1986), 16-23.

Goldstein, Jade and Roth, Steven F, Using aggregation and dynamic queries for exploring large data sets, *Proc. ACM CHI95 Conference: Human Factors in Computing Systems,* (1995), 23-29.

Greene, S. L., Devlin, S. J., Cannata, P. E., and Gomez, L. M., No IFs, ANDs, or ORs: A study of database querying, *International Journal of Man–Machine Studies 32* (March 1990), 303–326.

Hendley, R. J., Drew, N. S., Wood, A. S., Narcissus: Visualizing information, *Proc. IEEE Information Visualization '95,* (1995), 90-96.

Humphrey, Susanne M. and Melloni, Biagio John, *Databases: A Primer for Retrieving Information by Computer,* Prentice-Hall, Englewood Cliffs, NJ (1986).

Inselberg, Alfred, The plane with parallel coordinates, *The Visual Computer 1* (1985), 69-91.

Jerding, Dean F. and Stasko, John T., The information mural: A technique for displaying and navigating large information spaces, *Proc. IEEE Information Visualization '95,* 43-50.

Jog, Ninad and Shneiderman, Ben, Information visualization with smooth zooming on an starfield display, *Proc. IFIP Conf. Visual Databases 3,* Chapman and Hall, London (1995), 1-10.

Johnson, Brian, and Shneiderman, Ben, Tree-maps: A space-filling approach to the visualization of hierarchical information structures, *Proc. IEEE Visualization'91,* (1991), 284–291.

Keim, D. A. and Kriegal, H., VisDB: Database exploration using multidimensional visualization, *IEEE Computer Graphics and Applications* (September 1994), 40-49.

Korfhage, Robert, To see or not to see -- Is that the query?, *Communications of the ACM 34* (1991), 134-141.

Lamping, John, Rao, Ramana, and Pirolli, Peter, A focus + context technique based on hyperbolic geometry for visualizing large hierarchies, *Proc. ACM CHI95 Conference: Human Factors in Computing Systems*, (1995), 401-408

Laurini, R. and Thompson, D., *Fundamentals of Spatial Information Systems*, Academic Press, New York, NY (1992).

Marchionini, Gary, *Information Seeking in Electronic Environments*, Cambridge University Press, UK (1995).

Michard, A., A new database query language for non-professional users: Design principles and ergonomic evaluation, *Behavioral and Information Technology 1*, 3 (July–September 1982), 279–288.

Mitchell, Richard, Day, David, and Hirschman, Lynette, Fishing for information on the internet, *Proc. IEEE Information Visualization '95*, (1995), 105-111.

Mukherjea, Sougata, Foley, James D., and Hudson, Scott, Visualizing complex hypermedia networks through multiple hierarchical views, *Proc. ACM CHI95 Conference: Human Factors in Computing Systems*, (1995), 331-337 + color plate.

North, Chris, Shneiderman, Ben, and Plaisant, Catherine, User controlled overviews of an image library: A case study of the Visible Human, *Proc. 1st ACM International Conference on Digital Libraries* (1996), 74-82.

Pirolli, Peter, Schank, Patricia, Hearst, Marti, and Diehl, Christine, Scatter/gather browsing communicates the topic structure of a very large text collection, *Proc. ACM CHI96 Conference*, (1996), 213-220.

Plaisant, Catherine, Rose, Anne, Milash, Brett, Widoff, Seth, and Shneiderman, Ben, LifeLines: Visualizing personal histories, *Proc. ACM CHI96 Conference: Human Factors in Computing Systems*, (1996), 221-227, 518.

Rao, Ramana and Card, Stuart K., The Table Lens: Merging graphical and symbolic representations in an interactive focus + context visualization for tabular information, *Proc. ACM CHI94 Conference: Human Factors in Computing Systems*, (1994), 318-322.

Reisner, Phyllis, Query languages. In Helander, Martin (Editor), *Handbook of Human–Computer Interaction*, North-Holland, Amsterdam, The Netherlands (1988), 257–280.

Robertson, George G., Card, Stuart K., and Mackinlay, Jock D., Information visualization using 3-D interactive animation, *Communications of the ACM 36*, 4 (April 1993), 56-71.

Robertson George G. and Mackinlay, Jock D., The document lens, *Proc. 1993 ACM User Interface Software and Technology*, (1993), 101-108.

Sarkar, Manojit and Brown, Marc H., Graphical fisheye views, *Communications of the ACM 37*, 12 (July 1994), 73–84.

Shneiderman, Ben, Tree visualization with tree-maps: A 2-d space-filling approach, *ACM Transactions on Graphics 11*, 1 (January 1992), 92-99.

Shneiderman, Ben, Dynamic queries for visual information seeking, *IEEE Software 11*, 6 (1994), 70-77.

Spence, Robert and Apperley, Mark, Data base navigation: An office environment for the professional, *Behaviour & Information Technology 1*, 1 (1982), 43-54.

Spoerri, Anselm, InfoCrystal: A visual tool for information retrieval & management, *Proc. ACM Conf on Information and Knowledge Management* (1993).

Tufte, Edward, *The Visual Display of Quantitative Information*, Graphics Press, Cheshire, CT (1983).

Tufte, Edward, *Envisioning Information*, Graphics Press, Cheshire, CT (1990).

Tweedie, Lisa, Spence, Robert, Dawkes, Huw, and Su, Hua, Externalising abstract mathematical models, *Proc. ACM CHI96 Conference: Human Factors in Computing Systems*, (1996), 406-412.

Williamson, Christopher, and Shneiderman, Ben, The Dynamic HomeFinder: Evaluating dynamic queries in a real-estate information exploration system, *Proc. ACM SIGIR'92 Conference*, (1992), 338-346. Reprinted in Shneiderman, B. (Editor), *Sparks of Innovation in Human-Computer Interaction*, Ablex Publishers, Norwood, NJ, (1993), 295-307.

Wise, James A., Thomas, James, J., Pennock, Kelly, Lantrip, David, Pottier, Marc, Schur, Anne, and Crow, Vern, Visualizing the non-visual: Spatial analysis and interaction with information from text documents, *Proc. IEEE Information Visualization '95*, (1995), 51-58.

Wurman, Richard Saul, *Information Anxiety*, Doubleday, New York (1989).

Young, Degi and Shneiderman, Ben, A graphical filter/flow model for boolean queries: An implementation and experiment, *Journal of the American Society for Information Science 44*, 6 (July 1993), 327-339.

Supporting Creativity with Advanced Information-Abundant User Interfaces

Ben Shneiderman

Abstract

A challenge for human–computer interaction researchers and user interface designers is to construct information technologies that support creativity. This ambitious goal can be attained if designers build on an adequate understanding of creative processes. This chapter describes a model of creativity, the four-phase genex framework for generating excellence:

• Collect: learn from previous works stored in digital libraries, the Web etc.
• Relate: consult with peers and mentors at early, middle and late stages
• Create: explore, compose, discover and evaluate possible solutions
• Donate: disseminate the results and contribute to the digital libraries, the Web etc.

Within this integrated framework, there are eight activities that require human–computer interaction research and advanced user interface design. This chapter concentrates on techniques of information visualization that support creative work by enabling users to find relevant information resources, identify desired items in a set, or discover patterns in a collection. It describes information visualization methods and proposes five questions for the future: generality, integration, perceptual foundations, cognitive principles and collaboration.

33.1 Introduction

Ambitious visions can be helpful in shaping more concrete research agendas. Vannevar Bush's (1945) vision of a system to support memory expansion (memex) inspired researchers for a half century in the development of what has become the World Wide Web. Engelbart's goal of augmenting human intellect (Engelbart and English, 1968) led to innovations such as the mouse and windows. Later, Brooks's belief in the importance of toolmaking (Brooks, 1996) led to innovations such as haptic feedback in 3D graphical environments. Hiltz's recognition of the power of online communities (Hiltz, 1984), inspired early software development (Hiltz and Turoff, 1993) and the emergence of ideas such as the collaboratory (National Research Council, 1993). These inspirational visions were important predecessors for genex (generator of excellence), an integrated framework for creativity support tools (Shneiderman, 1998b, 1999).

33.1.1 Creativity Support

Supporting creativity is a bold ambition, but it is becoming feasible because of refined understandings of the creative processes (Rosner and Abt, 1970; De Bono, 1973; Boden, 1990; Mayer, 1992; Czikszentmihalyi, 1996; Couger, 1996) and the emergence of advanced user interfaces to support creativity (Massetti, 1996; Massetti *et al.*, 1999). While theories of creativity vary widely, common features describe a preparatory phase that deals with the need to find information, understand the problem and explore alternatives privately, followed by discussion with peers and mentors. These steps lay the basis for an incubation phase, and moments of inspiration to break a too rigid mind set. Then come the hours of perspiration to evaluate possibilities, refine potential solutions, implement the chosen solution and disseminate it.

The diverse theories contributed to the four phases in an integrated user interface framework, called genex:

• Collect: learn from previous works stored in digital libraries, the Web etc.
• Relate: consult with peers and mentors at early, middle and late stages
• Create: explore, compose, discover and evaluate possible solutions
• Donate: disseminate the results and contribute to the digital libraries, the Web etc.

Across these four phases, at least eight activities are opportunities for research in user interface design and human–computer interaction (Shneiderman, 1999) (Figure 33.1):

• Searching and browsing digital libraries
• Consulting with peers and mentors
• Visualizing data and processes
• Thinking by free associations
• Exploring solutions – "what if" tools
• Composing artifacts and performances
• Reviewing and replaying session histories
• Disseminating results

These activities are richly interwoven, for example, visualizing supports searching, exploring, reviewing etc. Each activity deserves consideration as part of a research agenda, but this chapter focuses on the third item – visualizing data and processes – and discusses its place in the broad array of genex activities.

World maps are especially rich information sources that enable designers to show complex relationships while allowing users to plan trips and make further discoveries. Mental maps of information spaces and special designs such as the periodic table of elements, monthly calendars or the Linnaean taxonomy of animal phyla also support creativity. By placing known information in an orderly compact structure they support users in solving problems, planning activities and making further discoveries.

33.1.3 Information Visualization

Human perceptual abilities are remarkable and still largely underutilized by the current graphical user interfaces. Computer-based visual presentations bring additional opportunities and dangers. Adding animations such as blinking, color shifts and movements enriches the possibilities for presentations but risks overwhelming readers. However, a great benefit of computing environments is the opportunity for users to rapidly revise the presentation to suit their tasks. Users can quickly change the rules governing proximity, linking, color, size, shape, texture, rotation, marking, blinking, color shifts and movements. In addition, zooming in or clicking on specific items to get greater detail increases the possibilities for designers and users (Bederson and Hollan, 1994). The simple process of viewing a year-long display and clicking on the month and then the day enables users to get an overview and quickly move to details. A picture is often said to be worth a thousand words. Similarly, an interface is worth a thousand pictures.

A reasonable expectation for the future of user interfaces is for the growth of larger, information-abundant displays. While small portable personal devices will proliferate, the attraction of large desk-mounted or projected displays will be great. Human perceptual skills are remarkable and largely underutilized in current information and computing systems. Based on this insight, designers at several leading research centers have developed advanced prototypes and a variety of widgets to present, search, browse, filter and explore rich information spaces (Card et al., 1999).

We can define information visualization as: a compact graphical presentation and user interface for rapidly manipulating large numbers of items (10^2–10^6), possibly extracted from far larger datasets. Effective information visualizations enable users to make discoveries, decisions or explanations about patterns (correlations, clusters, gaps, outliers,...), groups of items or individual items. This definition emphasizes the user interface for control of the presentation (location, color, size, rotation, shape, texture, blinking, movement, animation and other variables).

For the purposes of this discussion, information visualization deals with abstract multidimensional and multi-variate data and is quite different from scientific visualization or 3D modeling. Scientific visualization typically deals with three-dimensional real-world phenomena such as storms, crystal growth or human anatomy, and 3D modeling typically deals with mechanical parts, architectural walkthroughs or aircraft design.

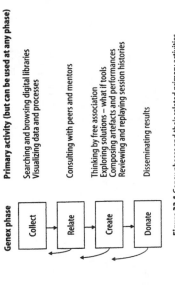

Genex phase	Primary activity (but can be used at any phase)
Collect	Searching and browsing digital libraries Visualizing data and processes
Relate	Consulting with peers and mentors
Create	Thinking by free association Exploring solutions – what if tools Composing artefacts and performances Reviewing and replaying session histories
Donate	Disseminating results

Figure 33.1 Genex phases and their related primary activities.

33.1.2 Visualizing as a Support for Creativity

Visualizing is one of the eight activities that support the genex framework because visual information processing is central to many problem-solving tasks and creative explorations. Information visualization can contribute to early stages of collecting information from vast digital resources, to exploring alternative solutions and to identifying appropriate people for consultations or dissemination.

Evolutionary needs have made the human visual system extremely well adapted to recognizing patterns, extracting features and detecting unexpected items. Humans can rapidly process enormous amounts of visual information and take action rapidly. The human perceptual apparatus integrates interpretation so that people can rapidly identify familiar faces or recognize threats.

Linear or tabular presentations of text, numbers and music extend human memory, enable transmission of information across time and space, and support creativity. The process of recording an idea facilitates innovation and discovery by compelling an author to produce a coherent presentation, develop a consistent notation and present a logical argument. The linear or tabular formats enable the author and others to review, edit, refine, compare and search presentations rapidly.

The goal for visual designers is to match the task to the presentation (Tufte, 1983, 1990, 1997). Bertin (1983) dramatically portrays the possibilities by showing one hundred different presentations of information about French provinces, each suited to a specific task.

Two-dimensional visual presentations such as drawings, tree structures, flowcharts and maps have additional advantages. They can present affinities among multiple items, enabling users to see relationships that might be difficult to discover in linear textual presentations. Proximity or links in two-dimensional presentations can show rich structural relationships. Coding by size and color are easily perceived and further coding by shape, texture, rotation or markings can highlight additional relationships.

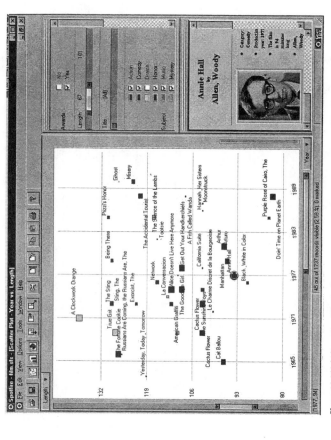

Figure 33.2 Multidimensional film database viewed with a two-dimensional starfield display in Spotfire. The x-axis contains the years and the y-axis is the popularity of the film. Color coding is film type (action, drama, mystery etc.), and larger dots indicate longer movies.

33.2 Examples of Information Visualization Supporting Creativity

One of our early visualizations was based on dynamic queries, which are animated user-controlled displays. These update immediately (no "run" button) in response to movements of sliders, buttons, maps or other widgets (Shneiderman, 1994). For example, in the HomeFinder the users see points of light on a map representing homes for sale (Ahlberg *et al*., 1992; Williamson and Shneiderman, 1993). As they shift sliders for the price, number of bedrooms etc. the points of light come and go within 100 milliseconds, offering a quick understanding of how many and where suitable homes are being sold. Clicking on a point of light produces a full description and, potentially, a picture of the house. A controlled experiment with 18 subjects confirmed the performance and preference advantages of dynamic queries over a natural language interface and a paper database.

A next step was the starfield display, which was created for the FilmFinder to provide visual access to a film database (Ahlberg and Shneiderman, 1994). The films were arranged as color-coded rectangles along the x-axis by production year and along the y-axis by popularity. Recent popular films were in the upper right-hand corner. Zoombars (a variant of scroll bars) enabled users to zoom in on a single axis in milliseconds to view the desired region. When fewer than 25 films were on the screen, the film titles appeared, and when the users clicked on a film's rectangle, a dialog box would appear giving full information and an image from the film. The commercial version of starfield displays became available late in 1996 (Figure 33.2) (http://www.spotfire.com/).

In our LifeLines prototype, we applied multiple timeline representations to personal histories such as medical records (Plaisant *et al*., 1996). Horizontal and vertical zooming, focusing, and filtering enabled us to represent complex histories and support exploration by clicking on timelines to get detailed information.

Information visualization supports creative work by enabling users to:

• find relevant information resources in digital libraries
• identify desired items in a set
• discover patterns in a collection

Figure 33.2 demonstrates how a digital library of films could be viewed in a way that presents large amounts of information in an orderly way. Users can understand the distribution of films in this library and find specific films to satisfy their needs. Similarly, in a legal information library, users may be seeking the relevant precedents to support their arguments. The West key number system organizes information in a hierarchy whose first three levels have 470 items, which then expands into a tree with 85 000 nodes. Figure 33.3 shows how the results of a search might be displayed to reveal where the cases fall within the key number hierarchy (Shneiderman *et al*., 1999). Additional information is supplied on the x-axis, currently organizing the cases by year, and by color coding, currently showing the region the case came from. This visualization makes it clear that the major topic is Criminal Law. This visualization enables users to find the relevant

resources that would be very difficult to discover in a typical paged list with 20 cases per page.

A second form of creativity support is to identify items in a set. The legal information library is an example of this as well, but the drug discovery task is more typical. In this example, 379 compounds are viewed at once, organized by the amount of carbon and oxygen, color coded by dipole moment and size coded by polarizability (Figure 33.4). The unusual compound (the selected square at the upper right) is clearly visible by its distinct color coding.

Important patterns can also be seen in visual displays. The familiar chemical periodic table of elements becomes more informative when color and size coding are added, and when users can make selections by moving the double box sliders. Figure 33.5 shows the usual layout, but the high electronegativity is immediately visible from the color coding. Figure 33.6 shows a strong correlation between electronegativity and ionization energy, with two dramatic outliers: helium and radon.

The three ways that information visualization interfaces support creativity are not a complete set, but they give designers some specific goals to work towards.

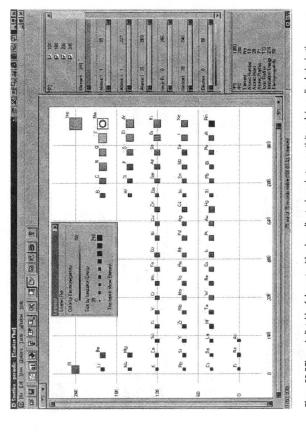

Figure 33.5 The periodic table of elements with color coding to show electronegativity and size coding by ionization energy.

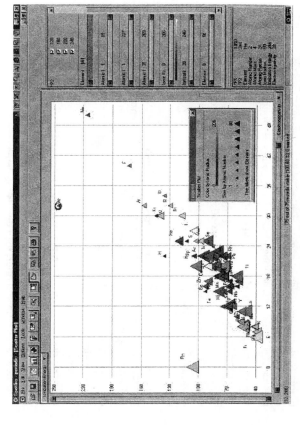

Figure 33.6 Chemicals organized by electronegativity and ionization energy, revealing a strong correlation and two outliers: helium and radon.

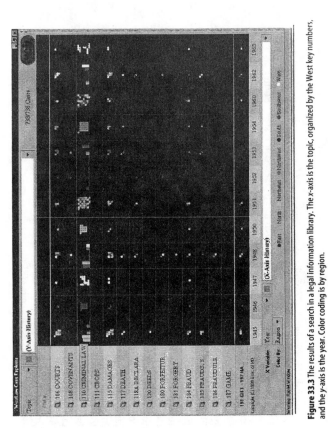

Figure 33.3 The results of a search in a legal information library. The x-axis is the topic, organized by the West key numbers, and the y-axis is the year. Color coding is by region.

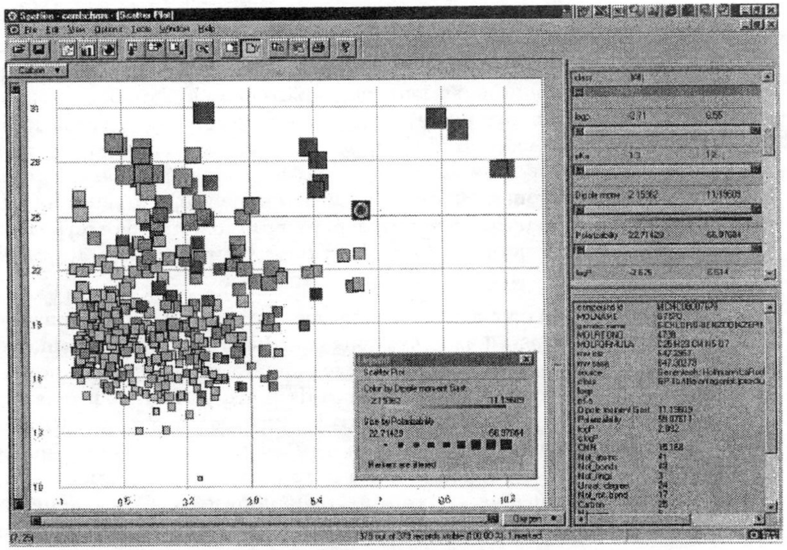

Figure 33.4 Information visualization of 379 chemical compounds. The x-axis is the amount of carbon and the y-axis is the amount of oxygen. Color coding is by dipole moment and size coding is by polarizability.

Cognitive principles: A solid theory for creativity support by way of information visualization would rest on a thorough understanding of cognitive principles to guide design (Card, 1996). Existing design principles such as direct manipulation have been demonstrated to be successful by empirical studies, and they have been widely applied in word processors, spreadsheets, drawing tools and many other environments:

• Visual representation of the "world of action"
 – Objects and actions are shown
 – Tap analogical reasoning by appropriate metaphors and icons
• Rapid, incremental and reversible actions
• Replace typing with pointing/selecting
• Continuous feedback

These principles are helpful to designers but need to be more rigorous if they are to provide predictive power. Another basic principle that has been applied for browsing and searching, might be summarized as the Visual Information Seeking Mantra:

Overview first, zoom and filter, then details-on-demand
Overview first, zoom and filter, then details-on-demand
Overview first, zoom and filter, then details-on-demand
Overview first, zoom and filter, then details-on-demand
Overview first, zoom and filter, then details-on-demand
Overview first, zoom and filter, then details-on-demand
Overview first, zoom and filter, then details-on-demand
Overview first, zoom and filter, then details-on-demand
Overview first, zoom and filter, then details-on-demand
Overview first, zoom and filter, then details-on-demand

Each line represents a project in which we struggled with a design only to rediscover this principle, and therefore I wrote it down as a continuing reminder. If we can design systems with effective visual displays, direct manipulation interfaces and dynamic queries, then users may be able to responsibly and confidently take on more ambitious tasks. However, empirical studies would be helpful in assessing the benefits.

Collaboration: A key phase of genex, and many creativity models, is the process of consultation with peers and mentors (Olson and Olson, 1997). Such consultations may occur at early, middle or late stages of a creative problem solving process. Users need to conference over some materials using an appropriate communications medium such as a face-to-face meeting, videoconference, telephone, email exchange or printed documents. Therefore creativity support and information visualization tools need to make it easy for users to save, extract, replay and annotate their activities.

33.4 Conclusions

Creativity support is a risky term because it may sound vague and difficult to evaluate. However, it can become a vigorous research topic if work focuses on more

33.3 Questions for the Future

The computing industry and the research community are moving ahead with a new generation of systems. In addition to our work, research on information visualization is emerging at key sites such as Georgia Tech's Graphics Visualization and Usability Center, Xerox's Palo Alto Research Center and Lucent Technologies (formerly AT&T Bell Labs) in Naperville, IL. Commercial activity ranges from expansion of existing statistical, spreadsheet, or database packages to include visualization capabilities, for example SPSS and SAS. Specialized visualization tools have emerged from new companies such as Inxight, Visual Insight, Visible Decisions and Spotfire. However, numerous questions remain that are the basis for this research agenda.

Generality: Many creativity support and information visualization tools are designed for a specific type of data and task, so generalization is an important issue. Since the range of information visualization situations includes at least 1D, 2D, 3D, multidimensional, temporal, hierarchical and network data types, it is not clear that a single tool can be useful to a wide range of users (Robertson *et al.*, 1993; Becker *et al.*, 1995; Shneiderman, 1998a). Tasks include presenting meaningful overviews, zooming in on desired items, filtering out undesired items, obtaining details-on-demand, showing relationships among items, extracting information for use in other programs and keeping a history of user actions to allow review and replay. Developing general purpose tools that support the range of data and tasks would be a major step forward.

Integration: Successful support for creativity and practical application of information visualization requires a smooth integration with other tools. The results of a Web or database search should be easily imported (for example by cut and paste) into a visual presentation. Then users should be able to filter the data appropriately and adjust the visualization features, such as x,y axes, color, size or other codings. When an interesting group of items is found, users should be able to select them and paste them into a spreadsheet or statistics package for further processing. At the next stage, the visualization and processed items should be embeddable in a written report, slide presentation, or email note. Email recipients should be able to manipulate the visualization or report still further (Roth *et al.*, 1996).

Perceptual foundations: A necessary foundation is an understanding of the perceptual principles concerning location, color, size, shape, animation and other codings (Rohrer *et al.*, 1999). While much is known about static displays, the dynamic environment of user interfaces is in need of extensive human factors analysis. Preconscious recognition of small numbers of items, simple patterns or outliers from a large group occurs very rapidly (less than 400 milliseconds), but recognition of more complex relationships involving multiple colors or shapes can take much longer. Strategies for rapid panning or zooming are beginning to be understood, but comparisons between these animated approaches, distortion-oriented (fisheye) and dual views would be very helpful (Plaisant *et al.*, 1995; Schaffer *et al.*, 1996). Another key comparison that deserves extensive study is between 2D and 3D visual presentations (Sutcliffe and Patel, 1996). Advocates of each style claim superiority, but the empirical evidence is still shallow.

identifiable user activities, such as the list of eight offered in Section 33.1.1. This chapter concentrates on the activity of visualizing and explores how information-visualization techniques can support creativity. Researchers will have to deal with at least five key questions in order to develop useful software: generality, integration, perceptual foundations, cognitive principles and collaboration.

However, implementation of novel tools is not a sufficient goal. New visualizations and their use must be subjected to rigorous empirical studies to get past the developer's bias and wishful thinking. Evaluations, ranging from controlled experiments to field trials with ethnographic observations, will validate or overturn hypotheses, refine theories, and sharpen our understanding of what to measure. Such studies are likely to be the rapid route to development of advanced information-abundant user interfaces.

Acknowledgments

I greatly appreciate my partners at IBM, NASA and WestGroup for partial support of this research. Thanks to Benjamin Bederson, David Ebert and Jenny Preece for their thoughtful comments on earlier drafts.

References

Ahlberg, C and Shneiderman, B (1994) Visual information seeking: tight coupling of dynamic query filters with starfield displays, in *Proc. ACM CHI'94 Conference: Human Factors in Computing Systems*, ACM, New York, pp. 313–321 and color plates.

Ahlberg, C, Williamson, C and Shneiderman, B (1992) Dynamic queries for information exploration: an implementation and evaluation, in *Proc. ACM CHI'92: Human Factors in Computing Systems*, ACM, New York, pp. 619–626.

Becker, RA, Eick, SG and Wilks, AR (1995) Visualizing network data, *IEEE Transactions on Visualization and Computer Graphics* 1(1), 16–28.

Bederson, BB and Hollan, JD (1994) PAD++: a zooming graphical user interface for exploring alternate interface physics, in *Proc. User Interfaces Software and Technology '94*, ACM, New York, pp. 17–27.

Bertin, J (1983) *Semiology of Graphics*, Madison, WI, University of Wisconsin Press.

Boden, M (1990) *The Creative Mind: Myths & Mechanisms*, New York, Basic Books.

Brooks, F, Jr (1996) The computer scientist as toolsmith II, *Communications of the ACM* 39(3), 61–68.

Bush, V (1945) As we may think, *Atlantic Monthly*, 76(1), 101–108. Also at http://www.theatlantic.com/unbound/flashbks/computer/bushf.htm.

Candy, L (1997) Computers and creativity support: knowledge, visualization and collaboration, *Knowledge-Based Systems* 10, 3–13.

Card, SC (1996) Visualizing retrieved information: a survey, *IEEE Computer Graphics and Applications* 16(2), 63–67.

Card, S, Mackinlay, J and Shneiderman, B (1999) *Readings in Information Visualization: Using Vision to Think*, San Francisco, CA, Morgan Kaufmann.

Couger, D (1996) *Creativity & Innovation in Information Systems Organizations*, Danvers, MA, Boyd & Fraser.

Csikszentmihalyi, M (1996) *Creativity: Flow and the Psychology of Discovery and Invention*, New York, HarperCollins.

De Bono, E (1973) *Lateral Thinking: Creativity Step by Step*, New York, Harper Colophon Books.

Engelbart, DC and English, WK (1968) A research center for augmenting human intellect, *AFIPS Proc. Fall Joint Computer Conference* 33, 395–410.

Hiltz, RS (1984) *Online Communities: A Case Study of the Office of the Future*, Norwood, NJ, Ablex.

Hiltz, RS and Turoff, M (1993) *The Network Nation: Human Communication via Computer*, rev. edn, Cambridge, MA, MIT Press.

Massetti, B (1996) An empirical examination of the value of creativity support systems on idea generation, *MIS Quarterly*, 20(1), 83–97.

Massetti, B, White, NH and Spitler, VK (1999) The impact of the World Wide Web on idea generation, in *Proc. 32nd Hawaii International Conference on System Sciences*, IEEE Press.

Mayer, RE (1992) *Thinking, Problem Solving, Cognition*, 2nd edn, New York, W. H. Freeman.

National Research Council – Committee on a National Collaboratory (1993) *National Collaboratories: Applying Information Technology for Scientific Research*, Washington, DC, National Academy Press.

Olson, GM and Olson, JS (1997) Research on computer supported cooperative work, in *Handbook of Human–Computer Interaction*, 2nd edn (eds. MG Helander, TK Landauer and PV Prabhu), Amsterdam, Elsevier, pp. 1433–1456.

Plaisant, C, Carr, D and Shneiderman, B (1995) Image-browser taxonomy and guidelines for designers, *IEEE Software* 12(2), 21–32.

Plaisant, C, Rose, A, Milash, B, Widoff, S and Shneiderman, B (1996) LifeLines: visualizing personal histories, in *Proc. of ACM CHI'96 Conference: Human Factors in Computing Systems*, New York, ACM, pp. 221–227, 518.

Robertson, GG, Card, SK and Mackinlay, JD (1993) Information visualization using 3D interactive animation, *Communications of the ACM*, 36(4), 56–71.

Rohrer, R, Ebert, D and Sibert, J (1999) A shape-based visual interface for text retrieval, *IEEE Computer Graphics and Applications*, 19.

Rose, A, Eckard, D and Rubloff, G (1998) An application framework for creating simulation-based learning environments, *University of Maryland Department of Computer Science Technical Report CS-TR-3907*.

Rosner, S and Abt, LE (eds.) (1970) *The Creative Experience*, New York, Dell Publishing.

Roth, SF, Lucas, P, Senn, JA, Gomberg, CC, Burks, MB, Stroffolino, PJ, Kolojejchick, JA and Dunmire, C (1996) Visage: a user interface environment for exploring information, in *Proc. Information Visualization '96*, Los Alamitos, CA, IEEE, pp. 3–12.

Schaffer, D, Zuo, Z, Greenberg, S, Bartram, L, Dill, J, Dubs, S and Roseman, M (1996) Navigating hierarchically clustered networks through fisheye and full-zoom methods, *ACM Transactions on Computer-Human Interaction*, 3(2), 162–188.

Shneiderman, B (1994) Dynamic queries for visual information seeking, *IEEE Software*, 11(6), 70–77.

Shneiderman, B (1998a) *Designing the User Interface: Strategies for Effective Human–computer Interaction*, 3rd edn, Reading, MA, Addison-Wesley.

Shneiderman B (1998b) Codex, memex, genex: the pursuit of transformational technologies, *International Journal of Human-Computer Interaction*, 10(2), 87–106.

Shneiderman, B (1999) Creating creativity for everyone: User interfaces for supporting innovation, *Univ. of Maryland Dept of Computer Science Technical Report*.

Shneiderman, B, Feldman, D and Rose, A (1999) Visualizing digital library search results with categorical and hierarchical axes, *University of Maryland Department of Computer Science Technical Report CS-TR-3992*.

Sutcliffe, A and Patel, U (1996) 3D or not 3D: is it nobler in the mind?, in *Proc. British HCI Conference*, pp. 79–94.

Tufte, E (1983) *The Visual Display of Quantitative Information*, Cheshire, CT, Graphics Press.

Tufte, E (1990) *Envisioning Information*, Cheshire, CT, Graphics Press.

Tufte, E (1997) *Visual Explanations: Images and Quantities, Evidence and Narrative*, Cheshire, CT, Graphics Press.

Williamson, C and Shneiderman, B (1992) The Dynamic HomeFinder: evaluating dynamic queries in a real-estate information exploration system, in *Proc. ACM SIGIR'92 Conference*, Copenhagen, Denmark, June, pp. 338–346. Reprinted in Shneiderman, B (ed.) (1993) *Sparks of Innovation in Human–Computer Interaction*, Norwood, NJ, Ablex, pp. 295–307.

Inventing discovery tools: combining information visualization with data mining[†]

Ben Shneiderman[1]

[1]Department of Computer Science, University of Maryland, College Park, Maryland, U.S.A.

Correspondence:
Ben Shneiderman, Department of Computer Science, Human-Computer Interaction Laboratory, Institute for Advanced Computer Studies, and Institute for Systems Research, University of Maryland, College Park, MD 20742 U.S.A.
E-mail: ben@cs.umd.edu

[†]Keynote for Discovery Science 2001 Conference, November 25–28, 2001, Washington, DC.

Abstract
The growing use of information visualization tools and data mining algorithms stems from two separate lines of research. Information visualization researchers believe in the importance of giving users an overview and insight into the data distributions, while data mining researchers believe that statistical algorithms and machine learning can be relied on to find the interesting patterns. This paper discusses two issues that influence design of discovery tools: statistical algorithms *vs* visual data presentation, and hypothesis testing *vs* exploratory data analysis. The paper claims that a combined approach could lead to novel discovery tools that preserve user control, enable more effective exploration, and promote responsibility.
Information Visualization (2002) **1**, 5–12. DOI: 10.1057/palgrave/ivs/9500006

Keywords: Information visualization; data mining; user interfaces; discovery; creativity support tools

Introduction

Genomics researchers, financial analysts, and social scientists hunt for patterns in vast data warehouses using increasingly powerful software tools. These tools are based on emerging concepts such as knowledge discovery, data mining, and information visualization. They also employ specialized methods such as neural networks, decisions trees, principal components analysis, and a hundred others.

Computers have made it possible to conduct complex statistical analyses that would have been prohibitive to carry out in the past. However, the dangers of using complex computer software grow when user comprehension and control are diminished. Therefore, it seems useful to reflect on the underlying philosophy and appropriateness of the diverse methods that have been proposed. This could lead to a better understanding of when to use given tools and methods, as well as contribute to the invention of new discovery tools and refinement of existing ones.

Each tool conveys an outlook about the importance of human initiative and control as contrasted with machine intelligence and power.[1] The conclusion deals with the central issue of responsibility for failures and successes. Many issues influence design of discovery tools, but this paper focuses on two: statistical algorithms *vs* visual data presentation and hypothesis testing *vs* exploratory data analysis

Statistical algorithms *vs* visual data presentation

Early efforts to summarize data generated means, medians, standard deviations, and ranges. These numbers were helpful because their compactness, relative to the full data set, and their clarity supported understanding, comparisons, and decision making. Summary statistics appealed to the rational thinkers who were attracted to the objective nature of data comparisons that avoided human subjectivity. However, they also hid interesting features such as whether distributions were uniform, normal, skewed, bi-modal, or distorted by outliers. A remedy to these problems was the presentation of data as a visual plot so interesting features could be seen by a human researcher.

The invention of times-series plots and statistical graphics for economic data is usually attributed to William Playfair (1759–1823) who published *The Commercial and Political Atlas* in 1786 in London. Visual presentations can be very powerful in revealing trends, highlighting outliers, showing clusters, and exposing gaps. Visual presentations can give users a richer sense of what is happening in the data and suggest possible directions for further study. Visual presentations speak to the intuitive side and the sense-making spirit that is part of exploration. Of course, visual presentations have their limitations in terms of dealing with large data sets, occlusion of data, disorientation, and misinterpretation.

By early in the 20th century statistical approaches, encouraged by the Age of Rationalism, became prevalent in many scientific domains. Ronald Fisher (1890–1962) developed modern statistical methods for experimental designs related to his extensive agricultural studies. His development of analysis of variance for design of factorial experiments[2] helped advance scientific research in many fields.[3] His approaches are still widely used in cognitive psychology and have influenced most experimental sciences.

The appearance of computers heightened the importance of this issue. Computers can be used to carry out far more complex statistical algorithms and they can also be used to generate rich visual, animated, and user-controlled displays. Typical presentation of statistical data mining results is by brief summary tables, induced rules, or decision trees. Typical visual data presentations show data-rich histograms, scattergrams, heatmaps, treemaps, dendrograms, parallel coordinates, etc. in multiple coordinated windows that support user-controlled exploration with dynamic queries for filtering (Figure 1). Comparative studies of statistical summaries and visual presentations demonstrate the importance of user familiarity and training with each approach and the influence of specific tasks. Of course, statistical summaries and visual presentations can both be misleading or confusing.

An example may help clarify the distinction. Promoters of statistical methods may use linear correlation coefficients to detect relationships between variables, which works wonderfully when there is a linear relationship between variables and when the data is free from anomalies. However, if the relationship is quadratic (or exponential, sinusoidal, etc.) a linear algorithm may fail to detect the relationship. Similarly if there are data collection problems that add outliers or if there are discontinuities over the range (e.g. freezing or boiling points of water), then linear correlation may fail. A visual presentation is more likely to help researchers find such phenomena and suggest richer hypotheses.

Hypothesis testing *vs* exploratory data analysis

Fisher's approach not only promoted statistical methods over visual presentations, but also strongly endorsed theory-driven hypothesis-testing research over casual observation and exploratory data analysis. This philosophical strand goes back to Francis Bacon (1551–1626) and later to John Herschel's 1830 *A Preliminary Discourse on the Study of Natural Philosophy*. They are usually credited with influencing modern notions of scientific methods based on rules of induction and the hypothetico-deductive method. Believers in scientific methods typically see controlled experiments as the fast path to progress, even though its use of the reductionist approach to test one variable at a time can be disconcertingly slow. Fisher's invention of factorial experiments helped make controlled experimentation more efficient.

Advocates of the reductionist approach and controlled experimentation argue that large benefits come when researchers are forced to clearly state their hypotheses in advance of data collection. This enables them to limit the number of independent variables and to measure a small number of dependent variables. They believe that the courageous act of stating hypotheses in advance sharpens thinking, leads to more parsimonious data collection, and encourages precise measurement. Their goals are to understand causal relationships, to produce replicable results, and to emerge with generalizable insights. Critics complain that the reductionist approach, with its laboratory conditions to ensure control, is too far removed from reality (not situated and therefore stripped of context) and therefore may ignore important variables that effect outcomes. They also argue that by forcing researchers to state an initial hypothesis, their observation will be biased towards finding evidence to support their hypothesis and will ignore interesting phenomena that are not related to their dependent variables.

On the other side of this interesting debate are advocates of exploratory data analysis who believe that great gains can be made by collecting voluminous data sets and then searching for interesting patterns. They contend that statistical analyses and machine learning techniques have matured enough to reveal complex relationships that were not anticipated by researchers. They believe that *a priori* hypotheses limit research and are no longer needed because of the capacity of computers to collect and analyze voluminous data. Skeptics worry that any given set of data, no matter how large, may still be a special case, thereby undermining the generalizability of the results. They also question whether detection of strong statistical relationships can ever lead to an understanding of cause and effect. They declare that correlation does not imply causation.

Once again, an example may clarify this issue. If a semiconductor fabrication facility is generating a high rate of failures, promoters of hypothesis testing might list the possible causes, such as contaminants, excessive heat, or too rapid cooling. They might seek evidence to support

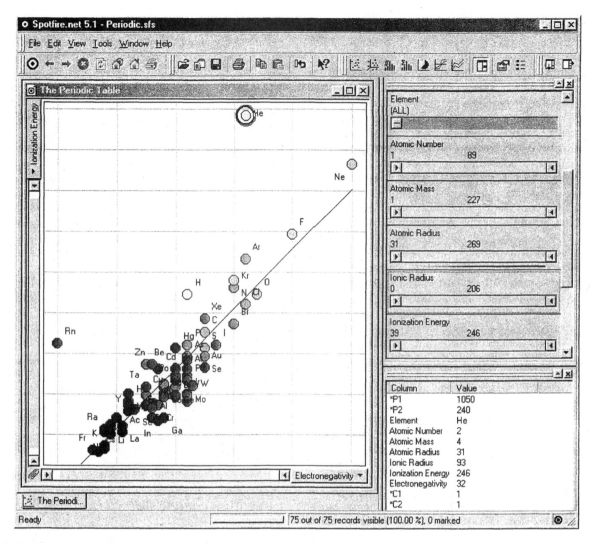

Figure 1 Spotfire (www.spotfire.com) display of chemical elements showing the strong correlation between ionization energy and electronegativity, and two dramatic outliers: radon and helium.

these hypotheses and maybe conduct trial runs with the equipment to see if they could regenerate the problem. Promoters of exploratory data analysis might want to collect existing data from the past year of production under differing conditions and then run data mining tools against these data sets to discover correlates of high rates of failure. Of course, an experienced supervisor may blend these approaches, gathering exploratory hypotheses from the existing data and then conducting confirmatory tests.

The new paradigms

The emergence of the computer has shaken the methodological edifice. Complex statistical calculations and animated visualizations become feasible. Elaborate controlled experiments can be run hundreds of times and exploratory data analysis has become widespread. Devotees of hypothesis-testing have new tools to collect data and prove their hypotheses. T-tests and analysis of variance (ANOVA) have been joined by linear and non-linear regression, complex forecasting methods, and discriminant analysis.

Those who believe in exploratory data analysis methods have even more new tools such as neural networks, rule induction, a hundred forms of automated clustering, and even more machine learning methods. These are often covered in the rapidly growing academic discipline of data mining.[4,5] Witten and Frank[6] define data mining as 'the extraction of implicit, previously unknown, and potentially useful information from data'. They caution that 'exaggerated reports appear of the secrets that can be uncovered by setting learning algorithms loose on oceans of data. But there is no magic in machine learning, no hidden power, no alchemy. Instead there is an identifiable body of simple and practical techniques that can often extract useful information from raw data'.

Similarly, those who believe in data or information visualization are having a great time as the computer enables rapid display of large data sets with rich user control panels to support exploration.[7] Users can manipulate up to a million data items with 100-ms update of displays that present color-coded, size-coded markers for each item. With the right coding, human pre-attentive perceptual skills enable users to recognize patterns, spot outliers, identify gaps, and find clusters in a few hundred milliseconds. When data sets grow past a million items and cannot be easily seen on a computer display, users can extract relevant subsets, aggregate data into meaningful units, or randomly sample to create a manageable data set.

The commercial success of tools such as SAS JMP (www.sas.com), SPSS Diamond (www.spss.com), and Spotfire (www.spotfire.com) (Figure 1), especially for pharmaceutical drug discovery and genomic data analysis, demonstrate the attraction of visualization. Other notable products include Inxight's Eureka (www.inxight.com) for multidimensional tabular data and Visual Insights' eBizinsights (www.visualinsights.com) for web log visualization.

Spence[8] characterizes information visualization with this vignette: 'You are the owner of some numerical data which, you feel, is hiding some fundamental relation... you then glance at some visual presentation of that data and exclaim 'Ah ha! – now I understand''. But Spence also cautions that 'information visualization is characterized by so many beautiful images that there is a danger of adopting a 'Gee Whiz' approach to its presentation'.

A spectrum of discovery tools

The happy resolution to these debates is to take the best insights from both extremes and create novel discovery tools for many different users and many different domains. Skilled problem solvers often combine observation at early stages, which leads to hypothesis-testing experiments. Alternatively they may have a precise hypothesis, but if they are careful observers during a controlled experiment, they may spot anomalies that lead to new hypotheses. Skilled problem solvers often combine statistical tests and visual presentation. A visual presentation of data may identify two clusters whose separate analysis can lead to useful results when a combined analysis would fail. Similarly, a visual presentation might show a parabola, which indicates a quadratic relationship between variables, but no relationship would be found if a linear correlation test were applied. Devotees of statistical methods often find that presenting their results visually helps to explain them and suggests further statistical tests.

The process of combining statistical methods with visualization tools will take some time because of the conflicting philosophies of the promoters. The famed statistician John Tukey (1915–2000) quickly recognized the power of combined approaches:[9] 'As yet I know of no person or group that is taking nearly adequate, advantage of the graphical potentialities of the computer... In exploration

they are going to be the data analyst's greatest single resource'. The combined strength of visual data mining would enrich both approaches and enable more successful solutions.[10] However, most books on data mining have only brief discussion of information visualization and vice versa. Some researchers have begun to implement interactive visual approaches to data mining[11–13] and a collection of papers has recently appeared.[14]

Accelerating the process of combining hypothesis testing with exploratory data analysis[15] will also bring substantial benefits. New statistical tests and metrics for uniformity of distributions, outlier-ness, or cluster-ness will be helpful, especially if visual interfaces enable users to examine the distributions rapidly, change some parameters and get fresh metrics and corresponding visualizations.

Case studies of combining visualization with data mining

One way to combine visual techniques with automated data mining is to provide support tools for users with both components. Users can then explore data with direct manipulation user interfaces that control information visualization components and apply statistical tests when something interesting appears. Alternatively, they can use data mining as a first pass and then examine the results visually.

Direct manipulation strategies with user-controlled visualizations start with visual presentation of the world of action, which includes the objects of interest and the actions. Early examples included air traffic control and video games. In graphical user interfaces, direct manipulation means dragging files to folders or to the trashcan for deletion. Rapid incremental and reversible actions encourage exploration and provide continuous feedback so users can see what they are doing. Good examples are moving or resizing a window. Modern applications of direct manipulation principles have led to information visualization tools that show hundreds of thousands of items on the screen at once. Sliders, check boxes, and radio buttons allow users to filter items dynamically with updates in less than 100 ms.

Early information visualizations included the Dynamic Queries HomeFinder (Figure 2) which allowed users to select from a database of 1100 homes using sliders on home price, number of bedrooms, and distance from markers, plus buttons for other features such as fireplaces, central air conditioning, etc.[16,17]

This led to the FilmFinder[18] and then the successful commercial product, Spotfire (Figure 1). One Spotfire feature is the View Tip that uses statistical data mining methods to suggest interesting pair-wise relationships by using linear correlation coefficients (Figure 3). The ViewTip might be improved by giving more user control over the specification of interesting-ness that ranks the outcomes.

While some users may be interested in high linear correlation coefficients, others may be interested in low

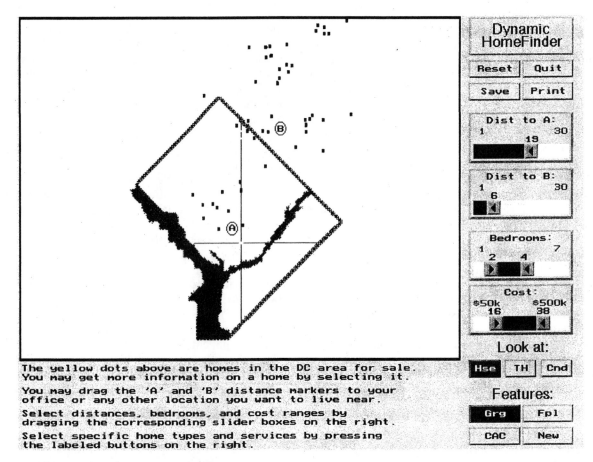

The yellow dots above are homes in the DC area for sale.
You may get more information on a home by selecting it.

You may drag the 'A' and 'B' distance markers to your
office or any other location you want to live near.

Select distances, bedrooms, and cost ranges by
dragging the corresponding slider boxes on the right.

Select specific home types and services by pressing
the labeled buttons on the right.

Figure 2 Dynamic Queries HomeFinder with sliders to control the display of markers indicating homes for sale. Users can specify distances to markers, bedrooms, cost, type of house and features.[16]

correlation coefficients, or might prefer rankings by quadratic, exponential, sinusoidal or other correlations. Other choices might be to rank distributions by existing metrics such as skewness (negative or positive) or outlierness.[19] New metrics for degree of uniformity, cluster-ness, or gap-ness are excellent candidates for research. We are in the process of building a control panel that allows users to specify the distributions they are seeking by adjusting sliders and seeing how the rankings shift. Five algorithms have been written for 1-dimensional data and one for 2-dimensional data, but more will be prepared soon (Figure 4).

A second case study is our work with time-series pattern finding.[20] Current tools for stock market or genomic expression data from DNA microarrays rely on clustering in multidimensional space, but a more user-controlled specification tool might enable analysts to carefully specify what they want.[21] Our efforts to build a tool, TimeSearcher, have relied on query specification by drawing boxes to indicate what ranges of values are desired for each time period (Figure 5). It has more of the spirit of hypothesis testing. While this takes somewhat greater effort, it gives users greater control over the query results. Users can move the

boxes around in a direct manipulation style and immediately see the new set of results. The opportunity for rapid exploration is dramatic and users can immediately see where matches are frequent and where matches are rare.

Conclusion and Recommendations

Computational tools for discovery, such as data mining and information visualization have advanced dramatically in recent years. Unfortunately, these tools have been developed by largely separate communities with different philosophies. Data mining and machine learning researchers tend to believe in the power of their statistical methods to identify interesting patterns without human intervention. Information visualization researchers tend to believe in the importance of user control by domain experts to produce useful visual presentations that provide unanticipated insights.

Recommendation 1: integrate data mining and information visualization to invent discovery tools. By adding visualization to data mining (such as presenting scattergrams to accompany induced rules), users will develop a deeper understanding of their data. By adding data mining to

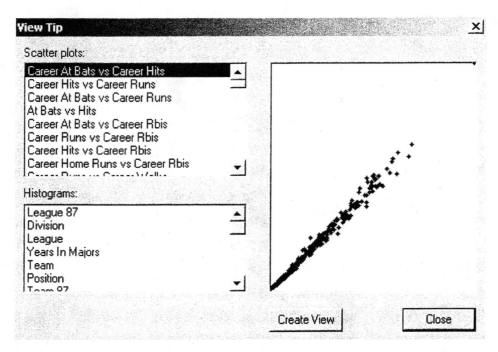

Figure 3 Spotfire View Tip panel with ranking of possible 2-dimensional scatter plots in descending order by the strength of linear correlation. Here the strong correlation in baseball statistics is shown between Career At Bats and Career Hits. Notice the single outlier in the upper right corner, representing Pete Rose's long successful career.

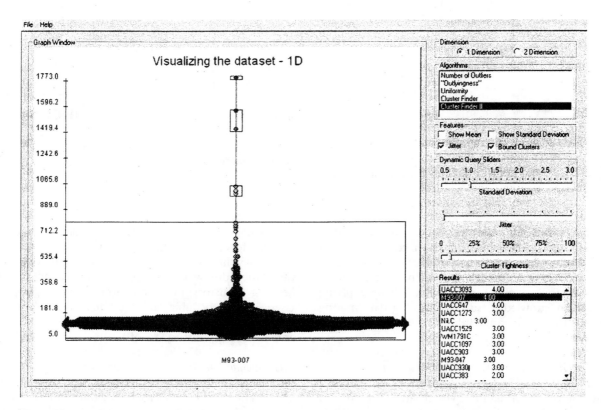

Figure 4 Prototype panel to enable user specification of 1-dimensional distribution requirements. User has chosen the Cluster Finder II algorithm that ranks all distributions according to the number of identifiable clusters, while allowing users to specify Cluster Tightness with a slider (Implemented by Kartik Parija and Jaime Spacco).

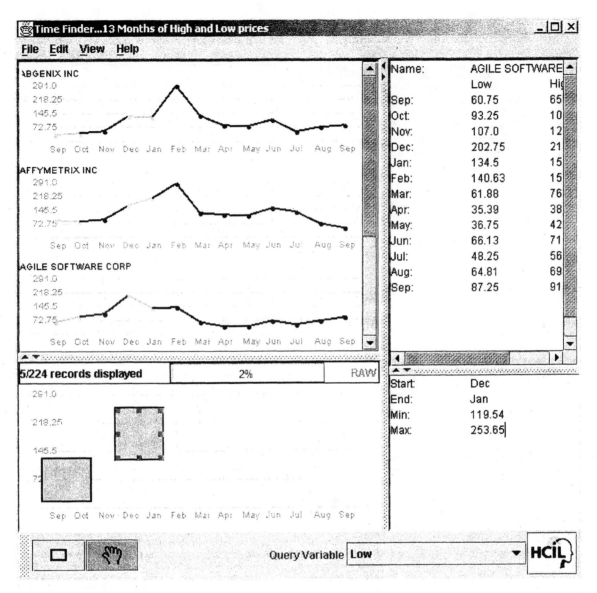

Figure 5 TimeSearcher allows users to specify ranges for time-series data and immediately see the result set. In this case two timeboxes have been drawn and five of the 224 stocks match this pattern.[21]

visualization (such as the Spotfire View Tip), users will be able to specify what they seek. Both communities of researchers emphasize exploratory data analysis over hypothesis testing. A middle ground of enabling users to structure their exploratory data analysis by applying their domain knowledge (such as limiting data mining algorithms to specific range values) may also be a source of innovative tools.

Recommendation 2: allow users to specify what they are seeking and what they find interesting. By allowing data mining and information visualization users to constrain and direct their tools, they may produce more rapid innovation. As in the Spotfire View Tip example, users could be given a control panel to indi-

cate what kind of correlations or outliers they are looking for. As users test their hypotheses against the data, they find dead ends and discover new possibilities. Since discovery is a process, not a point event, keeping a history of user actions has a high payoff. Users should be able to save their state (data items and control panel settings), back up to previous states, and send their history to others.

Recommendation 3: recognize that users are situated in a social context. Researchers and practitioners rarely work alone. They need to gather data from multiple sources, consult with domain experts, pass on partial results to others, and then present their findings to colleagues and decision makers. Successful tools enable users to exchange data, ask for consultations from peers and mentors, and report results to others conveniently.

Recommendation 4: respect human responsibility when designing discovery tools. If tools are comprehensible, predictable and controllable, then users can develop mastery over their tools and experience satisfaction in accomplishing their work. They want to be able to take pride in their successes and they should be responsible for their failures. When tools become too complex or unpredictable, users will avoid their use because the tools are out of their control. Users often perform better when they understand and control what the computer does.[22]

If complex statistical algorithms or visual presentations are not well understood by users they cannot act on the results with confidence. The author believes that visibility of the statistical processes and outcomes minimizes the danger of misinterpretation and incorrect results. Comprehension of the algorithms behind the visualizations and the implications of layout encourage effective usage that leads to successful discovery.

Acknowledgments

Thanks to Mary Czerwinski, Lindley Darden, Harry Hochheiser, Jenny Preece, and Ian Witten for comments on drafts.

References

1 Weizenbaum J. *Computer Power and Human Reason: From Judgment to Calculation.* W. H. Freeman and Co.: San Francisco, CA, 1976.
2 Fisher RA. *The Design of Experiments,* 9th edition. Macmillan: New York, 1971.
3 Montgomery D. *Design and Analysis of Experiments,* 3rd edn. Wiley: New York, 1991.
4 Fayyad U, Piatetsky-Shapiro G, Smyth P, Uthurusamy R. (eds). *Advances in Knowledge Discovery and Data Mining.* MIT Press: Cambridge, MA, 1996.
5 Han J, Kamber M. *Data Mining: Concepts and Techniques.* Morgan Kaufmann Publishers: San Francisco, 2000.
6 Witten I, Frank E. *Data Mining: Practical Machine Learning Tools and Techniques with Java Implementations.* Morgan Kaufmann Publishers: San Francisco, 2000.
7 Card S, Mackinlay J, Shneiderman B. (eds). *Readings in Information Visualization: Using Vision to Think.* Morgan Kaufmann Publishers: San Francisco, CA, 1999.
8 Spence R. *Information Visualization.* Addison-Wesley: Essex, England, 2001.
9 Tukey J. The technical tools of statistics. *American Statistician* 1965; **19**: 23–28. Available at: http://stat.bell-labs.com/who/tukey/memo/techtools.html
10 Westphal C, Blaxton T. *Data Mining Solutions: Methods and Tools for Solving Real-World Problems.* John Wiley & Sons: New York, 1999.
11 Hinneburg A, Keim D, Wawryniuk M. HD-Eye: Visual mining of high-dimensional data. *IEEE Computer Graphics and Applications* 1999; **19**: 22–31.
12 Ankerst M, Ester M, Kriegel H-P. *Towards an effective cooperation of the user and the computer for classification.* Proceedings of 6th ACM SIGKDD International Conference on Knowledge Discovery and Data Mining (2000), ACM: New York, 179–188.
13 Ware M, Frank E, Holmes G, Hall M, Witten IH. Interactive machine learning: Letting users build classifiers. *International Journal of Human-Computer Studies* 2001; **55**: 281–292.
14 Fayyad U, Grinstein GG, Wierse A. (eds). *Information Visualization in Data Mining and Knowledge Discovery.* Morgan Kaufmann Publishers: San Francisco, 2002.
15 Tukey J. *Exploratory Data Analysis.* Addison-Wesley: Reading, MA, 1977.
16 Williamson C, Shneiderman B. *The Dynamic HomeFinder: Evaluating dynamic queries in a real-estate information exploration system.* Proceedings of ACM SIGIR'92 Conference (1992), ACM Press: New York, 338–346.
17 Shneiderman B. Dynamic queries for visual information seeking. *IEEE Software* 1994; **11**: 70–77.
18 Ahlberg C, Shneiderman B. *Visual Information Seeking: Tight coupling of dynamic query filters with starfield displays.* Proceedings of ACM CHI '94 Human Factors in Computing Systems (1994), ACM Press: New York, 313–317.
19 Barnett V, Lewis T. *Outliers in Statistical Data,* 3rd edn. John Wiley & Son Ltd: Chichester, 1994.
20 Bradley E. Time-series analysis. In: Berthold M and Hand E. (eds). *Intelligent Data Analysis: An Introduction.* Springer: Berlin, 1999.
21 Hochheiser H, Shneiderman B. *Interactive exploration of time-series data.* Proc. Discovery Science. Springer: Berlin, 2001.
22 Koenemann J, Belkin N. *A case for interaction: A study of interactive information retrieval behavior and effectiveness.* Proceedings of CHI '96 Human Factors in Computing Systems (1996), ACM Press: New York, 205–212.

Appendix A
Videos

This appendix contains selections from the University of Maryland Human–Computer Interaction Laboratory Technical Videos Series related to information visualization. The HCIL video series (1991–2002) includes video reports and demonstrations from HCIL projects. Several of those video reports were subsequently reprinted in, or reedited for, the ACM SIGCHI video program. Those videos are marked with an asterisk (*). The series is edited by Catherine Plaisant (plaisant@cs.umd.edu).

Our purpose in producing these videos is to present our work to colleagues, preserve the ideas in a form that has proved to be more stable than the programming environments, and enable others to educate students and professionals. We see these as a form of technical report and endeavor to add references to previous work.

To recover some of the costs of production and distribution, we charge for the videotapes. Abstracts and prices (NTSC and PAL, shipping) are available online at *www.cs.umd.edu/hcil/pubs/video-reports.shtml*.

Requests for the tapes (VHS or PAL) may be sent to hcil-info@cs.umd.edu, or contact us at the following address:

Human–Computer Interaction Laboratory
UMIACS, A.V. Williams Building
University of Maryland
College Park, MD 20742
(301) 405-2769

Many HCIL videos are available free on the Web from Open Video: *www.open-video.org/collections/hcil.php*.

SELECTION FROM 1991 VIDEO REPORTS
Scheduling Home Control Devices*
Catherine Plaisant, Ben Shneiderman
Pie Menus
Don Hopkins
Three Interfaces for Browsing Tables of Contents
Rick Chimera

SELECTION FROM 1992 VIDEO REPORTS
Dynamic Queries: Database Searching by Direct Manipulation*
Ben Shneiderman, Chris Williamson, Christopher Ahlberg
Treemaps for Visualizing Hierarchical Information
Ben Shneiderman, Brian Johnson, Dave Turo
Three Strategies for Directory Browsing
Rick Chimera
Filter-Flow Metaphor for Boolean Queries
Degi Young, Ben Shneiderman
Remote Direct Manipulation: A Telepathology Workstation*
Catherine Plaisant and Dave Carr

SELECTION FROM 1993 VIDEO REPORTS
Dynamaps: Dynamic Queries on a Health Statistics Atlas
Catherine Plaisant and Vinit Jain
Hierarchical Visualization with Treemaps: Making Sense of Pro Basketball Data*
Dave Turo
TreeViz: File Directory Browsing
Brian Johnson

SELECTION FROM 1994 VIDEO REPORTS
Visual Information Seeking Using the FilmFinder*
Christopher Ahlberg, Ben Shneiderman
Organization Overviews and Role Management: Inspiration for Future Desktop Environments*
Catherine Plaisant, Ben Shneiderman
Visual Decisionmaking: Using Treemaps for the Analytic Hierarchy Process
Toshiyuki Asahi, Ben Shneiderman, David Turo
Visual Information Management for Satellite Network Configuration
Catherine Plaisant, Harsha Kumar, Marko Teittinen
Dynamic Queries Demos: Revised HomeFinder and Text Version Plus Health Statistics Atlas
Ben Shneiderman

SELECTION FROM 1995 VIDEO REPORTS
Introduction including FilmFinder
Ben Shneiderman
Using Dynamic Queries for Youth Services Information
Anne Rose, Ajit Vanniamparampil
Life-Lines: Visualizing Personal Histories
Brett Milash, Catherine Plaisant, Anne Rose
Dynamic Queries and Pruning for Large Tree Structures
Harsha Kumar
Browsing Anatomical Image Databases : The Visible Human*
Flip Korn, Chris North
BizView : Managing Business and Network Alarms
Catherine Plaisant, Rina Levy, Wei Zhao
WinSurfer: Treemaps for Replacing the Windows File Manager
Marko Teittinen

SELECTION FROM 1996 VIDEO REPORTS
Elastic Windows for Rapid Multiple Window Management
Eser Kandogan
Life-Lines: Visualizing Personal Histories (revised version)*
Brett Milash, Catherine Plaisant, Anne Rose

Designing Interfaces for Youth Services Information
Management
    Jason Ellis, Anne Rose, Catherine Plaisant
Query Previews in Networked Information Systems :
The Case of EOSDIS*
    Catherine Plaisant, Tom Bruns, Ben Shneiderman,
    Khoa Doan
Baltimore Learning Communities
    Gary Marchionini, Allison Gordon, Tracy Vitek,
    Horatio Jabari-Kitwala, Victor Nolet
Visual Information Seeking using the FilmFinder*
(Extract from the HCIL 1994 Video Report)
    Christopher Ahlberg, Ben Shneiderman

SELECTION FROM 1997 VIDEO REPORTS

Bringing Treasures to the Surface: Previews and
Overviews in a Prototype for the Library of Congress
National Digital Library
    Catherine Plaisant, Anita Komlodi, Gary
    Marchionini, Ara Shirinian, David Nation, Steve
    Karasik, Teresa Cronnell, and Ben Shneiderman
Viewing Websites Using a Hierarchical Table of
Contents Browser: WebTOC
    David Nation
Using Multimedia Learning Resources for the Baltimore
Learning Community
    Becky Bishop and Josephus Beale
Visual Data Mining Using Spotfire
    Ben Shneiderman

SELECTION FROM 1998 HCIL VIDEO REPORTS

LifeLines: Enhancing Navigation and Analysis of
Patient Records
    Catherine Plaisant and Jia Li
Pad++: A Zooming Interface
    Ben Bederson
Query Previews for NASA EOSDIS, An Update
    Ben Shneiderman and Catherine Plaisant
Genex: A Medical Scenario
    Ben Shneiderman

SELECTION FROM 1999 HCIL VIDEO REPORTS

Query Previews for EOSDIS (1999 Update)
    Catherine Plaisant and Maya Venkatraman
Design Space for Data and Label Placement for
Information Visualization
    Jia Li, Catherine Plaisant, Ben Shneiderman
Visualizing Legal Information: Hierarchical and
Temporal Presentations
    Bob Allen, Richard Feldman, Chandra Harris,
    Anita Komlodi, Ben Shneiderman
Snap-Together Visualization
    Chris North, Ben Shneiderman

2000 HCIL VIDEO REPORTS

The 2000 video is a compilation of the best of HCIL videos,
including many of the visualization demonstrations. See
special listing and abstracts at *www.cs.umd.edu/hcil/pubs/
video2000.shtml*

2001 HCIL VIDEO REPORTS

PhotoMesa: A Zoomable Image Browser
    Bederson, B. B.
Visual Specification of Queries for Finding Patterns in
Time-Series Data**
    Hochheiser, H., Shneiderman, B.
Fisheye Menus
    Bederson, B. B.
Visualization for Production Management: Treemap and
Fisheye Table Browser
    Plaisant, C., Babaria, K., Bederson, B. B., Betten, S.,
    Blowitski, J. Grosjean, J., Shneiderman, B.
Generalizing Query Previews
    Tanin, E., Plaisant, C., Shneiderman, B.

2002 HCIL VIDEO REPORTS

FishCal: A Calendar Interface for PDAs
    Bederson, B. B.
SpaceTree: A Novel Node-Link Tree Browser
    Grosjean, J., Plaisant, C., Bederson, B. B.
Interactive Information Visualization of a Million Items
    Fekete, J.-D.

Appendix B

Project Pages

The HCIL Web site includes a page on visualization
www.cs.umd.edu/hcil/research/visualization.shtml

Baltimore Learning Community
www.learn.umd.edu/

Census project: dynamic choropleth maps
www.cs.umd.edu/hcil/census/

CounterPoint zoomable presentations
www.cs.umd.edu/hcil/counterpoint

DateLens: A calendar interface for Pocket PC PDAs
www.cs.umd.edu/hcil/datelens/

Dynamic queries interfaces for the NASA EOSDIS
Information System
www.cs.umd.edu/hcil/eosdis/

Dynamic queries, starfield displays, and the
path to Spotfire
www.cs.umd.edu/hcil/spotfire/

Excentric labeling for information visualization
www.cs.umd.edu/hcil/excentric/

Fisheye Menus for selection within long menus
www.cs.umd.edu/hcil/fisheyemenu/

Generalized query previews
www.cs.umd.edu/hcil/qp/

Highway traffic management
www.cs.umd.edu/hcil/highway/

KidPad: Collaborative children's storytelling tools
www.cs.umd.edu/hcil/kiddesign/kidpad.shtml

Legal information interfaces
www.cs.umd.edu/hcil/west-legal/

Library of Congress National Digital Library
www.cs.umd.edu/hcil/ndl/

LifeLines for visualizing patient records
www.cs.umd.edu/hcil/lifelines/

Multidimensional clustering and outlier detection
www.cs.umd.edu/hcil/multi-cluster/

Network management: pointers to relevant HCIL papers
and past projects
www.cs.umd.edu/hcil/network-monitoring/history.shtml

PhotoFinder: Photo library project
www.cs.umd.edu/hcil/photolib/

PhotoMesa zoomable image browser
www.cs.umd.edu/hcil/photomesa/

SimPLE (Simulated Processes in a Learning
Environment)
www.isr.umd.edu/SimPLE/

Snap-Together Visualization
www.cs.umd.edu/hcil/snap/

SpaceTree node-link tree browser
www.cs.umd.edu/hcil/spacetree/

TimeSearcher for time-series data
www.cs.umd.edu/hcil/timesearcher/

Treemaps for space-constrained visualization
of hierarchies
www.cs.umd.edu/hcil/treemap-history

Treemap 3
www.cs.umd.edu/hcil/treemap

Visible Human Project (National Library of Medicine)
www.cs.umd.edu/hcil/visible-human/

Visualization for business network monitoring
www.cs.umd.edu/hcil/network-monitoring/

WebTOC: A tool to visualize and quantify Web sites
www.cs.umd.edu/hcil/Webtoc/

Zoomable User Interfaces (Jazz)
www.cs.umd.edu/hcil/jazz/

Appendix C

Software

Our software is typically developed in support of our research goals. The prototypes are polished for the purpose of demonstrating a principle or running empirical tests. Some programs go through enough refinement that we use them regularly ourselves and share them with others for education and research purposes. The most polished programs, for which there is a strong demand, are made available for licensing.

We typically make our software freely available in executable form to encourage use for education and research. Those desiring the source code for research purposes should contact us. Those seeking commercial licenses should contact The University of Maryland Office of Technology Commercialization at

Office of Technology Commercialization
University of Maryland
6200 Baltimore Avenue, Suite 300
Riverdale, MD 20737
Tel: (301) 403-2711
Fax: (301) 403-2717
otc@umail.umd.edu

Income from licensing is split into portions for the University of Maryland and the inventors, with a large fraction going to the support of students conducting further research. We like the idea of making modest incentives and rewards for innovators but are careful to avoid becoming too focused on commercial demands. Since there are limitations inherent in the university environment for software marketing (legal restrictions and difficulties in providing full customer support), we are happy to see companies building on our ideas and products.

A current list of our software products is maintained at *www.cs.umd.edu/hcil/pubs/products.shtml.*

CounterPoint (PC PowerPoint plug-in)

CounterPoint is a zooming presentation tool that acts as a plug-in to PowerPoint. It allows you to arrange PowerPoint slides on a zooming canvas that is provided by Jazz.
www.cs.umd.edu/hcil/counterpoint/

Dynamaps (Visual Basic application)

The Dynamap, or the Dynamic Query Maptool, is an interface designed to facilitate easier viewing and better analysis of map-related census data.
www.cs.umd.edu/hcil/census/

Dynamic Homefinder (PC application)

This is our classic 1992 DOS application that demonstrates the concept of dynamic queries in a familiar real-estate domain.
www.cs.umd.edu/hcil/pubs/products.shtml (select Dynamic HomeFinder)

Excentric Labeling (Java applet)

Excentric Labeling is similar to the infotip (or balloon help) but simultaneously reveals all the labels in the neighborhood of the cursor, allowing users to rapidly review the labels of hundreds of objects in data visualizations or maps.
www.cs.umd.edu/hcil/excentric/

Fisheye Menus (Java applet)

Fisheye Menus support fast selection of one item from a long list. By using graphical scaling of items, the "focus" region is presented full size while the periphery is smaller. This allows the entire list to be visible within a single view.
www.cs.umd.edu/hcil/fisheyemenu/

GRIDL—Graphical Interface for Digital Libraries (Java applet)

A hierarchical browsing tool with a two-dimensional display that uses categorical and hierarchical axes where each grid point shows a cluster of color-coded dots or a bar chart. Users can navigate through the hierarchy by clicking on axes labels.
www.cs.umd.edu/hcil/west-legal/gridl/

Hierarchical Clustering Explorer (PC application)

Four new interactive techniques enable users to explore the results of hierarchical clustering algorithms to better understand cluster and outlier patterns in multidimensional databases of many kinds, especially the results of DNA microarray studies.
www.cs.umd.edu/hcil/multi-cluster/

Jazz—Zoomable User Interfaces (Java toolkit)

Jazz is a freely available Java toolkit for building Zoomable User Interfaces. It is useful for building many types of graphical applications. Jazz is distributed under generous Open Source licensing.
www.cs.umd.edu/hcil/jazz/

LifeLines—Visualization of personal history data (Java applet)

This visualization software presents a compact graphical overview of temporal data and allows users to zoom, filter, and retrieve details about the events.
www.cs.umd.edu/hcil/lifelines/

PhotoFinder (Visual Basic application)

PhotoFinder enables you to organize, annotate, and browse your personal photo libraries. Its StoryStarter component allows you to export text and images to the Web.
www.cs.umd.edu/hcil/photolib/

PhotoMesa Image Browser (Java application)
PhotoMesa, a zoomable image browser for viewing multiple directories of images, uses a set of simple navigation mechanisms to move through the space of images.
www.cs.umd.edu/hcil/photomesa/

Piccolo—Zoomable User Interfaces (Java toolkit)
Piccolo is a freely available Java toolkit that supports the building of ZUIs. It is a successor to Jazz.
www.cs.umd.edu/piccolo

Query Previews (Java applet)
Generalized query previews form a user interface architecture for efficient browsing of large online data. Generalized query previews supply distribution information to the users on "multiple" attributes of the data, and they give continuous feedback about the size of the results as the query is being formed.
www.cs.umd.edu/hcil/qp/

SimPLE (Delphi Framework) / EquiPSim (PC application)
SimPLE is an application framework that supports the creation of simulation-based learning environments. EquiPSim is a simulation-based learning environment for teaching various semiconductor manufacturing processes.
www.isr.umd.edu/SimPLE/
www.cs.umd.edu/hcil/historian/

SpaceTree Node-Link Tree Browser (Java application)
SpaceTree is a novel tree browser that builds on conventional node-link diagrams. It adds dynamic rescaling of the tree branches to best fit the available screen space, optimized camera movement, and the use of preview icons summarizing the topology of the branches that aren't expanded.
www.cs.umd.edu/hcil/spacetree/

TimeSearcher (Java application)
Users can discover features and trends in time-series data with this tool that supports interactive querying and exploration. Users express their desired patterns with time-boxes: a powerful graphical, direct manipulation metaphor for the specification of queries.
www.cs.umd.edu/hcil/timesearcher/

Treemap 3.X (Java application)
Treemaps are a space-filling visualization for hierarchical structures that are extremely effective in showing attributes of leaf nodes by size and color coding. Treemaps enable users to compare sizes of nodes and of subtrees, and are especially strong in spotting unusual patterns.
www.cs.umd.edu/hcil/treemap3/

TreeViz (Macintosh application)
This is an early implementation of the treemap concept that allows users to view all the files and directories on a hard disk.
www.cs.umd.edu/hcil/pubs/treeviz.shtml

WebTOC (Java applet)
This is a tool to visualize Web sites using a hierarchical table of contents browser.
ftp.cs.umd.edu/pub/hcil/Demos/WebTOC/index.html

Appendix D

HCIL Technical Report Listing (1993–2002)

This is a list (in reverse chronological order) of all tech reports published by the HCIL between 1993 and 2002. It contains the tech report number (*e.g.*, HCIL-2002-23) as well as a list of other places the work has been published.

Papers included in this book are marked with the chapter and paper number in which they appear (*e.g.*, HCIL-2002-14 [2.4] means that tech report HCIL-2002-14 appeared in this book as the fourth paper in Chapter 2). Throughout the book, references to HCIL work are listed without the term HCIL, and if the paper is included in this book, it is also cited with the chapter in which it appeared (*e.g.*, 2002-14 [2.4]).

2002

Bederson, B. B., Bongshin, L., Sherman, R., Herrnson, P.S, Niemi, R. G.
  Electronic Voting System Usability Issues
  HCIL-2002-23

Ceaparu, I.
  Governmental Statistical Data on the Web: A Case Study of FedStats
  HCIL-2002-22

Hutchinson, H., Bederson, B. B., Plaisant, C., Druin, A.
  Family Calendar Survey
  HCIL-2002-21

Guimbretiere, F.
  On Merging Command Selection and Direct Manipulation
  HCIL-2002-20

Bessiere, K., Ceaparu, I., Lazar, J., Robinson, J., Shneiderman, B.
  Social and Psychological Influences on Computer User Frustration
  HCIL-2002-19

Bessiere, K., Ceaparu, I., Lazar, J., Robinson, J., Shneiderman, B.
  Understanding Computer User Frustration: Measuring and Modeling the Disruption from Poor Designs
  HCIL-2002-18

Guimbretiere, F.
  Measuring FlowMenu Performance
  HCIL-2002-17

Hutchinson, H., Bederson, B. B., Druin, A., Plaisant, C., Mackay, W., Evans, H., Hansen, H., Conversy, S., Beaudouin-Lafon, M., Roussel, N.,

Lacomme, L., Eiderbäck, B., Lindquist, S., Sundblad, Y., Westerlund, B.
  Technology Probes: Inspiring Design for and with Families
  HCIL-2002-16

Keogh, E., Hochheiser, H., Shneiderman, B.
  An Augmented Visual Query Mechanism for Finding Patterns in Time Series Data
  Proc. Fifth International Conference on Flexible Query Answering Systems, Copenhagen, Denmark (October 27–29, 2002), Springer-Verlag, in the series Lecture Notes in Artificial Intelligence.
  HCIL-2002-15

Shneiderman, B., Kang, H., Kules, B., Plaisant, C., Rose, A., Rucheir, R.
  A Photo History of SIGCHI: Evolution of Design from Personal to Public
  ACM Interactions 9, 3 (May 2002), 17–23.
  HCIL-2002-14 [2.4]

Farber, A., Druin, A., Chipman, G., Julian,D., Somashekhar, S.
  How Young Can Our Design Partners Be?
  HCIL-2002-13

Ceaparu, I., Shneiderman, B.
  Improving Web-based Civic Information Access: A Case Study of the 50 U.S. States
  Proc. 2002 International Symposium on Technology and Society (ISTAS 02), IEEE.
  HCIL-2002-12

Ceaparu, I., Lazar, J., Bessiere, K., Robinson, J., Shneiderman, B.
  Determining Causes and Severity of End-User Frustration
  HCIL-2002-11

Seo, J., Shneiderman, B.
  Understanding Hierarchical Clustering Results by Interactive Exploration of Dendrograms: A Case Study with Genomic Microarray Data
  Final version: Interactively Exploring Hierarchical Clustering Results, *IEEE Computer* 35, 7 (July 2002). 80–86
  HCIL-2002-10 [7.6]

Bederson, B. B., Czerwinski, M., Robertson, G.
  A Fisheye Calendar Interface for PDAs: Providing Overviews for Small Displays
  HCIL-2002-09 [7.5]

Golub, E., Shneiderman, B.
Dynamic Query Visualizations on World Wide Web Clients: A DHTML Approach for Maps and Scattergrams
HCIL-2002-08

Druin, A., Revelle, G., Bederson, B. B., Hourcade, J. P., Farber, A., Lee, J., Campbell, D.
A Collaborative Digital Library for Children: A Descriptive Study of Children's Collaborative Behavior and Dialogue
Forthcoming in the *Journal of Computer-Assisted Learning*.
HCIL-2002-07

Hochheiser, H., Shneiderman, B.
Visual Queries for Finding Patterns in Time-Series Data
HCIL-2002-06 [7.3]

Plaisant, C., Grosjean, J., Bederson, B. B. (April 2002)
SpaceTree: Supporting Exploration in Large Node Link Tree, Design Evolution and Empirical Evaluation
Proc. IEEE Conference on Information Visualization 2002, Boston (October 2002).
HCIL-2002-05 [6.6]

Kang, H., Shneiderman, B.
Dynamic Layout Management in a Multimedia Bulletin Board
HCIL-2002-04

Hourcade, J., Bederson, B. B., Druin, A., Rose, A., Farber, A., Takayama, Y.
The International Children's Digital Library: Viewing Digital Books Online
Short version appeared in *Proc. Interaction Design and Children International Workshop*, Eindhoven, Netherlands (August 28–29, 2002). Shaker Publishing, 125–128.
Full revised version forthcoming in *Interacting with Computers*.
HCIL-2002-03 [4.5]

Norman, K., Pleskac, T.
Conditional Branching in Computerized Self-Administered Questionnaires: An Empirical Study
HCIL-2002-02

Fekete, J., Plaisant, C.
Interactive Information Visualization of a Million Items
Proc. IEEE Conference on Information Visualization 2002, Boston (October 2002).
HCIL-2002-01 [6.5]

2001

Tang, L., Shneiderman, B.
Dynamic Aggregation to Support Pattern Discovery: A Case Study with Web Logs
Short version appeared in *Proc. Discovery Science: 4th International Conference 2001*, Springer-Verlag, Berlin, 464–469.
HCIL-2001-27

Norman, K.
Implementation of Conditional Branching in Computerized Self-Administered Questionnaires
HCIL-2001-26

Boltman, A., Druin, A.
Children's Storytelling Technologies
HCIL-2001-25

Boltman, A.
Children's Storytelling Technologies: Differences in Elaboration and Recall
University of Maryland, College of Education, Human Development, dissertation.
HCIL-2001-24

Kules, B., Kang, H., Plaisant, C., Rose, A., Shneiderman, B.
Immediate Usability: Kiosk Design Principles from the CHI 2001 Photo Library
HCIL-2001-23

Tanin, E.
Browsing Large Online Data Using Generalized Query Previews
University of Maryland, Computer Science Department, dissertation.
HCIL-2001-22

Montemayor, J., Druin, A., Farber, A., Simms, S., Churaman, W., D'Armour, A.
Physical Programming: Designing Tools for Children to Create Physical Interactive Environments
CHI 2002, ACM Conference on Human Factors in Computing Systems, CHI Letters 4, 1 (2002), 299–306.
HCIL-2001-21

Browne, H., Bederson, B. B., Plaisant, C., Druin, A.
Designing an Interactive Message Board as a Technology Probe for Family Communication
HCIL-2001-20

Mayer, M., Bederson, B. B.
Browsing Icons: A Task-Based Approach for a Visual Web History
HCIL-2001-19

Bederson, B. B., Shneiderman, B., Wattenberg, M.
Ordered and Quantum Treemaps: Making Effective Use of 2D Space to Display Hierarchies
ACM Transactions on Graphics (TOG) 21, 4 (October 2002), 833–854.
HCIL-2001-18 [6.4]

Shneiderman, B., Hochheiser, H.
Universal Usability as a Stimulus to Advanced Interface Design
Behaviour and Information Technology 20, 5 (Sept-Oct 2001), 367–376.
HCIL-2001-17

Shneiderman, B.
Inventing Discovery Tools: Combining Information Visualization with Data Mining
HCIL-2001-16 [8.4]

Konishi, M., Plaisant, C., Shneiderman, B.
Enabling Commuters to Find the Best Route: An Interface for Analyzing Driving History Logs
Proc. Interact 2001, IFIP IOS Press, (2001), 799–800.
HCIL-2001-15

Druin, A., Fast, C.
The Child as Learner, Critic, Inventor, and Technology Design Partner: An Analysis of Three Years of Swedish Student Journals
International Journal for Technology and Design Education.
HCIL-2001-14

Tanin, E., Shneiderman, B.
Exploration of Large Online Data Tables Using Generalized Query Previews
Revised Feb. 2002.
HCIL-2001-13

Plaisant, C., (ed.)
2001 Human–Computer Interaction Laboratory Video Reports
HCIL-2001-12

Hornbæk, K., Bederson, B. B., Plaisant, C.
Navigation Patterns and Usability of Zoomable User Interfaces with and without an Overview
Revised version, "Navigation Patterns and Usability of Zoomable User Interfaces With and Without Overviews,"
ACM Transactions on Computer-Human Interaction 21, 4 (October 2002), 833–854.
HCIL-2001-11 [3.4]

Bederson, B. B.
Quantum Treemaps and Bubblemaps for a Zoomable Image Browser
ACM Conference on User Interface and Software Technology (UIST 2001) as PhotoMesa: A Zoomable Image Browser using Quantum Treemaps and Bubblemaps, 71–80
HCIL-2001-10 [2.3]

Norman, K. L., Pleskac, T. J., Norman, K.
Navigational Issues in the Design of On-Line Self-Administered Questionnaires: The Effect of Training and Familiarity
HCIL-2001-09

Dang, G., North, C., Shneiderman, B.
Dynamic Queries and Brushing on Choropleth Maps
Proc. International Conference on Information Visualization 2001, IEEE Press, (July 2001), 757–764.
HCIL-2001-08 [1.5]

Chipman, G., Plaisant, C., Gahagan, S., Herrmann, J. W., Hewitt, S., Reaves, L.
Understanding Manufacturing Systems with a Learning Historian for User-Directed Experimentation
HCIL-2001-07

Shneiderman, B., Wattenberg, M.
Ordered Treemap Layouts
Proc. IEEE Symposium on Information Visualization 2001, IEEE Press, Los Alamitos, Calif. (October 2001).
HCIL-2001-06

Hochheiser, H., Shneiderman, B.
Visual Specification of Queries for Finding Patterns in Time-Series Data
Proc. Discovery Science 2001, Washington, D.C. (November 2001).
HCIL-2001-05

Suh, B., Bederson, B. B.
OZONE: A Zoomable Interface for Navigating Ontology
Proc. International Conference on Advanced Visual Interfaces (AVI 2002), ACM, Trento, Italy, 139–143.
HCIL-2001-04

Good, L., Bederson, B. B.
CounterPoint: Creating Jazzy Interactive Presentations
Zoomable User Interfaces as a Medium for Slide Show Presentations, *Information Visualization* 1, 1 (2002), Palgrave Macmillan, 35–49.
HCIL-2001-03 [3.3]

Hochheiser, H., Shneiderman, B.
Universal Usability Statements: Marking the Trail for All Users
ACM Interactions 8, 2 (March/April 2001), 16–18.
HCIL-2001-02

Shneiderman, B.
Bridging the Digital Divide with Universal Usability
ACM Interactions 8, 2 (March/April 2001), 11–15.
HCIL-2001-01

2000

Hochheiser, H.
Browsers with Changing Parts: A Catalog Explorer for Philip Glass' Website
Proc. ACM Designing Interactive Systems Conference.
HCIL-2000-26

Hochheiser, H., Shneiderman, B.
Coordinating Overviews and Detail Views of WWW Log Data
Proc. 2000 Workshop on New Paradigms in Information Visualization and Manipulation, ACM New York (November 2000).
HCIL-2000-25

Plaisant, C., (ed.)
2000 and 1999-1991 Retrospective: Human–Computer Interaction Laboratory Video Reports
HCIL-2000-24

Plaisant, C., Bhamidipati, P.
Vehicle Speed Information Displays for Public Websites: A Survey of User Preferences
Proc. Conference on Intelligent Transportation Systems' 2001 (CD ROM proceedings), ITS 2001, Washington, D.C., ITS America (June 2001).
HCIL-2000-23

Norman, K., Slaughter, L., Friedman, Z., Norman, K., Stevenson, R.
Dual Navigation of Computerized Self-Administered Questionnaires and Organizational Records
HCIL-2000-22

Kreitzberg, C. B., Shneiderman, B.
Making Computer and Internet Usability a Priority
Common Ground Anthology, Usability Professionals Association, 2000.
Revised version reprinted in Branaghan, R. J. (ed.),
Design by People for People: Essays on Usability,
Usability Professionals Association, 2001, Chicago, 7–20.
HCIL-2000-21

Christian, K., Kules, B., Shneiderman, B.,
Youssef, A.
A Comparison of Voice Controlled and Mouse Controlled Web Browsing
Proc. ACM ASSETS 2000 Conference, ACM Press, New York (November 2000).
HCIL-2000-20

Revelle, G., Druin, A., Platner, M., Weng, S.,
Bederson, B. B., Hourcade, J. P., Sherman, L.
Young Children's Search Strategies and Construction of Search Queries
Revised version: *A Visual Search Tool for Early Elementary Science Students, Journal of Science Education and Technology* 11, 1 (2002), 49–57.
HCIL-2000-19

Druin, A., Bederson, B. B., Hourcade, J. P., Sherman, L.,
Revelle, G., Platner, M., Weng, S.
Designing a Digital Library for Young Children: An Intergenerational Partnership
Revised version in *Proc. ACM/IEEE Joint Conference on Digital Libraries (JCDL),* Virginia (June 2001), 398–405.
HCIL-2000-18 [4.4]

Browne, H., Bederson, B. B., Druin, A., Sherman, L.,
Westerman, W., Bederson, B. B.
Designing a Collaborative Finger Painting Application for Children
HCIL-2000-17

Plaisant, C., Druin, A., Lathan, C., Dakhane, K.,
Edwards, K., Vice, J. M., Montemayor, J.
A Storytelling Robot for Pediatric Rehabilitation
Revised version in *Proc. ASSETS 00,* Washington, D.C. (November 2000), ACM, New York, 50–55.
HCIL-2000-16

North, C.
A User Interface for Coordinating Visualizations Based on Relational Schemata: Snap-Together Visualization
University of Maryland, Computer Science Department, doctoral dissertation
HCIL-2000-15

Tanin, E., Plaisant, C., Shneiderman, B.
Broadening Access to Large Online Databases by Generalizing Query Previews
Proc. Symposium on New Paradigms in Information Visualization and Manipulation—CIKM, 80–85.
HCIL-2000-14 [1.4]

Bederson, B. B., Meyer, J., Good, L.
Jazz: An Extensible Zoomable User Interface Graphics ToolKit in Java

UIST 2000, ACM Symposium on User Interface Software and Technology, CHI Letters 2, 2, 171–180.
HCIL-2000-13 [3.2]

Bederson, B. B.
Fisheye Menus
Proc. UIST 2000, ACM, New York, 217–225.
HCIL-2000-12 [7.1]

Kim, J., Oard, D. W., Romanik, K.
User Modeling for Information Access Based on Implicit Feedback
Proc. ISKO-France 2001 (July 5–6), Nanterre, France.
HCIL-2000-11

Norman, K. L., Friedman, Z., Norman, K.,
Stevenson, R.
Navigational Issues in the Design of On-Line Self-Administered Questionnaires
Behavior and Information Technology 20, 37–45.
HCIL-2000-10

Plaisant, C., Komlodi, A.
Evaluation Challenges for a Federation of Heterogeneous Information Providers: The Case of NASA's Earth Science Information Partnerships
IEEE 9th Intl. Workshops on Enabling Technologies (WETICE 2000) Evaluating Collaborative Enterprises, Gaithersburg, Md. (June 14–16), IEEE, Los Alamitos, Calif., 130–138.
HCIL-2000-09

Marchionini, G., Hert, C., Liddy, L.,
Shneiderman, B.
Extending User Understanding of Federal Statistics in Tables
HCIL-2000-08, CS-TR-4131, UMIACS-TR-2000-24

Kang, H., Shneiderman, B.
Visualization Methods for Personal Photo Collections: Browsing and Searching in the PhotoFinder
Proc. IEEE International Conference on Multimedia and Expo (ICME2000), New York.
HCIL-2000-07

Shneiderman, B., Kang, H.
Direct Annotation: A Drag-and-Drop Strategy for Labeling Photos
Proc. International Conference Information Visualization (IV2000). London, England.
Proc. International Conference on Information Visualization 2000, IEEE, Los Alamitos, Calif. (July 2000), 88–95.
HCIL-2000-06 [2.2]

North, C., Shneiderman, B.
Snap-Together Visualization: A User Interface for Coordinating Visualizations via Relational Schemata
Conference Proc. Advanced Visual Interfaces 2000, ACM, New York.
HCIL-2000-05 [7.7]

Semple, P., Allen, R. B., Rose, A.
Developing an Educational Multimedia Digital Library: Content Preparation, Indexing, and Usage
ED-MEDIA 2000, Montreal, and reprinted with

permission of Association for the Advancement of Computing in Education.
HCIL-2000-04

Gandhi, R., Kumar, G., Bederson, B. B., Shneiderman, B.

Domain Name Based Visualization of Web Histories in a Zoomable User Interface
Proc. 11th International Workshop on Database and Expert Systems Applications, includes *WebVis 2000: Second International Workshop on Web-Based Information Visualization*, IEEE Computer Society, Los Alamitos, Calif. (2000), 591–598.
HCIL-2000-03

Alborzi, H., Druin, A., Montemayor, J., Sherman, L., Taxen, G., Best, J., Hammer, J., Kruskal, A., Lal, A., Plaisant Schwenn, T., Sumida, L., Wagner, R., Hendler, J.

Designing StoryRooms: Interactive Storytelling Spaces for Children
Revised version in *Proc. ACM Desiging Interactive Systems* (DIS 2000), New York (August 2000).
HCIL-2000-02

Shneiderman, B.

The Limits of Speech Recognition: Understanding Acoustic Memory and Appreciating Prosody
Communications of the ACM 43, 9 (September 2000), 63–65.
HCIL-2000-01

1999

Plaisant, C., (ed.)
1999 Human–Computer Interaction Laboratory Video Reports
HCIL-99-34, CS-TR-4195

Zhang, Z., Basili, V., Shneiderman, B.
Perspective-Based Usability Inspection: An Empirical Validation of Efficacy
Empirical Software Engineering 4, 1 (March 1999), 43–69.
HCIL-99-33

Rose, A., Allen, R. B., Fulton, K.
Multiple Channels of Electronic Communication for Building a Distributed Learning Community
Proc. Computer Support for Collaborative Learning, CSCL 99, Stanford, Calif., 495–502.
HCIL-99-32

Fredrikson, A., North, C., Plaisant, C., Shneiderman, B.
Temporal, Geographical and Categorical Aggregations Viewed Through Coordinated Displays: A Case Study with Highway Incident Data
Proc. Workshop on New Paradigms in Information Visualization and Manipulation, Kansas City, Mo. (November 6, 1999), ACM, New York, 26–34.
HCIL-99-31 [1.3]

Hochheiser, H., Shneiderman, B.
Using Interactive Visualizations of WWW Log Data to Characterize Access Patterns and Inform Site Design

A revised version appeared in *ASIS 99 Proc. 62nd Annual Meeting of the American Society for Information Science, Annual Conference* 36 (October 31–November 4, 1999), 331–344.
Appeared also as "Understanding patterns of user visits to web sites: Interactive starfield visualizations of WWW log data," *Journal of the American Society for Information Science and Technology* 54, 4 (2001), 331–343.
HCIL-99-30

Tse, T., Vegh, S., Marchionini, G., Shneiderman, B.

An Exploratory Study of Video Browsing User Interface Designs and Research Methodologies: Effectiveness in Information Seeking Tasks
ASIS 99 Proc. 62nd Annual Meeting of the American Society for Information Science, Medford, N.J. (October 1999), 681–692.
HCIL-99-29

Benford, S., Bederson, B. B., Akesson., K., Bayon, V., Druin, D., Hansson, P., Hourcade, J., Ingram, R., Neale, H., O'Malley, C., Simsarian, K., Stanton, D., Sundblad, Y., Taxen, G.

Designing Storytelling Technologies to Encourage Collaboration Between Young Children
Proc. CHI 2000, The Hague, Netherlands (April 1–6), ACM, New York, 556–563.
HCIL-99-28

Bederson, B. B., Stewart, J., Druin, A.
Single Display Groupware
HCIL-99-27

North, C., Shneiderman, B.
Snap-Together Visualization: Evaluating Coordination Usage and Construction
Int'l Journal of Human–Computer Studies. Special issue on Empirical Studies of Information Visualization 53, 5 (November 2000), 715–739.
HCIL-99-26

Montemayor, J., Druin, A., Hendler, J.
PETS: A Personal Electronic Teller of Stories
Druin, A., Hendler, J. (eds.) *Robots for Kids: New Technologies for Learning*, Morgan Kaufmann, San Francisco, Calif., (2000).
HCIL-99-25

Hochheiser, H., Shneiderman, B.
Performance Benefits of Simultaneous Over Sequential Menus as Task Complexity Increases
International Journal of Human Computer Interaction 12, 2, 173–192.
HCIL-99-24

Druin, A.
The Role of Children in the Design of New Technology
Behaviour and Information Technology 21, 1 (2002), 1–25.
HCIL-99-23

Salter, R.
A Client-Server Architecture for Rich Visual

History Interfaces
HCIL-99-22

Chapman, R., Shneiderman, B.
Booksites as Web-Based Dynamic Supplements to Computer Science Textbooks
HCIL-99-21

Cailleteau, L.
Interfaces for Visualizing Multi-Valued Attributes: Design and Implementation Using Starfield Displays
HCIL-99-20

Fredrikson, A.
Temporal, Geographical and Categorical Aggregations Viewed Through Coordinated Displays: A Case Study with Highway Incident Data (Summer Project Report)
HCIL-99-19

Harris, C., Allen, R. B., Plaisant, C., Z Shneiderman, B.
Temporal Visualization for Legal Case Histories
ASIS 99 *Proc. 62nd Annual Meeting of the American Society for Information Sciences, Conference October 31–November 4, 1999* 36, 271–279.
HCIL-99-18

Shneiderman, B.
Universal Usability: Pushing Human–Computer Interaction Research to Empower Every Citizen
CACM 43, 5 (May 2000), ACM, New York, 84–91.
HCIL-99-17

Shneiderman, B.
Supporting Creativity with Advanced Information-Abundant User Interfaces
In Earnshaw, R., Guedj, R., Van Dam, A., Vince, J. (eds.), *Human-Centred Computing, Online Communities, and Virtual Environments*, Springer-Verlag, London (2001), 469–480.
HCIL-99-16 [8.3]

Zaphiris, P., Shneiderman, B., Norman, K. L.
Expandable Indexes Versus Sequential Menus for Searching Hierarchies on the World Wide Web
HCIL-99-15

Druin, A.
Cooperative Inquiry: Developing New Technologies for Children with Children
Proc. CHI 99, Pittsburgh (May 15–20), ACM, New York, 592–599.
HCIL-99-14

Druin, A., Montemayor, J., Hendler, J., McAlister, B., Boltman, A., Fiterman, E., Plaisant, A., Kruskal, A., Olsen, H., Revett, I., Schwenn, T. P., Sumida, L., Wagner, R.
Designing PETS: A Personal Electronic Teller of Stories
Proc. CHI 99, Pittsburgh (May 15–20), ACM, New York, 326–329.
HCIL-99-13

Ghosh, P., Shneiderman, B.
Zoom-Only vs. Overview-Detail Pair: A Study in Browsing Techniques as Applied to Patient Histories
HCIL-99-12

Plaisant, C., Rose, A., Rubloff, G., Salter, R., Shneiderman, B.
The Design of History Mechanisms and Their Use in Collaborative Educational Simulations
Proc. Computer Support for Collaborative Learning, CSCL 99, Palo Alto, Calif., 348–359.
HCIL-99-11

North, C., Shneiderman, B.
Snap-Together Visualization: Coordinating Multiple Views to Explore Information
HCIL-99-10

Potter, R., Shneiderman, B., Bederson, B. B.
Pixel Data Access for End-User Programming and Graphical Macros
HCIL-99-09

Hourcade, J. P., Bederson, B. B.
Architecture and Implementation of a Java Package for Multiple Input Devices (MID)
HCIL-99-08

Bederson, B. B., McAlister, B.
Jazz: An Extensible 2D+Zooming Graphics Toolkit in Java
[See updated report 2000-13 on the same topic.]
HCIL-99-07

Hochheiser, H., Shneiderman, B.
Understanding Patterns of User Visits to Web Sites: Interactive Starfield Visualization of WWW Log Data—Short Version
[See 99-30 (November 1999).]
HCIL-99-06

Combs, T., Bederson, B. B.
Does Zooming Improve Image Browsing?
Proc. Digital Libraries 99, ACM, New York (1999), 130–137.
HCIL-99-05

Murphy, E., Norman, K., Moshinsky, D.
VisAGE Usability Study
HCIL-99-04

Shneiderman, B., Feldman, D., Rose, A., Ferré Grau, X.
Visualizing Digital Library Search Results with Categorical and Hierarchial Axes
Proc. 5th ACM International Conference on Digital Libraries, San Antonio (June 2–7, 2000), ACM, New York, 57–66.
HCIL-99-03 [4.3]

Hochheiser, H., Shneiderman, B.
Understanding Patterns of User Visits to Web Sites: Interactive Starfield Visualization of WWW Log Data
[See 99-30 (November 1999).]
HCIL-99-02

Shneiderman, B.
Creating Creativity for Everyone: User Interfaces for Supporting Innovation
ACM Transactions on Computer-Human Interaction 7, 1 (March 2000), 114–138.
Also in Carroll, J. (ed.) (2001) *HCI in the Millennium*, ACM, New York.
HCIL-99-01

1998

Zhang, Z., Basili, V., Shneiderman, B.
An Empirical Study of Perspective Based Usability Inspection
Proc. Human Factors and Ergonomics Society 42nd Annual Meeting, Santa Monica, Calif., 1346–1350.
HCIL-98-18

Plaisant, C., Venkatraman, M., Ngamkajornwiwat, K., Barth, R., Harberts, B., Feng, W.
Refining Query Previews Techniques for Data with Multivalued Attributes: The Case of NASA EOSDIS
IEEE Forum on Research and Technology Advances in Digital Libraries (ADL 99), IEEE Computer Society, Los Alamitos, Calif., 50–59.
HCIL-98-17

Plaisant, C. (ed.)
1998 Human–Computer Interaction Laboratory Video Reports
HCIL-98-16, CS-TR-4007

Shneiderman, B.
Educational Journeys on the Web Frontier
EDUCOM Review 33,6 (1998), 10, 12–14.
HCIL-98-15

Stewart, J., Bederson, B. B., Druin, A.
Single Display Groupware: A Model for Co-present Collaboration
Proc. CHI 99, Pittsburgh (May 15–20, 1999), ACM, New York, 286–293.
HCIL-98-14, CS-TR-3966, UMIACS-98-75

Kandogan, E.
Hierarchial Multi-Window Management with Elastic Layout Dynamics
doctoral dissertation
HCIL-98-13

Meyer, J., Bederson, B. B.
Does a Sketchy Appearance Influence Drawing Behavior?
HCIL-98-12

Bederson, B. B., Boltman, A.
Does Animation Help Users Build Mental Maps of Spatial Information
Proc. InfoViz 99, IEEE, Los Alamitos, Calif., 28–35.
HCIL-98-11 [3.1]

Plaisant, C., Tarnoff, P., Keswani, S., Rose, A.
Understanding Transportation Management Systems Performance with a Simulation-Based Learning Environment
Proc. Conference on Intelligent Transportation Systems'

99, ITS 99, Washington, D.C., ITS America, Washington D.C. (1999), *www.itsa.org* (CD-ROM proceedings).
HCIL-98-10

Fekete, J.-D., Plaisant, C.
Excentric Labeling: Dynamic Neighborhood Labeling for Data Visualization
Proc. CHI 99, Pittsburgh (May 15–20, 1999), ACM, New York, 512–519.
HCIL-98-09 [7.4]

Plaisant, C., Mushlin, R., Snyder, A., Li, J., Heller, D., Shneiderman, B.
LifeLines: Using Visualization to Enhance Navigation and Analysis of Patient Records
Revised version in *1998 American Medical Informatic Association Annual Fall Symposium*, Orlando (Nov. 9–11, 1998), AMIA, Bethesda, Md., 76–80.
HCIL-98-08 [7.2]

Rose, A., Eckard, D., Rubloff, G. W.
An Application Framework for Creating Simulation-Based Learning Environments
HCIL-98-07

Hightower, R., Ring, L., Helfman, J., Bederson, B. B., Hollan, J.
Graphical Multiscale Web Histories: A Study of PadPrints
Proc. ACM Conference on Hypertext (Hypertext 98), ACM Press, 58–65.
HCIL-98-06 [5.3]

Li, J., Plaisant, C., Shneiderman, B.
Data Object and Label Placement for Information Abundant Visualizations
Proc. Workshop on New Paradigms in Information Visualization and Manipulation (NPIV 98), ACM, New York, 41–48.
HCIL-98-05

Shneiderman, B., Borkowski, E. Y., Alavi, M., Norman, K.
Emergent Patterns of Teaching/Learning in Electronic Classrooms
Educational Technology Research and Development 46, 4 (1998), 23–42
HCIL-98-04

Druin, A., Bederson, B. B., Boltman, A., Miura, A., Knotts-Callahan, D., Platt, M.
Children as Our Technology Design Partners
In Druin, A. (ed.), *The Design of Children's Technology: How We Design and Why?* Morgan Kaufmann, San Francisco, Calif. (1998), 51–72.
HCIL-98-03

Tanin, E., Lotem, A., Haddadin, I., Shneiderman, B., Plaisant, C., Slaughter, L.
Facilitating Network Data Exploration with Query Previews: A Study of User Performance and Preference
Behaviour and Information Technology 19, 6 (2000), 393–403.
HCIL-98-02

Marchionini, G., Plaisant, C., Komlodi, A.
Interfaces and Tools for the Library of Congress National Digital Library Program
Information Processing & Management 34, 5 (1998), 535–555.
A French version appeared in *Document numerique* 2, 1, Hermes, Paris (1998), 53–65.
HCIL-98-01

1997

Shneiderman, B.
A Grander Goal: A Thousand-Fold Increase in Human Capabilities
Educom Review 32, 6 (1997), 4–10.
HCIL-97-23

Plaisant, C., (ed.)
1997 Human–Computer Interaction Laboratory Video Reports
HCIL-97-22

Shneiderman, B.
Codex, Memex, Genex: The Pursuit of Tranformational Technologies
International Journal of Human–Computer Interaction 10,2 (1998), 87–106.
HCIL-97-21

Greene, S., Tanin, E., Plaisant, C., Shneiderman, B., Olsen, L., Major, G., Johns, S.
The End of Zero-Hit Queries: Query Previews for NASA's Global Change Master Directory
International Journal Digital Libraries 2, 2 + 3 (1999), 79–90
HCIL-97-20

Plaisant, C., Shneiderman, B., Muhslin, R.
An Information Architecture to Support the Visualization of Personal Histories
Information Processing & Management 34, 5 (1998), 581–597.
HCIL-97-19

North, C., Shneiderman, B.
A Taxonomy of Multiple Window Coordinations
HCIL-97-18

Shneiderman, B.
Relate-Create-Donate: An Educational Philosophy for the Cyber-Generation
Computers & Education 31, 1 (1998), 25-39.
HCIL-97-17

Greene, S., Marchionini, G., Plaisant, C., Shneiderman, B.
Previews and Overviews in Digital Libraries: Designing Surrogates to Support Visual Information-Seeking
Journal of the American Society for Information Science 51, 3 (2000), 380–393.
HCIL-97-16

Rose, A., Ding, W., Marchionini, G., Beale Jr., J., Nolet, V.
Building an Electronic Learning Community: From Design to Implementation

Proc. CHI 98, Los Angeles (April 18–23, 1998), ACM, New York, 203–210.
HCIL-97-15 [4.2]

Tanin, E., Beigel, R., Shneiderman, B.
Design and Evaluation of Incremental Data Structures and Algorithms for Dynamic Query Interfaces
Proc. the 1997 IEEE Information Visualization Workshop (1997), 81–86.
HCIL-97-14

Alonso, D., Rose, A., Plaisant, C., Norman, K.
Viewing Personal History Records: A Comparison of Tabular Format and Graphical Presentation Using LifeLines
Behavior and Information Technology 17, 5 (1998), 249–262.
HCIL-97-13

Oard, D. W. (1997)
Speech-Based Information Retrieval for Digital Libraries
HCIL-97-12

Ding, W., Marchionini, G.
A Study on Video Browsing Strategies
HCIL-97-11

Nation, D. A., Plaisant, C., Marchionini, G., Komlodi, A.
Visualizing Websites Using a Hierarchical Table of Contents Browser: WebTOC
Proc. 3rd Conference on Human Factors and the Web, Denver, Colorado (June 12, 1997).
HCIL-97-10 [5.1]

Doan, K., Plaisant, C., Shneiderman, B., Bruns, T.
Interface and Data Architecture for Query Preview in Networked Information Systems
ACM Transactions on Information Systems 17, 3 (July 1999), 320–341.
A short early version also appeared in *ACM SIGMOD Record* 26, 1 (March 1997) as "Query Previews for Networked Information Systems: A Case Study with NASA Environmental Data" by Doan, K., Plaisant, C., Shneiderman, B., Bruns, B., 75–81.
HCIL-97-09

Kandogan, E., Shneiderman, B.
Elastic Windows: A Hierarchical Multi-Window World-Wide Web Browser
Proc. ACM, UIST 97, ACM, New York (October 1997), 169–177.
HCIL-97-08 5.2]

Marchionini, G., Nolet, V., Williams, H., Ding, W., Beal Jr., J., Rose, A., Gordon, A., Enomoto, E., Harbinson, L.
Content + Connectivity => Community: Digital Resources for a Learning Community
HCIL-97-07

Lane, J. C., Kuester, S. P., Shneiderman, B.
User Interfaces for a Complex Robotic Task: A Comparison of Tiled vs. Overlapped Windows
HCIL-97-06

Shneiderman, B., Byrd, D., Croft, W. B.
Clarifying Search: A User-Interface Framework for Text Searches

D-Lib Magazine (January 1997). Condensed version published as "A framework for search interfaces" by Shneiderman, B., IEEE Software (March/April 1997), 18–20.

Revised and shortened version published as "Sorting out searching: A user-interface framework for text searches" by Shneiderman, B., Byrd, D., Croft, B., *Communications of the ACM* 41, 4 (April 1998), 95–98.
HCIL-97-05

Shneiderman, B.
Between Hope and Fear
Communications of the ACM 40, 2 (February 1997), 59–62.
HCIL-97-04

Alonso, D. L., Norman, K. L.
Apparency of Contingencies in Pull Down Menus
HCIL-97-03

Doan, K., Plaisant, C., Shneiderman, B., Bruns, B.
Query Previews for Networked Information Systems: A Case Study with NASA Environmental Data
ACM SIGMOD Record 26, 1 (March 1997), 75–81.
HCIL-97-02

Shneiderman, B.
Direct Manipulation for Comprehensible, Predictable, and Controllable User Interfaces
Proc. IUI 97, 1997 International Conference on Intelligent User Interfaces, Orlando (January 6–9, 1997), 33–39.
HCIL-97-01

1996

Plaisant, C., Bruns, T., Shneiderman, B., Doan, K.
Query Previews in Networked Information Systems: The Case of EOSDIS
Video in *CHI 97 Video program*, Atlanta (March 1997), ACM, New York, 22–27.
A two-page summary also appeared in *CHI 97 Extended Abstracts*, ACM, New York, 202–203.
HCIL-96-19

Tanin, E., Beigel, R., Shneiderman, B.
Incremental Data Structures and Algorithms for Dynamic Query Interfaces
Workshop on New Paradigms in Information Visualization and Manipulation, Fifth ACM International Conference on Information and Knowledge Management (CIKM 96), Rockville, Md. (Nov. 16, 1996), 12–15.
Also in *SIGMOD Record* 25, 4 (December 1996), 21–24.
HCIL-96-18

Kandogan, E., Shneiderman, B.
Elastic Windows: Evaluation of Multi-Window Operations
CHI 97, Proc., Atlanta (March 22–27, 1997), ACM, New York, 250–257.
HCIL-96-17

Plaisant, C., Marchionini, G., Bruns, T., Komlodi, A., Campbell, L.
Bringing Treasures to the Surface: Iterative Design

for the Library of Congress National Digital Library Program
CHI 97 Proc., Atlanta (March 22–27, 1997), ACM, New York, 518–525.
HCIL-96-16 [4.1]

Ellis, J., Rose, A., Plaisant, C.
Putting Visualization to Work: ProgramFinder for Youth Placement
Proc. CHI 97, Atlanta (March 22–27, 1997), ACM, New York, 502–509.
HCIL-96-15

Kolker, R., Shneiderman, B.
Tools for Creating and Exploiting Content
Getty Art History Information Program, Research Agenda for Networked Cultural Heritage, Santa Monica, Calif. (1996), 27–30.
HCIL-96-14

Shneiderman, B.
The Eyes Have It: A Task by Data Type Taxonomy for Information Visualizations
Proc. 1996 IEEE Conference on Visual Languages, Boulder, Colo. (Sept. 3–6, 1996), 336–343.
HCIL-96-13 [8.2]

Plaisant, C., (ed.)
1996 Human–Computer Interaction Laboratory Video Reports
HCIL-96-12

Alonso, D. L., Norman, K. L.
Apparency of Contingencies in Single Panel Menus
HCIL-96-11

Oard, D. W., Marchionini, G.
A Conceptual Framework for Text Filtering
Appeared as "The State of the Art in Text Filtering" in *User Modeling and User Adapted Interaction* 7, 3 (1997), 141–178.
HCIL-96-10

Marchionini, G., Plaisant, C., Komlodi, A.
User Needs Assessment for the Library of Congress National Digital Library
HCIL-96-09

Mahajan, R., Shneiderman, B.
Visual & Textual Consistency Checking Tools for Graphical User Interfaces
IEEE Transactions on Software Engineering 23, 11 (November 1997), 722–735.
HCIL-96-08

Rose, A., Ellis, J., Plaisant, C., Greene, S.
Life Cycle of User Interface Techniques: The DJJ Information System Design Process
HCIL-96-07

Greene, S., Rose, A.
Information and Process Integration from User Requirements Elicitation: A Case Study of Documents in a Social Services Agency
In Wakayama, T., et al., (eds.), "Information and Process Integration in Enterprises: Rethinking Documents," Kluwer, Boston (1998), 143–160.

Proc. IPIC 96: Information and Processes Integration Conference "Rethinking Documents," Sloan School of Management, MIT, Cambridge, Mass. (November 14–15, 1996).
HCIL-96-06

Shneiderman, B.
Designing Information-Abundant Websites
International Journal of Human–Computer Studies 47 (1997), 5–29.
Also *Designing the User Interface*, 3rd ed., Addison Wesley.
HCIL-96-05

Plaisant, P., Rose, A.
Exploring LifeLines to Visualize Patient Records
A short version of this report appeared as a poster summary in 1996 American Medical Informatic Association Annual Fall Symposium, Washington, D.C. (Oct. 26–30, 1996), AMIA, Bethesda, Md., 884.
HCIL-96-04

Paton, N. W., Doan, D. K., Diaz, O., Jaime, A.
Exploitation of Object-Oriented and Active Constructs in Database Interface Development
Proc. 3rd International Workshop on Database Interfaces (IDS3), Edinburgh, Scotland (July 1996), Springer Verlag, 1–14.
HCIL-96-03

Preece, J., Shneiderman, B.
Survival of the Fittest: The Evolution of Multimedia User Interfaces
ACM Computing Surveys 27, 4 (Dec. 1995), 558–559.
HCIL-96-02

Korn, F., Shneiderman, B.
Navigating Terminology Hierarchies to Access a Digital Library of Medical Images
HCIL-96-01

1995

Plaisant, C., Levy, R., Zhoa, R.
BizView: Managing Business and Network Alarms
Summary of the video available from HCIL as part of the 1995 HCIL video report.
HCIL-95-22

Pointek, J.
Data Structures for Dynamic Query Browsing of EOS Data Directories
Presentation abstract appeared in online *Proc. NASA Science Information Systems Interoperability Conference*, University of Maryland, College Park, Md. (Nov. 6–9, 1995).
HCIL-95-21

North, C., Shneiderman, B., Plaisant, C.
User Controlled Overviews of an Image Library: A Case Study of the Visible Human
Proc. 1st ACM International Conference on Digital Libraries, Bethesda, Md. (March 20–23, 1996), ACM, New York, 74–82.
In addition, the video "Browsing Anatomical Image

Databases: A Case Study of the Visible Human" appeared in *CHI 96 Video Program* with a two-page video summary in *ACM CHI 96 Conference Companion*, Vancouver (April 13–18, 1996), 414–415, 1995 HCIL Video report.
HCIL-95-20 [2.1]

Shneiderman, B., Alavi, M., Norman, K., Borkowski, E.
Windows of Opportunity in Electronic Classrooms
Communications of the ACM, Log on Education column 38, 11 (Nov. 1995), 19–24.
HCIL-95-19

Shneiderman, B., Rose, B.
Social Impact Statements: Engaging Public Participation in Information Technology Design
Proc. CQL96, ACM SIGCAS Symposium on Computers and the Quality of Life (Feb. 1996), 90–96.
Also in Friedman, B. (ed.), "Human Values and the Design of Computer Technology," CSLI Publications and Cambridge Univerity Press (1997), 117–133.
HCIL-95-18

Plaisant, C., Ed.
1995 Human–Computer Interaction Laboratory Video Reports
HCIL-95-17

Doan, K., Plaisant, C., Shneiderman, B.
Query Previews in Networked Information Systems
Proc. Third Forum on Research and Technology Advances in Digital Libraries, ADL 96, Washington, D.C. (May 13–15, 1996), IEEE CS Press, 120–129.
Abstract appeared as "Architecture of Dynamic Query User Interface for Networked Information Systems" in online *Proc. NASA Science Information Systems Interoperability Conference*, College Park, Md. (Nov. 6–9, 1995).
HCIL-95-16

Plaisant, C., Milash, B., Rose, A., Widoff, S., Shneiderman, B.
LifeLines: Visualizing Personal Histories
ACM CHI 96 Conference Proc., Vancouver, BC, Canada (April 13–18, 1996), 221–227, color plate 518, *www.acm.org/sigchi/sigchi96/proceedings*.
The paper also has a corresponding video in the *CHI 96 Video Program* ACM, New York. Video also available from HCIL in the 1996 HCIL video report.
HCIL-95-15

Kandogan, E., Shneiderman, B.
Elastic Windows: Improved Spatial Layout and Rapid Multiple Window Operations
ACM Proc. Workshop on Advanced Visual Interfaces, AVI 96, Gubbio, Italy (May 27–29, 1996), 29–38.
HCIL-95-14

Carr, D.
A Compact Graphical Representation of User Interface Interaction Objects
190-page doctoral dissertation CSC 949; see 94-09 for condensed version.
HCIL-95-13

Kumar , H. P., Plaisant, C., Shneiderman, B.
Browsing Hierarchical Data with Multi-Level Dynamic Queries and Pruning
International Journal of Human–Computer Studies 46, 1 (January 1997), 103–124.
HCIL-95-12

Plaisant, C., Shneiderman, B.
Organization Overviews and Role Management: Inspiration for Future Desktop Environments
IEEE Proc. 4th Workshop on Enabling Technologies: Infrastructure for Collaborative Enterprises, Berkeley Springs, W.V. (April 20–22, 1995), 14–22.
HCIL-95-11

Mahajan, R., Shneiderman, B.
A Family of User Interface Consistency Checking Tools
Proc. Twentieth Annual Software Engineering Workshop, SEL-95-004, Greenbelt, Md. (Dec. 1995), NASA Pub., 169–188.
HCIL-95-10

Slaughter, L., Norman, K. L., Shneiderman, B.
Assessing Users' Subjective Satisfaction with the Information System for Youth Services (ISYS)
VA Tech Proc. Third Annual Mid-Atlantic Human Factors Conference, Blacksburg, Va. (March 26–28, 1995), 164–170.
HCIL-95-09

Plaisant, C., Rose, A., Shneiderman, B., Vanniamparampil, A.
User Interface Reengineering: Low Effort, High Payoff Strategies
IEEE Software 14, 4 (July/August 1997), 66–72.
Also translated into Japanese in *Nikkei Computer*, Nikkei Business Publications, Inc., Tokyo, Japan, 430, 151–159.
HCIL-95-08

Rose, A., Shneiderman, B., Plaisant, C.
An Applied Ethnographic Method for Redesigning User Interfaces
ACM Proc. DIS 95, Symposium on Designing Interactive Systems: Processes, Practices, Methods & Techniques, Ann Arbor, Mich. (Aug 23–25, 1995), 115–122.
HCIL-95-07

Ellis, J., Tran, C., Ryoo, J., Shneiderman, B.
Buttons vs. Menus: An Exploratory Study of Pull-Down Menu Selection as Compared to Button Bars
HCIL-95-06

Shneiderman, B., Chimera, R., Jog, N., Stimart, R., White, D.
Evaluating Spatial and Textual Style of Displays
Proc. Getting the Best from State of the Art Display Systems, The Society for Information Display, Trafalgar Square, London (Feb. 21–23, 1995). Also in MacDonald, L., Lowe, A. (1997), *Display Systems: Design and Applications*, Chapter 5: Evaluating the spatial and textual style of displays,

John Wiley & Sons, 83–96.
HCIL-95-05

Asahi, T., Turo, D., Shneiderman, B.
Visual Decision-Making: Using Treemaps for the Analytic Hierarchy Process
Video in *CHI 95 Video Program*, ACM, New York. A two-page video summary also appeared in *ACM CHI 95 Conference Companion*, Denver, Colo. (May 7–11, 1995), 405–406.
Video also available through HCIL as part of the 1994 HCIL video report.
HCIL-95-04 [6.1]

Plaisant, C., Shneiderman, B.
Organization Overviews and Role Management: Inspiration for Future Desktop Environments
Video in *CHI 95 Video Program*, ACM, New York. A two-page video summary also appeared in *ACM CHI 95 Conference Companion*, Denver, Colo. (May 7–11, 1995), 419–420.
Video also available through HCIL as part of the 1994 HCIL video report.
HCIL-95-03

Shneiderman, B.
Looking for the Bright Side of User Interface Agents
ACM Interactions 2, 1 (Jan. 1995), 13–15.
HCIL-95-02

Shneiderman, B.
The Info Superhighway: For the People
Communications of the ACM, Inside Risks column, 38, 1 (Jan. 1995), 162.
HCIL-95-01

1994

Rosenfeld, A., Marchionini, G., Holliday, W. G., Ricart, G., Faloustos, Dick, J.P., Shneiderman, B.
QUEST: Query Environment for Science Teaching
Proc. Digital Libraries 94, Texas A&M University, College Station, Tex., 74–79.
HCIL-94-18

Plaisant, C., (ed.)
1994 Human–Computer Interaction Laboratory Video Reports
HCIL-94-17

Plaisant, C., Jain, V.
Dynamaps: Dynamic Queries on a Health Statistics Atlas
Video in *CHI 94 Video Program*, ACM, New York. A two-page video summary also appeared in *ACM CHI 94 Conference Companion*, Boston (April 24–28, 1994), 439–440. Video also available through HCIL as part of the 1993 HCIL video report.
HCIL-94-16

Turo, D.
Hierarchical Visualization with Treemaps: Making Sense of Pro Basketball Data
Video in *CHI 94 Video Program*, ACM, New York. A two-page video summary also appeared in *ACM*

CHI 94 Conference Companion, Boston (April 24–28, 1994), 441–442.

Video also available through HCIL as part of the 1993 HCIL Video Report.

HCIL-94-15 [6.2]

Ahlberg, C., Shneiderman, B.

Visual Information Seeking Using the FilmFinder

Video in *CHI 94 Video Program*, ACM, New York.

A two–page video summary also appeared in *ACM CHI 94 Conference Companion*, Boston (April 24–28, 1994), 433–434.

Video also available through HCIL as part of the 1994 HCIL video report.

HCIL-94-14 [1.1]

Marchionini, G., Barlow, D.

Extending Retrieval Strategies to Networked Environments: Old Ways, New Ways, and a Critical Look at WAIS

Journal of American Society for Information Science 45, 8, 561–564.

HCIL-94-13

Shneiderman, B.

The River Beyond the Rapids: Responsive Services for Responsible Users

Connecting the DOE Community: Partnerships in Information, Info Tech 94, Oak Ridge, Tenn. (Oct. 25–26,1994), 1–9.

Also appeared as "Comprehensible Predictable, and Controllable User Interfaces" in *American Programmer* 8, 4, 2–7.

HCIL-94-12

Barreau, D.

Context as a Factor in Personal Information Management Systems

Journal of American Society for Information Science 46, 5, 327–339.

HCIL-94-11

Kumar, H.

Browsing Hierarchical Data with Multi-Level Dynamic Queries and Pruning

105-page dissertation. [See 95–12 (CS-TR-3474) for condensed version.] ISR-MS-95-5.

HCIL-94-10

Carr, D., Jog, N., Kumar, H., Teittinen, M.

Using Interaction Object Graphs to Specify and Develop Graphical Widgets

HCIL-94-09

Asahi, T., Turo, D., Shneiderman, B.

Using Treemaps to Visualize the Analytic Hierarchy Process

Information Systems Research 6, 4 (Dec. 1995), 357–375.

HCIL-94-08

Kumar, H., Plaisant, C., Teittinen, M., Shneiderman, B.

Visual Information Management for Network Configuration

Part of this article was later published in *Next*

Generation Network Management Technology, by Atallah, G., Ball, M., Baras, J., Goli, S. Karne, R., Kelley, S., Kumar, H., Plaisant, C., Roussopoulos, N., Shneiderman, B., Srinivasarao, M., Stathatos, K., Teittinen, M., Whitefield, D., *Proc. 12th Symposium on Space Nuclear Power and Propulsion/Commercialization*, Albuquerque, N.M. (January 8–12, 1995), 75–82.

HCIL-94-07 [6.3]

Jog, N., Shneiderman, B.

Starfield Information Visualization with Interactive Smooth Zooming

IFIP 2.6 Visual Databases Systems Proc., Lausanne, Switzerland (March 27–29,1995), 1–10.

HCIL-94-06

Shneiderman, B., Plaisant, C.

The Future of Graphic User Interfaces: Personal Role Managers

People and Computers IX, British Computer Society's HCI 94, Glasgow, Scotland (Aug. 1994), Cambridge University Press, 3–8.

HCIL-94-05

Johnson, B.

Treemaps: Visualizing Hierarchical and Categorical Data

HCIL-94-04

Carr, D., Plaisant, C., Hasegawa, H.

Usability Experiments for the Redesign of a Telepathology Workstation

Based on "The Design of a Telepathology Workstation: Exploring Remote Images," *Interacting with Computers* 11, 1 (1998), 33–52.

HCIL-94-03

Plaisant, C., Carr, D., Shneiderman, B.

Image Browsers: Taxonomy, Guidelines, and Informal Specifications

IEEE Software 12, 2 (March 1995), 21–32.

HCIL-94-02 [8.1]

Shneiderman, B., Lewis, C.

Building HCI Partnerships and Infrastructure

Behavior and Information Technology 12, 2 (1993), 130–135.

HCIL-94-01

1993

Plaisant, C., (ed.)

1993 Human–Computer Interaction Laboratory Video Reports

HCIL-93-25, CS-TR-3530, CAR-TR-793

Plaisant, C., Carr, D. A., Hasegawa, H.

Exploring Remote Images: A Telepathology Workstation

Video in *ACM INTERCHI 93 Video Program*, Amsterdam, Netherlands (April 24–29, 1993).

Video available through *ACM SIGGRAPH Video Review* 88-89.

A one-page summary also appeared in *INTERCHI 93 Proceedings*, 518.

Video also available through HCIL as part of the 1992 HCIL video report.
HCIL-93-24

Potter, R.
Guiding Automation with Pixels: A Technique for Programming in the User Interface
Video in *ACM INTERCHI 93 Video Program*, Amsterdam, Netherlands (April 24–29, 1993).
Video available through *ACM SIGGRAPH Video Review* 88-89.
A one-page summary also appeared in *INTERCHI 93 Proceedings*, 530.
Video also available through HCIL as part of the 1992 HCIL video report.
HCIL-93-23

Norman, K., Wright, P.
HyperTools for HyperTexts: Supporting Readers of Electronic Documents
HCIL-93-22

Plaisant, C.
Facilitating Data Exploration: Dynamic Queries on a Health Statistics Map
Proc. Annual Meeting of the American Statistical Association of the Government Statistics Section, San Francisco (Aug. 1993), 18–23.
HCIL-93-21

Carr, D.
Specification of Interface Interaction Objects
ACM CHI 94 Conference Proc., Boston (April 24–28, 1994), 372–378.
HCIL-93-20

Potter, R., Maulsby, D.
A Test Suite for Programming by Demonstration
In Cypher, A. (ed.), *Watch What I Do: Programming by Demonstration*, MIT Press, Cambridge, Mass. (1993), 539–591.
HCIL-93-19

Potter, R.
Just-in-Time ProgrammingWatch
In Cypher, A. (ed.), *Watch What I Do: Programming by Demonstration*, MIT Press, Cambridge, Mass. (1993), 513–526.
HCIL-93-18

Marchionini, G., Crane, H.
Evaluating Hypermedia and Learning: Methods and Results from the Perseus Project
ACM Transactions on Information Systems 12, 1 (Jan. 1994), 5–34.
HCIL-93-17

Jain, V., Shneiderman, B.
Data Structures for Dynamic Queries: An Analytical and Experimental Evaluation
Proc. Workshop in Advanced Visual Interfaces, AVI 94, Bari, Italy (June 1–4, 1994), 1–11.
Previous version referenced as CAR-TR-685, CS-TR-3133, ISR-TR-93-73.
HCIL-93-16

Ahlberg, C., Shneiderman, B.
The Alphaslider: A Compact and Rapid Selector
ACM CHI 94 Conference Proc., Boston (April 24–28, 1994), 365–371.
HCIL-93-15

Ahlberg, C., Shneiderman, B.
Visual Information Seeking: Tight Coupling of Dynamic Query Filters with Starfield Displays
ACM CHI 94 Conference Proc., Boston (April 24–28, 1994), 313–317.
Also in Baecker, R. M., Grudin, J., Buxton, W. A. S., Greenberg, S., (eds.), *Readings in Human–Computer Interaction: Toward the Year 2000*, Morgan Kaufmann, San Francisco, Calif. (1995), 450–456.
HCIL-93-14

Shneiderman, B.
Preface to Sparks of Innovation in Human–Computer Interaction
In Shneiderman, B. (ed.), *Sparks of Innovation in Human–Computer Interaction*, Ablex (1993), *ACM Interactions* 1, 1 (Jan. 1994), 67–71.
HCIL-93-13

Shneiderman, B.
Declaration in Apple vs. Microsoft/Hewlett-Packard
In Shneiderman, B. (ed.), *Sparks of Innovation in Human–Computer Interaction*, Ablex (1993), 355-363.
HCIL-93-12

Chimera, R., Shneiderman, B.
User Interface Consistency: An Evaluation of Original and Revised Interfaces for a Videodisk Library
In Shneiderman, B. (ed.), *Sparks of Innovation in Human–Computer Interaction*, Ablex (1993), 259–273.
HCIL-93-11

Marchionini, G., Ashley, M., Korzendorfer, L.
ACCESS at the Library of Congress
In Shneiderman, B. (ed.), *Sparks of Innovation in Human–Computer Interaction*, Ablex (1993), 251–258.
HCIL-93-10

Chimera, R.
Evaluation of Platform Independent User Interface Builders
Complete paper version available with 100-page statistical data section.
HCIL-93-09

Osada, M., Liao, H., Shneiderman, B.
AlphaSlider: Development and Evaluation of Text Retrieval Method Using Sliders
9th Symposium on Human Interface, Kobe, Japan (Oct. 18–20, 1993), 91–94.
HCIL-93-08

Shneiderman, B.
Education by Engagement and Construction: Experiences in the AT&T Teaching Theater
AACE (Charlottesville, Va.), In Maurer, H. (ed.), *Education Multimedia and Hypermedia Annual* (1993), Ed-Media 93, Orlando (June 23–26, 1993), 471–479.
HCIL-93-07

Lindwarm, D., Norman, K.
Student Evaluation of the Software in the AT&T Teaching Theater
HCIL-93-06

Shneiderman, B.
Engagement and Construction: Education Strategies for the Post-TV Era
Computer Assisted Learning, International Conference on Computers and Learning, Wolfville, Nova Scotia, Canada (June 17–20, 1992), 39–45.
Also in *Journal of Computing in Higher Education*, Spring 1993, 4, 2, 106–116.
And in Shneiderman, B. (ed.), *Sparks of Innovation in Human–Computer Interaction*, Ablex (1993), 345–350.
HCIL-93-05

Sears, A.
Layout Appropriateness: Guiding User Interface Design with Simple Task Descriptions
113-page dissertation. [See 92-02 (CS-TR-2823) and 92-15(CS-TR-2997) for condensed version.]
HCIL-93-04

Shneiderman, B.
Beyond Intelligent Machines: Just Do It!
IEEE Software 10, 1 (Jan 1993), 100–103.
HCIL-93-03

Potter, R.
Triggers: Guiding Automation with Pixels to Achieve Data Access
In Cypher, A. (ed.), *Watch What I Do: Programming by Demonstration*, MIT Press, Cambridge, Mass. (1993), 360–380.
HCIL-93-02

Shneiderman, B.
Dynamic Queries: For Visual Information Seeking
IEEE Software 11, 6 (Nov. 1994), 70–77.
HCIL-93-01 [1.2]

Author Index

Key Terms Index